The IDG SECRETS™ Advantage

More Windows 3.1 SECRETS is part of the *InfoWorld SECRETS* series of books brought to you by IDG Books Worldwide. The designers of the SECRETS series understand that you appreciate insightful and comprehensive works from computer experts. Authorities in their respective areas, the authors of the SECRETS books have been selected for their ability to enrich your daily computing tasks.

The formula for a book in the SECRETS series is simple: Give an expert author a forum to pass on his or her expertise to readers. A SECRETS author, rather than the publishing company, directs the organization, pace, and treatment of the subject matter. SECRETS authors maintain close contact with end users through column feedback, user group participation, and consulting work. The authors' close contact with the needs of computer users gives the SECRETS books a strategic advantage over most computer books. Our authors do not distance themselves from the reality of daily computing, but rather, our authors are directly tied to the reader response stream.

We believe that the author has the experience to approach a topic in the most efficient manner, and we know that you, the reader, will benefit from a "one-to-one" relationship, through the text, with the author. The author's voice is always present in a SECRETS series book. Some have compared the presentation of a topic in a SECRETS book to sitting at a coffee break with the author and having the author's full attention.

And of course, the author is free to include or recommend useful software, both shareware and proprietary, in a SECRETS series book. The software that accompanies a SECRETS book is not intended as casual filler. The software is strategically linked to the content, theme, or procedures of the book. We expect that you will receive a real and direct benefit from the included software.

You will find this book comprehensive whether you read it cover to cover, section to section, or simply a topic at a time. As a computer user, you deserve a comprehensive and informative resource of answers that *More Windows 3.1 SECRETS* delivers.

— David Solomon
Publisher

INFO WORLD

MORE Windows 3.1 SECRETS™

by Brian Livingston

Software Editor
Margie Livingston

Technical Consultant
Davis Straub

Foreword by Amy Wohl

IDG BOOKS

IDG Books Worldwide, Inc.
An International Data Group Company

San Mateo, California ✦ Indianapolis, Indiana ✦ Boston, Massachusetts

More Windows 3.1 SECRETS

Published by
IDG Books Worldwide, Inc.
An International Data Group Company
155 Bovet Road, Suite 310
San Mateo, CA 94402

Library of Congress Catalog Card No.: 93-79178

ISBN: 1-56884-019-5

Printed in the United States of America

10 9 8 7 6 5 4 3 2 1

Distributed in the United States by IDG Books Worldwide, Inc.

Distributed in Canada by Macmillan of Canada, a Division of Canada Publishing Corporation; by Computer and Technical Books in Miami, Florida, for South America and the Caribbean; by Longman Singapore in Singapore, Malaysia, Thailand, and Korea; by Toppan Co. Ltd. in Japan; by Asia Computerworld in Hong Kong; by Woodslane Pty. Ltd. in Australia and New Zealand; and by Transword Publishers Ltd. in the U.K. and Europe.

For information on where to purchase IDG Books outside the U.S., contact Christina Turner at 415-312-0633.

For information on translations, contact Marc Jeffrey Mikulich, Foreign Rights Manager, at IDG Books Worldwide; FAX NUMBER 415-358-1260.

For sales inquiries and special prices for bulk quantities, write to the address above or call IDG Books Worldwide at 415-312-0650.

About the Author

Brian Livingston is the Window Manager columnist for *InfoWorld,* Contributing Editor of *Windows Sources* and *PC/Computing*, and a contributor to other publications. He is the author of *Windows 3.1 SECRETS* (IDG Books Worldwide, 1992), *Windows 3 SECRETS* (IDG Books Worldwide, 1992), and co-author with Margie Livingston of *Windows Gizmos,* (IDG Books Worldwide, 1993), which have more than a quarter million copies in print in 24 languages. He was a recipient of the 1991 Award for Technical Excellence from the Microcomputer Managers Association.

About IDG Books Worldwide

Welcome to the world of IDG Books Worldwide.

IDG Books Worldwide, Inc., is a division of International Data Group, the world's largest publisher of computer-related information and the leading global provider of information services on information technology. IDG publishes over 194 computer publications in 62 countries. Forty million people read one or more IDG publications each month.

If you use personal computers, IDG Books is committed to publishing quality books that meet your needs. We rely on our extensive network of publications, including such leading periodicals as *Macworld, InfoWorld, PC World, Computerworld, Publish, Network World,* and *SunWorld,* to help us make informed and timely decisions in creating useful computer books that meet your needs.

Every IDG book strives to bring extra value and skill-building instruction to the reader. Our books are written by experts, with the backing of IDG periodicals, and with careful thought devoted to issues such as audience, interior design, use of icons, and illustrations. Our editorial staff is a careful mix of high-tech journalists and experienced book people. Our close contact with the makers of computer products helps ensure accuracy and thorough coverage. Our heavy use of personal computers at every step in production means we can deliver books in the most timely manner.

We are delivering books of high quality at competitive prices on topics customers want. At IDG, we believe in quality, and we have been delivering quality for over 25 years. You'll find no better book on a subject than an IDG book.

John Kilcullen
President and C.E.O.
IDG Books Worldwide, Inc.

IDG Books Worldwide, Inc. is a division of International Data Group. The officers are Patrick J. McGovern, Founder and Board Chairman; Walter Boyd, President. International Data Group's publications include: **ARGENTINA's** Computerworld Argentina, InfoWorld Argentina; **ASIA's** Computerworld Hong Kong, PC World Hong Kong, Computerworld Southeast Asia, PC World Singapore, Computerworld Malaysia, PC World Malaysia; **AUSTRALIA's** Computerworld Australia, Australian PC World, Australian Macworld, Network World, Reseller, IDG Sources; **AUSTRIA's** Computerwelt Oesterreich, PC Test; **BRAZIL's** Computerworld, Mundo IBM, Mundo Unix, PC World, Publish; **BULGARIA's** Computerworld Bulgaria, Ediworld, PC & Mac World Bulgaria; **CANADA's** Direct Access, Graduate Computerworld, InfoCanada, Network World Canada; **CHILE's** Computerworld, Informatica; **COLOMBIA's** Computerworld Colombia; **CZECH REPUBLIC's** Computerworld, Elektronika, PC World; **DENMARK's** CAD/CAM WORLD, Communications World, Computerworld Danmark, LOTUS World, Macintosh Produktkatalog, Macworld Danmark, PC World Danmark, PC World Produktguide, Windows World; **EQUADOR's** PC World; **EGYPT's** Computerworld (CW) Middle East, PC World Middle East; **FINLAND's** MikroPC, Tietoviikko, Tietoverkko; **FRANCE's** Distributique, GOLDEN MAC, InfoPC, Languages & Systems, Le Guide du Monde Informatique, Le Monde Informatique, Telecoms & Reseaux; **GERMANY's** Computerwoche, Computerwoche Focus, Computerwoche Extra, Computerwoche Karriere, Information Management, Macwelt, Netzwelt, PC Welt, PC Woche, Publish, Unit; **HUNGARY's** Alaplap, Computerworld SZT, PC World; **INDIA's** Computers & Communications; **ISRAEL's** Computerworld Israel, PC World Israel; **ITALY's** Computerworld Italia, Lotus Magazine, Macworld Italia, Networking Italia, PC World Italia; **JAPAN's** Computerworld Japan, Macworld Japan, SunWorld Japan, Windows World; **KENYA's** East African Computer News; **KOREA's** Computerworld Korea, Macworld Korea, PC World Korea; **MEXICO's** Compu Edicion, Compu Manufactura, Computacion/Punto de Venta, Computerworld Mexico, MacWorld, Mundo Unix, PC World, Windows; **THE NETHERLAND'S** Computer! Totaal, LAN Magazine, MacWorld; **NEW ZEALAND's** Computer Listings, Computerworld New Zealand, New Zealand PC World; **NIGERIA's** PC World Africa; **NORWAY's** Computerworld Norge, C/World, Lotusworld Norge, Macworld Norge, Networld, PC World Ekspress, PC World Norge, PC World's Product Guide, Publish World, Student Data, Unix World, Windowsworld, IDG Direct Response; **PANAMA's** PC World; **PERU's** Computerworld Peru, PC World; **PEOPLES REPUBLIC OF CHINA's** China Computerworld, PC World China, Electronics International, China Network World; **IDG HIGH TECH BEIJING's** New Product World; **IDG SHENZHEN's** Computer News Digest; **PHILLIPINES'** Computerworld, PC World; **POLAND's** Computerworld Poland, PC World/Komputer; **PORTUGAL's** Cerebro/PC World, Correio Informatico/Computerworld, MacIn; **ROMANIA's** PC World; **RUSSIA's** Computerworld-Moscow, Mir-PC, Sety; **SLOVENIA's** Monitor Magazine; **SOUTH AFRICA's** Computing S.A.; **SPAIN's** Amiga World, Computerworld Espana, Communicaciones World, Macworld Espana, NeXTWORLD, PC World Espana, Publish, Sunworld; **SWEDEN's** Attack, ComputerSweden, Corporate Computing, Lokala Natverk/LAN, Lotus World, MAC&PC, Macworld, Mikrodatorn, PC World, Publishing & Design (CAP), Datalngenjoren, Maxi Data, Windows World; **SWITZERLAND's** Computerworld Schweiz, Macworld Schweiz, PC & Workstation; **TAIWAN's** Computerworld Taiwan, Global Computer Express, PC World Taiwan; **THAILAND's** Thai Computerworld; **TURKEY's** Computerworld Monitor, Macworld Turkiye, PC World Turkiye; **UNITED KINGDOM's** Lotus Magazine, Macworld, Sunworld; **UNITED STATES'** AmigaWorld, Cable in the Classroom, CD Review, CIO, Computerworld, Desktop Video World, DOS Resource Guide, Electronic News, Federal Computer Week, Federal Integrator, GamePro, IDG Books, InfoWorld, InfoWorld Direct, Laser Event, Macworld, Multimedia World, Network World, NeXTWORLD, PC Games, PC Letter, PC World Publish, Sumeria, SunWorld, SWATPro, Video Event; **VENEZUELA's** Computerworld Venezuela, MicroComputerworld Venezuela; **VIETNAM's** PC World Vietnam

Acknowledgments

Portions of this book were previously published in *InfoWorld* and *Windows* magazines. Contents that appeared in *InfoWorld* are copyright 1991, 1992, and 1993, by InfoWorld Publishing, Inc. and used with permission. The issues of *Windows* magazine in which contents appeared are copyright 1992, and 1993, by CMP Publications Inc.

The publisher would like to give special thanks to Patrick J. McGovern, without whom this book would not have been possible.

Credits

Publisher
David Solomon

Managing Editor
Mary Bednarek

Acquisitions Editor
Janna Custer

Production Manager
Beth Jenkins

Senior Editors
Sandy Blackthorn
Diane Graves Steele

Production Coordinator
Cindy L. Phipps

Acquisitions Assistant
Megg Bonar

Editorial Assistant
Patricia R. Reynolds

Project Editor
Sandy Reed

Technical Reviewer
Brian Moura

Production Staff
Tony Augsburger
Valery Bourke
Mary Breidenbach
Sherry Gomoll
Drew R. Moore
Gina Scott

Proofreader
Vicki West

Indexer
Sherry Massey

Book Design
University Graphics

Contents at a Glance

Table of Contents

Foreword

In the not very distant past, it was common to describe the computer market by saying, "IBM isn't the competition; it's the environment." We meant that IBM was so large and represented so great a percentage of so many different parts of the computer market that every one of its competitors had to consider IBM's enormous and pervasive influence as a condition of doing business, a simple fact of life. Of course, that was yesterday.

In the past 12 years, we have changed the world. Mainframes no longer rule, and with the diffusion of information processing power and information, IBM's power has waned too. Personal computers and microprocessor technology are the centerpiece of what we are building, but the large and complex systems we are building around them may require as much planning and support as the mainframes they replace.

We now live in an exciting, but chaotic and challenging, interregnum trying to decide where we want to keep our information, who we want to put in charge, and how to keep it all working. Moreover, there is no magic way to get from the old way of doing things to the new one. We'll have to live for many years with multiple generations and styles of computer systems working side by side — and compromising our ability to exploit new technology in order to continue to access the legacy systems that we cannot afford to abandon.

In today's world of personal computers, software rules supreme. On top of this software kingdom, the most important element in selecting, buying, and (most importantly) using computers sits Microsoft — not the competition, but the environment. How appropriate then, that it is Microsoft that provides the very environment — Windows — within which most business computing, now and in the foreseeable future, will occur.

But while Windows is intended to reduce complexity, and make computing accessible to ordinary business users, the fact is that Windows and the DOS operating system it employs can be confusing, even overwhelming. Worse, much of the complexity is sufficiently unpredictable so that Microsoft seems unable to supply adequate documentation to keep even well-behaved, manual-reading users out of trouble.

Enter Brian Livingston. Our Windows computers couldn't exist without a hefty assist from his clever, information-filled *Windows Secrets* series. They act as a highly readable extension to Microsoft's much-less-readable manuals in two ways: they make *what* you can do and *how* you can it much more easily understood. More important, they ferret out amazing information about Windows that makes the environment much more customizable and useful (and often much more sturdy and secure) and they tell you how to apply this information in a completely straightforward, non-computer-jargon way that even recent converts to the Windows environment can readily understand.

You (like me) will likely use Brian's newest book two ways: you'll browse through it and find some topics that are immediately interesting and useful and you'll use his careful directions to add function and power to your Windows system. Then you'll lean *More Windows 3.1 Secrets* against your computer (or, if you're neater than me you'll put it on the nearest bookshelf) to use as a very useful reference for a variety of Windows emergencies. There are thousands of computer reference books published every year. Only a few earn a place on your desk. This one will.

Amy D. Wohl
Wohl Associates

Amy D. Wohl is President of Wohl Associates, a consulting firm providing advice on computer industry trends, and Editor of *The TrendsLetter*, a monthly newsletter. She also writes several monthly columns and comments regularly on computer industry events.

Chapter 1
Read This First

If you spend five minutes reading this chapter, it's my hope that it will save you hours when you're looking for information in the rest of this book.

More Windows 3.1 Secrets is a treasure chest of all the undocumented and poorly documented features of Microsoft Windows that I've been able to find since the release of Windows 3.1.

This book is part of my "Windows Series." *More Windows 3.1 Secrets* is an important companion to *Windows 3.1 Secrets* — which shipped on April 22, 1992, the same day as version 3.1 of Windows itself — and *Windows Gizmos,* an encyclopedia of Windows software, which was published in January 1993. Together, these books provide over 2,200 pages of Windows knowledge, and more than 100 Windows freeware and shareware programs. But you do not need either of the two earlier books to get full value from *More Windows 3.1 Secrets.* It stands on its own as a book of "forbidden knowledge" in its own right. (For more information on any of these books, contact IDG Books Worldwide, 800-762-2974 and 415-312-0650 [orders] or 415-358-1260 [fax], at 155 Bovet Road, Suite 310, San Mateo, CA 94402.)

More Windows 3.1 Secrets is written for a slightly more advanced Windows user than *Windows 3.1 Secrets.* This is partly because most Windows users have become more sophisticated since Windows 3.1 was released. But it is also because I wanted to give you, the reader, the maximum possible value by including every trick I could — with as little duplication as possible between *More Windows 3.1 Secrets* and *Windows 3.1 Secrets.*

I never thought I would learn so many more undocumented features after the release of Windows 3.1. But in the long months since that promising but flawed environment shipped, the gems have just kept coming out. These secrets have required a lot more digging than before to uncover — but I think you'll agree that the effort was worth it when you examine the final product.

How to Use This Book

If you are a new Windows user:

I recommend you start by reading the "For New Windows Users" section of Chapter 49. Then return to this chapter and continue on to whatever chapters interest you.

If you are an experienced Windows user:

Jump right into *More Windows 3.1 Secrets,* after reading the tips in this chapter on how to get the most out of this book.

Getting Commands Right the First Time

You'll be able to use the secrets in this book faster if you know exactly how you should type the many Windows commands shown in the text. Some commands can be typed much faster than you can use a mouse to do the same thing.

Throughout this book, I've indicated many commands as shown in the following line:

```
NOTEPAD {/P} filename
```

In this command, *filename* is shown in *italics* to indicate that you should change *filename* to the actual name of the file you want to open in the Notepad text editor. The command /P is shown in curly braces {like this} to indicate that this *command-line switch* is optional. You should not type the curly braces if you decide to add /P to this command. Since Windows often uses square brackets [like this] to indicate the beginning of sections in initialization files, I do not use square brackets in this book to indicate optional switches. If you see a line that contains square brackets, you must type the square brackets along with the rest of the line.

If you want to print the SETUP.TXT file using Notepad, for example, you would click File Run in the Windows Program Manager or File Manager, type the following line, and click Enter:

```
NOTEPAD /P SETUP.TXT
```

When such a command appears in the body text of a paragraph, it usually appears in SMALL CAPITALS to indicate that it is a command, not a part of the discussion. Because this book includes a large number of DOS batch files and other material contributed by a variety of readers and Windows developers, every example in this book may not look exactly this way. Batch files, especially, are often easier to read when printed in lowercase letters. You should be able to use common sense to tell when to substitute your own text for a place holder in an example.

Whenever you see the term *filename* in italics, you can change it to any form of a valid file name that DOS or Windows will recognize, including drive letters and directory names. For example, if drive C is your current drive, any of the following names for the SETUP.TXT file are valid in this Notepad command:

```
NOTEPAD SETUP
NOTEPAD SETUP.TXT
NOTEPAD C:\WINDOWS\SETUP.TXT
NOTEPAD \WINDOWS\SETUP.TXT
```

I indicate special keys on your keyboard with an initial capital letter, like this: Enter, Tab, Backspace, Shift, Alt (alternate), Ctrl (control), and Esc (escape). When you see a phrase, such as "press Enter," you know not to type the keys *e, n, t, e,* and *r,* but to press the Enter key.

If one of the shift keys (Shift, Alt, or Ctrl) should be *held down* at the same time that you also press another key, the two keys are written with a plus sign between them. For example, "press Ctrl+A" means *hold down the Ctrl key, then press the A key, then release both.*

If you are supposed to *let up* on a key *before* pressing another one, those keys are separated by commas. If I say, "press Alt, F, O," this means *press and release Alt, then F, then O.* This sequence activates the main menu of a Windows application, then pulls down the File menu, then executes the Open menu item. This is the same as saying "click File Open."

In this book, I usually do not indicate a keyboard-only procedure every time I describe how to do something with your mouse. Saying "click File Open" always means *click the File and Open menu items with your mouse,* but can also mean *click the keys on your keyboard that represent the File and Open menu items.*

Finding the Good Parts

More Windows 3.1 Secrets uses the same icons as *Windows 3.1 Secrets* to lead your eye to those special passages that reveal hidden and little-understood facts about Windows.

Triangles point to summaries of each chapter. You can get most of the content out of this book in about one hour by scanning each chapter for these summaries.

Undocumented Features are items that are not explained in the Windows manual, or are described inadequately (if at all) in the SETUP.TXT file that comes with Windows 3.1. In some cases, Microsoft has written something about these features somewhere, but in other cases I had to dig them out through tips or trial-and-error.

Workarounds are procedures or temporary fixes that can help you solve a problem or add functionality to your Windows configuration. In some cases, this is a commercial product you can buy to fix some Windows limitation, but *workarounds* are usually free tricks that just take a little of your time and experimentation.

Error Messages Decoded are explanations of error dialog boxes that are confusing or even misleading. *Windows 3.1 Secrets* caught most of these — there is a special page in the Index to that book just to list all the decoded error messages. But I've found a few more and given you the lowdown on them here.

This Book's Overall Structure

More Windows 3.1 Secrets is organized into four sections:

Part I: Customization Secrets

This section covers tricks you can use to customize Drag-and-Drop, Program Manager, File Manager, your keyboard, and many other aspects of the Windows interface.

Part II: Setup Secrets

The Setup Secrets section includes tricks that I've learned since the release of Windows 3.1 — how to set up different Windows configurations for different users of a single PC, how to upgrade to new Windows drivers, how to deinstall Windows applications, and more. (See Chapter 17 of *Windows 3.1 Secrets* for complete Windows installation secrets, which are not duplicated here.)

Part III: Tips and Tricks

This section brings together several short techniques to improve Windows, as well as many imaginative fixes suggested by the readers of my columns in *InfoWorld* and *Windows Magazine:* easy ways to troubleshoot Windows, tricks that programming masters use, hidden keystrokes that let you cheat at Solitaire and Minesweeper, and more.

Part IV: Excellence in Windows Shareware

Wrapping up the book is complete documentation for more than two dozen of the best freeware and shareware programs I've been able to find since the publication of *Windows 3.1 Secrets* and *Windows Gizmos*. Since you might need to find a particular tool or program that appears in any of the three books in my Windows Series, I've listed in the introduction to the shareware section all the more than 100 programs in the entire set, broken into convenient categories.

Getting Technical Support

It is not possible for IDG Books to provide technical support for Windows or the many DOS and Windows applications that may cause conflicts within your system. Of course, if a diskette that comes with this book is damaged, or you need to exchange the 3½-inch diskette set for a 5¼-inch set, you should of course contact IDG Books, which is committed to providing you with a set in perfect condition. But for technical support, you will actually be better off contacting Microsoft directly — or using electronic support (which I'll describe in a moment).

First, Microsoft provides telephone technical support for its DOS and Windows products through the following numbers:

Microsoft Pay-Per-Call Support ($2 per minute to a maximum of $25)	900-896-9000 (in U.S.)
Microsoft General Support	206-454-2030
Microsoft Windows Environment	206-637-7098
Microsoft Windows Applications	206-637-7099
Microsoft International Support (for a referral to a non-U.S. office)	206-882-8080

Microsoft is, at this writing, planning to phase out its 206 area code support lines and offer technical support primarily through its 900-number paid lines and other international offices. Other software publishers, additionally, are reducing or eliminating their free telephone support. The best technical support, however, has *never* been provided on phone lines. Instead, the best help has always been provided (this is the secret) through electronic bulletin board systems (BBSs), especially the CompuServe Information Service, which is described in the next topic.

Accessing CompuServe Technical Support

The CompuServe Information Service (CIS) is a worldwide computer service that allows you to exchange messages with almost every other electronic mail address in existence. Almost all vendors of Windows products now maintain "forums" on CompuServe. A forum is a message area that technical support people monitor on a daily basis, answering questions and comments left by users of each vendor's products. By contrast, telephone support is considered expensive and boring to provide. But a company's top programmers often look in on its CompuServe forum, which is considered more convenient, since questions can be answered at night or any time.

To get electronic technical support from Microsoft on CompuServe, for example, you call a CompuServe local number with your modem, then type GO MICROSOFT at any CompuServe prompt. You then see a list of services, including several Microsoft forums supported in different languages and countries of the world. After choosing your language group, you then choose the forum for the product you need technical support for: DOS or Windows, Word for Windows, Excel, and so on.

If you need support from a vendor other than Microsoft, type GO SOFTWARE or GO HARDWARE. You will then see a listing of scores of companies, each with its own forum or forums filled with technical messages between company technicians and users.

Once you're in the forum for your particular vendor, choose the menu option "Announcements from Sysop." This displays a listing of system operators (sysops), along with the latest news about the forum: new program enhancement files you can copy (download) to your computer, for example. Write down the name and CompuServe number that corresponds to the sysop in your particular area of interest. Then switch to the "Messages" section of the forum, compose a detailed message about your problem, and address it to the number of the sysop you wrote down.

When you "post" a message in this way, it is seen not only by the sysop you addressed it to, but also by anyone else who reads the messages for that forum. Check the Messages section 24 to 48 hours later, and you'll probably find several responses. Some of them will likely be from people who are not employees of the vendor but are more expert users of the company's products than any employee!

At this writing, CompuServe charges fees of $6 per hour for access at 2,400 bits per second (bps), or $12 per hour for 9,600 or 14,400 bps. This can add up, but expert users of CompuServe have found many ways to reduce these fees to the bare minimum. The primary means of doing this is to run a program that takes your outgoing messages, dials CompuServe, spurts your messages into the appropriate forums, and retrieves any messages addressed to you — all within a fraction of the time that you could do this manually.

One of the best such programs is called WinCIS — a shareware Windows program from the Windows User Group Network (WUGNET). To get this program, type GO WUGNET, select the Libraries section, choose Library 12, and download the file named WC094A.ZIP. Decompress this file and read it for instructions on downloading a few other files. (The entire package is larger than CompuServe's limitation for file transmission.) To decompress this file, you must have the PKZip 2.0 program. You can obtain a shareware version of this program in Library 4 of GO WUGNET or by typing GO IBMNEW, Library 2, and downloading PK204G.EXE.

To gain access to CompuServe, call the Customer Service Dept. at 800-848-8990 in the U.S., or 614-457-8650 outside the U.S. Customer service is available 8 a.m. to 12 midnight, Eastern Time, Monday through Friday, and 12 noon to 10 p.m. Saturday and Sunday (except on U.S. holidays). CIS will send you a packet of information on how to find the closest local number in your area, and how to use the service.

If you don't already have a modem, I encourage you to buy the fastest modem that is available — 9600 bps or 14,400 bps (14.4 Kbps) or higher — and start taking advantage of BBSs for the excellent technical support and services they provide.

Happy Sailing!

I'd like to thank all the people who've sent me tips or dug out technical information for me — most of whom are credited in the text of this book (except for those who must remain anonymous so they can keep their jobs). And I'd like to thank you, my ever-curious readers, for supporting my efforts to pry the lid off the mysterious box we call Windows.

I hope you enjoy this book — may your mouse live to tell many a tail! (Grin.)

—Brian Livingston

Part I
Customization Secrets

Chapter 2
Make Drag-and-Drop Do Anything You Want

In This Chapter

▶ I describe a way to modify the Windows Drag-and-Drop technology so it does anything *you* want it to.

▶ I show you the specific language you can add to macros in Word for Windows and WordPerfect for Windows — and potentially *any* major application — to use this technique in a productive way: converting a formatted word processing file into a plain-text file simply by dragging the filename from the Windows File Manager and dropping it onto an icon.

In all my books and columns, I try to reveal undocumented and little-known features of Windows that can help you get more out of Microsoft's graphical environment.

Now, after several months of studying the inner workings of Windows 3.1, I've found a way to use a capability that is one of the least-understood aspects of Windows.

By taking advantage of one simple trick, you can redefine how Microsoft's Drag-and-Drop technology works. You can actually make Drag-and-Drop do anything you want, in almost any major Windows application!

What Drag-and-Drop Does For You

The old Windows 3.0 always had some Drag-and-Drop features. But these were limited to a few specific actions, such as dragging a file from one drive to another in the File Manager or moving an icon in the Program Manager.

Windows 3.1, however, introduced a significant enhancement to the functionality of Drag-and-Drop. Not only could you drag a filename out of the File Manager and drop it onto a Windows application's icon or window with 3.1, you could also drop a filename onto a minimized Print Manager icon — and the file would print itself to the current printer, assuming that the extension of the file was "associated" with a Windows application capable of printing. (The Print Manager must be "enabled" in the Control Panel's Printers dialog box for this to work. If not, you can also print a file by selecting it in File Manager and clicking File Print on the File Manager's main menu.)

Beneath the introduction of this seemingly simple feature was a somewhat controversial technology. The Windows 3.1 File Manager had gained the ability to pass information about dragged objects to other Windows applications. In Microsoft terminology, the File Manager was a Drag-and-Drop "server," while other applications could act as "clients." But Microsoft had chosen not to document its "server" methodology for developers of other Windows applications, such as third-party file managers. Only after repeated requests by programmers were declined during the beta period of Windows 3.1 (leading up to Windows 3.1's release in May 1992) did this information finally surface in an article in M&T Publishing's technical magazine, *Microsoft Systems Journal,* May-June 1993.

Now that both the "server" side and the "client" side of Drag-and-Drop are documented, most major Windows applications support Drag-and-Drop in some way. But even for those applications that do not support Drag-and-Drop explicitly, Windows users can still find ways to modify Drag-and-Drop behavior to accomplish almost anything you can imagine.

What You Can Make Drag-and-Drop Do

The key to understanding Microsoft's Drag-and-Drop functionality is to look again at what happens when you drop a filename from the File Manager onto a minimized Print Manager icon.

The Print Manager does not actually print your file. In fact, the Print Manager knows nothing about your word processor documents, spreadsheet grids, graphical images, or any other file type.

If you have "associated" a file type correctly with the appropriate Windows application, however, Print Manager has all the information it needs to cause your file to be printed. It simply relies on the File Manager to send a message to the affected application, commanding that app to open the document, print it, and terminate. You may see the application flash momentarily on the screen, but other than that, you need take little or no action.

Now imagine: what if you could control the message that the File Manager sends to each of your applications? With a few simple steps, you can do exactly that. Here are a few examples:

■ **Plain-text conversion.** Imagine a coworker calling you from a distant city, asking you to e-mail him several documents. The documents themselves are in a strange word-processing format he can't use. But instead of converting each file manually, you simply drop each document onto an icon, and a plain-text file automatically appears in the same directory — perfect for e-mail transmission.

■ **Spreadsheet charting.** Perhaps you have a spreadsheet that contains several financial charts. When your boss asks for a fresh set of printouts, you simply drag the appropriate spreadsheet filename onto an icon. The charts (not the whole spreadsheet) automatically print themselves.

■ **Graphics conversion.** Let's say that you often receive bitmapped graphics in a standard but incompatible format. Instead of opening them individually in a conversion program, you just drop each filename onto an icon, and the files are converted for you.

■ **Office automation.** You need to send documents to another office via a fax board every morning, not when you save those documents the previous evening. You can save the documents whenever convenient, and then fax them automatically when the other office opens in the morning by dropping your filenames onto an icon.

All these things and more are possible. The alternatives are limited only by your imagination.

To understand this concept, it may help to think of the term "printing" in a new way. Usually, when we say "print," we mean, "print to a printer." But we could also use the word "print" to mean "print to a file." In this case, the output of an application would be written to a disk file rather than to a printer port.

Another way we could use the word "print" would be to say, "print my document into a plain-text file." We could also say, "print my document into the fax board" or "print my .BMP files to .PCX files."

Once we have redefined the word "print" to mean "change the form of a file to another useful form," we can imagine a lot more possibilities for the files we drop on the Print Manager.

Now all you need is the means to modify the meaning of Drag-and-Drop in your very own copy of Windows.

Discovering the hidden Registration Editor

The key to Print Manager's ability to command applications to print their associated files lies in two features of Windows 3.1 that are not mentioned in your Windows manual: the Registration Database and the Registration Editor.

The Registration Database is a binary file, REG.DAT, that contains information on what File Manager should do with filenames that are associated with an application. When you double-click a filename, File Manager usually commands the associated application to open the file. When you drop a filename on the Print Manager icon it ordinarily prints the file.

The Registration Database also keeps track of Object Linking and Embedding (OLE) information. For example, you can embed a Paintbrush graphic into Windows Write. You do this by copying the graphic in Paintbrush, then clicking Edit Paste-Special in Write. Once the object has been pasted into Write in this way, you can double-click it. The graphic will appear in Paintbrush window, where it can be edited and then updated to reappear in the Write window in its new, edited form.

Information about associations and embedding was formerly stored in the [Extensions] and [Embedding] sections of WIN.INI in Windows 3.0. Windows 3.1 still maintains these sections of WIN.INI for older applications that look there for this type of information. But newer applications, and Windows itself, use the information written into the Registration Database, which overrides any information you might type into WIN.INI.

The Registration Editor is a program that acts as a front end to the Registration Database. No icon for the Registration Editor appears in the Program Manager, nor does it appear on any Windows menu. You must simply know about it to use it. Create an icon in the Program Manager with a command line of REGEDIT.EXE. To do this, click File New in the Program Manager, select Program Item, and click OK. In the dialog box that appears, type REGEDIT.EXE in the Command Line box and click OK. The RegEdit icon is shown in Figure 2-1. Double-click this icon, and you should see a dialog box like the one in Figure 2-2.

Registration
Editor

Figure 2-1: You can put the Registration Editor in your Program Manager by making an icon with the command line REGEDIT.EXE.

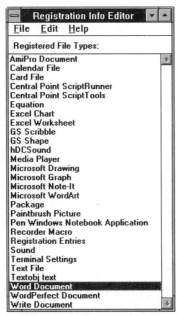

Figure 2-2: The Registration Editor shows the associations your File Manager knows about.

The Registration Editor dialog box contains a list of all applications that have "registered" their associated file types with Windows. Usually, major Windows applications that have been updated for Windows 3.1 automatically insert entries into this database when you install the application. Several Windows applets, such as Paintbrush and Write, however, are already present in the database when you install Windows 3.1.

The OLE information for each application is accessed in a slightly different way. To see this information, click File Run in Program Manager, then type REGEDIT /V. The "/V" switch stands for Verbose. This command displays a window similar to Figure 2-3. Each OLE-enabled application and its capabilities are listed in a complex tree structure.

It shouldn't be necessary to edit the OLE information, which is beyond the scope of this discussion. If you need more description about how the OLE structure works, click Help on the Registration Editor main menu.

Our principal interest in the Registration Editor is how to alter the meaning of the Drag-and-Drop interface, which we will now proceed to do.

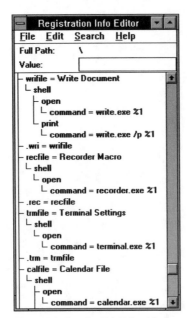

Figure 2-3: Starting RegEdit with the command REGEDIT /V displays a verbose listing of all file associations and Object Linking and Embedding (OLE) syntax, in a tree structure.

Modifying the RegEdit entries

To understand the entries in the Registration Database, first look at the entry for an application that everyone has: Windows Write. Run RegEdit, and double-click the Write Document line, which appears at the bottom of the dialog box.

A new dialog box should appear. The File Type in this dialog box says "Write Document." A box labeled "Action" shows two possibilities: Open and Print. When the Open button is checked, you should see a command line that says WRITE.EXE %1. This means that when you double-click a filename in File Manager that has the association "Write Document," File Manager will start WRITE.EXE with a command-line parameter — in this case, the filename you double-clicked, which is represented by the variable name %1.

If you click the Print button in this dialog box, you should see a command line that reads WRITE.EXE /P %1. This means that when you drop a Write file on a minimized Print Manager icon, the File Manager will start WRITE.EXE with two parameters: /P and %1. The /P switch is a convention used by most applications that are Windows 3.1-aware. It causes Write to automatically print the file represented by the %1 parameter.

You can see the action of the /P switch for yourself by clicking File Run in the Program Manager and typing WRITE /P WININI.WRI. Write will briefly open on the screen, and the WININI.WRI file (a documentation file for some WIN.INI settings) will print out on your current printer.

The existence of the Registration Editor, however, means that you can change the parameters that File Manager feeds each application when you double-click a filename or drop it on the Print Manager.

This means that you can cause the File Manager to run *any action* that can be defined in *any Windows application* that supports a macro language. Almost all major Windows applications, especially word processors and spreadsheets, now include some recording and playback macro facility. Now you can tap into these macro languages to run any process you want on files you have dropped onto the Print Manager.

An example: Converting documents to text

Every major Windows application with a macro language also supports some way to start a macro from the command line, or using Dynamic Data Exchange (DDE) commands. For example, Microsoft Word for Windows allows you to start the application and run any macro when you use the /M switch. The command line WINWORD.EXE /MFILENEW will start Word for Windows and automatically run its FileNew macro (which opens the File New dialog box).

To illustrate how you can edit the Registration Database to run any macros that you wish in your favorite applications, the following steps are designed to automatically convert any document file to a plain text file. The Listings later in this chapter for Word for Windows 2.0 and WordPerfect for Windows 5.2 give you the text of macros used in each of these products to perform the actual conversion. (This procedure will not work for Ami Pro 3.0, because it rewrites its entries in the Registration Database every time Ami Pro is launched. To make the procedure work with Ami Pro, you might try creating a different extension for Ami Pro documents and use RegEdit to associate the following steps with documents that have that extension. Ami Pro would not rewrite the entries in the Registration Database for this extension.)

STEPS

Converting to a Plain Text File in Word or WordPerfect

Step 1. Using the File Manager, find the file REG.DAT in your Windows directory. Click File Copy and make a copy of this file, called REG.ORI (for "original"). If anything goes wrong in this procedure, you can always copy REG.ORI over REG.DAT and restart Windows, and your system will be back the way it was. (If you *really* mess up, you can completely restore the Registration Database by clicking File Merge in RegEdit and selecting SETUP.REG in your System subdirectory, which contains the original data.)

Step 2. Click File Run and type REGEDIT. In the dialog box that appears, select the Registered File Type for your particular word processor, such as Word or WordPerfect, then click Edit Modify-File-Type. (If no Registered File Type for your application appears in the RegEdit dialog box, click Edit Add-File-Type and insert command lines into the dialog box that appears. Use the dialog boxes for Word or WordPerfect that accompany this procedure as a guideline.)

Step 3. In the Modify File Type dialog box for your application, click the Print button to switch to your application's commands to print a file. Change the command line so it includes switches necessary to make your application run a macro. If your macro to convert a document to a plain text file is called "SaveText," for example, you would do the following in each of these applications:

Word for Windows: Change the command line to read WINWORD.EXE %1 /MSAVETEXT. Notice there is no space between the /M switch and the word SAVETEXT.

WordPerfect for Windows: Change the command line to read WPWIN.EXE /M-SAVETEXT.WCM. Notice the hyphen between the /M switch and the full filename of the WordPerfect macro file.

Step 4. Click OK to close the dialog box and save your changes. Close RegEdit.

Step 5. In the File Manager, highlight a filename that has the extension that should be associated with your application. For Winword and WordPerfect, for example, this is probably DOC.

Step 6. Click File Associate on the File Manager's main menu. In the dialog box that appears, check that your file extension already matches the desired association. If not, select the association, such as "Word Document" or "WordPerfect Document," then click OK to save the link.

Step 7. Open the Control Panel, double-click the Printers icon, and make sure the check box that says "Use Print Manager" is on. If it is, you can use the Program Manager to run the Print Manager, then minimize it to an icon so you can drag files to it from File Manager. If not, you'll have to click File Print in the File Manager to do the same thing to files.

Step 8. Find the accompanying Listing for Winword or WordPerfect for Windows, and follow the instructions to insert the appropriate SaveText macro into your application.

Step 9. Once you've saved your macro, exit your application. Save any changes you are asked about as the application closes. For example, Winword asks, "Do you want to save global glossary and command changes?" You should answer, "Yes."

Step 10. Select a filename in File Manager that has an extension associated with your application. Drop the filename onto the Print Manager icon, or click File Print. If everything goes well, you should see your application flash on the screen momentarily. After the application closes, you should see a new file, with a .TXT extension, appear in your File Manager window.

Customizing the database for more flexibility

Dropping filenames from File Manager to the Print Manager icon has a few limitations you should be aware of.

Probably the most important is that only one file at a time can be dropped on the Print Manager icon (or selected in the File Print menu item in File Manager). If you try to drop multiple files on the Print Manager icon, you simply receive a File Manager error message saying you cannot print multiple files. Since multiple files could easily be queued up and fed to an application one at a time, hopefully Microsoft will add support for multiple file-dropping in the next version of Windows.

Second, when you modify the meaning of the Print settings in the Registration Database, you lose the ability to print a file to a printer by dropping its filename on the Print Manager icon. I don't mind this, because if I need to print a modified file, I'm usually already in the application that's doing the modifying, and I can easily print the file from there.

But if you want to have your cake and eat it too, there is a way to preserve your ability to drop files on the Print Manager icon and also gain other Drag-and-Drop abilities.

To do this, select your Registered File Type in the RegEdit dialog box, then click Edit Add-File-Type. In the dialog box that appears, type in a different Identifier and File Type (since no two Identifiers can be the same), but use the same commands appropriate to your particular application. Click OK to exit. Then, in the File Manager, create a filename with a bogus extension, such as .TX1, and click File Associate to associate that extension with your new identifier.

For example, if your word processor is Word for Windows, you could associate the extension .TX1 with the print command WINWORD %1 /MSAVETEXT. Then, to convert the file MYLETTER.DOC to MYLETTER.TXT, select MYLETTER.DOC in the File Manager, click File Rename, type *.TX1 to rename it MYLETTER.TX1, and then drop the .TX1 file onto the Print Manager icon to create MYLETTER.TXT. It's a few extra steps, but it preserves the original meaning of Drag-and-Drop while still giving you access to your application's macro features through Drag-and-Drop.

I'm sure you can be much more imaginative with your own documents than the examples I've described here. In the future, Microsoft might give us more actions in the Registration Editor than just Open and Print. Perhaps we'll see User-Defined1, User-Defined2, and so on in upcoming releases.

Or perhaps this is an opportunity for a small software vendor to develop icons that you can drop filenames on. The icons process different command lines, based on the extension (or other features) of the dropped filename.

In any case, experiment with this technique until you get it working exactly the way you want. The macro languages in most Windows applications are quite powerful (as well as somewhat confusing and cryptic, a problem that cannot be addressed in this limited space), and should allow almost any customization you can think of.

Modifying Drag-and-Drop for Word for Windows 2.0

Take the following steps to change the Drag-and-Drop actions of Word for Windows filenames:

STEPS

Creating the Save Text Macro in Word

Step 1. Run REGEDIT.EXE and modify the Print option of the Word Document dialog box (see Figure 2-4) so it contains the following Command line:

```
c:\ww\winword.exe %1 /mSaveText
```

Use the appropriate drive and directory name for WINWORD.EXE on your system, if necessary. Notice that there is no space between "/m" and "SaveText." (If there is no "Word Document" file type listed in REGEDIT.EXE, click Edit Add-File-Type and fill in the dialog box that appears, using the command shown above in the Print option, and C:\WW\WINWORD.EXE %1 as the command in the Open option.) Click OK to save your changes.

Step 2. In the File Manager, select a document with a Word for Windows extension (such as .DOC), then click File Associate on the File Manager menu. Make sure that "Word Document" is selected in the Associate With list that appears, and click OK to save the association.

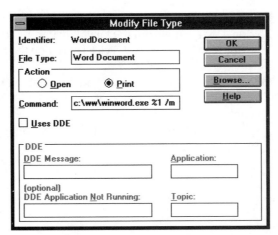

Figure 2-4: The Word for Windows default settings for Drag-and-Drop are modified in this dialog box of the Registration Editor.

Step 3. Start Word for Windows and click Tools Record-Macro.

Step 4. In the dialog box that appears, type SaveText as the Macro Name, and click OK. When asked whether to store the macro as Global or Template, select Global and click OK.

Step 5. When the dialog box closes, immediately click Tools Stop-Recorder.

Step 6. Click Tools Macro, then select the Macro Name "SaveText" in the dialog box that appears. Click Edit.

Step 7. You should see an editing window that contains only two lines:

Sub MAIN
End Sub

Replace these lines by typing in the lines shown in the "Word for Windows SaveText Macro" box in Listing 2-1. When finished, click File Save-All. Click "Yes" to save changes to Global: SaveText, then click "Yes" to save the "global glossary and command changes."

Step 8. Exit Word for Windows.

Step 9. In the File Manager, drag a filename with a valid Word for Windows extension from the File Manager and drop it on a minimized Print Manager icon. (Or click File Print on the File Manager menu.)

Step 10. You should see Word for Windows flash on the screen, and a message like, "File saved as C:\DIR\FILENAME.TXT." When you click OK, Word for Windows should close, and you should see your new plain-text file in the File Manager window, ready to use. Congratulations!

Listing 2-1:

```
' Word for Windows SaveText Macro — Public Domain — Brian Livingston 1993.
' Converts a fully-qualified filename (passed by DDE from File Manager) into a plain text file.

Sub MAIN
On Error Goto BYE
For i = Len(FileName$()) To 1 Step - 1              ' step through filename from right to left
        If Mid$(FileName$(), i, 1) = "." Then      ' if current character is a period,
                Goto SAVEIT                         ' break out of loop
        End If                                       ' i now equals position of period in filename
Next i                                               ' end For loop

SAVEIT:
newfile$ = Left$(FileName$(), i) + "TXT"            ' name is leftmost i characters plus TXT
FileSaveAs .Name = newfile$, .Format = 5           ' save as Format 5 (DOS Text With Breaks)
MsgBox "File saved as " + newfile$, "SaveText Macro" ' display completion message to user
FileExit 2                                           ' exit with no "save changes?" dialog box
BYE:

End Sub
```

You can modify this macro to take almost any action using Drag-and-Drop. For example, if you do not wish to see the "File saved as" message in the future (so the macro runs with no intervention), simply delete the line in the macro that starts with the word "MsgBox."

You can use DDE instructions directly, instead of command-line switches. For example, delete "%1 /mSaveText" from the Command line shown in Step 1. As a substitute, turn on the "Uses DDE" check box and put the line [FileOpen("%1")][SaveText] in both the DDE Message and DDE Application Not Running boxes. This accomplishes the same effect, without opening another instance of Winword, if a copy of Winword is already running.

In order to drop a filename on Print Manager while a copy of Word for Windows is already running (this starts another instance of Winword), you should have the command SHARE in your AUTOEXEC.BAT, a Winword requirement.

For more information on using Word for Windows macros, the very best source is *The Hacker's Guide to Word for Windows,* by Woody Leonhard and Vincent Chen (Addison-Wesley). My thanks to Mr. Leonhard for his help with this macro.

Modifying Drag-and-Drop for WordPerfect for Windows 5.2

Take the following steps to change the Drag-and-Drop actions of WordPerfect for Windows filenames:

STEPS

Creating the Save Text Macro in WordPerfect

Step 1. Run REGEDIT.EXE and modify the Print option of the WordPerfect Document dialog box (see Figure 2-5) so it contains the following Command line:

```
c:\wp\wpwin.exe %1 /m-savetext.wcm
```

Use the appropriate drive and directory name for WPWIN.EXE on your system, if necessary. Notice that there is a hyphen between "/m" and "savetext.wcm." (If there is no "WordPerfect Document" file type listed in REGEDIT.EXE, click Edit Add-File-Type and fill in the dialog box that appears, using the command shown above in the Print option, and c:\wp\wpwin.exe %1 as the command in the Open option.) Click OK to save your changes.

Step 2. In the File Manager, select a document with a WordPerfect extension (such as .DOC), then click File Associate on the File Manager menu. Make sure that "WordPerfect Document" is selected in the Associate With list that appears, and click OK to save the association.

Step 3. Start WordPerfect for Windows and click Macro Record.

Step 4. In the dialog box that appears, type SAVETEXT as the filename for the macro you are recording, and click Record.

Step 5. When the dialog box closes, press the Enter key once, then click Macro Stop.

Step 6. Click File Open. In the dialog box that appears, double-click the word "Macros" in the Quick List box. Select SAVETEXT.WCM in the Files list, then click the Open button.

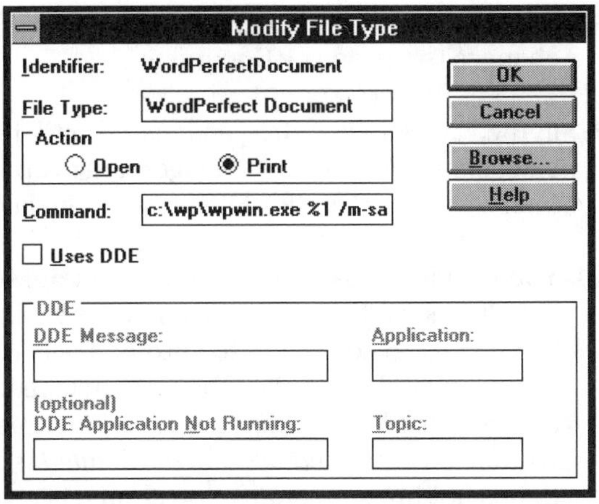

Figure 2-5: WordPerfect for Windows' default settings for Drag-and-Drop are modified in this dialog box of the Registration Editor.

Step 7. You should see a document that contains only two lines:

Application (WP;WPWP;Default;"WPWPUS.WCD")

HardReturn()

Delete the "HardReturn()" line, and replace it by typing in the lines shown in the "WordPerfect for Windows SAVETEXT.WCM Macro" box, Listing 2-2. When finished, click File Close, and click "Yes" to save changes to SAVETEXT.WCM.

Listing 2-2:
```
// WordPerfect for Windows SAVETEXT.WCM Macro — Public Domain — Brian Livingston 1993.
// Converts a fully-qualified filename (passed by DDE from File Manager) into a plain text file.

Application (WP;WPWP;Default;"WPWPUS.WCD")       // use WP functions defined in wpwpus.wcd
GetWPData (MacroVariable: filepath; SystemVariable: Path!)    // filepath = current document's drive and path
GetWPData (MacroVariable: docname; SystemVariable: Name!)     // docname = document's 8.3-format filename
StrPos (numchars; "."; docname)                  // numchars = number of chars through period
SubStr (shortname; 1; numchars; docname)         // shortname = first character through period
newfilespec := filepath + shortname + "txt"      // new name = path, short name, and TXT
FileSave (Filename: newfilespec;
    ExportType: ASCIIText!;
    Overwrite: Yes!)                             // save with new name as a plain text file
Prompt ("SaveText Macro"; "File saved as " + newfilespec; ; ;)   // display completion message to user
Pause                                            // wait for user to click OK or Enter
EndPrompt                                        // close if user clicks Macro Pause to unpause
```

Step 8. Exit WordPerfect. Click "No" when asked if you want to save changes to the empty Document1.

Step 9. In the File Manager, drag a filename with a valid WordPerfect extension from the File Manager and drop it on a minimized Print Manager icon. (Or click File Print on the File Manager menu.)

Step 10. You should see WordPerfect open on the screen, and a message like, "File saved as c:\dir\filename.txt." Click OK. WordPerfect has no macro command to automatically close the application, so you must double-click the System icon in the upper-left corner to exit WordPerfect. (The AppClose command described in the *WordPerfect for Windows Macros Manual* is a documentation error that is not implemented.) You should see your new plain-text file in the File Manager window, ready to use. Congratulations!

You can modify this macro to take almost any action using Drag-and-Drop. For example, you could change "txt" to "rtf," and change "ExportType: ASCIIText!" to "ExportType: WordRichTextFormat!" to convert files to a 7-bit format that you can send through e-mail services, but preserve formatting when the files are opened in applications that support RTF.

You cannot open a second instance of WordPerfect for Windows, so this Drag-and-Drop method works only when an instance of WordPerfect is not already running.

For more information on WordPerfect macros, a good book is *WordPerfect for Windows Power Tools,* by Gordon McComb (Bantam Computer Books). I'd like to thank Tom Creighton of WordPerfect for assisting with this macro.

Summary

In this chapter, I reveal a way to modify the meaning of Drag-and-Drop to perform almost any action that the macro language of a major Windows application is capable of.

▶ In the examples, you can see how Word for Windows, WordPerfect for Windows, and other applications can be made to save formatted files as plain text files when you drag a filename from the File Manager and drop them on the Print Manager icon.

▶ By modifying the example macros, you can modify Drag-and-Drop to take almost *any* action that an application's macro language is capable of.

Chapter 3
Mastering the Desktop Environment

In This Chapter

▶ I reveal several ways, some of them not documented in your Windows manual, to change the size and typeface of fonts used in the Windows system "shell" utilities.

▶ The first shell examined is the File Manager, which (in Windows 3.1) has a built-in ability in accommodate a variety of different fonts and sizes.

▶ Next, I describe several settings to change the look of the Program Manager, including changes you can put into your WIN.INI file that cannot be made through the Windows Control Panel.

Some of the new features of the File Manager and Program Manager in Windows 3.1 are as obvious as they are useful. For example, the new StartUp group in the Program Manager is visible as soon as you install Windows 3.1 — you simply drag icons into the group with your mouse.

Other new features of these two Windows "shell" programs are just as useful, but a lot more difficult to find out about.

Almost everyone, for instance, would benefit from using different fonts in the File Manager and Program Manager than the ones that Windows uses by default. But the best fonts (in my opinion) for these two essential utilities are mentioned nowhere in the Windows manual. Even Windows power users are usually in the dark about these hidden fonts.

Follow the steps in this chapter, and I think you'll find that you can make the File Manager and Program Manager even handier than ever.

First the Easy Part: File Manager

Making changes in the font that File Manager uses to display directories is fairly easy. You simply click Options Font on File Manager's main menu. This presents you with a Font dialog box, similar to the one that appears in many Windows applications.

When you install Windows 3.1, the File Manager defaults to an 8-point font named MS Sans Serif. This is a bitmapped font, which is identical to the old Helv screen font that was included in Windows 3.0.

MS Sans Serif is fine, but you may want to get more information in your File Manager windows than is possible with this font.

For this reason, I recommend that you scroll down through the list of fonts and select a typeface named Small Fonts. This typeface is small, indeed. It is available only in point sizes 4 through 7. Once you've selected this face, highlight "7" as the point size and click OK.

Although the resulting font in the File Manager is small, I think you'll find that it's easily readable (unless you have an old EGA monitor).

More importantly, you should find that you can get more data about each file into your File Manager windows. In one example (shown in Figures 3-1 and 3-2), you can get a whole additional column of information about each file. With the 8-point MS Sans Serif font, you can see only the filename, size and date for each file. Using 7-point Small Fonts, you can also see the last time each file was updated, or the file attributes (read-only, archive, and so on) — without needing to scroll through each window.

If you find 7-point Small Fonts a little too light for your tastes, try switching it to Bold instead of Regular. This makes it darker and more visible, although you lose the ability to display quite as many characters in a window.

Why did Microsoft include such a compact font with Windows 3.1 — and why don't we hear more about it?

The Small Fonts typeface was developed for those Windows applications that support a "Print Preview" function to display an entire page of a document on-screen. Since the type in these documents gets very small at the scale necessary to get a whole page on your monitor, Microsoft developed the Small Fonts typeface to represent characters as accurately as possible.

Small Fonts contains bitmapped fonts as small as 2 points, as you can see if you select "Small Fonts" in the Control Panel's Fonts dialog box. Applications can display these bitmapped fonts a lot quicker than they can scale a TrueType outline, such as Arial or Times New Roman. And because both Arial and Times look pretty much the same on your monitor at sizes below 8 point, nothing is lost on your Print Preview screen by using these tiny bitmaps. At 2-point size, actually, the Small Fonts resemble squashed ants more than recognizable letters. But that's fine when you're scanning a page layout in Print Preview mode.

Since the Small Fonts typeface isn't scalable, it's not very important in applications that print documents. But when you are primarily interested in getting as many characters as possible on-screen — as in File Manager or perhaps your spreadsheet program — Small Fonts can fill the bill perfectly.

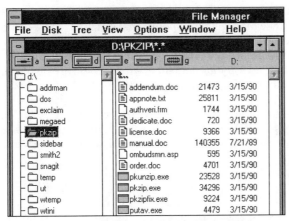

Figure 3-1: File Manager's default 8-point Sans Serif font allows only three columns in the right window.

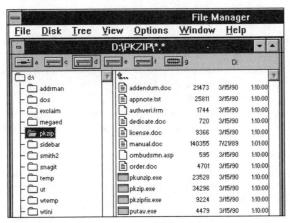

Figure 3-2: The little-known 7-point Small Fonts typeface fits a whole extra column in the right window.

You can select a variety of other fonts for use in File Manager, of course. Any text typeface you have installed, in fact, can become your display face for File Manager. (File Manager recognizes only typefaces that are marked as "text," however, so you can't play funny jokes on your friends by switching their File Manager windows to a symbol typeface like Wingdings!)

If you ever make presentations to meetings or audiences using Windows, you might want to set File Manager to 14-point Arial or larger. At 14-point size, Arial shows up on VGA screens in a thicker weight than the spindly characters that appear in Arial at 12 points and smaller. This makes the filenames in File Manager a lot easier to read for your audience, whether you are displaying Windows on a regular monitor or a large-screen projector.

Another typeface that comes with Windows that you might try is Courier Bold. This face is scalable in Windows 3.1, unlike Small Fonts. So you can make it as large as you want, if a fixed-width typeface would be preferable for your File Manager display.

The Next Step: Program Manager

How to change the fonts in Program Manager windows is even less well-understood than the fonts in File Manager. But if you use Program Manager as your primary Windows shell, changing fonts can pay off in benefits you'll notice every day.

The type font that appears under icons in Program Manager groups is that familiar 8-point MS Sans Serif that we met earlier in File Manager. For many people, this font is just too small and light to read clearly — especially when you're in a hurry to find that one icon you need.

The way this font can be changed to a better one, however, is not accessible through any of the Control Panel's dialog boxes. Nor is it documented anywhere in your Windows 3.1 manual.

In the following procedure, I'll explain each of the settings that control Program Manager's fonts. Some of these settings have been printed in Microsoft technical notes, but some have not. They work fine, however — they were simply left out of your documentation.

In the following example, we'll change the font used under icons in Program Manager groups from 8-point MS Sans Serif to a much clearer 10-point System font.

The System font is another typeface that you don't read much about. But it is installed automatically in every Windows setup. Windows uses the System font for the menu items in each Windows application. You may have noticed that Windows menus are easy to read, while Program Manager icon titles are small and indistinct.

Follow the procedure below, and your Program Manager icon titles will become easily readable.

STEPS

Changing Fonts Under Program Manager Icons

Step 1. In the File Manager, find the file WIN.INI in your Windows directory. Make a copy of this file, and call it WIN.OLD. If you make an error in the following procedure, you can always rename WIN.OLD to WIN.INI and restart Windows, and you'll be back exactly the way you started.

Step 2. Start Windows Notepad, and open the file WIN.INI. Scroll down until you see a section headed [Desktop], or click Search Find to search for [Desktop]. Insert three lines under that section heading, so it looks as shown below:

```
[Desktop]
IconTitleFaceName=System
IconTitleSize=10
IconTitleStyle=1
```

Step 3. Save the file, then exit and restart Windows. That's it!

You should notice that the icons in Program Manager now are much bolder and easier to read. Figure 3-3 shows Program Manager before the change, while Figure 3-4 shows Program Manager after the change.

These settings also affect the icons that appear at the bottom of your screen on the icon line.

In the [Desktop] section, the line that begins "IconTitleFaceName" specifies the typeface you want to use. In this case, we specified System, but this line could specify any typeface name you see in your Control Panel's Fonts dialog box.

"IconTitleSize" specifies the font size (10 points in this example). "IconTitleStyle" specifies normal or bold weight (0 means normal, 1 means bold). There is no setting for italic, but you can specify an italic face, such as Arial italic in IconTitleFaceName if you wish.

The first two settings are mentioned by Microsoft in its technical Resource Kit documentation, but the Style setting was left out. Nevertheless, each of these settings works with whatever fonts you have installed.

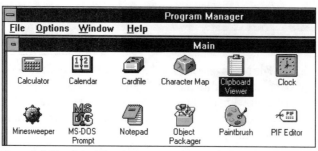

Figure 3-3: The default font in Program Manager is thin and hard to read quickly.

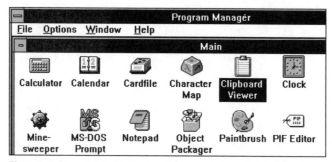

Figure 3-4: Changing to the System font can give you bolder icon titles.

The System font comes only in a 10-point bold weight, of course, so you get the same size and weight no matter what WIN.INI settings you specify. But these settings come in very handy if you choose a scalable font, such as Arial. You can make quite a dramatic-looking Program Manager if you specify Arial in, say, a 24-point bold weight. This might be useful if you make presentations to training groups or other audiences.

Once you've increased the size of your Program Manager icon titles, you may find that you need to increase the horizontal or vertical spacing between your icons. You can easily change the horizontal spacing. This setting is controlled by the Desktop dialog box in your Control Panel. Increasing this value adds more space between icons in your Program Manager to avoid icon titles running together. You may need to pull down the Options menu in Program Manager and turn *on* the Auto Arrange setting in order to make changes to the icon spacing take effect, but you don't need to restart Windows.

Since the horizontal spacing of Program Manager icons also determines the spacing of icons on your icon line, you may wish to take separate steps to configure both of these values. For example, you may want icons on your icon line to be close together (to get as many on the line as possible), but icons in Program Manager farther apart (so their titles don't run together). In this case, do the following.

STEPS

Changing Spacing Between Icons

Step 1. Change the Control Panel's Desktop dialog box to the value you want Program Manager icons to be spaced horizontally.

Step 2. Arrange your Program Manager groups the way you want them to appear.

Step 3. Save this layout in Program Manager by holding down your Shift key while you click File Exit with your mouse. Instead of exiting Windows, this saves your Program Manager configuration into your PROGMAN.INI file. This is an undocumented feature of Windows that was helpful to Microsoft testers who commonly set up new configurations, but works for everyone.

Step 4. Pull down the Options menu in Program Manager and turn *off* the Auto Arrange and Save Settings On Exit items. This way, changes to your Desktop will no longer affect your Program Manager layout.

Step 5. Return to the Control Panel's Desktop dialog box and set the Icon Spacing to the value you want for the icons on your icon line. When you click OK, your icon line and your icons in Program Manager will both space themselves according to the separate values you determined.

Changing the *vertical* spacing between Program Manager icons, however, cannot be accomplished using the Control Panel. Like the fonts themselves, the vertical spacing can only be accessed by making changes in WIN.INI that are documented only in obscure Microsoft technical papers.

If you need to change the vertical space between icons, open WIN.INI in Notepad and add a line to the [Desktop] section so it looks as follows:

```
[Desktop]
IconVerticalSpacing=75
```

Icons are usually 32 pixels high, and the titles under icons take up 30 to 40 pixels. Setting the IconSpacing value to 75, therefore, is normal for most systems. Save WIN.INI and restart Windows to see this change take effect. Make the number larger or smaller to change the vertical spacing to fit your particular font and display.

While you're changing the fonts used by Program Manager and your icon line, you may decide that you would prefer these fonts to be *smaller,* not larger. This might be the case if you want to get as many icons on your screen as possible.

In that case, you might want to specify Small Fonts as your "IconTitleFaceName," and 7 as your "IconTitleSize." As we saw when we used this bitmapped font in File Manager, the 7-point Small Fonts typeface is just about as small as you can make a typeface and still read it. But it may save you just enough space to get onto your screen those extra icons you need.

Hopefully, Microsoft will make the tuning of these Program Manager fonts easier in the next version of Windows. In the meantime, though, you can customize the selection of these fonts to make your system work for you — whether that means larger fonts for presentation purposes or smaller fonts to exploit every square inch of your display.

Summary

In this chapter, I describe ways to change the default fonts that File Manager and Program Manager use to display filenames, icon titles, and other information.

▶ The File Manager allows almost any installed Windows font to be used as its default font.

▶ The Program Manager requires a few undocumented lines to be edited into the WIN.INI file with a text editor.

Chapter 4
Program Manager Icons and Other Fixes

In This Chapter

I describe several fixes to icons and other aspects of the Windows interface.

▶ How to get more icons into the limited space of the Program Manager by eliminating the icon titles and displaying only the pictorial icons themselves.

▶ How to make an icon or set of icons appear in the Program Manager by typing a single command.

▶ How to move Windows or a Windows application to a new drive letter (to free up space on a crowded drive, for instance) without unnecessary labor to change all Program Manager icons manually to specify the new drive letter.

▶ How to quickly select multiple files and create "nested" directories in File Manager.

▶ How to change the "fixed" System and Notepad fonts.

▶ How to see the hidden "gang screens" that list all the developers of several Windows application packages.

▶ How to fix some irritating Microsoft Mail and Windows Terminal behaviors.

More than one person has asked me about turning the entire Program Manager into a button bar. These readers want to pack as many icons into one window as possible by eliminating the titles under the icons, leaving only the icons themselves.

Several people say they've already tried this, in fact, but have run into problems. First of all, if you try to leave the "Description" field blank in an icon's File Properties dialog box, Program Manager makes up a title using the filename in the "Command Line" field. The trick to getting an icon with *no* title is to type a *space* into the "Description" field. Program Manager accepts this as a valid string, and a blank space appears below each such icon. If you select one of these icons by clicking it once with your mouse, you may see a highlighted block of color beneath the icon (depending on the colors you have selected in the Control Panel). But otherwise these icons are title-less.

At this point, you can pack your Program Manager icons much closer together than you could with titles below each one. You can easily move the icons closer *horizontally* using the Icon Spacing setting in the Control Panel's Desktop dialog box. But to pack the icons closer together *vertically,* you need to use a setting described in the previous chapter that isn't in the Windows manual. Insert the line IconVerticalSpacing=36 (or any number of pixels) into the [Desktop] section of your WIN.INI file.

Once you restart Windows, another problem becomes apparent. The horizontal and vertical spacing of icons in the Program Manager also controls the icon line at the bottom of your screen. Now you can't see the titles under the icons of applications you've minimized.

One way to fix this is to save the configuration of your Program Manager icons and groups by holding down the Shift key and clicking File Exit-Windows. Then pull down Program Manager's Options menu and turn *off* Save Settings On Exit. Now you can set the horizontal and vertical spacing back to normal for your icon line, but still have the button-bar look you want in Program Manager.

This is when you run into the stickiest problem of all. If you press Ctrl+Esc to bring up the Windows Task List, you find that none of your running DOS applications show up! Windows 3.1 uses the icon *title* to make a DOS application's title bar. The Task List picks up each application's title bar. Therefore, the Task List shows a blank line for each DOS application that has no title under its icon. This makes it hard for you to switch to the one you want.

This problem can be fixed in two ways. The first way is to use a Windows Recorder macro to start each DOS application. In Program Manager, record Alt+F, R (File Run), then type DOSPRMPT.PIF, or whatever PIF runs the DOS app you want. Press Enter to run the PIF, then exit the DOS app and press Ctrl+Break to stop recording the macro. Finally, save the macro in a Recorder file.

You can make an icon run this macro with a tiny utility called Recrun. Save your macro with a key combination like Ctrl+Alt+F16 in the Recorder, then run this macro by making the command line of an icon look as follows: RECRUN FILENAME.REC CTRL+ALT+F16.

When you run a PIF in this manner, Windows uses the Window Title setting in the PIF as the title bar, thus making it visible in the Task List.

You can find Recrun in *Windows 3.1 Secrets*, or send $10 to Electron Image, Suite 252, 10342-107 St., Edmonton, Alberta, Canada T5J 1K2.

The second way to fix these blank lines in the Task List is to replace the Task List itself. Metz Task Manager 2.0a is a superior utility with many added functions, such as the ability to run commands. You can configure it to show running apps as names, icons with names, or just icons alone. This way you can see every application, even if it has a blank title. Task Manager sells for $49.95 plus shipping. You can get it by calling Metz Software at 800-447-1712 or 206-641-4525.

Personally, I find icons without titles to be more than a little confusing. But if you're one of the people who'd like to pack Program Manager as full of icons as the typical button bar, I hope I've given you the workarounds needed to do so.

Set Up Icons in Program Manager Groups Automatically

The Windows Setup program, SETUP.EXE, is kind of a programmer's oddity. It is both a Windows program and a DOS program. The Windows version executes when you click File Run and type SETUP, or click the Windows Setup icon in Program Manager. The DOS version is contained within the same file, in the place where most Windows applications simply run a short DOS program that displays the message, "This program requires Microsoft Windows."

One of the most interesting aspects of the Windows Setup program is its ability to add icons to the Program Manager *after* installing Windows. Click Options Set-Up-Applications, and you are given a choice of a) searching your system for any applications that Setup knows about, or b) specifying the name of a program. (This routine does not make icons for DOS applications without a valid PIF file.)

But even more intriguing are some Setup capabilities that don't appear in your Windows manual.

Clicking File Run in the Program Manager and typing SETUP /P has the effect of resetting the groups Main, Accessories, Games, and StartUp with the default icons they originally contained when you installed Windows 3.1. SETUP /P does not remove any icons from these groups. It merely ensures that all the icons that were originally supposed to be installed are, in fact, present in each group. If not, it adds them. (This *does* change the look of default icons you may have been using another icon file for.)

In Windows 3.0, SETUP /P does a "destructive" replace, removing any icons in these groups that are not on its list. And you must include a space before /P or the command won't work.

SETUP /P might be nothing but a curiosity — after all, how many times do you need to re-create Program Manager's default groups? But this can help you with a more pressing problem: how to add icons to different groups automatically on 10, 100, or 1000 users' machines.

To add a group window to a user's machine, you could always transfer a new group (.GRP) file to a diskette, copy it to the user's hard disk, click File New Program-Group OK, and then type in the group's filename. But you can't use this method to modify an existing group, such as the Main group, without wiping it out.

Here's a better way: SETUP /P gets its list of default groups and icons from a file in the System directory called SETUP.INF. This "information" file contains a wide variety of commands for the whole Setup program to carry out.

Make a backup copy of SETUP.INF. Then open it in DOS Edit or Windows Write. (In Write, click "No Conversion" when asked). SETUP.INF is a 57K text file that is too big for Notepad.

Search for "progman.groups" in this file. You will see the names of the four default groups, followed by several lines that define the icons in each group. Preceding each section are comments that explain the syntax of the lines.

Delete the lines in the [progman.groups] section, and the subsequent [Group*n*] sections of SETUP.INF. Insert new lines as follows:

```
[progman.groups]
Group1=Main
[Group1]
"My New Clock",clock,moricons.dll,80
```

Save SETUP.INF as a plain text file. (To do this in Write, click File Save-As, then make sure the "Save File As Type" box says "Text Files (*.TXT)" before clicking OK.) Then click File Run in Program Manager and type SETUP /P.

Voilà! Your Main group now contains an icon with the title "My New Clock," using CLOCK.EXE and the 80th icon from the MORICONS.DLL icon file.

Depending on your use of this technique, you may want to use the [new.groups] section of SETUP.INF instead of the [progman.groups] section. The [new.groups] section is designed to specify those icons that are written during a new install of Windows 3.1, while the [progman.groups] section is designed to specify those icons that are written when Windows 3.1 is installed over Windows 3.0.

The SETUP.INF file can also *delete* an icon. To do this, specify a title (such as "Clock") with nothing after it (no executable file name).

Sometimes SETUP /P doesn't restore the hourglass to a regular mouse pointer when exiting. Simply move your mouse to restore the pointer, if this occurs.

Copying a new SETUP.INF into a user's System directory, typing SETUP /P and then restoring the original file can save you hours that you might otherwise spend adding icons one at a time.

Moving a Windows Application Can Be *Almost* Pleasant

Many Windows users are gaining additional drive letters on their systems, and coming face to face with difficulties moving their Windows applications from a crowded drive letter to one with more room.

You might gain a new drive letter by a) adding a second hard drive to augment your original now-full one, b) installing a disk-compression utility that creates "phantom" drive letters, or c) partitioning a hard drive so it isn't all one big, impossible-to-find-anything C: drive.

In any case, moving Windows applications to a new drive letter isn't always a picnic. With DOS applications, you usually just moved a single subdirectory, perhaps edited your Path statement, and you were done. Thanks to the miracle of Windows, many things that were easy to do with DOS have become difficult or impossible. This is because Windows applications often reside in more than one directory, and usually hard-code information into one or more .INI files telling where to find everything.

Windows applications will write this information into only one of two places: (1) somewhere you will think to look, or (2) somewhere you won't.

Moving Windows itself turns out to be simpler than moving most Windows applications. Windows hard-codes very few drive letter specifications into its .INI files. It is assumed that the directory that contains WIN.COM will be on your Path. When you start WIN.COM, the program writes a variable ("winver") into the DOS environment. Using standard requests to Windows, applications can find the WIN.COM directory and the System subdirectory.

If you need to move Windows itself, therefore, you can usually use XCOPY /S at a DOS prompt to move all the files. You then make sure the new directory is on your Path. Finally, you must search CONFIG.SYS, AUTOEXEC.BAT, WIN.INI, SYSTEM.INI, and PROGMAN.INI (using DOS Edit or a similar text editor) and change any hard-coded references to the Windows directory. You should also run REG.EDIT and REG.EDIT_/V and change any hard-coded directory names in the Registration Database. (This is described in Chapter 2, "Make Drag-and-Drop Do Anything You Want.")

This leaves only one major file that you cannot edit manually, and it's a doozy. The *.GRP file (which the PROGMAN.INI file uses to load your application's group window) is not a plain text file and cannot be edited with a text editor. If you move a Windows application, any Program Manager icons that have an incorrect directory hard-coded into them revert to generic window icons and won't work any more. You have to re-create the icons by hand.

Windows doesn't hard-code the drive and directory names into most of its icons, such as Paintbrush, Control Panel, and so on. Windows simply says things like PBRUSH.EXE and finds these programs on the Path.

Many Windows applications, however, *do* hard-code drive letters into their icons. Moving these applications can result in hours of tedious make-work — unless you get one of two tools that have recently become available.

ChangeIt is a simple DOS utility written by Thom Foulks, the Business Fixtures columnist in *PC World.* If you have edited CONFIG.SYS, WIN.INI, and so forth, but face a troublesome group file in Program Manager, you simply run CHANGEIT MYAPP.GRP C: D:. All references to C: will be changed to D:. This will usually handle most cases, in which you change to a new drive letter but not a new directory name.

A more ambitious applet called Win Change will change drive letters *and* directory names, although the old and new directory names must be the same length. Win Change, a Windows application, will also edit multiple .INI and .GRP files with one click. Although backup files are made, this bulk editing is very dangerous and can cause lots of problems if you're not careful.

ChangeIt is a free utility; a copy of Change It appears on the diskettes that accompany *More Windows 3.1 Secrets;* see the Excellence in Windows Shareware section of this book. Win Change is $11 shareware. WCHG12.ZIP can be downloaded from CompuServe's WINSHARE forum, File Utilities library. (Future versions if this program will have a different filename on CompuServe.) CHGIT.ZIP can also be downloaded from this forum, if desired.

An Undocumented File Manager Feature Speedily Selects Files

I've found an undocumented feature of the Windows File Manager that can help you select multiple files in a File Manager directory window.

I've always felt that the documented way that File Manager makes you select multiple files is unnatural. If you wish to copy several text files to a backup disk, for example, you cannot simply click each one and drag the whole group to the backup disk drive icon. Every time you click a filename, all other filenames are deselected. Instead, these are the rules:

- To select multiple files, you must hold down the Ctrl key while clicking the second file, the third file, and so on. But don't hold down Ctrl while clicking the *first* filename! That has the effect of selecting not only the filename you clicked, but also any name that previously had been highlighted (usually the first name in that window). This can have disastrous consequences if you are selecting a few files to delete and wind up deleting an important file you had never consciously selected.

- To select a whole group of files (such as all the files that begin with the letter A), click the first filename in the group, then hold down Shift while you click the last filename in the group.

- To add a *second* group, you must hold down the Ctrl key while clicking the first filename in the second group. Then hold down Ctrl+Shift while clicking the last filename in the second group.

- You can't select multiple directories in a Tree window — only in a Directory window (this is a File Manager bug).

I don't know many people who can easily remember all these rules. I wish File Manager used a simpler method — just click all the filenames you want to select, and each one stays selected. (I've previously written that you can press the slash key to select all files in a directory window, or backslash to deselect all files — two other undocumented features.)

The easiest method, of course, would be for File Manager to allow users to select files by dragging a "rubber-band" over the desired filenames. As your mouse moved over the files, the ones you selected would change color — just as they do in the Macintosh Finder.

Until that day comes, we'll have to make do with this new trick I've found.

To see this trick work, start the File Manager and open a directory window for your Windows directory. Pull down the View menu and click Sort By Type. Find a file such as CALC.EXE (you should also see several other EXE files).

Now pull down the File menu, and click Select Files. Type "*.EXE" (without quotes) into the dialog box that appears, then click the Select button. You should see the CALC.EXE file selected in the directory window, along with any other files with an EXE extension.

The undocumented feature of File Manager is that you can type *any number* of file specifications into this dialog box, and clicking Select will select them. Type "*.EXE *.DLL" into the box and you'll see all EXE and DLL files selected.

Not only isn't this capability mentioned in the Windows manual, the Help text for the Select Files dialog box suggests that, to select multiple files, you should repeat the dialog box several times, typing a different spec each time.

Microsoft may not have documented this particular feature because the box doesn't use wildcards the same way as the plain old DIR command in DOS.

Try this: make a copy of CALC.EXE called CALC.EX. Then pull down the File menu, click Select Files, type "*.EX*," and click the Select button. CALC.EXE is selected, but CALC.EX is not. Nor do the file specs "*.EX?" or "*.E?*" select CALC.EX. But all these wildcard combinations do show the file in a DIR command at a DOS prompt.

If you can remember this bug — File Manager thinks "EX*" matches "EXE" but not "EX" — then the multiple-choice feature of the Select Files dialog box is a very convenient way to select a lot of different files quickly.

File Manager's nesting instinct

When the application I'm using doesn't allow me to save a file and create a new directory for it at the same time, it's irritating to have to switch to File Manager and make the directory before I can save the file.

Reader Jeff Pilch points out that you can use File Manager to make "nested" directories in a single command. To make several levels of directories, such as C:\CLIENTS\SMITH\DOCS, simply change to the root of the C: drive by clicking the C: drive icon and clicking the C:\ folder at the upper left of the Tree window. Then click File Create-Directory, and type CLIENTS\SMITH\DOCS. File Manager does the nesting for you, so you don't have to use the dialog box three times.

New Ways to Change System and Notepad Fonts

I've found a new, undocumented way to change the size and shape of Windows' menu and text fonts. This method is not mentioned in the Windows manual, Microsoft's Windows Resource Kit, nor in *Windows 3.1 Secrets*.

The bitmapped font that is used in Windows application menus is called the System font. I can think of three reasons you might want to change this font: 1) to make it smaller to fit in more text; 2) to make it larger so it is more readable; 3) or to change it to a fixed-pitch font rather than a proportional font.

The undocumented method to change the System font is to add a line to the [windows] section of WIN.INI as follows:

```
[windows]
SystemFont=coure.fon
```

This statement replaces the normal System font with a fixed-pitch Courier font. I don't actually recommend this — the System font works so well as a menu font precisely because it is proportional and bold, which Courier is not.

But you might have a good reason to change the *size* of the System font, rather than its pitch. In that case, you can try some other FON files that may be in your \Windows\System subdirectory.

If you installed Windows for a VGA system, the System font is probably called VGASYS.FON. You can make the System font smaller by changing your WIN.INI to specify EGASYS.FON, or larger by specifying 8514SYS.FON.

Fonts that don't match your screen resolution were probably never installed to your hard disk. You can decompress them off the Windows diskettes by copying EXPAND.EXE from Diskette 1 to your Windows directory (if it isn't already there), then typing a command like EXPAND A:\EGASYS.FO_ SYSTEM\EGASYS.FON at a DOS prompt in your C:WINDOWS directory. (Notice the underscore character in the compressed filenames.)

Windows 3.1 includes as many as 46 FON files on diskette, most of which you will never need. You may find some, however, that you prefer over the normal System font. Sets of fonts whose names end with E (as in COURE.FON) are VGA resolution. F signifies larger 8514 fonts, while B indicates smaller EGA fonts.

Another method to change bitmapped font sizes in Windows involves the [boot] section of SYSTEM.INI. If you installed Windows for a VGA system, this section probably looks as follows:

```
[boot]
fonts.fon=vgasys.fon
fixedfon.fon=vgafix.fon
oemfonts.fon=vgaoem.fon
```

The "fonts.fon" line determines the system font. (The SystemFont line in WIN.INI overrides this.) "Fixedfon.fon" determines the font used by Notepad and other fixed-pitch applications. "Oemfonts.fon" determines the font used by some applications that support the IBM PC-8 (line draw) character set.

If you'd like smaller text in Notepad, so you can see and edit more lines within one screen, change VGAFIX.FON to EGAFIX.FON. To make the text larger and more readable, use 8514FIX.FON.

You may need to use EXPAND.EXE, as described above, to decompress these files if they aren't already in Windows' System subdirectory.

Caution: Make these edits to SYSTEM.INI using SYSEDIT.EXE, which always creates a backup file with a SYD extension. If Windows doesn't find a valid FON file, it hangs, and you will need to copy SYSTEM.SYD over SYSTEM.INI to recover.

Windows Developers Are Getting the Whole Gang Involved

More and more Windows applications are emulating Microsoft's habit of including hidden screens showing the names of programmers and others who worked on the products. These displays — often quite colorful and animated — are called "credit screens," "gang screens," or "Easter eggs" (since you must hunt to find them).

I revealed in *Windows 3.1 Secrets* how to raise Microsoft's credit screen. For those who missed it, you click Help About in the Program Manager, then hold down Ctrl and Shift while you double-click the Windows logo in the upper-left corner of the About box. You must go through this whole procedure *three times* before you see an animation with Bill Gates or some other Microsoft character pointing at a scrolling list of developers' names.

PC Tools for Windows, version 1.0, has an undocumented feature that's similar. From the PC Tools Desktop application, click Help, then About Desktop. Hold down Ctrl+Shift and double-click *both mouse buttons* on the Desktop icon at the same time. It sometimes took me three or four times to get my mouse fingers coordinated well enough to make this work. But you only need to do the procedure once to see a window full of fireworks and developers' and support staff names.

Central Point Software, the publisher of PC Tools, has added a few nice wrinkles to the gang-screen scene. Double-clicking the screen makes it jump to the next scrolling section (to more quickly show your name to an impatient mom). Clicking once makes the fireworks seem to emerge from the area of the screen you clicked. And clicking once with the *right* mouse button makes the fireworks appear to emerge at random from the whole window. Thanks to Dennis Frazier of Pasadena, Maryland, for his help with this trick. (For information on PC Tools/W, call 503-690-8088.)

CorelDraw 3.0's credits screen is also accessed through the Help About box. Hold down Ctrl+Shift while you double-click the balloon logo. In the next window that appears, hold down your left mouse button, and a hot-air balloon rises with a banner listing the usual suspects.

But CorelDraw 4.0 has the best Easter egg of all. In the Help About box, you don't have to hold down Ctrl+Shift anymore — just double-click the balloon. Hold down your left mouse button to make the hot-air balloon rise. Then, click your right mouse button a few times, and *Flying Elvises* come parachuting out of the sky. This is reminiscent of Corel's stunt of hiring actual Flying Elvi for a promotion at Comdex/Fall 1992.

Finally, reader Mark Brady found a hidden screen in the new Borland Paradox for Windows. Pressing Shift+Alt+C in the Help About box scrolls the programmers' full names. And if you have a sound card, the credits play Peter and the Wolf when you get to Philippe Kahn's name!

Since these screens are so much fun to watch, I wish developers would simply put a Help Credits item on their menus. The names are always abbreviated (to keep pesky headhunters off the phones), so letting us see them couldn't hurt.

My Mail Runneth Over

Sales of Microsoft's Windows for Workgroups (WFWG) networking add-on are far below original projections. At this writing, only about 50,000 copies are reportedly selling per month, as opposed to a million-plus per month for Windows itself. This has led retailers who stocked up on the add-on to dub it Windows for Warehouses.

If you're using WFWG, however, you might like to know about an undocumented feature of the MS-Mail application that comes with the package. Since Mail doesn't clean up after itself very well, press and hold the Shift key while launching the app. A dialog box appears, which asks whether you want to recompress your mail (which takes a little while). "We've recovered many a megabyte of wasted space around here with this little goodie," says a reader.

Terminal Anxiety

People using the Windows Terminal application to connect to VAX/VMS minicomputers have been complaining. When they make a typing error and press Backspace, Terminal jumps to the beginning of the line and deletes the first character, instead of erasing the last character.

Michael Gordon passed along this fix, which was first posted on Internet by D.H. Frey of Agriculture Canada (frey@bcrsag.agr.ca). Make a backup copy of TERMINAL.EXE. Then, using a hexadecimal editor, look for hex 08 20 08 (backspace, space, backspace) around byte 166 in sector 80. Change this to hex 7F 00 00 (delete, nul, nul). VMS interprets this correctly as a destructive backspace.

You can use HexEdit, a program on the diskettes that accompany this book, to make this change.

Summary

In this chapter, I outline several workarounds for various problems and annoyances in Windows.

▶ Changing the Program Manager so it looks like a "button bar," with as many icons as you can cram into it.

▶ Setting up the SETUP.INF file so you can use it to insert icons into Program Manager on command.

▶ Utilities you can use to fix Program Manager groups after you've moved a Windows application, without having to change all the groups manually.

▶ Using File Manager tricks to select multiple files and create "nested" directories.

▶ Changing the "permanent" System and Notepad fonts to other fonts that may better suit your temperament.

▶ Finding the hidden "Easter eggs" in many Windows applications.

▶ Undocumented hacks for Microsoft Mail and Terminal.

Chapter 5
Making File Manager Your Own

In This Chapter

▶ I describe ways for you to get the most out of the File Manager in Windows 3.1.

▶ If you're still using Windows 3.0, I explain how to make a few simple changes that speed up the old File Manager to almost the same level as the new one.

▶ I show you a variety of ways to gain back in File Manager a number of DOS commands that are difficult or impossible to carry out in Windows — unless you know the secret.

Windows users have developed something of a love-hate relationship with the Windows File Manager. It seems that everyone who has ever used the File Manager either depends on it as their primary disk-management tool or avoids it at all costs.

There's no reason to go to extremes over the File Manager, though. When configured properly, it can be a useful tool — an accessory to be taken advantage of when appropriate, used alone or in conjunction with other utilities.

The File Manager in Windows 3.1 is greatly improved over the slow, ungainly File Manager in Windows 3.0. For this reason alone, it's worth exploring. And if you take a few minutes of your time to make the File Manager work the way *you* want it to, you may find that you'll want to join the ranks of PC users who use File Manager as their Windows home base. (The File Manager in Windows for Workgroups is even better, with its own button bar, and many of the techniques in this chapter work with that version of File Manager, too.)

Configuring File Manager

Even with the more-nimble File Manager that comes with Windows 3.1, a few changes are necessary to make this application truly work for you.

When you first install Windows 3.1 and start File Manager, it probably looks like Figure 5-1. The File Manager covers the screen and displays one window containing a single disk drive and its directories.

You can probably improve a great deal on this configuration. Before you make any changes, however, you should know how File Manager stores the configuration you choose.

Pull down the Options menu. You may see that the Save Settings on Exit menu choice is turned on. When it is, a small check mark appears beside the item, as shown in Figure 5-2.

At this point, click Save Settings on Exit once to remove the check mark and turn *off* the Save Settings option. After you finish fine-tuning your configuration, you'll save the new File Manager configuration using an undocumented feature. At that point, hold down the Shift key and click File Exit. You will notice that you don't exit File Manager. Instead, File Manager writes the positions of all open windows into a file called WINFILE.INI. This file will ensure that your preferred directory windows appear — in the arrangement you set up — the next time you start File Manager.

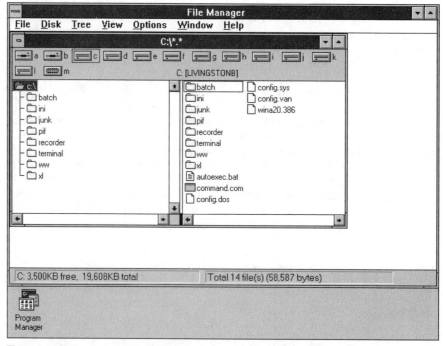

Figure 5-1: When you first install Windows 3.1, your File Manager probably looks like this. A single drive is displayed in a small window.

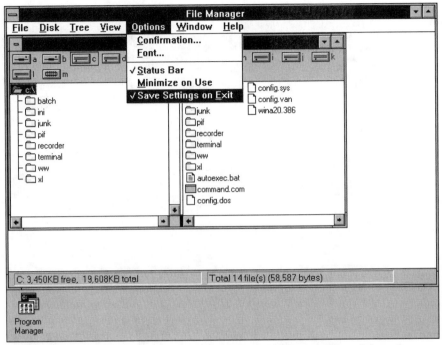

Figure 5-2: Before you start configuring the File Manager to suit your needs, pull down the Options menu and make sure the Save Settings on Exit item is turned *off.*

Turning off the Save Settings on Exit option prevents you from transforming a temporary arrangement you might have used in a Windows session into the permanent arrangement that File Manager uses to start subsequent sessions. Of course, you can use either method you prefer.

You will probably find that the most convenient working arrangement is two large windows side-by-side. This is because most people spend the majority of their file-management time comparing one directory with another, moving files from one directory or drive to another, and so on. This is also the common configuration used by successful DOS file-management utilities such as Norton Commander and Xtree.

If you open two windows in the Windows 3.1 File Manager and click Window Tile, however, you don't wind up with this arrangement at all. Instead, you get two stacked windows, as shown in Figure 5-3. This arrangement doesn't show much of the directory tree in either window, making it hard to compare two disk drives or two directories.

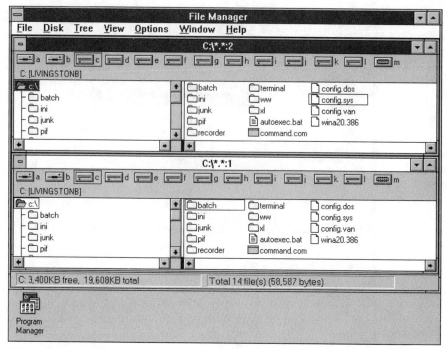

Figure 5-3: When you open two directory windows, then click Window Tile, the File Manager doesn't place them side-by-side, as you'd expect. It stacks them one on top of the other, like this — which may be less than convenient for your disk-management needs.

You can't configure two windows side-by-side using the Windows 3.1 File Manager's menu, but the following trick sets up the configuration easily.

First, start with a single directory window on-screen. Pull down the Window menu and click New Window. A smaller duplicate of your original window should appear.

Now hold down the Shift key and click Window Tile. At this point, the directory windows reshape themselves into a configuration with two on the left and two on the right, as shown in Figure 5-4. The Shift key used in conjunction with Window Tile is an undocumented feature of Windows 3.1 that makes two windows appear side-by-side, instead of stacked on each other. When you have three or more windows open, Shift Window Tile arranges your windows differently, depending on the number of windows. Try it to see how you like each arrangement.

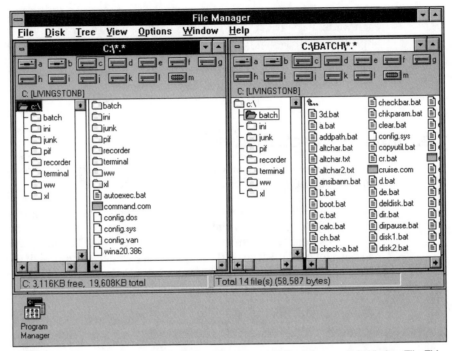

Figure 5-4: With two directory windows open, hold down Shift while you click Window Tile. This undocumented feature gives you two perfectly sized, side-by-side directory windows.

This Shift key behavior is supposed to be standard procedure for Windows applications that conform to the Multiple Document Interchange (MDI) developed by Microsoft. MDI principles are used in programs like Program Manager and File Manager, which can display more than one "child" window inside their boundaries. But this standard didn't get into the MDI libraries that shipped to developers of Windows 3.0 applications, and doesn't appear until a later version of those libraries. Meanwhile, even Microsoft Excel and Word for Windows, at this writing, don't support the Shift key's handy role-reversal of the Window Tile command.

A side-by-side layout in File Manager is a particularly convenient configuration when you are moving files from a floppy disk to your hard disk — or backing up hard disk files to a floppy. Simply click the icon for drive A: or B: and the contents of the diskette in that drive become visible in that window.

Once you've got the basic layout, customize it to fit your particular system. In the accompanying figures, each window contains a directory tree on the left, and a list of directories and file names on the right. In this view (obtained by pulling down the View menu and clicking Tree-and-Directory), you can drag each window's vertical "dividing line" to the left or right, so it divides the space appropriately between the two functions. When your mouse is positioned over this dividing line, your mouse pointer turns into a vertical bar with two bold "left-and-right" arrows on either side. Simply hold down your first mouse button and drag the dividing line to the place you want it.

Configuring for multiple windows

Once you've created two side-by-side windows, you might want to explore other configurations that could also suit your needs.

For example, you might commonly use only three or four directories on a regular basis. By sizing a window for each of these directories, and then placing an icon representing each directory at the bottom of the File Manager window, you can have immediate access to each directory whenever you wish to view it.

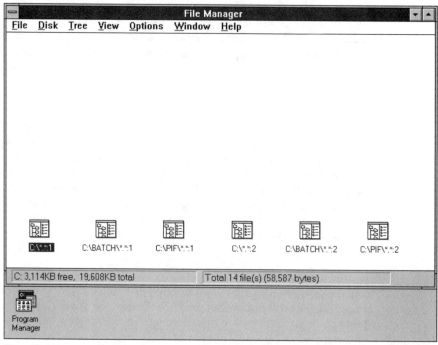

Figure 5-5: You can easily create minimized icons that represent directories that you often need to examine. When you double-click an icon, it expands to fill either the left half or the right half of the File Manager screen, as you've previously sized it (shown in the next figure).

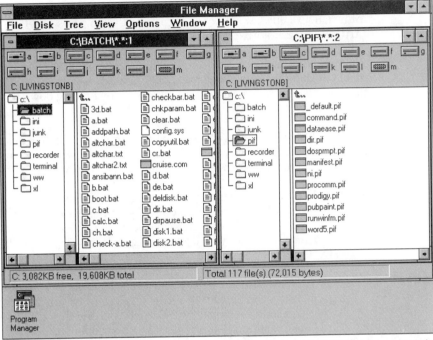

Figure 5-6: Double-clicking the icons for the C:\BATCH directory and the C:\PIF directory, shown in Figure 5-5, expands them to fill their respective places in the File Manager window. By careful planning, you can set up icons for each of your applications this way.

Look at Figure 5-5. In this illustration, I've created two windows for each of several directories, and then clicked the Minimize button to reduce them to icons. If I want to compare the contents of, say, the C:\BATCH directory with the C:\PIF directory, I simply double-click the two icons. Each window expands to fill the position that I earlier set for those windows, as shown in Figure 5-6.

Of course, you can do the same thing by changing the contents of two existing side-by-side windows to show the directories you want. My point is simply that you have many ways to configure the Windows 3.1 File Manager to fit the way you like to work.

Power shortcuts for File Manager

Almost everyone who uses File Manager learns quickly that clicking one of the drive icons with a mouse changes the current window to display a directory of that drive. But several other File Manager shortcuts are not nearly as well known.

If you happen to have your hands on the keyboard instead of on your mouse, for instance, a quick way to change to drive C: is to press Ctrl+C. Pressing Ctrl+D switches to drive D, and so on.

Whether you use the keyboard or the mouse, you can force File Manager to display all subdirectories when you switch to a new drive — no matter how many levels of subdirectories there may be — by holding down the Shift key when you select the drive.

If you click, say, the C: drive icon with your mouse while holding down the Shift key, File Manager displays all levels of subdirectories when it opens the window for drive C:. From the keyboard, Ctrl+Shift+C also displays all levels.

The fact that the File Manager in Windows 3.0 *always* searched hard drives for subdirectories before displaying even a top-level directory tree is the primary reason it got a reputation for being slow. Searching for subdirectories was necessary because the Windows 3.0 File Manager always displayed a little plus sign (+) on the icons of directories that had subdirectories.

This search process was turned off for the File Manager in Windows 3.1, representing a major gain in *apparent* performance. You can turn it back on, though, by clicking Tree Indicate-Expandable-Branches — and this will make File Manager 3.1 almost as slow as File Manager 3.0. In my opinion, it isn't worth the performance hit.

One trick that is definitely worth the effort, though, quickly redraws any directory window. For example, when you change a diskette in a floppy drive (in either version of File Manager), you don't have to reselect the drive with your mouse in order to update the window to show the new files. You can simply press F5, which does the same thing as clicking Window Refresh on the menu.

Many File Manager users are not completely familiar with the shortcuts available for selecting groups of files. You probably know that clicking a filename with your mouse selects (highlights) that file. And you may know that you need to hold down the Ctrl key while clicking the mouse in order to select additional files after the first one.

But did you know that you can click one file in a directory, and then select *all* the files in that directory simply by pressing the Slash key? To deselect all files in a directory (except the one that was originally highlighted), press the Backslash key. The File Manager menu says that the way to select and deselect all files is Ctrl+Slash and Ctrl+Backslash. But Slash and Backslash are the undocumented methods to do this, and they work exactly the same way as the documented methods (and save you keystrokes).

You can also select all the files from the currently selected file to the next filename you click by holding down the Shift key while clicking the mouse.

Even more important than selecting files is moving and copying them, because you can inadvertently "lose" files if you're not sure what happened when you dragged a group of files from one place to another.

When you drag a group of files within File Manager, Windows always *moves* the files from one directory to another if the source and the destination directories are on the *same* disk drive. But Windows *copies* the files if the source and destination directories are on *different* drives.

You can override this default behavior by using the Ctrl and Alt keys. When you hold down the Ctrl key while dragging files, that group of files is always *copied,* regardless of the source and the destination. (I remember this by recalling that both Ctrl and Copy begin with the letter C.) When you hold down the Alt key, files are always *moved* when dragged.

Customizing your File Manager fonts

One of the nicest new features of the Windows 3.1 File Manager is the ability to change the size and typeface of the filenames that appear in the application. You can make the listings larger or smaller, to make them more legible or pack more names into the same space.

To do this, pull down the Options menu and click Font. A dialog box appears, listing all the typefaces available on your system, as shown in Figure 5-7.

When you first install Windows 3.1, File Manager uses 8-point MS Sans Serif as the screen font. But a little-known trick, as described in Chapter 3, is to configure the File Manager instead to use a more compact font: 7-point Small Fonts. The Small Fonts file contains screen fonts that are intended to be used by applications when they display print-preview screens. But if your eyes are good, selecting Small Fonts will mean that more information will be displayed in each File Manager window than can be displayed by MS Sans Serif or TrueType fonts, such as 8-point Times New Roman.

Alternately, you can select a *larger* font, if you prefer legibility at a distance over the ability to see more files in each window.

Also be sure to pull down the View menu and configure each window to show filenames the way you prefer. For example, you can sort filenames alphabetically, or by date, size, or extension.

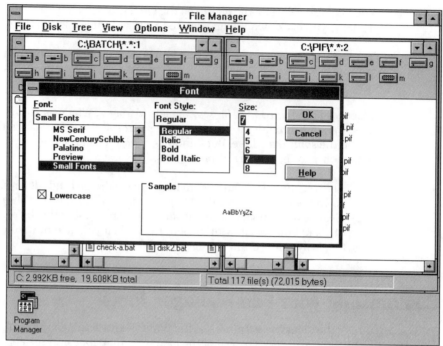

Figure 5-7: The Options Font item on the File Manager's main menu gives you access to all the text typefaces installed in your system. By choosing a compact face, such as 7-point Small Fonts, you can get more filenames to appear in each directory window on your screen.

Some people also use the View menu to get rid of the directory tree in each window, leaving only the filenames themselves. Since moving up and down the directory structure in a window shows the directories at each level (just as the directory tree window does), you may be able to save valuable space by eliminating the trees and leaving more room for the directories themselves.

Customizing the menu itself

The Windows 3.1 File Manager has an important capability that Windows 3.0's File Manager doesn't have — and it isn't mentioned in your Windows manual.

The File Manager's menu itself is customizable. You can add menu choices that carry out tasks you yourself determine, such as opening Notepad or starting a DOS prompt.

One software vendor that has taken advantage of this capability is Wilson
WindowWare with its File Commander application. When you install File Commander, it adds a Commander menu item to the File Manager's main menu, as
shown in Figure 5-8. The best thing about this drop-down menu is that it's fairly
easy for you to add *any* process you might want to keep handy.

File Commander comes with a "batch language" for Windows, which supports
some 200 or so commands. By stringing these commands together, you can
start Windows applications, change the size and color of objects, and automate
a variety of steps across applications.

This is a language functionally similar to WindowWare's earlier Windows products, Command Post and WinBatch. It's also the same as the batch language
built into the Norton Desktop for Windows.

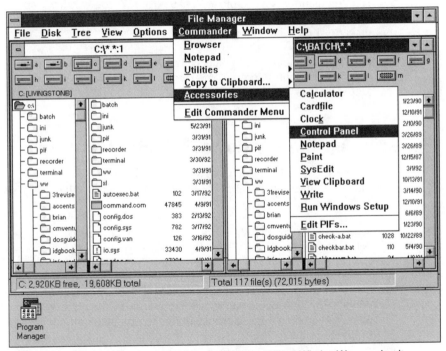

Figure 5-8: The File Commander, an add-on product from Wilson WindowWare, makes it
possible to add your own pull-down menus to the Windows 3.1 File Manager. You can easily
customize the list of commands to include any application you use, even DOS and Windows
batch files.

If you wanted to add a menu item, for example, that would load Notepad and open WIN.INI into it for editing, you would add lines like these to the text file that accompanies File Commander:

```
&Notepad WIN.INI

    run("notepad.exe","win.ini")
```

In this example, the ampersand (&) before the N in Notepad indicates that that character will be underscored in the pull-down menu. This acts as a keyboard shortcut, so the command can be run from the keyboard as well as with a mouse. The mention of "win.ini" in the RUN line acts as a parameter to the program that is being executed, NOTEPAD.EXE in this case. If you wanted to define a menu item that ran Notepad without loading a file, you would simply type nothing in between the second set of quote marks.

File Commander is available for $49.95 from Wilson WindowWare, 2701 California Ave. SW, #212, Seattle, WA 98116; 206-937-9335. It is also featured on the diskettes that accompany *Windows 3.1 Secrets*.

Another File Manager add-on is called WizManager. This program is described in its own chapter later in *More Windows 3.1 Secrets,* and is found on the diskettes that accompany this book.

Speeding up the Windows 3.0 File Manager

If your version of Windows is 3.0 rather than 3.1, you can actually speed up the old File Manager so it's almost as fast as the new one. All it takes is a short keystroke macro.

As we saw earlier, the Windows 3.0 File Manager is slower than the new one primarily because it must scan for subdirectories every time you open a window for a new drive.

The old File Manager needs to read a drive only once, when it first opens a window for that drive. If you keep windows open for each drive that you normally access, switching between those drives is almost instantaneous — just as it is in Windows 3.1.

You can make File Manager read these drives automatically, every time you start Windows 3.0, by recording and playing back a short, eight-keystroke macro using the Recorder application.

The following steps describe how to record such a macro. This macro will open windows for drives C: and D:, plus a window for a Directory Tree. If you don't have a drive D:, you can try this macro by substituting drive A: (with a diskette in the drive), or another directory on drive C: besides the root directory.

Before recording this macro, make sure that the RUN= line of your WIN.INI includes the filename WINFILE.EXE, which starts File Manager. Then restart Windows, and make sure that the File Manager is the foreground application, showing only the current drive (such as C:) in a window.

Next, start the Recorder by clicking File Run in the Manager File, typing RECORDER.EXE, and clicking ok. You should see an empty dialog box, similar to Figure 5-9. Pull down the Options menu, and make sure the following options are on: Control+Break Checking, Shortcut Keys, and Minimize On Use. Once these options are set, you can begin recording the actual macro.

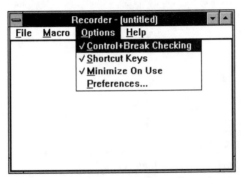

Figure 5-9: You can use the Windows Recorder to record a macro that speeds up the Windows 3.0 File Manager to be almost as fast as the one in Windows 3.1. When you start the Recorder, it displays this almost-empty dialog box with a simple menu bar.

Pull down the Macro menu and click Record. You should see a dialog box similar to the one shown in Figure 5-10. Fill in the form so it names your macro "Auto-arrange" and assigns the macro to the Ctrl+Shift+F16 key combination, as shown. (You can assign this macro to an imaginary key like F16 since you are going to run the macro automatically instead of pressing the key manually.)

Once you've filled in the dialog box, press Enter to start recording the actual macro. Type the following eight keystrokes. Their actions will occur in the current File Manager window.

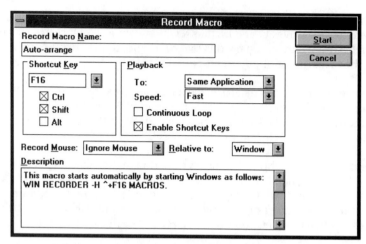

Figure 5-10: When you click Macro Record in the Recorder, you see this set of options for your macro. By setting the macro to work only in the Same Application, you can ensure that this macro will operate only on the Windows File Manager, not on other applications.

Keystroke:	Action:
Enter	Opens a window for the C: drive
Ctrl+Tab	Switches back to the Directory Tree
Ctrl+D	Displays the D: drive
Enter	Opens a window for the D: drive
Shift+F4	Tiles all open windows
Ctrl+Break	Stops recording the macro
Alt+S	Selects Save Macro
Enter	Confirms Save Macro

Now that you've recorded these keystrokes, use Recorder's File Save command to save the macro into a file in the Windows directory named MACROS. (the period at the end is important, so no extension is saved on this macro file).

You can now test the macro by starting Windows, loading the Recorder and running the macro. To do this, start Windows with the following command line from your DOS prompt:

```
win recorder -H ^+F16 macros.
```

This command line starts Windows and runs the Recorder application. The "-H" switch forces Recorder to look for a hotkey macro named Ctrl+Shift+F16 in the file MACROS. Again, the period at the end of "macros." is important, so Recorder looks for a filename with no extension.

If everything runs as expected, you should end up with a File Manager window that looks similar to Figure 5-11. Click on the title bar of the C: window, then click the D: window. Switching between the two is now almost instantaneous. The File Manager reads these drives when Windows first starts. This makes Windows take a little longer to load, but it should save you time nearly every time you use the Windows 3.0 File Manager during the day.

Using vs. replacing the File Manager

A variety of third-party replacements for the File Manager (as well as the Program Manager) have become available since the first shipment of Windows 3.0 in 1990. The best-known of these replacements is probably the Norton Desktop for Windows, but other substitutes are also making themselves known in the marketplace.

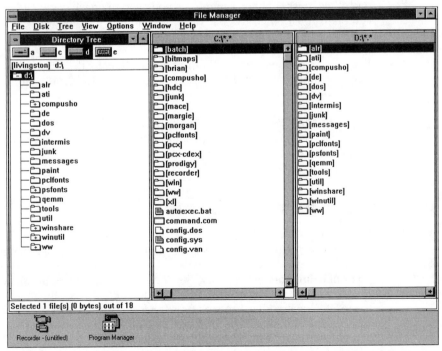

Figure 5-11: After running your macro in the Windows 3.0 File Manager, you should see a configuration like this, with two directory windows side-by-side. You can switch from one window to the other almost instantaneously, just as in the Windows 3.1 File Manager.

You may find that you prefer using one of these utilities in favor of the File Manager bundled with Windows. Each person has his or her own work habits, which different disk-management utilities try to emulate or support.

But — at least in Windows 3.1 — there is no reason not to configure the built-in File Manager to fit your work style as best it can.

Try it — you may like it.

Recovering Commands Microsoft Left Out of Windows

After all these years, there are still many things that are easy to do with a one-line command in DOS, but difficult or impossible to do in Windows.

People often ask me, for example, how to print a file listing from the Windows File Manager. You can see the filenames well enough on the screen, but there is no way to print a list of the filenames to a printer. And printing out such a list is one of the most common operations you need to do when cleaning up a disk, comparing the contents of one disk with another, looking over a list of files at home, and so on.

You could, I suppose, press Alt+Print Screen to copy the File Manager window into the Clipboard and then paste this graphic into Paintbrush and print it from there.

But that's a horrible prospect. In DOS, printing a directory listing is as easy as typing DIR>LPT1 at a command prompt. What's needed is a way to issue such a simple command in Windows.

Adding basic printing features

Until Microsoft adds directory listings and other basic features to Windows, you can use the following tricks to print file listings and do many other things.

To print a directory listing, click File Run in File Manager. (You can also use Program Manager or almost any other program that has File Run on its menu.) In the File Run box that appears, type the following line and click OK:

```
command /c dir c:\ > lpt1
```

This line starts a secondary copy of COMMAND.COM, which runs a DOS session under Windows. (The /C switch means "run the following Command.") The command DIR C:\, of course, creates a directory listing. The greater-than sign (>) redirects the output to your printer. In this case, the printer is on the LPT1 port, but you could use LPT2, COM1, or any other port with a text printer attached. You could also redirect the output into a text file by specifying C:\FILENAME.TXT or whatever, instead of LPT1.

When you click OK, Windows looks for a Program Information File called COMMAND.PIF. If it finds none, it uses instead a file called _DEFAULT.PIF (the first character is an underscore), which comes with Windows 3.*x*. The settings in the PIF file determine the characteristics of the DOS session: full-screen or windowed, etc.

When you run the command, a DOS session flashes on your screen for a moment, then disappears. If you want the DOS session to remain on screen after it runs your command, turn off the "Close Window On Exit" box in the PIF, using the PIF Editor.

You can do many other things with COMMAND/C, such as generating a complete listing of every directory and every subdirectory on a disk by typing the following in a File Run dialog box:

```
command /c tree c:\ > c:\filename.txt
```

This creates FILENAME.TXT, which uses line-draw characters to indicate the relationship among directories. You can also list every file, using lower-ASCII characters, by adding the switches /F/A after c:\ in the TREE command.

To print disk files containing line-draw characters (which Windows cannot), click File Run and type the following:

```
command /c copy c:\filename.txt lpt1
```

Notice that, in this case, there is no greater-than sign in the command. This is because LPT1 is the target of the COPY operation, and there is no need for the redirection symbol.

Comparing files in Windows

I often need to find out whether two files are exactly the same. If so, I can delete one. If not, I may be able to delete the older version.

In DOS 5.0 and higher, it's easy to compare files using the FC (File Compare) command. But in Windows, there is no way to do this at all — unless you start COMMAND.COM with the /C switch and employ FC. For instance, to compare two files in Windows using FC, click File Run and type:

```
command /c fc file1 file2
```

Replace "file1" and "file2" with the full names of two existing files, such as WIN.INI and WIN.BAK. When you click OK, a DOS session opens and you can read the output of FC. This will be a message like "No differences encountered," or a listing of the differences between the two files.

The FC command, unfortunately, closes the DOS session before you can read the output. To keep this window open, copy your _DEFAULT.PIF file to the name FC.PIF. Then use the PIF Editor to change the box Close Window On Exit so it is *off*. When you start the FC command, Windows will use the settings in FC.PIF, and its output will stay on the screen until you type EXIT to close the session.

Automating common commands

If you frequently use commands like those above, you may find that you wish to automate them. For example, the following command prints a list of every file in every directory on your disk:

```
command /c tree c:\ /f /a > lpt1
```

To place this command on a single key combination, use the Windows Recorder. I load a Recorder macro file just for this purpose every time I start Windows, and it's easy to record commands like TREE. Although Recorder cannot play keystrokes into a DOS session, you can play back any DOS command or start any batch file by using a File Run dialog box in this way.

STEPS

Recording Frequently Used Commands

Step 1. Make sure the Windows File Manager is running. (Or that you're running a program that has File Run on its menu.) Start the Recorder by clicking File Run and typing RECORDER.EXE. Minimize the Recorder window, make sure the File Manager window is the current window, then restore the Recorder window. This means that the File Manager will be the topmost window when you start recording.

Step 2. On the Recorder menu, pull down the Options menu. Make sure that Control+Break Checking, Shortcut Keys, and Minimize on Use are all *on*.

Step 3. Click Macro Record. In the dialog box that appears, give the macro a name like Print All Filenames. Assign a shortcut key, such as Ctrl+Alt+F. Set the Playback to the "Same Application," and Mouse to "Ignore Mouse." Then click Start to begin recording your macro.

Step 4. The File Manager should now be in the foreground. Do not use your mouse. Press Alt+F, R to pull down the File menu and use the Run command. Type the TREE command line COMMAND /C TREE C:\ /F /A > LPT1, then press Enter. When the command is finished, press Control+Break to stop recording. Press Alt+S, Enter to save the recording, then File Save in Recorder.

That's it. As long as your macro file is loaded and your File Manager or other shell is running in a window, you can use this key combination from any application. You can, of course, place these commands or batch files in icons, but then you must switch to the Program Manager to run them.

Shortcuts to internal DOS commands

If you need to use internal commands like DIR often, you can put them into PIF files and then run them without typing the whole command line.

To do this, open the PIF Editor from Program Manager by clicking File Run and typing PIFEDIT. In the Program Filename box, type the word %COMSPEC%. This is an environmental variable (you must include the percent signs) that always contains the location of COMMAND.COM. In the Optional Parameters box, type /C DIR > LPT1 (or whatever your command line is). When you save this PIF, click OK to ignore the "invalid extension" message you get. This error message is erroneous.

You can even make a PIF that allows you to specify *any* DOS command. In the Program Filename box, type %COMSPEC%, and in the Optional Parameters box, simply type a question mark (?). In the Window Title box, type "Type /C and any DOS command" (without the quote marks). Save this PIF file as DOS.PIF. Now any time you need to run a single DOS command, click File Run, type DOS, and click OK. A dialog box similar to the one in Figure 5-12 appears.

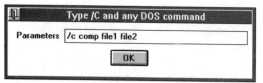

Figure 5-12: By correctly filling in the parameters to DOS.PIF, you can make a dialog box like this one appear by clicking File Run, typing DOS, and then typing /C and any DOS command you like — useful for internal commands and commands that require redirection.

You can type any DOS command into this box, and the command runs without requiring you to open a DOS session first. This trick is especially useful when you commonly need to run internal DOS commands and commands that require redirection (in other words, commands that use the greater-than [>], less-than [<], or pipe [|] symbols).

If you run commands that require you to read the output on the screen (such as FC, which closes the DOS window before you can read its File Comparison output), turn off the Close Window On Exit setting in your PIF file. This makes the session remain visible until you type EXIT to close it.

Ejecting the last page from a laser printer

If you run DOS commands like these that send output to a laser printer, you may notice that the last page of output doesn't emerge automatically. You can walk over to the printer, take it off-line and press the "form feed" button to eject the final page. However, this is inconvenient, especially if you are using a printer that is more than a few steps away, such as a network printer. Fortunately, there's an easier way to eject these pages.

To use this method, create a two-byte file called RESET.PRN. This file should contain nothing but an Escape character and a capital letter E. Esc-E is the command for a "printer reset" on all Hewlett-Packard LaserJet printers and compatibles. If a page is partially printed, but hasn't yet been ejected by the printer, the reset command ejects the page (as well as setting the printer back to its default values, in case the font or other settings were temporarily changed).

Sadly, Windows won't allow you to insert Escape or any other control characters into a file. You can't type a control character in any File Run dialog box. And you can't create a batch file containing such a character using Windows Notepad, either.

One way to create RESET.PRN is to use the Edit utility available in DOS 5.0 and higher. Edit ordinarily can't type control characters. You can, however, insert control characters into batch files with Edit by using the following undocumented feature: First press Ctrl+P, then hold down Alt while you type on your numeric keypad the number of the control character. Ctrl+A is Alt+1, Ctrl+L is Alt+12, Escape is Alt+27, and so on. In Edit, the Escape character looks like a left-pointing arrow, Ctrl+L looks like the scientific "female" symbol, and other control characters have their own symbols.

To create the necessary file in Edit, type Ctrl+P, Alt+27, E, Ctrl+P, Alt+26. This creates a file that contains Escape, E, and a Ctrl+Z character (the DOS end-of-file marker, which we will use in a minute). Then press Alt+F, S, save your file as RESET.TMP in a directory on your Path, and then press Alt+F, X to exit Edit. When you're typing the filename, your Edit screen should look like Figure 5-13.

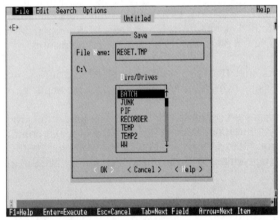

Figure 5-13: When you create a file in Edit that contains an Escape character, followed by E, Ctrl+L, Ctrl+Z, then click File Save, your Edit screen should look like this. The E with arrows around it in the upper-left corner of the editing window is the way Edit shows control characters.

Unfortunately, Edit always writes a carriage return-line feed combination to the end of files it saves. You must strip off this CR/LF, which is the purpose of the Ctrl+Z end-of-file marker in RESET.TMP. To do this, type the following command at a DOS prompt in the directory that contains RESET.TMP:

```
copy reset.tmp /a reset.prn /b
```

In this command, the /A switch tells COPY to treat the file RESET.TMP as an ASCII file (in other words, as a plain text file). In ASCII text files, a Ctrl+Z indicates the end of the file, so COPY reads no further. The /B switch tells COPY to treat the file RESET.PRN as a binary file, such as an executable file. Therefore, COPY adds no Ctrl+Z on to the end of that file when writing it.

This leaves us with RESET.PRN, a two-byte file that contains nothing but the characters Escape and E — exactly what we want.

As the last step in this procedure, create a one-line batch file that sends RESET.PRN to your printer, on whatever printer port your printer may be attached to. If your printer is attached to LPT1, for example, the form-feed batch file FF.BAT would look like this:

```
copy reset.prn lpt1
```

Open Notepad, type in this line, and save this file as FF.BAT in a directory on your Path. Once you've saved your FF.BAT file, simply click File Run in any Windows shell, type FF and click OK. You should see a DOS session flash on your screen for a second, and a page should emerge from the printer.

Of course, you can change FF.BAT to send a form feed to printers on LPT2, COM1, and so on by specifying that port in the COPY command.

Some users have suggested sending a Ctrl+L to LaserJet printers to force them to output a partially printed page, since Ctrl+L is the LaserJet command for a form feed. This method has drawbacks, however. If you type ECHO Ctrl+L>LPT1 to send a Ctrl+L to your printer, it appears at a DOS prompt like the following line:

```
echo Ctrl+L>lpt1
```

But, using this method, you get an extra blank line at the top of the next page of text sent to the LaserJet. This could interfere with the layout of that page. (The ECHO command always adds a carriage return-line feed combination to its output.)

Additionally, if you send a Ctrl+L to a LaserJet printer, and there is no partially printed page in the printer at the time, it outputs a blank page, wasting a sheet of paper.

The Escape-E method is better, because it ejects a page only if one is waiting inside the printer. And it doesn't leave extra blank lines at the top of the next text page, no matter how many times you use it.

Better LaserJet resets with Debug

An even better way to reset LaserJet printers remotely after sending them output from a DOS command is available if you're not afraid to create a little Debug script. The following script creates a tiny DOS program that sends out a Reset command (Escape E), ejecting pages in any LaserJet or compatible printer. Using Notepad or any text editor, create the following script file (call it RESET.SCR) in a directory on your Path:

```
e 100 b4 xx b0 1b ba yy 00 cd zz
e 109 b4 xx b0 45 ba yy 00 cd zz cd 20
rcx
14
n reset.com
w
q
```

You must replace the values *xx, yy,* and *zz* in the above script with the correct numbers for the type of port your printer is attached to — such as LPT1, COM1, and so on. Use the following chart to determine the correct values to insert in place of *xx, yy,* and *zz:*

	xx	**yy**	**zz**
LPT1	00	00	17
LPT2	00	01	17
LPT3	00	02	17
COM1	01	00	14
COM2	01	01	14
COM3	01	02	14
COM4	01	03	14

At a DOS prompt in the same directory as RESET.SCR, type the following to create RESET.COM:

```
debug < reset.scr
```

After redirecting DOS output to your printer, click File Run and type RESET to clear the printer on your specified port.

If you have more than one printer, you could create files named RESETLI.COM to reset the printer on LPT1, RESETCI.COM to reset the printer on COM1, and so on.

I'd like to thank Richard D. Minnick II for his suggestions on the RESET.PRN and RESET.COM methods of ejecting pages.

Summary

In this chapter, I lay out a number of ways to customize the Windows 3.1 and 3.0 File Manager.

▶ Making File Manager windows look and act the way you want them to.

▶ Making the Windows 3.0 File Manager as fast as the Windows 3.1 File Manager.

▶ Gaining back some DOS commands that have no equivalent in the Windows environment.

▶ Ejecting pages from LaserJet printers and compatibles — without having to walk over to the printer — after using a DOS command in File Manager that sends output to your printer port.

Chapter 6
Powering Up File Manager

In This Chapter

▶ I discuss a new feature of the Windows 3.1 File Manager, which allows you to add new commands to the File Manager main menu.

▶ I describe WizManager, a new program that takes advantage of this File Manager trick, along with a few tricks and gotchas that affect Microsoft's implementation of such File Manager extensions.

Those who wish that File Manager or Program Manager or both were more customizable will be heartened by a utility that adds all kinds of launching and scripting capabilities to the Windows 3.1 File Manager. This utility is called WizManager, and, with release 1.1, this tool has become a mature extension that you can use for a whole range of Windows customization needs.

WizManager takes advantage of an obscure capability of the Windows 3.1 File Manager that lies dormant in most Windows users' systems. If WINFILE.INI, which controls File Manager, contains an [AddOns] section, programs mentioned in that section can gain their own place on File Manager's main menu. The commands that may appear in the new drop-down menu are limited only by programmers' fertile imaginations.

To date, this capability has been tapped by only a few utility vendors. Examples of File Manager add-ons include the menu extension in Norton Desktop for Windows; the Launch add-on in Metz TaskManager; and Wilson WindowWare's File Commander (a shareware program found on the diskettes included with *Windows 3.1 Secrets*).

Even Microsoft's MS-DOS 6.0 has gotten into the act. If you choose to install the Windows versions of the new DOS Backup and Antivirus utilities, DOS adds a Tools item to the File Manager menu to give you access to these applets.

Therein lies a tale. Mike Kronenberg at Mijenix, the developer of WizManager, says the Windows documentation allows for up to five add-ons in WINFILE.INI. But the fifth add-on does not work — commands on the fifth menu bar are incorrectly passed to File Manager's Window drop-down menu instead.

The Windows API, which developers use to add lines to INI files, adds new lines to the *end* of a section. Hence, a newly installed extension may act weird if it is the fifth such program. MS-DOS 6.0, however, is apparently aware of this and inserts its Tools add-on line at the *beginning* of the AddOns section of WINFILE.INI. If you are suffering from this bug, add a semicolon to the beginning of one or more lines to cut your File Manager extensions down to four.

WizManager 1.1 takes extensions to new heights. Besides the drop-down menu it adds, WizManager also affixes a button bar to the top of the File Manager window. This bar is similar to the one that appears in the Windows for Workgroups version of File Manager, but WizManager provides many more buttons to choose from (such as a Run dialog box button).

WizManager's button bar also features a great command-line box. You can type in any DOS command, without starting a new DOS session. WizManager has duplicated all major DOS commands in Windows editions. Several shortcuts for power users are provided: If you prefer to run a real DOS command, say, in-stead of WizManager's version, simply precede the command with an equals sign. Instead of typing the current File Manager directory in a command, simply use a semicolon as a substitute.

You can also type into this command-line box any script file with a .WIZ exten-sion. WizManager will execute the instructions in the file. This includes all the usual commands plus several others. You can display dialog boxes for user input, run Control Panel dialogs, and so on.

Items on WizManager's drop-down menu include printing directories, trees, and search results; locking your system with a password; and much more.

Network administrators will love MERGEINI.EXE, a DOS utility provided when you register WizManager. You can put this into a batch file or logon script to insert or update lines in any .INI file.

WizManager is a shareware program featured in the Excellence in Windows Shareware section of this book. See the WizManager chapter in that section for complete address information and registration details.

Summary

In this chapter, the special ability of the Windows 3.1 File Manager to accept up to five (well, actually *four*) additions to its main menu is explained.

▶ The way that File Manager looks for an [AddOns] section in WINFILE.INI is described.

▶ The way DOS 6.0 and WizManager insert themselves into this [AddOns] section, including some problems when exactly five add-ons are inserted, is discussed.

Chapter 7

Replace Microsoft's Bland System Icons

In This Chapter

▶ I express my dissatisfaction with some of the generic icons Microsoft has subjected us to in Windows — specifically, the System Menu and Document Control Menu icons, one or both of which appear in the upper-left corner of nearly every Windows application.

▶ I announce the winners of my Incredible Indescribable Doohickies Contest, who successfully redesigned these icons to make them more understandable and useful.

When Microsoft copied the Macintosh interface to create Windows, it didn't duplicate everything exactly. Subtle changes were made. Several of these changes are improvements — for instance, when you click a Windows menu it stays down while you examine it. Mac menus flip back up unless you hold your finger on the mouse button.

In many cases, however, you could say that Microsoft didn't do much to improve on the Mac. To close a Mac application window, for example, you click a small square at the left end of the title bar. To close a Windows application, you click a small rectangle.

I call objects like these Indescribable Doohickies. The nondescript look of this little rectangular icon (and other bland tools) makes the job of supporting Windows users more difficult. The rectangle, as you may know, is called the System Menu or Control Menu icon. But when we're describing a procedure to a co-worker over the phone, we can't just say, "Double-click the Control Menu icon." Most Windows users have no idea what the anatomically correct names for the various Windows body parts are. Without immediately understandable visual symbols, we're reduced to saying things like, "Now double-click that thingie in the upper-left corner."

To make matters worse, most applications that allow multiple windows display near their menu another indescribable rectangle. This is called the Document Control Menu icon, which closes or manipulates a particular subwindow. The System Menu and Document Control Menu icons are shown in Figure 7-1.

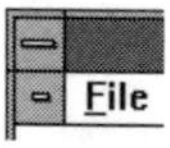

Figure 7-1: All Windows applications have a System Menu icon, shown on the title bar as a long rectangle, and many have a Document Control Menu icon, shown below the title bar as a short rectangle.

Lost in Windows' past is the reason why these icons have the blah shapes we see today. The keyboard shortcut to open the Control Menu is Alt+Spacebar. The shortcut for the Document Control Menu is Alt+Hyphen. The larger rectangle is supposed to look like a spacebar; the smaller one, like a hyphen.

I have asked several of my most knowledgeable Windows friends what these two icons symbolize. None of them knew, and I don't blame them. Spacebars and hyphens simply do not leap into your mind when you see these icons.

It's too bad that these two icons are so poorly understood. Depending on the application, they let you access the Task List and other important functions. And several utilities allow you to add almost any commands you want to the Control Menu. Such utilities include Power Launcher, from hDC Corp. of Redmond, and WinMacro, a part of WinBatch, from Wilson WindowWare of Seattle.

For the benefit of technical support people everywhere, I propose we change these two icons into something more symbolic and easier to understand. All it takes is ButtonMaker, a component of an inexpensive utility called Makeover, by Playroom Software. Makeover is a slim little package with modules that allow you to redraw the icons, pointers, and mouse cursors in Windows and almost any Windows application. You can also adopt predefined "looks" similar to the Mac, Next, Motif, or OS/2.

I don't lightly recommend changing the Windows interface. But if we all agreed to change the Control Menu icon to, say, a five-pointed star, you could easily say to users, "Click the Star," and they'd know what you meant.

The Incredible Indescribable Doohickies Contest

I invited my *InfoWorld* readers to come up with proposed replacements for the System Menu and Document Control Menu icons. The most commonly submitted entry for the System Menu (formally called the Control Menu) was to replace the gray dash with Microsoft's new, Windows 3.1 "window waving like a flag" logo. This presents problems, however. If the System Menu were represented by the Windows logo, we'd eventually have to say "Click the window." Our telephone caller, of course, would immediately reply, "Which window?" and we're back where we started.

For alternatives to the plain old System logo, Ken Rose of Softmart in Exton, Pennsylvania, definitely takes the cake for the most entries from a single reader. Mr. Rose submitted so many ideas that he had to break them into categories:

- **Informative.** The icon could be a number representing the Windows version, the percentage of Free System Resources, or Bill Gates' net worth, rounded to the nearest "bill"-ion.

- **Entertainment.** Your favorite team logo (for sports fans), a crash dummy's helmet (to protect you from what Windows usually does), or a smiley-face logo "to acknowledge the user's great insight in selecting the stupendous value known as Windows."

- **Cultural.** Depending on your religion, a cross or Star of David to invoke divine intervention against general protection faults, or the former USSR hammer-and-sickle ("After all, who else is using it?").

Another reader, noting that the System Menu can be used to close an application, suggested a large "X," meaning X-it, adding, "I expect *big bucks* for this one."

In the same vein, someone else suggested that the icon be a shirt, because "this is how you clothes the application."

Additional votes came in for the icon to be a stop sign. Natural enough, but having a bright red octagon glowing at me all day would drive me nuts.

A couple of respondents, including one from a financial firm, suggested replacing the System and Document Control icons with plus and minus signs. This would perhaps represent Wall Street's emphasis on profits and losses, but still isn't very descriptive.

Other entries included a steering wheel, a joystick, a light switch, the Space Shuttle, and a "horsie and duckie" (for the elementary school market, no doubt). While these all are useful Freudian symbols, they would be a little difficult to represent clearly in the 18 pixels allowed for each icon.

And the Winners Are...

Well, those are the runners-up — here are the winners (shown in Figure 7-2).

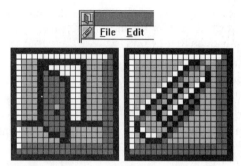

Figure 7-2: The winners of my Incredible Indescribable Doohickies Contest propose that Microsoft's bland icons be replaced with a door (to switch to another application) and a paper clip (to hold the parts of a document together).

Julie Schneider of Seattle, Washington, takes the prize for replacing the System Menu icon.

Ms. Schneider's proposal is to use a *door* as the picture for this icon. This is very symbolic, because the System Menu accesses the Task List to switch to other running applications. In some programs, the System Menu also includes a Run item, which allows you to type a command to start another application. And, of course, double-clicking the System Menu closes most applications, as you would close a door.

At least four other readers also suggested a door as the symbol: Chip Dicomo, Cynthia Frasz, Bill West, and David Harmon. These suggestions were received a few days after Ms. Schneider's, however.

Ms. Frasz sent an addition to her proposal a few days later, saying, "some companies might find a revolving door more appropriate."

Clay Fogler of Newport News, Virginia, submitted the most ingenious suggestion to replace the Document Control Menu icon (now a gray hyphen). This icon is used to close or move an individual document or window within Program Manager, File Manager, and most word processors.

Mr. Fogler would replace the hyphen with a *paper clip*. He points out this is "an internationally recognized temporary document holder."

Double-clicking the paper clip would put away all the various things that make up a document window. Clicking it once would pull down a menu that (in the future) could include helpful options.

I'd like to see these icons made much more powerful. For example, now that the Windows 3.1 File Manager is relatively fast, it could become the primary Windows shell. Clicking the System Menu (in File Manager and other applications) would reveal a list of all Program Manager groups. One more click would start the application or group you wished to use.

The System Menu could totally replace the Task List, too. A second column in the System Menu could show you a list of all running applications, available with a single click.

My wife, Margie, a computer art director and writer, created the icons shown in Figure 7-2. There isn't much you can do in 18 pixels. But we've converted our System Menu icons to these symbols, and (after getting used to the look) we like them a lot.

To change them yourself, you'll need Makeover, a resource-editing utility that's $39.95 from Playroom Software, 7308-C East Independence Blvd. #310, Charlotte, NC 28227; 704-536-3093. The company has made the door and paper clip icons two of the built-in selections you can choose in their package. With this utility, you'll be on your way to a whole new Windows.

As a special promotion for *More Windows 3.1 Secrets,* Playroom Software created a free version of Makeover, which allows you to edit the System and Document Control icons without purchasing the full Makeover package. The free version can be found on the *More Windows 3.1 Secrets* diskettes, and is documented in the Makeover chapter later in this book. I recommend that you still register to receive the full version of Makeover, which includes many other handy utilities, such as enhanced Windows calculators and a MIDI music software program. See the Makeover chapter for registration details.

My thanks to everyone who sent suggestions. Julie Schneider and Clay Fogler received free copies of the book co-written by Margie and me: *Windows Gizmos.*

Summary

In this chapter, I not only complain about a disappointing feature of Windows, I actually do something about it.

▶ The origin of the horribly bland System Menu and Document Control Menu icons is described.

▶ I show how, with the ingenuity of some of my *InfoWorld* readers, these boring, gray symbols can be replaced with pictures like doors and paper clips that suggest what these potentially useful icons really do.

Chapter 8
Windows and MS-DOS 6.*x*

In This Chapter

▶ I discuss some of the interactions between MS-DOS 6.0 and 6.2 (collectively referred to in this chapter as 6.*x*) and Windows 3.0 and 3.1.

▶ This chapter, however, will also be important even for readers who are *not* using DOS 6.*x*, because I also describe some improvements added to the version of SmartDrive that comes with Windows 3.1 (and how you can get the newer version and make it work with Windows and older versions of DOS).

▶ I describe steps you can take when using Windows swap files to make them run smoothly with DOS 6.*x*, especially when using DOS DoubleSpace disk-compression utility.

▶ Going further into reported problems with DoubleSpace, I summarize the entire controversy over the safety of using DoubleSpace, and report exactly what you can expect and what you should do to avoid problems.

With the release of MS-DOS 6.0 by Microsoft, disk-compression utilities — which were previously available only in the form of third-party products, such as Stacker from Stac Electronics — became a basic part of DOS.

Whether or not this is a good thing for Windows is unclear. Windows users, of course, probably need free disk space even more than most DOS users. But I have heard from many Windows users about various problems running Windows with MS-DOS 6.*x*, especially with the DoubleSpace utility, which compresses data on the fly.

These complaints include the usual new-DOS-version "gotchas," such as the fact that you must get DOS 6-aware upgrades to the Norton Utilities and other disk-optimization products, and that Windows NT 3.1 cannot read disks compressed with DoubleSpace, Stacker, and similar products. (By the time you read this, an NT driver may be available to allow compressed drives to be read by NT.)

But more serious complaints have arisen, such as findings that errors can be written into data files on a DoubleSpace-compressed disk under extremely fragmented or disk-full conditions. Microsoft released MS-DOS 6.2 to correct problems like this. The procedures I describe in this chapter apply to both DOS 6.0 and DOS 6.2.

MS-DOS 6.0 May Be a Corrupting Influence on Windows Users

The MS-DOS 6.0 utility DBLSPACE converts a normal disk into a compressed disk. (Do *not* try this while Windows is running.) If you compress, for example, drive C:, DoubleSpace skips four drive letters and creates a new, uncompressed drive H: on your system. Drive H: contains copies of the DOS hidden system files, plus other hidden files. One of these, DBLSPACE.000, is a huge file that contains the compressed contents of your entire drive C:.

Normally, the DBLSPACE utility detects the presence of a Windows permanent swap file and moves it correctly to the root of drive H:. Since Windows writes directly to permanent swap files in 386 enhanced mode, such files must not be compressed.

But if this step fails, as it has for some Windows users, you may find that Windows starts acting strangely. It may come up with the message "Corrupt Swap File," may hang at a black screen, or may exit to a plain DOS prompt.

If you get the "Corrupt Swap File" warning, it is fairly easy to recover by answering "Yes" when asked if you would like to delete the corrupted swap file. Under Windows 3.1, you would then start the Control Panel and use the 386 Enhanced dialog box's Virtual Memory option to recreate the swap file in a contiguous space on an uncompressed drive, such as H:. The DBLSPACE utility allows you to alter the ratio between the compressed and noncompressed portions of a drive if you need noncompressed space for a permanent swap file, although this occasionally has failed for some users, too.

If disaster strikes, and Windows hangs or drops out to DOS every time you try to start it, the following may help.

- A "permanent swap file" consists of two files: 386SPART.PAR, a large, hidden file in the root directory of the drive you created the swap file on, and SPART.PAR, a tiny file in the Windows directory that points Windows to the main file. In an emergency, you can use the DOS command ATTRIB -H -S -R 386SPART.PAR to make this file visible, then delete both files to try to get Windows to start. Windows 3.1 also includes the following lines in the [386Enh] section of SYSTEM.INI, which should be removed temporarily:

```
[386Enh]
PermSwapDOSDrive=x
PermSwapSizeK=nnnn
```

■ In Windows 3.0a, you cannot create a permanent swap file under MS-DOS 6.0 at all unless you patch SWAPFILE.EXE. To do this, you first copy SPATCH.BAT from the MS-DOS 6.0 diskettes. Then you run this command at a DOS prompt in the SWAPFILE.EXE directory:

```
spatch swapfile.exe
```

The MS-DOS 6.0 README.TXT file, which describes this procedure, incorrectly states that this will work with Windows 3.0. If you use Windows 3.0 (as opposed to 3.0a), you must change the line

```
set ADDR=2df2
```
in SPATCH.BAT to read
```
set ADDR=2dc0
```

according to a Microsoft technical document released April 22, 1993.

DoubleSpace Can Create Headaches for Windows Users _____

I've also found an example of repeatable errors by the DoubleSpace and Undelete utilities that come with MS-DOS 6.0. The errors affect Windows users, and you can reproduce the problem yourself by taking the following simple steps. (This should not harm your PC, but you should use a noncritical test system anyway.)

STEPS

Testing Undelete

Step 1. Make sure that MS-DOS 6.0 is installed on your system in a default configuration.

Step 2. Create a new, empty, compressed drive. Do so in one of two ways:

(A) Run the command DBLSPACE at a DOS prompt. Then type Alt, C, C to create a new compressed drive, using free space from an existing drive. If you select the free space on C: to convert into a compressed drive, DoubleSpace will create a compressed drive called H:.

(B) If you already have a free DoubleSpace drive, use the command DBLSPACE /FORMAT H to clear it of files. (Do this if you run this procedure a second time.)

Step 3. Exit DBLSPACE and start Windows 3.1. Open File Manager windows for C:\DOS and H:\. Copy the file C:\DOS\GRAPHICS.PRO to the root of H:. Then copy C:\DOS\README.TXT to H:\. You can copy these files with DOS commands instead, if you prefer.

Step 4. Delete the two files in H:\, using File Manager or DOS commands.

Step 5. Reboot. This is necessary because DoubleSpace does not save status information across warm boots.

Step 6. In Windows or DOS, copy C:\DOS\ATTRIB.EXE to H:\. This wipes out the space occupied by the first of the two deleted files, GRAPHICS.PRO.

Step 7A. If you are in DOS, change to H:\ and run the command UNDELETE. Provide the missing letter R in ?EADME.TXT (the first character was removed when DOS "marked" this file as deleted), and you will see the message "File successfully undeleted."

Step 7B. If you are in Windows, open a File Manager window for H:\, then click File Undelete. (The Undelete item was added to File Manager when you installed DOS 6.0.) In the dialog box that appears, highlight the filename ?EADME.TXT. A small gray status bar says, "All clusters are available, some may have been overwritten" — the same message you see every time you use this utility — but the main window reports that the condition of the file is "Excellent." Click the Undelete button and provide the missing letter R, and Undelete reports the condition of the file as "Recovered."

Step 8. Here's the problem — the README.TXT file hasn't been successfully recovered. The first several sectors of the file have been overwritten by garbage. You can see this in Windows by clicking File Run and typing WRITE H:\README.TXT. The beginning of the file is filled with control characters, which look like rectangular boxes. In DOS, use the command TYPE H:\README.TXT | MORE.

I used README.TXT in this example because it is easy to see the damage. But several other files also produce the problem. Instead of GRAPHICS.PRO, use SMARTDRV.EXE or MWAVDLG.DLL. Instead of ATTRIB.EXE, use EDIT.HLP, SYS.COM, or FORMAT.COM.

When undeleted files are reported as recovered successfully, but in fact are corrupted, it can cause serious problems. Say that you delete all the files in a directory, then realize you need a single file — such as an executable file — in that directory. When you try to run this file, your system would crash — or worse.

This corruption is being caused by an interaction between DOS 6's DoubleSpace and Undelete utilities. It does not occur on a Stacker compressed drive or a noncompressed drive that does not use DoubleSpace. This is a separate problem from the random, intermittent problems previously reported by *InfoWorld* and other computer publications when MS-DOS 6.0 was released. Because of the potential for software incompatibilities, I do not recommend using DoubleSpace compression.

DOS 6.0 provides no utility to remove DoubleSpace. Here's how to do that, if you followed the above procedure, or you installed DoubleSpace and compressed an entire drive letter.

If you created a new, compressed volume, as in the procedure above, you can simply delete all the test files and the volume itself. At a DOS prompt, change to the uncompressed drive, such as C:. In the root directory, type the command ATTRIB -H -S -R DBLSPACE.*. A directory of the root directory should now reveal a file named DBLSPACE.001. Delete this file, delete DBLSPACE.BIN and DBLSPACE.INI (if found), reboot, and everything on the compressed drive (typically, drive H:) should be gone.

If, however, you compressed an entire drive, you must take the following steps.

STEPS

Removing DoubleSpace Compression from a Drive

Step 1. At a DOS prompt (Microsoft provides no way to do this in Windows), change to the drive you wish to remove compression from, such as C:. Type the command DBLSPACE /LIST. The uncompressed "host" drive, and the hidden compressed file that stores your data, is listed. For example, it might show the file H:\DBLSPACE.000.

Step 2. Delete as many unneeded files as possible from C:. Then delete any unneeded files you have placed on the H: drive, such as the hidden Windows permanent swap file, 386SPART.PAR. (You can do this by setting your swap file to "None" using the Windows Control Panel's 386 Enhanced icon. You can re-create it later.)

Step 3.   On the compressed drive (C:), type the command DBLSPACE /SIZE. This reduces the hidden compressed file and frees space on the host drive (H:).

Step 4.   Use the DOS 6 MOVE command to move each directory from the compressed drive (C:) to the host drive (H:). For example:

```
move c:\directory\*.* h:\directory
```

Since the MOVE command cannot move subdirectories, you can alternatively use XCOPY /S and the new DELTREE command to copy and delete entire directory structures. In either case, leave at least 512K free on the host drive.

Step 5.   Repeat Steps 3 and 4 until all files have been moved. If you are removing DoubleSpace from your boot drive, make sure COMMAND.COM, CONFIG.SYS, etc., have been moved into the root directory of the host drive (H:).

Step 6.   Change to your host drive, such as H:. Run the command ATTRIB -H -S -R DBLSPACE.*. Delete the hidden file that previously held your compressed data, DBLSPACE.000.

Step 7.   Files on your host drive (H:) will be on your boot drive (C:) when you reboot. If this is the only drive letter that used DoubleSpace compression, delete DBLSPACE.INI, a text file that holds preferences, and DBLSPACE.BIN, which is loaded automatically if found in the root directory of your host drive (consuming about 43K of memory). A copy of DBLSPACE.BIN should remain in your DOS 6 directory, in case you ever wish to use DoubleSpace in the future. Also remove all DBLSPACE lines from CONFIG.SYS and AUTOEXEC.BAT on H:.

Step 8.   Reboot your PC. If everything worked, there will be no drive H:, and your files will now appear on C:. (When I did this procedure on a 30MB drive, it created five lost clusters, which had to be cleaned up with CHKDSK /F.)

When I sent information on the above problems to Microsoft, I received responses from Brad Chase, DOS 6 general manager, and Ben Slivka, DOS 6 development manager. Mr. Chase wrote, "Sounds like your true concern is that in this contrived case we report a file as recovered when it is not. This is a legitimate concern. I agree with you that this is bad. At the same time I do want to stress that this is not a problem customers are having.... By your definition all software, every single one on the market, has 'bugs.' This 'bug' does not even show up in the very long list of PSS [Product Support Services] calls customers are calling us about. Simply put, based on this data and all the data I have from CompuServe, customers are not experiencing this problem."

Avoiding problems with DoubleSpace

The most serious issues about the version of DoubleSpace included with MS-DOS 6.0 are those that involve actual data corruption under normal operating conditions. *InfoWorld* in its issues published on May 3 and May 10, 1993, chronicled its findings in testing DOS 6.0. Like many users, *InfoWorld*'s testers experienced data loss when they used DoubleSpace. However, many users and testers have been baffled in attempts to pinpoint what is causing these instances of data loss. The errors are difficult to reproduce in lab settings, and, lacking hard evidence of repeatable software problems, Microsoft publicly attributed the instances of data loss to user error.

In my research on this issue, full or fragmented disks have been suggested as one culprit in the missing data. In fact, Blossom Software Corp. has created a Windows utility that can detect conditions that lead to at least one of the causes of data loss when DoubleSpace is used.

Blossom, which developed the Lotus 1-2-3 add-ins Write-In and Allways, calls its utility DoubleCheck. It comes in a DOS version, but I've found the Windows edition more useful. It displays a signal like a traffic light. The signal is usually green but changes to yellow or red when the utility detects errors, disk-full conditions, or high levels of fragmentation on DoubleSpaced drives.

Disk-full and fragmentation conditions are important because of a repeatable flaw Blossom states it has identified in the DoubleSpace algorithm. DoubleSpace uses an "estimated compression ratio" to estimate the free space available on a compressed drive. When DoubleSpace writes 8K of compressed data, it requires 16 sectors of 512 bytes each, and those sectors must be contiguous. If contiguous sectors are not available, says the *DoubleCheck User's Guide,* this "causes a variety of symptoms, from lost disk clusters to unreported disk corruption, when space available on the disk becomes low or very fragmented."

As Allen Foyer, primary developer of DoubleCheck, explains: "DoubleSpace fails when a disk is fragmented enough that it can't find a new cluster for a file that's uncompressible." Files that can't be compressed include .ZIP and .GIF files, some .EXE files, and others.

Blossom developed a demo routine, BUST.EXE, which writes and deletes several test files, causing fragmentation. The company does not distribute this routine with DoubleCheck. But I obtained a copy and was able to reproduce the errors. When copying several files to fragmented, compressed drives, the COPY command (with VERIFY on) reported no errors. But each file that required 16 sectors was corrupted with intermittent NUL characters.

DoubleCheck is available for $29.95, plus shipping. Blossom also offers for $9.95 a 30-page booklet called the *DoubleSpace Reference Guide*. Both products provide essential reading, even if you never plan to use DoubleSpace. Contact Blossom at 1 Kendall Sq., Bldg. 600, Cambridge, MA 02139; 800-940-6163 or 617-738-1516.

Other issues can affect Windows users running on DOS 6. The TouchStone Software Corp., maker of the CheckIt Pro utility, is distributing a free app that tests disk sectors. The company states that the DOS 6.0 FORMAT command will "return to use some of the sectors that have been marked as part of a Bad Track at the low-level." On CompuServe, type GO IBMSYS, select the DOS Utilities library, and download DOSPR6.ZIP.

I asked Microsoft officials about both of these problems. Tony Audino, director of marketing for MS-DOS, replied, "Both can be characterized as real symptoms, but practically speaking, extremely remote in actual occurrence. However, just in case and for the record, both have been addressed in MS-DOS 6.2."

Windows users should watch out for many other conditions. In fairness, it should be said that some of the following "gotchas" are not actually DoubleSpace's fault. But since Windows is supposed to be "easy to use," ask yourself if you could intuitively figure out how to fix situations like these (all examples were confirmed by Microsoft Product Support Services [PSS]):

- When the Windows 3.1 File Manager makes a bootable system diskette, and you've compressed your C drive with DoubleSpace, the diskette will boot your machine but all your compressed hard disk data will have disappeared. After you recuperate from your heart attack, what would you do? Your hard disk data will appear again simply by rebooting without the diskette in drive A. File Manager neglects to copy DBLSPACE.BIN, a hidden file, to the root of the diskette, so DoubleSpace didn't load and your compressed files couldn't be seen. (File Manager could have launched SYS A:, which would work with any DOS version, but it doesn't.) You can't just copy DBLSPACE.BIN yourself. You must also create on the diskette a DBLSPACE.INI file, which is documented in the Microsoft DOS 6 Technical Reference manual.

- When you install DOS 6 after Windows 3.1, the Setup program always adds a Tools menu to the File Manager, even if you chose not to install any of the three optional Windows tools (Backup, Anti-Virus, and DoubleSpace Info). None of the menu items work, of course, if the utilities weren't installed.

- If you use DoubleSpace to compress data on a floppy disk, you may get an error message when you click the File Manager's DoubleSpace Info menu item for info on the compressed floppy. According to PSS, File Manager can't read a compressed floppy on some PCs that have only one floppy drive (not two), but the exact machines this occurs on have not been isolated as of this writing.

- Normally, you can use File Manager to disconnect from a LAN Manager 2.1 or 2.2 network drive. But if the drive letter is between C and the last drive letter DoubleSpace uses, the network drive icon turns into a floppy drive symbol and gives you a "no disk in drive" error message when you select it. To fix this, edit DBLSPACE.INI so LastDrive= and ActivateDrive= specify drive letters _before_ the network drive letter.

- Windows hangs at the logo screen in enhanced mode if you are running FTP Software's PC/TCP network software. You must move the DBLSPACE.SYS line in CONFIG.SYS _above_ the PROTMAN.SYS line. (DOS Setup usually places the DBLSPACE.SYS line _last_ in CONFIG.SYS.)

- If you create a permanent swap file (PSF) on a DoubleSpaced drive, every-thing seems OK, but you will soon get a "corrupt swap file" message. Microsoft warns people to use only noncompressed drives for PSFs. But you also should not place a _temporary_ swap file on a DoubleSpaced drive. DOS reports more space than is actually available on the drive, and even when no disk space is actually available, Windows will still think there is lots of virtual memory. For the same reason, don't SET TEMP= to a com-pressed drive.

- If you run on any of the following PCs, according to PSS, you need to patch DBLSPACE.BIN or get a BIOS upgrade: Acer 386-11/16SX and /20SX; AEG Olympia 386SX laptops (some models); Canon C-200 M-50 and M-55; Intel Above Board 2.0 or Snap-on 386; Microsolutions Compaticard; Positive PCs; Sharp 6700, 6781, 6785, 6800, and 6881; Texas Instruments TravelMate 2000; and Zeos 386s with a 9/15/89 AMI BIOS. DoubleSpace crashes, PSS says, when these machines process DoubleSpace's Interrupt 1A calls.

SmartDrive in Windows 3.1 has concerns similar to DOS 6.0

I've found that the disk cache program included with Windows 3.1, SmartDrive, has much the same behavior as the version included with MS-DOS 6.0. This is a cause for concern for Windows users as well as DOS 6 users.

InfoWorld first reported the appearance of cross-linked and corrupted files on DOS 6 DoubleSpace compressed volumes in its May 3 and May 10, 1993, issues. After investigation, many of these cases were traced to the new version of

SmartDrive in DOS 6. When machines running DOS 6 were cold-booted while no disk activity was occurring (but SmartDrive was waiting to write to disk), files on the DoubleSpace volume became corrupted.

Initially, this behavior was intermittent and thus impossible to reproduce and correct. Now I've found a way to make this behavior reproducible — you can even do it, safely, yourself.

SmartDrive (in Windows 3.1 and MS-DOS 6.0) defaults to a mode called "write caching." When you save a file, SmartDrive holds the information in memory and tells your application that the file is written. This makes your application seem to save data more quickly. In reality, SmartDrive waits up to 5 seconds before writing the data to disk in the background.

When write caching is enabled, SmartDrive also defaults to a mode called "request sorting." Data is written to the sectors of your disk in a specific order that minimizes head movements — not in the order that your application originally expected.

This is where SmartDrive can get you into trouble. If an application hangs before all the data is written, or you do a hard reset, or the power goes off, data that was supposedly written into one place may not actually be in that place at all.

This is bad for database products that provide "rollback" capabilities, such as Oracle, Gupta SQLBase, and many others. These programs keep track of disk writes for every transaction. If power is lost, a complete "rollback" is possible so no transaction is improperly written.

With SmartDrive's request sorting, however, this rollback feature is compromised. Data that the database package is sure was written (because it was informed that it was) actually was not.

The DOS file system is also a kind of database. When you write a file, DOS first edits its File Allocation Table (FAT). Only then does DOS update the directory entry for that file.

SmartDrive's request sorting, by contrast, can write several files in a row. The FAT, which is on a different part of the disk, may not be updated until much later in the process. During this period, disaster can strike.

There now exists a free utility you can use to see this for yourself. Jeopardy Detector changes the border of your display to a red color (in both DOS and Windows) when directory entries have been written, but the FAT has not yet been updated. Following the instructions in the included READ.ME file, switch off your power when the red border appears. Then reboot and run CHKDSK. You will see the message "Invalid file entries," fortunately affecting only one test directory. At this point, run CHKDSK/F to fix the test files, and you're fine.

Jeopardy Detector is available on CompuServe: GO PCVENA, Library 14, JPRDY.ZIP. It was developed by the PC-Kwik Corp., which makes disk cache software that competes with SmartDrive, but it's a valid utility in its own right. The instructions describe how to achieve the same results manually, without the utility.

If your power failed or an application hung your PC, but your operations were otherwise normal, you might never get a warning about the invalid file entries these situations can create. If you happen to write files to the affected disk sectors, the resulting data files become unrecoverable, cross-linked files — exactly the symptoms *InfoWorld* found.

Probably the most common error is caused when people exit a DOS application, say "Yes" to save files, and then turn off the power to their PC when they see a C prompt. Since no disk light is on, they reasonably assume this is safe — but SmartDrive may wait several seconds before writing to disk, and this is when disaster can strike.

To deal with this particular problem, Microsoft released an updated version of SmartDrive, which delays the appearance of a C prompt until all data has been safely written to disk. This should be called the Steve Gibson upgrade, since he revealed this problem in a series of his *InfoWorld* columns, but Microsoft calls it SmartDrive 4.2. (Windows 3.1 includes SmartDrive 4.0, and MS-DOS 6.0 includes SmartDrive 4.1 — both of which have the C prompt problem.)

To get the upgrade from CompuServe, if you have Windows 3.1 or DOS 6.0, type GO SML and download S14191.ZIP. If you don't have a modem, call 800-426-9400 and Microsoft will send it to you on a diskette for $7.50 plus tax.

This takes care of a leading cause of data loss. But to encourage DOS sales, Microsoft made SmartDrive 4.2 run only under DOS 6. This doesn't help Windows users who need the upgrade but are happy using DOS 3, 4, or 5.

Independent developer Gary Tessler suggests the following patch, which allows SmartDrive 4.2 to run under versions of DOS other than DOS 6.

STEPS

Running SmartDrive 4.2 Under Versions of DOS Other Than DOS 6

Step 1. Exit Windows, take the SMARTDRV line out of your AUTOEXEC.BAT, and reboot.

Step 2. Copy SMARTDRV.EXE to SMARTDRV.OLD, then rename SMARTDRV.EXE to SMARTDRV.BIN.

Step 3. At a plain DOS prompt, in the directory where SMARTDRV.BIN resides, issue the command DEBUG SMARTDRV.BIN. At Debug's hyphen prompt, type the following lines:

```
s 0 ffff 75 0f b4 30
e 6636
90 90
w
q
```

After the S command, you will see two four-digit numbers. The second number (probably 6636) is the number you must use in the E command. After the E command, you will see a prompt of numbers, at which point you type 90 (Space) 90 (Enter) and the rest.

If anything goes wrong, type Q at any hyphen prompt to quit Debug, then copy SMARTDRV.OLD to SMARTDRV.EXE and you'll be back the way you were.

If everything goes well, rename SMARTDRV.BIN to SMARTDRV.EXE. Use this new version in your AUTOEXEC.BAT. Microsoft (which knew people would apply this patch) left in the code the old routine that then tests for DOS 3.3 — the version that SmartDrive really requires.

If you don't want to patch SmartDrive, another way to run V4.2 is with a utility called VERS. This is a TSR, which helps you run programs that erroneously require a certain DOS version. The command VERS /T6.0 (inserted prior to the SMARTDRV line in AUTOEXEC.BAT) changes the "true" version of DOS to 6, so SmartDrive runs on DOS 3.3, 4, or 5.

VERS is part of Tessler's Nifty Tools, a set of 25 DOS utilities. I especially like DIR2BAT, which writes batch files to carry out commands on any filespec, and IFONSCRN, which takes action if specified characters appear on screen.

Send $19 for VERS, or $49 for the set, to TNT, P.O. Box 1791, San Ramon, CA 94583; CompuServe: 71044,542. Shareware files, VERS20.ZIP and TNT33.ZIP, are also available in IBMSYS, Library 1.

The version of SmartDrive that comes with DOS 6.0 contains some bug fixes over the version in Windows 3.1. For one thing, Microsoft PSS states that the Windows 3.1 SmartDrive has "minor problems" handling "bad sectors" on a hard disk, and may incorrectly handle "the Int 21 Function 68h (Commit File) carry flag." This function was added to DOS in version 3.3. This statement means that when an application has requested that a change to a file be written immediately to disk (in other words, commit the file), the SmartDrive in Windows 3.1 may incorrectly respond if the "carry" bit is set to 1, indicating there was an error condition when the write was attempted. No further information on this situation is available from Microsoft.

For these reasons, I recommend that Windows 3.1 users obtain SmartDrive version 4.2 or higher — by downloading it from CompuServe or using the version in DOS 6.2 — and apply one of the patches described above, if Windows 3.1 is running on DOS 3.3, 4, or 5.

By itself, SmartDrive 4.2 removes one important cause of invalid directory entries — users shutting off power to their PCs when they see a C prompt, reasonably believing it is safe. SmartDrive 4.2, as discussed earlier, withholds the C prompt after you exit a DOS application until SmartDrive has written all data to disk.

Unfortunately, the type of write caching used in SmartDrive 4.2 does not remove the biggest problem: your PC losing power or being hung by an application while SmartDrive is in a "jeopardy period" — a state during which directories and File Allocation Table (FAT) entries are being written to disk out of order.

If an error occurs while an application is writing files, and SmartDrive has updated directory entries before the files first and then the FAT entries (the opposite of the normal sequence), you might never know that something unusual had occurred. The files look normal in File Manager and when you type DIR. But the files may have become La Brea Tar Pits on your disk. Any new files that are written into those sectors of your disk become cross-linked files, and are virtually unrecoverable.

PC-Kwik Corp. officals launched this topic by posting their Jeopardy Detector utility on CompuServe (JPRDY.ZIP, GO PCVENA, Library 14). They have an interest, of course, in protecting sales of their Super PC-Kwik cache program. But they are criticizing not only SmartDrive. They claim in text files accompanying JPRDY.ZIP that Norton Utilities 7.0's Ncache2 and PC Tools 8.0's PC-Cache also have "jeopardy periods" during which data is written out of order.

Let me emphasize that it is not "write caching" *per se* that causes problems. Write caching (using RAM to buffer data being written to disk) can actually reduce the period during which your data is at risk from a power outage.

The problems are caused by "request sorting" (writing sectors out of the order in which they were received), "elevator seeking" (writing to cylinders only in the order they appear on the disk), and "time delay" (making applications look faster by postponing disk writes for a few seconds).

I asked the affected vendors about PC-Kwik's charges. Jim Streater, Norton lead developer, confirmed that Ncache2 and Norton Speed Drive default to time delay and request sorting. Specifically, FAT entries are written *last.* He felt, however, that this could be safer in the event of a power outage, since data files would be written first, and (if the FAT was corrupted) could be pieced together with Norton Disk Doctor.

An engineer for Central Point Software, developers of PC Tools, confirmed that the version of PC-Cache that is available as of this writing defaults to elevator seeking. This also has a bias toward writing FAT entries last.

Another product, Cache86 5.0 from the Aldridge Co. of Houston, Texas, claims to always update the FAT first, then directory entries, then the data. According to the company, Cache86 5.0 defaults to what it calls "no staged writes" (no write caching), but can be configured for a 1 to 3 second time delay.

Which cache is best for Windows users? If cache products have a "jeopardy period," how long is it? What is the worst that can happen? It is impossible for me to resolve all these questions in this chapter. In the future, we must ask that magazine reviewers test caches with an emphasis on reliability, rather than speed, so these issues can be resolved in a controlled, lab setting.

Meanwhile, Super PC-Kwik and Cache86 appear to be the only major products that default to a safe, first-in-first-out method of caching disk writes, without unnecessary time delays. Unless you have an uninterruptible power supply — and stable applications that never crash — I recommend that Windows users disable request sorting and time delays in other caches you may be using.

In SmartDrive 4.*x*, you cannot turn off request sorting and time delay without disabling write caching. To do this, add your hard drive letters (C D E and so on) to the end of your SMARTDRV command line. Hopefully, Microsoft will some-day provide us with a version of SmartDrive that allows the benefits of write caching without the risks of request sorting.

Setting Up Swap Files Faster

It is well known that Windows requires contiguous free space on a hard disk drive in order to create a permanent swap file. You create this contiguous space by running a file defragmentation utility, which moves all the files on a disk, leaving a single, unbroken open space on the drive. Into this open space, you can create a permanent swap file by opening the Windows 3.1 Control Panel's 386 Enhanced dialog box, clicking the Virtual Memory button, and then clicking the Change button.

Usually, I don't recommend that you rely on a permanent swap file. I would prefer that you install enough RAM in your system that Windows never needs to swap anything to disk.

(Here's a way you can tell whether Windows has swapped anything to disk. First, open all your applications in Windows. Then press Alt+Esc to switch to each application in turn, and watch your disk drive light. If the light goes on when you switch to an application, it means that Windows had swapped that app to disk — and you should get more RAM.)

But there are cases where only a permanent swap file will help you. Perhaps you are limited to 2MB of RAM and your company won't buy more. In that case, I would recommend that you make a permanent swap file large enough to give you at least 5MB total (2MB physical memory plus a 3MB permanent swap file, for example). There usually is no benefit to making a permanent swap file larger than 4MB in size, but some applications — such as LaserMaster Corp.'s high-resolution WinJet printer driver — require an 8MB permanent swap file or they refuse to run.

For those of you who create permanent swap files in the course of your work, I've found an undocumented feature of Microsoft's MS-DOS 6.0 that should speed up the process.

Many third-party vendors offer defragmentation utilities — Symantec's Norton Utilities, Central Point's PC Tools, and others come to mind — but for the first time, Microsoft has included a defragger in DOS: DEFRAG.EXE.

Normally, DEFRAG rearranges each file's clusters into consecutive order, and also makes all files contiguous, leaving one large open space on the drive. This is good for creating a permanent swap file. But DEFRAG is notably slow.

Imagine you've been given the task of adding permanent swap files to, say, 100 PCs in your company. Waiting for DOS 6's DEFRAG to give you contiguous space on all these PCs could take days.

But not if you know the undocumented switch that speeds up DEFRAG. Run the command DEFRAG /Q at a plain DOS prompt (with Windows *not* running).

The /Q switch stands for Quick. When you run DEFRAG /Q, the utility does not bother to move each file's clusters into consecutive order. Instead, it simply moves all the disk clusters so they reside at the beginning of the drive, leaving one contiguous space on the disk — perfect for creating a permanent swap file.

After making your swap file (a process that takes only a few seconds in Windows), you may wish to defragment all the files completely, since this does give the user somewhat faster disk access. In that case, start a full defrag with the command DEFRAG /F *after* exiting Windows. Now you can tell the user that he or she can start using their PC again after the DEFRAG screen has ended — and you can go on to the next PC.

The /Q switch is not mentioned in the Microsoft MS-DOS 6 Technical Reference, nor in the on-line text that appears when you type HELP DEFRAG. Two managers at Microsoft told me that the company had been having discussions with Symantec (which provided the DEFRAG code) about which features would and would not be provided for the money Microsoft was paying. The Quick feature was left out of the documentation, but actually did make it into the product.

Summary

In this chapter, I describe a few anomalies that affect Windows users who also use MS-DOS 6.0 and 6.2.

▶ If your permanent swap file is not correctly placed on a noncompressed drive letter when you install DoubleSpace, there are steps you can take to get the correct configuration.

▶ If you use DoubleSpace and the Undelete utility in DOS 6.*x* or the Windows 3.1 File Manager, you may get confusing results in some cases.

▶ If you need to remove DoubleSpace, I describe the correct procedure.

▶ The most serious criticisms of DoubleSpace involve errors that occur when a compressed drive is full or in a highly fragmented condition, and I describe a utility, DoubleCheck, that you can use to detect when you should defragment DoubleSpaced drives to avoid problems.

▶ I quote Microsoft's Product Support Services about differences in SmartDrive versions that cause me to recommend that Windows 3.1 users obtain SmartDrive 4.2 from CompuServe, or the version of SmartDrive in DOS 6.2, and use one of two methods to allow these newer versions of SmartDrive to run with Windows on older, more stable versions of DOS.

▶ Finally, if you need to defragment a DoubleSpace drive to create room for a permanent swap file, it may be possible to save a significant amount of time with the undocumented DEFRAG /Q switch.

Chapter 9
Dealing with DOS

In This Chapter

▶ I describe some of the most important ways to improve the performance of DOS under Windows, using a few simple tests to determine the best settings for multitasking on your particular system.

▶ I enumerate some new and little-known capabilities that DOS sessions have gained under Windows 3.1.

▶ I review new versions of some useful utilities that can make DOS run with new power under Windows — or allow you to run a window that acts like DOS while consuming only 14 percent as much memory.

▶ I show some simple ways to capture and print DOS application screens in Windows documents, including those PC line-draw characters that are otherwise impossible to reproduce in Windows.

▶ I warn about the consequences of running DOSX.EXE and several other commands under standard- or enhanced-mode Windows.

▶ I bring you up-to-date on the latest in ZIP file compression, both as it works (and doesn't work) under Windows, and show you how to harness ZIP files in a totally Windows environment.

Of all the capabilities that Windows acquires in 386 enhanced mode, none seems as mysterious as its ability to multitask DOS applications.

I'm not going to spend any time debating whether or not this is "true" multitasking. But I do think it's worthwhile to discuss how to get the best performance for DOS applications under Windows.

When you start a DOS session, the performance of that session — whether it's simply a DOS prompt or a full-blown application — is controlled by a *Program Information File* (PIF). You may never have set up a PIF file, but your DOS sessions are controlled by PIFs nonetheless.

If you don't start a DOS session from a particular PIF, Windows uses the settings in a file called _DEFAULT.PIF (the underscore character is part of the filename). Unfortunately, Microsoft's default settings in this PIF are designed for the worst possible case. This is almost guaranteed to harm the performance of your DOS sessions.

Improving the Performance of DOS Sessions Under Windows

To correct this, pull down the File menu in your Windows shell and click Run. In the dialog box that appears, type PIFEDIT _DEFAULT.PIF and click OK. Windows opens the PIF Editor application and loads _DEFAULT.PIF automatically. Click the Mode menu item and make sure the PIF Editor is in 386 Enhanced mode.

You may notice that the _DEFAULT.PIF file specifies C:\COMMAND.COM as the filename that it runs. This filename is just a place holder. Although _DEFAULT.PIF must contain a valid filename in this box, Windows actually substitutes the filename of any DOS application you run.

Establishing the best default settings

Click the PIF Editor's Advanced button, and the Advanced Options window opens. This is where the important multitasking settings appear. (See Figure 9-1.)

The first group of settings controls the priority that your DOS sessions receive. I change the Foreground Priority to 10000 (ten thousand). This is the maximum foreground setting, which gives any DOS session you are currently working in as much CPU time as it wants. However, when the DOS session falls idle — if it is merely waiting for you to press a key — the 10000 setting allows Windows to give some CPU time to any programs you may have loaded in the background, such as E-mail or fax-board programs.

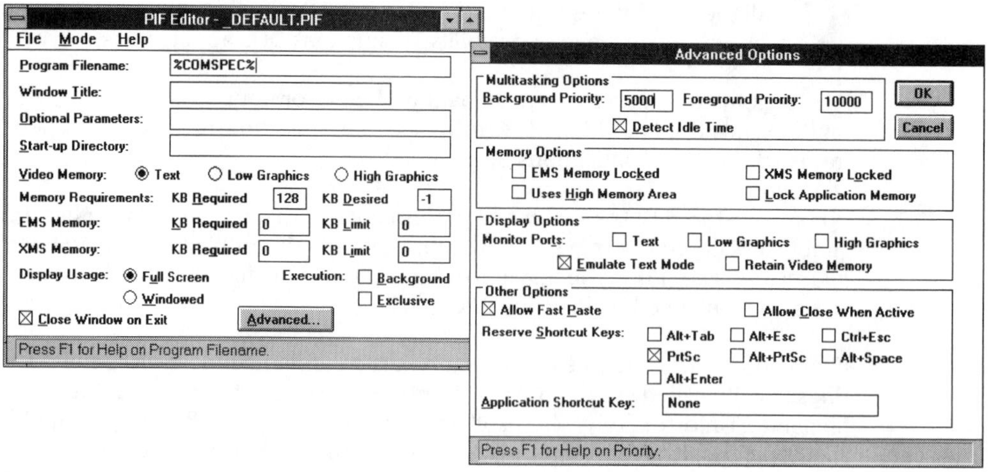

Figure 9-1: The PIF Editor's multitasking settings.

I find this preferable to setting the PIF Editor's Exclusive Execution box on. When set to Exclusive, a DOS session suspends every background process, including Windows. (Even a Foreground Priority of 10000 may be too high to allow a background task to stay alive, so you may have to reduce this if it interferes with important background tasks.)

The next group of settings controls Memory Options. For most programs, you can turn all these options (such as Uses High Memory Area) off, and set Expanded and Extended Memory Required to zero. If you have any DOS programs that use expanded or extended memory, these programs should have their own PIFs.

Finally, change the Display Options settings. It's especially important to turn off all of the Monitor Ports options. These options are designed to monitor ill-behaved EGA applications. But they can cause serious harm to the performance of DOS applications that don't require such monitoring. Set the Video Memory option to Text, since most DOS graphics programs start out in text mode and can easily switch to graphics mode if necessary. And make sure the Emulate Text Mode option is turned on. This setting allows Windows to use faster text-mode calls, which work fine with almost all programs.

If you're curious about any PIF Editor setting, click your mouse in any box and press F1. An informative, context-sensitive help screen appears.

After you've done all this, click OK to close the Advanced Options box. Then click File Save to write your changes into the _DEFAULT.PIF file.

Setting options for multitasking

Now that you've set up your _DEFAULT.PIF for running DOS applications in general, make a copy of it, using File Manager or your favorite utility. Call the copy COMMAND.PIF.

Open the PIF Editor and load COMMAND.PIF. Click the Mode menu item and make sure the PIF Editor is in 386 Enhanced mode. Then make the following changes.

First, change the Window Title to DOS Session, and change the Optional Parameters box to /E:512. The /E switch allows your DOS sessions to have an environment size of 512 bytes – large enough to hold environmental variables you may need to use later.

Next, make sure the Exclusive Execution check box is off, and the Background Execution box is on. I'd normally leave the Background box off (since a simple DOS prompt is unlikely to do any background processing, which can slow the performance of Windows applications). But background execution will be necessary for our experiment.

Now change the Display radio button from Full Screen to Windowed — again for the purpose of our experiment.

Finally, click the Advanced button. Set the Multitasking Options as follows: Background Priority 50, Foreground Priority 100. Set all the boxes in the Memory Options section off or to zero. In the Display Options section, set Video Memory to Text, turn off all Monitor Ports boxes, and make sure the Emulate Text Mode box is on. Click OK to close the Advanced Options window, then File Save to save your new COMMAND.PIF.

Now that you have this PIF, change the DOS Session icon in your Program Manager window so it starts COMMAND.PIF instead of running COMMAND.COM directly. To do this, highlight the DOS Session icon by clicking it once with your mouse, then click File Properties in the Program Manager menu and edit COMMAND.COM to say COMMAND.PIF.

Improving the refresh rate of DOS windows

Since we're going to be using DOS sessions in a smaller, moveable window instead of full-screen, let's improve the refresh performance of these windows. To do this, open your SYSTEM.INI file with Notepad or any plain-text editor. Locate the section headed [386Enh]. Insert a line under this heading that reads as follows:

```
[386Enh]
WindowUpdateTime=200
```

Ordinarily, Windows gives a priority of only 50 to refreshing the screen area of a windowed DOS session. Increasing this priority to 200 can make a noticeable difference in how quickly commands like DIR scroll output on the display. This effect is much more striking in Windows 3.0 than Windows 3.1, but it still may make a difference for you in either version. Unfortunately, the only way to find the best setting for your PC is to try several settings, restart Windows each time, and see which one gives you the best windowed DOS performance. (This setting can be increased all the way to 999, but I've found that values higher than 200 don't provide additional benefit. Try 25, 50, 100, and 200 on your system to see what happens.)

You must exit and restart Windows for the SYSTEM.INI changes to take effect. Start Windows with the command WIN /3, if necessary, to ensure that you will be working in 386 enhanced mode.

After Windows loads, double-click your DOS Session icon. You should see the DOS prompt, but in a small window with a title bar, just like every other Windows application. Go back to Program Manager and double-click DOS Session again. You should see another DOS window open, just like the first one.

Testing the Minimum Timeslice

With your COMMAND.PIF set for a Foreground Priority of 100, and a Background Priority of 50 (as described above), you're ready to test an obscure control over your Windows performance: the Minimum Timeslice.

The default Minimum Timeslice value of 20 milliseconds means that a DOS session under Windows can run for 1/50 of a second before Windows may pass control to another session or Windows application. This value was determined by Microsoft to allow sufficient time for each session on a slow 386. I'm convinced that a Minimum Timeslice of 20 is too high for today's faster systems.

The Minimum Timeslice value is controlled by opening the Control Panel from its icon in the Main group of Program Manager, then double-clicking the 386 Enhanced icon. (This icon appears in the Control Panel only if Windows is currently in enhanced mode.) The Minimum Timeslice value can be set as low as 1, and I've in fact run fast 386 systems set to 1 for days on end with no ill effect. But the following procedure should help you find the best value for your particular configuration of hardware and software.

One way to test the proper value for yourself is by typing in the batch file shown in Listing 9-1. (If you prefer another benchmark, of course, run it instead, but the following procedure does not require that you buy a separate, third-party benchmark program.) Call the file LOOP1.BAT, and place it in any directory on your Path. Then replace "loop1" with "loop2," and save the file as LOOP2.BAT.

Listing 9-1: LOOP1.BAT

```
@echo off
echo Loop1 is running...
echo. | date | c:\loop1\find "Current" >> c:\loop1\loop1.txt
echo Settings: %1 %2 %3 %4 %5 %6 %7 %8 %9 >> c:\loop1\loop1.txt
:LOOP
echo. | time | c:\loop1\find "Current"
echo. | time | c:\loop1\find "Current" >> c:\loop1\loop1.txt
goto :LOOP
```

Before running these batch files, create two directories called C:\LOOP1 and C:\LOOP2. Then copy FIND.EXE from your \DOS directory into *both* of these directories (you can't open the same file from two different DOS sessions).

Now close all windows, except Program Manager. Next, open two windowed DOS sessions by double-clicking your DOS Session icon, which runs COMMAND.PIF. Position these two windows so you can see as much of each window as possible.

At the DOS prompt in the "front" window, type the command LOOP2 SLICE=20 FOREGROUND. Don't press Enter yet. Click your mouse in the *other* DOS window and type LOOP1 SLICE=20 BACKGROUND. (The parameters echo the current settings into the output files.) At this point, start LOOP1, then LOOP2, as close to the same moment as possible.

Note when Loop2 displays the first timestamp on the screen and, after 60 seconds have elapsed, stop Loop2 by pressing Ctrl+Break. Then click the other DOS window and stop Loop1 the same way.

Now you have two text files. Each records the number of loops that each batch file could perform in the time available. (Count only lines written within the 60 seconds that Loop2 was running.)

By changing Minimum Timeslice to 20, 10, 5, and 1 using the Control Panel's 386 Enhanced dialog box, I obtained the results in the following table (on a 386/33 with 8MB RAM):

Timeslice	20	10	5	1
Background Loops	73	69	57	30
Foreground Loops	88	93	100	90
Total	161	162	157	120

Notice that the default value of 20 did not result in the best foreground performance. By reducing the Minimum Timeslice to 5, we improved the number of loops from 88 to 100 (at the expense of the background process) while executing almost the same number of total loops.

You should also run this test with both batch files running in full-screen mode instead of windowed. To switch between these windows, press Alt+Tab or Alt+Esc. Use the results from whichever test best reflects the way you actually use DOS sessions under Windows — full-screen or windowed.

After you've determined the optimum timeslice value, you can perform further experiments by increasing the Foreground Priority value in COMMAND.PIF (from 100 in increments of 1000 all the way up to 10000).

Several people I know have tried the Loop1 and Loop2 batch files. The optimum setting obtained by these users varied from 25 down to 5. But the majority of responses indicated that a setting of 5 or 10 was the best overall for most 386 and 486 systems.

Some testers worried that they weren't able to get the batch files to produce as many loops on their system as I seemed to be getting on my test 386/33. I wouldn't worry about the absolute number of loops. These batch files were developed only to test performance within a single system, not to compare the performance of two different PCs.

Loop1 and Loop2 do nothing except write a line to the screen and a line to a disk file, repeatedly. As such, they test nothing but the speed of your video BIOS and the speed of disk writes to a single sector. Windows does not use the video BIOS (it writes directly to video RAM). Nor do most Windows applications write to disk a single sector at a time.

To determine the best setting for your system, you should add to these batch files some operation that is typical of the actual work you do, such as a DOS application that you can program to carry out a set of tasks automatically.

One reader did find a setting that significantly improved his DOS performance. He changed VirtualHDIRQ=ON to VirtualHDIRQ=OFF in the [386Enh] section of his SYSTEM.INI file. This keeps Windows from "virtualizing" (managing) the hard disk interrupt-request line, so Windows is forced to access the hard disk through the system BIOS.

This change doubled the number of loops he was able to perform in his DOS sessions. One reason is that he was using PC-Kwik Corp.'s Super PC-Kwik disk cache instead of SmartDrive. The Super PC-Kwik documentation states that VirtualHDIRQ=OFF should be added to SYSTEM.INI so disk access can be cached by the utility.

You can add VirtualHDIRQ=OFF in the [386Enh] section of your SYSTEM.INI if you want to test its impact on your system's performance. But if a statement like this already appears in your SYSTEM.INI, don't blithely change it to VirtualHDIRQ=ON. Some disk drivers aren't compatible with Windows' virtualization, and they may have written this line into your SYSTEM.INI for a reason.

Some of the Best Windows 3.1 Secrets Are DOS Capabilities

Some of the best new features of Windows 3.1, ironically, are the capabilities that DOS applications gain under Windows.

If you have a 386-based system or higher, you've probably already run a windowed DOS session, and discovered the new DOS session fonts.

To see these fonts, if your DOS sessions start out full-screen, press Alt+Enter to shrink the session to a small window. Next, pull down the Control menu from the left-hand side of the window's title bar, then click Fonts. You should see several choices of font sizes for text-mode DOS apps, including the DOS prompt itself.

Displaying 50 lines in a DOS session

But the choicest DOS capabilities are two little-known features worth trying.

The first is a method to change the number of lines that appear in a DOS session from the standard 25 lines to 50 lines. This convinces many DOS commands, and even some DOS applications, to switch to 50-line mode themselves.

The method to accomplish this text-mode magic is simple. Add the following to the [NonWindowsApp] section of your Windows 3.1 SYSTEM.INI file:

```
[NonWindowsApp]
ScreenLines=50
```

When you restart Windows and start a windowed DOS session, your DOS prompt appears in a window that accommodates 50 text lines. You may need to change the DOS font to a smaller size to see the entire window at the particular resolution your monitor supports.

Once your windowed DOS fonts are adjusted to your liking, try the command DIR/P in a directory with a lot of filenames. DIR displays a full page of listings — stopping only after all 50 lines in your window are filled.

Many applications, of course, will force the screen to their usual display mode, no matter how many lines your screen can handle. But you'd be surprised at the utilities that take to your new mode just fine. DOS 5's EDIT program, for example, runs in a 50-line window with no fuss, and even supports a mouse under Windows (if you load a MOUSE.COM driver in your AUTOEXEC.BAT before starting Windows).

You can also set the screen to 43 lines, using the setting ScreenLines=43. Most VGA adapters support 25-, 43-, and 50-line modes, although if yours doesn't, changing the setting won't change anything. A 43-line display takes up less room on your Windows display than a 50-line display while still giving you a lot more information than the bad old 25-line display.

Creating a distinct prompt for DOS sessions

The other new feature is a way to set a prompt inside DOS sessions under Windows that is different than the normal DOS prompt you see when Windows isn't running.

Windows 3.1 prevents you from starting another instance of itself if you type WIN at a DOS prompt while Windows is already running. (If you try, it just displays a warning message.)

But you still might find it desirable to remind yourself — in full-screen DOS sessions — that Windows is already running. For example, you shouldn't start a disk-optimizer program, or other program that directly modifies File Allocation Tables, under Windows. Windows doesn't detect these activities, so you might scramble valuable data.

You can warn yourself that Windows is active by adding a line to your AUTOEXEC.BAT after your normal SET PROMPT statement. This line might look like the following: "SET WINPMT=Press ALT+ENTER or type EXIT to return to Windows.$_$_PG". (The "$_" symbols insert blank lines between your message and the normal Path and Greater-than signs used in most prompts.)

After rebooting, so this AUTOEXEC.BAT is executed, you should be able to start Windows, and see your new prompt inside DOS sessions — but not at the DOS prompt *after* you exit Windows.

If you type SET by itself in a DOS session under Windows, you can see what's happening. The SET command displays the contents of the DOS environment. In DOS sessions, Windows reverses the meaning of SET PROMPT and SET WINPMT. While Windows is running, therefore, SET WINPMT is equal to PG (or whatever your normal prompt setting is), and SET PROMPT is equal to your longer message.

This crude but effective method can be used to create any DOS prompt you like under Windows — at least until Microsoft decides how it wants to implement this feature in the next major release.

Enhanced DOS in Enhanced Windows Mode

Most Windows users have learned something about the differences between standard mode and 386 enhanced mode. Among other things, enhanced mode can run more than one DOS session, and each session can work in the background. Standard mode can support only one DOS session, and that session is suspended when placed in the background.

Under Windows 3.0, applications typically ran 10 to 20 percent slower in enhanced mode than in standard mode. However, Windows 3.1 has largely closed that gap, so there is no longer a good reason to avoid enhanced mode for performance reasons.

But there is another feature of enhanced mode that is almost unknown to Windows users.

In 386 enhanced mode, Windows supports *virtual device drivers*. These drivers, known as VxDs for virtual (unknown or X) device drivers, often appear in Windows filenames with extensions like .VXD or .386 — but they can just as easily be files named .EXE, .DLL, or any other extension.

Virtual device drivers are examples of full 32-bit programming code. These little programs run in 386 protected mode, use 32-bit instructions, and have several capabilities that normal, 16-bit Windows applications do not.

Most Windows applications cannot directly affect a PC's hardware and memory — they must request these services from Windows itself. But VxDs can do anything that is permitted of Windows.

In enhanced mode, Windows itself is made up of many VxDs. They attach themselves to the Windows kernel and, in effect, become part of the kernel, with all its privileges.

Although VxDs are usually written using Microsoft's Windows Device Driver Kit (DDK), they are not limited to the functions associated with DOS device drivers. Instead, they can directly influence Windows, and even DOS applications running under Windows. In his book *Undocumented Windows* (Addison-Wesley), Andrew Schulman, formerly a programmer for Phar Lap Software, writes, "Some programmers have even come to regard VxDs and the DDK as the 'real' Windows API [Application Programming Interface]."

Adding new commands to DOS sessions

This information is significant for PC managers because of a VxD called Enhanced DOS. By simply installing this small program into Windows, all your DOS sessions under Windows gain some remarkable powers.

Enhanced DOS, or EDOS for short, actually adds internal commands to DOS. *Internal commands*, as you recall, are statements such as DIR and COPY that are built into COMMAND.COM. By contrast, *external commands* — such as XCOPY.EXE — are separate executable files in your DOS directory.

When EDOS is installed, every DOS session in enhanced mode gains several new commands, such as ALARM, CLIPBOARD, and EXCLUSIVE. There are no executable files with these names on your disk, yet the power of these "enhanced" commands can be surprising.

If you have an important meeting coming up in an hour, for example, you can simply type ALARM 3600 in a DOS session and minimize it. Exactly one hour (3600 seconds) later, the DOS session will display a Windows dialog box to remind you of the alarm you set.

How is it that a DOS session can display a Windows dialog box, complete with a title bar and OK button? That's the magic of VxDs.

With another command, CLIPBOARD /VIEW, you can display in a DOS session any text that happens to be in the Windows Clipboard. By adding ">LPT1" to redirect the output to your printer, you can print the Clipboard — something even Windows 3.1's Clipboard Viewer can't.

As programmer Michael Maurice notes, the routines that give EDOS its power can easily be adapted to other applications. Any DOS application, therefore, could gain the ability to display alarms in Windows or print the Windows Clipboard.

EDOS also allows you to specify all PIF settings in batch files. This eliminates maintaining multiple PIFs. You can even add more memory to a DOS session than it started with.

Tuning your performance with BOXTIME

But the monitoring and timing functions of EDOS are perhaps its most useful features.

As a 386 virtual device driver (which runs only in enhanced mode Windows), EDOS has the same access to your hardware that Windows itself does. This allows EDOS to set timers that not only record the total elapsed time (the time you see on a stopwatch), but also record the CPU time that each DOS session is allocated by Windows.

I've spent a lot of time tuning different PIF settings for particular DOS applications. I wish I'd had EDOS then.

With EDOS's new BOXTIME command (one of the internal commands that it adds seamlessly to DOS), this kind of tuning becomes a snap.

When you first type BOXTIME (or run it in a batch file), it resets its timers. When you run it again, it reports to you the total elapsed time, as well as the time (in seconds, and as a percentage of elapsed time) that the current DOS session was allowed by Windows to run.

To test how well a DOS application such as Lotus 1-2-3 runs under Windows, you could start a DOS command line from a PIF and run the following batch file:

```
BOXTIME
123
BOXTIME
```

By running a macro that performs the same actions in 1-2-3 every time, you can use this batch file to get very precise information. For example, you could evaluate running 1-2-3 under various foreground and background priority settings.

You can even learn useful data about Windows performance using plain old DOS commands. The following DOS command generates a DIR listing of a large disk directory, sorts it alphabetically, sorts it in reverse, then outputs it to the screen:

```
dir \windows | sort | sort/r
```

On the 386/33 system that I tested, this command received about 99 percent of the CPU's time when it ran with the Exclusive PIF option on. It also received 99 percent with the Foreground priority set to 10000 (the maximum) and Exclusive off. But this figure dropped to only 33 percent when the batch file was run in a DOS session that was windowed. In each case, several Windows applications were idle in the background. Apparently, even Windows 3.1 steals a major slice of time from windowed DOS apps — whether the other apps need any time or not.

In addition to PIFs, you should also test the following performance variables in the [386Enh] section of your SYSTEM.INI: FileSysChange, MinTimeslice, WindowUpdateTime, WinExclusive, and WinTimeslice.

The current version of EDOS has been significantly upgraded from the early shareware version that is on the diskettes accompanying *Windows 3.1 Secrets*. That version wouldn't work with some clone PC BIOSes, but extra code has been added to EDOS that allows it to work with almost all flavors of PCs. Registering with the publisher of EDOS brings you the current, updated version.

EDOS is $69.95, which includes 2-day UPS delivery, from Mom's Software, 32345 SW Arbor Lake Dr., Wilsonville, OR 97070; 800-248-0809 (orders), 503-694-2221 (information and technical support).

EDOS and users of Novell's DR DOS

If you use DR DOS 6.0 from Digital Research and Novell, a few EDOS features don't work — specifically, DR DOS does not allow EDOS to use "installable commands" to add new internal commands to DOS. This is true even if you have obtained the "Business Update" that was released by Digital Research in an April 1992 patch to make DR DOS 6.0 capable of running Windows 3.1.

In technical terms, DR DOS does not support DOS function call AE, subfunctions 00 and 01. These functions were added to MS-DOS 3.3, but their first known use by a program was in the DOSSHELL application included with DOS 4.0. These functions are described in the Command Interpreters chapter of *Undocumented DOS* (Addison-Wesley).

There is a workaround, if you use DR DOS and want to try EDOS: obtain an enhanced DOS command interpreter called 4DOS from J.P. Software. Use this command processor instead of the COMMAND.COM file that comes with DR DOS 6.0, and all EDOS functions will be supported. You can order 4DOS, at this writing, for $69 by calling 800-368-8777 or 617-646-3975.

Exclaim Adds Capabilities to DOS Under Windows

Another utility, Exclaim from Terratech Inc., almost completely replaces the need for a DOS session in Windows. Exclaim is one of the most ambitious shareware programs (for its size) I've seen. It emulates all the major DOS internal commands (DIR, COPY, and so on) in a graphical window that you can resize, scroll, and use like any other window. Yet Exclaim uses only 76K of memory, unlike ordinary 640K DOS sessions, which actually use over 550K.

This means that you can put Exclaim on the Load= line of your WIN.INI file, or in the StartUp group of Windows 3.1, and have a DOS prompt handy whenever you need one. Or you can click File Run in Program Manager and simply type "!" — because Exclaim is really a Windows program named "!.EXE." And as a genuine Windows application, you can feed "!" keystrokes from a Recorder macro, unlike DOS sessions.

Exclaim does have several differences from COMMAND.COM, the DOS command-line interpreter. For example, Exclaim does not support SET, FORMAT, and a few other DOS commands. And when you start a batch file from Exclaim, the batch file starts running in a separate DOS window. (You can override this, though.)

Although Exclaim does not support every possible DOS command and feature, it offers many commands that are not available in DOS. You can move files to a different location, change the color of your command-line window without strange escape sequences, and write IF...THEN...ENDIF statements. Funny that a single programmer, working at home, can provide these features when Microsoft hasn't been able to put them into DOS for more than a decade.

You can even start Windows applications from the Exclaim command line. Type NOTEPAD, for example, and Notepad appears in its own window.

Exclaim is a shareware program featured in *Windows Gizmos.* Order Exclaim by sending $25 to Terratech, 19817 61st Ave. SE, Snohomish, WA 98290. The company isn't yet taking phone or credit card orders, but I think you'll find Exclaim worth cutting a check for.

Printing the DOS Character Set in Windows Applications

Although my primary focus is Windows, I find myself (perhaps like you) spending a lot of my time dealing with good ol' DOS.

I have long recommended that companies converting from DOS to Windows also spend the money to convert all their applications to Windows. Eliminating DOS applications saves many costly headaches related to incompatibilities, use of memory, and so on.

But those companies fortunate enough to be able to make a full conversion to Windows applications are few. I was recently giving a Windows seminar, and I asked the audience of 800 for a show of hands on how many companies used all Windows applications, and how many still used some DOS applications under Windows. No one responded to the first question, but almost 100 percent raised their hands to the second.

Several people have asked me how to capture a DOS screen shot and print it in a Windows application. This is important to people who use Windows apps to document DOS programs or commands.

The question is complicated by the odd fact that Windows does not support the so-called PC-8 character set that DOS uses. In particular, Windows cannot display the line-draw characters that often appear in DOS apps as borders.

The only method that preserved these lines was a clumsy workaround:

STEPS

Capturing and Printing a DOS Screen Shot

Step 1. With a DOS application running full-screen under Windows, press Alt+Print Screen to copy the DOS characters into the Windows Clipboard.

Step 2. From Program Manager, start the Clipboard Viewer. This should display the text of the DOS screen.

Step 3. On the main menu, click Display OEM-Text. This changes the Clipboard's font so it accurately displays the DOS PC-8 character set. (Clipboard uses a Windows screen font with a name like VGAOEM.FON or similar.)

Step 4. Size the Clipboard Viewer window so all the DOS text is visible. Finally, press Alt+Print Screen to transfer the Clipboard Viewer window itself into the Clipboard.

Step 5. Start Windows Paintbrush. Click Edit Paste to paste the contents of the Clipboard into the drawing area. You can then erase the Clipboard's window border, leaving just the DOS area. This can, in turn, be pasted into a Windows word processor and printed as a graphic.

As I said, this is a kludge. I've recently found a better way to print the PC-8 character set, which doesn't involve printing DOS windows as graphics.

Using VTS fonts to print screens

Video Terminal Screen (VTS) is a new typeface for Windows. It includes all the upper-ASCII characters, plus symbols for control characters like Ctrl+L.

The typeface is shareware, and is featured in the Excellence in Windows Shareware section of *More Windows 3.1 Secrets*. You can also obtain VTS, in both TrueType and PostScript Type 1 versions, on CompuServe. Type GO DTPFORUM, select Libraries, then select PC Fonts (Library 9). Download the file VTSR-T.ZIP for a TrueType font or VTSR-P.ZIP for a PostScript Type 1 font (which requires Adobe Type Manager or Zenographics' SuperPrint type scaler).

If you find these fonts work for you, it's just $10 to register them with their creator, E.A. Behl. This is a good idea, because you also receive two other fonts, "bold" and "italic" versions of VTS. These are not really bold and italic, but are needed to print some characters that you cannot access in Windows using the Alt key and the numeric keypad, such as control characters (Alt+1 to Alt+31).

Many upper-ASCII characters are converted incorrectly when pasted from the Clipboard into a Windows application. To avoid this, first save a DOS screen to a text file. If you don't have a DOS screen-capture utility, the best way to do this is with the Windows Clipboard. To do this, follow these steps:

STEPS

Capturing a DOS Text Screen into a Text File

Step 1. Run your DOS text-mode application full-screen under Windows. Press Alt+Print Screen to copy the screen to the Clipboard. (I recommend elsewhere in this book that you reserve the Print Screen key for the DOS application, not Windows. Therefore, I recommend Alt+Print Screen be used to copy DOS full-screen text to the Clipboard.) Switch back to Windows with Alt+Tab and start the Clipboard Viewer from the Main group in Program Manager. Something like your DOS text should be visible in the Clipboard Viewer window. Click File Save-As and save the contents of the Clipboard into a file named MYSCREEN.CLP or whatever.

Step 2. Now open this file in such applications as Windows Write (specifying the "No Conversion" option) and Word for Windows (specifying "Text Only," not "DOS Text"). In word processors like these, the file MYSCREEN.CLP will contain a one-line header (which looks like garbage), followed by a copy of your DOS text, a separator line, and another copy of the text. You should delete the header, the separator, and everything after the separator. (The text after the separator is your DOS text *after* its line-draw characters and other special characters have been converted into plain keyboard characters that Windows supports.) At this point, formatting the remaining text in the VTS font displays the correct characters. All line-draw and special upper-ASCII characters should appear exactly as they did in your DOS application.

Send $10 for VTS to E.A. Behl, 2663 Red Oak Ct., Clearwater, FL 34621-2319. The author's CompuServe account number is 70413,1073.

Solving DOSX.EXE Problems Under Enhanced-Mode Windows

One of my readers, Scott Hanselman, reports a problem he had with DOSX.EXE, a standard-mode Windows file. While running Windows in enhanced mode, he was looking through directories with Norton Commander. His finger accidentally hit Enter with DOSX.EXE highlighted, which caused the file to be run. Loading DOSX.EXE with Windows in enhanced mode hung the system and corrupted files that other applications happened to have open. (Several other shells, including Windows' own File Manager, also allow you to run a highlighted program by pressing Enter.)

Since users often double-click filenames in File Manager "just to see what they do," you might want to guard against this destructive possibility.

 Don't delete DOSX.EXE — you'll need it if you ever have to start Windows in standard mode someday. Instead, mark it Hidden and System using the File Manager's File Properties dialog box, or the DOS command ATTRIB +H +S DOSX.EXE. Windows will still start in standard mode, even though DOSX.EXE isn't visible.

Protecting Windows Files from Dangerous DOS Commands

Microsoft's release of DOS 5.0 made available a little more memory to DOS applications under Windows than DOS 3 or 4. But it didn't solve other problems I've always had running DOS sessions in the Windows environment.

Several DOS commands, for example, are dangerous when run in a DOS session under Windows. One such command is the check disk utility, CHKDSK.COM. Issuing the CHKDSK command by itself in a DOS session is perfectly harmless, just as it is when run from an ordinary DOS prompt. You not only receive a warning of file errors on your hard drive, you also get a count of how much RAM is available — a statistic that is often useful when running DOS applications in a window.

If you check your hard drive, however, with a switch that also "fixes" disk errors, as when you type CHKDSK /F, you are in serious danger of losing files if you're running Windows 3.0 in standard mode.

Preventing CHKDSK disasters

CHKDSK, a relic that is largely unchanged since its introduction in DOS 1.0, correctly rewrites "lost" file fragments into visible chunks that you can delete (reclaiming disk space), if you run it at the DOS prompt. But if you run CHKDSK /F in a DOS session under Windows 3.0 in standard mode, CHKDSK incorrectly interprets files that Windows applications have open as "lost files" and rewrites them. This has the disastrous effect of chopping your open documents into a series of files with names like FILE0000.CHK, FILE0001.CHK, and so on. Each of these files is 2,048 bytes in size (or whatever size the clusters on your hard drive are), and no undelete utility can put them back together again. You'll have to reinstall or restore such files from any backups you may have prepared.

It's inexcusable that this nasty behavior wasn't corrected in DOS 5.0, since it was released more than a year after the success of Windows 3.0. But rather than adding a few dozen bytes to CHKDSK's code to test for Windows before running destructive routines, Microsoft added a line to page 382 of the DOS 5 manual stating, "Avoid using CHKDSK from another program or Microsoft Windows."

This is corrected in DOS 6.0 and Windows 3.1. But because CHKDSK /F can cause problems when run in a DOS "shell" under DOS applications such as Lotus 1-2-3, you may want to replace CHKDSK.COM with a batch file that tests for Windows and other programs that can "shell out" to DOS. If all is clear, the batch file can then execute CHKDSK normally.

To test for Windows from a batch file, type the Debug script shown in Listing 9-2 into a text file named ISWIN.DEB. Be sure to type a carriage return after the "Q" in the last line, and two returns after "INT 21." Once this file is saved, type the command DEBUG<ISWIN.DEB at a DOS prompt. This creates a small executable file called ISWIN.COM, which sets the DOS Errorlevel to zero if Windows is not running, and a positive number if Windows is running.

Listing 9-2: Type this Debug script into a text file named ISWIN.DEB.

```
N ISWIN.COM
A 100
MOV AX,4680
INT 2F
XOR AL,80
MOV CL,AL
MOV AX,1600
INT 2F
AND AL,7F
OR  AL,CL
CMP AL,80
JZ  011A
MOV AH,4C
INT 21

MOV AX,1605
XOR BX,BX
MOV ES,BX
XOR SI,SI
MOV DS,SI
XOR CX,CX
MOV DX,0001
MOV DI,0300
```

```
INT 2F
CMP CX,+00
JNZ 0139
MOV AX,1606
INT 2F
MOV AL,80
OR  AL,CL
MOV AH,4C
INT 21
R CX
41
W
Q
```

Watch out for other destructive commands

Other DOS commands in DOS 5.0 can be dangerous or confusing to Windows as well. Take the old DOS APPEND command, which makes data in a particular subdirectory appear to actually be in the current directory (for applications that can't change directories). If such a command is in effect, Windows may think that a file it found on your disk is actually located in the current directory, and may display an error message or write inaccurate information to that file later in your workday.

Another command that can be useful for older DOS applications, but confusing to Windows, is SUBST. This command makes a particular subdirectory, such as C:\DATA, appear to be the root directory of a fictitious drive, such as E:\. Many microcomputer managers use this command to create short aliases for long directory names, allowing them to place more directories in the Path than would be allowed by the Path's 127-character limit.

If you use SUBST to do this while Windows is running, however, Windows applications that expect drives to really *be* drives may act improperly. The Windows 3.0 Setup program, which installs Windows, is especially sensitive to fake drives. If a SUBST command is in effect, Setup thuds gracelessly to a halt during the process of scanning all your hard drives for applications. This is fixed in Windows 3.1, but you still should not run SUBST in a DOS session under Windows.

In any case, you should definitely prevent destructive commands like CHKDSK /F from being run under Windows. This includes any command that rewrites your file structure directly, such as disk optimizers, interleave utilities, and undelete programs. (Some versions of disk utilities — like Norton Utilities 6.0 and higher — detect when they are being run in a DOS session under Windows, and refuse to perform these activities until Windows has been exited.)

Batch files that test for Windows

To keep these commands from mistakenly being started inside Windows, you should run such commands from batch files that test for Windows. To protect yourself from accidentally running CHKDSK /F under Windows, for example, change to your DOS directory and rename CHKDSK by typing the command REN CHKDSK.COM CHKDSK!.COM. (I use an exclamation point when I modify a DOS filename; the symbol reminds me that there is something dangerous about that program.) Then create the batch file in Listing 9-3, CHKDSK.BAT, in a directory on your Path.

Listing 9-3: CHKDSK.BAT can keep you from accidentally running CHKDSK /F under Windows.

```
echo off
if "%1"=="" goto :OK
  iswin
  if not errorlevel 1 goto :OK
    echo.
    echo You can't use CHKDSK options in Windows.
    echo.
    goto :END
:OK
  chkdsk! %1 %2 %3
:END
```

CHKDSK.BAT executes the renamed CHKDSK!.COM command as usual if you typed CHKDSK with no switches, or if Windows is not running. CHKDSK.BAT uses ISWIN.COM to test for Windows.

If you started the batch file by typing CHKDSK /F, and Windows is running, you receive a message that you can't use parameters to CHKDSK under Windows, and CHKDSK.BAT quits. Like any batch file, there must be a space between CHKDSK and /F for the DOS command processor to detect that there are any switches at all. If you forget the space, the batch file runs CHKDSK without any parameters, which is harmless whether or not Windows is running.

ISWIN.COM sets the DOS Errorlevel variable. After you use ISWIN.COM, the Errorlevel will be zero if Windows is not running, and a positive value if Windows is running. The following chart shows these values:

Status of Windows	Errorlevel
Windows is not running	0
Windows/386 2.x is running	1
Windows 3.x is in 386 mode	3
Windows 4.x is in 386 mode	4
Windows/386 2.x is running	127
Windows 3.x is in real mode	128
Windows 3.x is in standard mode	255

CHKDSK.BAT, as written above, simply exits if the Errorlevel is 1 or higher. But you can create a more sophisticated batch file, if you wish, that takes different actions depending on which mode or version of Windows is running.

Batch files that test for other programs

To test for programs other than Windows, start these DOS programs from a batch file. In the batch file, set an environmental variable before and after running the program. For example, to test for Lotus 1-2-3, use this batch file to start the program:

```
@echo off
set LOTUS123=y
123
set LOTUS123=
```

In the CHKDSK.BAT program, you can add the line IF NOT "%LOTUS123%"=="y" GOTO :OK to test for Lotus 1-2-3 before running CHKDSK with switches like /F.

I would like to thank Fran Finnegan, who developed this program at Finnegan O'Malley & Company Inc. in San Francisco, the firm responsible for E-Mail Manager, a commercial Windows application. An earlier version of this script was made public in the March 1991 *Microsoft Systems Journal*, which also showed a way to do the same thing in a C program.

Using PKZip 2.x and Similar Programs Under Windows

To reduce the disk-space demands of Windows applications, Windows users often turn to various compression alternatives. One of the most popular is PKZip, a shareware program that compresses multiple files into a single ZIP file, often saving 50 percent or more of the space required by the original files.

A major upgrade to PKZip, called Version 2.04c, was released to bulletin boards and other shareware distributors in early 1993. According to Douglas Hay, a co-developer of PKZip, this version was called 2.04c instead of simply 2.0 because bulletin boards received fake programs (some with viruses) calling themselves PKZip 2.0, 2.01, and 2.05.

Since PKZip 2 has several puzzling interactions with Windows, this section is devoted to helping you troubleshoot these situations, even though PKZip is a DOS, not a Windows, program.

PKZip 2.04c was released in January 1993 with much fanfare. To correct a few problems, a later version with some Windows fixes, called release 2.04e was announced later that month. But the one that Windows users should really have is Version 2.04g, which started appearing on bulletin boards just a few weeks later.

You may have Windows users in your company who heard the publicity about PKZip 2.04c and immediately downloaded it and started using it. If so, and they use it in a DOS session under Windows, you may see messages like "This application has violated system integrity and will be closed."

Maddeningly, this message does not appear the first time PKZip is used. Mr. Hay says it only occurs after you use PKZip several times and then run some *other* command.

PKZip 2.04e and 2.04g correct this problem in *most*, but not all, cases. Mr. Hay says PKWare received more than 500 calls about this in Version 2.04c, but only five or six for Version 2.04e and later.

The cause of the "system integrity" error, according to Mr. Hay, is the Windows 3.1 extended memory manager for DPMI — the DOS Protected Mode Interface. Mr. Hay says there is no problem with PKZip 2.04g using extended memory under QEMM or 386Max at a DOS prompt — only under Windows, when Microsoft's DPMI manager is in control.

You can eliminate the error messages by adding the line DPMI=Disabled to the file PKZIP.CFG, which should be in the same directory as PKZip. To fix PKUnzip, a companion program, the line SET PKUNZIP=-) should be in your AUTOEXEC.BAT.

The value after the equals sign in this line is a hyphen followed by a closed parenthesis mark, which is a PKWare command-line switch. (Mr. Hay says PKZip has run out of letters for switches and must now use symbols.)

Another anomaly that will affect many users is that PKZip 2 uses a different ZIP format than Version 1.1. PKWare says the new version compresses files faster and about 10 to 15 percent smaller than before. But Version 1.1 cannot decompress Version 2.0 files — and there is no command-line switch that allows Version 2.0 to make Version 1.1 ZIP files.

Phil Katz, president of PKWare, told me this was to keep the code size of PKZip small. Additionally, he said, anyone can get the new PKZip 2.0 by downloading it from a variety of bulletin boards.

However, this will cause problems for those using only PKZip 1.1, or versions of Windows unzip programs that were originally featured in *Windows Gizmos:* Windows Unarchive and Zip Tools for Windows.

By now, both of those programs have been revised to support both the old PKZip 1.1 format and the newer 2.0 format. The upgraded version of Windows Unarchive is available by sending $15 to James Hughes, 1100 Fair Park Blvd. #2, Little Rock, AR 72204; CompuServe: 73777,3273. The new Zip Tools is available by sending $64.50 to Richard Patterson, P.O. Box 270492, Houston, TX 77277; CompuServe: 70771,1336.

Until everyone has switched to upgraded versions of PKZip and other such programs, I recommend you not delete PKZip 1.1, if you already have it. Use it to create ZIP files you distribute to others who don't have PKZip 2.0, and use PKZip 2.0 to exchange files with people who have that version.

Summary

In this chapter, I cover many of the necessary tricks you'll need to handle the operating system we can't live with, but can't live without: DOS.

▶ First, optimizing the performance of DOS multitasking is described, including setting the Foreground and Background Priorities and the poorly understood Minimum Timeslice value.

▶ Some of the new DOS capabilities that have been gained under Windows 3.1 are explored.

▶ Powerful DOS and DOS-like utilities, such as EDOS and Exclaim, are reviewed and their functionality explained.

▶ Printing DOS text screens, including the elusive PC-8 line-draw and upper-ASCII characters, is detailed, including a discussion of the Video Terminal Screen (PC-8) font that can be found on the *More Windows 3.1 Secrets* diskettes.

▶ Commands that are dangerous under Windows 3.0 and 3.1 in standard or enhanced modes are listed, and workarounds suggested.

▶ The somewhat shaky shift from PKZip format 1.1 to 2.0 is examined, in context with true Windows utilities that handle both the old and new ZIP file formats.

Chapter 10
Print Screen Secrets

In This Chapter

In this chapter, I'll show you the following secrets about using the Print Screen key in Windows:

▶ How to regain the Print Screen function in DOS sessions under Windows, while retaining the ability to copy information to the Clipboard.

▶ How to print the screen in Windows, using a few simple but poorly understood steps.

▶ How to automate those steps, so you can print your screen from Windows with a single keystroke combination.

If you're a regular Windows user, you've probably noticed that Windows makes some things a lot easier but it makes other things a lot more difficult than DOS.

A Windows word processor, for example, usually makes it a lot easier for you to format a page of type compared to the same job in a DOS word processor.

But when you want to send to your printer a quick snapshot of what's on your screen, the plain old DOS Print Screen key does the job a lot faster than anything in Windows.

In DOS, when you press the Print Screen key on your keyboard, the text on your screen is immediately sent to the printer on your first printer port (LPT1). If you have DOS 5.0 or higher, you can even extend this ability to graphics screens by first running a memory-resident program called GRAPHICS.COM (described in your DOS manual).

Windows, unfortunately, suffers from a decision made by Microsoft long ago to use the Print Screen key for another function. When you press the Print Screen key in Windows, nothing is sent to your printer. Instead, a copy of your screen is sent to the Windows Clipboard — an area of memory set aside to hold text and graphics that you cut and paste between programs. And Microsoft "forgot" to give the Clipboard any way to print its contents — you need a separate application.

To add insult to injury, the Print Screen key is actually *disabled* even for plain old DOS applications you may be running under Windows.

Regaining Print Screens in DOS

One of the simplest improvements you can make is restoring the Print Screen capability that Microsoft took away from DOS applications running under Windows. You can easily do this, while preserving the ability to copy data from a DOS application to the Windows Clipboard when necessary.

All DOS sessions that you start in Windows are controlled by a Program Information File (PIF). If you have a PIF file with the same name as the DOS application you are starting (such as 123.PIF for a DOS version of Lotus 1-2-3), Windows uses the settings you've specified in that PIF. If not, Windows uses the settings in _DEFAULT.PIF (the first character of the filename is an underscore).

You change the settings in these PIF files using an application included with Windows called the PIF Editor. I recommend that you customize a PIF file for every DOS program you use under Windows. But first you'll need to edit Windows's _DEFAULT.PIF file, which most people use (without being aware of it) every time they start a DOS prompt or DOS application.

STEPS

Editing Windows' _DEFAULT.PIF

Step 1. In the Program Manager, double-click the PIF Editor icon, or click File Run and type PIFEDIT. In the PIF Editor window that appears, click File Open. Double-click the filename _DEFAULT.PIF (you'll usually find this file in your C:\WINDOWS directory, but it may be placed in any directory on your DOS Path).

Step 2. If you are running Windows in standard mode, you'll see a section in the PIF Editor window labeled Reserve Shortcut Keys, and a box titled PrtSc. In 386 enhanced mode, you must click the Advanced button to see this section. In either case, click the box to turn *on* the "X" by the PrtSc label. This reserves the use of the Print Screen key for any DOS prompt or application you start from _DEFAULT.PIF, and stops Windows from using it to copy the screen to the Clipboard.

Step 3. Click File Save to write your changes into _DEFAULT.PIF. This changes the Print Screen setting for DOS sessions running under either Windows standard mode or 386 enhanced mode. (Windows 3.0 has a bug that disables the Print Screen key in DOS sessions under standard mode, no matter *how* you set your PIF files. This bug was corrected in Windows 3.1.)

Step 4. Open any other PIF files you use for DOS applications. Set the Print Screen box *on* in these PIF files as well, and save the changes.

Now that you've taken these steps, start a DOS session and try your Print Screen key. Make sure you are starting a DOS session from one of the PIF files you edited. If you aren't sure, click File Run in the Program Manager and type _DEFAULT.PIF. Windows will interpret this as a command to run this PIF file, including all its settings.

If you use a dot-matrix printer, pressing the Print Screen key at this point should print a few lines of text. If you use a laser printer, you should see the Form Feed light go on, but nothing come out of the paper tray. This is because most laser printers wait until a full page is printed before ejecting the paper.

You can walk over to the printer and eject the page manually. Or you can *make* your laser printer eject the page by running a small program that you can create with the DOS Debug utility. I describe a complete procedure to do this in the "Better LaserJet Resets with Debug" section of Chapter 5, "Making File Manager Your Own."

If you ever need to copy text from a DOS application running under Windows to the Windows Clipboard, press Alt+Print Screen instead of just Print Screen. Alt+Print Screen commands Windows to copy the active window to the Clipboard. If your DOS application is running full-screen, its active window is synonymous with the whole screen, and that's what goes into the Clipboard. If your DOS application is running windowed, press Alt+Enter to switch it to full-screen mode before pressing Alt+Print Screen.

On some keyboards that have Print Screen on a separate, independent key, it is possible to defeat Windows' usual control over the Print Screen key by holding down the Shift key while pressing Print Screen. Windows interprets this as a different key than pressing Print Screen by itself. On keyboards where there is no dedicated Print Screen key, and you access the Print Screen function by pressing Shift plus one other key, this trick won't work, of course.

Printing the Screen Manually in Windows _____

After you've taken the steps above, you'll probably want to print screens from Windows itself.

This is a rather complex process, because Microsoft provides no way for the Clipboard to send its contents to the printer. You need to paste the contents into another application that *can* send files to your printer.

You can, of course, buy any one of several programs that specifically support printing Windows screens. But, rather than buying another application, you can print your screens by using the free (but limited) Paintbrush program included with Windows.

Take the following steps, which you can use to print any Windows screen to any graphics printer.

STEPS

Printing Windows Screens to a Graphics Printer

Step 1. In Windows, press the Print Screen key to copy the entire screen to the Clipboard, or Alt+Print Screen to copy only the active window.

Step 2. Start the Paintbrush program. Double-click its title bar to maximize the application to full-screen.

Step 3. Click Options Image-Attributes on the Paintbrush main menu. In the Image Attributes dialog box that appears, click the Pels button to specify your screen in pixels, rather than inches or centimeters. Change the Width and Height boxes so they represent about 20 *more* pixels than the width and height of your actual display. If you use a 640 x 480 VGA display, for example, set the Image Attributes dialog box to 660 x 500. If you use 800 x 600 Super VGA, set the box to 820 x 620. Set your attributes to black-and-white or color (depending on your monitor), then click OK to save these changes.

Step 4. Click File New to start an empty, white drawing area in Paintbrush with these new dimensions.

Step 5. Click View Zoom-Out. You should see the drawing area reduce itself so it fits completely within the Paintbrush window, with no hidden areas.

Step 6. Click Edit Paste to paste the contents of the Clipboard into this drawing area. You will see a gray, hatched outline, which represents the image you pasted. If you copied the whole Windows screen and want to edit it, you may want to drag this image with your mouse so it is centered in the drawing area.

Step 7. Click one of the Scissors tools in the tool palette at the left of the Paintbrush window. This "sticks" the Clipboard image down on the drawing area. It can no longer be dragged to a new position.

Step 8. Click View Zoom-Out. Then click File Print and click OK to send your image to your current printer.

This sounds like a lot of steps just to print the screen, and it is. Each step is necessary — if you don't zoom out the drawing area, the right side and bottom of your image will be cut off if it's larger than Paintbrush can display.

But these steps become almost automatic after you've done them once. And you can make them *completely* automatic by recording them into a self-running macro, as I describe in the next section.

Automating Print Screens from Paintbrush ____

You can completely automate the steps necessary to print screens from Windows by using the little-understood Recorder application. This application, which is included with Windows, has many limitations. You can't edit macros it records, so if you make a mistake you must start over. But for simple tasks, such as printing the Clipboard through Paintbrush, it's perfect.

To record this macro, first start Recorder by double-clicking the Recorder icon in the Program Manager. A large, empty dialog box appears. Pull down the Options item on the Recorder's main menu. Make sure the following menu items have a check mark beside them, indicating that they are turned on: Control+Break Checking, Shortcut Keys, and Minimize on Use. Then press the Print Screen key so you have an image in the Clipboard (or the following macro won't work).

Now you're ready to click Macro Record on the Recorder main menu. A Record Macro dialog box appears. In this dialog box, you need to fill in a few choices:

Type "Prints Clipboard Graphics" as the Macro Title.

Specify Ctrl+Shift+P as the Shortcut Key. (You can't redefine the Print Screen key in the Recorder, and if you could you'd lose the ability to copy things to the Clipboard anyway.)

Specify "Same Application" for the Playback, and "Recorded Speed" for the Speed. (If your macro works, you can change its properties later so it runs "Fast," instead of at the speed you originally recorded it.) Make sure the Continuous Loop box is off, and the Enable Shortcut Keys box is on.

Finally, in the Record Mouse box, specify "Ignore Mouse."

You are now ready to record the actual steps in your macro. During the recording, you must not use the mouse — set it aside and don't touch it. All Recorder actions will take place exclusively from the keyboard.

To start recording the macro, click the Start button. The Recorder window disappears, but the Recorder icon blinks on the icon line to indicate that a macro is being recorded. You are returned to the Program Manager window, from which you started the Recorder application.

STEPS

Recording a Macro to Print the Clipboard through Paintbrush

Step 1.   Press Alt+F, R to start the File Run menu item in Program Manager.

Step 2.   In the dialog box that appears, type PBRUSH and press Enter to start Paintbrush.

Step 3.   When you see the Paintbrush window, press Alt+Spacebar, X to Maximize Paintbrush.

Step 4.   Press Alt+O, I to run the Options Image-Attributes dialog box. When this box appears, press Alt+U for Units, and press the down-arrow key until the choice "Pels" is highlighted. Press Alt+W and type the Width of the image in pixels, then press Alt+H and type the Height (make these at least the width and height of your monitor's resolution). Press Alt+O to specify colors in the image, then press the cursor-down key until "Black & White" or "Colors" is highlighted. Perform these steps even if the choices already appear correctly in this dialog box, because the macro will need to set these options every time. Finally, press Enter to close the dialog box.

Step 5.   Press Alt+F, N (File New) to clear the drawing area to the correct size.

Step 6.   Press Ctrl+O to zoom out.

Step 7.   Press Alt+E, P to Edit Paste the image from the Clipboard into Paintbrush.

Step 8.   Press the Tab key to select the Scissors tool, then press the Insert key on your cursor keypad to "stick" the image down on the drawing area.

Step 9. After the image has redrawn itself, press Ctrl+N to zoom in.

Step 10. Press Alt+F, P (File Print). In the Print dialog box that appears, set the options as you like, which will probably be as follows: Press Alt+U to use the current printer resolution. Press Alt+S and type 200 to set the printer Scaling to 200% (or whatever the best size printouts for your printer would be). Press Enter to send the job to the printer.

Step 11. After the Print dialog box closes, press Alt+F, X (File Exit) to close Paintbrush. Press N to answer "No" to the question "Save current changes?" Your print job should have finished by now, and you should see a run up copy of your Windows screen, just as you put it in the Clipboard.

Step 12. The Recorder icon should still be blinking on the icon line, so now you must halt the macro recording process. To do this, press Ctrl+Break. A Recorder dialog box appears, enabling you to stop or pause recording. Press Alt+S to save the macro, and Enter to close the dialog box. At this point, you can return to using your mouse. Double-click the Recorder icon, and click File Save on the Recorder window's main menu. Give your macro file a name like MACROS.REC, or, if you already have a file with that name, save your new macro in the same macro file. Later, you can also record other macros into this same file, if you like. You can also add macros from one file into another file, using the Recorder's File Merge menu item.

Each macro must be saved with a different hotkey combination, so you can run each of them at any time. Avoid combinations that consist of Alt or Ctrl plus a letter — these combinations are used by many Windows applications. Instead, use Ctrl+Shift plus a letter. Almost no Windows applications reserve these key combinations.

You can try out your macro by pressing Print Screen to put something new into the Clipboard, then pressing Ctrl+Shift+P (or whatever key combination you originally defined for this macro). If it works as expected, click Macro Properties on the Recorder main menu and change the Speed from Recorded Speed to Fast. If your machine displays an error message when you run the macro set to Fast, you'll have to set it back to run at your Recorded Speed for reliability's sake.

A few cautions are in order so that you can depend on this macro to work for you every time:

■ Program Manager must be running (and not minimized) whenever you press Ctrl+Shift+P to start the macro.

■ Since Recorder and this macro file must be loaded to run the macro, you must make sure that both are properly loaded on the icon line every time you start Windows. In Windows 3.0, a good way to do this is to place the statement MACROS.REC in the LOAD= line of WIN.INI. Windows interprets the .REC extension as a command to start Recorder (minimized) and load its MACROS.REC file. In Windows 3.1, its easier to place an icon in Program Manager's Startup group to load Recorder and this file every time.

Print screen alternatives

These methods should make it possible for you to print virtually any DOS or Windows screen to your printer. But if you print screens very often, you might find it worthwhile to invest in a commercial program that captures screens.

Two useful but inexpensive programs are Paint Shop Pro and SnagIt. In addition to copying the whole screen or a window, Paint Shop Pro can copy any area you select with a mouse. The program is particularly good at converting Clipboard images into a wide variety of graphic formats, including MAC (Macintosh), GIF (CompuServe), TIFF (gray scale), and WPG (WordPerfect Graphics). You can order Paint Shop Pro for $49 plus shipping from JASC, Inc., 17743 Evener Way, Eden Prairie, MN 55346, or by calling the Public (Software) Library at 800-242-4775 or 713-524-6394.

SnagIt also allows you to copy any area of a window. Even better, you can capture screens into a different bitmap file every time you copy an image, without having to use the Paintbrush to save each file. SnagIt is $79 plus shipping and handling from TechSmith Corporation, 1745 Hamilton Road, Suite 300, Okemos, MI 48864; 517-347-0800.

Shareware versions of Paint Shop and SnagIt are also featured in *More Windows 3.1 Secrets*.

Capturing DOS line-draw characters

You can capture a DOS application that is running in full-screen text mode under Windows into the Clipboard by pressing Alt+Print Screen. If you look at the Clipboard Viewer at this point, however, you'll see that line-draw characters have been converted into rough text equivalents. You can fix this by clicking Display OEM-Text on the Clipboard menu. Your DOS text is converted to the IBM PC-8 character set, complete with line-draw boxes. You can then press Alt+Print Screen to capture the Clipboard display, then paste *that* into a Windows application as a graphic — boxes and all.

You can also print line-draw characters using the Video Terminal Screen font found on the diskettes accompanying *More Windows 3.1 Secrets*. See the "Using VTS fonts" section of Chapter 9, "Dealing with DOS" or the chapter on VTS in the shareware section.

Summary

In this chapter, I go into various aspects of using the Print Screen function in DOS sessions under Windows, and printing Windows screens using the Paintbrush applet.

▶ Reserving the original Print Screen function for DOS applications, using settings in a PIF file allows this key to operate as users have come to expect, while letting users copy DOS screens into the Clipboard, if necessary, by pressing Alt+Print Screen.

▶ Printing Windows screens by pasting them into Paintbrush is the simplest way to obtain a graphical Print Screen function, without purchasing separate screen-capture utilities.

▶ If you need this kind of functionality often, you can automate the whole Paintbrush procedure by recording the steps in a Recorder macro.

▶ Finally, several professional Windows programs are available to print screens, with far more control over the printing process than is available through Paintbrush alone.

Chapter 11
Mighty Macro Recorder

In This Chapter

If you know some of the undocumented secrets of the Windows Recorder, which I explain herein, you can:

▶ Redefine almost any key on your keyboard.

▶ Record and play back actions in applications that don't have their own macro recorder.

▶ Develop a macro that you can run whenever you press a key combination or double-click an icon in the Program Manager.

▶ Create an automatic startup routine for Windows that acts like the AUTOEXEC.BAT function does for DOS (a feature Windows lacks).

One of the applications bundled with Windows that "don't get no respect," as Rodney Dangerfield says, is the Windows Recorder. This little application is often dismissed as a weak macro-recording facility, and, as a result, is ignored.

But I myself load and use the Recorder every day. I think almost every Windows user can find something helpful that this little app can do for them, running quietly in the background.

Although the Recorder does have its limitations, it's free, so it won't cost you a penny to try out the following ideas.

Finding Worthy Tasks for the Recorder

First, ask yourself what you want to accomplish with the Recorder. The Recorder can play back almost any sequence of keystrokes to Windows applications (but not DOS applications), so the only limitation here is your imagination. For the sake of illustration, let me suggest a simple but irritating problem that anyone who uses Windows in an office might face.

In a working environment, people often share their PC with someone else. This could be someone who doesn't have a PC of his or her own, or someone who works a night shift and uses the same desk that you use during the daytime. If anyone is left-handed, you might have to run the Control Panel every day in order to switch your mouse between left-handed and right-handed after your PC has been used by one of your co-workers.

Wouldn't you like it if you could automatically switch the mouse from a left-handed to a right-handed mouse, just by pressing a single key? This is easily within the capabilities of the Recorder. In fact, with the procedure I'm about to describe, you can reconfigure almost *any* Control Panel setting with a single keystroke.

In addition to the letters A-Z, the Recorder can redefine any function key, and "gray" keys (shaded, nonalphabetic keys on your keyboard) such as Delete, Escape, and Home. Since you probably don't want to lose important keys like "A" or "Escape," Recorder allows you to require that the keys Shift, Alt, and/or Ctrl be held down for a macro to run.

Since many Windows applications use up all the possible Ctrl and Alt combinations (such as Ctrl+B for bold text), I usually recommend that all your key redefinitions start with Ctrl+Shift or Ctrl+Alt, such as Ctrl+Alt+F5. In Windows 3.1, you don't need to worry that you'll accidentally hit Ctrl+Alt+Delete and reboot your PC, because Windows catches this combination and gives you a chance to change your mind. Therefore, I place most of the macros I use on some combination of Ctrl+Alt with one other key.

The exception to this rule is an underutilized function key that I *like* to redefine. That's the F10 key. This key was originally reserved for early Windows users who didn't have a mouse. In virtually every Windows application, pressing F10 highlights the first choice on the main menu. You can then move among the other menu items with the arrow keys. But since almost every Windows user now has a mouse, this key seems ripe for redefinition.

Now that we've chosen our task and a key to put it on, let's use this example to see how to set any Control Panel function with a keypress.

STEPS

Configuring Control Panel with a Single Key

Step 1.   Start the Recorder application. Do that by double-clicking its icon in the Program Manager. You should see a large, empty window with a menu bar. Pull down the Options menu, and make sure the following items have a check mark beside them, indicating they are *on:* Control+Break Checking, Shortcut Keys, and Minimize on Use. If any items are not checked, click them once to set them on. Then pull down the Options menu and click Preferences. In the dialog box that appears, set the following values. Playback To: Same Application; Speed: Fast; Record Mouse: Ignore Mouse; and Relative To: Window. Click OK to save these preferences.

Step 2. You are now ready to record your macro. Pull down the Macro menu and click Record. A new Record Macro dialog box appears. This box should already reflect the preferences you previously set, such as Speed: Fast. About all you still need to do is give your macro a name, assign a shortcut key, type a description, and go.

In the Record Macro Name box, type something like "Reverse Mouse Buttons." In the Shortcut Key box, scroll through the choices and select F10. Make sure the boxes for Ctrl, Shift, and Alt are *off*. Also make sure the box for Enable Shortcut Keys is *on*, and Continuous Loop is *off* (or your macro will run over and over, which is great for demos but poor for configuring the Control Panel). Finally, type within the Description box something like, "Runs Control Panel's Mouse dialog box, swaps mouse buttons, and exits." Once all these settings are to your liking, click the Start button to begin recording your macro.

Step 3. The Recorder window should automatically reduce itself to an icon on the icon line. The icon blinks to indicate that you are currently recording your actions. At this point, remember one important rule: Don't perform any actions with your mouse. The Recorder can play back mouse actions only to the same position where you originally recorded them, and they might not work if any of the windows have moved. This is why we set Recorder earlier to "Ignore Mouse," so it wouldn't cause any problems. Set your mouse aside and don't touch it while you record this macro.

The Program Manager should now be the foreground application in Windows. (If it isn't, something is wrong. Press Ctrl+Break to stop recording, and be sure you start Recorder from a Program Manager icon. Unfortunately, if you make a mistake, you can't change a Recorder macro, only record it again.)

Press Alt+F to pull down Program Manager's File menu. Then press R to open the Run dialog box. In this dialog box, type:

```
CONTROL MOUSE
```

and press Enter to close the dialog box and run the command.

This command requires a bit more explanation. It's an undocumented feature of the Windows 3.1 Control Panel that you can feed it a parameter on the command line like this. You can feed it any word that appears underneath a Control Panel icon. This includes COLOR, FONTS, PRINTERS, DATE/TIME, and so on. If you have a network running, you can use the parameter NETWORK to open that dialog box. These dialog boxes are all parts of the MAIN.CPL file, which determines most of the icons that appear in the Windows 3.1 Control Panel.

If you're running Windows in enhanced mode, you can also open the 386 Enhanced dialog box. This is controlled by a different file, however, so you would type CONTROL CPWIN386.CPL.

Finally, you may have icons in your Control Panel that correspond to additional control files. In Windows 3.1, it's common to find Drivers and Sound icons, which are accessed by the commands CONTROL DRIVERS.CPL and CONTROL SND.CPL.

If you have Windows 3.0, these command lines won't work. But you can still open Control Panel dialog boxes without using your mouse. Type CONTROL by itself in the File Run dialog box, then press Alt+S, M, which pulls down the Settings menu and clicks the Mouse menu item.

Step 4. The Control Panel's Mouse dialog box should be open at this point. Press Alt+S, which turns on and off the Swap Left/Right Buttons box. Press Enter to close this dialog box.

Step 5. Your macro is done. Press Ctrl+Break to stop recording. A Recorder dialog box appears. Press Alt+S to save your macro, then press Enter to close the dialog box.

You can now use your mouse again, since you are no longer recording. But beware. Your mouse may seem to have hung. In fact, it only appears that way because you have reversed the mouse buttons on yourself. Your right mouse button now does what your left button used to do, and vice versa.

This is a good time to test your macro. Press the F10 key, and see whether the Mouse dialog box comes up and re-configures itself. If so, congratulations. If not, try the above steps again and carefully check your work.

Step 6. Double-click the minimized Recorder icon to restore its application window. Save your macro by clicking File Save-As. Give your file a name like MACROS.REC. Windows will probably save this file into your Windows directory automatically — but you may prefer to save it into any other directory that is on your DOS Path.

Step 7. To keep your macro available at all times, put the command MACROS.REC in the LOAD= line of your WIN.INI file. Or, if you have Windows 3.1, put an icon in your Startup group with the command line MACROS.REC. The next time you start Windows, it automatically associates the .REC extension with Recorder, and loads Recorder and any macros in that file.

When you press F10 to run your macro, you'll probably notice that the Program Manager pops up over whatever application you may have been using. This happens because we defined your macro to play back into the "Same Application," and Program Manager is the application we used to start the Control Panel in the first place. After the macro has run its course, and your mouse buttons are re-configured, simply click anywhere in your original application to return to it. (Remember that your buttons are reversed.) This macro won't work unless Program Manager is running non-minimized.

By the way, if you modify F10 to switch between left- and right-handed mice, be sure to tell your co-workers about it.

Setting Up Other Hotkeys _____

The above steps can be modified to perform several other configuration tasks in the Control Panel (or in many other applications). For example, you could set up hotkeys to switch the current printer from portrait to landscape and back. Of course, you need to test such macros carefully. Not all Control Panel functions use a simple toggle switch, such as Alt+S to swap mouse buttons. You might have to define *two* different key combinations, one for portrait and one for landscape orientation. Not all printer drivers use the same keystrokes to set their orientation, either.

But once you have the idea, you should be able to find many functions that previously took many steps, but are a single key combination away with the Recorder.

One of the best ways to exploit the Recorder is in applications that don't have their own macro language. You could record a macro, for instance, to start Notepad from the File Run menu of Program Manager, and then configure Notepad's default values. In Notepad's File Page-Setup dialog box, Notepad defaults to printing the filename and page number on every page. But there's no reason you couldn't make a macro change these defaults to include your own name or the name of your company.

Placing a Recorder Macro on an Icon

If you manage other people's PCs, one of the best Recorder tricks is to set up macros that work for them whenever they click an icon in their Program Manager window. To make an icon play a macro requires another simple, undocumented feature of the Recorder.

You could, for example, design an icon that reverses people's mouse buttons. Simply click File New in a Program Manager window, and give your new icon the following properties:

Description:	Reverse Mouse
Command Line:	recorder -H F10 c:\windows\macros.rec
Working Directory:	{blank}
Shortcut Key:	None
Run Minimized:	Yes

When you click OK, a new icon appears in Program Manager. It bears the Recorder icon, but you can easily change this to any icon you like with the Change Icon button in the File Properties dialog box. The file MORICONS.DLL, which comes which Windows 3.1, contains numerous icons. And all the icons found in the Control Panel can be selected by specifying MAIN.CPL (or any of the other Control Panel files mentioned earlier) as the icon file. In Windows 3.0, CONTROL.EXE itself contains these icons.

The command line in the above example requires some explanation. The -H switch on the Recorder command line forces Recorder to run the F10 macro in the MACROS.REC file, just as though you had actually pressed the F10 hotkey. If your hotkey includes the Shift, Alt, or Ctrl keys, you must precede the hotkey with these symbols: Shift (+), Alt (%), and Ctrl (^). For example, if you placed a macro on Ctrl+Shift+F10, your command line would read RECORDER -H ^+F10 C:\WINDOWS\MACROS.REC.

Although this feature has been written about for some time, Microsoft still does not document it in the Windows 3.1 manual.

One reason for this lack of documentation is a bug in Recorder that hasn't been fixed, even in Windows 3.1. Placing a macro on an icon in this way *doesn't work if Recorder is already running*. If Recorder is running, nothing happens or you get an error message when you double-click the icon.

The best way to get around this is with a small utility called Recrun. By placing the command RECRUN in front of Recorder command lines, you make your macro run correctly, whether or not the Recorder is already running in the background.

Recrun is shareware, which means you can try it free before you register it with the author. If you have a modem and are a member of the CompuServe Information Service, you can download the file RECRUN.ZIP from Library 13 of the GO WINADV forum. (You must also have the utility PKUNZIP.EXE to decompress this file.) Or you can obtain Recrun in the book *More Windows 3.1 Secrets* from IDG Books. Finally, you can order it directly from the author by sending $20 in U.S. funds to: Recrun, Electron Image, Inc., Suite 250, 10342-107 Street, Edmonton, Alberta T5J 1K2, Canada. There is no telephone support, and none should be needed for this very simple tool.

Making an Autoexec for Windows

The last secret you need to know about Recorder is its ability to run a sequence of commands every time you start Windows. This ability is similar to the commands in AUTOEXEC.BAT, which runs every time you boot up DOS. But unlike AUTOEXEC.BAT, which is a cryptic text file, the macro you play when you start Windows consists of actions you recorded, just like our mouse-button macro.

You could use this undocumented feature of the Recorder to open and position several windows the way you like them, every time Windows starts. Or you could configure your applications in a certain way, by playing back keystrokes into their own menus. Just remember that you should use your keyboard, not your mouse, when recording these actions. If you want to move and re-size a window, for example, press Alt+Spacebar to pull down an application's System Menu, then press M for Move or S for Size, followed by pressing arrow keys to indicate the direction you wish to move or re-size the window.

To play back a Recorder macro when Windows starts, you use a command line similar to the one we placed in a Program Manager icon earlier. The difference in this case is that, instead of placing the command line in an icon, you place it in the WIN command line that starts Windows itself. Using a batch file to start Windows, the WIN command line would look like the following:

```
WIN RECORDER -H F10 C:\WINDOWS\MACROS.REC
```

Again, the -H switch forces the Recorder to play back the F10 macro in the MACROS.REC file, just as though you had pressed that hotkey after you started Windows. Placing the Recorder command line after the command WIN causes Windows to load Recorder and feed it the parameters you specified. (Placing any commands on the WIN command line also makes the Program Manager start up minimized, if you use Program Manager as your check Windows shell.)

If you use this method, you can take advantage of some of the special function keys that Recorder supports. Since some computer terminals have 16 function keys instead of 12, Recorder allows you to define macros on F13 through F16, as well as F1 through F12. Since you can never press F16 on a keyboard that doesn't have such a key, it makes a good hotkey for a Recorder "autoexec" routine. This way, you don't use up a good hotkey that you might want to use while Windows is running.

Beyond the Recorder

If you should tire of the Recorder's limitations, and its lack of Windows documentation, there *are* a few alternatives. One is WinBatch — a complete batch language for Windows with over 100 functions. WinBatch can be found in *More Windows 3.1 Secrets* (IDG Books), is included in Norton Desktop for Windows, or you can obtain it for $69.95 from Wilson WindowWare by calling 800-762-8383 or 206-937-9335.

Summary

In this chapter, I summarize the undocumented features that allow you to use the Windows Recorder to automate almost any kind of Windows activity.

▶ How to redefine keys on your keyboard.

▶ How to make an icon run a Recorder macro automatically.

▶ How to use Recorder to give Windows an AUTOEXEC.BAT-like capability, which it sorely lacks.

Chapter 12
Fixing Your Windows Dialog Boxes

In This Chapter

▶ I delve into some obscure but very handy ways to change the File Open dialog boxes of various Windows applications to show what *you* want them to show.

▶ This includes ways to change Notepad to list all files (*.*) in its File Open dialog box, instead of just *.TXT files, Paintbrush so it lists all *.BMP *and* *.PCX files, instead of just *.BMP, and Word for Windows so it lists all files instead of *.DOC or whatever.

Many people ignore the handy little word processor called Windows Write. It's easy to forget about this modest application, but it has some capabilities that come in handy. You can use it to open files that are larger than the 50K Notepad maximum, and you can even use it to edit Windows executable files and fix irritating behaviors.

In my work, I often open "README" text files in Notepad. It's always frustrating, however, that the File Open dialog box in Notepad shows only files with a TXT extension. A text file can have any extension, such as README.DOC, README.1ST, and so on. You can manually override the Notepad defaults, but it requires separate steps every time you want to open a file.

Changing the Default File Extensions in Notepad

Fortunately, you can use Windows Write to edit Notepad so it shows *all* files in the current directory. I would never suggest that Write is a good hexadecimal editor. But Write's search-and-replace ability makes Windows customization possible for anyone who uses Windows, not just those who are familiar with Debug and other byte-level editors.

The following procedure edits the Windows 3.1 Notepad so it displays all files when you use its File Open dialog box.

STEPS

Displaying All Files in Notepad

Step 1. Make a copy of the NOTEPAD.EXE file in your Windows directory. You can use File Manager or your favorite utility. Call the duplicate copy NOTEPAD.DUP. Do not edit NOTEPAD.EXE directly.

Step 2. Start Windows Write and click File Open. Then open the NOTEPAD.DUP file you just created. Write asks if you want to convert the file to Write format. Click "No Conversion," and Write opens the file as is. You will see several lines of garbage characters, similar to Figure 12-1. The cursor should be located at the beginning of the file.

Step 3. Pull down the Find menu and click Replace. A dialog box appears. Type "*.TXT" (without the quotation marks) into the Find What field, then Tab down and type "*.*(space)(space)" into the Replace

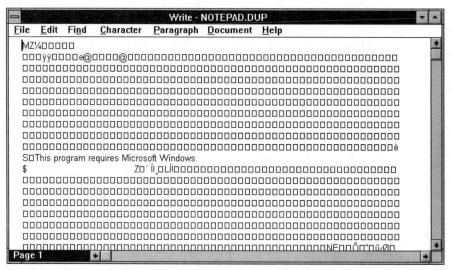

Figure 12-1: When you open NOTEPAD.DUP in Windows Write and click "No Conversion," the file initially looks like random characters.

With field. It is important that you press the spacebar twice after typing star-dot-star so you don't change the length of the search string. Click the Find Next button. Write highlights the string "*.TXT" in the middle of the file. Click the Find Next button to skip over this selection. This is not the spot you want to change. When the search procedure stops on the *second* instance of *.TXT, click the Replace button. You should see "*.TXT" change to "*.* ", as you specified. That is the only instance you want to change. There are others, but leave them alone. Double-click the Control Bar in the upper-left corner of the Find Replace dialog box to close it. Then click File Save on Windows Write's main menu and you're done. (Don't use File Save-As, because it changes the size of the file.) Exit Write.

Step 4. Check the size of NOTEPAD.EXE and your new NOTEPAD.DUP file with File Manager. If the two files are the same size, rename NOTEPAD.EXE to NOTEPAD.ORI ("ori" as in "original"), and rename NOTEPAD.DUP to NOTEPAD.EXE. Start this new NOTEPAD.EXE, and click File Open. You should see that the dialog box now uses "*.*" as the default, and lists *all* files in the current directory. If this *doesn't* work, copy NOTEPAD.ORI over NOTEPAD.EXE and you've restored Notepad to its original condition.

There is one little "gotcha" about this procedure. The File Open dialog box will, in fact, show "*.*" in the Filename box, and will show all files in a directory, not just *.TXT files (although the Show Files As Type box will still show "Text Files" as the default). This is handy, but when you click File Save-As to give a file a different name, you will have to type in the ".TXT" part of the filename yourself. Notepad no longer assumes that "*.TXT" is the default pattern for files you save without specifying an extension.

If you're using the Windows 3.0 version of Notepad, NOTEPAD.EXE contains *two* instances of "*.TXT" in the file. Be sure to replace only the *first* instance. After successfully replacing the first "*.TXT" with "*.*(space)(space)," close the Change dialog box, click File Save and you're done.

Don't think that this little trick means you can start using Write to edit any old program, however. You can't use Write to make Word for Windows' or WordPerfect's File Open dialog boxes default to "*.*", for example. For a method that *does* work on Word for Windows, see the section below entitled "WordBasic Macros."

Making Paintbrush Support Your Preferred Filenames

I've always wondered why Microsoft distributes the bitmaps that are bundled with Windows in .BMP format. The same files, loaded into Paintbrush and saved as .PCX files, usually require significantly less disk space. This is because the .PCX format includes a certain amount of compression.

In case you try loading .BMP files into Paintbrush and saving them as .PCX files, you should know that the conversion doesn't *always* save space. It depends on the size and complexity of the original file. And one flaw of Paintbrush is that it only saves .PCX files with the same number of colors as your display. If you load a 16-color .PCX file and save it as a .PCX file while using a 256-color display, Paintbrush will create a 256-color .PCX file. The only way around this is to switch to the 16-color mode of your graphics adapter to save 16-color .PCX files. (Note: Paintbrush also has problems saving .PCX files while a 32,000-color ["high color"] graphics driver is in use.)

Additionally, the Control Panel doesn't accept .PCX files as wallpaper — it accepts only .BMP or RLE files as wallpaper. (RLE files are a special compressed form of bitmap that some graphics programs create.) So we can't just convert all our .BMP files to .PCX files and expect everything to work.

But as a general rule, I prefer to save graphics in .PCX format, rather than .BMP format, when I plan to print them only from Paintbrush or other programs that support .PCX files.

Therefore, it irritates me that when I run Paintbrush's File Open dialog box, it always lists only .BMP and .DIB files. (.DIBs are device-independent bitmaps, which may contain several bitmaps concantenated together — for use in animation, for example.)

It takes only a few mouse clicks, of course, to switch the dialog box to .PCX, or any extension you wish. But I've found a way to avoid those extra clicks and make Paintbrush show .PCX files every time you run its File Open dialog box. The following procedure requires the Windows 3.1 version of Paintbrush.

STEPS

Displaying .PCX Files in Paintbrush's File Open Dialog Box

Step 1.   In File Manager, make a copy of PBRUSH.EXE. Call it PBRUSH.ORI ("ori" for "original").

Step 2.   Open the file PBRUSH.EXE in Windows Write. When asked if you want to convert the file to Write format, click "No Conversion."

Step 3. On the Write main menu, click Find Replace. In the Find What box that appears, type "*.BMP;*.DIB" (without the quotation marks). In the Replace With box, type "*.BMP;*.PCX" (without quotes). It's important that you type these strings in all capital letters. You must also type the semicolon in each string *without* a space after it.

Step 4. Leave the other defaults in the Replace dialog box as they are. Click the Replace All button. There is only one instance of the specified string in the file, so Write should finish the search-and-replace operation fairly quickly. When it is completed, click the Close button to exit the dialog box.

Step 5. On the Write main menu, click File Save. Don't use File Save-As. That option changes the length of the file, which must remain its original length to work. Then exit Write.

That's it. Run your new PBRUSH.EXE to make sure it works. Click Paintbrush's File Open command. You should see "*.BMP;*.PCX" in the filename list box. Either .PCX files or .BMP files will appear, whichever the current directory contains. You have the best of both worlds. If your new Paintbrush doesn't work, copy PBRUSH.ORI over PBRUSH.EXE and you're back to the original version.

This little change saves me several steps each day, since I frequently work with .PCX screen shots and other graphics embedded in documents. Try it.

WordBasic Macros

Unfortunately, I've heard from several people who can't figure out how the heck to modify the File Open macros in Word for Windows to show their preferred defaults: *.* instead of *.DOC.

These are intelligent microcomputer managers — not novices. The problem isn't with their understanding of Windows. It lies in WordBasic itself: the "easy, English-like" language that is showing up in more and more Microsoft products.

The following macro, for example, controls the File Open menu function in Word for Windows. My correspondents can be forgiven for loading this into the macro editor and thinking that it looks more like Greek than English:

```
Sub MAIN
Dim dlg As FileOpen
GetCurValues dlg
Dialog dlg
Super FileOpen dlg
End Sub
```

The above macro creates (dimensions) a File Open dialog box named "dlg," fills it with defaults, displays it, and gives the user a chance to change the default values and click OK before running it.

I'm no expert on designing computer languages. But if Microsoft wanted its Windows macro languages to be easy to use, its programmers could have designed WordBasic so the above macro would read:

```
Begin Macro
Create FileOpen box
FillDefaultsInto box
Display box
Start FileOpen box
End Macro
```

I suppose Microsoft wanted to preserve some cherished jargon from DOS' GW-Basic (Gates, William–Basic), such as "Sub" for a subroutine. But WordBasic is so different from DOS Basic anyway — it's virtually impossible to convert a DOS Basic program into WordBasic without rewriting the thing — that perhaps we could have taken a step toward really using the English language rather than inventing a new one. The second version of the macro isn't significantly longer than the first (for those programmers who hate to type); it's just more readable to more people.

In any case, the following procedure allows you to force Word for Windows 1.*x* and 2.*x* to use *.* in its File Open dialog box (showing all files in the current directory), instead of *.DOC. You should also use a similar procedure to change Winword's Insert File dialog box.

Using Winword, click File Open, select Document Template *.DOT as the file type, and open your NORMAL.DOT document template, from the directory where your *.DOT files are stored. Click Tools Macro. Make sure the Show box is set to Global, then select FileOpen in the list of built-in macros and click Edit. Insert three lines, as shown below in bold, which add your desired filename defaults and some necessary error trapping:

```
Sub MAIN
Dim dlg As FileOpen
GetCurValues dlg
On Error Goto BYE
dlg.Name = "*.*"
Dialog dlg
Super FileOpen dlg
BYE:
End Sub
```

Double-click the document icon to close the macro. Click "Yes" when asked if you want to save your changes to Global: FileOpen. Then open the InsertFile macro and make the same changes. Finally, exit Winword and answer "Yes" when asked if you want to save "global glossary and command changes." This rewrites your NORMAL.DOT template file.

To learn more about WordBasic programming, get *The Hacker's Guide to Word for Windows* (Woody Leonhard and Vincent Chen, Addison-Wesley) from any computer bookstore.

Summary

In this chapter, I delineate the exact steps required to change the File Open dialog boxes of various Windows applications so they list the files you want them to list, instead of the limited default file extensions that these applications were originally limited to.

▶ You can change Notepad's defaults from listing just *.TXT files to all files (*.*).

▶ You can change Paintbrush so it lists *.BMP *and* *.PCX files, not just *.BMP.

▶ And you can change Word for Windows so it lists all file types instead of defaulting to *.DOC for everything.

Chapter 13
Fixing Notepad's Margins

In This Chapter

▶ I take on a subject similar to the one in the last chapter, which discussed how to change the File Open dialog box in several Windows applications, including Notepad.

▶ Besides File Open, you may find it very desirable to change the File Page-Setup dialog box, so you don't have to change the left and right print margins from 0.75 inches to 0.00 inches every time you want to print a normal text file on an ordinary printer.

I often use Windows Notepad to display and print 80-column text files that document one program or another. But only after I've printed several pages of unusable garbage do I remember that Notepad is hard-coded to force a 3/4-inch margin on both sides of the printout.

These margins are too wide to print an 80-column document using most printers' built-in Courier font. So I have to click File Page-Setup to manually set the margins to zero and print the document again. (It's also irritating that Notepad can't fit all 80 columns of a text file into the width of a plain VGA screen — another argument for 800-by-600 displays or better — but that's another topic.)

Since this is annoying, I've edited my copy of Notepad to default to zero margins instead of 0.75 inches. This makes Notepad print a quarter-inch from the left edge of the paper on a LaserJet — exactly what I want.

You, too, can make this change in Notepad. In the previous chapter, "Fixing Your Windows Dialog Boxes," I describe a way to force Notepad's File Open dialog box to default to *.* instead of *.TXT. Changing the default margins is just as easy.

The following steps that change Notepad's default margins can be performed using Windows Write or any byte editor.

STEPS

Changing Notepad's Default Margins

Step 1. Make a copy of NOTEPAD.EXE and call it NOTEPAD.ORI ("ori" for "original"), using File Manager or your favorite utility.

Step 2. Start Windows Write and open the file NOTEPAD.EXE. Write asks if you want to convert the file to Write format. Click "No Conversion" and Write opens the file as is. You will see several lines of garbage characters. The cursor should be located at the beginning of the file.

Step 3. Pull down Find on the main menu and the click the Find item. As the text to search for, type ".75" (without the quotation marks) into the dialog box that appears. Click Find Next. This takes you to the section of the executable file that contains Notepad's left and right .75-inch margin settings. Double-click the Control Menu icon to close the Find dialog box. In the text of the file, replace .75 with .00 in both instances. (It's important to preserve the two decimal places, because you must not change the length of any string in the Notepad executable file.)

Step 4. Click File Save and you're done. Don't use Write's File Save-As option, because it changes the size of the edited file, which won't work. After you exit Write, use File Manager to check that NOTEPAD.ORI and your new NOTEPAD.EXE file are still the same length — they should be.

You now have an updated version of Notepad. Run this copy and load a text file. Confirm that the left and right margins in the File Page-Setup dialog box default to .00 inches, then print a file. If the document prints appropriately on your printer, congratulations! If some problem occurs, copy NOTEPAD.ORI over NOTEPAD.EXE and you're back to normal.

During the above procedure, you might be tempted to change some of Notepad's other Page-Setup defaults near the left- and right-margin defaults. Proceed with caution. The numbers "1" and "1" immediately after the .75 settings, for example, represent the top and bottom margins, in inches. But you probably can't change these in any meaningful way.

Here's why. You can't edit the top and bottom margins from 1 to .5 or similar, because you can't change the length of these strings. You might desire 0 margins at the top and bottom of each printout, thinking this would work like setting the left and right margins to 0. But it doesn't.

With a document set to a zero top margin, Notepad overlaps the first two lines when printing to a LaserJet printer. And the first line may not appear at all when printing to a PostScript printer. These printers require a top margin of at least .25 inches.

Perhaps in a future version of Windows, Microsoft will correct these glitches, and provide us with settings in WIN.INI to override Notepad's hard-coded defaults.

Summary

In this chapter, I add Notepad's File Page-Setup dialog box to the Windows defaults that you can easily change with Windows Write or any byte editor.

▶ Since 80-column text files require a full 8 inches to print in the default font of almost every ordinary text printer, it's irritating to have to set Notepad manually to use 0.0-inch left and right margins (so the document prints with 0.25 inches of margin on the left and right sides of the paper).

▶ By using a procedure in Windows Write, it's a simple matter to change the margin defaults from 0.75 to 0.00, although few other Notepad defaults can be changed because the length of the old string and the new string in the file must match.

Chapter 14
Tweaking Toolbars

In This Chapter

▶ I discuss the use of "toolbars" and "button bars" in various Windows applications.

▶ I show you ways to add your own, customized button bars to these applications — or add specialized button bars of your liking to *any* Windows application, even ones that don't support toolbars.

Before Windows, the user interface provided by most DOS applications was a command line. The user memorized the meaning of several commands and typed them to carry out specific operations. These commands worked only with a keyboard and didn't support a mouse.

Windows 1.0 introduced a new user interface: pull-down menus. Users no longer had to memorize commands. Anyone could pull down each of the menus in an application and read in plain English what each command did. The menus supported both keyboard and mouse input.

Recently, a new interface has been added to Windows applications: the button bar or toolbar. In some ways, this new way of issuing commands brings us full circle. Because the buttons are too small for illustrations that are perfectly clear, users must memorize what each button means. Most button bars have no text below the buttons to remind the user what each does. And most toolbars work only with a mouse and cannot be accessed directly from the keyboard. All these things slow down most users.

One of the first applications that sported the current style of toolbar was Lotus 1-2-3 for Windows. Lotus' toolbar became somewhat famous for cramming so many buttons into such a small space (with no text labels) that it gave birth to a new cliché: "icon overload." With all the buttons, almost no one could remember what they all did, much less use them effectively.

Applications in other categories have gotten in on the button-bar act, especially word processors. WordPerfect for Windows and Ami Pro developed button bars, and a while back Microsoft Word for Windows sprouted one, too.

WordPerfect's button bar is almost an ideal implementation. The buttons can be configured by the user to show both a picture and a text label, just the picture, or just the text. (The latter choice is my personal favorite, since a single word in a small space can be clearer than most tiny icons.)

WordPerfect's toolbar can also be positioned at the top or along the sides of the display; Winword's is stuck at the top. And WordPerfect's button bar is customizable by the user, while Winword's is limited to the icons that come with the package.

Not All Button Bars Can Be Customized — Or Can They?

Technically speaking, this last point is not entirely accurate. You *can* make up an entirely new button bar for Winword 2.0, but this feature is undocumented.

The story goes that the Ford Motor Co. was considering a large purchase of Winword, but refused because it was unable to change the application's toolbar. To make the sale, Microsoft agreed to put a line in WIN.INI that causes Winword to load a toolbar from an external binary file in place of its internal toolbar. But instead of shouting about this feature from the rooftops (to counter WordPerfect's competitive advantage), Microsoft never told users, probably because Winword provides no method for average users to create such a binary file.

You can, in fact, create your own Word for Windows toolbar using Woody's Office Power Pack, which you can obtain for $49.95 plus shipping by calling 800-659-4696 or 314-965-5630. The package includes a Toolbar Editor as well as dozens of other routines: Duplex Printing (on regular printers), File Delete, Super Scripts, and so on. It discloses the secrets of Winword's WIN.INI settings that make a customizable toolbar possible, as well as many other tricks.

But what about other applications for which we might wish to create a customized button bar? Fortunately for Windows users, utilities that make it possible for you to do this have begun to appear.

One such product is Power Toolboxes from the hDC Computer Corporation. This product creates button bars that "float" horizontally or vertically over your other applications. Figure 14-1 shows such a toolbar for Windows Write. Global actions are on the left buttons, while Write-specific actions (making fonts smaller and larger, for example) are on the right buttons.

Figure 14-1: hDC Computer Corp.'s Power Toolboxes product creates toolbars that "float" over applications.

When you change to a different application, the global buttons remain the same, but the application-specific buttons change. You can modify the global and application buttons to suit the way you work.

The buttons can be programmed with hDC's "Enhanced Command Language." In addition to ordinary Windows commands, such as NOTEPAD README.TXT, this language supports numerous parameters. These options allow you to start an application at a certain size, with certain keystrokes or DDE instructions fed into it, and so on.

Power Toolboxes lists for $40. A related product, Power Launcher, lists for $100. The more expensive product includes all the functionality of Power Toolboxes plus customizable keyboard and mouse definitions, a "virtual desktop" that expands your screen area, and a "power bar" that appears above all your application windows. Power Toolboxes and Power Launcher can be ordered from hDC, 6742 185th Ave. NE, Redmond, WA 98052, or by calling 800-321-4606 or 206-885-5550.

SmartPad, which is shown in Figure 14-2, has additional features that make it interesting. SmartPad, from Softblox Inc., has the ability to make its button bars appear to be part of the affected application. In the illustration, Windows Write gains a toolbar directly beneath its menu. Documents you open in Write display themselves beneath this toolbar, instead of being covered up by it.

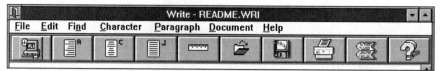

Figure 14-2: Softblox Inc.'s SmartPad can make toolbars that appear to be an integral part of each application, just beneath its main menu.

You can also make SmartPad's button bar attach to the side of an application window, or float separately. And you can customize the actions and look of the buttons themselves.

SmartPad's approach to customization is unique. To change the location of a button, hold down Shift and drag it with your mouse. To change the actions launched by a button, open the macro editor and drag pictures that represent actions from one point to another. The actions are also represented by text descriptions, which makes them easy to understand.

SmartPad lists for $60, and is available from Softblox Inc., 58 Oakwood Road, Huntington, NY 11743; 516-424-8851.

Summary

In this chapter, I describe ways to customize toolbars in applications that don't allow customized icons, and add toolbars to applications that don't have them.

▶ While WordPerfect for Windows and Ami Pro provide flexible toolbars that you can customize, Word for Windows 2.*x* lagged behind with a toolbar that is limited to only those icons that are provided with the package. Fortunately, this can be changed by using an undocumented feature of Word for Windows that is exploited by Woody's Office Power Pack.

▶ hDCs Power Toolboxes and Softblox's SmartPad allow you to provide a similar level of user-selectable button bars for *any* application, whether or not that application supports a toolbar feature.

Chapter 15
Add Character to Your Documents

In This Chapter

▶ I describe a hidden method that Microsoft provided in Windows to allow users to type many characters in the Windows character set which do not appear on most keyboards with only one or two keystrokes.

▶ I list tools that allow you to work on documents containing different languages, and provide a list of common English words that require characters that do not appear on U.S. keyboards.

You may know that Windows 3.1 provides a broad array of characters that do not appear on your keyboard. These characters include fractions, footnote superscripts, copyright and trademark symbols, and many others. But you probably are *not* aware of a hidden method that Windows provides to give you easy access from your keyboard to these characters.

This method is not mentioned in the Windows manual, nor is it accessible through the Control Panel's Keyboard dialog box. But it is a method developed and supported by Microsoft, nonetheless.

When you use this trick, you need only press a simple two-key combination to insert symbols such as © into text in any Windows application. I include in Chapter 16, "Characters and Fonts," a complete list of every character available in the TrueType fonts that Microsoft ships. But most methods to access these characters are awkward.

For example, you can always start the Character Map applet that ships with Windows 3.1, select a symbol, and insert it into your word processing document. But this requires that you leave your application.

You can also turn Num Lock on, hold down your Alt key, type a number on your numeric keypad, then release the Alt key. Alt+0169, for instance, inserts the © symbol.

You might try placing characters like these on common key combinations using the Windows Recorder applet. But you would soon find that Recorder has no way to record the insertion of a special character, such as Alt+0169.

But a much more handy method (literally) allows you to type characters like these directly into your documents using only one or two keystrokes. Best of all, you can switch this ability on and off at any time, and use it in conjunction with the Character Map applet or the Alt+*number* method whenever you wish.

This method requires what Microsoft calls the "U.S. International" keyboard layout. Most Windows users in the U.S., of course, use the plain old U.S. keyboard layout. This layout corresponds with the keys on typical U.S. keyboards. Each key inserts a lowercase letter and an uppercase letter, and that is it. There are no keys for extra symbols or accented letters, such as the *é* in *café*.

When you switch to the U.S. International keyboard layout, however, most of the keys on a plain U.S. keyboard gain a third or a fourth meaning. The plain *C* key, for example, gives you access to the copyright symbol (©) and cent sign (¢), as well as the normal uppercase *C* and lowercase *c*.

To switch to the U.S. International keyboard layout, open the Control Panel and run the International dialog box. In the box marked "Keyboard Layout," select "US-International." You may be asked to insert one of the original Windows diskettes, so Windows can copy a small, 1,641-byte file (KBDUSX.DLL) to your hard disk. But you won't need to restart Windows or any of your Windows applications for the change to take effect. The change is applied immediately to all applications.

While the U.S. International keyboard layout is in effect, the *right* Alt key on your keyboard is turned into an "Alternate Character" key. When you hold down this key (alone or with the Shift key), most of the keys on your normal U.S. keyboard gain new meanings.

For the rest of this chapter, I will refer to this Alternate Character key as AltChar. The location of this key on extended, 101-key keyboards, and the meaning of each of the keys in the U.S. International keyboard layout, is shown in Figure 15-1. The normal character is shown on the left of each key, while the character inserted when you hold down AltChar or Shift+AltChar is shown on the right.

The U.S. International keyboard layout

Alternate Character
(AltChar) key

Figure 15-1: The layout of keys when the U.S. International keyboard is selected in the Control Panel's International dialog box. The characters on the right side of the keys are inserted when the keys are pressed while holding down AltChar or Ctrl+Alt. Capital letters are inserted with Shift+AltChar or Ctrl+Shift+Alt held down. Copyright 1992 Alki Software Corp. Reprinted with permission.

What You Can Do With This Keyboard Layout __

You gain many categories of characters by switching to the U.S. International keyboard. For clarity's sake, I break them into the following groups:

- Legal characters, such as the copyright symbol (©), registered trademark (®), and the section mark (§) and paragraph mark (¶) used by lawyers.

- Currency symbols, such as the British pound (£), Japanese yen (¥), the cent sign (¢), and the international generic currency symbol (¤).

- The fractions one-fourth (¼), one-half (½), and three-fourths (¾), and the degree symbol (°), useful when typing recipes (bake at 350° F.) or addresses like 120 ½ Main St.

- Superscripts from one to three (^{123}), useful for inserting footnotes into a page of text, or for expressions like x^2. Windows 3.1 doesn't offer superscript numbers higher than three, but Windows NT provides a full set of superscript and subscript numbers, from 0 to 9.

- True multiplication and division symbols ($\times \div$), so you don't have to use a lowercase x and a forward slash (/) in your documents.

- Open and closed quote marks (' '), also called "smart quotes," which look like the quote marks used in professionally typeset books, magazines, and newspapers.

- Accented characters, so you can correctly spell words like *résumé* and *mañana*.

The U.S. International keyboard actually provides two different ways to insert accented letters into your documents. This ability is becoming more important as more Americans have names that include accented letters, such as Frederico Peña, who is at this writing the U.S. Secretary of Transportation.

The first way is to hold down the AltChar key and press one of the letters on your keyboard that has an accented alternate character. For example, AltChar+E produces the accented *é,* while AltChar+N produces the accented *ñ.*

The second way is to use what are called *dead keys.* These are keys that do nothing until another key on the keyboard is pressed.

Using Dead Keys

On the U.S. International keyboard, five keys are converted into dead keys. These five:

- The *circumflex* or "hat" over the "6" key (^), which is used in words like *crêpes Suzette;*

- The *back quote* (`), which produces a *grave accent* (*grave* rhymes with "Slav" or "slave") in words like *à la carte;*

- The *tilde* (~), used in words like *jalapeño;*

- The *apostrophe* ('), which produces an *acute accent* in words like *exposé;* and

- The *double-quote* ("), which produces an *umlaut* or *dieresis* in words like *naïve.*

When you press one of these dead keys, Windows shows nothing on your screen until you press another key. Then, if that key is a letter that has an accented form, such as most vowels, the appropriate accented letter is inserted into your document. If not, such as the letter *t,* both the accent and the *t* are inserted, one after the other. If you want to insert just an accent itself, you press the corresponding dead key, followed by the spacebar, and Windows inserts just the accent.

This behavior produces a small irritation when using the apostrophe and double-quote key on your keyboard. When you press the apostrophe, which is common in contractions like *don't* and possessives like *Brian's,* you don't see the apostrophe until the second letter is typed. But you don't get an apostrophe at all if you type an unusual contraction, such as Hallowe'en. With the U.S. International keyboard, pressing the apostrophe and then *e* produces the letter *é,* unless you remember to press the spacebar after the apostrophe.

This is a very minor problem, because most English contractions end in *s* or *t,* not in vowels. But it is a more serious problem with the double-quote key, which is used to begin sentences that are quotations, such as "Are you there?" Sentences often begin with *A, E,* and other vowels, and you must remember to press the spacebar after the double-quote key when typing any such sentence.

If you ever use symbols or accented characters, the advantages of using the U.S. International keyboard far outweigh the slight disadvantage of remembering how to use the quotation marks. But because it *is* irritating, I wish Microsoft hadn't used the apostrophe and double-quote key as dead keys. Instead, they should have used the colon (:) and the semicolon (;). The colon looks like an umlaut, and the bottom of the semicolon resembles an acute accent mark. Since colons and semicolons are always followed by spaces or carriage returns in normal English usage, you wouldn't need to remember to press the spacebar before pressing a vowel after these keys. If a letter immediately followed a colon or semicolon, you could be sure that it was meant to be an accented letter.

Perhaps Microsoft will change these dead keys in Windows 4.0 from the apostrophe and double-quote to the colon and semicolon. Or perhaps some third-party developer will come up with an improved DLL that allows you to swap or modify these keys.

In any case, using the U.S. International keyboard is usually better for users of U.S. keyboards than switching to an entirely different keyboard layout to type in another language, such as French. You can use the Control Panel's International dialog box, of course, to change from the U.S. layout to French, German, or other languages used on keyboards in the corresponding countries. But this almost always moves some alphabetical keys to new positions that are customary in those locales. For example, the top row of alphabetical keys on keyboards sold in France starts out with the letters AZERTY, not QWERTY, as on U.S. keyboards. Unless you're a touch typist who learned to type on keyboards in a non-U.S. country, it's better for U.S. typists to stick with the U.S. International keyboard layout.

If You Don't Have an Extended Keyboard_____

For users with older 84-key keyboards (the ones on the original IBM AT, with 10 functions keys on the left side), the U.S. International keyboard provides another way to access alternate characters. This is necessary, of course, because 84-key keyboards do not have two Alt keys and therefore cannot convert one into an AltChar key.

Holding down Ctrl+Alt while pressing a letter is the same as holding down the right Alt key (the AltChar key) while the U.S. International keyboard is in effect. Shift+Ctrl+Alt does the same thing as Shift+AltChar.

Unfortunately, these parallel methods are in force even if you are using a new, 101-key extended keyboard. This means that you must take care when using the Windows Recorder or a macro language in your word processor to redefine Ctrl+Alt keys or Shift+Ctrl+Alt keys to run macros. These macro definitions overrule the meaning of letters that have an alternate form when used with the AltChar key. In other words, a macro that has been defined to run when you press Ctrl+Alt+A will take precedence over AltChar+A. The macro will execute instead of AltChar+A inserting *á* into your document.

Microsoft should have made the U.S. International DLL check to see whether an 84-key or a 101-key keyboard was set up in the current configuration. Then the AltChar key could be used without being overruled by macros that have been redefined on Ctrl+Alt and Shift+Ctrl+Alt combinations. Perhaps this is another oversight that could be corrected in Windows 4.0.

Using Multiple Languages

Many North American companies routinely use different languages in their documents. Companies in the southern half of the U.S. often produce documents containing both English and Spanish text, while Canadian documents often include both English and French.

If you find yourself using different languages frequently, you should probably obtain one or more of Alki Software Corp.'s Proofing Tools packages. The packages' manuals alone are valuable for their extensive charts showing the location of Windows characters and the layout of every different keyboard language supported by Windows. More importantly, each Proofing Tools package provides a spelling checker, thesaurus, and hyphenation utility for a different language supported by Microsoft Word for Windows.

In Word for Windows 2.0 and higher, text may be marked with the language it belongs to. By default, text in Winword documents is marked as the language you have selected in the Control Panel. But one section could be marked "English," while another section is marked "French," for example. Text as small as a single word or character can be marked as a particular language.

The ability to mark sections of text as different languages can be very important when spell-checking, hyphenating, and using a thesaurus. Word for Windows automatically uses the appropriate utility when operating on any section of text, if utilities in that language are installed.

Alki offers Proofing Tools packages for the following languages: Danish, Dutch, English-British, Finnish, French, French-Canadian, German, Italian, Norwegian, Portuguese, Portuguese-Brazilian, Spanish, and Swedish. (The Finnish and Portuguese packages contain spelling and hyphenation utilities but not a thesaurus.)

Each package has a list price of $99.95, but is $89.95 if obtained directly from Alki. The company also sells a Comprehensive Thesaurus for Word for Windows (list $79.95, $39.95 from Alki), which contains three times the synonyms of the thesaurus that comes with Winword, and a Comprehensive Spelling package (list $79.95, $69.95 from Alki), which adds 74,000 medical, legal, and business terms to Winword's spell-checker.

Alki Software Corp. may be reached at 300 Queen Anne Ave. N., Suite 410, Seattle, WA 98109; 800-669-9673 or 206-286-2600.

Using Accented Letters

Since it isn't very useful to have access to accented characters if you don't know *when* to use them, I've prepared the chart in Table 15-1 with some words in common English usage that contain accents. Many of these words started out as phrases in languages other than English, but became an accepted part of the English vocabulary long ago. Spelling these words correctly (accents and all) can make a positive impression in business, especially when you write words such as *résumé*.

Windows provides many ways to access different symbols and characters when you write — it's up to us to find ways to use these characters more expressively in our documents.

Words and Phrases		Proper Names	Major Place Names
à la carte	fête champêtre	Condé Nast	Ascunción, Paraguay
à la mode	fiancé	Crédit Suisse	Belém, Brazil
adiós	fiancée	Crédit Lyonnais	Bogotá, Colombia
appliqué	jalapeño	Dom Pérignon	Brasília, Brazil
après ski	lamé	Estée Lauder	Córdoba, Argentina
attaché	maître d'hôtel	Hermès	Curaçao, Lesser Antilles
au révoir	mañana	Lancôme	Düsseldorf, Germany
bête noire	moiré	Lazard Frères & Co.	Genève, Switzerland
café	naïf	Les Misérables	Medellín, Colombia
cause célèbre	naïve	Moët & Chandon	México
coup d'état	naïveté	Nestlé	Montréal, Canada
coup de grâce	negligée	Plaza Athénée	Québec, Canada
crème de menthe	passé		San José, Costa Rica
crème fraîche	pâté		São Paulo, Brazil
crêpe	pièce de résistance		Tiranë, Albania
crêpes Suzette	pied à terre		Valparaíso, Chile
débridement	piña colada		Zürich, Switzerland
déclassé	protégé		
décolletage	raison d'être		
décolleté	répondez s'il vous plaît (RSVP)		
décor			
découpage	résumé		
déjà vu	risqué		
déshabillé	roman à clef		
discothèque	sautéed		
émigré	soufflé		
exposé	tête-à-tête		
fête	très chic		

Table 15-1: Some accented words in common English usage. This is only a partial listing, leaving out many prominent individuals' names and smaller company and place names.

Summary

In this chapter, I reveal some tricks you can perform with a special keyboard layout that isn't in your Windows manual, but is provided and supported by Microsoft.

▶ The U.S. International keyboard provides convenient access to special characters, such as the copyright symbol, fractions, and superscript numerals, while at the same time making available accented characters to users of U.S. keyboards that lack keys for these characters.

▶ Companies that create documents with a mix of two or more languages can benefit from spell-checkers, hyphenation dictionaries, and thesauri in various languages from Alki Software Corp.

▶ U.S. users of Windows should be aware of common English terms that are correctly spelled with accented characters, such as résumé, requiring the use of the full Windows character set.

Chapter 16
Characters and Fonts

In This Chapter

▶ I reveal the entire hidden character set of the Windows 3.1 environment, plus more than 1,000 virtually unknown symbol characters available in Microsoft's scandalously low-priced TrueType Font Pack, which started a revolution in the font business.

▶ I disclose the secrets behind an entirely new kind of font technology that offers Windows users a choice of millions of fonts for the low price of a single diskette of software.

▶ I tell LaserJet users how they can improve the appearance of Hewlett-Packard's PCL5 underlined fonts by making a simple change to a mere four bytes of their Windows print driver.

The addition of TrueType capabilities to Windows 3.1 gave us all one big benefit. For the first time, you could make a typeface like Times Roman as big or as small as you wanted, and it would display and print perfectly — without the extra purchase of Adobe Type Manager, Bitstream FaceLift, Zenographics SuperPrint, or other type-scaling products.

Almost all Windows 3.1 users quickly learned that they could now scale type and print it directly from Windows to their favorite laser or dot-matrix printer. This is a welcome change from the old days of Windows 3.0, when there was seldom any connection between the characters you saw on your screen and the typefaces that happened to be in your printer.

But you may be unaware of many *secret* benefits lurking in the shadows of Windows 3.1's TrueType capabilities.

For one thing, every TrueType face that comes with Windows 3.1 includes more than twice as many characters as there are letters on your keyboard. It's easy to insert these extra characters into your documents (as I'll explain in a moment). But most people don't even know they are there, because the Windows 3.1 manual doesn't include any chart or listing of these characters.

Another little-known benefit of Windows 3.1 is that it includes a bundled typeface — containing several clip art-like characters — that isn't mentioned anywhere in the manual. This face is called Wingdings, and it can definitely add interest to your documents once you know what characters are there to be used.

Finally, Microsoft reports that most of the Windows users who upgraded from version 3.0 to 3.1 in the first few months of the new release also took advantage of a reduced-price offer to get an additional *44* TrueType faces. This set, called the Microsoft TrueType Font Pack, consists mainly of typefaces similar to the 35 that are found in PostScript printers. But buried beneath these familiar typefaces are four unusual fonts, each with more than 200 symbols — one of which might be just perfect to make a point in your next newsletter, fax, or spreadsheet. (The special offer has expired, but the Font Pack is still available from many software dealers at substantial discounts off the $99 list price.)

Accessing Hidden Characters

The truth of the matter is that *every* Windows 3.1 user has access to hundreds of characters that are not visible on any keyboard. And the *majority* of Windows 3.1 users (those with the TrueType Font Pack) have access to more than 1,000 symbols, bullets, arrows, and other designs that printers call "dingbats." But there's almost no way for the average person to know which characters are available.

To be fair, it must be said that Microsoft tried to help people access these symbols by providing a new applet with Windows 3.1. It's called the Character Map, represented by an icon in the Program Manager. When you start this map, it displays all 224 characters that appear in a Windows TrueType face. You can select the typeface to view, and you can even copy characters, one or several, to the Clipboard (after which you can paste them into any other Windows application).

Unfortunately, the Character Map window is small (and can't be resized), so it's difficult to use it to browse through your type collection.

For this reason, I've collected all the characters available to Windows 3.1 users into two charts. Figure 16-1 is for all Windows 3.1 users, while Figure 16-2 is for those who have the TrueType Font Pack. These charts are suitable for copying and tacking onto the nearest bulletin board, for the next time you need just the right symbol.

In these charts, about half the characters can be inserted into a document by pressing a key on your keyboard. Pressing the "w" key, for example inserts character number 119 into your document. If you're using a text typeface, such as Windows 3.1's Arial, the inserted character is, in fact, a "w." But if you're using Wingdings, the same keystroke inserts a diamond-shaped bullet (◆).

The Windows 3.1 Character Set

Windows 3.1 includes three kinds of TrueType faces: Text typefaces (Times New Roman, Arial, and Courier New), Symbol, and Wingdings. To access characters that cannot be typed directly from the keyboard:

1) Make sure the Num Lock light is *on.*
2) Hold down the Alt key while typing the appropriate number on the numeric keypad.
3) Release the Alt key.

Text character set
Symbol character set
↓ ↓ Wingdings character set
Character Number → 98 b β ♌

32				64	@	≅	🖎	96	`	‾	♊	0128			⓪	0160			
33	!	!	🖉	65	A	Α	✌	97	a	α	♋	0129			①	0161	¡	ϒ	○
34	"	∀	✂	66	B	Β	🖏	98	b	β	♌	0130	‚		②	0162	¢	′	⭕
35	#	#	✁	67	C	Χ	👍	99	c	χ	♍	0131	ƒ		③	0163	£	≤	🞅
36	$	∃	👓	68	D	Δ	👎	100	d	δ	♎	0132	„		④	0164	¤	⁄	🞆
37	%	%	🕭	69	E	Ε	☜	101	e	ε	♏	0133	…		⑤	0165	¥	∞	◎
38	&	&	🕮	70	F	Φ	☞	102	f	ϕ	♐	0134	†		⑥	0166	¦	ƒ	🔿
39	'	∍	🕯	71	G	Γ	☝	103	g	γ	♑	0135	‡		⑦	0167	§	♣	▪
40	(	(	🕿	72	H	Η	☟	104	h	η	♒	0136	ˆ		⑧	0168	¨	♦	◻
41	)	)	✆	73	I	Ι	🖐	105	i	ι	♓	0137	‰		⑨	0169	©	♥	🟂
42	*	∗	🖂	74	J	ϑ	☺	106	j	φ	🙰	0138	Š		⑩	0170	ª	♠	✦
43	+	+	🖃	75	K	Κ	😐	107	k	κ	🙵	0139	‹		⓿	0171	«	↔	★
44	,	,	📪	76	L	Λ	☹	108	l	λ	●	0140	Œ		❶	0172	¬	←	✶
45	-	−	📫	77	M	Μ	💣	109	m	μ	🔾	0141			❷	0173	-	↑	✴
46	.	.	📬	78	N	Ν	☠	110	n	ν	■	0142			❸	0174	®	→	✹
47	/	/	📭	79	O	Ο	🏳	111	o	ο	□	0143			❹	0175	¯	↓	✵
48	0	0	🗀	80	P	Π	🏱	112	p	π	🞐	0144			❺	0176	°	°	⯐
49	1	1	🗁	81	Q	Θ	✈	113	q	θ	❑	0145	‘		❻	0177	±	±	⌖
50	2	2	🗎	82	R	Ρ	☼	114	r	ρ	❒	0146	’		❼	0178	²	″	⟡
51	3	3	🗏	83	S	Σ	💧	115	s	σ	⬧	0147	“		❽	0179	³	≥	⌑
52	4	4	🗐	84	T	Τ	❄	116	t	τ	⧫	0148	”		❾	0180	´	×	⯑
53	5	5	🗄	85	U	Υ	🕆	117	u	υ	◆	0149	•		❿	0181	µ	∝	✪
54	6	6	⌛	86	V	ς	✞	118	v	ϖ	❖	0150	—		🙢	0182	¶	∂	✰
55	7	7	🖮	87	W	Ω	🕈	119	w	ω	⬥	0151	–		🙠	0183	·	•	🕐
56	8	8	🖰	88	X	Ξ	✠	120	x	ξ	⌧	0152	˜		🙡	0184	¸	÷	🕑
57	9	9	🖲	89	Y	Ψ	✡	121	y	ψ	⮹	0153	™		🙣	0185	¹	≠	🕒
58	:	:	🖳	90	Z	Ζ	☪	122	z	ζ	⌘	0154	š		🙞	0186	º	≡	🕓
59	;	;	🖴	91	[	[	☯	123	{	{	🏵	0155	›		🙜	0187	»	≈	🕔
60	<	<	🖫	92	\	∴	ॐ	124	|	|	🏶	0156	œ		🙝	0188	¼	…	🕕
61	=	=	🖬	93	]	]	☸	125	}	}	🙶	0157			🙟	0189	½	⏐	🕖
62	>	>	✇	94	^	⊥	♈	126	~	∼	🙷	0158			·	0190	¾	⎯	🕗
63	?	?	✍	95	_	_	♉	127			▯	0159	Ÿ		•	0191	¿	↵	🕘

0192	À	ℵ	🕙	0224	à	◊	🡪
0193	Á	ℑ	🕚	0225	á	〈	🡩
0194	Â	ℜ	🕛	0226	â	®	🡫
0195	Ã	℘	⮰	0227	ã	©	🡬
0196	Ä	⊗	⮱	0228	ä	™	🡭
0197	Å	⊕	⮲	0229	å	∑	🡯
0198	Æ	∅	⮳	0230	æ	⎛	🡮
0199	Ç	∩	⮴	0231	ç	⎜	🡸
0200	È	∪	⮵	0232	è	⎝	🡺
0201	É	⊃	⮶	0233	é	⎡	🡹
0202	Ê	⊇	⮷	0234	ê	⎢	🡻
0203	Ë	⊄	🙪	0235	ë	⎣	🡼
0204	Ì	⊂	🙫	0236	ì	⎧	🡽
0205	Í	⊆	🙕	0237	í	⎨	🡿
0206	Î	∈	🙔	0238	î	⎩	🡾
0207	Ï	∉	🙗	0239	ï	⎪	⇦
0208	Ð	∠	🙖	0240	ð		⇨
0209	Ñ	∇	🙐	0241	ñ	〉	⇧
0210	Ò	®	🙑	0242	ò	∫	⇩
0211	Ó	©	🙒	0243	ó	⌠	⬄
0212	Ô	™	🙓	0244	ô	⎮	⇳
0213	Õ	∏	⌫	0245	õ	⌡	⬁
0214	Ö	√	⌦	0246	ö	⎞	⬀
0215	×	⋅	⮘	0247	÷	⎟	⬃
0216	Ø	¬	⮚	0248	ø	⎠	⬂
0217	Ù	∧	⮙	0249	ù	⎤	🢬
0218	Ú	∨	⮛	0250	ú	⎥	🢭
0219	Û	⇔	⮈	0251	û	⎦	🗶
0220	Ü	⇐	⮊	0252	ü	⎫	✔
0221	Ý	⇑	⮉	0253	ý	⎬	🗷
0222	Þ	⇒	⮋	0254	þ	⎭	🗹
0223	ß	⇓	🡨	0255	ÿ		⊞

Figure 16-1: The Windows 3.1 Character Set

You use the numeric keypad to access characters that don't correspond with keyboard keys. With the NumLock light on, hold down the Alt key and type 119 on the keypad, and the same letter "w" (or alternate character) appears.

The Microsoft TrueType Font Pack Character Set

The TrueType Font Pack includes four TrueType faces with numerous special characters: Lucida Bright Math Extension, Math Italic, and Math Symbol; and Monotype Sorts. To access characters that cannot be typed directly from the keyboard:

1) Make sure the Num Lock light is *on*.
2) Hold down the Alt key while typing the appropriate number on the numeric keypad.
3) Release the Alt key.

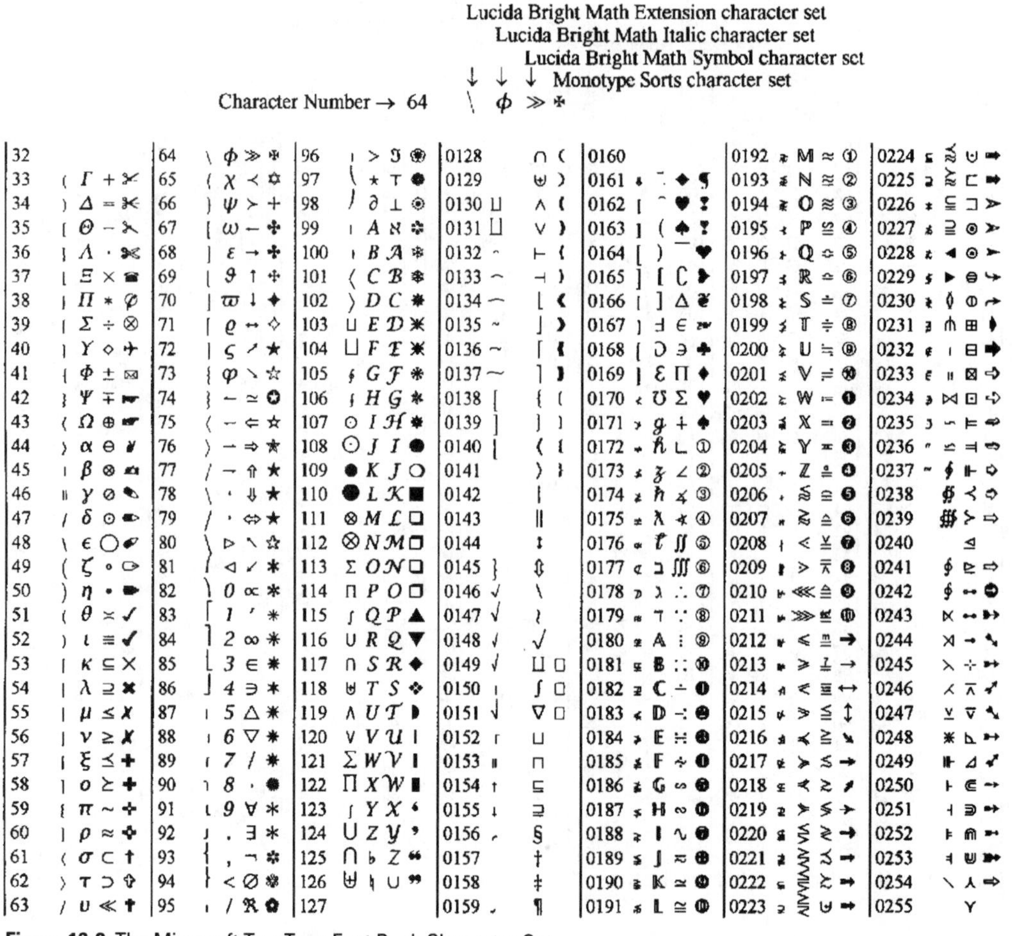

Lucida Bright Math Extension character set
Lucida Bright Math Italic character set
Lucida Bright Math Symbol character set
Monotype Sorts character set

Character Number → 64

Figure 16-2: The Microsoft TrueType Font Pack Character Set

This is most useful when you want a character that doesn't have its own key. Alt+0189, for example, inserts a one-half symbol (½) in Arial, Times New Roman, and other text typefaces.

You must add a leading zero — as in "0189" — when using this method to insert characters numbered 128 through 255. This is because Windows is downward compatible with the IBM PC-8 character set, which is used by DOS applications. The PC-8 character set already uses the Alt+*number* method, and Windows allows you to enter characters in this way, too. For example, Alt+171 inserts a one-half symbol in both DOS and Windows. (Characters in the PC-8 character set that do not exist in Windows, such as line-draw characters, are ignored or converted into other keyboard characters.)

I use many of the higher-numbered special characters all the time. Windows makes it easy for me to use a long dash for emphasis — like this — by typing Alt+0150. Bullets to set off paragraphs are found at Alt+0149. And many word processors, such as Word for Windows, allow you to use the "curly quote" characters numbered 0145 through 0148, by adding a macro that comes with the application.

The Wingdings character set takes these special symbols much, much farther. Many Wingdings characters are pictorial. This includes keyboard and mouse symbols, Alt+55 and Alt+56, and electronic mail symbols, Alt+42 through Alt+47. You can easily use these symbols in documents as clip art, merely by increasing the point size of an individual Wingdings character up to 127 points (the maximum in applications like Microsoft Word for Windows 2.0), or even 999 points (the maximum in Ami Pro).

Finally, Microsoft's Font Pack contains a whole grab bag of symbols: Monotype Sorts, with more than 200 arrows, pointing hands, and bullets from a grand old type foundry; and three math symbol fonts from the upstart Lucida typographers (who also created Wingdings).

All these characters are laid out for you in Figures 16-1 and 16-2. Look through them with an eye for a particular character that you might use in your work. Chances are, you'll find it.

Microsoft isn't the only source for fonts, of course. More symbols (and even better TrueType faces) are available from a variety of vendors. Agfa Compugraphic has an excellent "Discovery Font Pack," with elegant Wile Roman, Shannon, and other text typefaces, for a list price of a remarkably low $49.95 at this writing. Afga has also converted many trademark and corporate images into TrueType format (call 800-424-8973 or 508-658-0200). Casady & Greene offers Keycap faces for computer documentation, as well as a range of Russian and other language sets (call 800-359-4920 or fax 408-484-9218). For more vendors, see the Fonts category in the Windows Showcase catalog that comes with Windows 3.1, or call Microsoft at 206-882-8080 for a copy of the catalog.

The Technology of a Million Faces

I've recently purchased a house, and moles have quickly made their presence known in my front yard. I can imagine them underground, stepping on each other and passing along sizable mounds of dirt.

It reminds me of Comdex/Fall, that technological molehill of a computer conference that some 130,000 of us descend into each year. Whether or not you attend, I'd like to share with you a look at a product I first saw previewed behind closed doors at a recent Comdex exposition, and which you might actually benefit from.

One of the most interesting developments I've seen is a revolutionary font technology that will change the way all fonts are packaged and sold.

Called Font Chameleon, this technology was developed under tight wraps by Ares Software of Foster City, California. Ares is best known in the Mac market for its utilities that convert PostScript fonts to TrueType, and vice versa. But in the recent past, it has also released its FontMonger and FontMinder utilities in Windows versions as well.

Font_Chameleon isn't a font utility, but an actual font. The difference between Chameleon and ordinary font files, however, is spectacular. Ares Software has found a way to pack almost every text typeface you can think of into a single file. This means that you can install typefaces like Avant Garde Gothic and Bookman *on demand*.

Even better, you can modify typefaces, or combine two different faces into an original creation of your own design. Much like the "morphing" effect you see in special-effects movies, you can tell Font Chameleon to give you a typeface that's "80 percent Avant Garde and 20 percent Bookman." You can watch the effect change as you tweak the settings.

Programmers who worked on the project say you'll be able to create more than 4 *billion* different typefaces using Chameleon. Yet it ships on a single 720K floppy, and lists for $295 (with a street price around $175).

I've long complained about the price of PostScript type. When Adobe Systems had a monopoly on the PostScript language, it priced individual PostScript font families higher than some major applications.

Then Microsoft created a price war among type vendors by pricing the 44 faces in its TrueType Font Pack below $50 (during the Windows 3.1 introductory upgrade period). In response, other TrueType vendors began selling their faces as libraries, rather than individually. Now, Ares will shift type sales toward single, low-cost files from which you can create as many typefaces as you like.

Ares has figured out the essential characteristics of all text typefaces. All type designs start with the outline of a basic alphabet, then dress it up with serifs and so on. But far from merely copying the outlines of other type vendors, Ares has generated its own master outline, and manipulates it endlessly. They call this *parametric* technology.

I call it something that will shoot a big hole in Adobe's Multiple Master type technology. Multiple Master allows a magazine designer to distort one or two typefaces into enough shapes to fill a whole publication. But only three Multiple Master families are currently available, and they're expensive. When a designer has 4 billion faces to choose from, that's a selection.

Multiple Master fonts are used in Adobe's Acrobat product, which allows you to create documents that look the same on your PC as well as on a PC that has only a few basic fonts. Besides Acrobat, other players that strive for leadership in the "portable document" market include Common Ground and Digital Paper. But I predict that parametrics will ultimately play a determining role in this battle. Parametric technology will soon trickle down into desktop applications. You'll be able to tell your word processor to generate a font that's say, 2 percent smaller, so your newsletter will fit into 16 pages instead of 16 1/2. And electronic publishers will distribute magazines on disks, with Font Chameleon providing the fonts.

Contact Ares Software at 561 Pilgrim Dr., Suite D, Foster City, CA 94404; 415-578-9090 for more information.

Regaining True Underlining on LaserJets under Windows 3.1

One of the changes that Windows 3.1 brought is a set of new printer drivers. In general, all Windows 3.0 printer drivers require updates to become true Windows 3.1 drivers. (This is also true of video drivers.) Without these updates, these drivers won't work with TrueType and other 3.1-specific features.

One of the side benefits of this wholesale updating of Windows drivers is that the new drivers contain some undocumented features we can take advantage of.

 Underlining is a perfect case in point. Underlining has not always been handled properly by Windows, and it still isn't, but at least we can patch this behavior in Windows 3.1 under certain circumstances.

First, a little background. Every traditional print shop uses two kinds of horizontal lines in typesetting. The first is the kind that you might use when composing a mail-in coupon, with lines extending horizontally from headings like Name,

Address, and so on. This kind of line is called a *baseline rule* or an *underscore.* On a PC keyboard, it is represented by the underscore character, which is just above the hyphen.

The second kind of line runs beneath text that is supposed to be emphasized. This is called an *underline,* and it is usually added to text in Windows word processors by clicking a "U" icon or pressing Ctrl+U.

When the early Hewlett-Packard LaserJet printers were being designed, both an *underscore* and an *underline* capability were programmed in. HP calls the baseline rule a *fixed* underline (because the line is fixed at just a few pixels below the baseline on which the characters sit). And it calls the true underline a *floating* underline (because it "floats" just beneath the descender of lowercase characters like "g" and "y").

Why care about underlining? After all, if you're using a typeface that allows italic and bold — as all the new TrueType text faces included with Windows 3.1 do — you should almost always use italic and bold to indicate emphasis, rather than underlining text.

But there are several cases in which underlining is important to the readability of a document. In law firms, as well as in any company that frequently revises documents, underlining is commonly used to indicate text that has been added to a draft and which other reviewers must approve. In a table of figures, you should underline the headings of related columns of numbers, and so on.

It is usually pretty easy to use the two types of underlining correctly in DOS word processors, such as Microsoft Word, which allow you to edit their printer driver tables. By specifying the Escape codes that should be sent to the printer, any type of underlining, boldfacing, or other printer capabilities can be added quickly to the DOS application's printer support.

But the LaserJet printer drivers for Windows 3.0 seemingly ignored the difference between baseline rules and underlines. All underlines were jammed up against the baseline, cutting through the descenders of g's and y's and making underlined revisions in documents hard to read.

At the time, I complained to Hewlett-Packard's LaserJet staff in Boise, Idaho, about the loss of true underlines in Windows 3.0. There was no way for Windows technical staff like myself to edit the driver and regain a feature that our users had come to expect from their DOS word processors.

HP promised me that a way to add this feature back into the Windows 3.1 printer driver would be found, and so it was. All it requires is a change of one byte in the Windows 3.1 LaserJet III printer driver, which takes no more than a minute.

In order to make this change, it helps to know one thing about how the LaserJet family of printers handles underlines. Ordinarily, if an application wants a LaserJet to start using a floating underline under words, it sends to the printer a series of Escape codes. The exact sequence is ESC&d3D, where "ESC" represents the Escape character. To start a baseline rule, which HP calls a *fixed underline,* the sequence is ESC&d0D — the same as before, but with a zero instead of a 3.

In the Windows 3.0 LaserJet drivers (and in the Windows 3.1 LaserJet II driver), this sequence was incorrectly coded as ESC&dD — no zero or 3. The printer interprets the lack of a number as a zero and starts printing a baseline rule onto all words. But there is no way to switch to true underlining — you cannot simply insert a 3 into the sequence because the driver cannot be allowed to change from its original size, by even one byte.

This problem does not exist in the Windows 3.1 LaserJet driver, fortunately. The underline sequence is present in its expanded form, and can be revised to a true underline by changing the zero to a 3.

If you haven't installed the LaserJet III driver, use the Control Panel's Printers dialog box to do so. You can edit the driver with any byte editor, but I'll use Windows Write here since it works and I know all Windows users have it.

STEPS

Adding True Underlining to LaserJet printers

Step 1. In Windows Write, print some underlined text in one of the LaserJet III's proportional typefaces, such as 12-point CG Times. Print words with a lot of descenders, such as "wysiwyg," so you can see the difference in underlining later. Close Windows Write.

Step 2. Using the File Manager or your favorite utility, select the LaserJet III driver file, HPPCL5A.DRV, in the Windows \SYSTEM subdirectory. Click File Copy and make a copy named HPPCL5A.BIN. (You can make these changes while Windows is running, but not while printing, OK?)

Step 3. Open Windows Write, click File Open, and load the file HPPCL5A.BIN. When Write asks whether you want to convert the file to Write format, click "No Conversion."

Step 4. When the file is displayed, click Find Find. In the dialog box that appears, type "&d0D" (ampersand-d-zero-D) as the text to search for. Click Find Next, and this string in the file is highlighted for you on-screen. Press the Esc key to close the Find dialog box.

Step 5. Type "&d3D" (without quotes) to replace the old string with your new string. *Case is important* — the first "d" must be lowercase, the second one uppercase.

Step 6. Click File Save. Don't use File Save-As, because this menu item changes the length of the file, which won't work. Close Windows Write.

Step 7. Returning to File Manager, select HPPCL5A.DRV and click File Rename to change its name to HPPCL5A.ORI ("ori" as in "original"). Then select HPPCL5A.BIN and rename it to HPPCL5A.DRV.

Step 8. In Windows Write, print the same underlined text you tried earlier. The underline should now touch the bottom of the descenders, instead of cutting through them. If you have any problems, rename HPPCL5A.ORI to HPPCL5A.DRV to go back to your original driver.

This works not only with the built-in LaserJet III typefaces, but also with PCL5 scalable outline typeface cartridges.

Unfortunately, it doesn't change TrueType faces, which have their underline stroke fixed in place toward the baseline. You can correct this only by requesting typefaces with true underlining from vendors of TrueType.

Summary

In this chapter, I disclose some of the more exotic secrets of the Windows environment's font handling potential.

▶ With my two charts on the entire Windows 3.1 character set, and the more than 1,000 little-known symbols in the Microsoft TrueType Font Pack, you should never again be at a loss for just the right symbol to highlight that important document, spreadsheet, or presentation.

▶ With new Font Chameleon technology, you should be able to find — or, more interestingly, *create* — exactly the right typeface for the mood you want to convey.

▶ With my little one-byte LaserJet print driver hack, you can improve the appearance of all the scalable fonts you underline using HP's PCL5 standard.

Chapter 17
Getting Fonts and Characters to Say What *You* Want

In This Chapter

▶ I describe the frustration of trying to create documentation to explain Windows' arcane keystroke combinations to novice computer users, and illustrate a special TrueType font that's been created just to solve this problem.

▶ I review a free Windows utility that allows you to insert long character strings (such as a corporate name) or special characters (such as the "©" copyright symbol) into any Windows document with only two or three keystrokes.

When documenting Windows applications for the average user, you might find yourself wondering how to represent certain keystrokes that the user is supposed to press.

Windows is full of important key combinations that are, frankly, hard to remember. I usually indicate such key combinations by capitalizing the first letter of special keys on the keyboard. For example, to bring up the Windows Task List, I would say, "press Ctrl+Esc." To switch among running applications, "press Alt+Esc."

But one of my readers, Elizabeth Johnston, finds that this isn't enough, and has actually done something about it. She teaches a microcomputer literacy course to beginners, and says, "My students just didn't 'get it' when I wrote ENTER or [Enter] or <Enter>, no matter how carefully I explained it." Some of her students mistakenly typed *e, n, t, e, r,* instead of pressing the Enter key. So she created her own TrueType and e, which show every key on the keyboard as a tiny keycap.

There are many retail versions of fonts that show the PC keyboard, of course. But Ms. Johnston didn't find them useful, because they were too "arty." By rendering each keycap as a three-dimensional object, or with an artistic shadow border, these keycap characters actually become too small to read clearly when inserted into 10-point or 12-point type — the same size as the body copy of Ms. Johnston's documentation.

Ms. Johnston's fonts, shown in Figure 17-1, are simple, two-dimensional shapes that reproduce well at small sizes.

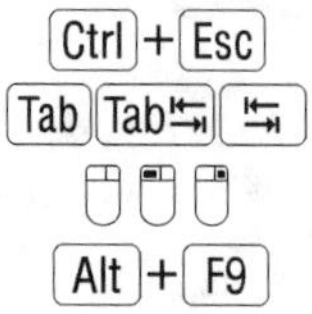

Figure 17-1: Examples of characters in the RRKeyCaps TrueType face.

One font, RRKeyCaps, includes all the "gray keys" on a typical PC keyboard. Different variations are provided for certain keys, such as Tab. Sometimes the word "Tab" is printed on the key, sometimes a double-headed arrow, sometimes both. The variations allow you to choose the Tab key that looks like the one on the keyboards in your company.

Another font, RRKeyLetters, includes key caps for punctuation marks, such as periods and commas. When you register, you receive a complete set of both fonts, with all the letters of the alphabet.

A shareware version of RRKeyCaps is featured on the diskettes that accompany this book. For more information, including a complete character map, see the Excellence in Shareware section. Shareware copies are also available on CompuServe. To download these fonts from CompuServe, type GO DTPFORUM. Select the PC Fonts library, then download RRKEYT.ZIP (TrueType) or RRKEYP.ZIP (PostScript).

To register, or to obtain both font formats and printed documentation by mail, send $54 (Louisiana residents add tax) to: Elizabeth Swoope Johnston, RoadRunner Computing, P.O. Box 21635, Baton Rouge, LA 70894; CompuServe: 76436,2426.

Redefine Keys Into Any Character String

I'm always looking for ways to save a few more keystrokes in Windows. Oft-repeated names and phrases can be a pain to type, and I often have to look up the oddly spelled names of companies and friends that I work with, which takes even more time.

I have sometimes used the Windows Recorder to place long, frequently typed names on various key combinations, such as Ctrl+Alt+F12. This has a few drawbacks, though. It takes away a key combination I may someday need in a Windows application. And the Recorder has a strange limitation: it cannot record the use of Alt and the numeric keypad. This means that I cannot, for example, record Alt+0169 in order to place the copyright symbol (©) on some easier-to-remember key combination, such as Ctrl+Alt+C.

The answer to these Windows redefinition problems is a free utility called Compose. This tiny Windows application allows you to insert virtually any character or character string into your documents by pressing just two or three keys on your keyboard.

In its default configuration, Compose uses the Right Ctrl key as its "compose" key. You press and release your Right Ctrl key, then press and release any combination of keys that are defined.

Compose comes with more than 100 such sequences defined for you. For example, pressing Right Ctrl, the letter Y, and an equals sign inserts a Japanese Yen symbol (¥) into your document. You can type "Y" and "=" in any order, in upper- or lowercase. Or you can change these options, to insert a different character when you change the order or the case.

As you might expect, Compose is easily capable of handling all of Windows's so-called upper ANSI characters. It is much easier to remember the predefined Compose sequences for these characters — Right Ctrl, the letter e, and an apostrophe produces the accented *é* in *café,* for instance — than the equivalents (Alt+0233, in this case).

You can make the Compose shortcut include up to five characters, so acronyms can be expanded easily to any reasonable length. Because Compose was created within the Digital Equipment Corp. by Jerry Cummings, the sequence Right Ctrl, D, E, C, is predefined for you to insert "Digital Equipment Corporation." This can be changed, if you prefer.

Other defaults are more useful. Pressing Right Ctrl, D, and a space inserts into your documents the current date, T and a space inserts the current time, and DT inserts both. For some reason, these assignments can't be changed, but you *can* determine the format used for the date and time. Compose picks up these formats from the preferences you set in the Control Panel's International dialog box.

The only other combination you can't change is Right Ctrl followed by two spaces. This brings up a scrolling box that allows you to insert any character from any typeface you have installed. It's much easier to make out each character in this resizable box than it is in the Character Map applet included with Windows 3.1 — especially when you're choosing from a symbol font such as Wingdings.

Compose is available on CompuServe in the WINSHARE forum, Library 6 (General Win Utilities). Download the filename CMPOSE.ZIP, a 66K file. Place the unzipped files in any directory, then make a Compose icon in your StartUp group. (It was not possible to include Compose on the diskettes that accompany this book because of legal and licensing restrictions.)

You can use Compose's Options menu to switch from the Right Ctrl key to other compose keys, such as Alt+F12. Using the Print Font Samples item on the File menu, you can also use Compose to print a sample of any or all type fonts you have installed — a very handy feature.

All in all, Compose is a cool tool.

Summary

In this chapter, I describe alternative ways to represent key combinations in Windows documentation, and make key combinations expand to long names or special characters.

▶ RRKeyCaps and Elizabeth Swoope Johnston's other related TrueType faces are excellent fonts to represent keystrokes in the text of 10- and 12-point documentation.

▶ Compose is a handy, free utility that expands nearly any combination of two or three keystrokes into full phrases or Alt+keypad characters.

Chapter 18

Using Undocumented CD-ROM Functionality

In This Chapter

▶ I delve into some of the mysterious workings of CD-ROM drives, those handy devices that store 600 megabytes of data on a convenient, shiny disk.

▶ I focus on CorelSCSI and other products that can improve your CD-ROM performance, along with some intriguing background on the ways Microsoft has and has not documented the DOS interface to CD-ROMs and other external drives.

More and more Windows users are working with CD-ROM drives and other high-capacity peripherals. That means more and more PC systems are using the Small Computer System Interface (SCSI, pronounced "scuzzy").

SCSI was a great idea invented several years back. Its purpose was to allow computer users to connect as many as seven devices to a single adapter board. This would avoid the need for a separate board (and slot) for each device. Peripherals as diverse as CD-ROMs, tape drives, data cartridges, and flatbed scanners now wave the SCSI banner. The SCSI protocol gained popularity with peripheral manufacturers because it promised high throughput rates for devices that could be used in different environments, like DOS, Mac, and Unix.

But the SCSI standard never seemed to work as well in practice as in theory. Apple invented its own low-performance version of SCSI. (Back then, they thought no one would ever want to transfer data faster than a Mac I.) Devices from different manufacturers wouldn't always work together, even on the Apple variant, until vendors agreed to a SCSI 2 standard.

And lately, with more "multimedia Windows" hardware becoming available, I've been noticing a number of manufacturers that have been shipping "SCSI" boards that work only with *their brand of peripherals*. I call these "bastard SCSI" boards, or B.S. boards for short.

I know one heavy PC user who has five SCSI peripherals, all using different add-in boards. Since he doesn't have that many free slots, he takes one board out and inserts another whenever he needs to use his scanner.

He isn't the only person who thinks this state of affairs is foolish. The Corel Corporation, best known for its CorelDraw graphics software, also produces a product called CorelSCSI to bring some sense to this market. CorelSCSI 1.1 ($99) is the basic product, and CorelSCSI Pro ($495) also provides graphically based backup and other bundled apps. Both products are software only. Inside the box, you get diskettes that support DOS, Windows, NetWare, OS/2, and Unix machines.

Corel claims it has developed a driver capability for virtually every SCSI peripheral available. They defend this claim with a huge listing of supported CD-ROMs (including jukeboxes for network storage), WORMs, hard drives, optical erasable drives, and so on.

I tested CorelSCSI with three devices: a NEC CDR-74 CD-ROM drive, a Bernoulli Transportable 90 cartridge drive, and an Insite 20-megabyte Floptical diskette drive.

Initially, each drive came with its own SCSI board. I installed all three boards into a single 386, and verified that they each worked. Then I removed two of the boards, and daisy-chained all three devices into the remaining board — an Adaptec 1520 (a full-featured SCSI board). When I turned the power on, the device drivers for the two "orphaned" devices booted up with error messages like "Host adapter not found."

Inserting the CorelSCSI diskette and typing INSTALL completely cured this. CorelSCSI found all three SCSI devices and inserted its own device drivers into the CONFIG.SYS file. All three devices worked as well as they had with their own, proprietary boards.

The SCSI standard still has its quirks, of course. To get the original configuration working in the first place:

- SCSI devices come with "terminators" and you must enable only two of them.

- I.D. numbers (0 through 7) must be set to a different value on each device.

- SCSI boards use an interrupt, an upper memory block, and an I/O base address, which must be set to *not* match any other device in your system.

SCSI doesn't configure any of this automatically. (The Bernoulli handled this best, with easy-to-use pushbuttons instead of jumpers to set.) But, if you have CorelSCSI, at least you won't need to deal with multiple SCSI boards.

CorelSCSI's device driver for CD-ROM drives, CORELCDX.COM, has several advantages over the CD-ROM driver that has been distributed for years by Microsoft, MSCDEX.EXE:

■ MSCdex (Microsoft CD-ROM Extensions), which consumes 35K, cannot be removed from memory. CorelCDX, by comparison, comes with a CDOFF utility which totally recovers the memory when used with Mark and Release utilities. (The Mark and Release utilities are available on CompuServe: type GO PCVENB, go to the TurboPower library, and download TSRCOM.ZIP).

■ MSCdex caches only two CD-ROM sectors. CorelCDX can cache up to eight sectors, with the switch /DATABLK:n (where n is 2 to 8). This can improve your CD-ROM performance.

There is one thing that CorelCDX cannot do, however. It cannot, at this writing, share CD-ROM drives across machines that are running Windows for Workgroups (WFWG).

Dave Madden, CorelSCSI product manager, says this is because "Microsoft hasn't documented the API that's used for the network redirector" in DOS, and repeated requests to Microsoft did not produce the information. Madden also can't duplicate MSCdex's Kanji support, which limits Corel's market in Japan.

In Chapter 19, "Uncovering Undocumented Windows," I describe eight different cases of undocumented features of DOS and Windows that have been used in Microsoft applications and utilities before being released to competitors. MSCDEX.EXE is one of these examples. The undocumented nature of DOS is keeping at least one vendor from selling a utility with equivalent features (CorelCDX).

Andrew Schulman, co-author of *Undocumented DOS* (Addison-Wesley), states, "Microsoft has never documented the redirector," which is needed to run any non-DOS file system, not just CD-ROMs. His book includes a whole chapter on the API: DOS's undocumented Interrupt 2F, Function 11h. But he says the next edition of *Undocumented DOS* will include even more material, since his co-authors have found many more functions that Microsoft left out of its documentation.

Schulman writes, "The problem isn't that they [Microsoft] have some Machiavellian conspiracy against the rest of the software industry, but instead that they have an extremely informal approach to documentation, and to Windows itself, that is out of touch with their near-monopoly position in the industry.... Their absolutely wretched documentation is getting intolerable given their importance in the industry."

If you need to share CD-ROM drives across a Microsoft network, you need to use a /S switch with MSCdex, which does not appear in the Windows for Workgroups User's Manual:

```
MSCDEX /S {options}
```

MSCdex is included in WFWG, and a better version (which requires less memory to load high) is in MS-DOS 6. But there is no mention of the /S switch in the paperback that comes with the MS-DOS 6 upgrade, either. In fact, Microsoft provides no reference guide to DOS syntax with that upgrade at all. Instead, you get a "Road Map" to installing DOS. You must buy what is called a DOS 6 Technical Reference for $22.45 postpaid to get what we used to know as the DOS manual. (Call 800-426-9400 or 206-882-8080 to order it.)

I hope Microsoft documents the redirector interface to DOS so we can all see better products for Windows and CD-ROMs. And I hope the decision to remove the manual from the MS-DOS 6 upgrade is just a temporary aberration that doesn't spread to Windows or other applications.

For information on CorelSCSI and CorelCDX, Corel Corp. can be reached at 613-728-8200.

At least two other CD-ROM enhancements are also available:

Online Computer Systems sells CD-ROM server software called OptiNet, with a client module that can load and unload MSCdex at will. Pricing varies by network, with a 100-user license priced at $1495, including all server, client, and MSCdex licenses. Contact Online at 800-922-9204 or 301-428-3700.

CD Net is a similar product from Meridian Data, 5615 Scotts Valley Dr., Scotts Valley, CA 95066; 408-438-3100. According to Meridian engineer Ed Smiley, CD Net can multitask several DOS or Windows CD-ROM applications, each using the same drive letter for the CD-ROM. This allows you to conserve drive letters and maintain consistent drive mappings, unlike MSCdex, he says.

Summary

In this chapter, I describe some alternatives to improve your CD-ROM performance and features.

▶ Products from Corel, Online Computer Systems, and Meridian Data support features that are not available from MSCDEX.EXE, the Microsoft CD-ROM driver.

▶ Even more vendors should be able to create drivers to enhance the functionality of CD-ROMs and other external drives if good documentation for the "network redirector" services of MS-DOS becomes available.

Chapter 19
Uncovering Undocumented Windows

In This Chapter

▶ I describe some of the undocumented programming calls that are hidden in Windows and show how you can use them in your own programs written in Visual Basic, WordBasic, and many other languages.

▶ I examine in detail the charges that Microsoft has withheld programming calls like these from Windows and DOS programmers, using eight specific examples to illustrate the issues, how programmers feel about them, and how Microsoft responds to them.

In my books, I try to reveal undocumented features that can be employed by the widest variety of Windows users, from novices to experienced PC managers.

There is also a book that does the same thing for Windows programmers: *Undocumented Windows,* by Andrew Schulman, a former Phar Lap Software developer, and David Maxey, a former Lotus developer. This team, and others, in 1990 also brought us *Undocumented DOS* (both published by Addison-Wesley).

Schulman and Maxey's earlier, DOS, book was largely about writing stable terminate-and-stay-resident (TSR) programs. About TSRs, they write, "you must use undocumented DOS functions; you simply have no choice."

Undocumented Windows charts new ground by describing programming functions that were first used in Microsoft's Windows applications (and some others), but did not appear in Windows 3.0's Programmer's Reference.

How the Plumbing Works _____

Because Windows is marketed as an operating system (it now says so right on the box), we can forgive a certain number of secret functions. There are, after all, certain things that only an operating system should do.

But you may be surprised to learn that Schulman and Maxey have uncovered *more than 200* undocumented functions and messages in Windows 3.0 and higher. They learned many of these features by running Microsoft Excel and Word for Windows, and laboriously noting (with utilities included in the book) exactly what they do.

For example, both Excel and Word for Windows, according to Schulman/Maxey, use the undocumented calls SetSystemTimer() and KillSystemTimer(). These calls, unlike the documented SetTimer() function, allow an application to get timer services from Windows, even when Windows reports that all timers are already busy.

At this point in the book, Schulman and Maxey describe the Federal Trade Commission's investigation of Microsoft, adding, "Using these functions but not documenting them certainly gives the appearance of an unfair advantage over Microsoft's competitors."

Yet there is evidence that a few programmers outside Microsoft did manage to learn about the same features that *Undocumented Windows* describes. Schulman and Maxey themselves detail at least 10 undocumented Windows calls made by various modules of Norton Desktop 1.0, marketed for Windows 3.0 by Symantec Corp. It's interesting to wonder how long it took the developers of Lotus 1-2-3 for Windows and WordPerfect for Windows to find out similar calls that they, too, needed.

There's nothing wrong with a company maintaining trade secrets. It *is* a no-no, however, for a company with a monopoly-like position to unfairly restrict competition. This issue forms a major part part of the FTC's antitrust investigation of Microsoft, which was turned over to the U.S. Department of Justice for final disposition. In a different case, IBM got into antitrust problems with the Department of Justice in the '60s, and eventually had to "untie" its dominant mainframe sales from its software sales, to allow competition.

To its credit, Microsoft decided some time ago to document system features needed by application competitors. Some information appears in TOOLHELP.DLL (a Windows 3.1 program that software vendors can freely distribute to users of Windows 3.0), which makes many function calls available. Other information is part of Microsoft's "Open Tools," which are intended to allow other companies to develop Windows-compatible compilers and debuggers.

If you're a C programmer, don't write another line of code until you get *Undocumented Windows*. It's $39.95 plus shipping from Addison-Wesley, 800-447-2226 or 617-944-3700.

Meanwhile, even average, non-C computer users can take advantage of these functions, as described in another book. Windows users owe a debt of gratitude to a Coloradan named Woody Leonhard. His book, appropriately entitled *Windows 3.1 Programming for Mere Mortals* (Addison-Wesley), opens up Windows' application programming interface (API) to those who program in Visual Basic,

GFA-Basic, Realizer, WordBasic, and similar graphical languages. His book is chock full of programming code that can help you do in one line things that you might otherwise have assumed weren't possible at all.

Complementing this book are two of Leonhard's other works: an add-on called "Woody's Office Power Pack for Word for Windows 2.0" (WOPR, pronounced "whopper"), and *The Hacker's Guide to Word for Windows,* also published by Addison-Wesley. *The Hacker's Guide* is an 800-page manual to undocumented features of WordBasic for Winword 2.0, plus many other treats.

It was in *The Hacker's Guide* that I learned Winword's undocumented ExitWindows command. This is one of my favorites, because you can use it in a macro that's only four lines long:

```
Sub MAIN
FileSaveAll 0
ExitWindows
End Sub
```

When you run this macro, Winword (1.1 or 2.0) will ask if you want to save each unsaved document. After Winword closes, all *other* Windows applications will ask if you want to save *their* unsaved documents. Then you drop out to a DOS prompt. (Change the 0 into a 1 in the second line of this macro, if you want to force all Winword documents to be saved without asking.)

You can easily place this routine on a menu or the Winword 2.0 button bar, for a clean and quick exit from Windows at the end of your workday.

Undocumented Windows is an important companion to Leonhard's works. You can utilize many of the 200 undocumented Windows API calls revealed in *Undocumented Windows* by using the Basic "Declare Function" command, as Leonhard describes in *Windows 3.1 Programming for Mere Mortals.*

For example, instead of using WordBasic's own ExitWindows command, you could access from WordBasic the documented ExitWindows() API function, or other undocumented functions, as explained in *Undocumented Windows.* ExitWindows() accepts parameters that either cause Windows to exit and re-start, or cause your whole system to reboot. This can be very handy if your macro has made changes in WIN.INI or AUTOEXEC.BAT that require restarting Windows or your system.

One problem common to all Windows applications is dealing with limited memory and System Resources. Leonhard says that some Word for Windows macros tend to fail when System Resources fall to 30 percent free or lower. ("System Resources" refers to 128K of memory used by Windows Graphics Device Interface and User modules.)

The following WordBasic code checks the status of these resources before running large macros. Written for Windows 3.1 and Winword 2.0, this illustrates how to tie into Windows' USER.EXE module using WordBasic's "Declare Function" statement. The macro either runs a large procedure or displays a message box, depending on whether the variable "free" is greater than 30 percent.

```
Declare Function GetFreeSystemResources Lib "user"(wflags As Integer) As Integer

Sub MAIN
free = GetFreeSystemResources(0)
If free > 30 Then
  BigMacro
Else
  Msg$ = "Less than 30% Free System Resources. Close"
  Msg$ = Msg$ + " some windows and try again."
  MsgBox Msg$, "Low Resources", 16
End If
End Sub
```

In this macro, replace the line "BigMacro" with the name of the large procedure you conditionally wish to run. If you merely want to display the Free System Resources (rather than branching between two different actions), replace all the lines from the "If" statement to "End If," inclusive, with the following line:

```
MsgBox "Free System Resources:" + Str$(free), "Resources", 64
```

In case you're using Windows 3.0, Leonhard's book also suggests a way that you can get the percentage of Free System Resources using the undocumented GetHeapSpaces() function described in *Undocumented Windows*.

At this point, a few warnings are in order. Leonhard and the authors of *Undocumented Windows* correctly point out that no one should use undocumented functions without a good reason. Since the undocumented GetHeapSpaces() function may actually disappear in future versions of Windows, you should always use the documented GetFreeSystemResources() function instead, if you have Windows 3.1. Use undocumented functions only when they are the sole method to accomplish your task.

You should also realize that not all Windows API functions can be handled properly in every language. Many API calls, for example, expect to be passed a pointer to a callback function. This is simple in C, but is difficult or impossible in Visual Basic or WordBasic.

Additionally, Visual Basic is designed to handle only signed arithmetic where, say, a one-byte integer represents a value from -127 to +127. Numerous API functions, however, use unsigned integers, where a byte represents 0 to 255. This is a severe limitation of Visual Basic, which is not easily overcome. Other graphical Basics, such as Realizer and GFA-Basic, provide more power and may be preferable.

WOPR 2.0 is $49.95 plus shipping from Pinecliffe International, 800-OK-WINWORD or 314-965-5630. It includes a Winword 2.0 Toolbar Editor and numerous ready-to-run macros.

Windows 3.1 Programming for Mere Mortals is $34.95, and *The Hacker's Guide to Word for Windows* is $39.95, plus shipping, from Addison-Wesley, 800-447-2226 or 617-944-3700.

Another good reference, which includes many tips by Woody Leonhard and others, is the Word for Windows Macro Developers' Kit, $9.95 postage-paid from Microsoft at 800-323-3577 or 206-882-8080.

Undocumented Windows Calls

The subject of undocumented system calls in Windows and DOS brings up a much larger question: Does Microsoft use knowledge of its operating systems to retard competition? Or it is just a smart development manager?

We may never know the true nature of the U.S. government's investigation into the Microsoft Corporation, until the Department of Justice (which took over the case from the Federal Trade Commission in mid-1993) decides to go public with its case, if ever. But based on accounts by developers, a composite of parts of the government's potential case against Microsoft can be drawn.

Research and interviews have revealed at least half a dozen cases where Microsoft allegedly withheld information on functions of DOS or Windows from outside developers, for periods ranging from six months to several years. During these periods, Microsoft's own developers appear to have used these functions in applications or utilities that competed with ones eventually developed by independent software vendors, according to programmers who have examined the code.

In only one case (involving a version of Microsoft Excel) do the undocumented functions appear to have given a Microsoft application a performance advantage. But, in each case, the lack of documentation of the functions may have given Microsoft applications a time-to-market lead of six months or more before similar features could be incorporated into competing developers' applications, according to critics of the company.

What is the government interested in?

The government refuses to comment on pending cases (or even confirm that Microsoft is the subject of an investigation). Lacking hard facts, observers have assumed that investigators are interested in possible anti-competitive behavior that Microsoft may have engaged in when marketing DOS, OS/2, and Windows.

The tone of recent interviews sponsored by government attorneys, however, suggests that the investigation has moved into a slightly different area: enforcing federal laws against unfair competition.

Microsoft enjoys at least a near-monopoly in the market for its two main products: MS-DOS and Windows. Market analysts indicate that Microsoft controls over 80 percent of the market worldwide for DOS-compatible operating systems, with most of the rest sold by Novell and Digital Research's DR DOS (mainly in Europe and Asia). Microsoft's shipments of Windows amount to 100 percent of the market for Windows 3.1-compatible operating systems. Whether this market dominance has been taken advantage of by Microsoft is hotly disputed between Microsoft and its critics in the software industry.

Federal antitrust laws do not prohibit one company from "benignly achieving an overwhelming share of a market," according to Gerry Elman, CEO of Elman, Wilf & Fried, a Philadelphia law firm that represents software companies. The Federal Trade Commission Act, however, does prohibit "unfair methods of competition." This includes improper activities by companies that have a monopoly on a particular market, says Elman, who worked for 6 years in the Antitrust Division of the U.S. Department of Justice.

Because the relevant act is broad, the U.S. Supreme Court in 1972 clarified the definition of *unfair competition*. The Court upheld an FTC policy against practices that are: (1) prohibited by "common law, statutory or other established concept of unfairness"; (2) "immoral, unethical, oppressive, or unscrupulous"; or (3) cause "substantial injury to consumers (or competitors or other businessmen)."

This definition is still quite broad. According to Elman, "the court interpreted congressional intent as granting the FTC wide discretion in identifying unfair behavior in the marketplace."

A defining issue: What's an operating system?

Software developers do not complain about Microsoft reserving functions of its operating systems solely for the internal use of those systems. An operating system must, in fact, keep a certain number of functions to itself. Otherwise, applications using these functions could make the system unstable.

It is only when Microsoft's *utilities* and *applications* use "undocumented" functions that competing vendors complain.

Software vendors often make substantial amounts of revenue by selling utilities that supplement Microsoft's. Such products as the Norton Utilities, Mace Utilities, and PC Tools have been tremendous financial successes. Vendors use these revenues to fund the development of other applications, which may compete with Microsoft more directly. For Microsoft to use undocumented functions that outside vendors cannot easily obtain would cut off a vital flow of cash for software development.

Consider MS-DOS. The DOS operating system consists of two hidden files that are installed on a PC's hard disk. In DOS 5.0, these files are called IO.SYS and MSDOS.SYS. These files provide all Disk Operating System functionality.

Microsoft also sells utilities, such as COMMAND.COM, which act as "shells" for DOS, but are not the operating system itself. COMMAND.COM is replaceable, and competes with 4DOS, by J.P. Software; NDOS, a part of the Norton Utilities (which is based on 4DOS); and several other DOS shells.

Similarly, other Microsoft utilities, such as FORMAT.COM, are not the operating system, but are run by the operating system. These "external" utilities compete with Digital Research's DR DOS, and other vendors trying to sell operating systems compatible with MS-DOS.

Windows (which Microsoft markets as an operating system) also has operating-system components and utilities. The operating system consists of three components: USER.EXE, GDI.EXE, and KRNL*X*86.EXE. Shells, such as Program Manager and File Manager, are not part of the Windows operating system. These shells can be replaced by other shells, which are run by Windows' three essential components. Program Manager and File Manager compete with Norton Desktop for Windows, WinTools, and numerous other products.

The distinction between the kernel of an operating system and utilities that are *bundled with* that operating system is often unclear, even within Microsoft. "What are the areas that third parties can and should market?" asks Cameron Myhrvold, former product manager for the Windows Software Development Kit (SDK). "The shell is not something we have encouraged a lot of people to replace, because of the importance of a consistent interface."

But DOS and Windows, like most computer operating systems, are clearly made up of an essential OS kernel, and simple but useful utilities that use the functions of that kernel. "Every operating system works that way," says Steve Gibson, the developer of SpinRite and other utilities. "You have a core operating system, and utilities that can't function without that core."

On top of its two operating systems and the utilities bundled with them, Microsoft develops and sells applications. These applications usually compete with those of other vendors, who would like to make money selling similar or superior products.

If Microsoft withholds information about important features of its operating systems and then uses these features in applications or utilities that compete with other vendors, is it practicing unfair competition, or merely managing its business well?

Developers themselves are of different minds. "My own attitude toward the undocumented functions is it's sort of a witch-hunt," says Paul Yao, who leads Power Programming workshops for International Systems Design of Bellevue, Washington. "Yes, there are undocumented calls. But at the end of one chapter of my book (Chapter 5 of *Peter Norton's Windows 3.0 Power Programming Techniques,* by Peter Norton and Paul Yao, Bantam), there is a statement not to use these calls." Yao feels developers who use these functions run the risk of their applications not working in a later operating system version.

With all these legal and technical issues, what is the government looking for in its investigation of Microsoft? The following details, organized into points that might figure in a Justice Dept. challenge to Microsoft, provide clues to the government's thinking.

Point 1: Did Microsoft use undocumented features of DOS?

To understand the roots of the current controversy, it is necessary to go back to the release of DOS 2.0.

It is often said that DOS is a single-user, single-tasking operating system. That is only partially true. DOS 2.0 (and later versions) has the ability to run more than one task or process at a time — as programmers who looked carefully soon learned.

To a programmer, the behavior of DOS 2.0's PRINT.COM utility was unusual. A user was able to type a command, such as PRINT BIGFILE.TXT, and almost immediately return to the DOS prompt. Users could start and run another program, such as Lotus 1-2-3 or WordStar, while DOS sent Bigfile.txt to the printer *in the background.* PRINT.COM knew how to terminate, yet stay resident in DOS — it was the first Terminate and Stay Resident (TSR) program.

Even today, the DOS 5.0 manual hints at the way PRINT.COM performs this trick. For example, the following DOS command gives PRINT.COM 25 CPU clock ticks for its background processing — about 10 percent of a possible 255 clock ticks for all applications:

```
PRINT /S:25 bigfile.txt
```

Although the DOS manual doesn't say so, the "S" in /S:25 stands for *Slices*. DOS 2.0 was capable of allocating time slices of a PC/XT processor to different applications in turn. This is called *preemptive multitasking*.

How did PRINT.COM continue to run even when the DOS prompt had returned and another program had been started? PRINT.COM had found a way to terminate itself, but stay resident in DOS, doing useful work.

The function calls that allowed PRINT.COM to multitask were not described in Microsoft's reference books on DOS. In fact, many other function calls were not documented, either.

From its earliest days, Microsoft Windows has relied on the background-processing feature of DOS to multitask applications. The Windows environment (and Quarterdeck DESQview, a Windows competitor) can run on top of DOS only because DOS is a crude multitasking operating system.

Since it is a highly desirable feature for a program to be able to work in the background, programmers outside Microsoft began to puzzle out how this magic was accomplished. One result was a TSR called SideKick, released in 1984 by a tiny company named Borland International.

SideKick was a remarkable success, and was soon imitated by other programmers. Unfortunately, because Microsoft hadn't documented several functions necessary to write a reliable terminate-and-stay-resident program, many of these TSRs left out important safeguards. They crashed when more than one was loaded, or, worse, interfered with normal foreground applications.

Under fire from Borland and other companies, Microsoft representatives in 1986 began to discuss publicly some of the secret functions. But the effort was too late. Swamped with mysterious problems, many PC managers adopted policies forbidding the use of TSR programs. Other than SideKick, no TSR became a commercial best-seller for an independent software vendor.

Yet Microsoft released its own utilities that depended on undocumented TSR function calls. For example, Microsoft's CD-ROM Extension program, MSCDEX.EXE, released in 1987, allows files on a compact disk to appear in the standard DOS file system. Microsoft spokesman Tony Rizzo said in the September 1987 *Microsoft Systems Journal,* a programmers' magazine currently published by M&T Publishing, that MSCDEX used something called the DOS "network redirector." But this capability remained undocumented and unavailable to developers of competing file-system products. (Technically speaking, MSCDEX uses undocumented Function 11 of DOS Interrupt 2F. For more on this subject, see Chapter 18, "Using Undocumented CD-ROM Functionality.")

Undocumented functions were also used by Microsoft debuggers, including Debug and CodeView. These debuggers call Interrupt 21, Function 4B, Subfunction 01. Microsoft's technical documentation listed only Subfunctions 00 and 03, until recently. Knowing the missing subfunction is a requirement for any company trying to write a competing debugging environment for programmers.

Programmers outside Microsoft kept digging. Their findings were posted piecemeal in programmers' haunts, such as the IBM.DOS/SECRETS forum on the Byte Information Exchange and *Dr. Dobb's Journal*. In 1990, this information was collected into a book called *Undocumented DOS* (Addison-Wesley), edited by Andrew Schulman — at that time a software engineer with Phar Lap Systems — with contributions from Tim Paterson (the author of DOS 1.0) and others. The book explained the functions used by MSCDEX, as well as many other aspects of DOS that had remained unclear to programmers for years.

Although *Undocumented DOS* became popular in the programming community, it never provoked the controversy that *Undocumented Windows* did. Partly, this is because many of the events surrounding early DOS occurred when Microsoft did not have the near-monopoly in operating systems and environments that it does today. When DOS 2.0 was released, other contenders for the desktop — such as an "improved" CP/M, Unix, and others — were still considered plausible. Therefore, there was no FTC interest in the matter. While programmers could complain about Microsoft's secretiveness, there was little they could do.

Point 2: Did Microsoft use undocumented features in Excel?

Today, Microsoft Excel is by far the number-one selling graphical spreadsheet. Lotus 1-2-3 for Windows did not appear until a year and a half after Windows 3.0, and Quattro Pro for Windows wasn't finished until October 1992, more than two-and-one-half years later.

But Microsoft was well-positioned to take the market leadership in Windows applications. Even before Windows 3.0, competing vendors questioned what they saw as a close relationship between Microsoft application developers and system software developers. They pointed out that, in 1989, Microsoft upgraded Windows from version 2.1 to version 2.11. Windows 2.11 was released at the same time as Microsoft Word for Windows 1.0, which required the exact fixes present in that Windows upgrade. Meanwhile, vendors complained that fixes they needed to support their products were left out.

By 1990, with all its strengths in operating systems, Microsoft had not succeeded in publishing a market-leading DOS application. Microsoft MultiPlan, an early spreadsheet program, was far outsold by Lotus 1-2-3. Microsoft Word for DOS, meanwhile, sold far fewer copies than WordPerfect.

Today, Word for Windows is arguably the number-one selling graphical word processor, and Microsoft Excel the number-one graphical spreadsheet. WordPerfect for Windows was not released until February 1992, almost two years after Windows 3.0. Lotus 1-2-3 for Windows and Borland Quattro Pro for Windows also shipped long after Windows 3.0. As a result, Microsoft enjoyed a tremendous marketing lead over those companies.

Microsoft points out that it had focused its programming efforts on Windows, while other companies concentrated on developing applications for OS/2 (which proved to have a much smaller market). Does this account for the lateness to market of competing applications? Or did Microsoft's knowledge of undocumented Windows functions contribute to the lag, as some vendors allege?

With its now-dominant place in the market, it's easy to forget that Excel originally *did* have stiff competition. Under Windows 2.*x*, Excel had to face well-financed spreadsheet rivals known as Wingz and Full Impact.

The failure of these products was widely attributed to their slower performance, compared with Excel. Numerous published reviews of that era showed Wingz and Full Impact lagging behind Excel.

Tim Paterson, the author of DOS 1.0, revealed an important reason for this difference in a two-part article, "Managing Multiple Data Segments Under Microsoft Windows," published in the February and March 1990 issues of *Dr. Dobb's Journal* (San Mateo, California). Paterson and fellow programmer Steve Flenniken described undocumented function calls in Windows 2.*x* that allowed Excel to access large amounts of extended memory rapidly.

Specifically, Excel used undocumented functions of Windows 2.*x* named *DefineHandleTable*. Without these functions, Paterson and Flenniken wrote, an application's data was limited to "not more than 300K under the best conditions." However, they wrote, "Microsoft's own Windows applications use all of the techniques discussed here . . . to build Windows applications with virtually unlimited data capacity."

The *DefineHandleTable* functions in Windows 2.*x* were documented by Microsoft in the Windows 3.0 SDK. But developers charge that this was too late, since the functions are no longer needed in Windows 3.0's protected mode.

Point 3: Did Microsoft use undocumented features in Quick C?

On Aug. 31, 1992, Microsoft released an 8-page statement and a 10-page White Paper on 16 undocumented Windows 3.0 functions used by Microsoft applications. These functions were revealed earlier that month in *Undocumented Windows*.

In its statement, Microsoft said: "Microsoft applications derive no unfair advantage from the few undocumented APIs that they call." Additionally, "Microsoft has also provided at least 26 ISVs (independent software vendors) with the information on undocumented calls in Windows."

 Regarding some of the undocumented functions used by Microsoft applications, the White Paper describes four of these functions as "documented in the Windows Software Development Kit (SDK), version 3.1," six as obsolete in Windows 3.1, and six more as undocumented but with "documented equivalents" or "entirely useless."

For example, the White Paper describes the Windows 3.0 function *GetTaskQueue* as "undocumented," with "no equivalent, but useless." Another Windows 3.0 function call, *DirectedYield,* is described as being documented in the Windows 3.1 SDK.

Undocumented Windows co-author Schulman charges, "It's dishonest for Microsoft to tag as 'Documented in SDK' functions that have only recently been documented in the 3.1 SDK, but that Microsoft (and others) were using long before 3.1. Timing is everything in this industry."

Schulman says that *GetTaskQueue* and *DirectedYield* are essential to the working of Microsoft's Quick C for Windows and are, in fact, "crucial to writing an integrated development environment or debugger for Windows."

By disassembling QCWIN.EXE, the main executable file in Quick C for Windows, Schulman says he found at least three instances of the following code:

```
if (GetTaskQueue(hTask != 0)
   PostAppMessage(hTask, ...);
DirectedYield(hTask);
```

The first line of code determines whether a C application running in Quick C's development environment has set up a "Task Queue" for messages. If so, the second line posts a message to that queue. Finally, Quick C yields control to the application, so it can process the message. This routine is necessary because sending a message to an application before it's ready can cause strange system crashes.

"We needed five undocumented calls to write debugging devices for Windows 3.0," says one developer for a major software firm, who spoke only on condition of anonymity. "Meanwhile, Microsoft came out with these devices, and it wasn't until six months after the release of their debuggers that Microsoft provided the information."

Point 4: Did Microsoft withhold the "secret sauce"?

One of the most controversial uses of undocumented functions by Microsoft in Windows 3.0 products was by the Windows 3.0 Software Development Kit itself. Until the release of the Windows 3.1 SDK nearly two years later, most developers outside Microsoft had no documentation of the function calls necessary to compile a Windows program.

According to *Undocumented Windows,* several undocumented calls — known among developers as the "secret sauce" — were used to build Windows programs by Microsoft's own Windows 3.0 SDK, which Microsoft began selling in 1989. Competitors such as Borland, Zortech/Symantec, and other C language vendors could not create their own standalone Windows compilers, which did not require Microsoft's SDK, without conducting a major project to disassemble Windows and discover these secrets.

After much criticism by competitors, several of these crucial, undocumented functions — including *InitApp, InitTask,* and *WaitEvent* — were finally unveiled by Microsoft. Most of the information came out April 9, 1991, in Microsoft's "Open Tools" binder, as well as being documented in the Windows 3.1 SDK later that year.

The Open Tools effort, initiated by Microsoft just before it announced that it was the subject of an FTC antitrust investigation, was accompanied by a few conditions. According to *Windows Watcher* editor Jesse Berst, "The Open Tools agreement required that companies agree that any code they discussed with Microsoft employees became the property of Microsoft." Several companies refused to sign the agreement under these conditions, Berst says, adding that large companies such as Lotus and Borland simply asserted their right to attend Microsoft's Open Tools meetings and took the information without signing. Many smaller companies, however, did without the Open Tools materials until the same information appeared later in the Windows 3.1 SDK documents.

Unfortunately for Microsoft's major competitors in the heated C-language marketplace, Microsoft had already shipped more than 48,000 copies of its SDK compiler by the time the Open Tools release took place. Critics of Microsoft argue that this gave the company a tremendous lead with corporate and commercial programmers, who were actively purchasing tools to create Windows applications.

Microsoft's Cameron Myhrvold argues that, far from giving Microsoft an advantage, the extra effort that Zortech and Borland put into their compilers increased their market share, at Microsoft's expense. "Zortech was the first (standalone) compiler to ship for Windows in August of 1990, then Borland," says Mr. Myhrvold. "The first Microsoft C compiler that didn't need the SDK didn't ship until around Windows 3.1." As a result, Mr. Myhrvold says, Borland and Zortech now outsell Microsoft in C language compilers.

Point 5: Did Microsoft developers get advance OLE code?

A hot new feature of Windows 3.1 is Object Linking and Embedding (OLE). OLE allows users to double-click a graphic in a document, edit that graphic, then return the edited graphic to the document. This capability is highly desirable in, say, a presentation package that can use clip art from various other applications.

Microsoft's documentation of the OLE 1.0 specification was released to developers in December 1990 at a developers' conference in Bellevue.

But Microsoft PowerPoint 2.0, which was shipping to paying customers six months earlier in June 1990, already had support for OLE between its graphing and display modules, developers point out. PowerPoint had OLE hard-coded into it, rather than relying on external OLE libraries, as became possible later.

Mr. Myhrvold said, "I don't know how to call that one. PowerPoint (developers) went ahead and shipped something before it was final, probably version 0.8 or something like that." He explained that Microsoft is trying to work more closely with independent software vendors on the upcoming OLE 2.0 specification, beta copies of which were shipped to several dozen vendors in October 1992, well before the final implementation of OLE 2.

Point 6: Did Microsoft withhold details of Drag-and-Drop?

Windows 3.1 allows users to drag filenames from the File Manager window and "drop" them onto other applications. The applications then automatically open or print the dropped documents.

Microsoft documented how a "client" application should respond to a file being dropped on it. But despite repeated requests from independent software vendors, Microsoft pointedly refused to give outside developers any information about how the Windows 3.1 File Manager acts as a "server" for the file names dragged *out* of its window. This prevented developers of competing file managers from adding Drag-and-Drop functionality to their products to coincide with the release of Windows 3.1 on April 6, 1992, without extensive reverse-engineering efforts.

During the beta-test phase of Windows 3.1, many developers had requested information from Microsoft on the Drag-and-Drop function calls. These requests included angry demands by developers at Microsoft's "Open Tools Summit" in 1991, as well as messages from developers to Microsoft's CompuServe forum during the Windows 3.1 beta testing period.

Reflecting the company's policy, Steve Fait (a Microsoft developer-support coordinator) on Feb. 15, 1992, sent one of several messages to Windows 3.1 beta-test developers, saying, "We are not documenting the server end of DragDrop with this version of Windows." Microsoft's reason was that the company planned to change the Drag-and-Drop method in the next version of Windows. "We use the method," Mr. Fait continued, "but when the next version of Windows comes out, we can easily replace the component (File Manager) that implements it with the new version. We will document it most likely in the next version."

Microsoft's own Windows 3.1 File Manager existed in a working form as early as November 1990, when it was first developed to answer criticism of Windows 3.0's slow file utility, according to developers within Microsoft. Outside developers didn't get access to the documentation necessary to write similar features until 18 months later.

The information needed for competing vendors to develop their own Drag-and-Drop servers remained undocumented until an article by Jeffrey Richter — the author of *Windows 3.1: A Developer's Guide* (M&T Publishing) — appeared in the May-June 1992 issue of the *Microsoft Systems Journal*. Even then, the information appeared only after attempts by Microsoft officials to suppress the article, and after another magazine had threatened to print it. "The *Microsoft Systems Journal* article by Jeffrey Richter was stalled by Microsoft for months because of resistance in the company to publishing this article," says Andrew Schulman. Mr. Richter confirmed this, saying "It was held up by a Windows 3.1 product manager," whom he declined to identify.

"There were a number of vendors who figured out Drag-and-Drop," Mr. Myhrvold states. "With certain issues, we aren't going to sue Norton (Desktop) or stop them, but we're not going to assist them in doing a shell." Server Drag-and-Drop "wasn't implemented robustly in Windows 3.1, and we wanted to improve it (in a later version). It's important for consistency for the user."

Point 7: Windows NT and the future

Considering the lead time necessary to write successful Windows applications, do developers outside Microsoft face impossible hurdles to competition?

Some developers interviewed for this chapter felt that Microsoft had an insurmountable advantage only over programmers who assume that all the functions they need are described in Microsoft's documentation.

One developer who asked not to be named said, "Their (Microsoft's) apps guys sit down with systems and say that they need something, they direct that development and plan applications strategy in concert with systems strategy. It seems unfair, but it won't make the difference between being successful or not." He added, "Microsoft doesn't support their undocumented calls. They don't really tell us about them. It's up to the developers to find these things."

Meanwhile, new developments at Microsoft are raising additional questions about the relationship between Microsoft's systems developers and application developers.

 Outside developers have found parts of Windows NT that were undocumented, but were being used in Microsoft utilities that competed with utilities they would like to sell. Even when NT was still in beta-testing, several vendors were already selling NT development toolkits to numerous commercial and corporate sites.

Microsoft's Win32 Software Development Kit (required for developing NT applications) includes a utility called PVIEW. This tool lets developers look at the tasks assigned to one or more processors. The utility uses functions like *NtQuerySystemInformation, NtQueryPerformanceCounter,* and *NtQueryInformationThread,* according to Schulman. These functions, although contained in NTDLL.DLL — which is included in the shipping version of NT — were all undocumented.

"If NT is to be successful," says Mr. Schulman, "won't it need the same kind of active third party-utilities market that DOS and Windows have? So won't developers need to be able to write their own utilities, such as PVIEW?"

Microsoft always did intend to provide this information to developers, Mr. Myhrvold said. "We're going to document the NT API. Some of it is in the NT DDK (Device Driver Kit)," which shipped to developers in November 1992. "We're also looking at producing a Technical Reference, or putting it in the MSDN (Microsoft Developer Network CD-ROM). That will be forthcoming near or just after NT ships." The NT API calls did, in fact, appear in NT developer documentation around that time.

Point 8: Is it simply good business?

Is Microsoft's use of undocumented functions in applications and utilities that compete with independent software vendors something that developers (or the FTC) should complain about? Or is it simply good business?

For whatever reasons, Microsoft has become by far the world's largest software company. In the fiscal year ending Sept. 30, 1992, Microsoft had sales of $3.0 billion and net income of $773 million. Microsoft's sales in that period represented only 7 percent of all sales made by U.S. companies in the "computer software and data processing" category, according to Media General Financial Services, a market analysis firm. But Microsoft's net income represented 25 percent of all profits made by those same firms — a fact that causes resentment among other developers.

Whether its share of the operating systems market has given Microsoft an unfair advantage in marketing MS-DOS and Windows *applications* is open to dispute. What is certain is that Microsoft is now selling over 60 percent of all Windows applications, according to Jesse Berst, editor of the *Windows Watcher* newsletter, which tracks software sales.

Because of this dominance, some vendors argue that Microsoft should be broken into separate companies responsible for systems, languages, and applications. These "Baby Bills," like the 1980s breakup of AT&T into "Baby Bells," would presumably improve competition. Is this what the government seeks, or a much milder change? Since the present Justice Department investigation of Microsoft will wind slowly through the courts — if the agency takes any action at all — it may be years before anyone knows the final outcome.

Summary

In this chapter, I provide an in-depth analysis of the issues surrounding Microsoft's alleged use of undocumented features in Windows and DOS to gain advantages for Microsoft applications and utilities that compete with those of independent companies.

▶ I review two books, *Undocumented Windows* and *Windows 3.1 Programming for Mere Mortals,* which describe undocumented programming calls in Windows and how you can use them in programs of your own.

▶ I summarize more than a decade of controversy over features of DOS and Windows that independent software developers claim were used to gain unfair competitive advantages for Microsoft applications. These issues are now being analyzed by the U.S. Department of Justice, which may either drop the investigation or eventually present charges before a court of law.

Part II

Setup Secrets

Chapter 20
Private Windows

In This Chapter

▶ I describe a way around a situation in which two or more people need to use Windows on the same PC, but one set of people — parents using a PC at home, perhaps — need some protection from another set of people — kids or "helpful" friends — who might "improve" their Windows icons or files.

▶ For situations in more heavily used office PCs, I detail a special DOS program and batch file combination that can provide separate Windows configurations for up to 26 different people.

I often hear about the problems of home-office Windows users who have children around the house. Most Windows aficionados have collected at least a few games — and children, naturally, want to play these games. In fact, if you work around any adults, they probably want to play on your Windows PC, too.

Unfortunately, little hands often do not leave your Windows configuration looking exactly the way you'd expect.

At least Windows users don't have some of the problems common to owners of Macintosh systems. I've heard stories about kids who dragged file after file into the Mac's trash can icon, just because they liked to watch the sides of the can expand and then contract when they "emptied" the trash.

How to Child-Proof (or Friend-Proof) Your Windows Setup

But children (and co-workers) can do just as much damage to your precious applications and data in Windows, even without a trash can beckoning them. Pressing a PC's Delete key in File Manager, after all, deletes files much faster than dragging icons into the garbage.

Protecting your particular configuration from your kids (or other loved ones) is much easier in Windows NT. This is because NT allows you (if you log on as Administrator) to set up accounts for different users. These users have to log on to Windows with their own names, and NT allows them access only to the directories that you specify. Bobby and Susie won't even be able to *see* your résumé, much less delete it.

But we can do something like this in plain old Windows, and I'll show you how, step-by-step.

Setting up different configurations

This method requires that you establish different Program Manager groups for your different users. After doing this, you can keep them from accessing groups they shouldn't get into.

Let's take a simple example, with two users, you and Heather. You want to allow Heather to play Solitaire and Reversi on your Windows PC but you don't want her to use any of your applications or change any files.

The following steps will set up different configurations for two users. Once you've followed this procedure, you can easily repeat it to make three, four, or more configurations.

STEPS

Creating Different Configurations for Two Users

Step 1. Open the Control Panel and set your Date and Time exactly. You will be creating several files in this procedure, and correct date/time stamps are useful.

Step 2. Organize the Program Manager exactly the way you like it. Arrange the icons as you prefer, and minimize or restore the group windows just as you want to see them. This will be the configuration that *you* see when you start Windows.

Step 3. Create a new group window. Click File New, then "Program Group" in the dialog box that appears, and then click OK. In the next dialog box, type a description for this new window, such as "Heather's Menu," and click OK. You don't have to type a filename in the Group File box that appears — Program Manager automatically creates a filename using the first eight letters of your description.

Step 4. Place the Solitaire and Reversi icons into your new, empty group window. Also place any other icons here that you want Heather to have access to. To do this, hold down Ctrl while you drag each icon from one of your own windows into Heather's window. Using the Ctrl key in this way creates a duplicate of your icon, so you have one in both groups. (If you don't hold down Ctrl when you drag an icon to a new group, it removes the original from your group.) When you're finished, minimize this group.

Step 5. Finish configuring Program Manager the way you want to see it. Then, hold down your Shift key and double-click the System Menu icon (the square at the left end of Program Manager's title bar). You would expect this to exit Windows, but it does not. Thanks to an undocumented feature of Windows, holding down the Shift key forces Program Manager to save a copy of its configuration. This is precisely what we want. (Pressing Shift+Alt+F4 in Program Manager also saves its configuration.)

Step 6. Look in your Windows directory for a file called PROGMAN.INI. You can use the Windows File Manager or your favorite utility. PROGMAN.INI is the configuration (initialization) file that Program Manager just wrote. The file should have the current date and time. If File Manager isn't displaying the date and time for each filename, click PROGMAN.INI once with your mouse to highlight it, then click File Properties. You will see the exact date and time the file was last saved.

Step 7. With PROGMAN.INI highlighted, press F8 to make a copy of it. In the dialog box that appears, type in a name to give the copy. If your name is Tom, you might name the copy PROGMAN.TOM, for example. Click OK to close the dialog box. Then press F8 again, and make another copy of PROGMAN.INI this time called PROGMAN.HEA for Heather

Step 8. Start Notepad and open file PROGMAN.HEA. In this file, you should see a [Groups] section, followed by several lines like MAIN.GRP, Group 2=STARTUP.ARP, etc. Place a semicolon (;) at the beginning of each such line, except the one that loads HEATHER.GRP. The semicolon keeps these groups from loading, so Heather sees only her own group window. Save PROGMAN.HEA and exit Notepad. You have completed separate configuration files for you and Heather.

You are now ready to select the best way to switch between your configuration and Heather's.

Selecting your configuration

Using this procedure, a different Windows configuration comes up when you hold down "shift keys" such as the Ctrl key or the Alt key (or no key) while Windows is starting.

This method requires that you start Windows using a DOS batch file, which checks the state of these keys before starting Windows. Starting Windows from a batch file is actually a good idea — because it allows you to define other Windows behaviors, if you like — and it's very easy. I'll describe each of the steps.

STEPS

Starting Windows with a Different Configuration

Step 1. Create a small, 10-byte utility to test for shift states. To do this, use Notepad or any plain text editor (such as the EDIT command in DOS) to create a short assembly-language script file. The text should look exactly like the following (notice the difference between the letter "l" used in "al," and the numeral "1" in 100, 16, and 21):

```
a 100
mov ah,02
int 16
and al,0f
mov ah,4c
int 21

rcx
a
n shiftest.com
w
q
```

Step 2. Check your text file before you save it. It's important that you press Enter *twice* after "INT 21" to create the blank line above "RCX." It's also essential that you press Enter after the "Q" in the final line, so the text file ends with a carriage return.

Step 3. Save this text file into a directory that is on your DOS Path. This might be a C:\BATCH directory you use for batch files, or just your drive C:\ root directory. You can see which directories are on your DOS Path by looking in your AUTOEXEC.BAT with Notepad for a line that starts with PATH. All the directories on that line (which should include C:\, C:\BATCH, C:\DOS, and so on) are in your Path, which DOS (and Windows) searches for commands.

Step 4. Save your script. Name the file SHIFTEST.SCR and place it in your C:\BATCH directory (or whatever other directory on your Path you selected).

Step 5. Start a DOS session in Windows, or exit to DOS. Change to the directory that contains SHIFTEST.SCR. If this directory is C:\BATCH, you would do this at a DOS prompt by typing the following commands:

```
c:
cd \batch
```

Step 6. Assuming that the DOS directory itself is on your Path, you can create the 10-byte utility SHIFTEST.COM by typing the following command:

```
debug<shiftest.scr
```

This command uses the DOS Debug utility to compile your assembly-language script into a working program. Notice the less-than sign (<) between DEBUG and SHIFTEST.SCR. This symbol *must* be pointing toward the word DEBUG, not toward SHIFTEST.SCR, for this command to work. You will see several lines of garbage scroll up your screen as Debug does its work. If you see any error messages, or if Debug doesn't return you to a plain DOS prompt, press Q and then Enter to quit the Debug utility. Then check your work and try again.

Step 7. With SHIFTEST.COM completed, you're ready to make a short batch file to start Windows. Return to Windows (by typing EXIT) to use Notepad, or use the DOS 5.0 EDIT text editor to create a batch file called WIN.BAT with the following lines:

```
@echo off
echo Press the Enter key to start Windows.
pause>nul
shiftest
rem Shiftest sets Errorlevel=1 if Left Shift is down.
rem Shiftest sets Errorlevel=2 if Right Shift is down.
rem Shiftest sets errorlevel=4 if Ctrl is down.
rem Shiftest sets errorlevel=8 if Alt is down.
set NAME=hea
if errorlevel 4 if not errorlevel 5 set NAME=tom
if errorlevel 8 if not errorlevel 9 set NAME=sue
copy c:\windows\progman.%NAME% c:\windows\progman.ini
c:\windows\win %1 %2 %3 %4 %5 %6 %7 %8 %9
copy c:\windows\progman.ini c:\windows\progman.%NAME%
if not %NAME%=hea copy c:\windows\progman.hea
c:\windows\progman.ini
set NAME=
```

If your Windows directory is named something other than
C:\WINDOWS, change the directory name in the above batch file to
the correct directory name.

Step 8. The SHIFTEST.COM program sets a variable called the DOS
Errorlevel. This variable is set to 4 if the Ctrl key is down at that
moment, and 8 if the Alt key is down. SHIFTEST also sets the
Errorlevel to 1 for the Left Shift key, and 2 for the Right Shift key.
And the value set by SHIFTEST is additive — if Ctrl and Alt are
both down, the Errorlevel is set to 12, because Ctrl=4 and Alt=8.
You could potentially use SHIFTEST to create many different user
configurations — but if you need more than two or three, you'll
probably want to use a better method described in the "Good
Fences Make Good Co-Workers" section later in this chapter.

This batch file uses an environmental variable called NAME to
determine which Windows configuration to use. The routine
copies the file PROGMAN.TOM over PROGMAN.INI if you press
Ctrl+Enter to start Windows. It copies PROGMAN.SUE over
PROGMAN.INI if you press Alt+Enter (assuming you've saved a
configuration for Sue). But Heather, or anyone who just presses
Enter, will get PROGMAN.HEA — your most limited Program Manager group.

To make sure of this, the batch file copies PROGMAN.HEA over PROGMAN.INI, if necessary, *after* the batch file detects that you've exited Windows. This makes your most limited Program Manager group the default if someone manages to start Windows without using this batch file.

You should also guarantee that your most limited configuration remains the default, even if someone exits Windows by rebooting (therefore bypassing the line at the end of your WIN.BAT file). To do this, add the line COPY C:\WINDOWS\PROGMAN.HEA C:\WINDOWS\PROGMAN.INI anywhere in your AUTOEXEC.BAT file. This resets PROGMAN.INI to your default settings every time someone starts your PC.

Of course, if your PROGMAN.INI files are in a directory other than C:\WINDOWS, use the correct directory name in your batch files.

Step 9. Make sure that users start Windows with the batch file. To do so, save the text as C:\BATCH\WIN.BAT, and ensure that the directory C:\BATCH appears *before* the directory C:\WINDOWS in your Path statement.

For example, if the Path statement in your AUTOEXEC.BAT looks like this:

```
path=c:\windows;c:\dos;c:\batch;c:\
```

edit your AUTOEXEC.BAT in Notepad so the C:\BATCH directory comes first, like this:

```
path=c:\batch;c:\windows;c:\dos;c:\
```

This makes DOS find your WIN.BAT file before finding WIN.COM. The first directory in the Path takes precedence in almost every case. (The exception is if the C:\WINDOWS directory is actually the current directory when the user types WIN to start Windows.) You must reboot your PC for these changes in AUTOEXEC.BAT to take effect.

When Windows starts, it reads PROGMAN.INI. Program Manager then loads only the group windows that are named in that file, and no others.

By saving different files for different users, you can completely determine which groups and icons they will see when they start Windows. Best of all, you can see their groups, too (if you set up your Program Manager with a copy of each group). Any changes you make to their groups are immediately reflected when they start Windows again. This is because Program Manager automatically saves any changes you make to any group window when you drag a new icon to it, or you press Shift+Alt+F4.

The existence of different configurations for different people won't prevent a knowledgeable user from pulling down the File Run menu and starting File Manager, of course. And it assumes that you need configurations for just three or four users (or types of users, such as "parents" and "kids," or "support staff" and "vice-presidents").

If your needs are more complex, you might need more elaborate security restrictions. These are discussed in the next topic.

Good Fences Make Good Co-Workers

As Windows becomes more popular, computers running Windows are being used by more and more people. Unfortunately for you, it often seems like your computer is the *only* one running Windows when Bob "just needs to look at a Paintbrush file for a minute" or Sue "has to have this report printed for the boss in Times Roman."

If multiple people use your PC — or any PC running Windows — it may be time to create a separate configuration for each user. That way, if one of your buddies decides to redesign your desktop while using your machine, you won't have to spend all day with the Control Panel trying to change it back.

In the previous section, I described a simple way to do this for two different people, such as a parent and a child. The method involved creating two different PROGMAN.INI files (which control the icons in Program Manager) and using a batch file to switch to the correct one to start Windows.

In this section, I'll lay before you a slightly more sophisticated method, which allows you to store configurations for up to *26* different users. And with this method, you have peace of mind over more than just the location of icons in your Program Manager. Almost every aspect of Windows that can be customized can also be personalized — with each person running a Windows environment that can be changed with little or no effect on other's environments.

Windows doesn't yet allow one user to be totally insulated from another. For that, we'll have to look to Windows NT, which allows you to log on as Administrator and set up different user accounts. When users log on with their own password, they can't even *see* files that don't belong to them.

In Windows, nothing prevents someone from firing up File Manager — or a DOS session, for that matter — and deleting every file you've ever created. But, assuming that you don't work with totally destructive psychos — just the normal office chowder heads — the following will probably provide you with all the protection your Windows setup needs.

Creating separate configurations

This method requires that you create (on the PC that is used by multiple workers) a separate directory for each person. This directory will contain all the files that control the customization of Windows.

Most people install Windows using one of the prescribed methods in the Windows Setup procedure. In other words, you probably have a main Windows directory (such as C:\WINDOWS) and a System subdirectory below that (such as C:\WINDOWS\SYSTEM).

When you start Windows, using the WIN command, you are actually running the WIN.COM program in the main Windows directory. This program looks in the same directory for your WIN.INI and other .INI files. If you use Program Manager as your Windows shell program, it looks in the same directory in turn for your group windows files, MAIN.GRP, STARTUP.GRP, and so on.

By moving these files into their own directory, and creating separate directories for each different user, you gain quite a bit of insulation between each person. Changes one person makes to Program Manager icons, File Manager settings, desktop colors, fonts, and so on, do not affect the other users. When these other people start Windows, they see the same icons and colors, etc., that they did when they last ran Windows.

Take the following steps to implement this kind of insulation.

STEPS

Creating a Separate Directory for Each Person

Step 1. Make your directories. Let's say you want separate configurations for Bob, Sue, and Ren. Somewhere on the PC's hard drive (it makes no difference where), create three directories. Perhaps these could be called C:\BOB, C:\SUE, and C:\REN. You can create these using the Windows File Manager, by highlighting a directory and clicking File Create-Directory. Or if, for some reason, you can't use Windows, you can change to the root directory of your C: drive and make these directories with the following DOS commands:

```
c:
cd \
md bob
md sue
md ren
```

Step 2. Copy your personal files. From the main Windows directory, copy WIN.COM, all *.INI files, all *.GRP files, REG.DAT and WINVER.EXE into each of the directories you just created for Bob, Sue, and Ren. For this to work, you must also remove the original files from the main Windows directory. Rather than deleting them, you can simply rename them. The following DOS commands, which change the last character of each filename to "$," would accomplish this:

```
c:
cd \windows
ren win.com win.co$
ren *.ini *.in$
ren *.grp *.gr$
ren reg.dat reg.da$
ren winver.exe *.ex$
```

If anything goes wrong, you can rename these files back to their original names, and everything will be exactly as it was before.

In each directory, you must open the PROGMAN.INI file with the DOS Edit utility or Windows Notepad and change references like GROUP1=C:\WINDOWS\MAIN.GRP to GROUP1=C:\BOB\MAIN.GRP or GROUP1=C:\SUE\MAIN.GRP, or whatever names you used for the new directories you created. If you don't do this, Program Manager won't be able to find the group files in the new locations.

Step 3. Set up your selection process. Now that you have three different subdirectories, each with its own initialization and group files, you need a way for each person to start Windows with his or her own configuration. One simple way to accomplish this would be to have Bob press the letter "B" when starting Windows, Sue press "S," and Ren press "R." The following script file produces a tiny, 12-byte program called GETALPHA, which can distinguish any letter of the alphabet that a person presses. A variety of programs circulated on electronic bulletin boards can do this; I've looked at them all and created my own simple version. Using Notepad (or any plain-text editor), type the following lines into a file on your Path called GETALPHA.SCR:

```
e 100 b4 00 cd 16 24 df 24 3f b4 4c cd 21
n getalpha.com
rcx
c
w
q
```

Be sure to press the Enter key after the line containing the letter "Q." This script file must end with a carriage return in order to work. Also, notice that all the "0" characters in this script are zeroes, except for the letter *"o"* in the COM extension of GETALPHA.COM.

Step 4. Start a DOS session in Windows, or exit Windows to get to a plain DOS prompt. This is necessary to do something that Windows can't. At the DOS prompt, change to the directory that contains GETALPHA.SCR. If that directory is C:\UTIL, for example, you could do this with the following DOS commands:

```
c:
cd \util
```

Assuming that your DOS directory is also on your Path, type the following line. This feeds the text of GETALPHA.SCR into the Debug utility, which comes with DOS:

```
debug < getalpha.scr
```

Notice that the "less-than" symbol in this line must be pointing *toward* the word DEBUG for this command to work. You should see several lines of garbage on your screen while DEBUG compiles your script into a working program. If you aren't returned to a plain DOS prompt after a few moments, or if any other errors occur, press Q and then Enter to quit the Debug utility. Then check your work and try again.

If everything works as expected, you should now have a 12-byte GETALPHA.COM utility. This program is used in a batch file to determine which of the 26 letters of the alphabet a user pressed, then branch to the appropriate action.

Step 5. Set up your batch file. This method requires that everyone start Windows from a batch file, instead of running WIN.COM directly. To accomplish this, create a file called WIN.BAT in a directory on your Path. This directory must appear on your Path *before* the directory that contains Windows. For example, if you keep batch files in a directory called C:\BAT, your Path statement in AUTOEXEC.BAT should look like this:

```
path=c:\bat;c:\windows;c:\;c:\dos;etc.
```

Your WIN.BAT file will ask each person who types WIN to also type a letter representing the appropriate configuration. Using Bob, Sue, and Ren again as examples, you might create a WIN.BAT file that looks like this:

```
@echo off
set THE_USER=
:TOP
echo Press B, R, or S to start Windows, or Esc to quit.
getalpha
if errorlevel 27 goto END
if errorlevel 2 if not errorlevel 3 set THE_USER=c:\bob
if errorlevel 18 if not errorlevel 19 set THE_USER=c:\ren
if errorlevel 19 if not errorlevel 20 set THE_USER=c:\sue
if "%THE_USER%"=="" goto TOP
set OLD_PATH=%PATH%
path=%THE_USER%;%PATH%
%THE_USER%\win.com %1 %2 %3 %4 %5 %6 %7 %8 %9
path=%OLD_PATH%
set THE_USER=
:END
```

The WIN.BAT file does several things. After @ECHO OFF, it sets a DOS environmental variable, THE_USER, equal to nothing. This blanks the contents of this variable, if it was used before. (Since this erases the value of any such variable, I use the underscore symbol in my variables, which users are unlikely to have used in batch files of their own.)

After the label :TOP, WIN.BAT displays a message asking the user to press B, R, or S to start Windows. (You can make this message as elaborate as you like, of course.)

The next line runs GETALPHA.COM. GETALPHA displays nothing, but simply halts the batch file until a key is pressed. When that occurs, GETALPHA.COM sets a variable called the DOS Errorlevel. This variable is set equal to 1 if the key was A, 2 for B, and so on up to 26 for the letter Z. GETALPHA is not case-sensitive, so it doesn't matter whether Shift or CapsLock was on when the letter was pressed. GETALPHA also sets the Errorlevel to zero if the Spacebar was pressed, or 27 if Esc was pressed. The next line of the batch file, in fact, allows the user to press Esc to exit if the choices are not understood.

The next three lines of WIN.BAT set the variable THE_USER equal to the directory that corresponds to Bob, Sue, or Ren. The statement IF ERRORLEVEL 2 IF NOT ERRORLEVEL 3, for example, determines whether the Errorlevel is at least 2, but not 3 or higher. If both of these cases are true, then the letter B must have been pressed, and THE_USER is set equal to C:\BOB. (If you have more than three cases, create more Errorlevel tests, up to IF ERRORLEVEL 26 IF NOT ERRORLEVEL 27.)

At this point, one of the three letters should have been pressed, and the batch file should know which directory to use to start Windows. If a letter other than B, R, or S was pressed, no value will have been assigned to THE_USER. The next line of WIN.BAT detects this, and sends the batch file back to the top to ask the question again. The user may either press one of the three letters or press Esc to exit.

If one of the correct three letters was pressed, the batch file moves on to the next line. This line, SET OLD_PATH=%PATH%, saves the current DOS Path into another environmental variable.

Next, the directory represented by THE_USER is tacked on to the front of the current Path. The statement PATH=%THE_USER%;%PATH% adds C:\BOB, C:\SUE, or C:\REN to the beginning of the Path — whichever is appropriate.

Finally, WIN.BAT runs C:\BOB\WIN.COM, C:\SUE\WIN.COM, or C:\REN\WIN.COM. The batch file replaces THE_USER with the directory name that was previously set in one of the IF statements.

The WIN.COM line includes "replaceable parameters," such as %1, %2, and so on. These parameters allow the user to start Windows with such commands as WIN /S or WIN CLOCK, if desired. The whole command line is passed to WIN.COM.

After Windows is exited by the user, and control returns to this batch file, each of the environmental variables is cleaned up. The original Path is restored by the statement PATH=%OLD_PATH%. And the variable THE_USER is reset by the statement SET THE_USER=.

This batch file still works correctly if people exit Windows by pressing Ctrl+Alt+Delete or turning off the power. In that case, the computer (when restarted) clears the environment and runs AUTOEXEC.BAT, which re-establishes the original Path.

Step 6. Test your configurations. After saving these files, be sure to test each of the different configurations you've established. Log on as Bob, Sue, and Ren, and see that a change to the desktop colors in one environment doesn't affect the colors in another.

This method works because Windows applications look on the Path to find WIN.INI and any .INI files they create for themselves. Finding these files in, say, C:\BOB is enough to initialize these programs. The remaining Windows files these applications need are also on the Path, in the C:\WINDOWS directory. As long as both directories are OK, everything runs fine. I use separate directories like this on my own machine every day, just so I can switch among different configurations for testing purposes. You may ned to add C:\WINDOWS\SYSTEM to you Path, after C:\WINDOWS, if necessary for Windows to find system files.

You need to watch for a couple of things. First, saving all these environmental variables may cause you to get the message "Out of environment space" from DOS. This is because DOS normally sets aside only 160 bytes of RAM for environmental variables. You should raise this to at least 512 bytes, by placing the following line at the beginning of your CONFIG.SYS file:

```
shell=c:\command.com c:\ /e:512 /p
```

This line specifies that COMMAND.COM is in your C:\ directory, that you want to reserve 512 bytes for your environment, and that you want COMMAND.COM to load itself "permanently."

Second, you must make sure that your Path statement does not exceed 127 characters (including the characters PATH=). Any characters after 127 are ignored, which can cause problems.

Third, you should watch what happens when you install a new application under Windows, while one of your directories is currently the one that contains WIN.INI. If the application writes a section into WIN.INI, you need to add that section to the end of each WIN.INI (if you want the other people to be able to use that application). For this reason, it's better for applications to create their own .INI files, instead of writing into WIN.INI. If BigApp creates BIGAPP.INI when you install it, you can simply move BIGAPP.INI from your C:\BOB directory to your C:\WINDOWS directory. The next time you start BigApp, it finds BIGAPP.INI on your Path in the C:\WINDOWS directory — no matter whose personal directory is current. (Conversely, you can copy BIGAPP.INI to every personal directory, and each person can configure BigApp to his or her liking.)

Finally, applications often ask you to tell them (during their installation procedure) the location of "your Windows directory." This almost always means the directory that contains WIN.COM, WIN.INI and the like — not the directory that contains the standard Windows executable files. If you are asked this question, you should answer "C:\BOB," or whatever is currently your personal directory. Again, if an application installs files there, instead of in the main Windows directory, you'll need to move them in order for everyone to use that application.

Beyond individual .INI files

If you need even more control over your Windows configurations for different users, you should investigate MERGEINI.EXE. This program makes changes to .INI files under the control of a separate script file, which you can program for various users. Using the same .INI files for everyone but modifying them dynamically as different people start Windows might be a good plan if you often install new software that needs to modify WIN.INI settings and copy special files into the Windows directory. MERGEINI.EXE comes with the registered version of WizManager, a shareware program featured in its own chapter in the Excellence in Windows Shareware section of *More Windows Secrets*.

Another option is INI.EDIT, a separate shareware program also featured in the shareware section of this book. INI.EDIT allows you to enable and disable individual line in .INI files (by switching them into comments and back) for different users.

The effort involved in separating each person's configuration files should pay off for you in the time you'll save by not arguing over what shade of purple everyone's Windows desktop will be. On the other hand, maybe everybody would happier if you just bought each user their own, personal 486 to run Windows.

Summary

In this chapter, I detail a variety of ways to create multiple configurations of Windows for different users of the same PC.

▶ For PCs with two or three users, such as co-workers in an office or parents and children in the same family, I outline a simple Debug script and batch file procedure to enable you to switch between two or three different Windows configurations, each with some protection from the other.

▶ For PCs in a more complex office environment, with up to 26 different users, I provide a Debug script and batch file example that can be expanded to handle this many configurations, or perhaps perform other configuration tasks when users press a key A through Z.

Chapter 21
Installing Windows 3.1 Without Pain

In This Chapter

▶ I provide a few additional details to the "Installing and Configuring Windows" chapter of *More Windows 3.1 Secrets,* which you should peruse if you have to install Windows on several machines.

▶ I list several tricky aspects of memory managers, disk cache utilites, virus-detection utilities, screen savers, and using different versions of HIMEM.SYS when installing Windows on a PC for the first time.

Hard disks are getting larger, but not as quickly as Windows. You'll need between 8MB and 10.5MB of your hard disk to install Windows 3.1 on a 386 (a bit less on a 286) — as much as 5MB more than Windows 3.0. You'll want to make sure you have enough free disk space before you install your new copy of Windows.

If you use a 386 memory manager, make sure you're using a compatible version. Quarterdeck Office Systems states that any QEMM386 version of 5.11 or later will work, although version 7.02 or higher is recommended. Meanwhile, Qualitas — the maker of 386Max — defines 386Max version 5.1 as the oldest you can use with Windows (version 6.01d or higher is recommended).

I used to suggest that you strip your PC down to the bare minimum CONFIG.SYS and AUTOEXEC.BAT possible before running Windows Setup. With Windows 3.1, however, that's not always the best course.

Windows 3.1 performs several inspections before Setup installs the graphical interface. If it finds certain drivers and memory-resident programs (TSRs), it upgrades them or removes them with a warning message about their incompatibilities with Windows.

If 386Max is in memory when you run Setup, for example — and the memory manager is older than version 6.0 — Setup automatically copies into your 386Max directory the new "virtual device driver" that 386Max needs to work with Windows 3.1. If you removed 386Max before installing Windows, this driver upgrade won't take place and 386Max won't support Windows except in standard mode.

It's particularly important to have Microsoft's MOUSE.COM in your AUTOEXEC.BAT. If you don't have a mouse driver in memory, Setup doesn't copy Windows 3.1's new MOUSE.SYS or MOUSE.COM files to your hard drive. This is particularly aggravating since these new mouse drivers are necessary to use a pointing device in DOS applications under Windows 3.1.

There are several things you *shouldn't* have in memory when you run Setup, however. You should probably remove all disk-cache programs, anti-virus watchdogs, and screen savers.

To ferret out some hardware and software items that conflict with Setup, open and read the file SETUP.TXT on Windows Diskette #1, *before* trying to install.

Other problems can be caused by third-party device drivers that work fine with Windows 3.0, but haven't yet been updated to work with Windows 3.1. Almost all printer drivers and video drivers that worked with Windows 3.0 are problematic under 3.1. If Windows 3.1 doesn't include a driver for your display or printer, you'll need to obtain a new version from the vendor. To find the names of products that have new Windows 3.*x* drivers, see Chapter 28, "License to Upgrade — Help for Expired Drivers."

Windows 3.1 and DOS 6.*x* come with new versions of HIMEM.SYS, EMM386.EXE, and SMARTDRV.EXE, which are installed automatically and should be used instead of the versions that came with DOS 5.0 or Windows 3.0. (See Chapter 8, "Windows and MS-DOS 6. *x* if you are using Smart Drive with DOS 6. *x* .) HIMEM.SYS now supports up to 16 different methods that various "PC compatibles" use to access extended memory — including six methods used by similar but not identical models of IBM-brand PCs. The HIMEM.SYS in DOS 5.0 supports only 14 flavors of extended memory access, while the HIMEM.SYS in Windows 3.0 supports only eight.

The 16 variations are cited in the Optimizing chapter of the Windows manual, so I won't list them here. In almost all cases, Windows 3.1's HIMEM.SYS correctly detects which machine it's running on, and which extended memory "handler" to use. But HIMEM.SYS can't accurately determine that it's running on an Acer 1100, IBM 7552, or Wyse 286/12.5. If you have one of these machines, you need to add an "/M" parameter to the end of the HIMEM.SYS line in your CONFIG.SYS. The correct parameters are /M:ACER1100, /M:IBM7552, and /M:WYSE, respectively. If you have a system other than these, and HIMEM.SYS won't work with it, the setting that is most compatible with the greatest number of systems is /M:PTLCASCADE, as explained further in the "Computers" chapter of *More Windows 3.1 Secrets*.

Summary

In this chapter, I add a few findings I've made on the installation process for Windows since the time I released *More Windows 3.1 Secrets:*

▶ Aspects of memory managers, disk cache utilities, virus checkers, and screen savers that affect the Windows installation process are described.

▶ The various flavors of HIMEM.SYS and how you can make it compatible with the widest variety of systems are defined.

Chapter 22
Password-Protecting Windows

In This Chapter

▶ I describe a way to make Windows start up with a dialog box asking for a password, so someone who plays with your mouse or keyboard while you are away can't easily get into your Windows environment.

▶ I use this as an example of how to automatically run at Windows start-up *any* DOS or Windows program that requires parameters on its command line, when you want such a program to run *before* the items in the Program Manager StartUp group.

There are times when it is advantageous to place a program on the LOAD= or RUN= line in WIN.INI, instead of in the Windows 3.1 StartUp group.

First, StartUp has the nasty habit of loading all Windows programs first, and then going back and loading the DOS apps. If you want a DOS program to load first, you must put it on the LOAD= line.

Second, anyone can keep the programs in your StartUp group from running by holding down the Shift key until the Program Manager has loaded. This would concern you if you used a trick that's been making the rounds to password-protect Windows by putting a screen saver in your StartUp group.

In both of the above cases, you can't take a program out of the StartUp group and put it on the LOAD= line if the program requires a parameter. Any spaces in the LOAD= line are interpreted as a new program name. Parameters are not passed to the program that needs them.

I've found a way to use any parameters you want with programs on your LOAD= line. I'll illustrate this by describing a password-protection trick in a way that doesn't require the StartUp group and can't be bypassed with the Shift key.

STEPS

Password Protection Using a Screen Saver

Step 1. Add a space and SCR to the PROGRAMS= line in your WIN.INI file. It's not mentioned in the Windows manual, but this makes it possible for you to run screen savers, just as you run any EXE file. Restart Windows after this change.

Step 2. Use the Control Panel's Desktop dialog box to select the Marquee screen saver (or any screen saver that supports password protection). Click the Setup button, turn on Password Protection, and type in a password. Click OK to save your changes.

Step 3. In Program Manager, make an icon with the command line SSMARQUE.SCR /S. The /S switch tells the screen saver to "save now." (If you leave off this switch, you just get a dialog box that configures your screen saver.) Click OK to save this icon. Double-click the icon to confirm that the command SSMARQUE.SCR /S does, in fact, start your screen saver and require your password to get back into Windows.

Step 4. In File Manager, click File Run and type REGEDIT. This starts an undocumented Windows Registration Editor that maintains a Registration Database on OLE and other file associations. (I don't have space here to explain this applet, but you can learn about it by clicking Help and reading the topics contained therein. There is also more information about the Registration Database in Chapter 2, "Make Drag-and-Drop Do Anything You Want.")

Step 5. In RegEdit, click Edit Add-File-Type. In the dialog box that appears, fill in the following information:

```
Identifier: ScreenSaver
File Type:  Screen Saver
Command:    SSMARQUE.SCR /S
Uses DDE:   Off
```

Step 6. Still in RegEdit, click the Print button and fill in the same information. But this time leave off the /S switch in the command line.

Step 7. Click OK to save this listing, and exit RegEdit.

Step 8. Make a small text file called SCRNSAVE.ZZZ in any directory. In File Manager, highlight this file and click File Associate. In the dialog box that appears, scroll through the list of file types, and select Screen Saver. Click OK to associate the extension ZZZ with your screen saver.

Step 9. In WIN.INI, add C:*dir*\\SCRNSAVE.ZZZ to the front of your LOAD= line and save WIN.INI, where *dir* is the name of the directory where you placed your .ZZZ file.

Step 10. The next time you start Windows, it will try to "load" SCRNSAVE.ZZZ. This will, in fact, execute the command line SSMARQUE.SCR /S, which runs your screen saver. Don't forget your password!

You can also double-click any .ZZZ file to execute your screen saver. And you can drop any .ZZZ file on a Print Manager icon (or select it and click File Print in File Manager) to bring up its configuration dialog box. That's why we left off the /S in Step 6.

You can use this procedure to run *any* program that requires parameters on the LOAD= or RUN= lines of WIN.INI. Using a Windows 3.1 screen saver with a password in this way doesn't mean that you have foolproof security, of course. There are ways to get around the password by editing files in DOS, and anyone can delete all your files from DOS if they prevent Windows from trying to loading in the first place. But for casual protection against curious co-workers in an office, this method should provide you with a modicum of privacy for your Windows configuration.

Summary

In this chapter, I define a way to gain password protection for your Windows start-up, and how to run any DOS or Windows program that requires parameters but you want to start up before the regular StartUp group.

▶ By adding SCR to the list of Programs in WIN.INI, you can turn your password-protected screen saver into a Password dialog box that comes up whenever someone starts your Windows system when you're not there.

▶ You can use a similar trick to run *any* program that requires command-line parameters, and even make such programs do special tricks when you drag certain filenames from the File Manager onto the Print Manager icon.

Chapter 23
Using WIN.INI's Compatibility Bits

In This Chapter

▶ I tell you the meanings of the mysterious "Compatibility" section that appeared in WIN.INI without explanation in the upgrade from Windows 3.0 to 3.1.

▶ More importantly, I describe how you can use the esoteric meanings of the "compatibility bits" that are referenced in this section to work around bugs in applications that have compatibility problems with Windows 3.1.

With all the differences, major and minor, that exist between Windows 3.0 and Windows 3.1, at least you can be assured that all your Windows programs that ran under Windows 3.0 are guaranteed to run under Windows 3.1 — not!

There are, in fact, many differences that "break" Windows applications. These programs ran perfectly under Windows 3.0 (or at least passably), but exhibit weird behavior or don't run at all under Windows 3.1.

Originally, Microsoft intended Windows 3.1 to be 100 percent downward compatible with Windows 3.0 programs. I attended Microsoft Developer Forums in 1991, in which the speakers explained that Windows developers would finally enjoy a new version of Windows that didn't require them to rewrite any of their applications.

That idealistic goal, in retrospect, was not completely achieved. Although Microsoft expended a concerted effort to ensure compatibility with Windows 3.0 applications, a decision was made several months before Windows 3.1 was released to stop trying to make every Windows 3.0 application run perfectly under Windows 3.1.

Some of the applications that have problems under Windows 3.1 do things that Microsoft loudly said "will not be supported in future versions." Other errant applications do things that their developers couldn't have known would be changed in Windows 3.1.

Whatever the reason, it isn't useful to assign blame now. Windows programs are very complex, and every Windows developer I know is working furiously to build improved versions that take advantage of every feature of Windows 3.1 possible.

Fixing 'Broken' Applications

In any case, if you're responsible for managing Windows on several PCs, sooner or later you may run into a program that worked fine under Windows 3.0, but is quirky or worse under Windows 3.1.

To avoid such difficulties, several Windows programs were upgraded for Windows 3.1 compatibility. You should use at least the version number indicated, or later, of the following products: Norton Desktop 2.0, NewWave 4.0, Lotus Ami Pro 2.0, Microsoft PowerPoint 3.0, Bitstream FaceLift 2.0, Adobe Illustrator 4.0, Aldus Freehand 3.1, and hDC FirstApps Memory Viewer 1.1.

These and other programs that require "tweaks" to work under Windows 3.1 are described in a file called APPS.HLP. When you set up Windows 3.1, this file is installed on your hard disk. To see it, click File Run in Program Manager, type WINHELP and click OK. When the Windows Help application appears, click File Open, type APPS and click OK. You should read through the list of 20-odd programs that are displayed.

Contrary to some printed reports, all these applications do not have "bugs" — the help file just suggests tweaking the performance settings for some of the applications.

But many more applications than those listed in APPS.HLP do have difficulty with Windows 3.1. The two-year gap between Windows 3.0 and 3.1 gave Microsoft's programmers plenty of time to find performance enhancements in Windows' code — and most of these shortcuts broke one Windows application or another that depended on the original behavior.

Rather than take out the performance gains, Microsoft worked around the ailing apps by building features into Windows 3.1 known collectively as AppHacks.

If you look into WIN.INI after installing Windows 3.1, you'll see a section headed [Compatibility]. This section looks as follows:

```
[Compatibility]
AMIPRO=0x0010
APORIA=0x0100
_BNOTES=0x24000
CCMAIL=0x0008
CHARISMA=0x2000
CP=0x0040
DESIGNER=0x2000
DRAW=0x2000
ED=0x00010000
EXCEL=0x1000
GUIDE=0x1000
JW=0x42080
MCOURIER=0x0800
MILESV3=0x1000
NETSET2=0x0100
NOTSHELL=0x0001
PACKRAT=0x0800
PIXIE=0x0040
PLANNER=0x2000
PLUS=0x1000
PM4=0x2000
PR2=0x2000
REM=0x8022
TME=0x0100
TURBOTAX=0x00080000
VB=0x0200
VISION=0x0040
W4GL=0x4000
W4GLR=0x4000
WINSIM=0x2000
```

In this section, you find cryptic lines such as EXCEL=0x1000 and
WPWINFIL=0x0006. These lines set flags, in hexadecimal code, that change Windows 3.1's behavior — but only if program modules with these specific names
are running.

The EXCEL=0x1000 flag, for example, fixes the fact that Excel developers hard-
coded the bitmapped font names "Tms Rmn" and "Helv" into their tutorial. With
the flag set, Windows 3.1 supplies Excel with the old names it needs, instead of
the new names "MS Serif" and "MS Sans Serif." (Microsoft changed the names at
the request of Linotype, the owner of the trademarked names Times Roman and
Helvetica.)

The WPWINFIL=0x0006 flag partially corrects a WordPerfect for Windows module's inability to print graphics on landscape-oriented pages.

WordPerfect for Windows 5.1 has another problem, however, that isn't fixed by this line. When you change Windows printer drivers, WPWin 5.1 can make you wait a full minute or more, especially on dot-matrix printers. If you are using the original version of WPWin 5.1 — dated 11/7/91 — you should change the line in WIN.INI so it reads WPWINFIL=0x1206, according to Kevin Adamson, WordPerfect's manager of Windows testing. This works with all printers.

A later release of WordPerfect for Windows fixed these problems, as well as adding features like drag-and-drop text. The new release is still called 5.1, but you can tell the two versions apart by looking for a May 1992 date on the files. WPWin 5.2 and later versions also correct this problem, of course.

The old 5.1 version of WordPerfect for Windows, however, provides a perfect example of how a problem with a pre-Windows 3.0 program may be corrected by changing a line in the [Compatibility] section of WIN.INI.

Changing the Compatibility Bits

I don't recommend that you change settings at random in the [Compatibility] section, just because some application displays a behavior you don't like.

But the range of problems that the [Compatibility] section *can* solve is so broad that I think it's useful for you to know about them. For that reason, this chapter contains an explanation of each of the settings in the Windows 3.1 [Compatibility] list.

If you open WIN.INI with Notepad, you can easily find the [Compatibility] section and read lines like WIN2WRS=0x1210. This particular line refers to a module of WordPerfect called WIN2WRS. It means that this module requires certain compatibility "flags" to be set — specifically, the hexadecimal bits 1000, 0200, and 0010. These flags force Windows 3.1 to change its behavior slightly when this module is running.

These compatibility bits are largely required because of bugs in Windows 3.0. These bugs were not apparent to end users, but made it necessary for Windows application developers to code around the bugs to get their applications to work.

When Windows 3.1 changed the original buggy behavior, some of these applications couldn't automatically adjust. The [Compatibility] section fixes that.

When a newer version of such an application is installed, it can delete the relevant line in the [Compatibility] section if the fix is no longer needed.

Alternately, an application can be "marked" by its developers as version 3.1 - aware, and Windows 3.1 will then ignore the compatibility bits for that app.

In the following paragraphs, I describe each of the compatibility bits defined so far, and the applications that Microsoft has determined are affected. The prefix "0x," which specifies a hexadecimal number, and some leading zeros are left out of these descriptions for brevity.

- **Bit 0001** works around a bug in the Microsoft C 6.*x* run-time installation library. This affects the Setup programs in Microsoft Publisher, Money, Works, and other applications that were similarly compiled. Setting bit 0001 fixes the "NOTSHELL" module of the Setup routine in these applications (for example, NOTSHELL=0x0001).

- **Bit 0002** fixes applications that have problems with the way Windows 3.1 combines text and graphics on printouts. (This is a performance enhancement). This fix assists the WPWINFIL module of WordPerfect and the REM module of Freelance.

- **Bit 0004** tells Windows 3.1 to print landscape graphics in one large chunk, rather than several. This tweak, like the previous one, is also required by WordPerfect's WPWINFIL module. The statement WPWINFIL=0x0006 in your WIN.INI shows how different values can be added together in a single statement (for example, 0002+0004=0006, even in hex numbers).

- **Bit 0008** fixes applications that can't handle other apps that try to remain visible at all times (called "topmost" windows). You couldn't always start another Windows 3.1 app from ccMail, for example, if this bit wasn't set in WIN.INI. ccMail assumes the app it just started will always be the top window, even if another window is making itself topmost. This causes a General Protection Fault (a UAE under another name). Setting the bit prevents the problem.

- **Bit 0010** forces Windows 3.1 to give applications a list of TrueType faces in a way indicating that those typefaces are actually resident in the current printer. They aren't, but this flag helps some apps print the correct face.

- **Bit 0020** instructs Windows 3.1 to print graphics in multiple bands. If enough memory is available, Windows 3.1's new universal printer driver (which many devices rely on) tries to optimize printing by placing all text and graphics in a single, page-long band. But this confuses Freelance's REM module, which is fixed by the statement REM=0x8022.

- **Bit 0040** causes Windows 3.1 to send window-repaint messages to every running application when a new window is opened. Windows 3.0 always did this, but Windows 3.1 tries to gain performance by messaging only those windows it thinks need redrawing. Some apps use these messages for other purposes, however. Therefore, lines in the [Compatibility] section restore the old behavior for Pixie, ObjectVision, and the CP module of Cricket Presents.

- **Bit 0080** relates to a Windows 3.0 bug, which converted text passed to an application's File Open dialog box into all capitals. Windows 3.1 fixed this, but apps like JustWrite compensated for the bug and can display the wrong extension in File Open boxes without this workaround in the [Compatibility] section.

- **Bit 0100** changes the allocation of 4 bytes in a memory structure that was accessible by applications under Windows 3.0, but not Windows 3.1. Setting this bit allows the original behavior for apps like Aporia, the TME module of Compton's Multimedia Encyclopaedia, and the NETSET2 module of ExploreNet.

- **Bit 0200** corrects a problem that exists because, in Windows 3.1, a TrueType face can be represented on-screen by either a scalable outline or (at smaller sizes) a pre-installed bitmap. Specifying this bit in the [Compatibility] section eliminates any confusion for Visual Basic's VB module and WordPerfect for Windows' WIN2WRS module.

- **Bit 0800** deals with another bug in Windows 3.0, affecting serial communications on COM2, which applications like Packrat and Microcourier depended on and coded around.

- **Bit 1000** handles applications that hard-wired the Windows 3.0 font names Helv and Tms Rmn into their code. Because the owner of the trademarked names Helvetica and Times Roman (Linotype Corp.) objected, Microsoft changed the names of these fonts in Windows 3.1 to MS Sans Serif and MS Serif. Setting bit 1000 allows applications like Excel, Guide, Spinnaker Plus, WordPerfect's WIN2WRS module, and Milestones, Etc.'s MILESV3 module to still "see" the old names until upgrades are available.

- **Bit 2000** allows some applications to recognize TrueType faces as scalable, even though the current printer cannot scale type. This aids Charisma, PageMaker 4.0, Micrografx Designer and Draw, JustWrite, AccPac's WINSIM module, Persuasion's PR2 module, and Ascend's PLANNER module.

- **Bit 4000** affects applications that display drop-down lists inside dialog boxes (to show a list of disk drives, for example). Setting this bit ensures that such boxes overlap other boxes properly in Windows 3.1, as they did in Version 3.0. The WAGL and WAGLR modules of Ingres and the _BNOTES module of Lotus Notes 2.0 and 2.1 benefit from this fix.

- **Bit 8000** forces Windows 3.1 to print TrueType faces as graphics output — rather than downloadable printer fonts — for certain applications. This accommodates the REM module of Freelance.

- **Bit 10000,** as seen in WIN.INI in the line ED=0x00010000, controls the way Windows 3.1 delivers information to Windows applications. Due to a programming bug in Windows 3.0, Windows would sometimes send to an application an invalid set of coordinates for rectangles that needed to be redrawn. Windows 3.1 fixes this, but some Windows applications worked around the behavior by correctly handling the incorrect information that Windows 3.0 passed in certain situations.

Setting Bit 10000 re-introduces the Windows 3.0 behavior into Windows 3.1, specifically for the ED module of Microsoft Draw. Without this line in WIN.INI, some MS Draw objects are not properly redrawn in Word for Windows.

- **Bit 20000** affects a message that Windows sends to an application after its window has been moved by the user. Windows 3.0 always sent the application a message to recalculate its window size. Since this is more important when a window is created (not just moved), Windows 3.1 usually doesn't send this message after a mere move. This is one of many ways that Microsoft slightly improved Windows' performance.

  Some applications, however, depend on receiving the recalculate message when their window moves. The _BNOTES module of Lotus Notes, for example, has bit 20000 set in WIN.INI so the Navigator bar in Notes is always redrawn properly.

- **Bit 40000** changes the way Windows 3.1 processes a mouse double-click on the System Menu icon, which closes an application window. Just Write handles these messages differently if one of its multiple child windows is maximized than when the window is not maximized. Setting bit 40000 enables Just Write to react to these double-clicks in Windows 3.1 the same way it did in Windows 3.0.

- **Bit 80000** alters the way that Windows 3.1 calculates PostScript character widths for certain applications. TurboTax benefits from this setting, which allows it to print 1040 tax forms using its old assumptions about Windows' behavior.

That's it for the settings in the [Compatibility] section of WIN.INI. Now for the good part — using your knowledge of these settings to help fix minor incompatibilities.

If you use a particular Windows app — and it ran fine under Windows 3.0 but has a minor glitch under Windows 3.1 — one of the settings I've described in this chapter will almost certainly fix it.

As I've said above, you shouldn't change [Compatibility] settings unless advised to do so by a vendor's technical support department. There are too many delicate Windows behaviors that these settings affect to change them at random.

But if you can isolate and reproduce a specific misbehavior that your favorite app is exhibiting under Windows 3.1, the publisher of that application may be able to recommend a WIN.INI line that will clear up the problem immediately.

If you're interested in more technical information on the settings in the [Compatibility] section, you can download the file COMPAT.ZIP from the CompuServe WINSDK forum, Library 3.

Summary

In this chapter, I shed light on the entire [Compatibility] section of WIN.INI, which appeared in Windows 3.1 with no explanation in your Windows manual.

▶ Each number in the compatibility strings in this section is defined, with examples showing how each setting changes the behavior of Windows slightly to prevent intereference with some Windows applications.

▶ I suggest ways that you can ask vendors of software that worked fine under Windows 3.0 but has one or more difficulties under Windows 3.1 how to work around this with a specific setting in the [Compatibility] section.

Chapter 24
Controlling WIN.INI and SYSTEM.INI

In This Chapter

▶ I describe a handy utility that gives you a convenient front-end to the settings in your WIN.INI and SYSTEM.INI files.

▶ I also describe a unique, Windows-driven hypertext system that allows you to search through a complete database of Windows configuration lore.

O ne of the most arcane aspects of Windows 3.0 and 3.1 is the way that many settings must be edited manually in Notepad. Windows 3.0 introduced us to the concept of separate INI files for different functions, such as WIN.INI for personal preferences and SYSTEM.INI for hardware drivers. But the way settings are described in these files is anything but clear.

Someone back in early Windows development decided that ordinary users would never need to look in these INI files. Therefore, these files are full of techno-jargon like VirtualHDirq, 386grabber, and CoolSwitch, instead of plain English words.

Of course, many of these settings can be changed in the Windows Control Panel, but not all. Sometimes, the easiest or the only way to make a change is to manually edit WIN.INI, SYSTEM.INI, or another file. But as soon as you open these files, finding what you want amid the jargon is daunting.

An attempt to tame this jungle has been made by the Windows User Group Network (WUGNET), a group in Media, Pennsylvania, that publishes technical information on our favorite GUI. After months of mostly volunteer efforts, WUGNET has completed System Engineer, a front-end to almost every setting in WIN.INI and SYSTEM.INI.

Most of the settings are described using the same jargon found in the INI files themselves. But, then, this isn't a utility for novices — it's intended for professionals who support Windows and want to know the messy details of how it works.

System Engineer's Undocumented Desktop Tricks

One example of the usefulness of System Engineer is a dialog box called Desktop. Windows 3.1 allows the titles of icons on the desktop to wrap around on more than one line. But the Control Panel gives users no way to change the font used for icon titles, nor to adjust the vertical spacing (if you turn title wrapping off, for example).

All of these things can be done by manually setting lines in WIN.INI, but the information has been described only tersely in the Windows Resource Kit, where most INI settings are documented. (This Kit is almost a requirement for serious use of Windows and the System Engineer. It's only $19.95, and I recommend you get it by calling Microsoft at 206-882-8080.)

In the System Engineer's Desktop dialog box, you can see a preview of changes to your icon titles before making them. Not only can you change the spacing, size, and typeface used for icon titles. You can also make the titles bold for added readability — an undocumented feature of WIN.INI that didn't make it into the Windows Resource Kit.

When you install Windows 3.1, it defaults to icon titles of 8-point MS Sans Serif, with vertical spacing of 72 pixels from the top of one icon to the top of the next. If you use System Engineer to change this to, say, 9-point Arial Bold, it writes several lines into the [Desktop] section of your WIN.INI, as follows:

```
IconTitleFaceName=Arial
IconTitleSize=9
IconVerticalSpacing=72
IconTitleStyle=1
```

The line "IconTitleStyle=1" turns icon titles bold (if the font supports bold). Changing 1 to 0 makes the titles revert to normal weight.

System Engineer also has many other useful features, such as backing up your configuration files: *.INI, *.GRP, AUTOEXEC.BAT, and so on. WUGNET is distributing System Engineer free of charge to members, who also receive the monthly Windows Journal. Membership is normally $150 per year; System Engineer separately is $79.95. The address and phone for WUGNET are at the end of this chapter.

Getting the Windows Resource Kit On-Line ____

WUGNET has also produced another tool that may be of interest to an even larger number of people. That tool is Microsoft's *Windows Resource Kit,* a 500-page book of Windows 3.1 technical information — converted electronically into nearly 2MB of on-line Help files.

I've written elsewhere about the potential for the Windows Help engine to provide you with more than just a quick-reference card to a program. (See the chapter "Hypertext Help" for details.) The Windows Help application, WINHELP.EXE, is practically a free hypertext environment — especially the improved Windows 3.1 version. You can display words, graphics, text that jumps to related sections, buttons that perform actions, and even icons that run other applications. A help file could be a good choice for a company telephone book, a parts catalog (complete with illustrated specifications), or any information-rich document.

WUGNET's electronic edition of the Windows Resource Kit, known as WRK Help, goes much further than most programs in exploiting these features. The version I examined has such innovations as an Index and Glossary that display themselves in separate windows from the main Help text. This brilliant idea allows you to click an item in one window, and the other window automatically changes to show you a complete explanation. You don't have to click one window, and then the other, to see the information you need.

The Index and Glossary work together in other ways. All the terms in the Glossary are also present in the Index, which leads to each reference in the text. And the top of the Index displays an alphabetic "keypad": click on any button and you are immediately transported to listings beginning with that letter.

Because WINHELP.EXE can execute other programs, WRK Help includes icons for Windows Write (so you can open NETWORKS.WRI and other Windows documentation), SysEdit, File Manager, and so on. And imagine my surprise when clicking the Help button in a static screen-shot actually brought up Help for that topic.

As one minor, but important, enhancement, WRK Help changes the color of its highlighted text from the default, pale green, to a bold blue. This is intended to aid users of monochrome laptops (such as field engineers), but is a good idea for everyone. You can make the same change in Windows Help files by editing or inserting the following lines in your WIN.INI file:

```
[Windows Help]
Jumpcolor=0 0 128
Popupcolor=0 0 128
```

I usually prefer browsing through a good book to reading it on-line, especially when it's as dense as the WRK. But WRK Help is a strong alternative, which you'll appreciate when you electronically search for (and find) a topic you need.

WRK Help also adds several new touches to the 4.5 MB of Word for Windows 2.0 text and graphics that make up the original file. The book's elaborate trouble-shooting charts are included, for example. But WRK Help adds Yes/No buttons that lead support personnel through the most common problems.

WRK Help was produced by Jack DeLand of Adam Charles Consulting, 313-482-1600. For development, he used RoboHelp 1.0, $495 from Blue Sky Software, 619-459-6365. He converted the files with Doc-to-Help 1.1, a $295 package from WexTech Systems, 212-949-9595.

Getting the WRK book from Microsoft is still a good idea. It's only $19.95, and is available by calling 206-882-8080.

Membership in WUGNET, which includes the monthly Windows Journal, is $150 per year. WUGNET can be reached at 126 E. State St., Media, PA 19063; 215-565-1861, CompuServe: 76702,1356.

Summary

In this chapter, I describe two efforts by the Windows User Group Network (WUGNET) to make Windows more configurable and technically accessible.

▶ System Engineer gives you a graphical interface to the settings in your .INI files, as well as providing other tools to help you manage Windows.

▶ WRK Help, a hypertext file that incorporates the knowledge in the Microsoft Windows Resource Kit, is a unique way to jump through this large databank of Windows arcana to look for items that might affect your Windows systems.

Chapter 25
Finding the Windows Directory

In This Chapter

▶ I describe a problem that afflicted users of Windows 3.0 and was never corrected in Windows 3.1: Both versions set an environmental variable that shows which directory contains WIN.COM, but batch files cannot use this variable.

▶ I provide a pair of short batch files that can be used to test for the current Windows directory, or detect that Windows 3.x is not running, from a DOS session — and also establish an environmental variable that future batch files in that session *can* test.

Several readers have asked for a procedure that allows a batch file to find the Windows directory — the directory that contains WIN.COM, WIN.INI, and other such files.

The solution is by no means straightforward.

A full-blown Windows program can always find the directory that contains WIN.COM by asking Windows through a published Application Programming Interface (API) call.

But you may need to find the Windows directory from a lowly batch file for a variety of legitimate reasons. Perhaps you wish to use a batch file to distribute a new DLL you have written in-house or to update a Windows driver in every user's disk drive.

The developers of Windows created an environmental variable specifically to meet this need in batch files. If you open a DOS session under Windows, and type SET by itself (no parameters), you'll see the current DOS environment strings. One of them should be something like "windir=C:\WIN." This variable's value is the directory that contains WIN.COM — the directory C:\WIN, in this case.

Unfortunately, this variable is of little use in its original form. This is because DOS always treats the names of environmental variables as ALL CAPS. You might try to use the "windir" variable in a batch file, as in this line:

```
COPY A:\MY.DLL %WINDIR%\MY.DLL
```

DOS looks for a variable named WINDIR, which should have the value C:\WIN. But Windows names its "windir" variable in all *lowercase*. Therefore, there is no match. A DOS batch file can't "see" the variable at all.

Although I (and others) complained about this problem under Windows 3.0, it wasn't corrected in Windows 3.1. Fortunately, we can work around it.

First, the brute force method: You can use a byte editor to change the string "windir" to "WINDIR" in WIN.COM and WIN.CNF. (Setup uses WIN.CNF to rebuild WIN.COM when you change your settings.)

But if you'd rather not perform this surgery on every Windows installation, you *can* write a batch file that uses the value of "windir" correctly.

The following batch-file fragment tests for the existence of the string "windir=" in the DOS environment, and jumps to the label NOWIN if it isn't found:

```
SET|FIND "windir=">C:\TEMP_1.BAT
COPY C:\TEMP_1.BAT C:\TEMP_2.BAT
IF NOT EXIST C:\TEMP_2.BAT GOTO :NOWIN
C:\TEMP_2.BAT
:NOWIN
DEL C:\TEMP_1.BAT
ECHO Windows is not running.
```

The first line pipes the output of the SET command into FIND, which is case-sensitive. FIND writes the line it finds into a temporary file. If no line contains "windir=", this will be a 0-byte file.

The second line copies the temporary file to a new name. Due to a bug in COPY (which thousands of batch files now rely upon), if the first file is a 0-byte file, the second file will not be created.

The third line, therefore, tests for the existence of the second file. If there is none, no "windir=" was in the environment (Windows was not running).

If the batch file was run in a DOS session under Windows, however, TEMP_2.BAT will contain a single line:

```
windir=C:\WIN
```

Running TEMP_2.BAT executes this line, which runs a file called WINDIR.BAT and feeds it a single parameter: the directory name. (DOS considers a single equals sign to be a blank, so this line looks like WINDIR C:\WIN to DOS.)

WINDIR.BAT, which you must create yourself, does your *real* work with lines such as the following:

```
SET WIN-DIR=%1
COPY A:\MY.DLL %WIN-DIR%\MY.DLL
DEL C:\TEMP_2.BAT
```

The replaceable parameter "%1" has the value C:\WIN. Just what we want. This batch file leaves an environmental variable, %WIN-DIR%, available for future use (until this DOS session is terminated or the PC is rebooted).

Of course, if Microsoft ever fixes this variable in a future version of Windows, these batch files will no longer be necessary — nor will they work! Fortunately, that isn't likely.

Summary

In this chapter, I describe an irritation that affects Windows 3.0 and 3.1 users.

▶ The "windir" environmental variable was never switched to uppercase in Windows 3.1 so batch files in DOS sessions could easily test whether Windows was running and, if so, which directory contains WIN.COM (and presumably WIN.INI and other Windows configuration files).

▶ With two small batch files, you can test for Windows and establish an environmental variable that *does* work in batch files in a DOS session.

Chapter 26

When Worlds Collide: Solving Memory Conflicts

In This Chapter

▶ I provide a complete explanation of the mysterious "Upper Memory Blocks" that DOS and Windows use, and how you can get more out of them.

▶ I detail a comprehensive trouble-shooting procedure to help you isolate and cure problems you may be having when Windows and other software or hardware in your system have conflicts over upper memory address space.

▶ I explain a little-known conflict between the memory managers in DOS 5 and Windows 3 and show you an undocumented feature of the DOS expanded memory manager that allows you to fix the problem.

Memory is a valuable commodity, especially when you're running Windows. You probably know that Windows runs better as you add more memory (up to a point). DOS applications that you run under Windows may run better with access to more memory, too. But, unlike Windows, DOS applications that use conventional memory do not necessarily benefit when you add memory above 1MB to your system. Instead, you can give DOS applications under Windows more memory only by understanding how Windows itself allocates memory.

In this chapter, I'll explain some of the more obscure, little-understood methods that Windows uses to manage memory, and how you can take advantage of specific Windows features to optimize that memory.

Why Bother with Memory?

You might ask, "What difference does it make how Windows uses memory? I have (fill in the blank) 4MB/6MB/8MB, etc..."

The answer is that, even if you have a lot of memory, you may not have it configured properly for Windows or for DOS applications running under Windows.

I've found that almost every company using Windows also has some DOS programs that people run in DOS sessions under Windows. Even though these programs may appear to run fine, many DOS programs will run faster or more reliably when given access to more conventional memory. And one of the biggest problems reported by companies using Windows is that certain DOS programs cannot run under Windows because not enough conventional memory is available in a DOS session.

Therefore, a knowledge of how Windows uses memory can pay off in better performance or the prevention of problems that you may be experiencing or may experience in the future.

The PC memory map

To understand Windows memory management, it's necessary to know a few details about the memory in every 286 PC and higher. Figure 26-1 shows a simple memory map that applies to all 286s, 386s, and 486s.

We are primarily concerned with three types of memory for use by Windows: conventional memory, Upper Memory Blocks, and extended memory. DOS applications also use a fourth type of memory, expanded memory.

- *Conventional memory* is the first 640K of memory in your PC. DOS applications run in this memory. Windows also uses this memory when it switches to "real mode" in order to access some DOS device drivers and PC hardware.

- *Upper Memory Blocks* (also called UMBs) are theoretical locations where hardware devices and software drivers may be accessed by DOS and Windows. Exactly 384K of space is reserved for Upper Memory Blocks, and it is always located just above the first 640K of conventional memory.

- *Extended memory* (also called XMS, for eXtended Memory Specification) is the memory above conventional memory and the Upper Memory Blocks. It begins at the 1MB line, which is the same as 1024K (640K + 384K). If you have 2MB of RAM in your system, the first 640K is conventional memory, and the rest begins at the 1024K line and is counted upward from there. The first 64K of extended memory (minus 16 bytes) is called the *High Memory Area* (HMA), and is used by DOS, Windows, and a few other programs.

- *Expanded memory* (also called EMS, for Expanded Memory Specification) is a special type of memory that requires at least 64K of address space, usually in the Upper Memory Blocks, no matter how much expanded memory is installed in a PC. On a 286, expanded memory is often provided by an add-in memory board. On a 386 and higher, expanded memory is usually provided by an *expanded-memory manager*, a program that converts extended to expanded memory as required. In either case, expanded memory requires a 64K "page frame" somewhere below the 1MB line in order to function. The EMM386.EXE file provided by DOS and Windows is an expanded memory manager. Additionally, QEMM, 386Max, NetRoom, and other products are available from other software vendors, which provide more functionality than the Microsoft utility.

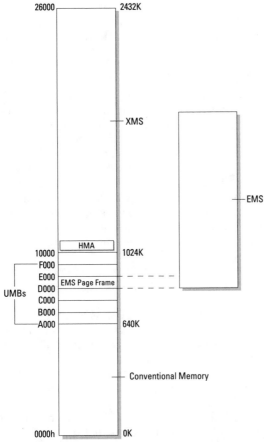

Figure 26-1: This diagram shows a PC with 2MB of RAM on the motherboard (640K of conventional memory + 1408K of extended memory = 2048K plus 384K of Upper Memory Blocks, for a total of 2432K), plus an add-in expanded memory board with another 1MB installed.

We will primarily be discussing the Upper Memory Blocks in this chapter. This is because you can increase the amount of conventional memory available under Windows by moving device drivers and DOS itself from conventional memory into Upper Memory Blocks.

Upper Memory Blocks from A to F

The 384K of Upper Memory Blocks can be thought of as six separate areas, each of which is 64K in size. These six blocks are known as A, B, C, D, E, and F. The address of the beginning of A block is called A000 (pronounced "A thousand") in hexadecimal numbering; the beginning of the B block is B000, and so on.

The A block is used for the addresses of the RAM on your VGA or higher video board. When the board is in graphics mode (as opposed to text mode), the 64K of address space at A000 is used by Windows to write information into the RAM on the board. No matter how much RAM the board has physically installed — 256K, 512K, or more — the same 64K block is used to write to all video memory.

The B block is used for two purposes. The first 32K, which begins at B000, is used when a VGA or higher board is in monochrome graphics mode. These memory addresses would be used, for example, if you were using a monochrome monitor and the Windows VGA monochrome driver. The second 32K, from B800 to BFFF, is used for VGA or higher text mode. A portion of this address space is used when you are at a DOS prompt and type a command. The DOS output is written to B800, where it appears on your screen as text characters.

The C block is used for the read-only memory (ROM) chip that is present on all VGA and higher adapters. This chip always begins using address spaces at C000. From that point, the chip may claim 16K, 24K, or more, depending on the complexity of the adapter and how many video modes it supports.

The/D block has no reserved function, but often is claimed by memory managers for the 64K page frame required for the use of expanded memory.

The E block is often unused on AT-bus and EISA-bus machines, but is usually claimed by machines with a Micro Channel Architecture (MCA) bus. MCA machines include a unique set of ROM chips that reside at addresses starting at E000 and continue toward EFFF. These chips contain instructions in ROM that are used when OS/2 is running. For those people who are not using OS/2, many memory-manager programs can claim these memory addresses for other purposes.

Finally, the F000 block is reserved on all PCs for the ROM chips that hold the basic input-output system (BIOS) — instructions that run low-level functions, such as writing to disk drives.

Knowing the purpose of each Upper Memory Block can help you claim more memory for Windows and DOS applications running under Windows.

Loading upper memory support

Windows has certain features that require memory addresses in conventional memory and Upper Memory Blocks. How these features are allocated to these memory addresses can determine how much memory is left over for other applications.

Before changing the way Windows allocates conventional and UMB memory, you should ensure that your overall system memory is configured properly for the Windows modes you typically run.

In standard mode, Windows uses only extended memory and cannot provide expanded memory to DOS applications running under Windows. In this case, if you have DOS applications that require expanded memory, you must set aside a certain portion of memory as expanded before Windows starts. You typically do this using switches or software provided with memory add-in boards, or with 386 memory management software on 386s with all memory located on the motherboard.

In enhanced mode, Windows uses all extended memory, but also can convert extended to expanded memory on-the-fly for DOS applications running under Windows. If you always run Windows in enhanced mode, and have DOS applications that require expanded memory, you should configure all your system memory as extended and let Windows and memory-management software convert it to expanded as required. Unless stated otherwise, the remainder of this chapter will assume you are using a 386 or higher with Windows in enhanced mode.

DOS 5.0 and higher and Windows 3.1 and higher provide tools to manage memory on 386 PCs and higher. With Windows 3.1, your CONFIG.SYS file probably contains lines similar to the following:

```
device=c:\windows\himem.sys
dos=high,umb
device=c:\windows\emm386.exe
```

The first line loads HIMEM.SYS, a driver that enables extended memory management. The second line loads most of COMMAND.COM, the DOS command interpreter, into the so-called high memory area (HMA, the first 64K of extended memory) instead of into conventional memory, and enables the use of Upper Memory Blocks. The third line loads the expanded memory manager that provides expanded memory and UMB services to applications.

If you have Windows 3.1 and DOS 5.0, you should use the versions of HIMEM.SYS and EMM386.EXE that come with Windows, not the versions that come with DOS 5.0. Alternatively, if you have Windows 3.1 and DOS 6.x, you should use the drivers that came with DOS 6.x, not the Windows 3.1 versions. In each case, the newer drivers provide better features.

Other vendors also provide 386 expanded memory managers. Typical drivers include QEMM386, from Quarterdeck Office Systems, 386Max, from Qualitas, Inc., and NetRoom. If you use one of these drivers, your CONFIG.SYS file probably starts out with a line loading that file instead of Microsoft's HIMEM.SYS and EMM386.EXE.

How Windows uses memory blocks

When Windows loads in enhanced mode, it looks for space in the Upper Memory Blocks for two different purposes:

- It places an expanded memory page frame, 64K in size, in an unused area above 640K. If an expanded memory manager was loaded in CONFIG.SYS, Windows "inherits" the settings for that EMS page frame.

- Windows claims another area, approximately 16K in size, for DOS translation buffers. These buffers are used by Windows to transfer data to and from real-mode devices such as disk drives. If there is not enough space left in Upper Memory Blocks, Windows takes the equivalent amount of space out of conventional memory.

The fact that Windows uses these two chunks of memory can reduce the amount of conventional memory available to DOS applications under Windows. In some cases, certain DOS applications will refuse to run under Windows, simply because they don't have quite enough memory.

To free up more conventional memory, DOS memory managers and those of third parties provide ways to move drivers that would usually consume conventional memory into UMBs instead. Using DOS's HIMEM.SYS and EMM386.EXE, you would load a device driver into UMBs in CONFIG.SYS with a line like the following:

```
devicehigh=c:\dir\filename.sys
```

In AUTOEXEC.BAT, memory-resident programs are typically loaded into UMBs instead of conventional memory with a line like this:

```
loadhigh c:\dir\filename.com
```

If EMM386.EXE or another memory manager has already claimed a 64K page frame, however, these command lines may not find free UMB space and may fail to load the drivers or memory-resident programs into UMBs. Additionally, Windows may fail to load its translation buffers into UMBs, eating up even more conventional memory.

Claiming the space used by the page frame

If you have large DOS programs that need lots of conventional memory but don't require expanded memory, you can get more memory for these programs by disabling the creation of a 64K page frame in upper memory.

If you are using EMM386.EXE, you can do this by adding FRAME=NONE to the command line in CONFIG.SYS, as in the following example:

```
device=c:\windows\emm386.exe frame=none
```

This parameter also works with QEMM386, but varies with other memory managers. The parameter FRAME=NONE is undocumented for EMM386.EXE, and does not work in some configurations. It usually frees a little more memory than putting NOEMS on the EMM386 command line. But if FRAME=NONE does not work in your system (Windows won't start in enhanced mode, for example), you must use the NOEMS parameter instead.

If you eliminate the page frame in your memory manager in CONFIG.SYS, you should also prevent Windows from creating one when you start Windows in enhanced mode. To do this, place a line in the [386Enh] section of your SYSTEM.INI file with Notepad, as follows:

```
[386Enh]
NoEMMDriver=TRUE
```

Eliminating the page frame in both CONFIG.SYS and SYSTEM.INI guarantees that Windows will not create a page frame — even if you take the EMM386.EXE line out of your CONFIG.SYS in the future for whatever reason.

By preventing the creation of the 64K page frame in EMM386 and in Windows, you open up this much space to load additional device drivers and memory-resident programs into Upper Memory Blocks. Drivers that wouldn't load high before you reconfigured your memory managers may now fit just fine.

Claiming the space used by translation buffers

The 16K used by the DOS translation buffers can be a little trickier to manage. At present, there is no utility in Windows that allows you to determine whether these buffers are taking up conventional memory or are loaded into Upper Memory Blocks.

One way to check this is to start Windows as you normally do, then start a DOS session under Windows. At the DOS prompt, type the command MEM (which works in DOS 4.0 and higher). Write down the amount of available RAM reported by this command.

Next, exit Windows and restart it with the following command:

```
win /d:x
```

The switch /D:X places Windows in a so-called debugging mode and excludes all Upper Memory Blocks from use by Windows. In this situation, Windows is forced to locate its translation buffers conventional memory, because UMBs are not available. (For an explanation of this and other switches, see Chapter 33, "Troubleshoot Windows à la Mode.)

After starting Windows in this way, start a DOS session and type MEM. Note the difference in available memory from your previous session. If available memory has gone down 8 to 16K or so, this is the amount of space Windows is setting aside for translation buffers. If available memory shows no change, something is preventing Windows from placing the translation buffers into UMBs under normal circumstances. You might be able to get more RAM for DOS applications under Windows by loading a small driver into conventional memory instead of Upper Memory Blocks. Even a 1MB device driver might be taking up a 16K address space that could be used for Windows translation buffers.

One other thing might be preventing Windows from finding a free 16K space in Upper Memory Blocks. If an expanded memory manager claims all UMBs, Windows may find there are none for it to use. If Windows is forcing its translation buffers into conventional memory, try excluding a 16K area of UMBs from your expanded memory manager. EMM utilities usually allow you to do this by adding the switch /X or X to their command line in CONFIG.SYS, followed by an equals sign and the exact addresses to exclude. For example, if you are using QEMM and wish to exclude the last 16K of the D000 block, you would use the following line in CONFIG.SYS:

```
device=c:\qemm\qemm386.sys /x=dc00-dfff
```

One way to see what programs are loaded into Upper Memory Blocks is to start your PC normally, but without starting Windows. At the DOS prompt, type MSD. This starts a Microsoft Diagnostic program that is included with Windows 3.1 but not discussed in the Windows manual.

The MSD utility provides screens that show the use of upper memory and any devices that are loaded there. Microsoft uses this utility when people call for technical support. Strangely, MSD can provide unreliable information when used in a DOS session under Windows, so run it from a plain DOS prompt instead. For more information on MSD, see Chapter 32, "MSD: The MisSing Documentation."

Getting the best of conventional and upper memory

If you have fit the translation buffers and page frame into upper memory as well as you can, and your DOS programs are still not getting enough conventional memory to run, you can add another trick to your arsenal: claiming the monochrome UMB area.

If you run Windows with a VGA or Super VGA color driver, it's likely that no program is using the memory area that starts at B000 at all. Additionally, DOS text-mode programs rarely use all of the text-mode memory that starts at B800 and continues to C000. (IBM XGA adapters, however, do use the B000 area to store information, so don't use the following technique with them.)

Even if you have a monochrome monitor, or a laptop with a monochrome display, you may be able to use this technique. Instead of using the "VGA with Monochrome Display" driver that comes with Windows, try switching to the color "VGA" driver. Many monochrome displays simply use shades of gray when color information is output, and will work fine with color VGA drivers.

To give your expanded memory manager access to the monochrome B000 area, use an "include" parameter in CONFIG.SYS similar to the following:

```
device=c:\windows\emm386.exe i=b000-b7ff
```

This statement instructs your memory manager to use the entire block between B000 and B800 (the address B7FF is one lower than B800, in hexadecimal numbering). This block is often avoided by memory managers, since VGA adapters can be switched into monochrome mode by programs at any time. But if you don't use such programs, this area can be managed safely by your 386 memory manager.

If you give access to this area to your memory manager in CONFIG.SYS, you should also specify this for the Windows memory manager, 386 memory manager (which takes over when Windows starts in enhanced mode). To do this, add an "include" line to the [386Enh] section of SYSTEM.INI with Notepad, as follows:

```
[386Enh]
EMMInclude=B000-B7FF
```

When you restart Windows and run MEM in a DOS session, you may find that a substantially larger amount of conventional memory is now available. This is because more room is available to locate the translation buffers and page frame (if you use one).

If you see the error message, "Windows cannot set up an Upper Memory Block at segment B000," when you start Windows in enhanced mode, there may be a conflict between your video adapter and your memory manager, which can easily be fixed. In this case, start Windows in standard mode with the command WIN /S. Then add one of two lines into your SYSTEM.INI file.

■ If you are using QEMM386, add a line that loads a driver called MONOUMB2.386, which is a file that comes with Windows 3.1. Place the following line into the [386Enh] section of SYSTEM.INI:

```
[386Enh]
device=monoumb2.386
```

■ If you are using EMM386.EXE, you must obtain a driver called MONOUMB.386 from Microsoft, and load it with a line in SYSTEM.INI like the following:

```
[386Enh]
device=monoumb.386
```

This file was not finished when Microsoft shipped Windows 3.1. Instead, it is part of the Microsoft Windows Driver Library (WDL), a set of drivers that became available later. You can obtain this file by calling Microsoft at 800-426-9400 or 206-882-8080.

Alternatively, you can download a file called MONO.EXE for free (except for phone charges) by calling Microsoft's bulletin board system at 206-936-6735 with your modem set to 8 data bits, 1 stop bit, and no parity. Place this file in a separate directory (*not* the one containing Windows), then change to that directory at a DOS prompt and type MONO. This file is a self-extracting file that creates MONOUMB.386 and a text file with instructions.

Another way to obtain the file MONO.EXE, if you have access to CompuServe or GEnie, is to download it from those services.

On CompuServe, type GO MSL (for the Microsoft Software Library). Select Libraries, then download MONO.EXE.

On GEnie, select Computing Services, then IBM PC/Tandy Roundtables, then Microsoft Roundtable, and finally Software Library. Select Search File Directory, search for "WDL," then download MONO.EXE from the indicated library.

For more information on the Windows Driver Library, see Chapter 28, "License to Upgrade — Help for Expired Drivers."

Managing memory with Windows can be a tricky process, but it can pay dividends by providing additional memory for Windows and DOS applications. Good luck in finding those extra kilobytes you need.

Troubleshooting Memory Conflicts _____

An experience I had with a colleague shows how tricky it can be to troubleshoot some Windows memory-management quirks.

I was visiting the office of a friend who had just purchased one of the latest 4-pound notebook 386 computers. Although the system's gray-scale VGA screen was quite suitable for running Windows, DOS programs wouldn't start under Windows on the notebook without immediately exiting back to Windows.

I was able to fix the situation by changing a line in the notebook's SYSTEM.INI file. But if my acquaintance, a woman who runs a respected computer training company, couldn't figure out this problem, I assume there must be thousands of other people who are having problems like this as well.

The tip-off that helped diagnose this malady was the fact that the problem occurred only in enhanced mode. This usually suggests that Windows has a memory conflict with some device in the system.

In 386 enhanced mode, Windows relocates some extended memory from addresses above 1MB to UMB addresses between 640K and 1MB. The memory relocated into this area can be used by Windows to provide an expanded memory page frame, buffers for file transfers, and other services.

Problems occur when Windows relocates memory into a block that is also used by a device like a video board or a network adapter. Boards like this require some address space between 640K and 1MB to operate. Windows attempts to identify all the Upper Memory Blocks that are in use, but this attempt is not always successful.

The addresses between 640K and 1MB that Windows relocates memory into are referred to in hexadecimal numbering as A000 to EFFF. One way to test whether some form of memory conflict is causing a problem in enhanced mode is to force the built-in expanded memory manager to stop using these memory addresses. This can be accomplished by opening the SYSTEM.INI file with Notepad, finding the section headed [386Enh], and inserting the following lines:

```
[386Enh]
EMMExclude=A000-AFFF
EMMExclude=B000-B7FF
EMMExclude=B800-BFFF
EMMExclude=C000-C3FF
EMMExclude=C400-C7FF
EMMExclude=C800-CBFF
EMMExclude=CC00-CFFF
```

```
EMMExclude=D000-D3FF
EMMExclude=D400-D7FF
EMMExclude=D800-DBFF
EMMExclude=DC00-DFFF
EMMExclude=E000-E3FF
EMMExclude=E400-E7FF
EMMExclude=E800-EBFF
EMMExclude=EC00-EFFF
```

If the problem goes away when you restart Windows with these lines in SYSTEM.INI, a memory conflict was definitely present. Only one or two of the lines is actually needed to resolve the problem, however — not all of them.

To determine which lines are necessary, comment out the bottom eight lines (by placing a semicolon in front of "EMMExclude") and restart Windows. If the problem recurs, comment out only the bottom *four* lines, and so on. By this method, you should be able to isolate the culprit within only about four trials (if just one line is at fault). This is faster than trying all 15 lines, one at a time.

It's unfortunate that there aren't more foolproof ways to pinpoint and prevent memory conflicts like this. (The notebook's setup routine and the other diagnostic utilities that we tried didn't identify the specific areas of memory in question.) The Windows manual says nothing about EMMExclude — you must read about it in the SYSINI.WRI file located in your Windows directory.

But thank heavens the developers of Windows provided a means to correct these situations once they're understood.

DOS 5.0 and Windows 3.0 Problems

Microsoft's introduction of memory-management features in DOS 5.0 was not entirely trouble-free. If you are still using that version of DOS, and Windows 3.0, there are some incompatibilities with the early versions of EMM386.EXE provided with those products. (This was corrected in Windows 3.1.)

To illustrate, let's say you wanted to provide additional memory for a DOS program that didn't have quite enough memory to run under Windows. With DOS 5, you might provide this application with additional room by loading DOS itself into extended memory. You might also install EMM386.EXE, and use DOS 5's DEVICEHIGH command to load your ANSI.SYS display driver into UMBs, thereby saving another few K.

To do this, the first four lines of your CONFIG.SYS would look as follows:

```
device=c:\dos\himem.sys
dos=high,umb
device=c:\dos\emm386.exe
devicehigh=c:\dos\ansi.sys
```

Under DOS 5, this is a perfectly legitimate configuration. If you reboot your 386 this way, however, you may find that Windows 3.0 has difficulty loading in 386 enhanced mode, and won't start in standard mode at all.

The problem is that the EMM386.EXE memory manager in DOS 5.0 is not compatible with the 286 protected-mode instructions that Windows 3.0 uses in standard mode. Once EMM386.EXE has been called upon to load a program into UMBs, or provide a DOS application (such as a disk cache) with expanded memory, Windows in standard mode cannot "inherit" or reclaim the memory managed by EMM386.EXE. (This problem also affects the older EMM386.SYS driver provided with Windows 3.0.)

To start Windows 3.0 in 386 enhanced mode after utilizing EMM386.EXE memory, you may need to use an undocumented feature of EMM386.EXE. This feature is called the /Y switch ("Y" as in, "Yes, I'm using Windows.")

If you add a /Y switch, an equals sign, and the full path name of EMM386.EXE, Windows is able to locate DOS 5's memory manager and cooperate with it. After this change, the EMM386.EXE line in your CONFIG.SYS would look like this:

```
device=c:\dos\emm386.exe ram /y=c:\dos\emm386.exe
```

Microsoft isn't quite certain at this time which 386 machines need this switch, and which don't. But this interaction with Windows is a known feature, which is mentioned in section four of the README.TXT file included on the DOS 5 distribution diskettes.

A similar problem with Windows 3.0's standard mode affects old versions of the 386Max memory manager from Qualitas, Inc. By far the best solution, of course, if to upgrade from Windows 3.0 to 3.1 or higher, if you haven't already done so.

Summary

In this chapter, I delve into the arcane world of upper memory management — a dry subject, but one that can pay off if you can find additional memory for your applications or remove the source of a conflict.

▶ The entire PC memory map, including conventional memory, Upper Memory Blocks, the High Memory Area, extended memory, and expanded memory, is laid out and described.

▶ Conflicts that can occur between Windows and other software and hardware are described, and a trouble-shooting process that can help you find and eliminate these conflicts is given.

▶ A bug that affects the expanded memory manager in DOS 5 and Windows 3 is detailed, with an explanation of an undocumented switch that can clear up the problem.

Chapter 27
Stormy Com Ports

In This Chapter

▶ I identify conflicts between PC communication (com) ports under Windows, and show you how to fix them.

▶ I describe two software products that allow you to get around some of the communications limitations.

Since the subject of PC communications apparently wasn't confusing enough under DOS, Windows has come along to muddy the waters even more.

One problem that Windows creates is its limit on the throughput of all four communications, or com, ports. You can use the Control Panel to set any bits-per-second rate you want for COM1 through COM4, as long as that rate is 19,200 bps or less. Today, you can buy high-speed modems with compression features that accelerate throughput up to bursts of 38,400 bps. And many DOS file-transfer packages allow speeds up to 115,200 bps. This makes the strict 19.2-Kbps limit in Windows seem a little dated.

Equally frustrating is the fact that Windows doesn't allow Windows or DOS apps to communicate with most systems' COM3 or COM4 in enhanced mode at all.

Both of these problems can be fixed, more or less. Let's first deal with support for COM3 and COM4.

In standard mode, Windows communicates with all four com ports through a device driver called COMM.DRV. If you look in the [boot] section of your SYSTEM.INI file, you should see the line COMM.DRV=COMM.DRV, which loads this driver.

In enhanced mode, Windows employs an internal driver known as the Virtual Communications Driver (VCD). The [386Enh] section of your SYSTEM.INI probably says DEVICE=*VCD. The asterisk indicates that the VCD driver is internal, not an external file in the System directory like COMM.DRV.

To handle input and output for com ports, your CPU uses a logical address. This is called the ports' *base I/O address*.

Everyone seems to agree that the I/O address for COM1 is 03F8 (in hexadecimal numbering), and COM2's is 02F8 hex. When DOS 3.3 introduced COM3 and COM4, most (but not all) communications software assumed these ports would be located at 03E8 and 02E8 hex, respectively — exactly one memory "paragraph" lower.

The Windows COMM.DRV driver follows this convention, but the Virtual Communications Driver in Windows 3.0 did not. The Windows 3.0 VCD used the addresses 2E8 and 2E0 for COM3 and COM4, respectively. When you run communications software in Windows 3.0 enhanced mode, the software doesn't match the I/O addresses Windows is using, and there is no communication.

You can correct this by adding the following two lines — undocumented in your Windows manual — to the [386Enh] section of the SYSTEM.INI file for Windows 3.0:

```
[386Enh]
COM3Base=3E8h
COM4Base=2E8h
```

This problem was "corrected" in Windows 3.1 — COM3 and COM4 are given the base I/O address that most communications programs expect. But that isn't the end of the problems with COM3 and COM4, by any means.

Because of ISA-bus limitations dating back to the original IBM PC-1, you cannot use a device on COM1 at the same time as one on COM3. Nor can you use COM2 while COM4 is in use. Most serial ports use Interrupt 4 for both COM1 and COM3, and Interrupt 3 for both COM2 and COM4 — and two devices cannot use the same interrupt simultaneously on an ISA-bus machine. You can have a modem on COM1, a serial mouse on COM2, and a serial printer on COM3. But you can't print to the serial printer while using the modem. And since mice use interrupts constantly, you can't have anything on COM4 at all. (The current version of Microsoft's mouse driver does not seen to support serial mice on ports other than COM1 or COM2, either.)

Even though AT-class machines and higher have up to 15 interrupts, most serial-board vendors simply haven't designed their hardware to allow configuration for the higher interrupts. However, if you *do* find a serial port that allows a port to be assigned to an interrupt other than 3 or 4 (interrupts 10, 11, 12, and 15 are almost always available on AT-class and higher systems), you can tell Windows to use a different interrupt for that port by adding a line to your SYSTEM.INI file. For example, if your COM3 serial port can be assigned to interrupt 11, add the following to the [386Enh] section of SYSTEM.INI and restart Windows:

```
[386Enh]
COM3IRQ=11
```

You can also insert the line COM*x*IRQ=-1 (where *x* is the number of the com port) to disable a com port. This might be necessary if serial-port hardware is interfering with some other device in your system.

MicroChannel (MCA) and EISA machines solve the ISA-bus limitation by allowing *shareable hardware interrupts*. This means that any MCA and EISA serial boards can support COM3, COM4, and up, in any combination. This is one of the benefits of these advanced buses, though I rarely see it mentioned. Windows automatically detects MCA and EISA systems, if you are using one.

Once you've set up COM3 and COM4 properly, you can solve the Windows 19.2-Kbps limitation by upgrading your COMM.DRV to a driver called TurboCom ($52.50 postpaid, plus tax in California). This product allows you to use any port up to COM4 (in any combination, if you have a special four-port serial board). And can program Windows to accept rates up to 57.6 Kbps or higher. Contact Bio-Engineering Research Labs at 2831 7th St., Berkeley, CA 94710; 510-540-8080.

And if you need more than four ports, you can obtain a driver called W3COM9 ($99 postpaid), which supports up to nine. This product requires the purchase of a special eight-port serial board, such as ones manufactured by DigiBoard, Comtrol, and others. The software supports up to 64 ports. Contact Cherry Hill Software at Meetinghouse Square, Suite 215, Hainesport-Mt. Laurel Rd., Marlton, NJ 08053-9468; 609-983-1414.

Summary

In this chapter, I try to shed some light on the black art of data communications under Windows:

▶ How you can configure COM1, COM2, COM3, and COM4 under Windows to avoid conflicts between mice, serial printers, modems, and other devices that use com ports.

▶ What you can get out of TurboCom, a software product that programs Windows to communicate at rates up to 57.6 Kbps, and W3COM9, a driver that allows you to install more than the normal four com ports on a single PC.

Chapter 28
License to Upgrade: Help for Expired Drivers

In This Chapter

▶ I reveal that — of the software driver files included with Windows 3.1 for printers, video boards, network adapters, and other peripherals — there have been literally *hundreds* of upgrades that can improve the performance and reliability of your Windows system, if only you knew about their existence.

▶ I list every upgraded driver that was available at press time, how you can get them, and how you can stay up-to-date on these important Windows enhancements in the future.

Every Windows user wants to improve the performance and reliability of Windows. The easiest way to do that is to upgrade to new versions of Windows driver files that may affect your system.

What are driver files? Windows is made up of hundreds of files known as *dynamic link libraries* (DLLs). A DLL is an executable program that is called upon to perform services by other Windows programs. For example, COMMDLG.DLL is a "common dialog box DLL" provided with Windows 3.1, which several Windows applications use to display their File Open, File Save, and a few other dialog boxes for routine functions. This is why the File Open dialog boxes in, say, Windows Notepad and Windows Write look exactly the same.

DLL files may have the extension .DLL or they may have any extension.

Printer drivers are DLLs that control output to your printer, and they usually have the extension .DRV. Display drivers, which control your video adapter, also have the extension .DRV.

Screen-saver modules and Control Panel icons, on the other hand, are also DLLs but have the extensions .SCR and .CPL, respectively. Finally, programs that control DOS functions in 386 enhanced mode usually have the extension .386.

What can these programs do for you? They may, in fact, be responsible for several slight incompatibilities plaguing your system. If your Windows configuration sometimes crashes, exits to DOS unexpectedly, or exhibits other random behavior, updating to a new device driver may fix the problem.

Even if you aren't experiencing a specific problem now, it's a very good idea to learn whether a new driver has been released for one of your hardware components, and to upgrade to that driver. It's often free or very inexpensive (the cost of a phone call).

The Humongous Driver List

The fact is that Microsoft has released literally *hundreds* of updated Windows drivers since Windows 3.1 shipped in April 1992. The fact that these drivers exist is not a secret — Microsoft places each new driver into a set of files called the Windows Driver Library (WDL). But Microsoft sponsors no advertising or publicity about the existence of these files. You have to know where to look and how to find them.

Because I feel it is so important for Windows users to have the latest, most stable versions of all their driver software, I obtained the entire Windows Driver Library from Microsoft and sorted the whole set by vendor. The result, based on Microsoft's on-line documentation for these files, is printed in Table 28-1 at the end of this chapter.

Look through this table for the names of any vendors whose hardware you use in your system. Perhaps you have a display adapter from ATI, Tseng, or Western Digital/Paradise, or a printer from Epson, Hewlett-Packard, or IBM. You will find new drivers for all of these vendors and many more.

I'll explain the significance of some of the gems in this table , and then describe exactly how you can get these drivers and install them in your system.

A driving passion

Where did Microsoft get the hundreds of drivers that now make up the Windows Driver Library? Most of these drivers exist because time did not stand still when Windows 3.1 was shipped. The master diskettes for Windows 3.1 were sent to Microsoft's disk duplicators on March 10, 1992 (hence the 3/10/92 date on the files that come with Windows 3.1), and any driver that wasn't fully ready on that date simply didn't get into the box.

Microsoft doesn't write all the DLLs that ship with Windows 3.1. Many drivers are written by the vendors responsible for each piece of hardware that is supposed to work with Windows. Drivers written outside Microsoft that were finished after Windows 3.1 shipped are in the WDL.

Unfortunately for users, many of the drivers that *did* ship with Windows 3.1 had subtle bugs. The tweaks and fixes to these drivers also show up in the new versions in the WDL.

Goodies galore

As a top priority, everyone who prints should upgrade to the newest version of the universal printer driver. Downloading UNIDRV.EXE and running it once to decompress this file provides you with UNIDRV.DLL and UNIDRV.HLP. Run UNIDRV.EXE once at a plain DOS prompt in its own separate directory. (Do *not* decompress this file in the Windows directory while Windows is running, because you may wipe out files with the same name.) You can then copy the resulting UNIDRV.DLL and UNIDRV.HLP files into the correct directory while Windows is not running. Alternatively, you can backup and delete your old UNIDRV.DLL file, then open the Control Panel's Printers dialog box, click Install, and provide the name of the drive and directory where the new driver file is located. This will copy it to your Windows System subdirectory. These universal printer driver files have each gained about 10K of code since Windows 3.1 first shipped, and solve several minor but annoying quirks.

If you use a PostScript printer, you should also download PSCRIP.EXE, which contains the new PSCRIPT.DRV file. The current version at this writing, 3.56, is the sixth release of a new PostScript driver since the launch of Windows 3.1, and each time Microsoft gets the driver a little closer to working perfectly.

Those who use the Generic/Text Only printer driver — perhaps for printing output in plain-text format from any application — will also benefit from downloading GENDRV.EXE.

Besides printer drivers, display drivers, and network adapter drivers (which make up about 90 percent of the files in the WDL), there are also several other gems and goodies, including

- Microsoft developed a special speaker driver which can play sounds on most internal PC speakers without requiring the purchase of a Sound Blaster or other add-in board. This driver is available in the WDL in a self-extracting file called SPEAK.EXE.

- Better versions of SYSINI.WRI and WININI.WRI, which document the settings in SYSTEM.INI and WIN.INI, respectively, are available in a file named WRI.EXE.

- The Access Pack, a keyboard and mouse driver that makes these devices easier to use for people with limited dexterity, is available in the file ACCP.EXE. Even people with average dexterity might appreciate this driver, which makes it possible to press Ctrl+A by pressing each key sequentially, for example, instead of having to hold down both keys at the same time.

- Some gems that were left out of Windows 3.1 or 3.0 for disk space reasons have achieved immortality in the WDL. Here you will find the Reversi game from Windows 3.0, the MS-DOS Executive (a fast, text-only file manager that came from Windows 2.x), and several wallpaper, sound, and screen saver files. The old Windows 3.0 CGA driver — for those who are stuck with 1980s hardware — shows up here, too.

How to get updated Windows drivers

Microsoft distributes the Windows Driver Library files via public bulletin boards and by an in-house bulletin board system.

Public bulletin boards from which you can obtain drivers include CompuServe, GEnie, and others. On CompuServe, type GO MSL to access the Microsoft Software Library. On GEnie, select Computing Services, the IBM PC/Tandy Round Tables, then select the Microsoft Round Table, and finally the Software Library.

If you do not subscribe to services such as CompuServe and GEnie, you can call Microsoft's internal bulletin board system, which is available free of hourly charges (you pay only for the telephone call). With your modem set to 8 data bits, no parity, and 1 stop bit (8N1), dial 206-936-6735 and follow the prompts.

Whichever of these bulletin boards you use to access the Windows Driver Library, you should first download and print a file called WDL.TXT. It is formatted so Windows Notepad can print it out perfectly.

WDL.TXT contains a list of all drivers in the library. Unfortunately, at the time of this writing, Microsoft included in WDL.TXT only the date of the *self-extracting file* stored in the library, not the date of the driver file that you might wish to upgrade. Therefore, you cannot easily compare the dates in WDL.TXT with the dates of your driver files to determine whether or not you need an upgraded driver. However, if WDL.TXT lists a driver that came with Windows 3.1, you can be almost certain that there are improvements in the version in the library that could make the driver worth downloading.

After reading the table at the end of this chapter, you should make a point to download WDL.TXT every month or two, just to see if any vendors have updated their drivers without notifying anyone. It's amazing how often drivers are updated — sometimes as often as once a month. These updates may fix vexing problems with Windows, but you rarely hear anything about the existence of these improvements. You would think the vendors would be shouting from the rooftops about how they improved the stability of their products with Windows, but they don't.

In addition, software and hardware vendors sometimes make new drivers for their products available on their own in-house bulletin board systems. Usually, these upgrades make it into Microsoft's Windows Driver Library, but in some cases they don't. The only way to know for sure is to contact the vendors whose products you rely on and ask them to provide you with details on their upgrade strategy.

Installing your new drivers

Each file in the WDL is in a self-extracting format. You must copy each file into a separate directory, and then, at a DOS prompt (not within Windows) type the name of the file, such as SPEAK for the SPEAK.EXE speaker driver.

Don't do this in the Windows directory, since the decompressing files will very likely have the same name as a file that Windows already depends on, and it may crash. For safety's sake, exit Windows and decompress all your files from a plain DOS prompt. (Why Microsoft doesn't provide upgraded files in a Windows self-extracting format, which correctly asks the user to name a temporary directory other than the Windows directory, I don't know. Maybe one day they'll get this together.)

Once you have decompressed each file, look for a documentation file, usually with a TXT extension, such as SPEAKER.TXT. You can read this in DOS using the command MORE<SPEAKER.TXT. (Notice that the less-than symbol points *toward* the word MORE. If you get it turned around, you'll wipe out the SPEAKER.TXT file you just downloaded.) This file should describe any steps you must take to install the driver.

At this point, it's a good idea to make a back-up copy of any files you are going to install the new driver over. Simply copy them to a floppy, or to a directory named something like ORIGINAL under your Windows directory.

Most drivers can be installed by restarting Windows and running the Control Panel or the Setup utility. You then run a dialog box, such as Printers, and click the Add button to add an "Unlisted or Updated Driver." When prompted, type the name of the directory where you decompressed the new drivers. The Control Panel or Setup will install them and make the necessary changes in WIN.INI and SYSTEM.INI, if any.

Some drivers, unfortunately, do not have a convenient install routine. These drivers require that you simply copy them over the old version, using a DOS command.

In a perfect world, there would be no need to constantly upgrade to better versions of software. But this isn't a perfect world, and certainly Windows isn't perfect yet. Until that day comes, we have the Windows Driver Library to forage in. Happy hunting!

Table 28-1:   The entire Windows Driver Library

	Download Filename	File Date
Software Applications		
Access Pack (eases keyboard and mouse actions)	ACCP.EXE	03/12/93
Arches Wallpaper	ARCHES.EXE	10/27/92
C and D printer fonts	CDFONT.EXE	07/10/92
Chitz Wallpaper	CHITZ.EXE	10/27/92
Chord Sound File	CHORD.EXE	10/27/92
Marble Wallpaper	MARBLE.EXE	10/27/92
MONOUMB.386	MONO.EXE	07/10/92
MSCDEX	CDEXT.EXE	07/10/92
MS-DOS Executive	MSEXE.EXE	08/12/92
Microsoft Mail Help	MMHELP.EXE	10/27/92
Microsoft Schedule Plus Help	SPHELP.EXE	10/27/92
Mystify Screen Saver	SSMYST.EXE	10/27/92
Novell NetWare & MS IPX Upgrade Utility	NOVELL.EXE	07/10/92
Reversi	REVERS.EXE	07/10/92
SYSINI.WRI	WRI.EXE	07/10/92
TADA Sound File	TADA.EXE	10/27/92
Tartan Wallpaper	TARTAN.EXE	10/27/92
VPD.386	VPD386.EXE	07/10/92
WININI.WRI	WRI.EXE	07/10/92

Audio Drivers

Artisoft Sounding Board - ISA, MCA	ARTIS.EXE	06/19/92
Creative Sound Blaster Pro, Pro Basic	CREAT.EXE	06/19/92
IBM M-Audio Adapter AT BUS, MCA	IBM.EXE	06/29/92
PC-Speaker Driver	SPEAK.EXE	06/19/92
Thunderboard	THUNDR.EXE	06/19/92

Display Drivers

Super VGA Driver		
256 colors at 640 x 480, 800 x 600, 1024 x 768	SVGA.EXE	04/30/93
CGA Driver	CGA.EXE	06/19/92
MCGA Driver		
VGA (320 x 200, 256 colors)	MMDISP.EXE	06/19/92
Palletized (Multimedia) VGA Driver		
VGA (640 x 480, palettized 16 colors)	MMDISP.EXE	06/19/92
VGAGRAY Driver		
VGA (640 x 480, 16 grays)	MMDISP.EXE	06/19/92
Appian RGDI & Compatibles	RGDI.EXE	06/19/92
ATI		
8514/Ultra, Graphics Ultra, Graphics Vantage, VGA Wonder, VGA Wonder XL, VGA Wonder Plus	ATI.EXE	06/19/92
Chips & Technology CHIPS 655XX	CHIPS.EXE	10/27/92
Cornerstone		
MC168Ci, PC168Ci, MC128Ci, PC128Ci	CORNST.EXE	08/19/93
DGIS 3.00 & Compatibles	DGIS30.EXE	10/08/92
HP UltraVGA V1.6	HPULT.EXE	02/03/93
S3 & Compatible Cards	S3.EXE	06/19/92
Tseng ET4000		
16 colors 640 x 480	TSEN1A.EXE	06/19/92
16 colors 800 x 600	TSEN1B.EXE	06/19/92

(continued)

	Download Filename	File Date
16 colors 1024 x 768	TSEN1C.EXE	06/19/92
16 colors 1280 x 1024	TSEN1D.EXE	06/19/92
256 colors 640 x 480	TSEN2A.EXE	06/19/92
256 colors 800 x 600	TSEN2B.EXE	06/19/92
256 colors 1024 x 768	TSEN2C.EXE	06/19/92
32,000 colors	TSENG3.EXE	06/19/92
64,000 colors	TSENG4.EXE	06/19/92
Western Digital/Paradise		
90C30-based boards	WD9030.EXE	02/03/93
90C31-based boards	WD9031.EXE	02/03/93

Printer Drivers

	Download Filename	File Date
Generic Printer Driver 1.68	GENDRV.EXE	02/03/93
Universal Printer Driver 3.1.2	UNIDRV.EXE	10/08/92
Microsoft PostScript Driver 3.56	PSCRIP.EXE	07/01/93
Agfa Compugraphic Genics	HPPCL.EXE	08/31/93
Apple		
LaserWriter Pro 600 & 630, Personal LaserWriter NTR	APPLE.EXE	07/01/93
Apricot Laser	HPPCL.EXE	08/31/93
Brother		
HJ-100, HJ-770, HL-4, HL-8, HL-8D, HL-8e	BROHL.EXE	10/08/92
M-1309, M-1809, M-1909	BRO9.EXE	10/08/92
M-1824L, M-1324, M-1924L	BRO24.EXE	10/08/92
Bull		
Compuprint 4/12, 4/14, 4/22, 4/23, 4/40, 4/41, 4/51, 4/52, 4/54, 4/64, 4/66, 4/68, 922N, 923, 924, 924N, 970, 1070, PageMaster 411, PageMaster 721, PageMaster 821, PageMaster 1021	BULL.EXE	10/08/92
Compuprint PM 201	JP350.EXE	12/09/92

	Download Filename	File Date
Canon		
Bubble-Jet BJ-10sx	BJ10.EXE	04/30/93
Bubble-Jet BJ-230	BJ230.EXE	04/30/93
Bubble-Jet BJ-10ex, BJ-130, BJ-20, BJC-800	CANON.EXE	10/08/92
Bubble-Jet BJ-300	CANON2.EXE	10/20/92
Bubble-Jet BJ-200, BJ-330	CANON3.EXE	12/09/92
Citizen		
120D, 120D+, 180D, 200GX, 200GX/15, HSP-500, HSP-550, Prodot 9, Prodot 9x, Swift 9, Swift 9x	CIT9.EXE	10/08/92
124D, 224, GSX-130, GSX-140, GSX-140+, GSX-145, PN48, Prodot 24, Swift 24, Swift 24x, Swift 24e	CIT24.EXE	10/08/92
PROjet	JP350.EXE	12/09/92
Diconix 150 Plus	DICONX.EXE	10/20/92
Compaq Pagemarq 15 & 20	COMPAQ.EXE	04/30/93
Digital		
DEClaser 1100, DEClaser 2100/Plus, DEClaser 2200/Plus, DEClaser 3200, LA70, LA75, LA75 Plus, LA324, LJ250/252, LN03/PLUS	DEC1.EXE	02/03/93
MultiJET 1000, 2000	JP350.EXE	12/09/92
Epson AP-3250, AP-5000, AP-5500, LQ-100, LQ-570, LQ-870, LQ-1070, LQ-1170, SQ-870, SQ-1170, Stylus 800	EPSON.EXE	06/24/93
DLQ-2000, L-750, L-1000, LQ-200, LQ-400, LQ-450, LQ-500, LQ-510, LQ-800, LQ-850, LQ-860, LQ-950, LQ-1000, LQ-1010, LQ-1050, LQ-1060, LQ-1500, LQ-2500, LQ-2550, SQ-850, SQ-2000, SQ-2500, SQ-2550	EP24.EXE	10/08/92
DFX-5000, EX-800, EX-1000, FX-80, FX-80+, FX-85, FX-86e, FX-100, FX-100+, FX-105, FX-185, FX-286, FX-286e, FX-800, FX-850, FX-1000, FX-1050, JX-80, LX-80, LX-86, LX-400, LX-800, LX-810, LX-850, LX-850+, MX-80, MX-80 F/T, MX-100, RX-80, RX-80 F/T, RX-80 F/T+, RX-100, RX-100+, T-750, T-1000	EP9.EXE	03/12/93

(continued)

	Download Filename	File Date
ActionLaser II, EPL-4000, EPL-7000	EPLZR.EXE	10/08/92
AP-3250 ESC/P 2, AP-5000 ESC/P 2, AP-5500 ESC/P 2, ESC/P2, LQ-100 ESC/P 2, LQ-570 ESC/P 2, LQ-570 Scalable Font, LQ-870 ESC/P 2, LQ-870 Scalable Font, LQ-1070 ESC/P 2, LQ-1070 Scalable Font, LQ-1170 ESC/P 2, LQ-1170 Scalable Font, SQ-870 ESC/P 2, SQ-1170 ESC/P 2	ESCP2.EXE	01/15/93
Fujitsu		
PrintPartner 10, 10/W (2MB)	FJ10W2.EXE	07/01/93
PrintPartner 10, 10/W (2MB+)	FJ10W3.EXE	07/01/93
Breeze 100, 200	JP350.EXE	12/09/92
DL 900, DL 1100, DL 1100 Colour, DL 1200, DL 3350, DL 3450, DL 3600, DL 4400, DL 4600	FUJI24.EXE	12/09/92
DX 2100, DX 2200, DX 2300, DX 2400	FUJI9.EXE	10/20/92
HP		
DeskJet, DeskJet Plus, DeskJet Portable, DeskJet 500, DeskJet 500C (monochrome), DeskJet 550C (monochrome)	HPDJET.EXE	07/01/93
LaserJet, Plus, 500+, 2000, II, IID, IIP, IIP Plus	HPPCL.EXE	08/31/93
LaserJet III, IIIP, IIID, IIISi	HPPCL5.EXE	11/16/92
LaserJet 4/4M, 4Si, 4Si MX	HPCL5E.EXE	06/24/93
PaintJet, PaintJet XL	HPPJET.EXE	10/08/92
QuietJet, QuietJet Plus	HPQJET.EXE	10/08/92
IBM		
Laser Printer 4029	IB4029.EXE	02/03/93
Personal Printer II 2380, 2381, 2390, 2391	IB2390.EXE	10/08/92
Proprinter X24, X24e, XL24, XL24e	PROP24.EXE	10/20/92
Proprinter, II, III, XL, XL II, XL III	PROP9.EXE	10/08/92
QuickWriter 5204	IB5204.EXE	11/16/92
QuietWriter III	QWIII.EXE	11/16/92

	Download Filename	File Date
Kyocera		
F-Series (USA), F-5000 (USA)	HPPCL.EXE	08/31/93
Linotronic		
100, 200/230, 300 v47.1, 300 v49.3, 330, 500, 530, 630	LINO.EXE	12/09/92
Mannesmann Tally		
MT 130/24, 130/9, 131/24, 131/9, 230/18, 230/24, 230/9, 290, 330, 340, 730/735, 81, 82, 90, 91, 92, 92C, 93, 94, 98/99	MANNT.EXE	10/08/92
Minolta		
SP1000, SP1500	MINOLT.EXE	04/30/93
NEC		
Pinwriter CP6, CP7, P2plus, P5XL, P6, P6plus, P7, P7plus, P9XL, P2200, P5200, P5300	NECP24.EXE	02/09/93
Pinwriter P3200, P3300, P6200, P6300, P9300	NECPIN.EXE	10/08/92
Silentwriter LC 860 Plus	HPPCL.EXE	08/31/93
Okidata		
LaserLine 6	HPPCL.EXE	08/31/93
ML 380, 390, 390 Plus, 391, 391 Plus, 393, 393 Plus, 393C, 393C Plus	OKI24.EXE	10/08/92
OL-400, OL-800	OKILED.EXE	10/08/92
OL-830	OK830.EXE	07/01/93
Olivetti		
DM 124 C	OLIVE.EXE	02/03/93
ETV 5000, PG 108, PG 208 M2, PG 308 HS	HPPCL.EXE	08/31/93
JP 150, JP 350, JP 350S	JP350.EXE	12/09/92
PG 108, PG 208 M2	HPPCL.EXE	10/08/92
PG 306, PG 308	OLIPG.EXE	11/16/92
Panasonic		
KX-P1081, KX-P1180, KX-P1695, KX-P2180	PAN9.EXE	02/09/93

(continued)

	Download Filename	File Date
KX-P1123, KX-P1124, KX-P1124i, KX-P1624, KX-P2123, KX-P2124, KX-P2624	PAN24.EXE	12/09/92
KX-P4420	HPPCL.EXE	08/31/93
KX-P4450, KX-P4450i	PANKX.EXE	10/20/92
QMS		
PS 2000, PS-2200	PS2000.EXE	07/01/93
QuadLaser I	HPPCL.EXE	08/31/93
Royal CJP 450	OLIVE.EXE	02/03/93
Seiko (Generic Printer Driver)		
CH 5504, CH 5514, CH 4104	SEIKO.EXE	02/03/93
Seiko (Postscript Driver)		
CH 5504 (PS)	SEIKO2.EXE	07/01/93
CH 5514 (PS)	CH5514.EXE	07/01/93
CH 4104 (PS)	PS4104.EXE	07/01/93
Sharp		
JX-9300, JX-9500, JX-9500E, JX-9500H, JX-9700	SHARP.EXE	10/08/92
Star		
Laserprinter 4, Laserprinter 8, Laserprinter 8 DB, Laserprinter 8 DX, Laserprinter 8 II, NB24-10, NB24-15, Rainbow, NX-1500, NX-2400, NX-2410, NX-2415, NX-2420, NX-2420 Rainbow, NX-2430, SJ-48, XB-2410, XB-2415, XB-2420, XB-2425, XR-1000, XR-1020, XR-1500, XR-1520	STAR.EXE	10/08/92
Tandy LP-1000	HPPCL.EXE	08/31/93
Tegra Genesis	HPPCL.EXE	08/31/93
Tektronix		
Phaser 2200e 17, Phaser 200e 39, Phaser 200i	TEKTRO.EXE	07/01/93
TI		
Omnilaser 2108, Omnilaser 2115	TIOMNI.EXE	07/01/93
Toshiba		
ExpressWriter 420, ExpressWriter 440	EXPRSS.EXE	10/08/92
PageLaser12	HPPCL.EXE	08/31/93

	Download Filename	File Date
P351, P1351	TOSH24.EXE	08/12/92
P351SX	P351SX.EXE	10/08/92
Unisys		
AP-1324, AP-1337, AP-1339	UNI24.EXE	10/08/92
AP-1371	UN1371.EXE	10/08/92
AP-9205/AP-9210	UNILZ.EXE	10/08/92
AP-9210	HPPCL.EXE	08/31/93
Wang LDP8	HPPCL.EXE	08/31/93

Network Adapter Drivers

3Com		
EtherLink, EtherLink/MC 32	3COM.EXE	11/16/92
EtherLink 16 (3C507)	ELNK16.EXE	04/02/93
EtherLink III (3C509), EtherLink EISA (3C579)	ELNK3.EXE	04/02/93
EtherLink II (3C503), EtherLink II/16 TP (3C505 16-TP)	ELNKII.EXE	04/02/93
EtherLink MC (3C523)	ELNKMC.EXE	04/02/93
EtherLink Plus (3C505-B)	ELNKPL.EXE	04/02/93
TokenLink III (3C619), TokenLink III (3C629)	IBMTOK.EXE	04/02/93
Accton Technology		
EtherCoax-16 (EN1642), EtherCombo-16 (EN1640), EtherPair-16 (EN1641)	NE2000.EXE	04/02/93
Advanced Micro Devices		
AM2100, PCnet-ISA Ethernet Controller	AM2100.EXE	04/02/93
Alta Research EtherCombo-16 T/C	NE2000.EXE	04/02/93
Allied Telesis		
AT1500T, AT1500BT, AT1500FT	AT1500.EXE	03/12/93
Apricot		
LS 386SX-20 w/i82592, XEN-LS 486SX-20 w/i82592	ETH592.EXE	03/12/93
LS PRO w/i82596	ETH596.EXE	03/12/93

(continued)

	Download Filename	File Date
Cabletron		
E2000 Series DNI, E2100 Series DNI	CTRON.EXE	04/02/93
E3000 Series DNI, E3100 Series DNI	CTETH.EXE	04/02/93
T2015 Token Ring DNI, T3015 Token Ring DNI	CTTOK.EXE	04/02/93
Compaq		
32-bit DualSpeed Token Ring, 32-bit NetFlex Controller	NETFLX.EXE	03/12/93
Compex ENET16/U	COMPEX.EXE	10/27/92
Crescendo Communications C321M	CRESDO.EXE	03/12/93
Digital Communications Associates (DCA)		
10-Net, 10-Net Fiber Optic, 10-Net Twisted Pair, 10-Net MCA	DCA586.EXE	10/27/92
IRMAtrac Token-Ring Convert	IRMA.EXE	03/12/93
Digital Equipment Corporation		
Etherworks LC, Etherworks MC, Etherworks Turbo, DEPCA	DEPCA.EXE	04/02/93
WaveLAN AT	WAVELN.EXE	04/02/93
Everex SpeedLink /PC16 (EV2027)	EVEREX.EXE	10/27/92
Gateway Communications G/Ethernet 16 Combo	GETHER.EXE	03/12/93
HP		
EtherTwist MCA (HP27246)	HPLAN2.EXE	03/12/93
PC LAN Adapter/8 TL (HP27250), PC LAN Adapter/8 TP (HP27245), PC LAN Adapter/16 TP (HP27247A), PC LAN Adapter/16 TL Plus (HP27252), PC LAN Adapter/16 TP Plus (HP27247B), Ethertwist EISA LAN 32-HP27248	HPLAN.EXE	10/28/92
IBM		
PC Network Adapter II, II/A, Baseband Adapter, Baseband Adapter/A	IBMNET.EXE	10/27/92
PCMCIA-NIC	IBMPCM.EXE	10/27/92
Token Ring, Token Ring /A, Token Ring II, Token Ring 4/16, Token Ring 4/16 A	IBMTOK.EXE	04/02/93
ICL EtherTeam 16	NOKIA.EXE	03/12/93

	Download Filename	File Date
Intel Corporation		
EtherExpress 16, 16 TPE, 16C, 16TP, MCA, MCA TP	EXP16.EXE	04/02/93
EtherExpress TPE Hub Adptr	INTHUB.EXE	10/27/92
Token Express MCA 16/4, EISA 16/4, ISA 16/4	OLITOK.EXE	04/02/93
Madge		
Smart 16/4 XT RingNode, AT RingNode, EISA RingNode, MC RingNode	MADGE.EXE	10/27/92
National SemiConductor		
At/Lantic EtherNODE 16*AT3, EtherNODE *16AT	NE2000.EXE	04/02/93
PCMCIA Ethernet, Sonic EISA-DP83932EB	NATSEM.EXE	04/02/93
NCR		
StarCard (8-bit)	NCRSTR.EXE	10/27/92
StarLAN 16/4 Token MC NAU	STRN.EXE	04/02/93
WaveLan AT Adapter, WaveLan MC Adapter	WAVELN.EXE	04/02/93
Novell		
NE1000	NE1000.EXE	04/02/93
NE/2, NE2000, NE2000T	NE2000.EXE	04/02/93
Olivetti		
Olicom 16 bit EISA 16/4, ISA 16/4, MCA 16/4	OLITOK.EXE	04/02/93
Proteon		
ISA Token Ring 1340, 1342, 1346, 1347	PRO4.EXE	03/12/93
ISA Token Ring 1346, 1347	PRO4AT.EXE	03/12/93
ISA Token Ring 1390, 1392	P139X.EXE	04/02/93
MCA Token Ring 1840	PRO4.EXE	03/12/93
ProNET-4/16 p1892	PROTEO.EXE	04/30/93
Proxim RangeLAN Wireless	PROXIM.EXE	03/12/93
Pure Data		
PDE9025-32 16/4, PDI9025-16 4, PDuC9025 16/4	OLITOK.EXE	04/02/93
PDI8023-16, PDI8023-8, PDuC8023	PDIETH.EXE	10/27/92
PDI90211 (Wireless), PDuC90211 (Wireless)	WAVELN.EXE	04/02/93

(continued)

	Download Filename	File Date
Racal-Datacom		
ES3210, NI5210/8, NI5210/16, NI9210, Interlan ILANAT	RACAL.EXE	10/27/92
NI6510	NI6510.EXE	04/02/93
Standard Microsystems		
SMC 3000 Series	SMC3.EXE	04/02/93
SMC PC130, SMC PC130E, SMC PC130W, SMC PC130WS	SMCARC.EXE	04/02/93
SMC 8003E/A, SMC 8003EP, SMC 8003EPC, SMC 8013EPC, SMC 8003EWC, SMC 8003WC	SMCMAC.EXE	04/02/93
Thomas Conrad		
TC6042, TC6045, TC6142, TC6145, TC6242, TC6245	TCCARC.EXE	03/12/93
Token Ring Adapter	TCCTOK.EXE	10/27/92
Tiara EtherStar LanCard/E	TIARA.EXE	10/27/92
Tulip NCC-16	TULIP.EXE	10/27/92
Ungermann-Bass		
NIC/ps, NIU (All Types), NIUpc (PC2030), NIUpc/3270, NIUpc/EOTP (PC4035), NIUps (PC3030), NIUps/EOTP (PC3035), pcNIU, pcNIU/ex 128K, pcNIU/ex 512K	UB.EXE	03/12/93
Xircom		
Pocket Ethernet I, Pocket Ethernet II	XIRCOM.EXE	03/12/93
Zenith Data Systems		
Z.Note 325L Notebook PC	IMLM.EXE	04/02/93

Summary

In this chapter, I explore the almost-unknown Windows Driver Library — a vast storehouse of improved drivers for printers, video boards, network adapters, and many other types of peripherals — and describe how you can take advantage of it, once you've learned about it.

▶ I describe how dynamic link libraries (DLLs) can affect the performance and reliability of your system, and how you can safely install them in your Windows configuration.

▶ I publish an extensive list, sorted by vendor, of every driver available in the Windows Driver Library, including many that enhance Windows independently of any particular peripheral, such as the speaker driver that allows PCs without special multimedia hardware to play sound files.

Chapter 29

The *Real* Cost of Switching to Windows

In This Chapter

▶ I examine the hidden costs of converting DOS PCs to Windows-capable PCs so you can avoid unpleasant and unplanned economic surprises when you upgrade multiple systems.

▶ I describe a detailed report on the dollars-and-cents of Windows upgrades and tell how you can get your own copy, complete with diskette.

Most Windows managers have, by now, become aware of the fact that converting the PCs in your company from an all-DOS operating system to a Windows environment costs more than the $49 or so that you spent for the Windows diskettes.

But how *much* more, exactly, does the conversion actually cost your company? And is the cost justified by specific gains?

One organization has taken a commendable stab at answering these questions with hard facts. Rather than making guesses about all the hardware and software costs involved in an upgrade, the Microcomputer Managers Association (MMA) — a New York-based national organization — polled PC managers who had already gone through much of the conversion process.

The MMA sent its poll to about 900 members, and received back about 46 percent of the printed surveys. A dollar bill was enclosed to encourage responses, but this can't explain the high level of feedback. Anyone who has ever dealt with polling recognizes that this is a phenomenal rate of return. PC managers seem to have very strong feelings about the conversion to Windows, which they don't mind sharing.

While the response may have been broad, it should also be remembered that the survey reflects the findings of companies that are larger than average. About one-fourth of the companies surveyed had 1992 sales of $1 billion or more. In terms of number of PCs, 23 percent of the survey respondents were responsible for more than 500 PCs, 44 percent for 100 to 500 PCs, and 33 percent for fewer than 100 PCs.

Larger companies, of course, may make larger expenditures. But even considering the size of the companies surveyed, the results should be relevant, whether you are planning to upgrade 100 PCs or 1,000.

The survey found that the median costs for converting PCs to Windows (half of the companies spent more than this, while half spent less) were as follows:

Hardware	$1,020
Software	776
Training	497
Service/Support	471
Total	$2,764

The MMA did not ask the respondents to include the cost of networking hardware or software, reasoning that companies would have added such items eventually, whether or not they moved to Windows. More significantly, the MMA did not ask respondents to quantify the cost of switching in-house development to a graphical rather than a DOS-based environment, or other long-term costs.

You would expect to find a high cost for adding hardware and software when converting PCs to Windows. But a surprising cost that is often overlooked is training and support, which amount to several hundreds of dollars per user.

Despite these costs, the MMA found that only 10 percent of respondents are trying to measure the cost savings that might result from Windows. This is probably because the respondents strongly felt that graphical interfaces are a "strategic platform" for their companies, and were ultimately less expensive than trying to continue to use character-mode systems.

One of the most notable parts of the MMA's report is a diskette that allows you to calculate your own costs and projected benefits. Whether your company has already converted many PCs, or only a few, I recommend you try out this disk.

The MMA sells its report, *The Real Cost of the Graphical User Interface*, as a fundraiser for the organization for $50. But a better deal is to join the organization for $75, which gets you an interesting newsletter plus the report for free.

For more information, contact: MMA, P.O. Box 4615, Warren, NJ 07059; 212-787-1122. You can charge membership and the report to an American Express or Optima credit card.

Summary

In this chapter, I cite specific numbers that quantify the DOS-to-Windows conversion cost in a wide variety of companies.

▶ The average cost per PC was over $2,750, more than one-third of which was for training and support. The total doesn't count the cost of networking or the expense of switching in-house developers from character-based to graphical programming tools.

▶ A complete report is available from the Microcomputer Managers Association, which includes its publication in the cost of membership.

Chapter 30

Unwelcome Guests: Uninstalling Windows Applications

In This Chapter

▶ I walk you step-by-step through a procedure to examine and delete unwanted old Windows applications from your hard disk in order to free valuable storage space.

▶ I describe a much easier way, which involves an inexpensive utility that does almost all the work for you.

One of the most difficult things to do with a Windows application, after installing it and learning it, is to uninstall it.

It used to be so easy to uninstall an application. DOS applications usually install themselves into a single directory, perhaps with a few subdirectories below that. If a DOS application made any changes to your system, it usually limited itself to adding a line to your AUTOEXEC.BAT file. When you wanted to delete the application, you could do so by simply deleting the application's directory and all its subdirectories, and removing references to it in AUTOEXEC.BAT.

Windows apps are not quite so simple. It seems that Windows applications love to spread files all around your disk. How do you know what can be deleted and what's needed by Windows? What's worse, Windows users have a more serious problem with "disk full" conditions, and thus a greater need to delete unused software, because Windows applications tend to be much larger than DOS apps.

In this chapter, I'll provide a step-by-step approach to deleting unused Windows applications so you can reclaim valuable hard disk space. First, I'll describe a method that's totally *free*, but requires some detective work on your part. Second, I'll tell you about a utility that will do a lot of the work for you for as little as $19.

The Way It Oughta Be

Of course, nothing on uninstalling Windows apps should ever be written without a few choice words for software developers who don't include an easy-to-use Uninstall option one or two levels down in their menu structure. With the complexity of Windows software today, it's more important than ever that users be able to access some sort of Uninstall menu item. (Grammatically, Uninstall should really be called Deinstall. But since the whole computer industry has adopted terms like "uninstall" and "unformat," I'll follow the same terminology in this chapter.)

For those software developers who ask, "Why should I create an Uninstall menu item, when I want people to *use* my software, not delete it?", I have a simple answer. More people will install and try your application if they know that they can easily remove the program and reclaim their hard disk space after their testing is complete. Since the people who most often install, test, and delete software packages are volume software buyers for large companies (and writers of computer books), software vendors should see the wisdom of giving these users (and everyone else) a quick way to install and uninstall all applications. This includes a menu item that allows users to delete unneeded modules — such as drawing routines, symbol fonts, and Help systems — to free precious megabytes of storage.

Windows 3.1 is a good example of a program that has become much better in its support for uninstalling components of itself. If you choose the Custom setup over the Express setup when you first install Windows (which I recommend for everyone, even if you simply select the default installation), the Setup program allows you to define those components (wallpaper and so on) that you do or do not wish to copy to your hard disk.

After you've installed Windows, you can still run Setup and use it to delete various components. To do this, double-click the Windows Setup icon in Program Manager, or click File Run and type SETUP. Once the Setup window is running, pull down its Options menu and click Add/Remove Windows Components. The dialog box that appears gives you several choices of accessories and other components to delete — all the way down to deleting individual files.

If you're not sure whether or not to delete an individual file in Windows, the Windows manual actually gives you some guidance on several files you can remove without affecting Windows' essential operations. Check the chapter of the manual entitled Optimizing Windows. The manual's suggestions break into roughly two categories: deleting all files with a BMP extension (which are bitmaps used for wallpaper), and deleting a list of accessories you probably don't use, such as CALENDAR.EXE and its help file, CALENDAR.HLP. However, I don't recommend you delete WRITE.EXE, one of the suggestions, because many utilities and shareware applications depend on Windows Write to display and print their documentation for you.

In case the Windows manual isn't specific enough for you, a complete list of the files that come on the Windows 3.1 diskettes is described in the Windows Resource Kit, a 500-page book with technical information about Windows. This book is available for $19.95 by calling Microsoft at 206-882-8080.

Deleting Applications You Don't Need

Let's say that you've already deleted all the Windows accessories you don't use, but you still are short of hard disk space. You decide to delete an old Windows app that you never use any more, but you don't have any record of what files it installed and the app has no Uninstall option.

The following steps are my recommended procedure for removing any such application from your hard disk:

STEPS

Deleting Old Windows Applications

Step 1. Examine the application's main directory. Most applications install most of their files into a single directory. This might have been a directory you specified when you installed the application. Or it might have been determined for you by the application automatically.

In either case, open the Windows File Manager and open a directory window showing the application's main directory. If you don't know which directory that is, look in the Program Manager for an icon for that application. Highlight the icon by clicking it once, then click File Properties on Program Manager's menu. Chances are that the application's main directory shows up in the command line for that icon, such as C:\MYAPP\MYAPP.EXE.

Once you have changed to C:\MYAPP in a File Manager window, click View Sort-By-Date to see the files displayed in order from newest to oldest. If you can't see specific dates of the files in the window, enlarge the window and click View All-File-Details so the dates show up.

Write down any dates that seem to be common to several files. (Developers usually give all the files in an application the same date every time they release a major upgrade.) We will look for files with these dates in other directories later, in order to weed out unneeded files that may have been written to these other directories.

If you like, you can print out a listing of the files in date order, for later reference during this procedure. The Windows File Manager, strangely, has no way to print a file listing. But you can print out a list of the files in approximate date order by typing a single command. In the File Manager, click File Run and type the following command:

```
COMMAND /C DIR x:\directory | SORT /+24 > LPT1
```

Replace *x:\directory* with the main directory for your application. This command starts a DOS session, pipes a directory listing into the SORT command, sorts it on the 24th column, and sends the output to the printer on your LPT1 port.

If your text printer is on another port, such as COM1, replace LPT1 in this command with COM1.

If you have your PC set up for a language in which directory date strings appear in day-month-year order (as in Europe) instead of month-day-year (as in the U.S.), use the following command to sort on the month and year:

```
COMMAND /C DIR x:\directory | SORT /+27 > LPT1
```

In either case, these commands will create a rough sort of the file dates. The SORT command, in the U.S. date order sorts only the month and day (since they come first in the listing). Years like '92 and '93 sort in random order. But this sort should be accurate enough for the work we will do in the next few steps.

Step 2. Back up your files, then delete the directory. If your application's main directory, or any subdirectories, contains documents or other data files you've created, this is the time to copy those files to a diskette or other backup medium. That way, if you delete the application, but later decide you need to use a particular document, you can reinstall the app and open the desired file.

After backing up or moving any such data files, delete the application's main directory and any subdirectories. The easiest way to do this is to highlight the main directory in a File Manager window, then click File Delete and respond to any confirmation messages you receive.

If you're afraid to actually delete the application's directory at this point, you can rename the directory by clicking File Rename in File Manager. A few days later, after you reassure yourself that none of the files in that directory are really needed by any other Windows application, you can finally delete the renamed directory.

Step 3. Delete icons from Program Manager. Switch to the Program Manager and delete any icons or group windows created by the now-defunct application. This is a good point to check the File Properties of a few icons to see if any other directories contain files that you should also delete.

Step 4. Delete files from other directories. Beyond the application's own main directory, applications typically install files into some or all of the following locations:

The Windows directory, such as C:\WINDOWS.

The System subdirectory, such as C:\WINDOWS\SYSTEM.

The root directory, normally C:\.

To find files that should be deleted from these directories, change to each directory in the File Manager, and view each directory sorted by date. Using the dates you noted in Step 1, look for files that stick out with dates that are not shared by other files in the same directory.

For example, in the C:\WINDOWS directory, most of the files that correspond with Windows 3.1 have a file date of March 10, 1992 (3/10/92, the date Windows 3.1 went into the diskette manufacturing process — a little Microsoft internal joke, "three one oh," get it?). If you see files with dates other than March 10, 1992 in this directory, and they match the dates in your application's main directory, you have good reason to suspect that these files are part of the old application and can be scrapped. The same goes for files you find in the C:\WINDOWS\SYSTEM directory and the C:\ root directory.

Unless you're absolutely sure about these files, however, you are better off temporarily moving them rather than immediately deleting them. That way, if you start Windows and get an error message like "Cannot find file MYAPP.DLL," you can still move the file back to its original location.

Therefore, create a directory called HOLD under the directory you are examining, and move suspect files into that directory, rather than deleting them. Make a note to yourself to delete these files a few days or weeks from now. If you're really paranoid, copy these files to a floppy for safekeeping before deleting them entirely.

Be careful moving files that don't have the name of the deleted application (or an acronym) within them. Some applications install files that are also required by other applications. Visual Basic applications, for example, may install VBRUN200.DLL or similar files into the Windows directory. If you install another Visual Basic app, it will see the existence of VBRUN200.DLL and not install it again. But if you delete the first Visual Basic application and also VBRUN200.DLL, the second Visual Basic application will refuse to run.

Besides VBRUN*x*00.DLL, other files that are commonly required by multiple applications are COMMDLG.DLL and TOOLHELP.DLL. Don't delete or move files with these names from the Windows or System directories. (If you find these files in an application's main directory, however, it's OK to delete them, since they must have been used only by that application. In any case, you don't need more copies of these files than one, if they are located in the proper Windows directory.)

Step 5. Remove unneeded lines in WIN.INI, SYSTEM.INI, other INI Files, CONFIG.SYS, and AUTOEXEC.BAT. You can open and edit WIN.INI, SYSTEM.INI, and other configuration files with NOTEPAD.EXE or SYSEDIT.EXE (an editing utility that comes with Windows). You can save a bit of memory in Windows and slightly improve its loading time by removing sections that your deleted application wrote in WIN.INI. You may also find some drivers that your application wrote into SYSTEM.INI, which now will cause "File Not Found" errors if the lines refer to files that existed in directories that no longer exist.

In WIN.INI, it is fairly easy to locate lines written by old applications. This is because Windows applications tend to locate these lines in sections headed by the name of the application itself.

For example, if you had an application called My Spreadsheet, you may find a section in WIN.INI that looks like the following:

```
[My Spreadsheet]
configuration=1
options=2 3 4
```

When you find such lines, the safest way to remove them is to first turn them into remarks that are not loaded by Windows. To do this, add a semicolon (;) and a space to the beginning of each line. (The space is simply for readability.) Windows ignores anything after a semicolon in WIN.INI, SYSTEM.INI, and other INI files. This change would make the above section look as follows:

```
; [My Spreadsheet]
; configuration=1
; options=2 3 4
```

By remarking out these lines, you can find out the next time you start Windows whether any application really did need these statements. If you see a message like, "Can't find configuration information — using defaults," you can restore the lines to full effect by removing the semicolons and the leading space.

The same principle holds true for SYSTEM.INI. You may find a line like the following:

```
device=c:\myapp\driver.drv
```

The reference to the C:\MYAPP directory is a tip-off that this line was probably installed by the application you just deleted. Re-marking out this line can help you find out whether it is actually needed by more than one application.

When you remove lines from WIN.INI and SYSTEM.INI, you run the risk that you will do something that keeps Windows from running properly, or even loading at all. For this reason, before you edit them to files named WIN.OLD and SYSTEM.OLD or similar. (SysEdit automatically creates files called WIN.SYD, SYSTEM.SYD, and so on, if you make any changes in these files using SysEdit.) That way, if Windows won't start, you can restore these files to their original condition by changing to the Windows directory at a DOS prompt and typing commands like the following:

```
C:
CD \windows
COPY WIN.OLD WIN.INI
COPY SYSTEM.OLD SYSTEM.INI
```

If Windows won't start, but you *didn't* make backups first, you can also restore these files (if you're using DOS 5.0) by typing EDIT WIN.INI and using the DOS 5 Edit utility to remove the semi-colons from lines you remarked out.

Uninstalling the Easy Way

If the steps I've described above seem complicated, they are. These steps are an exhaustive process to look for every file and setting — in every place they might be located.

A much easier way to uninstall Windows applications, but one that requires a little forethought, is to use a shareware application called Uninstall for Windows, Version 1.1. This program is a utility that you run at a DOS prompt before installing a Windows application. After the app is installed, you run Uninstall for Windows again, and it creates a list of changes that were made to directories and files. To uninstall the application, you reverse the changes that Uninstall for Windows found.

Uninstall for Windows, interestingly, is a DOS program, not a Windows program. This is because some applications do not write all their settings until they are run once and then closed. Even some of Windows own applications, such as Program Manager, write some changes when they are closed. By running Uninstall for Windows before and after a Windows installation session, you are assured that these types of changes have been recorded.

Since Uninstall for Windows has a very simple menu, with only five choices, it really doesn't need a Windows interface anyway. The menu choices are: Do System Survey, Compare Old System to New, Look At Report, Help, and Quit. What could be simpler? For those who want to run the utility under Windows, the developer, It's Your Money, Inc., provides a customized PIF file and an Uninstall icon to place in Program Manager. The utility works fine under Windows, except for those cases I mentioned earlier where some changes are not written until Windows is exited.

Each time you compare your old system to your new one, Uninstall creates the file REPORT.TXT. Looking in this file (from the menu or with the included text editor) will give you an exact listing of changes to your files and INI settings. You are responsible for saving this report under a different name after viewing it, since Uninstall uses the same filename every time it runs (which is one weakness in this utility).

Using Uninstall for Windows is a major improvement over the guesswork involved if you try to look through all of your Windows directories and INI files manually. And, best of all, the cost is low. It's only $19 postpaid from It's Your Money, Inc., 3 Floyd Drive, Mt. Arlington, NJ 07856. If you have a CompuServe account, a shareware copy of the utility is available in the GO IBMSYS forum; select Libraries, then choose the Multitasking library, and download the file UN4WIN.ZIP. You need PKUNZIP or another program that decompresses files to expand UN4WIN.ZIP into its usable components. It's Your Money, Inc., provides technical support via CompuServe account 72621,2222 and America OnLine account IYM.

Until the day when all Windows applications include Uninstall options on their menus, uninstalling applications manually or using utilities like this one is a necessary chore. Good luck.

Summary

In this chapter, uninstalling Windows applications is examined.

▶ We see that a detailed, five-step process can help isolate and eliminate files that Windows applications have installed into a variety of different directories on your hard disk.

▶ Although this method is usually successful, for an investment of only $19, Uninstall for Windows can automate almost all of the detective work that would ordinarily be involved.

Chapter 31
Networking Windows Tips

In This Chapter

▶ I discuss tips about running Windows on network configurations, both in general and on specific networks.

▶ Novell NetWare, Banyan Vines, and Microsoft LAN Manager all have specific settings and files that should be used for compatibility with Windows.

I've been traveling frequently to speak at Windows seminars, so I've been on a lot of planes lately.

Due to some recent air safety incidents where passengers couldn't manage to get out the exit doors, the Federal Aviation Administration passed new regulations. Anyone seated in a row with an exit must be capable of opening the doors and understanding English well enough to follow instructions to do so. The airlines must also inform anyone seated in these rows of these requirements.

To comply, United Airlines printed a plastic card, which it placed in the seat pockets. The card begins, "If you are sitting in an exit row and you cannot read this card, please tell a crew member."

Perhaps you've heard of the rural county where they have a similar approach to flood-control emergencies. A large lake in the area threatens to burst its dike and flood the town below when the water level reaches a certain height. The authorities in the area sank a pole into the lake bottom and posted a sign atop the pole. It reads, "If this sign is under water, call Flood Control at 555-3344."

Well, if you're the kind of person who can follow directions on cards you can't read, or dial phone numbers printed on signs that are hidden under water, then you're fully qualified to follow Microsoft's obscure instructions on how to manage Windows across a network.

It's not that there's *no* information on networking Windows. The Windows manual contains four pages called "Putting Windows on a Network," which describe how to decompress the files from the Windows diskettes to a network drive. Then there is NETWORKS.WRI, a Windows Write file tucked away in the Windows directory, which you should print and read. Finally, Microsoft includes a 28-page section called "Networks and Windows" in the Windows Resource Kit, which documents how Windows interacts with various vendors' network software. (The kit is available for $20 by calling 800-642-7676 or 206-882-8080, and you should obtain it immediately.) A similiar resource kit is also available for Windows for Workgroups (WFWG). It includes tips such as how to disable WFWG's peer-to-peer features, if these are not necessary in your environment but you want to use WFWG's new File Manager toolbar and other enhancements to the Windows interface.

It's just that there is no comprehensive, step-by-step guide that takes you by the hand and shows you why and how you can get the maximum benefit out of networking Windows in your company.

I covered many of these steps in *Windows 3.1 Secrets* (especially the Networking and Converting Your Company to Windows chapters), so I won't duplicate that here. But it's a shame that the esoteric knowledge of how to network Windows isn't more widely available and understood, because the benefits can be so great.

Let me clear up a few myths right away: Windows does *not* run more slowly on a network than any other application, if it's set up using one or two tricks (described in this chapter). And Windows users are *not* necessarily hard to manage on a network.

Quite the contrary. Almost every setting that controls Windows is contained in a few files such as WIN.INI. You can locate these files in network subdirectories, and place the appropriate subdirectory on each user's Path. Then it requires only a few minutes for a supervisor to batch-edit new features into each person's WIN.INI — when you need to put a new utility on the LOAD= line, for example. Compare this to the days or weeks that are required to walk around and make a change to AUTOEXEC.BAT files in every local hard drive in your company.

Novell actually produces one of the best Windows networking guides, useful for managers of almost any network. This publication, *NetWare Application Notes* (January 1991) is available for $10 by calling 801-429-5511. See the Resources section later in this chapter for additional information.

Getting all the configurations right to run Windows across networks is a hassle, I admit. But once you've got it working, and you can edit *.INI files for people without having to hike all over your company, I think you'll agree it's worth it.

The Fine Art of Networking _____

Over the past 10 years, local area networks (LANs) have gradually become an accepted part of computing in companies around the world. And during the past few years, Microsoft Windows has become an accepted computing environment as well.

Now, many companies are grappling with the art of combining the two technologies into a single, functioning whole.

The benefits of installing and running Windows across a network, as opposed to installing it one copy at a time on individual PC hard drives, can be enormous.

Case studies in firms that have tried it both ways find that the labor costs alone of supporting standalone installations can be 3 to 10 times higher than labor costs for supporting networked installations.

When Windows is installed on individual hard drives in a company's PCs, a simple change — such as adding a single utility command to each user's WIN.INI file — requires that support personnel travel to each machine to perform the edit. If these files are stored on a network server's drives, by contrast, a network administrator can add the command to each WIN.INI by running a batch editor from a single workstation.

The costs of software licensing can amount to even greater differences. When software is installed onto the hard disks of individual PCs, copyright law requires that a license fee be paid for every copy made. When software is installed on a network hard drive, however, a company can use "concurrent licensing" to legally pay only for the number of copies of the software *in use* at any one moment.

The number of users who actually run a piece of software at the height of a typical business day can easily be as few as one-half or one-third of the total number who *ever* need to run the software. This translates directly into licensing costs only one-half to one-third as much as that of standalone installations.

These benefits of networking Windows, however, do not come without serious planning. Windows, more than most software, writes directly to PC hardware. Microsoft's graphical environment, therefore, turns up incompatibilities among different, supposedly compatible peripherals more readily than other PC software.

Even this exposure of incompatibilities can be turned into an asset by astute network managers, however. Windows provides an excellent reason for a company to retire aging PC components that would otherwise linger on users' desktops for years.

Windows conversion considerations

The early adopters of Windows on a network have found that the process is a little more difficult than simply decompressing the Windows files onto their server drives, as described in the NETWORKS.WRI file that comes with Windows.

After the decompression step comes a series of steps that must be developed and tested for reliability by each adopting company. Some of these steps are the same, regardless of the company's network configuration.

Most companies, for instance, find it necessary to upgrade some or all of their PCs to improve Windows' performance and reduce the number of different components that must be supported. Certain changes in Windows' WIN.INI and SYSTEM.INI files are also implemented by most network managers. For example, settings in the SYSTEM.INI file that determine where Windows locates its 386 paging file, and the maximum paging file size, are usually necessary when running Windows across a network. (These steps are described later in this chapter.)

Making your network safe for Windows

After software management issues have been resolved, hardware and network "shell" issues must be tested. Again, Windows can unearth potential problems that many companies could have or should have dealt with earlier — Windows simply provides a reason to fix these situations once and for all.

The amount of memory required for DOS applications to run under Windows, for example, can act as an incentive for a company to upgrade to a newer version of DOS or their network shell — a step that otherwise might be put off indefinitely.

Newer operating systems, such as Microsoft's MS-DOS 5.0 or 6.x, or Novell's DR DOS 6.0 or 7.0, can move programs (including DOS itself) into Upper Memory Blocks (UMBs) above 640K, thereby freeing significant chunks of conventional PC memory located below 640K. Additionally, third-party memory managers such as QEMM386 by Quarterdeck Office Systems and 386Max by Qualitas can provide benefits above and beyond those included with both versions of DOS.

Network interface cards (NICs) can cause their own conflicts. Almost all NICs use some upper memory block addresses for buffer RAM chips located on the board. When users load their network software before starting the Windows environment, Windows can usually detect that this memory is in use, and no problems occur. If users start Windows and then open a DOS window and try to load the network software, however, the RAM on the adapter can come into play unexpectedly, hanging the PC. (You should never logon to a network from within a DOS session under Windows.)

Other conflicts can be more subtle. Microsoft's language compilers use the PC I/O address of 2E0 hex to call screen-scrolling functions. Some network interface cards can also be configured to use this I/O address, which guarantees a dispute with Windows over turf. The solution is to change the NIC's I/O address to another selection, using switches or software provided with the board. Until this conflict is diagnosed, however, network users with boards configured in this way will experience problems every time Windows is started. (At least they don't get far enough to cause any real damage.)

Finally, certain changes fall into the category of network-specific issues. Microsoft officially supports network operating systems as diverse as Novell NetWare, Banyan Vines, and LAN Manager. Additionally, networks with smaller markets, such as DEC Pathworks, DCA 10Net, and Artisoft LANtastic are supported. Each of these networks has its own set of configuration settings and steps necessary to prepare network users for Windows.

The following sections describe some of the issues commonly confronted by users of NetWare, Vines, and LAN Manager.

Novell NetWare

One of the most important issues facing NetWare administrators is the need to upgrade to a version of the NetWare shell programs (NETX.COM and other files) that support Windows. After Windows 3.0 was released in May 1990, Novell distributed at least five new versions of these shell programs in the succeeding six months — version 3.01 revision A, B, C, D, and E — and the pace has hardly slowed since then.

If you are running Novell NetWare, it is essential that you upgrade to the newest network-driver software when new versions are released. The latest shell files can be downloaded from Novell's forum on CompuServe. (CompuServe users can access this forum by typing GO NOVFILES at a system prompt.)

Using NetWare shells with MS-DOS 5.0 presents other issues. Novell recommends that network administrators *not* use the NET5.COM program provided on the DOS 5.0 diskettes. This version of the shell has known incompatibilities with WordPerfect and "load high"-type programs, according to Doug Knight, a Novell senior systems engineer. Instead, Novell distributes a version of the shell that works with all versions of DOS, including 5.0, known as NETX.COM. (IBM never included a NetWare driver in its version of PC-DOS 5.0, so NetWare users of IBM DOS 5 need to download the shell programs anyway.)

After the shell has been upgraded for all workstations, certain changes are required for each user's SHELL.CFG or NET.CFG configuration file. Although SHELL.CFG was originally used as the configuration file, Novell now uses a new file, named NET.CFG, which supports commands that are not available in SHELL.CGF.

Whether SHELL.CFG or NET.CFG is used, specific statements need to be inserted to increase the number of file handles reserved by DOS, and to force NetWare to support DOS convention of using a single dot (.) for the current directory and two dots (..) for the parent directory. Additionally, applications that communicate using the Netbios protocol usually require two other statements. These statements are illustrated in the following example:

```
FILE HANDLES=60
SHOW DOTS=ON
NETBIOS BROADCAST COUNT=5
NETBIOS BROADCAST DELAY=10
```

The FILES= statement in each user's CONFIG.SYS file must agree with the one in SHELL.CFG or NET.CFG, as follows:

```
FILES=60
```

Certain changes should also be made in the SYSTEM.INI files of Windows users running NetWare. When the Windows Setup routine detects a NetWare workstation, it writes the following line into the [386Enh] section of SYSTEM.INI:

```
[386Enh]
network=*vnetbios,vnetware.386,vipx.386
```

The VIPX.386 file is a driver loaded from the Windows \SYSTEM subdirectory to support programs that issue NetWare IPX calls, such as 3270 emulation programs. Due to incompatibilities, Novell states that you must delete the ",vipx.386" portion of this line in SYSTEM.INI, to prevent VIPX.386 from being loaded. Instead, it is preferable to support IPX-type programs by using a TSR provided by Novell called TBMI.COM (Task Switched Buffer Manager for IPX). The use of this program is described in a TBMI.DOC file that accompanies the TSR.

Other settings in SYSTEM.INI that affect Novell networks are contained in a section headed [NetWare]. By default, SYSTEM.INI uses the following values for this section:

```
[NetWare]
RestoreDrives=yes
NWShareHandles=no
```

The RestoreDrives setting resets all network drive mappings when you exit Windows (if you made any changes within Windows). If you want mappings made within Windows to remain in effect when you exit Windows, change this setting to "no."

The NWShareHandles setting keeps drive mappings you make in one DOS session under Windows from affecting other DOS sessions. If you want changes in one session to affect all other sessions, change this setting to "yes."

Finally, network administrators may want to customize the NETWARE.INI file that is created when a Windows workstation is first run under NetWare. Statements in this file determine which utilities are available when users click the Network icon in the Control Panel.

To allow a user to run the System Configuration Utility (SYSCON) from the Control Panel, for example, a network administrator might define a Windows PIF file for this DOS utility and place the following in NETWARE.INI:

```
[MSW30-Utils]
System Configuration Utility=SYSCON.PIF
```

All the above settings are described in much greater detail in a useful, 68-page *NetWare Application Note* called "NetWare and Microsoft Windows Integration." This paper is available for $10 by calling 801-429-7550.

Finally, Windows users should be aware of a problem called the "Black Screen of Death" that affects NetWare. If you start a DOS application under Windows but you only get a blinking cursor in the upper left corner of a black screen, you have this problem. To correct it, download the file BSDUP1.ZIP from CompuServe's GO NOVFILES forum. Read the text file and install the new drivers included in this ZIP file.

Banyan Vines

The first release of the Banyan Vines network operating system that supports Windows 3.0 is Vines 4.0. This release requires a minor upgrade diskette known as "patch 0 hex." When this patch is applied, Vines reports its version number as 4.0(0).

Vines 4.0 does not fully support some Windows File Manager functions, such as dragging files with a mouse from a local hard disk directory onto a network directory.

Additionally, Vines users who need to print to network printers require a TSR that provides Netbios support for interrupt 2A, which controls printing. Vines administrators usually provide this support by including a patch TSR, known as TSR2AP.COM, in a file named WINSTART.BAT. When Windows finds a file with this name in the Windows directory, it loads the commands in this file before starting in 386 enhanced mode. TSRs loaded in WINSTART.BAT take up only extended memory, instead of consuming valuable conventional memory. (The presence of WINSTART.BAT, in some cases, causes Windows to hang when exiting to DOS. This seems to be configuration dependent, and Microsoft has not determined the exact configurations affected.)

Releases of Vines version 4.1 and later fully support Windows's File Manager and printing functions. TSRs such as TSR2AP.COM are not required under Vines 4.1 and higher.

LAN Manager

A variety of flavors of Microsoft LAN Manager are available, including LAN Manager 1.x, 2.x Basic and 2.x Enhanced, 3Com 3+Open LAN Manager 1.x, 3+Open LAN Manager 2.x, and so on. Windows accommodates each flavor in slightly different ways.

When Windows Setup detects Microsoft LAN Manager 1.x, it automatically installs the LANMAN10.386 driver required in SYSTEM.INI. The WINPOPUP.EXE utility supplied with LAN Manager 1.x, which displays network messages in Windows, is not compatible with Windows, however, and must be disabled in the LANMAN.INI file. To solve this problem, obtain an updated version of WINPOPUP.EXE, or upgrade to LAN Manager 2.x.

3Com 3+Open LAN Manager 1.x is set up the same way as Microsoft LAN Manager 1.x, unless the XNS protocol is being used. In that case, you must install Windows 3.0 for the 3+Open 1.x network in order for SYSTEM.INI to be written with the correct settings. Additionally, Microsoft states that Windows enhanced mode is not compatible with 3Com's 3C505 network interface card when running 3Com Link Plus software, which must be disabled.

When Windows Setup detects Microsoft LAN Manager 2.0 Basic, it installs the driver MSNET.DRV in SYSTEM.INI. For 2.0 Enhanced, however, it installs the driver LANMAN.DRV. In both cases, these drivers support all Windows functionality.

Windows Setup also installs LANMAN.DRV for 3Com 3+Open LAN Manager 2.0. It is necessary for network administrators to manually add the following statements in the [386Enh] section of SYSTEM.INI in order for 3+Open LAN Manager 2.0 to operate properly:

```
[386Enh]
TimerCriticalSection=10000
UniqueDOSPSP=true
PSPIncrement=5
```

Microsoft states that LAN Manager 1.x network software cannot be loaded into the High Memory Area (HMA), the first 64K of extended memory, under DOS 4.0. Additionally, when using DOS 5.0, it is necessary to use the LAN Manager driver that ships on the DOS 5.0 distribution diskettes.

Resources

The following technical papers and books provide detailed information on the installation and management of Windows on company-wide networks.

The Windows Resource Kit, Microsoft Corp., 1 Microsoft Way, Redmond, WA 98052-6399; 800-642-7676 or 206-882-8080. $20. A valuable collection of technical notes gained from Microsoft's experience with thousands of telephone support calls. Includes a software diskette with Windows utilities. A Windows for Workgroups Resource Kit is also available.

Challenges in Migrating to the Windows Environment, Corporate Software Inc., 275 Dan Road, Canton, MA 02021-9879; 617-821-4500. A 44-page study of 14 corporations that switched whole departments to Windows during 1990, the year of the Windows 3.0 rollout.

NetWare Application Notes: NetWare and Microsoft Windows Integration Special Issue, January 1991; Novell Inc., AppNotes Subscription Dept., 122 East 1700 South C-25-1, Provo, UT 84606-6194; 801-429-7550. $10. A 68-page description of the process of networking Windows that is essential for NetWare administrators and helpful to the managers of other networks as well.

Windows 3.1 Secrets, by Brian Livingston; IDG Books, 155 Bovet Road, San Mateo, CA 94402; 800-282-6657 or 415-358-1250. $39.95 plus shipping. A 990-page field guide to Windows' behaviors and numerous undocumented features. Includes three diskettes with 45 Windows shareware applications.

Summary

This chapter covers the concepts of running Windows across a network. More details are covered in the Networks chapter of *Windows 3.1 Secrets*. In this chapter, I touch on:

▶ Performance and management issues that affect the decision to run Windows on a network.

▶ A few specific steps that are necessary when running Windows with Novell NetWare, Banyan Vines, and Microsoft LAN Manager networks.

Part III
Tips and Tricks

Chapter 32
MSD: The MisSing Documentation

In This Chapter

▶ I document the almost-invisible Microsoft Diagnostics (MSD) program, a very useful troubleshooting program that is hidden within every copy of Windows 3.1.

▶ In addition to documenting the various commands and screens of this utility, I describe several ways you can put MSD to good use in your system immediately.

To help computer users troubleshoot problems with Windows, Microsoft in 1992 quietly began shipping a free diagnostic utility in all boxes of Windows 3.1. An updated version of this utility now appears in MS-DOS 6.x, as well. But there is no explanation of this utility in the Windows manual or the User's Guide that comes with the MS-DOS 6 upgrade.

This utility is called MSD, which you might think stands for MisSing Documentation. In fact, it means MicroSoft Diagnostics, and everyone who uses Windows should be familiar with how this complex and powerful utility can help you prevent or correct problems in your PC.

In the first half of this chapter, I have written the printed MSD documentation that Microsoft forgot. In the second half, I build on this framework with some specific examples of how this tool can be used to minimize or eliminate conflicts that can keep Windows from running smoothly.

Running Microsoft Diagnostics

Although MSD.EXE was introduced as a part of Windows 3.1, it is ironic that it is a character-based DOS application, and you should *not* run it under Windows. You must exit Windows, and then type MSD at a plain DOS prompt. Otherwise, you may get inaccurate information from MSD. (It would, at a minimum, be limited to the memory settings in the _DEFAULT.PIF file that comes with Windows, and you want MSD to be able to diagnose all possible memory locations.)

The complete parameters for MSD are as follows:

```
msd {color} {ignore}
```

where *{color}* may be /B for black-and-white or /M for monochrome displays, and *{ignore}* may be /I to "ignore" your hardware configuration. The /B and /M switches are useful if you have a portable computer and MSD is hard to read on your portable's monochrome display in the software's normal, color mode. The /I switch is useful if MSD hangs while it is examining your system when it starts up.

For example, the following three command lines start up MSD in black-and-white mode, in monochrome mode, and bypassing its initial hardware detection routine, respectively:

```
msd /b
msd /m
msd /i
```

Besides displaying diagnostic information on your screen, it is also possible for MSD to print the same information directly to a printer or a text file. MSD has three ways to do this, illustrated by the following three examples:

```
msd /f filename
msd /p filename
msd /s {filename}
```

The command MSD /F, followed by a filename (which may include a complete path, such as C:\WINDOWS\REPORT.TXT), creates a File with a complete report of MSD's examination of your system's hardware and running software. You are first prompted to enter your name, company, address, phone number, and any remarks, which become a part of the output file for future reference. You can then print this file, with a DOS command such as COPY REPORT.TXT LPT1, and refer to it while troubleshooting your system.

The command MSD /P *filename* immediately writes a complete report to the filename you specify, without Prompting you for your company information, as with MSD /F *filename*.

The command MSD /S *{filename}* prints only a 10-line Summary of your hardware and running network software, if any. If you omit the optional filename parameter, MSD writes this summary on your screen.

Because MSD is located in your Windows 3.1 directory, which must be on the DOS Path (or in your DOS 6 directory, which also must be on the Path), you should not need to add a drive and directory name in front of the MSD command in order for it to run.

Interpreting the MSD Screen

When you run MSD, the first thing you see (after MSD inspects your system for installed hardware and software) is the Summary Screen, shown in Figure 32-1.

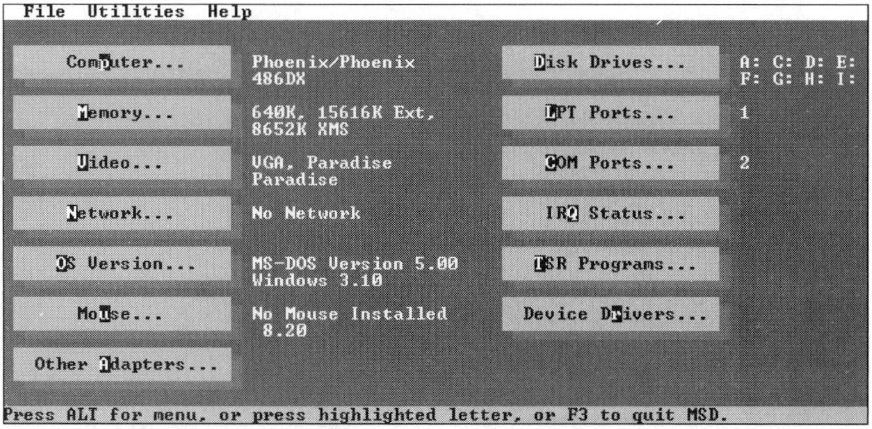

```
 File   Utilities   Help

    Com[]uter...        Phoenix/Phoenix      []isk Drives...    A:  C:  D:  E:
                        486DX                                   F:  G:  H:  I:

    []emory...          640K, 15616K Ext,    []PT Ports...      1
                        8652K XMS

    []ideo...           UGA, Paradise        []OM Ports...      2
                        Paradise

    []etwork...         No Network           IR[] Status...

    []S Version...      MS-DOS Version 5.00  []SR Programs...
                        Windows 3.10

    Mo[]se...           No Mouse Installed   Device D[]ivers...
                         8.20

  Other []dapters...

Press ALT for menu, or press highlighted letter, or F3 to quit MSD.
```

Figure 32-1: The MSD Opening Screen.

This screen contains three pull-down menus and 13 buttons for various diagnostic options. If you have a mouse, you will find MSD easier to use if you load your mouse driver — in most cases, MOUSE.COM — at a DOS prompt (or in your AUTOEXEC.BAT) before starting the utility. That way, you can use a character-block mouse pointer to run the menus and buttons in MSD. Otherwise, you must press keyboard keys to activate these features. (Press Alt+F to pull down the File menu or press M to access the Memory diagnostic, for example.)

The File menu contains items that allow you to find disk files with names you specify, print customized MSD reports, examine such configuration files as AUTOEXEC.BAT, and exit MSD.

The Utilities menu allows you to display the location of software loaded into memory, browse upper-memory locations for text messages in BIOS chips, insert standard configuration statements into CONFIG.SYS and AUTOEXEC.BAT, and send test samples to various text and PostScript printers.

The Help menu merely displays the version number of the MSD utility you are running. In Windows 3.1, this is Version 2.0. In Windows for Workgroups, it's Version 2.00a, while in DOS 6.0, it's Version 2.01. One change between Version

2.0 and 2.00a is the Help menu in the earlier version. When you clicked the Help item, thinking you would see some information about how to use MSD, you instead saw only an About item. When you clicked About, and then pressed F1 for help, you received the message box (shown in Figure 32-2) saying, "No Help Available (so leave me alone)"! Microsoft cleaned up this message (by deleting it), without actually providing any Help option within MSD 2.00a or 2.01.

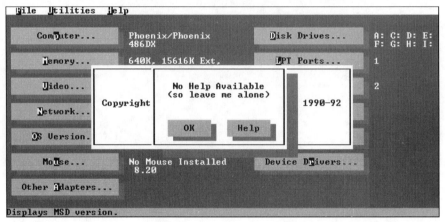

Figure 32-2: The message you might get, depending on the version of MSD, when you press F1 in the Help About screen.

The meat of MSD is contained in the screens that appear when you click one of the 13 buttons on the summary screen (or press the highlighted letter on each button). These buttons provide information in the following categories: Computer, Memory, Video, Network, Operating System Version, Mouse, Other Adapters, Disk Drives, LPT Ports, COM Ports, Interrupt Request Line (IRQ) Status, Terminate-and-Stay-Resident (TSR) Programs, and Device Drivers.

Understanding MSD Information Screens

The Computer screen (see Figure 32-3) displays information about your system's manufacturer, BIOS type and date, CPU type, and other basic hardware. MSD gets this information by reading text strings in your ROM BIOS chips, or by running diagnostics (to determine whether your machine is a 286 or 386, for example).

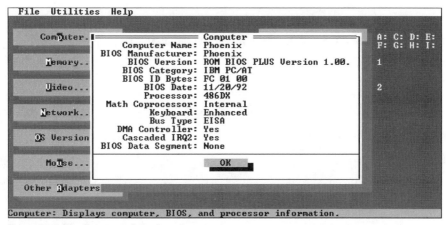

Figure 32-3: The Computer Screen.

The Memory screen (see Figure 32-4) shows a quite useful map of hardware devices and software drivers that are using space between 640KB and 1MB. This analysis includes hex addresses C000 to FFFF. These addresses are above the normal video RAM addresses (A000-BFFF), which is where many Upper Memory Block conflicts occur. It's unfortunate that MSD doesn't include the video RAM addresses in its display, since the B000-B7FF addresses are commonly used by "load-high" utilities.

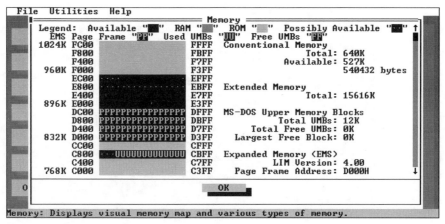

Figure 32-4: The Memory Screen.

The Video screen (see Figure 32-5) displays information on your video adapter manufacturer and video BIOS date. MSD obtains this information by reading the ROM BIOS chip located on your video adapter.

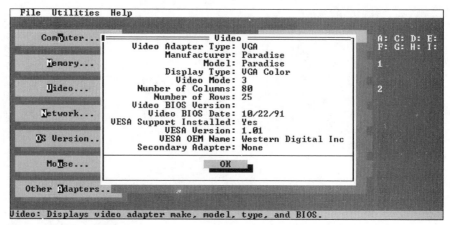

Figure 32-5: The Video Screen.

The Network screen (see Figure 32-6) reports which network shell, if any, you are currently running.

```
 File  Utilities  Help

     Computer...       Phoenix/Phoenix      Disk Drives...    A: C: D: E:
                       486DX                                  F: G: H: I:

     Memory...         640K, 15616K Ext,    LPT Ports...      1
                       8652K XMS

     Video...          UGA,  ═══ Network ═══ M Ports...       2
                       Parad  Network Detected: No

     Network...        No Ne        OK            Status...

     OS Version...     MS-DOS                     rograms...
                       Windows 3.10

     Mouse...          No Mouse Installed   Device Drivers...
                       8.20

  Other Adapters...

 Network: Displays network information.
```

Figure 32-6: The Network Screen.

The OS Version screen (see Figure 32-7) identifies your version of DOS, the letter of your boot drive (usually C:), and whether DOS is loaded into the High Memory Area. One interesting feature of this screen is the "Internal Revision" line. Some DOS 5.0 users see an internal revision number of 00, while others see 01. The latter revision is a version of DOS 5.0 that Microsoft slipstreamed into the market without an announcement. It merely makes a minor change to NetWare drivers bundled with DOS 5, which are obsolete with DOS 6.0 now, anyway. But this internal revision number is intriguing to watch under DOS 6 to see if any improvements in the product are being made.

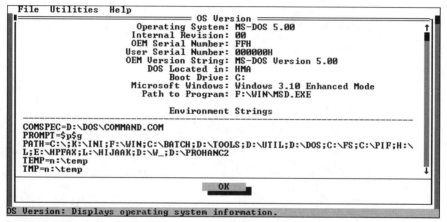

Figure 32-7: The OS Version Screen.

The Mouse screen (see Figure 32-8) displays information on your mouse hardware and driver, if you have a mouse and mouse software installed.

The Other Adapters screen (see Figure 32-9) reports whether you have a game port installed (for a joystick, for example).

The Disk Drives screen (see Figure 32-10) shows the size of any disk drives and partition letters present in your system, including floppy drives and hard drives.

The LPT Ports screen (see Figure 32-11) specifies the existence and location in your system of parallel ports LPT1 through LPT3, and the status of any attached devices (paper out, etc.).

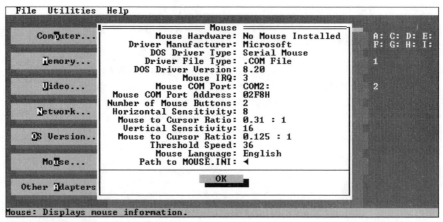

Figure 32-8: The Mouse Screen.

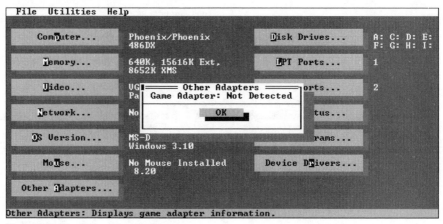

Figure 32-9: The Other Adapters Screen.

The COM Ports screen (see Figure 32-12) indicates the presence of serial ports, including their current baud rate and transfer settings, plus the type of chip used to support serial communications (the older 8250 chip vs. the buffered 16550 series).

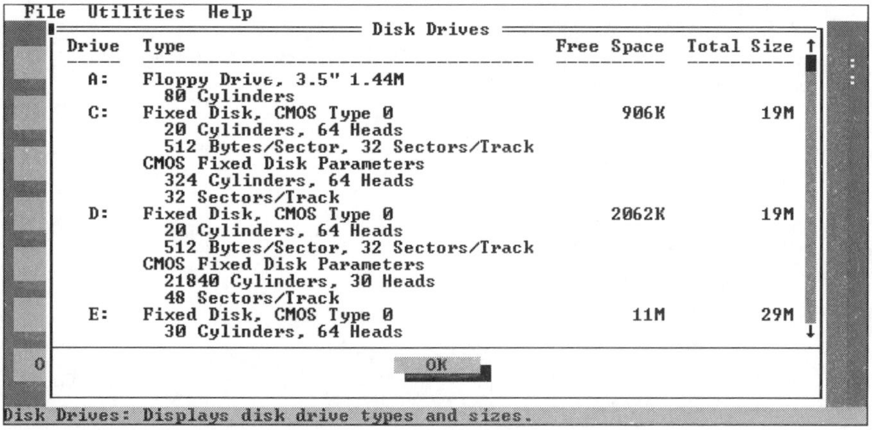

```
 File  Utilities  Help
 Drive  Type                                 Free Space  Total Size ↑
 ─────  ────                                 ──────────  ──────────
   A:   Floppy Drive, 3.5" 1.44M
          80 Cylinders
   C:   Fixed Disk, CMOS Type 0                 906K        19M
          20 Cylinders, 64 Heads
          512 Bytes/Sector, 32 Sectors/Track
        CMOS Fixed Disk Parameters
          324 Cylinders, 64 Heads
          32 Sectors/Track
   D:   Fixed Disk, CMOS Type 0                2062K        19M
          20 Cylinders, 64 Heads
          512 Bytes/Sector, 32 Sectors/Track
        CMOS Fixed Disk Parameters
          21840 Cylinders, 30 Heads
          48 Sectors/Track
   E:   Fixed Disk, CMOS Type 0                 11M         29M
          30 Cylinders, 64 Heads            ↓
                          ┌─────────┐
                          │   OK    │
                          └─────────┘
Disk Drives: Displays disk drive types and sizes.
```

Figure 32-10: The Disk Drives Screen.

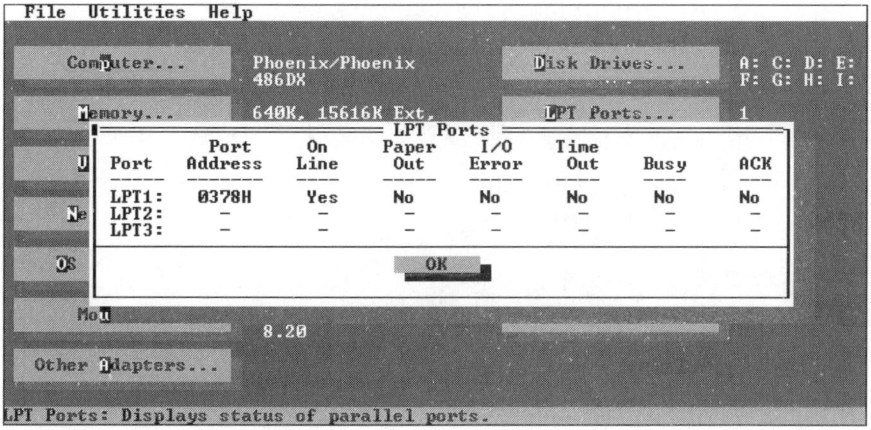

```
 File  Utilities  Help
     Computer...        Phoenix/Phoenix          Disk Drives...    A: C: D: E:
                        486DX                                      F: G: H: I:
     Memory...          640K, 15616K Ext.        LPT Ports...      1
                        ┌──────────── LPT Ports ────────────────────────┐
                        │        Port     On    Paper   I/O    Time      │
     U                  │ Port  Address  Line    Out   Error   Out  Busy  ACK │
                        │ ────  ───────  ────   ─────  ─────  ────  ────  ─── │
     Ne                 │ LPT1:  0378H    Yes     No     No     No    No   No  │
                        │ LPT2:   -        -      -      -      -     -    -   │
     OS                 │ LPT3:   -        -      -      -      -     -    -   │
                        │              ┌─────────┐                        │
                        │              │   OK    │                        │
     Mo                 │              └─────────┘                        │
                        └─────────────────────────────────────────────────┘
                                   8.20
     Other Adapters...
LPT Ports: Displays status of parallel ports.
```

Figure 32-11: The LPT Ports Screen.

The IRQ Status screen (see Figure 32-13) displays how the 16 interrupt request lines (IRQs) are being used in your system. The "Description" column stays the same on all systems, while the "Detected" column changes to indicate devices that MSD has determined are actually connected.

The TSR Programs screen (see Figure 32-14) charts the size and location of memory-resident programs that you have loaded in CONFIG.SYS, AUTOEXEC.BAT, or in other ways.

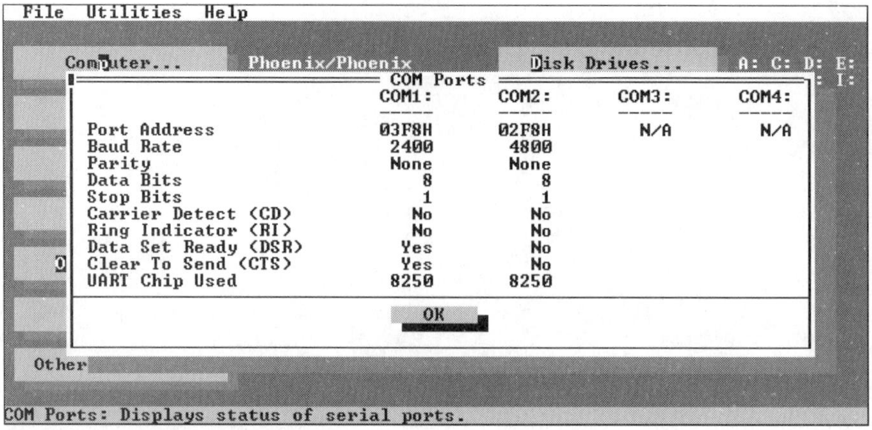

```
 File  Utilities  Help

   Com uter...      Phoenix/Phoenix        Disk Drives...   A: C: D: E:
  ┌──────────────────────── COM Ports ──────────────────────┐  : I:
  │                         COM1:     COM2:     COM3:   COM4:│
  │                         ─────     ─────     ─────   ─────│
  │   Port Address          03F8H     02F8H      N/A     N/A │
  │   Baud Rate              2400      4800                  │
  │   Parity                 None      None                  │
  │   Data Bits                 8         8                  │
  │   Stop Bits                 1         1                  │
  │   Carrier Detect (CD)      No        No                  │
  │   Ring Indicator (RI)      No        No                  │
  │   Data Set Ready (DSR)     Yes       No                  │
  │ 0 Clear To Send (CTS)      Yes       No                  │
  │   UART Chip Used          8250      8250                 │
  │                                                          │
  │                    ▆▆▆▆▆ OK ▆▆▆▆▆                        │
  │                                                          │
  └──────────────────────────────────────────────────────────┘
  Other
 COM Ports: Displays status of serial ports.
```

Figure 32-12: The COM Ports Screen.

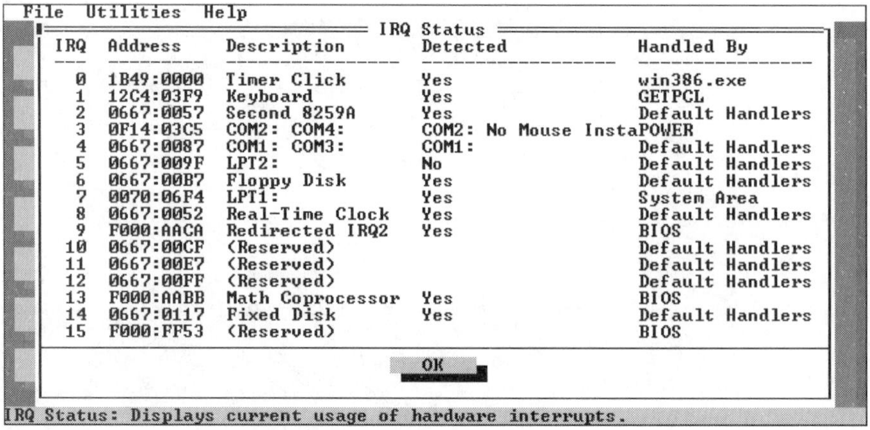

```
 File  Utilities  Help
  ┌──────────────────────── IRQ Status ─────────────────────┐
  │  IRQ Address   Description      Detected        Handled By│
  │  ─── ───────── ─────────────── ─────────────── ──────────│
  │   0  1B49:0000 Timer Click     Yes             win386.exe │
  │   1  12C4:03F9 Keyboard        Yes             GETPCL     │
  │   2  0667:0057 Second 8259A    Yes             Default Handlers│
  │   3  0F14:03C5 COM2: COM4:     COM2: No Mouse InstaPOWER  │
  │   4  0667:0087 COM1: COM3:     COM1:           Default Handlers│
  │   5  0667:009F LPT2:           No              Default Handlers│
  │   6  0667:00B7 Floppy Disk     Yes             Default Handlers│
  │   7  0070:06F4 LPT1:           Yes             System Area│
  │   8  0667:0052 Real-Time Clock Yes             Default Handlers│
  │   9  F000:AACA Redirected IRQ2 Yes             BIOS       │
  │  10  0667:00CF (Reserved)                      Default Handlers│
  │  11  0667:00E7 (Reserved)                      Default Handlers│
  │  12  0667:00FF (Reserved)                      Default Handlers│
  │  13  F000:AABB Math Coprocessor Yes            BIOS       │
  │  14  0667:0117 Fixed Disk      Yes             Default Handlers│
  │  15  F000:FF53 (Reserved)                      BIOS       │
  │                                                           │
  │                    ▆▆▆▆▆ OK ▆▆▆▆▆                         │
  │                                                           │
  └───────────────────────────────────────────────────────────┘
 IRQ Status: Displays current usage of hardware interrupts.
```

Figure 32-13: The IRQ Status Screen.

Finally, the Device Drivers screen (see Figure 32-15) specifies the existence of reserved device names in your system. This includes reserved names that appear automatically every time you reboot your system, such as CON (the console, or keyboard and monitor as a unit) and LPT1 (the first parallel port). But it also includes device drivers that you optionally load, such as HIMEM.SYS and EMM386.EXE.

After you have MSD up and running, you can use the following techniques to diagnose various aspects of your system.

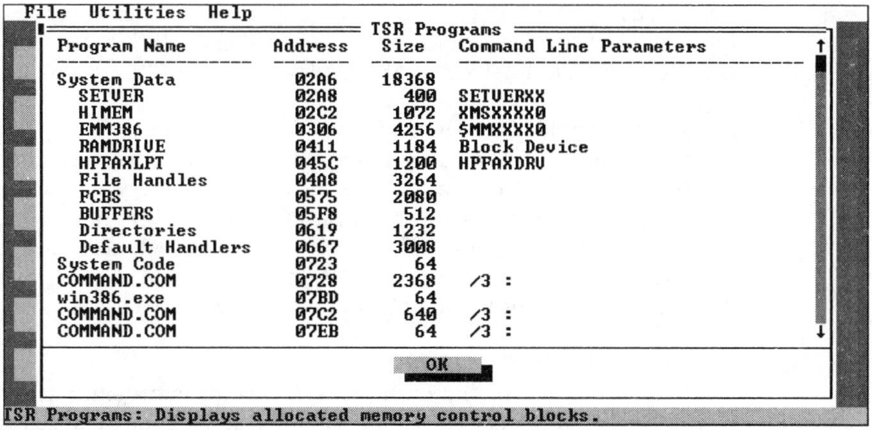

```
 File  Utilities  Help
                              ═══ TSR Programs ═══
   Program Name          Address   Size   Command Line Parameters       ↑
   ─────────────────────────────────────────────────────────────────────
   System Data           02A6     18368
     SETVER              02A8       400   SETVERXX
     HIMEM               02C2      1072   XMSXXXX0
     EMM386              0306      4256   $MMXXXX0
     RAMDRIVE            0411      1184   Block Device
     HPFAXLPT            045C      1200   HPFAXDRV
     File Handles        04A8      3264
     FCBS                0575      2080
     BUFFERS             05F8       512
     Directories         0619      1232
     Default Handlers    0667      3008
   System Code           0723        64
   COMMAND.COM           0728      2368   /3 :
   win386.exe            07BD        64
   COMMAND.COM           07C2       640   /3 :
   COMMAND.COM           07EB        64   /3 :                            ↓

                             ▓▓▓ OK ▓▓
 TSR Programs: Displays allocated memory control blocks.
```

Figure 32-14: The TSR Programs Screen.

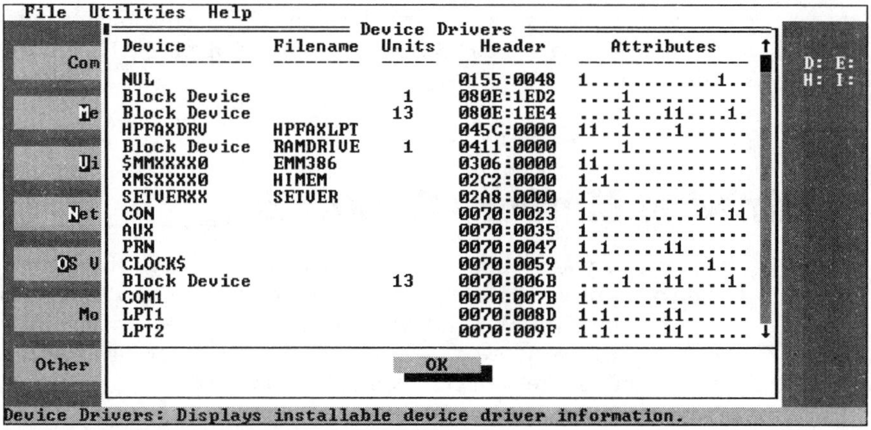

```
 File  Utilities  Help
              ═════════════ Device Drivers ═════════════
 Com   Device        Filename   Units    Header      Attributes      ↑     D: E:
       ──────────────────────────────────────────────────────────          H: I:
       NUL                               0155:0048  1............1..
       Block Device              1       080E:1ED2  .....1..........
 Me    Block Device              13      080E:1EE4  ....1...11....1.
       HPFAXDRV      HPFAXLPT            045C:0000  11..1.....1.....
 Ui    Block Device  RAMDRIVE    1       0411:0000  ....1...........
       $MMXXXX0      EMM386              0306:0000  11..............
       XMSXXXX0      HIMEM               02C2:0000  1.1.............
       SETVERXX      SETVER              02A8:0000  1...............
 Net   CON                               0070:0023  1.........1..11
       AUX                               0070:0035  1...............
       PRN                               0070:0047  1.1.....11......
 OS U  CLOCK$                            0070:0059  1..........1...1.
       Block Device              13      0070:006B  ....1...11....1.
       COM1                              0070:007B  1...............
 Mo    LPT1                              0070:008D  1.1.....11......
       LPT2                              0070:009F  1.1.....11......   ↓
 ─────
 Other                         ▓▓▓ OK ▓▓
 Device Drivers: Displays installable device driver information.
```

Figure 32-15: The Device Drivers Screen.

Updating Your ROM BIOS

One irritating problem with PCs from various manufacturers is that the ROM BIOS chips they use for compatibility with the IBM standard may be updated with little or no notice to users. Older BIOS chips may have subtle incompatibilities with Windows. Often, these incompatibilities are not obvious, but result in small errors that show up in Windows only intermittently as General Protection Faults or other messages.

You can easily check the age and make of your BIOS chips using MSD. Click the Computer button of MSD, and a window showing the BIOS manufacturer and date (among other information) is displayed.

Microsoft has published a list of known BIOS problems in Chart 1.4 of the Windows 3.1 Resource Kit (a booklet available for $20 by calling Microsoft at 206-882-8080). In general, any BIOS dated earlier than 1988 should be updated by contacting the manufacturer of your PC. But Microsoft has also made specific recommendations on BIOS versions that have been upgraded to work well with Windows. For example, Microsoft states that the Award BIOS, used in PCs from several different manufacturers, should be at least Version 3.05, and preferably 3.1.

You may be able to find out even more interesting information about your BIOS chips by using MSD. Click the Utilities item on MSD's main menu, then click Memory Browser. This displays a screen that allows you to search your ROM BIOS and video BIOS for specific text strings. Select the line that says, "ROM BIOS," then search for the string "Copyright" (without the quote marks). This almost always finds a line in the BIOS code with the copyright date and BIOS manufacturer's name, which may be different from the manufacturer of your PC. (Many PC makers buy BIOS chips from suppliers like Phoenix, AMI, Award, and others.)

Eliminating Memory Conflicts

Windows, as you probably know, uses areas of memory above the 640KB line. When other programs and devices also use such memory, called Upper Memory Blocks (UMBs), and Windows does not detect and avoid using these memory areas, Windows may crash or exhibit weird behavior. These problems are often intermittent and difficult to troubleshoot.

One of the best ways to avoid this type of problem is to ensure that Windows does *not* accidentally use an area of memory that is already claimed by another piece of software or hardware. This problem is particularly troublesome on PCs that have a network adapter board. Network adapters almost always have some RAM chips that use UMBs. However, this RAM may not be visible to memory managers (including Windows) until the network software is actually active. This can cause such memory managers to claim some upper memory, which will later also be claimed by your network adapter, with disastrous results.

To work around this problem, load all the software drivers and memory-resident programs you usually use (but not Windows). Then start MSD and click the Memory button. This will produce a display similar to the one shown in Figure 32-4.

Upper Memory Blocks are generally numbered A000 (pronounced "A thousand"), B000, C000, D000, E000, and F000. Windows and most other memory managers ordinarily avoid using the A000 and B000 areas. Therefore, MSD shows you a picture that includes only C000 and above.

Look in this diagram for memory areas marked "ROM" or "RAM." Areas marked this way by MSD are almost always ROM or RAM chips that are located on add-in boards, such as network adapters, scanner boards, SCSI adapters, and so on.

You can ensure that Windows does not accidentally use any of these in-use UMBs by specifically excluding these areas. You do this by adding parameters in CONFIG.SYS to any memory manager you use, and in the [386Enh] section of SYSTEM.INI for Windows. (Windows should automatically inherit any such parameters you put on the command line of your memory manager in CONFIG.SYS. But I recommend that you put these parameters in both places, in case your memory manager in CONFIG.SYS — such as EMM386.EXE — later changes or is no longer needed.)

Let's say you find ROM chips from C800 to CBFF in MSD's display. You can exclude this area from use by the EMM386.EXE memory manager by adding an /X parameter in CONFIG.SYS, as follows:

```
device=c:\windows\emm386.exe x=c800-cbff
```

Other memory managers use a similar syntax. Check the documentation for your memory manager to find the exact syntax for their "exclude" switches.

To exclude this memory area from accidental use by Windows, add an EMMExclude statement in the [386Enh] section of SYSTEM.INI, as follows:

```
[386Enh]
EMMExclude=c800-cbff
```

These upper memory areas use hexadecimal numbering, in which numbers run from 0 to 9 and then A to F, so they are difficult to figure out. There are only four possible areas that you might need to exclude between C800 and CBFF. These are C800-C8FF, C900-C9FF, CA00-CAFF, and CB00-CBFF. C800 to C8FF represents 4K of upper memory, C800 to C9FF represents 8K, and so forth. This numbering system is the same in the other UMBs: D000 to DFFF, E000 to EFFF, etc. By carefully reading MSD's Memory display, you should be able to identify those specific 4K areas that are in use.

Windows and other memory managers automatically exclude the F000-FFFF area, since this is where your main ROM BIOS are always located. For this reason, you don't need to manually exclude this area.

You can get additional information about software that is using Upper Memory Blocks by clicking Utilities on the MSD main menu, then clicking Memory Block Display. This brings up a window that displays the name and location of every memory-resident program between C000 and FFFF. This can help you determine which memory-resident programs you want to load into upper memory using the DEVICEHIGH command in your CONFIG.SYS, or the LOADHIGH command in your AUTOEXEC.BAT (in DOS 5.0 and higher).

Avoiding Interrupt Conflicts

Another irritation for Windows users comes from hardware devices that conflict when using your PC's Interrupt Request lines (IRQs). Every 286 and higher system has 16 IRQs available, but no two devices may use the same IRQ at the same time.

Because Windows machines usually include a mouse, and often include a modem port and several printer ports, Windows users can find themselves running out of IRQs. This is because mice, modems, and the like always require an interrupt to themselves. Other devices that use interrupts include add-in boards for scanners, external disk drives, tape drives, and the like.

Before you add a board (or any other hardware device) to your PC, I recommend that you start MSD and click the IRQ Status button. This displays a window like the one shown in Figure 32-13.

The first column in this window lists the 16 available interrupts (numbered 0 to 15). The second column shows the address in memory where the handler (the program that manages this interrupt) resides. The third column lists the typical uses that each IRQ is called upon to serve: the COM ports and LPT ports, your fixed disk and math coprocessor (if you have one), and so on.

The important column is the fourth one, which is headed "Detected." The third column never changes, no matter what you have installed in your PC. But the fourth column shows you the hardware that MSD has detected on each of the valuable IRQs in your system.

If you have a mouse using COM1, for example, MSD will report "Serial Mouse" on that port. COM1 usually takes control of IRQ 4. If you have no COM2, on the other hand, the fourth column of this window will show "No" as its status. This means that your IRQ 3 is probably free, and can safely be used by another add-in board that needs its own IRQ.

When you install such a board, configure it to use an IRQ that shows up in MSD's IRQ Status window as unused. (Check the documentation that came with the board to determine the proper switch settings or software to use to do this.) Other devices may also require proper IRQ settings. A bus mouse, as opposed to a serial mouse, usually is set at the factory to use IRQ 5, but may be switched to other IRQs instead.

If you have used up all the IRQs numbered 3, 4, 5, 6, and 7, you must look to the other IRQs for one that is available.

Some add-in boards will work properly when assigned to IRQ 2. This interrupt request line shows up in MSD as "Second 8259A," but this doesn't mean that no device can use this interrupt. The 8259A is a chip that uses interrupt 2 to send data to the higher interrupts, numbered 8 through 15. It does this by "redirecting" IRQ 2 to IRQ 9, but you may be able to use either of these IRQs for other devices as well. Many network adapter boards are configured at the factory to use IRQ 2, for example.

LPT1 is usually assigned to IRQ 7, and LPT2 (if your PC has a second parallel printer port) is usually assigned to IRQ 5. Again, this does not necessarily mean that you cannot use these IRQs for other devices. The parallel ports will conflict with other hardware devices using IRQ 7 or IRQ 5 only if you have unusual software that communicates with printer ports using hardware interrupts. Most software actually communicates with printers by writing directly into the appropriate "input/output port address" for each printer port. If you need a spare IRQ for a device, try IRQ 5, and then IRQ 7, and test your printer to see if there is any conflict.

Finally, you may be able to assign newer add-in boards to IRQs 8 through 15. Although MSD describes IRQ 10, 11, 12, and 15 as "Reserved," this really should say "Available." If you do not see any device in the "Detected" column for one of these IRQs, you should be able to assign a new add-in board to one of them safely. Newer network adapters, such as the 3Com Etherlink III, for example, come from the factory pre-configured to use IRQ 10. This produces the fewest conflicts in today's PCs, which often have the lower eight IRQs filled up with COM ports, mice, tape drives, and whatnot.

Some Caveats About MSD

This discussion can only scratch the surface of the uses of MSD, because it is capable of so many complex diagnostics. Many of the screens, moreover, present even more technical information than those I have already described.

Of interest to programmers, for example, is the Device Drivers screen in MSD. When you click this button, you get a display similar to that shown previously in Figure 32-15.

This screen shows various device drivers that have been installed since you rebooted your PC. Included are several that are always present, such as CON (your console, also known as the keyboard and screen) and NUL (a nonexistent device useful for testing purposes). It also includes device drivers installed by lines in your CONFIG.SYS or AUTOEXEC.BAT, or features of the operating system, such as the DoubleSpace (DBLSPACE) file compression driver in MS-DOS 6.0.

The "Attributes" column in this display refers to the header of each device, which indicates whether the device driver is a real-time clock device, the NUL device, or has other characteristics. The meanings of the 16 attributes in this window are described in the Device Drivers chapter of the *Microsoft MS-DOS Programmer's Reference,* a technical manual available from Microsoft Press.

A few other cautions about MSD should be observed. I've already mentioned that MSD should not be run in a DOS session under Windows. You may not be *able* to do this anyway, if you have a serial mouse on your COM1 port, since MSD is likely to hang if you start it in this situation.

If you have a disk drive that has been divided into more than one logical drive letter (C:, D:, E:, etc.), MSD will try to report information on each logical *partition.* Unfortunately, the disk drive type and related information will be correct only for the primary partition (C:) and will be incorrect for drive letters in the extended partition (D:, E:, etc.). Microsoft says in its technical support document Q81745 that this is due to the way MS-DOS stores the partition information, which MSD cannot read correctly. This does not affect MSD's report on the size and free space on each drive letter, however, which should be correct.

If you have created a phantom com port using a DOS utility or DEBUG, MSD will always report that port as having a 16550AF chip, when in fact there is no communications chip (and no port at all). It also reports that port as being set to 8 data bits, 2 stop bits, and other erroneous information.

Other than these minor glitches, you should be able to use MSD on systems of all descriptions to gain valuable insight into their inner workings. Good hunting!

Summary

In this chapter, I take apart the Microsoft Diagnostics program, screen by screen, to show how you can use it to improve reliablity and eliminate conflicts in your PC.

▶ Each menu and screen in MSD is defined and their functions are described.

▶ Most important, practical examples are presented, showing how to use MSD to overcome three typical problems: determining the date or developer of an older ROM BIOS that might need to be updated, searching for memory conflicts between TSR programs loaded into upper memory, and eliminating interrupt-sharing conflicts among different hardware components.

Chapter 33
Troubleshoot
Windows à la Mode

In This Chapter

▶ I describe powerful troubleshooting tools that are built into Windows — but that few Windows users know about or know how to exploit.

▶ After describing the special "debugging" modes built into Windows, I provide a complete listing of error codes that Windows might output while in one of these modes, and what you can do to clear them up.

Just when things look bleakest — when your copy of Windows won't start and you don't have a clue as to why — take heart! You may be able to find the problem and correct it with several little-known options that put Windows into a special diagnostic mode.

The cause of most Windows hangs, I find, is the powerful capabilities that are available in 386 enhanced mode. This mode is usually preferable to standard mode: You can run DOS applications in the background or in sizable windows, for example. And the 15 percent performance advantage that standard mode enjoyed over enhanced mode in Windows 3.0 has been essentially eliminated in Windows 3.1. So there is little reason to use standard mode if you have a 386 or higher processor and enough RAM to run enhanced mode.

But 386 enhanced mode does "touch" more of your hardware than standard mode does, which makes Windows more, well, "touchy" — it uses Upper Memory Blocks (UMBs) above 640K, it uses 386-chip tricks to run DOS applications under Windows, and so on.

If you find that Windows hangs in 386 enhanced mode, or that you can start Windows in standard mode by typing WIN /S but not in enhanced mode (and you have well over 2MB of memory), try the following techniques.

Using the Windows Debug Mode

The following procedure requires that you disable any expanded memory managers (EMM) you may have in your CONFIG.SYS file. These managers are usually present to provide expanded memory to DOS applications. When Windows is running DOS applications, Windows takes over expanded memory management from any EMM products you may have in CONFIG.SYS.

For troubleshooting, temporarily remark out any lines in CONFIG.SYS that contain EMM386, QEMM386, 386MAX, or similar managers. (Place the word REM and a space at the beginning of any line in CONFIG.SYS you want to temporarily disable. Don't disable HIMEM.SYS — it's required by Windows.)

Try rebooting and see if Windows will start normally. If so, your EMM may be causing the problem. Check the documentation for the product to see if it is configured improperly.

If you still have the problem, start Windows with the following command line:

```
win /d:xfvs
```

The /D switch puts Windows into a Debug or Diagnostic mode, for this one session only. The colon and the letters following the colon (in this case, XFVS) modify Windows behavior. Each letter affects a different aspect of Windows, making it a little more reliable and less likely to "touch" certain hardware.

If this command line makes your Windows problem go away (you can now run Windows without it crashing, for example), then you need to run WIN /D with each individual option to see which one relates to the problem.

I suggest you try each option in the following order, taking into consideration my suggestions for what to do if one particular option indicates the trouble spot.

WIN /D:X

The command line WIN /D:X has the effect of Excluding all Upper Memory Blocks (UMBs) from Windows' use. This means that Windows will not be allowed to use any of the memory addresses known as A000 to FFFF, which correspond to 640K to 1,024K in your system.

What to do: If this command line makes your problem go away, you probably have a conflict between Windows and some other hardware or software that is using an upper memory block that Windows cannot detect. When Windows uses the UMB for some purpose, it collides with the other product that is also trying to use that UMB, and Windows crashes.

The statement WIN /D:X is the same as adding the following line to the [386Enh] section of your SYSTEM.INI file:

```
[386Enh]
EMMExclude=A000-FFFF
```

You could put this line into your SYSTEM.INI and restart Windows normally, but I wouldn't recommend it. Windows can use memory more efficiently when some Upper Memory Blocks are available to it. And providing expanded memory to DOS applications under Windows is only possible when Windows has access to UMBs.

Instead, I strongly recommend that you find the exact location in upper memory that is causing the conflict. This can pay off later by helping you to identify the individual hardware or software component that is affected.

To do this, you can use a variety of diagnostic programs that are available to locate upper-memory conflicts, such as WinSleuth or System Sleuth from Dariana, or the MSD.EXE utility that is included with Windows 3.1, which I covered in the preceding chapter.

Or you can try a few individual settings in the [386Enh] section of SYSTEM.INI to see which one corrects the problem.

Windows never uses the F000-FFFF area of upper memory, since this is occupied on all PCs by the system ROM BIOS chips. Additionally, Windows avoids the A000-AFFF area on VGA and higher systems, since this area is used by video RAM. So we can eliminate these areas from consideration.

 That leaves the rest of upper memory to test. I suggest you start with the following lines in the [386Enh] section, *one at a time,* to see if they correct the problem:

```
EMMExclude=B000-BFFF
EMMExclude=C000-CFFF
EMMExclude=D000-DFFF
EMMExclude=E000-EFFF
```

If one of these lines makes the problem go away, you must reduce the excluded area down to the actual problem spot. If the problem area is C000-CFFF — a 64K upper memory block which is a very common conflict zone — you can exclude only a 32K area with *one* of the following lines:

```
EMMExclude=C000-C7FF
EMMExclude=C800-CFFF
```

Finally, if one of these lines corrects the problem, reduce the excluded area to 16K, the smallest UMB that Windows uses. To do this in the C000-CFFF area, use one of the following lines at a time:

```
EMMExclude=C000-C3FF
EMMExclude=C400-C7FF
EMMExclude=C800-CBFF
EMMExclude=CC00-CFFF
```

Because these Upper Memory Blocks are numbered in hexadecimal code, it is difficult to calculate the settings. But you can use similar numbers in the UMBs other than C000; for example, the first 16K of the D000 memory block is D000-D3FF.

When you find the UMB that is causing the problem, add an exclude statement to the CONFIG.SYS line that loads your expanded memory manager, and re-enable your EMM in CONFIG.SYS. For example, if the C800-CBFF area needs to be excluded in the [386Enh] section of SYSTEM.INI, you should also place the switch X=C800-CBFF on the line that loads EMM386. (Check the documentation for the proper exclude statement if you use an EMM other than the EMM386.EXE that comes with Windows.)

WIN /D:F

The command WIN /D:F corrects problems with the 32-Bit Disk Access option that is provided with Windows 3.1. The "F" stands for Fixed disk, and it forces Windows to use standard BIOS methods to access your hard disk, rather than the newer 32-Bit Disk Access methods.

You normally turn 32-Bit Disk Access on and off in the Control Panel's 386 Enhanced dialog box. When you click the Virtual Memory button, and then the Change button, you will see a check box labeled "32-Bit Disk Access" if your computer is capable of supporting this feature. (If not, the box will not appear.)

This option is not, contrary to popular belief, primarily intended to make disk access faster. Instead, it allows you to run more DOS applications under Windows, with a given amount of extended memory.

When you turn this option on and restart Windows to enable it, everything may seem to be running fine, but your system may crash as soon as some disk access takes place. In that case, how can you get back to the Control Panel to turn 32-Bit Disk Access off?

What to do: The WIN /D:F command is the answer. If this switch corrects your problem, immediately turn off 32-Bit Disk Access in the Control Panel and restart Windows normally.

Alternately, you can find the line 32BitDiskAccess=TRUE in the [386Enh] section of your SYSTEM.INI file, and change it with a text editor to read 32BitDiskAccess=FALSE. If this line does not appear in the [386Enh] section, do not put it in manually, because it means that Windows previously determined that your system is not compatible with this disk access method.

WIN /D:V

The command WIN /D:V is another option that affects hard drives, in particular SCSI (Small Computer System Interface) drives. The "V" stands for "virtual," and this command line in effect says to Windows, "Don't *virtualize* the hard drives — access them using normal BIOS routines."

What to do: If this command line fixes your problem, then Windows is not able to write to your particular hard drives when it "virtualizes" (takes direct control of) them. You can correct this permanently by adding the following line to the [386Enh] section of SYSTEM.INI:

```
[386Enh]
VirtualHDIRQ=FALSE
```

This line forces Windows not to virtualize the hard disk interrupt request line (IRQ). It should make Windows more reliable with any disk drives that have this problem.

WIN /D:S

The command line WIN /D:S prevents Windows from searching ROM in upper memory between F000 and FFFF for an instruction called a "system break point," which is used for reboots.

What to do: WIN /D:S does the same thing as inserting the following line in the [386Enh] section of SYSTEM.INI:

```
[386Enh]
SystemROMBreakPoint=OFF
```

Ordinarily, Windows can use the normal break point, but memory managers like QEMM386 and 386MAX require that this be set OFF. These EMMs should write this line into SYSTEM.INI themselves, but you may need to add it manually if WIN /D:S corrects a problem you are having.

Serious Troubleshooting: Using BOOTLOG.TXT

If the preceding switches did not help you locate the problem, you are ready for a heavy-duty troubleshooting mechanism known as BOOTLOG.TXT.

To use this method, look in the directory that contains WIN.COM for a file named BOOTLOG.TXT, and rename it to BOOTLOG.001 or similar. Then start Windows with the following command:

```
win /b
```

The "B" switch causes Windows to write into BOOTLOG.TXT a complete record of all the files it loaded during its startup process, and whether each file loaded successfully. This can be an invaluable aid in finding the source of a problem. (It was necessary for us to rename the original BOOTLOG.TXT because Windows creates this file when you install Windows, and appends information to this file every time you run the command WIN /B.)

Even if Windows hangs when you start it, you will find a copy of BOOTLOG.TXT in the Windows directory. The last line of BOOTLOG.TXT will contain a description of the last file that loaded, successfully or unsuccessfully.

Figure 33-1 shows a fragment of BOOTLOG.TXT in the Windows Notepad. In this case, I moved the file WINGDING.FOT out of the Windows directory temporarily to create the error message "LoadFail = WINGDING.FOT Failure code is 02." Messages like this can instantly pinpoint problem areas for you. In fact, it's a good idea to run WIN /B and examine BOOTLOG.TXT every once in a while. For one thing, Windows gives you no error message when a font file that is specified in WIN.INI (such as the Wingdings TrueType FOT file) is not actually found — but you can learn this with BOOTLOG.TXT.

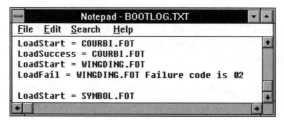

Figure 33-1: When you run WIN /B, the file BOOTLOG.TXT may indicate the exact problem your Windows setup is having.

The possible failure codes you may see in BOOTLOG.TXT, and some steps you can take to deal with them, follow.

0 Out Of Memory. Add extended memory or remove device drivers from conventional or upper memory to see if you can eliminate this error.

2 File Not Found. The file may have been moved or deleted. You may need to decompress the original file off the Windows diskettes using a command like EXPAND A:\FILENAME.EX_ C:\WINDOWS\FILENAME.EXT. Notice that the last character of a compressed file on the Windows diskettes is an underscore (_), but you must provide the correct filename and directory for the decompressed file. (EXPAND.EXE is installed in your Windows directory when you install Windows 3.1.)

3 Path Not Found. A directory that previously existed may have been deleted, and you will have to re-create it.

5 Attempt To Dynamically Link To A Task. The file may have been corrupted, and you may need to EXPAND it off the diskettes.

6 Library Requires Separate Data Segments For Each Task. Same as 5.

8 Insufficient Memory To Start Application. Increase extended, conventional, or upper memory.

10 Incorrect Windows Version. You may have some Windows files from an older version of Windows. Reinstall Windows into the same directory.

11 Invalid .EXE File. This may be a non-Windows .EXE file or a corrupt Windows file. Replace it or EXPAND the original off the diskettes.

12 OS/2 Application. Replace the OS/2 application with one that runs under Windows.

13 MS-DOS 4.0 Application. This may refer to a "family mode" application. This was an old idea for character-mode applications that would run under both DOS 4.0 and OS/2 1.0. These applications will not run under Windows.

14 Unknown .EXE File Type. Replace or eliminate the .EXE file, which may be corrupt.

15 Attempt In Protected Mode (Standard Or 386 Enhanced) To Load An .EXE File Created For An Earlier Version Of Windows. Update the application.

16 Attempt To Load A Second Instance Of An .EXE File Containing Multiple Writeable Data Segments. Remove duplicate instances of this application from the StartUp group in the Program Manager, and the LOAD= and RUN= lines in WIN.INI.

17 Attempt In A Large-Frame EMS Mode To Load A Second Instance Of An Application That Links To Certain Nonshareable DLLs Already In Use. Same as 16.

18 Attempt In Real Mode To Load An Application Marked For Protected Mode Only. You should not see this error in Windows 3.1, which has no real mode, but in Windows 3.0 you can correct it by removing the application from the LOAD= and RUN= lines of WIN.INI.

All the above techniques can help you quickly identify problem areas with Windows. By adding these to your arsenal, you may be able to pinpoint an error that otherwise would take hours or days of trial-and-error to isolate.

Summary

In this chapter, I disclose the background behind the Windows "debug" modes, which can quickly point out specific problem areas, saving you hours of trial-and-error.

▶ The Windows debug modes, when used to isolate upper memory problems, disk drive incompatibilities, ROM BIOS traps, and other conditions, alter the behavior of Windows temporarily so you can determine whether one of these problems is affecting your system.

▶ Most important, the BOOTLOG.TXT file that Windows can generate is a unique way to identify problems affecting individual Windows files that are not loading properly — even when these problems cause no other visible error messages.

Chapter 34
Brainteasers and Brainstorms

In This Chapter

▶ I provide a grab-bag of my favorite tips and tricks from readers.

▶ Included are workarounds and undocumented features that can help you print better-looking characters, fix mice on IBM PS/2s, print to network workstation printers, use line-draw characters in Windows, load memory-resident programs in DOS sessions, keep Word for Windows from grabbing all your CPU time while it prints — and other much-needed ammo for your Windows war chest.

Workarounds for Windows Annoyances _____

Several of my readers have asked about or suggested various fixes for Windows behaviors. In the following sections, I relate some of these problems and their workarounds.

Driver madness

One reader, Dr. John Toppins, sent a message that TrueType looked "wavy" on his Toshiba dot-matrix printer. After a little investigation, we figured out that the TOSHIBA.DRV driver for Windows 3.1 was forcing the printer to use bidirectional printing. In other words, the print head would first print from left to right, then from right to left.

This looks fine for dot-matrix text characters. But when printing graphics (which is what TrueType is on dot-matrix printers), the print head can't perfectly line up one dot with another when it's going in alternating directions. Unidirectional printing produces more precise printouts, although it's slightly slower.

 The code that Toshiba printers use to start bidirectional printing is ESC< (Escape followed by a less-than symbol). This is hard-coded into TOSHIBA.DRV. I suggested changing the driver with a byte editor to read ESC> instead, which starts unidirectional printing.

This change immediately improved the look of TrueType. Because the print head was positioned more precisely with each pass, the vertical strokes of the TrueType characters lined up exactly.

If you have a technical manual for your printer, and the Windows printer driver is forcing some behavior you don't like, you may be able to change escape codes like this yourself. It's impossible to say what will work for every printer. But you should be safe if you follow these rules:

1. Work only on a copy of the printer driver file, not the original.

2. When you've edited your copy, exit Windows, rename the two files, then restart Windows.

3. If your edited driver doesn't work, immediately return to the original.

IBM printers and PS/2s

Other readers were the source of tips about IBM hardware. Users of the IBM 4019 laser printer found a bug in the Windows 3.1 driver. The first copy of a document prints fine on a 4019, but subsequent print jobs are garbled.

A workaround for this behavior may be possible. Open the Control Panel's Printers dialog box, select the 4019 driver, and click Setup. In the dialog box that appears, select the "Universal" font option. This enables Windows 3.1's universal-printer support. Save your changes and try printing. If that doesn't solve the problem, try turning on the "TrueType Fonts as Graphics" option in the dialog box. You also may be able to download a new 4019 driver; see Chapter 28, "License to Upgrade: Help for Expired Drivers."

A different problem affects users of IBM's 386-based PS/2s. Some BIOS revisions for these PS/2s have difficulty exiting Windows in enhanced mode if MOUSE.SYS or MOUSE.COM is loaded. The PS/2 appears to hang, but it actually does exit Windows as much as a minute later.

The fix is an undocumented feature of SYSTEM.INI. Insert the following line into the [386Enh] section if your PS/2s exhibit this behavior:

```
[386Enh]
InitPS2MouseAtExit=False
```

Mousing around

Speaking of mice, I often recommend that you use the Windows 3.1 MOUSE.COM file rather than MOUSE.SYS because it has slightly better support for saving your mouse settings — the acceleration rate and so on. (For more information, see the Windows 3.1 README.WRI file.)

Some readers who have seen this advice couldn't find MOUSE.COM in their Windows subdirectory. The problem is that Windows does not install MOUSE.COM, unless it finds a Microsoft Mouse driver already loaded in your AUTOEXEC.BAT file.

To install MOUSE.COM, first copy the file EXPAND.EXE from the Windows diskettes to your Windows directory. Then, at a DOS prompt, type the command EXPAND A:\MOUSE.CO_ C:\WINDOWS\MOUSE.COM. At that point, you can add mouse support for your DOS programs by inserting the line C:\WINDOWS\MOUSE /Y into your AUTOEXEC.BAT. (The /Y switch tells the mouse driver to use a character-mode cursor in character-mode DOS programs, instead of a graphics character, when using Video Seven and similar graphics adapters.)

By the way, you should check out Version 9.0 of the Microsoft Mouse driver, an improved release available from Microsoft for a list price of $19.95. It adds several handy features to Windows, such as a selection of different mouse pointers.

Use that hourglass

You can actually "click" your hourglass icon (the "wait" symbol) on menu items and dialog boxes, while you're waiting to get your mouse pointer back. Windows stores your mouse clicks until the hourglass disappears — then it plays them all back at once, executing whatever commands you clicked.

I sometimes edit a few pixels of a bitmap file in Paintbrush and, while printing a copy of the result, want to shave off a few more pixels before printing again. The secret is that the "hotspot" of the hourglass is in the *center* of the icon, not the upper left, as with the usual mouse pointer.

This doesn't work in every application, but when it does work it makes me feel like I'm getting more done and waiting for Windows less. Perhaps the hourglass will disappear for good in the multi-threaded Windows NT — but until then, I'll take every shortcut I can get.

Excel-*ent* tips

After writing about some tips about Microsoft Excel in *Windows 3.1 Secrets*, a friend of mine at Microsoft contributed some more pointers, which weren't in the Excel manual at the time.

You probably know that you can type EXCEL *filename* and Excel will load a particular spreadsheet. But you may not know that the command EXCEL /R *filename* loads that file as read-only — safe from accidental changes.

Other switches include EXCEL /P *path,* which starts Excel with a particular drive and directory current; EXCEL /M, which starts Excel with a blank macro sheet; and EXCEL /E, which starts Excel with no Sheet1 (in other words, Empty).

Printing and workstations

Writing about how to improve printing performance under Windows spawned a discussion with readers about other printing-related problems besides speed.

I once stated, for example, that Windows does not support printing to printers that are attached to a networked workstation, as opposed to printers that are attached directly to a print server.

Reader Joe Healy reports, however, that he has been successful in getting Windows to print to such a workstation-connected printer. The secret is to attach the printer, through the Windows Control Panel, to a port called LPT1.OS2 instead of LPT1.

This trick has nothing to do with OS/2. When you have an entry like LPT1.OS2 in the [ports] section of your WIN.INI, Windows thinks you are printing to a file instead of a printer port. It therefore uses the ROM BIOS to output the information, instead of sending it directly to the LPT1 hardware port, where it can't be "seen" by the software that is supposed to direct it to the workstation-attached printer. DOS handles the data by sending it to LPT1 anyway, because you can't name a file the same as a reserved device name.

Good work, Mr. Healy. I hope other network users benefit from this trick, too.

Windows 3.0 and memory

Here's a puzzler for you: Someone who tries to start Windows Write gets the message "Can't find TEMP.WRI." Windows then complains about "Insufficient memory," although the system has plenty of memory.

Give up? This problem is caused by the SET TEMP statement in the AUTOEXEC.BAT file. This statement looks like SET TEMP=C:\TEMP, but there is a *space* between the TEMP and the carriage return at the end of the line. This space, of course, is invisible, so no one has noticed it before. But it creates this maddening error with Write and some other Windows functions.

This problem is fixed in Windows 3.1, but my thanks to the reader who pointed this out to me in case anyone else is vexed by this situation under Windows 3.0 or 3.0a.

Loop logic

In some of my batch file examples, I include a structure like the following:

```
:LOOP
{instructions here}
GOTO :LOOP
```

A.M. of New Mexico expresses his view that this is an illogical expression, because the GOTO that refers to the label :LOOP does not require the colon.

I hate to bite that hand that reads me, but in this case I prefer the style as shown. It doesn't say so in your DOS manual, but reference books show that the syntax of the GOTO statement is GOTO [:]LABEL. The colon is optional, not an error. My staff and I decided as long ago as 1986 that the extra colon makes the two statements look similar enough that it's easier for the eye to jump from one line to the other, and we've used it ever since.

Now I'd like someone to tell me why — after more than 10 years — DOS doesn't have a simple If-Then-Else or While batch command so we could get rid of GOTO statements.

This Is Your Brain on Windows — Any Questions?

If you're hooked on Windows, as I am, you probably have a lot of questions. Windows is a complex environment. It's like we've all traded in our old stick-shift DOS cars for new, shiny, automatic-transmission Windows models. But when the Windows engine is overheating, you could fry an egg on the hood.

So this section is devoted to inquiries you've sent me — straight from your brain to these pages. I'd like to especially thank Jeffrey Katz, Ed York, and Rich Abel for their input.

Drawing the line

Q. How can I get the line-draw characters in a DOS character-mode screen to show up in a Windows application?

A. Pressing the Print Screen key while running a DOS session full-screen under Windows copies the screen into the Clipboard. Windows applications use the ANSI character set instead of IBM's PC-8, which has characters for drawing boxes. But you can switch the Clipboard Viewer to display these characters by clicking Display OEM-Text. Then press Alt+PrintScreen to copy just the Clipboard window. This display is now a graphic that you can paste (Shift+Insert) into Paintbrush or Windows Write, or any word processor that supports graphics.

When you paste captured screens into Paintbrush, remember to click Options Image-Attributes and size the drawing area *larger* than your normal screen area in pixels (Pels). Then click File New and View Zoom-Out before pasting. Paintbrush can't paste into a part of the drawing area that's not visible.

Accelerating the repeat rate

Q. I accelerate my keyboard's repeat rate using a memory-resident TSR in AUTOEXEC.BAT. But when I start a DOS session under Windows, the keyboard goes back to its old repeat rate. The repeat setting is as high as possible in the Windows Control Panel, but this doesn't affect DOS.

A. Not all DOS utilities work as expected when Windows is in protected mode. One thing you can try is to start DOS sessions from a batch file that re-installs your TSR just for that session. Use the PIF Editor to create a file called COMMAND.PIF. Make this PIF file run MYDOS.BAT. The trick to starting a DOS session from a batch file is to make COMMAND the last line of the batch file, like this:

```
@ECHO OFF
c:\utility\mytsr.com
COMMAND
```

The COMMAND line starts a temporary command processor (another instance of COMMAND.COM). This makes the DOS prompt remain available, instead of closing the window as soon as the batch file is completed. Don't use any parameters to COMMAND, as might be necessary in a SHELL= statement in your CONFIG.SYS.

Sometimes utilities don't function when you start more than one instance of them. If that is the case, you might get relief by using Qualitas's 386Max 5.1 or Quarterdeck's QEMM386 6.0 (or higher) memory managers, which support multiple "instancing" of TSRs.

Multitasking in Winword

Q. Why can't I switch to another task while Word for Windows is printing? Isn't Windows multitasking?

A. This problem occurs if Winword is running full-screen when you start printing. Winword ignores you while it continues printing, even when you click the Minimize icon to switch to another application. But Windows is still "listening" for mouse events — it's just that Winword is absorbing them all.

Try "restoring" Winword to a partial-screen window before you do a File Print. Then double-click any minimized icon on the icon line. You should find that Windows recognizes the mouse action and switches to that application, while Winword continues to print in the background. This time, your mouse click was intercepted by Windows itself, not Winword.

Worthless Windows Tips

You may have seen the headline "201 Windows Secrets" on the February 1992 cover of a newsstand magazine about PC computing.

Actually, only 12 of the tips contained in the article relate to Windows itself. The other 189 items, far from being undocumented "secrets," are simple functions of such applications as Microsoft PowerPoint and Adobe Type Manager, virtually all of which are straight out of the manuals that ship with those products.

But several people — assuming because I have written a work with a very similar name that I had something to do with the preparation of this material — have contacted me with the question, "Why can't I get many of these tips to work?"

My responses to these questions may be useful to a number of readers, since the answers illustrate some useful features of the Windows environment.

Generating the copyright symbol

■ The article states that you can insert a copyright symbol (©) into text in a Windows application by holding down the Alt key and typing 169 on the numeric keypad. It also suggests 174 for a registered trademark symbol (®), 165 for a Yen symbol (¥), and 163 for the Pound Sterling symbol (£).

If you actually try this tip, however, you only get some accented characters from the IBM PC-8 Line Draw character set.

The real way to get the copyright symbol is to press Alt+0169. The trademark symbol is Alt+0174, and so on. (Note that NumLock must be on.)

The reason the writer got these keystrokes wrong is that he saw these numbers on a chart listing the entire Windows character set — such as one I published in *Windows 3.1 Secrets* and in the "Characters, Fonts, and Fast Printing" chapter of this book — and assumed that the leading zero wasn't important. Omitting the zero, however, completely changes the meaning of the keystroke combination.

Faster loading

■ The article suggests that you can "speed up the process" of Windows loading by editing "superfluous lines" out of your WIN.INI and SYSTEM.INI files. It specifically recommends removing all blank lines with a text editor.

This "tip" seemed so absurd that I actually tested it several times (after rebooting each time to ensure a fair comparison).

In fact, removing the blank lines in your .INI files doesn't make any difference in loading time at all. The few carriage returns in most people's .INI files are such a small percentage of the total number of characters Windows must read in these files that any difference is imperceptible. Don't mess with your WIN.INI for such an illusory benefit. (The writer of this suggestion was thinking of batch files, which *do* run slightly slower when many blank lines are included.)

You'd get a bigger speedup in loading time — about one second — by using the undocumented command line WIN F7 (WIN followed by a space and the F7 key, which looks on-screen like WIN ^@). This eliminates the Windows advertising screen.

Selecting all files

■ The article states that a shortcut to select all the files in a File Manager directory window is Shift+Backslash.

This key combination actually does nothing. The correct shortcut to select all files is simply to press the Slash key. Press Backslash to deselect them.

Loading multiple apps

■ In a description of how to add applications to the LOAD= line of WIN.INI, it's explained that you should separate different application names by semicolons.

This tip will confuse novices a great deal when they can't get more than one app to load. Any experienced user knows that semicolons start comments in WIN.INI. It's *spaces* that are used to separate application names.

Tracking spreadsheet versions

■ One tip claims that you can keep track of the current version of several spreadsheet printouts by including the following formula in a cell in Microsoft Excel:

```
="Printed "&TEXT(NOW(),"Mmmm d, yyyy hh:mm")
```

The article states that every time the worksheet is printed, the current date and time will also be printed, allowing you to easily find the most recent printout.

This is a nice idea, but the formula shown simply doesn't work. It prints the last time the worksheet was changed (if automatic calculation is on) or recalculated (if automatic recalculation has been turned off), which may be nowhere near the time the worksheet was printed.

Another way to try to print the current date and time (but it would be wrong) would be to place the formula =NOW( ) into a cell by itself, then format that cell as "Mmmm d, yyyy h:mm am/pm." But this has the same problem — again, the NOW( ) function does not update itself every time the worksheet is printed.

This discrepancy, of course, will surely convince your co-workers of the accuracy of the other formulas in your spreadsheet model.

The best way to add the actual date and time of printing to your spread-sheets is to insert the text "Printed &d, &t" into the header or footer of the worksheet, using Excel's File Page-Setup dialog box. This actually does update itself whenever you print.

I could go on with more examples, but you get the idea. Every blunder could have been caught if someone had tried each tip even once before publishing it.

Summary

In this chapter, my readers provide or inquire about a number of secrets that can help you fix problems or take advantage of quirks in the Windows environment.

▶ With just minor tweaks, these readers are now printing better-looking type on dot-matrix printers and IBM 4019 printers, expanding the DOS-based mouse drivers off the Windows distribution diskette set, using the irritating "hourglass" symbol to actually get some work done, troubleshooting esoteric TEMP variable problems, and many other little quality-of-life improvements.

Chapter 35

Secrets of the Word Processing Masters

In This Chapter

▶ I give you the good parts of a scathing book that shows bugs and limitations in Microsoft's flagship word processor, Word for Windows, and how you can work around them.

▶ I show you ways to access unused and undocumented key combinations in Word for Windows, WordPerfect for Windows, and Ami Pro.

Once in a great while, book authors come along who understand the awful truth about computer software: that it *never* works exactly the way it says in the software's manual.

Woody Leonhard and Vincent Chen are such authors, and they have written a book that tells the truth about at least one Windows software package: *The Hacker's Guide to Word for Windows* (Addison-Wesley). I wouldn't have believed this until I saw it myself, but practically every page of this 800-page book describes a bug or "undocumented feature" of Microsoft Word for Windows 2.0. For example:

■ Open a Winword document that includes several paragraphs. Select several paragraphs between the first paragraph and the last one, and format them as "Hidden Text." In the Tools Options View dialog box, turn off the display of Hidden Text, so those paragraphs do not appear on-screen. Then place your insertion point at the beginning of the first non-hidden paragraph after the hidden text, and delete a few characters or words. Turn the display of Hidden Text back on, and you'll see that Winword deleted *all the hidden text,* not just the words you thought you deleted. This can be catastrophic in a document that contains hidden and non-hidden text, such as a price list with retail and (hidden) wholesale prices.

■ Open another document, and make a duplicate copy of it with a different name. Add and delete characters here and there in one copy of the document. Save the file, then click Tools Compare-Versions to compare it with the other document on disk. You should see your changes marked throughout the document. Now, say you change your mind and you click the Undo Revisions button to restore your document to its original version. Surprise! Winword deletes *every paragraph* that changed, even if the change was only a single character.

- Insert part of one document that contains paragraph styles into another document that contains different styles. Intermittently, some of the fonts in the inserted document will magically be changed by Winword into fonts that don't exist in either document! This happens randomly, but with such regularity that it even has a name: the Phont Phunnies. Mr. Leonhard and Mr. Chen's book includes several steps you can take to 1) reproduce the bug, and 2) try to avoid it.

- Once you open a non-Winword file and do simple things like insert text from the Clipboard, you cannot save the file to its original format and filename (such as saving plain-text files with their original name).

- In WordBasic, Val("-123") returns a value of -123, but Val("+123") returns 0 and Val("1,234") returns 1 (among other weird behaviors).

- When creating a dialog box for a macro, you must test it in four different screen resolutions so you know the text will fit, due to Winword's weird spacing conventions. But if you load your painstakingly created dialog box into Winword's Dialog Editor, it truncates your text boxes into "standard" sizes, making them unreadable.

I could go on, but it would take several chapters for me to mention all the "features" of Winword revealed in this book. Every section exposes a museum of "gotchas" in Winword. Mr. Leonhard and Mr. Chen have painstakingly tested every single Winword menu and command, and describe the results — which often vary enormously from the descriptions in the official manual.

The best part of the _Hacker's Guide_ (the book is named for _hackers_ in the sense of "ultimate power users," unrelated to _crackers_ who break into dial-up systems) is its collection of tips on using undocumented features. The authors have found at least 72 undocumented commands in the WordBasic language!

Mr. Leonhard and Mr. Chen found these commands the way much of the book was discovered: they actually tested every possible use of every command and noted the results. All computer books should benefit from this kind of research, but very few do.

The 72 undocumented WordBasic commands are created by adding a dollar sign ($) to the end of standard commands. For example, if you use the standard command "CharColor" in a macro, it asks the user to type a number, 0 to 15, representing a color for selected text. But "CharColor$" asks the user to type a color _name,_ such as red, green, and so on. This is _much_ more useful.

The _Hacker's Guide_ also provides many brilliant remedies for common Word for Windows problems. For example, you may wish to create a dialog box that accepts a name and address for a personalized letter. Unfortunately, Winword provides no way for the Enter key to be used at the end of lines in a multi-line text box. Pressing Enter automatically clicks OK or some other button, and there has been no way to alter this behavior. But the _Hacker's Guide_ reveals an elegantly simple way to allow Enter to end lines in such boxes, using an undocumented parameter to Winword's Dialog macro command.

The book also provides a disk of useful add-ons to Winword, including their WordBasic source code so you can easily customize them. The disk includes a way to insert hypertext "jump to" buttons into Winword documents, a much better Envelope feature than the one on Winword's toolbar, and more.

Additional valuable tips are found in Guy Gallo's *Take Word for Windows to the Edge* (Ziff-Davis Press). Mr. Gallo covers some of the same bugs as the *Hacker's Guide*. But Mr. Gallo adds a few new gotchas, such as the fact that changing the style of footnotes and annotation references doesn't change any existing text in those styles, unlike all other Winword styles.

Why are books like these necessary? Because Microsoft has never produced Version 1.0 of any software product that was rock solid. DOS 1.0? Pathetic. Access 1.0? Bugs that lose data. Windows 1.0? Get real.

And the truth is that there's a lot of old Winword 1.0 code still inside Winword 2.0 (even in Winword 2.0c — the fourth version of the product released within a 13-month period). Sources say that Microsoft developers found the cause of the Phont Phunnies in the old font-mapping engine from Winword 1.0, and created a fix for it. But putting the fix into Winword 2.0 beta code broke so many other things that they had to leave out the fix until the next complete rewrite.

I asked Microsoft representatives about the numerous bugs discussed in the *Hacker's Guide* and *Take Word for Windows to the Edge*. Winword marketing manager Eric Levine said, "These are things we know about," but could not say whether individual behaviors would or would not appear in the next release of the product. He did say, however, that the undocumented feature that allows the Enter key to end multiple text lines in dialog boxes (and not activate an OK button) would be removed from future releases.

I hope Microsoft provides *documented* ways to do this and other things. For instance, now that Windows 3.1 traps Ctrl+Alt+Delete, it is no longer necessary to avoid Ctrl+Alt key combinations for macros. But neither Winword 2.0 or the new WordPerfect 5.2 for Windows allows this. In the following sections, I'll show you how.

Using Ctrl+Alt Combinations for Winword Macros

Windows 3.1 introduced a handy new feature called "local reboot." This means that when you press Ctrl+Alt+Delete in Windows enhanced mode, your PC does not immediately restart. Instead, Windows displays a text box that gives you a choice of returning to Windows, terminating a hung application (if one is in that state), or really rebooting. (If you don't like this feature, and want Ctrl+Alt+Delete to reboot your PC immediately, you can put the line LocalReboot=OFF in the [386Enh] section of SYSTEM.INI.)

Local reboot means that it is no longer risky for us to place keyboard macros on Ctrl+Alt key combinations. If a user accidentally hits the Delete key while holding down Ctrl and Alt, a Windows text screen appears and the user can continue working, if desired.

For this reason, I was surprised when Microsoft Word for Windows 2.0 and WordPerfect 5.2 for Windows came out. These applications allow you to assign macros to certain key combinations — but not to any combination that includes Alt, Ctrl+Alt, or Shift+Alt!

It's particularly important to be able to redefine Ctrl+Alt key combinations, because almost every key combination involving Ctrl+Shift and Shift+Alt is already being used by one application or another. So let me make clear to software vendors Livingston's Law of User Customizability:**Leave all Ctrl+Alt combinations for the user to redefine!**

Having said that, I'd like to give you a way to place macros on *any* key combination in Word for Windows — even undocumented key combinations. (We'll look at WordPerfect in a later section.)

STEPS

Placing Macros on any Word for Windows Key Combination

Step 1.   In Winword 2.0, click Tools Record-Macro. Type in the name AutoAssignToKey and click OK. Assign the macro to the Global level when asked. Without pressing any other keys, click Tools Stop-Recorder. You've just recorded the shortest possible macro.

Step 2.   Click Tools Macro, select AutoAssignToKey, and click Edit. You should see a macro editing window containing only two lines: Sub MAIN and End Sub. Type between these lines the contents of the AutoAssignToKey macro shown in Listing 35-1. Once your window looks the same as this macro, click File Close and save the changes when asked.

Listing 35-1: AutoAssignToKey macro:

```
Sub MAIN
On Error Goto BYE
name$ = InputBox$("Type the macro name to assign to a key")
number$ = InputBox$("Type the key number from Using WordBasic")
num = Val(number$)
If num < 8 Or num > 2014 Then
MsgBox "Number of the key must be 8 to 2014."
Else
ToolsOptionsKeyboard .Name = name$, .KeyCode = num, .Context = 0
End If
BYE:
End Sub
```

Now you can assign *any* Winword macro to *any* key combination — even ones not permitted by Winword's Tools Options Keyboard dialog box. Let's start by assigning the AutoAssignToKey macro *itself* to a key combination, so it's easily accessible when you need it.

STEPS

Assigning the AutoAssignToKey Macro to a Key Combination

Step 1. Click Tools Macro, select AutoAssignToKey, and click Run. You should see a dialog box that asks you for a macro name to assign. Type in the name AutoAssignToKey. Click OK, and you should see another dialog box, this one asking you for a key number. Type in 1288 to assign it to Ctrl+Alt+Backspace, and click OK.

Step 2. After the dialog box closes, try out your new key definition. Press Ctrl+Alt+Backspace, and the AutoAssignToKey dialog box should appear, ready for you to define any other key definitions you like.

By the same method, type in the AutoUnassignToKey macro, shown in Listing 35-2 so it's ready when you need to undo any key redefinitions. (One time I accidentally redefined the Alt key itself, and *boy* does that make it hard to use Winword!)

Listing 35-2: AutoUnassignToKey macro:

```
Sub MAIN
On Error Goto BYE
number$ = InputBox$("Type the key number to unassign from Using WordBasic")
num = Val(number$)
If num < 8 Or num > 2014 Then
MsgBox "Number of the key must be 8 to 2014."
Else
ToolsOptionsKeyboard .KeyCode = num, .Context = 0, .Delete
ToolsOptionsKeyboard .KeyCode = num, .Context = 0, .Delete
BYE:
End Sub
```

To find the key codes for any particular key, use the accompanying Key Codes listed in Table 35-1. To assign a key with Ctrl held down, add 256 to the number shown. Add 512 for Shift, and 1024 for Alt. These values can be added together to indicate more than one shift key. The Backspace key, for example, has a key code of 8, so Ctrl+Alt+Backspace is 1288 because 256+1024+8=1288.

Bksp.	8	5	53	l	76	F1†	112	Keypad 0	96	Keypad 5	
Tab	9	6	54	m	77	F2†	113	Keypad 1	97	(NumLock off)	12
Enter	13	7	55	n	78	F3	114	Keypad 2	98	Pause	19
Esc	27	8	56	o	79	F4	115	Keypad 3	99	Scroll Lock	3 or 145
Space	32	9	57	p	80	F5	116	Keypad 4	100	; (semicolon)	186
PgUp	33	a	65	q	81	F6	117	Keypad 5	101	= (equals sign)	187
PgDn	34	b	66	r	82	F7	118	Keypad 6	102	, (comma)	188
End	35	c	67	s	83	F8	119	Keypad 7	103	- (hyphen)	189
Home	36	d	68	t	84	F9	120	Keypad 8	104	. (period)	190
Ins	45	e	69	u	85	F10	121	Keypad 9	105	/ (slash)	191
Del	46	f	70	v	86	F11†	122	Keypad *	106	' (backquote)	192
0	48	g	71	w	87	F12†	123	Keypad +	107	[(left bracket)	219
1	49	h	72	x	88	F13	124	Keypad ,	108	\ (backslash)	220
2	50	i	73	y	89	F14	125	Keypad -	109	] (right bracket)	221
3	51	j	74	z	90	F15	126	Keypad .	110	' (apostrophe)	222
4	52	k	75			F16	127	Keypad /	111		

Table 35-1: Word for Windows Key Codes

† Windows forces Alt+F1 and Alt+F2 to have the same meaning as F11 and F12.

Most of these codes are listed in *UsingWordBasic,* Microsoft's latest attempt to document the WordBasic language — but not all. Each of the keys from Pause to Apostrophe are undocumented by Microsoft, although I've written about them since 1991. And, as Woody Leonhard and Vincent Chen point out in the *Hacker's Guide*, not all the combinations that are documented actually work.

Due to bugs, some combinations simply do not function as expected. *Using WordBasic* states, for example, that Numeric Keypad 5 — with Num Lock off, when it ordinarily does nothing — can be redefined by specifying key code 12. But this does not work, unless you specify a Ctrl or Alt key in conjunction with Keypad 5. For example, Shift+Alt+Keypad 5 can be assigned to a macro successfully, but Keypad 5 and Shift+Keypad 5 cannot.

The Scroll Lock key is another oddity. Along with Pause, this is a great key to redefine, because it has no function in Winword or most other programs. But sometimes the Scroll Lock key acts like it has a value of 145, at other times (specifically, when the Ctrl key is involved in the combination) a value of 3! The Pause key can't be redefined with Ctrl involved at all. Test these keys carefully when you assign them.

Additionally, according to the *Hacker's Guide,* many combinations involving the numeric keypad and directional-arrows keypad do not work well. The authors tested every single combination — another example of the extensive research that went into their book. It seems that the numeric keypad doesn't like to be reassigned with the Shift key involved, nor the arrow keypad unless Alt is involved. Check the book.

Be aware that Windows pre-empts Ctrl+Alt+Delete and key combinations involving Ctrl+Escape. Finally, you should know that Windows forces Alt+F1 and Alt+F2 to mean the same thing as F11 and F12, in case you're still using a keyboard with only 10 function keys.

Armed with this knowledge, you should now have plenty of macro keys on hand.

Using Winword add-ons and fixes

I mentioned earlier that using Winword's Undo Revisions feature can delete every paragraph that has even a single change in a document that has revisions marked using the Compare Documents feature. It's better to avoid Winword's limitations entirely by using DocuComp, a product that marks specific changes from one document to the next, instead of just flagging whole paragraphs. (Advanced Software Inc., $199.95, 800-346-5392 or 408-733-0745.)

Another problem is embedded graphics. Winword converts each graphic into a "metafile," with enormous overhead. Inserting a 146K bitmap into one page of text resulted in a 1,326K document on my disk. This is corrected by Quicture, a product that inserts place holders into documents and compresses the bitmaps, saving tremendous amounts of space and making screen scrolling much faster. (WexTech Systems Inc., $59, 212-949-9595 ext. 1.)

Difficulties opening or saving files in non-Winword formats can be overcome using Word for Word, from the people who produced some of the original file filters for Microsoft. The Winword add-in version is $79.95 and supports some 50 formats, including import/export filters for older applications that may still be important in your office, such as Multimate 4.1, Office Writer, and Pro Write. The stand-alone application (which can batch-convert files) is $149 and supports over 100. (Mastersoft Inc., 800-624-6107 or 602-277-0900.)

Finally, the best all-around add-in is probably MasterWord, with more than 500 customizable color toolbar buttons, and the best File Open and File New dialog boxes I've seen. (Alki Software Corp., $59; 800-669-9673.)

Using Ctrl+Alt Combinations for WordPerfect Macros

Earlier in this chapter, I showed a method to assign Ctrl+Alt key combinations to macros in Word for Windows. In the next few pages, I'll do WordPerfect for Windows.

WPWin 5.2 includes several features that are not found in Winword. For example, character styles can be applied to less than a whole paragraph, and multiple columns on a page can be different widths. My method for assigning Ctrl+Alt keys takes advantage of another convenient feature of WordPerfect: the ability to switch from one keyboard layout to another at any time.

WordPerfect 5.2 provides several keyboard layouts, including one similar to WordPerfect 5.1 for DOS, and one that uses the Windows Common User Access (CUA) guidelines. The following procedure assumes the CUA layout, stored in a WordPerfect .WWK file.

STEPS

Assigning Macros to WordPerfect Ctrl+Alt Key Combinations

Step 1. If you wish to assign a macro to a key combination, you must first run the macro once, which "compiles" it.

Step 2. Click File Preferences Keyboard. Click the Default (CUA) button, then click Create. Click the Save As button, type in CUA.WWK, and click the Save button to save this file. Then click OK. (If you use a non-CUA layout, simply select your existing .WWK file.)

Step 3. Click the Edit button to edit your .WWK file. Pull down the Item Types list and select Macros. Click the Add button. In the list of macros that appears, select the name of the macro you wish to assign to a Ctrl+Alt key, then click the Import button. The macro name appears in the Keyboard Editor window.

Step 4. If the key combination you wish to assign this macro to is Ctrl+Alt+A, press Ctrl+A, then click the Assign button. (We will change this to Ctrl+Alt+A later.) Then click the Save As button, type in an alternate filename, such as CUA1.WWK, and click Save.

Step 5. You are returned to the Keyboard Editor window. Click the OK button. Click the Select button, highlight your original file (such as CUA.WWK), then click Select. Repeat Step 3, selecting the same macro name as before. Then repeat Step 4, but this time turn on the check box titled Allow Reassigning of ABC. Press the letter A, then click the Assign button to assign your macro to the plain letter A. Click the Save As button, pick a new alternate filename, such as CUA2.WWK, and click Save.

Step 6. Click OK twice, and exit WordPerfect. Start a DOS session and change to the directory that contains your files. Issue this DOS command:

```
fc /b cua1.wwk cua2.wwk
```

This file-compare (FC) command should produce a line of output such as 00005213: 08 00. These are hexadecimal numbers representing the location of the Ctrl key (08) or no Ctrl key (00) in your two files. If you see more than one line of output, something went wrong.

Step 7. Use the Windows Calculator to add 100 in hex to the location. Remember that 5213 plus 100 hex would be 5313, but 5913 plus 100 hex would be 5A13.

Step 8. At the DOS prompt, type DEBUG CUA1.WWK. When you see Debug's hyphen prompt, type these lines:

```
d 5313
e 5313 18
w
q
```

The D command should output "08" as the first byte. (If it doesn't, press Q to quit.) The E command changes one byte in the file from 08 (Ctrl) to 18 (Ctrl+Alt). Now start WordPerfect and test CUA1.WWK. Success! If it doesn't work, go back to CUA.WWK and try again.

You can currently change only one key reassignment per round for this to work. Fortunately, WordPerfect plans to support Ctrl+Alt keys in its next release, and your edits will continue to run.

Using Ctrl+Alt Combinations for Ami Pro Macros

Interestingly, Ami Pro by Lotus is one word processing application that has no trouble supporting Ctrl+Alt keys.

It's ironic that applications that work fine get less ink in my writings than apps with problems. That's because I try to tell you ways to do things that Windows apps *can't* usually do, not what they *can* do easily.

If you have Ami Pro, here is the method to assign a macro or command to a Ctrl+Alt key combination:

Click Tools Macro Playback. Select the file AMIMENUS.SMM. Select "Customize Ami Pro Menus" and click OK. In the dialog box that appears, click "Assign Key Commands." Click either Ami Pro Macro or Function. Then select any macro or function, and assign it any Ctrl, Shift, or Alt combination you like.

Summary

In this chapter, I examine perhaps the most popular Windows application category — word processing — with an eye toward weaknesses and workarounds.

▶ The groundbreaking book, *The Hacker's Guide to Word for Windows,* was one of the first to go through a major Windows application, command by command, and document all of its bugs, flaws, and broken promises. The authors provide many ways to fix Winword problems, as well as showing how to do things you never imagined you could pull off.

▶ Now that Windows 3.1 protects users from pressing Ctrl+Alt+Delete accidentally, there's no reason not to use Ctrl+Alt plus a letter to represent macros — but it's difficult or impossible to assign such a combination to macros in Winword and WordPerfect for Windows, unless you know the secret.

Chapter 36
Hypertext Help

In This Chapter

▶ I reveal how easy it can be for you, a Windows user with a little ambition, to create your own Windows help file, containing your résumé, your company's catalog, or anything you like.

▶ I show you tools that can ease the creation of help files with hypertext links to related information — even make it fun — and undocumented WIN.INI settings to make your hypertext links more visible on-screen.

Some of the best features of Windows aren't the obvious ones that you first see, such as the Program Manager and File Manager. Instead, I believe that some of the most interesting aspects of the graphical environment are those that you appreciate gradually, over time.

One of these features is the Windows help engine, which provides a quickie online manual for almost every Windows program now shipping. Most Windows applications no longer include their own separate help engine. For the most part, applications now take advantage of WINHELP.EXE, the help application that is included in Windows 3.1 and 3.0, Windows for Workgroups, and Windows NT.

Application developers like using the services of WINHELP.EXE, because it provides impressive text-handling capabilities. Under Windows 2.x, help windows tended to be boring black-and-white, text-only explanations. But starting with Windows 3.0, and improved in Windows 3.1, help text became much more than boring text. Today, help files can display information in any size and in almost any format. Help files can include colored words or graphics that "jump" to related sections of text when clicked with a mouse.

In Windows 3.1, it's even possible to include colored buttons that run other programs. For example, a help file can now launch Paintbrush and load an image, possibly for a tutorial on bitmap graphics.

With all these capabilities, most Windows users still don't realize that they can create help files of their own. It requires a few specialized tools and some clear design work. But a help file may be just what you need to distribute time-sensitive information that wouldn't be quite the same in print.

How Help Files Can Help You

The problem with help files is that we have allowed ourselves to think of them only as copies of printed computer manuals. Of course, help files are very useful as replacements for manuals. But that's probably their least interesting use.

More intriguing is the use of help files for any body of information that is visual and detailed. The Windows help engine is actually a kind of *hypertext* environment. This means that you can jump from any part of the text to any other part. When you've found the information you need, you can jump back to where you began.

This is possible with a printed book, of course. But books are bulky and hard to update. If you wanted to send out a new edition every month, it would be quite an expense to print 12 new volumes a year. Sending out a new diskette containing a help file every month, however, would be relatively cheap and convenient. And placing a new file on a network every month, for use by all employees of a company, would be very simple indeed.

The portability and ease of updating qualities of help files can inspire us to think of new ways we can use the Windows hypertext engine. Consider these possibilities:

■ A warehouse could distribute a huge auto-parts catalog in the form of a help file. The help file could include bitmap graphics of each individual part, engine assemblies, and so on. Clicking such a part would display detailed specifications, prices, and ordering information.

■ A company could maintain its entire employee telephone directory in the form of a help file. Every month (or every day!) an updated copy of this file could be placed on the corporate network. From there it would be accessible from an icon in each user's Program Manager. Clicking a person's name and phone number might display mail-stop or address information. It could even dial the person's phone, if desired.

■ A group working on a joint document might access each person's contributions as part of a large help file. At the end of each day, a coordinator might collect the latest version of each person's text, and merge the pieces into a single file. The next day, each contributor could see how his or her work looked, and jump to related sections in other contributors' chapters.

These are just a few ideas. I'm sure you can be much more creative in imagining even better applications.

Tools for Designing Your Own Help

Windows application developers are accustomed to making help files for their programs with the Microsoft Windows Software Development Kit (SDK). This bundle of resources includes a Help Compiler (HC.EXE) and documentation on the requirements for preparing raw help text.

Microsoft requires that help text be written in Rich Text Format (RTF). This format defines a special kind of text file, which uses only the first 127 characters in the ASCII character set to describe all aspects of a document. This includes such things as paragraph styles, bold and italic text, and any special characters that may be required.

Few word processors produce RTF files, but Microsoft Word for Windows does a good job of it. Unfortunately, even when you have a word processor that supports RTF, preparing help files by hand can be quite time-consuming.

To ease this burden, WexTech Systems of New York City distributes a package of templates for Word for Windows 2.0 and higher, called Doc-To-Help. These templates allow a developer or corporate PC manager to prepare a relatively simple document containing help text, rather than typing in arcane RTF codes by hand. Macros provided with Doc-To-Help automatically translate Winword files into the required RTF output. This file is then fed into Microsoft's Help Compiler, which results in a working .HLP file. Doc-To-Help also has the great feature of being able to produce, from the same input document, printed documentation. The resulting manual includes all the text but leaves out "jump colors" and the like, which are appropriate in hypertext, but not in print.

Doc-To-Help 1.1 lists for $295, which includes the Help Compiler, but does not include a copy of Word for Windows. For more information, contact WexTech Systems, 60 E. 42nd St., Suite 1733, New York, NY 10165; 212-949-9595 or 212-949-4007 (fax).

For those without Winword, an alternate solution is provided by a product called QDHelp. This application includes a text converter and several sample files, which allow you to produce "Quick and Dirty Help." The product is a shareware program, which means you can download it from a service such as CompuServe and try it before obtaining a license. If you decide to use it long-term, the license costs $35, plus $3 shipping (plus an additional $2 shipping outside the U.S.).

The sample files included with QDHelp provide a sort-of "fill in the blanks" approach to making your own help files. See Figures 36-1 and 36-2 for examples. By following the outline that author Phil Allen has provided, it's possible for anyone with a little programming knowledge to get a small help file working — complete with jump words and graphics — in only a few hours. Figure 36-3 shows one result.

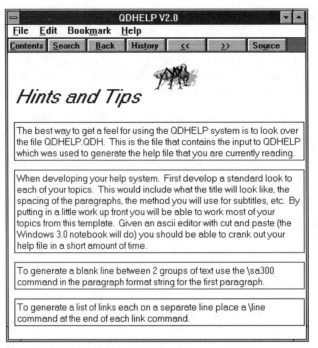

Figure 36-1: The QDHelp package lets you prepare Windows .HLP files by substituting your own text in sample files. This QDHelp help file was created using QDHelp itself. For another view of the same text, see Figure 36-2.

To download QDHelp when accessing CompuServe, use the command GO WINSDK, select the Libraries menu, and choose Library 16. Download the file named QDHELP.LZH from this library. (For information on how to access CompuServe with your modem, call 800-848-8990 in the U.S., or 614-457-8650 outside the U.S.)

Allen also offers assistance to professional developers who must create help files for commercial applications. Download the file QDTOOL.LZH from the same library, which contains QDMenu. This program creates a basic help text file by reading the menu structure within any Windows .EXE file. You fill out this file by adding a description of each menu item, which is simpler than creating the entire help file from scratch.

```
┌─────────────────────────────────────────────────────────────┐
│ ⊟              Notepad - HINTS.QDH                      ▼ ▲  │
├─────────────────────────────────────────────────────────────┤
│ File  Edit  Search  Help                                     │
├─────────────────────────────────────────────────────────────┤
│ /topic HINTS                                              ▲  │
│                                                           █  │
│     /title hints and tips                                 █  │
│     /keywords hints;tips                                  █  │
│     /browse index,AUTO                                    █  │
│                                                           █  │
│     /para \sa300                                             │
│         /text \b\i\fs40,Hints and Tips                      │
│         /bitmaplink INDEX,live.bmp                          │
│     /endpara                                                 │
│                                                             │
│     /para \box\sa150                                        │
│         The best way to get a feel for using the QDHELP system│
│         is to look over the file QDHELP.QDH.  This is the file│
│         that contains the input to QDHELP which was used to │
│         generate the help file that you are currently reading.│
│     /endpara                                                 │
│                                                             │
│     /para \box\sa150                                        │
│         When developing your help system.  First develop a standard│
│         look to each of your topics.  This would include what the│
│         title will look like, the spacing of the paragraphs, the│
│         method you will use for subtitles, etc.  By putting in a│
│         little work up front you will be able to work most of your│
│         topics from this template.  Given an ascii editor with cut│
│         and paste (the Windows 3.0 notebook will do) you should be│
│         able to crank out your help file in a short amount of time.│
│      /endpara                                               │
│                                                             │
│     /para \box\sa150                                        │
│         To generate a blank line between 2 groups of text  │
│         use the \\sa300 command in the paragraph format    │
│         string for the first paragraph.                    │
│     /endpara                                                │
│                                                             │
│     /para \box                                             │
│         To generate a list of links each on a separate line place│
│         a \\line command at the end of each link command.  │
│     /endpara                                                │
│                                                             │
│ /endtopic                                                 ▼ │
├─────────────────────────────────────────────────────────────┤
│ ◄ ▓▓▓                                                   ► │
└─────────────────────────────────────────────────────────────┘
```

Figure 36-2: This text file shows the same text as the help window in Figure 36-1, but in the Rich Text Format required by Microsoft's Help Compiler.

To use either of the files QDHELP.LZH or QDTOOL.LZH, you must have a program to decompress the files. You can do this with LHA.EXE, a free program that compresses and decompresses files. On CompuServe, use the command GO IBMSYS, choose the File Utilities library, and download the file LHA213.EXE. Run this program once from a DOS command line. It extracts itself into several files, including LHA.EXE and LHA213.DOC. The .DOC file explains the use of LHA.EXE to decompress files in DOS. For example, to extract QDHELP.LZH, change to the directory that contains that file, and type the following command:

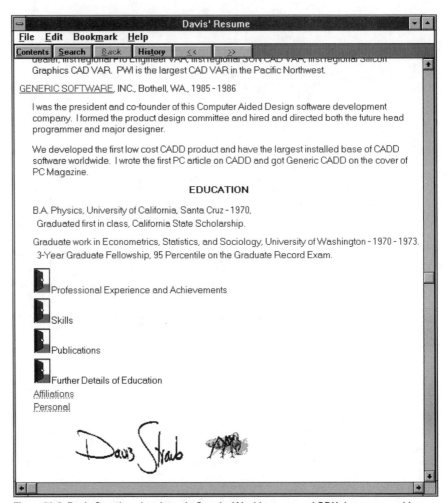

Figure 36-3: Davis Straub, a developer in Seattle, Washington, used QDHelp to convert his résumé into a Windows help file. Clicking one of the doors or underlined words leads to more information. The "bug" graphic was copied from the QDHelp sample help file.

```
C:\directory\LHA E QDHELP.LZH
```

You may also obtain QDHelp and QDMenu by sending the $35 registration (plus shipping) directly to: Phil Allen, 1185 Lowell Dr. #5, Oconomowoc, WI 53066. Specify the size of disk you prefer (5 ¼- or 3 ½-inch disks).

Additionally, you need the Microsoft Help Compiler to convert the output of QDHelp into a working .HLP file. At this writing, you can download the latest copy of the compiler from CompuServe's WINSDK forum, Library 16, filename HCP.ZIP. (To decompress this file, you'll need to get PKZip by downloading PK204G.EXE from the IBMNEW forum, Library 2. The version numbers in this filename may change in the future, but the location of the file should remain the same. Run PK204G.EXE once at a DOS command line, and it extracts itself into several files. Use the command PKUNZIP HCP.ZIP to decompress the Help Compiler.)

Since the file HCP.ZIP is a bug-fix version of the compiler found in the Windows 3.1 SDK, it may change its location or availability in the future. If it's no longer located in that library, the compiler is also available in Microsoft's Visual Basic Professional, Borland's C++ package, Doc-To-Help, or it may be purchased directly from Microsoft.

Don't jump to the conclusion that making your own help files is a piece of cake. Like any executable Windows program, a complex help file requires quite a bit of work. Writing one should be part of a process that starts with a clear design, proceeds with well-thought-out development, and finishes with a rigorous testing procedure before distribution.

Brian Moura, who developed a help file as assistant city manager of San Carlos, California — and is an accomplished Windows expert who served as a technical reviewer of *More Windows Secrets* — says interested PC users shouldn't shy away from creating their own hypertext help files. "The creation of a Windows help file can be easy with a tool like DocToHelp, so even a non-programmer can do it. On the other hand, it is very time consuming. Our 'Doing Business in San Carlos' help file took many hours, most of which was taken up by typing in text, creating diagrams, and formatting. However, by using DocToHelp, we were rewarded by both a printed guide to opening a business in San Carlos as well as a Windows help file of same."

To learn more about the ins and outs of Windows help file creation, check out the "Help Authoring Guide," a help file that acts as a resource to a number of tricks and traps. It is available from the Windows User Group Network (WUGNET) on CompuServe: GO WUGNET, Library 9, download HAG.ZIP.

If you find that making help files is too much work, many companies now specialize in doing it for you. One company with experience in this area, including help files that launch applications and display multimedia presentations, is Adam Charles Consulting, 737 Kewanee, Ypsilanti, MI 48197; 313-482-1600 or 313-482-6460 (fax); CompuServe: 70571,1632.

But you may find that developing your own Windows help files provides you with excellent experience you can use to distribute almost any information you care to place on a disk. Try it for yourself.

Undocumented Ways to Change Color Settings

The Windows manual does not explain the undocumented method you can use to change the colors for jump words in the help text. Many people can benefit by changing the default faded-out green color of these words — especially users of laptops and other monochrome displays. Help colors are defined using the same red-green-blue values seen in the Control Panel's Color dialog box. If you want to change the jump and keyword colors to dark, bold red, for example, add the following section to your WIN.INI:

```
[Windows Help]
Jumpcolor=127 0 0
Popupcolor=127 0 0
```

Another way to change the Windows help jump colors is to use the More Control program featured in the Excellence in Windows Shareware section of *More Windows Secrets*.

Summary

In this chapter, I put forth a variety of tools and techniques to make Windows help files accessible to ordinary Windows users.

▶ Retail applications like Doc-To-Help are available for producing help files from Word for Windows documents, but the most economical way to get started is to use QDHelp, a quick-and-dirty help utility.

▶ Once you've made your own help files, or you've contracted with a firm like Adam Charles Consulting to make them for you, you can make them more readable on all displays, especially portables, by using undocumented features of WIN.INI to change the colors in the [Windows Help] section of the file.

Chapter 37

Getting a Grip on Graphics

In This Chapter

▶ I describe a way to reduce the size of the bitmap wallpaper files you use, taking advantage of an undocumented feature of Windows that allows fat .BMP files to be reduced to compressed .RLE files and still work.

▶ Even better, you can use this knowledge to replace the Microsoft advertising logo that comes up when you start Windows with your *own* favorite logo — whether it's your company's trademark or a picture of your kids.

The graphics files that make the Windows visual environment useful can be a mixed blessing. Graphics are very bulky compared with text. The CHESS.BMP bitmap wallpaper file that comes with Windows 3.0 is over 150K, for example.

And the bitmap formats that Windows supports — .BMP and .PCX in Windows Paintbrush — are not always compatible with the formats of other environments. These include WordPerfect Graphic files (.WPG), CompuServe's Graphics Interchange Format (.GIF), Digital Research's GEM image format (.IMG), Pictor/PC Paint's PIC format, MacPaint's MAC format, and the Tagged Image File Format (.TIF) generated by many gray-scale and color scanners.

Into this welter of graphics standards comes Paint Shop Pro (PSP), a clever Windows utility whose author, Robert Voit, keeps producing upgrades. PSP opens and converts files among all the above formats.

In addition to converting files from other sources into Windows-compatible bitmaps, PSP allows you to change the original image in many ways. Once you have opened a file in one of the supported formats, you can rotate, mirror, resize, or crop the image, as well as changing its color values (if any).

PSP also allows you to capture any part of the screen and save it to any file format. When capturing a portion of the screen, your mouse pointer changes into a crosshair, and a text box shows the exact size (in pixels) of the area you are selecting. This is very useful if you have a Super VGA display (800 x 600) and you want to save an image only as large as, say, plain VGA (640 x 480).

One of the real benefits of Paint Shop Pro, though, is its support for several "flavors" of each graphics standard. The Windows .BMP bitmap format (among others) supports several "modes," although you won't find this in the Windows manual.

Compressing Windows Bitmaps: Looks Great, Less Filling

Bitmap files can be compressed, for example. The Windows .BMP format allows at least two types of *run-length encoding* (RLE). An ordinary bitmap file describes pixel information bit-by-bit, which might sound like "red red red, blue blue blue, green green," and so on. A run-length encoded (.RLE) file would describe the same pixels as "3 reds, 3 blues, 2 greens," and so forth.

If you compress your Windows bitmaps into .RLE files, you can still use them as wallpaper in Control Panel, *and* they take up much less space on your hard disk. Paint Shop Pro reduces CHESS.BMP to fewer than 35,000 bytes, for example — a 75 percent savings.

Another utility that compresses bitmaps is called WinGIF. It supports just four formats: .GIF, .BMP, .PCX, and .RLE. But it also supports most of the same image-manipulation capabilities as Paint Shop for those formats — and it's only $15.

Since these utilities are worth far more than they cost, I recommend you get both. The easiest way to order Paint Shop Pro with an American Express card is to call the Public Software Library at 800-242-4775 or 713-524-6394. Ask for product number 10286. The cost is $69 plus $5 shipping ($16 for express delivery outside the U.S. and Canada). Or you can use MasterCard or Visa, or mail a check for the same amount to JASC, Inc., 10901 Red Circle Dr., Suite 340, Minnetonka, MN 55343. Telephone: 612-930-9171, fax: 612-930-9172. (Minnesota residents add $4.49 sales tax.)

WinGIF is available by sending $15 to SuperSet Software Corp., P.O. Box 1036, Orem, UT 84059.

Earlier versions of both programs are featured in *Windows 3.1 Secrets,* and shareware versions are available on CompuServe, but I recommend that you order the updated, registered versions to get the best combination of features and support.

You may be interested to know that the Windows startup logo itself is a compressed .RLE bitmap. You can demonstrate this by opening Control Panel's Desktop icon and typing in C:\WINDOWS\SYSTEM\VGALOGO.RLE as your wallpaper file. (If you don't use a VGA or higher display, look in your System subdirectory for an .RLE file that begins EGA, CGA, or HERC.) The next time you start Windows, the Windows logo should become your wallpaper.

But instead of Microsoft's Windows logo, it's much more interesting to display your *own* logo when you start Windows.

To explain how do to this, it's necessary to say a little about WIN.COM, the Windows loader. You may notice that the Windows 3.1 and 3.0 diskettes do not contain a program called WIN.COM, even in compressed form. This is because running Setup creates on-the-fly a WIN.COM program appropriate for your system.

When you type WIN, this program does three things: 1) it determines whether your system is capable of running in standard or enhanced mode, 2) it changes to a supported graphics resolution for your display (EGA, VGA, etc.), and 3) it displays the Windows advertising screen in that resolution. After these three steps, WIN.COM exits, turning control over to the Windows kernel.

Setup creates WIN.COM by combining three files. The first file, WIN.CNF, is the part of WIN.COM that determines the Windows capabilities you can run — standard or enhanced. (You must have 2MB of RAM and a 386 processor or higher for Windows to start in enhanced mode.) The second file, if you have a VGA display, is VGALOGO.LGO, a program that switches graphics adapters into 640-by-480 mode. The last file, VGALOGO.RLE, is the actual bitmap, compressed using run-length encoding. When you install Windows, these three files are placed in the System subdirectory under Windows.

You can eliminate the Windows logo entirely by copying a file in your Windows System subdirectory, WIN.CNF, to a file in your Windows directory called WI.COM. (Dropping the "N" helps you remember that something is missing from this file.) Then create a W.BAT file that starts Windows by running WI.COM instead of WIN.COM. This is especially useful in network installations where different workstations have various graphics adapters. Since WI.COM simply detects your memory configuration and passes control to the Windows kernel (without changing into a particular graphics mode), the same WI.COM can be used on machines of any video type.

It's a lot more fun to add your own logo, though. You can do this by creating a 16-color .BMP file in Paintbrush the size of your display (640 x 480 or whatever). Make a backup copy of your WIN.COM file called WIN.OLD (in your Windows directory) and copy your VGALOGO.RLE file to VGALOGO.OLD (in your System subdirectory). Then use Paint Shop Pro or WinGIF to convert your .BMP file into a compressed .RLE file called VGALOGO.RLE in your System subdirectory. Finally, make your own version of WIN.COM exactly the way Setup does it by issuing a command like the following at a DOS prompt in the System directory:

```
COPY /B WIN.CNF+VGALOGO.LGO+VGALOGO.RLE x:\windows\WIN.COM
```

The /B switch in this COPY command ensures that DOS treats each file as a binary file, rather than text. The plus signs add together, or *concatenate,* the three files into a single file, WIN.COM, in your Windows directory. (Replace *x:\windows* in this command line with the actual drive and directory that contains your old WIN.COM.)

If everything goes all right, you'll see your own graphic the next time you start Windows. If not, you can copy your backup copy of WIN.COM and revert to normal.

In either case, Microsoft's copyright notice is still preserved in the Help About box — as with all Windows applications — for the legally minded who might be concerned that we are eliminating the one in the startup screen.

There is one significant technical restriction. The code in WIN.COM cannot grow larger than 64K in size. This means that your .RLE file must compress to less than 55K, or it won't work. Graphics with random splotches of color don't compress very well. If your .RLE file is too large, reduce your logo and place it in the middle of a solid color, such as black or green. The solid background compresses to a much smaller size than a "busy" graphic does.

Perhaps in a future version of Windows, Microsoft will include a way to specify in WIN.INI the startup bitmap you wish to display.

Compressing Graphics Files with Hijaak for Windows

Many retail programs convert graphics files from one format to another. One of the most popular ones is Hijaak for DOS, which converts over two dozen bitmap and vector formats into encapsulated PostScript files, fax output, or almost any format you can think of.

Inset Systems also publishes Hijaak for Windows, with the same features as the DOS version, plus support for Object Linking and Embedding (OLE). After installing Hijaak, you can double-click a graphic in any Windows application that supports OLE. If the picture is in a format that Hijaak supports, Hijaak automatically loads the graphic and allows you to manipulate it.

In the previous section, I described the fact that Windows accepts run-length encoded (.RLE) files as wallpaper in the Control Panel's Desktop dialog box, as well as any bitmap (.BMP) file. And I discussed saving disk space by converting your wallpaper files to run-length encoded files with Paint Shop Pro. But Hijaak for Windows allows this, too.

Pull down Hijaak's File menu and click Command. In the dialog box that appears, type +BMPFLAV=RLE and click OK. The plus sign is an undocumented feature of Hijaak that writes the rest of the line into a file called HJWIN.SET. Now Hijaak can compress any .BMP file; simply use an .RLE extension when you save the file.

Hijaak for Windows lists for $249 from Inset Systems, 71 Commerce Dr., Brookfield, CT 06804; call 800-828-8088 or 203-740-2400.

Summary

In this chapter, I bring together all the pieces to help you compress your bitmaps and re-place the Microsoft advertising screen with one of your own.

▶ The crucial information is the fact that the Control Panel accepts run-length encoded (.RLE) files as well as uncompressed bitmap (.BMP) files when you establish the Wallpaper setting in its Desktop dialog box.

▶ Using Paint Shop Pro, WinGIF, or Hijaak, you can easily convert your own graphics into .RLE files and use them in place of the Windows logo in VGALOGO.RLE.

Chapter 38
Finding Secret Hotkeys

In This Chapter

▶ I show you how to assign hotkeys so you can launch a screen saver (perhaps with password protection), maximize and restore Windows, and many other actions, with a single keystroke.

▶ Even better, I share with you a method I found that allows you to gain 16 extra function keys on your keyboard (in addition to F1 through F12), by assigning macros to each of the keys on your numeric keypad, which Windows users who aren't bookkeepers never touch.

O ne of the pleasant little additions to Windows 3.1 is the Control Panel's screen-saver feature. By accessing the Control Panel's Desktop dialog box, you can choose from among five different effects that blank your screen (after a period that you specify) and display a moving image.

Screen savers were originally designed to prevent ghostly images from permanently "burning in" on monochrome monitors that displayed the same application day after day. The "rotated-L" of Lotus 1-2-3 spreadsheets, for example, might still be visible even after you'd exited the program.

Today's color monitors don't have burn-in problems (as quickly as monochrome monitors do). But screen savers still have their uses. I like to blank my own screen when I leave the room, or when someone walks in, if the document I'm working on is at all confidential or personal. I'll even blank the screen just to be able to clear my mind for a few moments without my work staring me in the face. (If I'll be gone for several minutes, I turn off the monitor's power, which does the same thing as a screen saver and also saves energy, but requires a longer recovery time when I return to my document.)

Since all these uses for a screen saver require an immediate response time (rather than waiting 30 minutes or whatever for the saver to kick in), I've always found it irritating that Windows 3.1 provides no easy way to launch its screen saver instantly from a hotkey combination, as do retail screen savers like Intermission and After Dark.

A Hotkey for Screen Savers

You can, of course, start the screen saver by opening the Control Panel's Desktop dialog box and clicking Test — the saver will then begin. But I've found a much faster method, which isn't in the Windows manual. If you've obtained any compatible savers from companies other than Microsoft, the following steps should work with them, too.

STEPS

Quickly Launching Your Screen Saver with a Hotkey

Step 1.   In the Windows 3.1 File Manager, change to your Windows directory, then click View Sort-By-Type to arrange the filenames by their extensions. Scroll down to the .SCR (screen saver) extensions. You should see SCRNSAVE.SCR, SSFLYWIN.SCR, and any other savers you may have.

Step 2.   Click one of the .SCR filenames once to highlight it. Then click File Associate to see if the .SCR extension is already associated with an application. (Some communications programs, for example, allow you to run their script [.SCR] files by double-clicking them.) If you find an existing association, and you can live without it, click "None" in the File Associate dialog box to revoke the association. This deletes it from Windows 3.1's Registration Database, and from the [Extensions] section of WIN.INI. If you find no existing association, simple cancel out of the dialog box.

Step 3.   Open your WIN.INI file in Notepad. In the [windows] section, add SCR to the list of extensions in the PROGRAMS= line. This should make it look something like the following:

```
Programs=com exe pif bat scr
```

This tells Windows that .SCR files are executable programs. Screen savers are simply Dynamic Link Libraries (DLLs) in an new executable format, and therefore can be executed by Windows. Save your changes in WIN.INI, and restart Windows so the changes take effect.

Step 4.   Locate a saver, such as SSMARQUE.SCR, in the File Manager window, and double-click it. You should see a dialog box, which allows you to configure the saver's options (if any). Make any desired changes, then click OK.

Step 5. In the Program Manager, click File New to create a new program item. Type in a command line such as SSMARQUE.SCR /S (the /S switch stands for Save Now). As a DLL, each saver file contains its own icon for your use, or you may select an icon from MORICONS.DLL or any other Windows file.

Step 6. Double-click in Program Manager the program item you just created. You should see your saver immediately start up. Whatever configuration you've set in the Control Panel (password, etc.) should still be in effect.

Windows 3.1 allows you to define a Ctrl+Alt hotkey combination when you set the properties for this icon. But such a hotkey works only when Program Manager is your foreground application.

If you want to define a hotkey that works in *any* application, you can use the Windows Recorder. To do this, start the Recorder from the Program Manager window. Pull down the Options menu, and make sure "Minimize On Use" is on. Click Macro Record, and set the macro to playback to the "Same Application" (Program Manager). Press Alt+S to start recording. Record the keystrokes Alt+F, R (to start the File Run dialog box), SSMARQUE.SCR /S, and Enter. Press Ctrl+Break to end recording, and save the macro to a file. (If you already have a Recorder file, such as MACROS.REC, record this macro and save it in that file. If not, click File Save to save your macro into a file.) As long as Recorder is running this file in the background, the hotkey you selected will switch to the Program Manager from any application and run your command, starting your screen saver. (Program Manager must be running in a window, not as an icon, for Recorder to play back to it, however.)

You can also launch your screen saver every time you start Windows by placing its icon in the StartUp group.

The Windows 3.1 screen-saver feature has very weak password protection (you can bypass it with a reboot, unlike some other screen-saver packages). So I don't recommend you rely on it as system security. Windows screen savers also won't launch automatically if a DOS session is running. But by using a hotkey you define, you may find these screen savers to be sufficient for simple privacy needs. For more complicated situations, see Chapter 22, Password-Protecting Windows.

Maximize and Restore Any Application with a Hotkey

You may know that the Alt+Enter key combination switches a DOS session in Windows enhanced mode between a full-screen and a windowed display. But there is no similar key combination to switch Windows applications between their "maximized" and "restored" states. To make matters worse, instead of correcting this omission in Windows 3.1, Microsoft inconsistently assigned the Alt+Enter combination to the File Properties dialog box in the Program Manager.

I've found you can switch any Windows application between maximized and restored, with a single keystroke, using the Windows Recorder. Many people avoid the Recorder due to its limitations — but it's free, so I like it. (You can get more power with WinBatch, a Windows batch language available by calling 206-938-1740, but it costs more.)

It would be ideal to use Alt+Enter to resize both DOS and Windows applications. Unfortunately, that isn't possible in this case. If you redefine Alt+Enter in the Recorder, it disables that key combination's usual meaning to windowed DOS sessions.

My recommendation, instead, is that you redefine the F10 key. This key was set aside in the early days of Windows for users who had no mouse. F10 highlights the first choice on the main menu, so you can move to other menu choices using your arrow keys. Since virtually every Windows user now has a mouse, F10 is fair game for redefinition.

STEPS

Redefining the F10 Key to Resize Windows

Step 1. Start Recorder from the Program Manager. You see an empty Recorder window. Minimize this window for the moment.

Step 2. Start Notepad from Program Manager, and maximize it.

Step 3. Hold down the Alt key and press Tab repeatedly until you see "Recorder," then let up on the Alt key. The Recorder window should reappear.

Step 4. Pull down Recorder's Options menu, and make sure the items Control+Break Checking, Shortcut Keys, and Minimize on Use have a check mark beside them to indicate they are *on*.

Step 5. Click Macro Record. A dialog box appears. Establish the following settings: Macro Name: "Maximize or Restore." Shortcut Key: F10. Ctrl, Shift, and Alt: Off. Playback To: Any Application. Speed: Fast. Continuous Loop: Off. Enable Shortcut Keys: On. Record Mouse: Clicks + Drags. Relative To: Window. Finally, click Start to begin recording your macro.

Step 6. The Recorder window should disappear, and you should see just your maximized Notepad window. Double-click your mouse at the left end of the Notepad title bar, just to the right of the System Menu icon. This double-click on the title bar is an undocumented feature that always maximizes or restores Windows applications. Performing the double-click on the extreme left end of the title bar is necessary because the Recorder will play this mouse action back to the same exact spot later, and we want this macro to work no matter how small the title bar may be at that time.

Step 7. Press Ctrl+Break on your keyboard to stop recording. Press "S" to save your macro, then click OK.

Step 8. Press F10 to test your macro. Every Windows application should maximize or restore when you do this.

Step 9. Click File Save on the Recorder menu and give your macro file a name like MACROS.REC. Make sure this file loads in the background every time you start Windows, by placing the command C:\WINDOWS\MACROS.REC on the LOAD= line of your WIN.INI file, or in your StartUp group in Windows 3.1.

I'm sure you can think of many other keys to place shortcuts on. Since it's easy to click Help with a mouse, I've even redefined my F1 key. It now plays back Alt+Spacebar, N to minimize any Windows application I wish to set aside. You could play back Alt+F4 instead, if you wish to close applications. Enjoy.

Add 16 Extra Function Keys to Your Keyboard

When IBM brought out its first PCs, the keyboards had their function keys on the left, and an integrated numeric and cursor-arrow keypad on the right.

In 1985, IBM moved the function keys above the top row of characters (where they would be as far as possible from user's hands). At the same time, IBM added a separate numeric keypad on the right, for bookkeepers who learned 10-key data entry. For the other 98 percent of us, this new keypad covers up that annoying extra desk space we used to have.

I always use the separate arrow keys to move my cursor, and never use the numeric keypad for anything. At the same time, I've always wanted more function keys. Now, I've found a way you can re-define all 16 of the numeric keypad keys — and many other keys — into any Windows functions you want.

As you may have read in the previous topic, I routinely load a small Recorder file that re-defines some of my keys. For example, the F10 key performs the same function in all Windows applications (it activates the first choice on the menu, just like pressing and releasing Alt). So I've redefined F10. This way, I get rid of one trivial function and replace it with a better one.

One of Recorder's many limitations, however, is that it cannot redefine the numeric keypad. Besides A-Z and 0-9, it only allows you to redefine certain keys in its Macro Properties drop-down box (Backspace, Delete, and so on), with combinations of Ctrl, Alt, and Shift.

What I've found is that you can replace the keys in this drop-down box with any other keys you want (such as the numeric keypad).

If even the 16 keypad keys aren't enough, you might want to redefine other keys that aren't available through the Windows Recorder, such as the period, comma, and slash.

It's very unlikely, of course, that you would ever want to change the meaning of your period key (unless you write only run-on sentences). But it can be very useful to place a macro on Ctrl+Period, which is easy to press, instead of a hand-twister like Ctrl+Shift+P.

Another reason to redefine punctuation keys is to produce accented letters. The reader who got me started on this topic, Carl Herup, originally used this method to fix Microsoft's own accented keyboard driver for Windows.

Mr. Herup commonly types documents that include accented letters in various languages. For this reason, he used the Control Panel's International dialog box to switch his keyboard layout from "US" to "US-International."

The U.S.-International keyboard layout, which is not documented in the Windows manual, has the very useful purpose of providing you with a way to type accented characters. When you press the tilde, caret, or a quote mark key, followed by the relevant letter key, you get the accented version of that letter. (For complete documentation on the U.S.-International keyboard layout, see Chapter 15, "Add Character to Your Documents.")

Mr. Herup didn't like redefining his quote mark keys in this exact way. So he used the Recorder to move the accented "dead keys" to other locations that he preferred.

Don't ask more about this, because there's an easier way. A firm in Quebec produces a keyboard driver for Windows that accesses all accented letters, as French-Canadian typewriters do. The cost is only $19.95 plus tax from PM Informatique, 514-446-1775.

Other keys you might find handy to redefine include the useless Pause key and the keypad 5 (a blank key when your NumLock light is off).

The Pause key was an undocumented feature in Windows 2.*x*. When you pressed it, it "paused" Windows' control over the keyboard; the next key combination you pressed was sent through to DOS memory-resident programs. This was useful for things like flushing DOS disk caches, for example. This function was removed in Windows 3.0, however. Now the Pause key does absolutely nothing, so redefine it as you wish.

To do this, you'll need an editor that allows you to type hexadecimal numbers. Several hex editors are available in such products as Norton Utilities and PC Tools. If you don't have these, you can get a handy Windows shareware hex editor by sending $10 to Al Funk, 42 Parkwyn Dr., Delmar, NY 12054; CompuServe 71505,1277. HexEdit is also featured in the Excellence in Windows Shareware section of *More Windows Secrets*.

First, make a copy of RECORDER.EXE and call it RECORDE2.EXE. Open this copy in your hex editor. Near the end of the file, you should see a section that starts with "Backspace" and ends with "F16." This section determines the strings that will appear in the Recorder's drop-down box as keys that can be re-defined.

After each string, such as F1, is a hex number representing the keycode for that key. The keycode for F1 is 70, F2 is 71, and F16 is 7F. (Remember, the keycode is hex.) After each keycode is the hex value 00, which is a "null" that ends the string.

In Figure 38-1, a portion of the RECORDER.EXE file is shown in Hex Edit. In the left half of the screen, the numbers 4 6 3 1 7 0 0 0 represent the four bytes that match up the string "F1," shown on the right half of the screen, with hex keycode 70, which appears as the letter "p" to the right. The "null" character that ends this key definition appears on the left as the number 00, and on the right as a period (.).

You must change the hex keycode values to the correct ones for each key. For example, the keycode for F1 is 70 hex, as I described earlier. To change this keycode to the keycode for N1, you would change the hex number 70 to the hex number 61, as shown in Table 38-1a.

You must also replace the strings from F1 to F16 with N1, N2, and so on, representing the numeric keypad keys. Each string must retain its original length. The string that replaces "F16," for example, must be exactly three characters long. Add spaces at the end of the new strings, if necessary, to make them the right length.

```
┌─────────────────────────────────────────────────────────────────────┐
│ ─                            Hex Editor                          ▼ ▲  │
├─────────────────────────────────────────────────────────────────────┤
│ File   Edit   Options                                          Help   │
│  37312 [ 07536176652 04173  054D6572 6765 044F ]  [ .Save As.Merge.O ]│
│  37328 [ 70656E0000000000  0000000000000000 ]  [ pen.............. ] │
│  37344 [ 817000FFFF000000  0000000000000000 ]  [ .p............... ] │
│  37360 [ 4261636B73706163  6508004361707320 ]  [ Backspace..Caps   ]│
│  37376 [ 4C6F636B14004465  6C6574652E00446F ]  [ Lock..Delete..Do  ]│
│  37392 [ 776E2800456E6423  00456E465720D00 ]  [ wn(.End#.Enter..  ]│
│  37408 [ 4573631B00486F6D  652400496E736572 ]  [ Esc..Home$.Inser  ]│
│  37424 [ 742D004C65667425  004E756D204C6F63 ]  [ t-.Left%.Num Loc  ]│
│  37440 [ 6B90005061676520  446F776E22005061 ]  [ k..Page Down".Pa  ]│
│  37456 [ 6765205570210052  6967687427005363 ]  [ ge Up!.Right'.Sc  ]│
│  37472 [ 726F6C6C204C6F63  6B91005370616365 ]  [ roll Lock..Space  ]│
│  37488 [ 2000546162090055  702600 4631700046 ]  [ .Tab..Up&.F1p.F  ]│
│  37504 [ 3271004633720046  3473004635740046 ]  [ 2q.F3r.F4s.F5t.F  ]│
│  37520 [ 3675004637760046  3877004639780046 ]  [ 6u.F7v.F8w.F9x.F  ]│
│  37536 [ 313079004631317A  004631327B004631 ]  [ 10y.F11z.F12{.F1  ]│
│  37552 [ 337C004631347D00  4631357E00463136 ]  [ 3|.F14}.F15~.F16  ]│
│  37568 [ 7F00416C74120042  7265616B0300436F ]  [ ■.Alt..Break..Co  ]│
│  37584 [ 6D6D612C00437472  6C11005368696674 ]  [ mma,.Ctrl..Shift  ]│
│  37600 [ 1000000000000000  0000000000000000 ]  [ ................. ]│
│  37616 [ E001340056535F56  455253494F4E5F49 ]  [ ..4.US_VERSION_I  ]│
│  37632 [ 4E464F00BD04EFFE  000001000A000300 ]  [ NFO.............. ]│
│  37648 [ 670000000A000300  670000003F000000 ]  [ g.......g...?.... ]│
│  37664 [ 0000000001000100  0100000000000000 ]  [ ................. ]│
│  37680 [ 0000000000000000  7201000053747269 ]  [ ........r...Stri  ]│
│  37696 [ 6E6746696C65496E  666F00005E010000 ]  [ ngFileInfo..^.... ]│
│  37712 [ 3034303930344534  0000000027001700 ]  [ 0409 04E4....'... ]│
└─────────────────────────────────────────────────────────────────────┘
```

Figure 38-1: In a hexadecimal editor, the ASCII text in a file is shown on the right, and the hex equivalent is shown on the left. To change the F1 key in Recorder to Numeric Keypad 1, you would change the string "F1" (highlighted in gray on the right) to "N1," and change the hex value "70" (highlighted on the left) to "61."

Table 38-1 shows every hexadecimal keycode I know of that can be patched into Recorder using a hex editor.

Table 38-1: Hexadecimal Keycodes

Key	Keycode
5 (NumLock off)	0C
Pause	13
Semicolon (;)	BA
Equals sign (=)	BB
Comma (,)	BC
Hyphen (-)	BD
Period (.)	BE
Slash (/)	BF
Backquote (')	C0
Left Bracket ([)	DB
Backslash (\)	DC
Right Bracket (])	DD
Apostrophe (')	DE
N0	60
N1	61
N2	62
N3	63
N4	64
N5	65
N6	66
N7	67
N8	68
N9	69
N*	6A
N+	6B
N,	6C
N-	6D
N.	6E
N/	6F

Readers have asked how to redefine the keypad Enter key. Alas, Windows traps that key and gives applications the same keycode number as the main keyboard Enter key. So I make use of the keypad Enter without redefining it. After I've clicked some options in a dialog box with my mouse, I press the keypad Enter key with my right thumb. That way, I don't have to move my mouse over to the OK button. (Every shortcut helps.)

Additionally, readers have asked what the keypad comma (N,) key is. A comma appears on the numeric keypad of only a few PC keyboards. If yours doesn't have one, you can't produce this keystroke, of course.

After you save your changes, you can create macros in RECORDE2.EXE and assign them to numeric keypad key combinations. Any macros you create in this way work fine when loaded and run by the original, unaltered Recorder.

I've redefined several keypad keys to insert long text strings that I must commonly type. You might redefine Numeric Keypad 1 to type your name and address, Numeric Keypad 2 to type your company's slogan, and so on.

Of course, most word processors allow you to define frequently used phrases. But using the Recorder, these phrases are also available in Write, Notepad, and other Windows applications that lack macro languages. (Unfortunately, the Recorder does not allow you to record the higher-ANSI characters shown in Windows 3.1's Character Map applet. This means you can't define a macro to insert, for example, true fractions from the Windows character set.)

Launching a series of Windows macro actions from a numeric keypad key is even more useful than inserting text strings into your documents. The Recorder can record just about any action you can perform with the keyboard in one or more Windows applications.

If you'd like to record some new functions onto your numeric keypad keys with your edited copy of the Recorder, here's a simple example. We'll redefine the numeric keypad 0 key to minimize the current application.

STEPS

Redefining the Numeric Keypad

Step 1. Open your new Recorder and minimize it to an icon. Then open an applet like Windows Write.

Step 2. Double-click the Recorder icon to open its window. Make sure the following items on the Options menu have a check mark to indicate they are on: Control+Break Checking, Shortcut Keys, and Minimize On Use. Then click Options Properties and establish the following defaults: Any Application, Fast, and Ignore Mouse. Then click OK.

Step 3. Click Macro Record. In the dialog box that appears, pull down the Shortcut Key list box and select the N0 (numeric keypad 0) item you previously edited into your new copy of Recorder. Turn off Ctrl, Shift, and Alt, so your macro will redefine the 0 key itself. (You can change this later, if you like.) In the Record Macro Name box, type "minimize application." Click the Record button.

Step 4. You should see the Recorder window reduced to an icon, blinking to indicate that you are recording. The Write window should now be the foreground window. Don't use your mouse to minimize this applet. Instead, press Alt+Spacebar, N. This pulls down the System Menu and selects Minimize. Write should reduce itself to an icon.

Step 5. Press Ctrl+Break to stop recording. Press Alt+S to save the macro, then Enter. Double-click the Recorder icon to restore its window. You should see your macro, named "minimize application," in the macro list. Open a few applications, then press 0 on your numeric keypad to demonstrate that your macro is working.

You can record many other actions and place them on your numeric keypad keys in this way. The important thing to remember is to use the keyboard instead of the mouse to record macros. Mouse actions won't necessarily play back to the same spot on the screen when repeated later, while keystrokes will.

As I've mentioned before, the Recorder has many limitations. You can't edit a macro, only re-record it. And you can't play a macro into a DOS session.

But you should be able to find many actions that Recorder macros can be useful in performing on your keypad.

Summary

In this chapter, I go into some very technical areas of the Windows keyboard interface to show you how to assign actions to keys that you may rarely or never use.

▶ By taking advantage of the little-used F10 key, for example, you can launch your screen saver instantly, maximize and restore applications, and automate many other actions.

▶ If you're a power user who isn't afraid to get up to your elbows in hexadecimal code, you can hack the Windows Recorder so it allows you to record macros on your under-utilized numeric keypad keys, or even *verboten* key combinations like Ctrl+Period, 5 with NumLock off, and Pause.

Chapter 39
The Shifty Shift Key

In This Chapter

▶ I unveil some little-known and undocumented behaviors of the Shift key when used in Windows Program Manager, File Manager, Paintbrush, and Word for Windows.

▶ I show how to overcome a PC's habit of inserting *lowercase* letters when you have Caps Lock on and you press Shift and a letter — the opposite of what you wanted — and how to play other tricks, such as reversing the Ctrl and Caps Lock keys on awkward keyboards where the Ctrl key is not adjacent to the "A" key.

Behold the lowly Shift key. You hold it down while you type, and all you get is a capital letter, right? Not quite. Beneath the Shift key's humble reputation lies a world of undocumented functionality.

Many Windows users know the most basic ways the Shift key has been redefined. One of the first lessons for a new Windows user, for example, is the fact that holding down the Shift key in a word processor while pressing an arrow key actually highlights text, instead of just moving the cursor. Holding down Shift while clicking your mouse in text also highlights everything between the current insertion point and the place you clicked (in most Windows word processors).

Other functions of the Shift key, while adequately documented in the Windows manual, are much less well known. When you use the straight-line tool in Paintbrush, for example, holding down Shift forces the line you draw to be perfectly horizontal or vertical. Similarly, when you use the box or oval tools, Shift forces these shapes into perfect squares or circles, respectively.

Still more functions seem to be known only by true enthusiasts: When you start a program by double-clicking an icon in Program Manager — or a filename in File Manager — holding down Shift forces the application to start as a mini-mized icon instead of in a window. This lets you do things such as starting a background DOS session, for immediate access later.

And if you have re-defined any application menu items — by writing a Word for Windows macro to modify the File Print routine, say — you can often force the app to revert to the original, built-in procedure by holding down Shift while clicking that menu choice. (To defeat Winword's AutoExec macro, however, you must start the application with the command WINWORD /M.)

Stalking the Esoteric Secrets of the Humble Shift Key

But there are many undocumented functions for the Shift key that I've found aren't in any manuals at all.

These functions were added to Windows 3.0 or 3.1 by harried Microsoft programmers who wanted a quick way to test various features without exiting and restarting their whole Windows environment every time.

Windows 3.1, for example, added a convenient StartUp group window in the Program Manager. Icons placed in this group are automatically loaded by Windows every time you start it. But if you hold down Shift when you see the Windows logo — and keep it down until Program Manager has finished initializing — the StartUp group is completely ignored! This is *very* handy if something in the StartUp group is hanging Windows. Or you might try this just to get Windows up and running quickly for some short task.

Windows 3.1 also makes it possible for you to automatically save your preferred window arrangement in Program Manager and File Manager, by turning on the menu item Options Save-Settings-on-Exit. But what if you've just perfected your window arrangement in File Manager, and don't want to exit just to save?

Simply hold down Shift while you double-click the System Menu icon. Instead of closing the File Manager application, you have just saved your window configuration into WINFILE.INI. Now you can turn off Save-Settings-on-Exit, but your preferred arrangement will show up the next time you start Windows and File Manager.

This function also works when you Shift+Double-Click the System Menu icon in Program Manager. A new PROGMAN.INI is written, saving your window preferences without exiting Windows. This is convenient if you're a PC manager setting up a series of slightly different group windows to be used by other people in your company. Copy each new PROGMAN.INI file to a temporary name, then give the appropriate file to the different users later.

In both File Manager and Program Manager, you can also save the current configuration by pressing Shift+Alt+F4.

Another hidden feature of the Shift key is used in the File Manager. First, a little background: the File Manager in Windows 3.0 insisted on reading every directory so it could display tiny plus signs (+) on those folders that contained subfolders. This was disabled by Microsoft in Windows 3.1 to make the version 3.1 File Manager much faster.

You can make the new version almost as slow as the older one by turning this feature back *on*. To do this, pull down the Tree menu and click Indicate Expandable Branches.

A better way, however, is to use the Shift key to display the existence of subdirectories only when you *care* to see them.

You probably know that clicking, say, the C: drive icon with your mouse displays the top-level directories of that drive. You can also press Ctrl+C to display drive C:.

But it's undocumented that holding down the Shift key while clicking the drive icon forces File Manager to display all levels of directories on that drive. (In one step, this does the same thing as clicking the drive icon, then clicking Tree Expand-All.)

The Shift key works as a keyboard shortcut, too. When you press Ctrl+Shift+C, File Manager changes to the C: drive and displays all subdirectories, and so forth.

One of the *worst* features of the Shift key in Windows, however, is that Microsoft repeated a mistake that IBM made with its first DOS PCs.

On an old IBM Selectric typewriter (and virtually every typewriter in the world), pressing the Shift key releases your Caps Lock key, if was already on. This is because, after typing a heading in all caps, you probably want to start a new paragraph with a capital letter, then continue typing lowercase letters, as usual. Millions of touch-typists do this without thinking.

The IBM PC, however, does this wrong. If you have the Caps Lock key on, and press the Shift key, you get a *lowercase letter*. This is because the BIOS uses the Shift key to reverse the state of any key that is pressed, and no one at IBM checked to see what would happen if Caps Lock was on at the same time.

While this is an obvious and simple mistake to correct, no other PC manufacturer has ever done so, because of Livingston's Law of Compatibility: the dumber the mistake that IBM built into the original PC, the more slavishly it will be copied by compatible makers.

After years of putting up with this foolishness, I've finally found a utility that can return the Shift key to its time-honored and intuitive function, in every Windows application.

It's called WinKey and it's just $15. Lest you think reprogramming the Shift key isn't much functionality for a utility, WinKey has plenty of other features.

Besides returning Shift to its original Selectric behavior, WinKey allows you to configure the Shift key so it *doesn't* turn off Caps Lock if you press a non-alphabetical key, such as a numeral or an underscore. This is great when you're typing API functions such as WM_COMMAND in C programs, or spreadsheet functions such as @SUM.

You can also use WinKey to switch the Ctrl and Caps Lock keys, if you're subjected to a keyboard that doesn't give you freedom of choice on those keys. (Since there's always room for two keys to the left of the "A" key, I don't know why more companies don't put Caps Lock and Ctrl, in that order, to the left of "A," as DEC does on some keyboards.)

Finally, you can use WinKey to force NumLock and ScrollLock on or off. ScrollLock enables cursor keys to be used to scroll the screen in Excel, and invokes DEC-style VT-100 function keys in Windows Terminal.

Send $15 to DataGem Corp., 1420 NW Gilman #2859, Issaquah, WA 98027; 206-391-4415; CompuServe 75540,762. You can also find an unregistered, shareware version of WinKey in *Windows Gizmos.*

Summary

In this chapter, a few of the odd and secret effects of the Windows Shift key are described, and some of them fixed.

▶ Undocumented features of the Shift key in Program Manager, File Manager, Paintbrush, and Word for Windows are explained.

▶ A useful, set-it-and-forget-it utility, WinKey, is recommended for Windows users who've been frustrated by the IBM PC's tendency to reverse the Caps Lock state of a character when Shift and a key are pressed, instead of automatically providing a capital letter, as the user would expect.

Chapter 40
The Forgotten Mouse Button

In This Chapter

▶ I give you several ways, documented and undocumented, to actually use the right (or second) mouse button in Windows, which usually goes unused.

▶ One undocumented feature of the right mouse button, for example, is a way to copy text from a windowed DOS session into the Windows Clipboard with a single click.

One of the differences between Windows and the Macintosh — albeit a minor one — is that all Microsoft-compatible mice have two buttons, while the Mac ships with a one-button mouse.

Since all Windows users, therefore, have access to at least two mouse buttons (three with certain third-party mice), it's ironic that Windows makes no documented use of the second mouse button.

I've found an undocumented use for the second mouse button, however, that can make life a little easier for those of you who need to transfer information between DOS and Windows programs.

A few Windows applications *do* exploit the right mouse button. (If you're left-handed and switched the mouse buttons using the Control Panel, the second mouse button for you will be the left one.)

Windows Paintbrush, for example, uses the right mouse button to select the background color for drawing and filling, while the left mouse button is for selecting the foreground color.

Word for Windows makes little use of the right mouse button except in tables. You use the left mouse button to select entire columns in a table, but you must place the mouse pointer in the first table row for this to work. Using the right mouse button, though, you can select entire columns no matter what row the mouse is in.

The right mouse button in Winword can also move a selection of text to a new location. After highlighting the text you want to move, hold down the Ctrl key and click the right mouse button at the location the text should move to. If you hold down both Shift and Ctrl, the right mouse click *copies* the selection into the new location, rather than moving it. (In Winword 2.*x*, you can move a selection to a new location by dragging it, or copy it by holding down Ctrl while you drag.) I've heard reports that this does not work on some systems with the new MOUSE.COM 9.0 — a version that was developed after Windows 3.1 and is available for sale from Microsoft — so your results may vary.

Finally, you can select a rectangular area of text by dragging your mouse over the area with your right mouse button held down. This allows you to select, and then delete, for example, several spaces at the beginning of several lines of text.

Aside from these exceptions, and a few others in various Windows applications, the right mouse button is mainly a useless appendage. There is no consistent rule as to how the right mouse button should be implemented.

The *undocumented* behavior of the right mouse button, however, suggests that this little clicker can play a valuable role in copying information to the Windows Clipboard.

Try the following experiment if you have a 386 and enough RAM to start Windows in 386 enhanced mode: Start Windows in enhanced mode. Open the Clipboard application, then start a DOS session. (If the DOS session opens full-screen, press Alt+Enter to reduce it into a window.) Position the DOS session and the Clipboard so the DOS session is in the foreground, but you can still see a portion of the Clipboard window.

Type the command DIR at the DOS prompt to put a few lines of text on the screen. If you are using Windows 3.1, click the System Menu icon in the upper-left corner of the DOS window. On the System Menu that appears, click Edit, then Mark. (If you are using Windows 3.0, you don't need to click Edit Mark.) Then, using the left mouse button, drag your mouse over a few of the lines in the DOS window. You should see the lines change color, indicating that you are selecting these lines.

After selecting, click the *right* mouse button anywhere within the DOS window. The selected rectangular area immediately appears in the Clipboard window. You have effectively copied your entire selection into the Clipboard. This selection can now be pasted into any other application under Windows (even another DOS application).

You could accomplish this same copying action, of course, by pulling down the System Menu of the DOS window, clicking Edit, and then clicking Copy. Or you could press the Enter key, which also copies your selection. But both of these documented methods require more steps (or require that you take your hand off the mouse) than the simple right-button click.

This feature can be very handy (no pun intended) for anyone who regularly runs DOS programs under Windows and wants to transfer information into other applications. Using the left mouse button to select an area of text, then the right mouse button to copy it to the Clipboard, becomes a fast and easy maneuver.

I'd like to thank my friends at Microsoft technical support, who wanted to share this trick.

Summary

In this chapter, the forgotten right mouse button gains its 15 minutes of fame.

▶ Several things you may never have known you could do with the right mouse button are explored.

▶ Neat tricks, like copying marked text from a windowed DOS session into the Windows Clipboard, are explained.

Chapter 41
Genetically Engineered Mice

In This Chapter

▶ I explore the frontiers of mouse-dom, looking at mice that can help you work faster and better by providing you with new mouse metaphors or more mouse manueverability.

▶ The Gliffic Plus, for example, is a mouse-and-pen combination that allows you to pick up one or the other without restarting Windows, while the ProHance series of mice bristles with as many as 40 programmable mouse buttons.

Personally, I can't work without at least a three-button mouse, like the ones that come with ATI graphics boards. I use GenSoft Development Corp.'s Whiskers utility (featured in *Windows 3.1 Secrets*) to turn the middle mouse button into a Delete key, which I use often on my tortured prose.

But the rodent state of the art has evolved far past this level.

Appoint, a maker of many meritorious mice, has developed a great idea — Gliffic Plus, a mouse pad that supports both a mouse and a pen. Windows responds to whichever device you are currently using. You can use the mouse for simple menus, then pick up the pen for finer detail, such as positioning desktop publishing objects. Since the pad's own cord plugs into your COM port, the mouse and pen are blessedly cord-free.

I tested the pen under Microsoft's Windows for Pens, a set of routines that installs on top of Windows. The stylus-based environment automatically recognized my pen-printing as text. I can envision vertical applications that would use a monitor and this pen/pad combo as the whole interface, dispensing with the need for a keyboard. In a hospital, for example, a workstation mounted in a hall could be used by medical personnel to check off patients' conditions and so on. (Microsoft's block-printing recognition isn't sufficient to replace keyboards for touch typing, though.)

The Gliffic mouse is about half the size of Microsoft's, allowing it to be held like an artist's chalk for greater control, as well as flat on the mouse pad. Appoint also sells this mouse as a corded, stand-alone unit called the Gulliver ($99 list). The Gliffic Plus pen/mouse/pad is $299.

You can contact Appoint at 800-448-1184 or 510-463-3003.

If you need to switch between a mouse and a pen interface, and you already use a Wacom or Calcomp tablet, you can get a driver in the Fractal Design Painter application that does the same thing ($299 from Alexander & Lord, 800-647-7443.) Wacom owners can get such a driver free by calling 206-750-8882 or by dialing 408-982-2737 with your modem and downloading WACOM.ZIP.

A mouse of a different color is sold by ProHance Technologies, Inc., which specializes in mice with buttons built around the normal left and right mouse buttons. The most popular model, the PowerMouse/100, looks like a mouse on steroids — it has a total of 40 buttons. ProHance's president, Kirk MacKenzie, says this model ($175 list) is purchased heavily by spreadsheet jockeys, since the mouse supports an entire numeric keypad, so you never have to remove your hand from the mouse to enter data.

ProHance also makes 12- and 17-button mice ($99 and $125), and a 40-button trackball ($175). Mr. MacKenzie claims to have invented "toolbars" before they began appearing in Windows applications. He simply placed his toolbars on top of his mice. Talk about information at your fingertips!

ProHance can be reached at 415-967-5774.

Neither the Gliffic Plus nor the PowerMouse will be everyone's cup of miced tea. The Gliffic's mouse pad, for example, uses *absolute* rather than *relative* positioning. This means that each point on the pad represents a specific point on the screen, which you may or may not like. (A relative-positioning driver is in development.) And the PowerMouse takes time to learn.

But these specialized mice might be just what you need if you've outgrown the two-button varieties.

Summary

This chapter tests the outer limits of what you can do with a mouse under Windows.

▶ For those who benefit from drawing with a pen as well as pointing with a mouse, the Gliffic Plus gives you the ability to switch at will between the two devices (owners of Wacom and Calcomp tablets can get drivers that allow this, too).

▶ For those who feel constrained by having only two mouse buttons, ProHance Technologies comes to the rescue with its line of 12-, 17-, and 40-button mice and trackballs.

Chapter 42
Gang Screens, Solitaire, and Minesweeper

In This Chapter

▶ I discuss the Windows 3.1 "gang screen," that scrolling list of developers featuring Bill Gates, Steve Ballmer, and other luminaries at Microsoft.

▶ For those who've played the Windows Solitaire and Minesweeper games (and who hasn't), I reveal tricks that allow you to cheat — with an explanation of why you might want to, and why you might not.

After you've used Windows 3.1 for a while and evaluated some of its obvious features, you'll probably want to try some of its *undocumented* features — such as the "gang screen" that credits Microsoft's programmers and support staff.

To see this screen, open the Help About box in any Windows 3.1 applet (Program Manager, Write, Notepad, etc.).

Notice the icon in the upper-left corner of the dialog box. Hold down the Ctrl and Shift keys simultaneously while you double-click the icon with your mouse. The first time you do this, nothing happens. Click OK to close the dialog box. Pull down Help About a second time and Ctrl+Shift+Double-click the icon again. This time, a small Windows flag appears (the Republic of Windows?) with a text message about the hard-working people who brought you Windows 3.1. But you're not done yet.

Close this dialog box and click Help About a third time. When you Ctrl+Shift+Double-click this time, a completely different display appears. A cartoon figure appears, pointing to a scrolling list of the usual suspects: programmers, marketers, and support staff. (In Windows 3.1, the people who demonstrate the product to corporate buyers are identified as "Marketing," instead of "Penguin Trainers," as in Word for Windows 1.*x*'s gang screen.)

For more information on secret credits in other Windows applications, see the gang screen topic in Chapter 4, "Program Manager Icons and Other Fixes," and the "Secrets of the Windows Applets" chapter of *Windows 3.1 Secrets*.

Bill, Steve, Brad, and T-Bear

The four figures who appear at random in this display are Microsoft chairman Bill Gates, co-president Steve Ballmer (he's the bald one), Windows- and DOS-product manager Brad Silverberg (the one with the beard), and a fuzzy teddy bear. This latter character requires some additional explanation.

In Microsoft jargon, a "bear" is something that comes along and bonks a programmer after he or she has introduced a bug into a Windows module in development that must be corrected before the product can ship. It's kind of a Microsoft mascot, like Smokey the Bear, who "crushes your butts."

Besides the scrolling credits, T-Bear is memorialized in another obscure function of Windows 3.1, as well. Start a DOS session under Windows 3.1 in 386 enhanced mode, and press Alt+Enter to reduce the session from full-screen to a smaller window (if necessary). Pull down the Control Menu from the upper-left corner of the window. Click the Fonts menu item, and you see one of the best new features of Windows 3.1 — different-sized screen fonts that you can choose for each DOS application you run.

Choose the "6 x 8" font. As a sample of the font you've selected, you see a small DOS directory listing (see Figure 42-1). There, under WIN.COM, is the file BEAR.EXE. There is, of course, no BEAR.EXE file in the Windows directory. It's just a nod to Microsoft's bonking Bear.

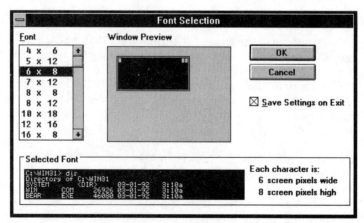

Figure 42-1: In the last line of the DOS "selected font" example is a listing for the nonexistent BEAR.EXE file — a nod to the Microsoft mascot.

Cheating at Solitaire _____

But the undocumented feature that everyone *really* wants to know is how to cheat at Solitaire.

Confirmed SOL.EXE addicts know that once you've started a Draw Three game you can't switch to a Draw One game. If you try (using Game Options), Solitaire ends your current game and deals you a new hand.

We've all had that sinking feeling when we've drawn three cards, and the exact card we need is just underneath the one at the top of the pile.

 When this happens to you, click Game Undo to return the three cards to the deck. Then hold down the Ctrl, Alt, and Shift keys simultaneously when you click the deck. Miraculously, only one card turns over. You can go through the entire deck this way — three times.

If you can't win at Solitaire now, I don't know how else I can help you.

Minesweeper's Back Door_____

A "back door" is also programmed into Minesweeper, the other game that comes with Windows 3.1.

 First, use the Control Panel to change your Desktop color to black in order to see this trick. Minimize all your applications so the upper-left corner of your screen is visible. Then start a new Minesweeper game. Move your mouse pointer into the playing area, then (on your keyboard) type "xyzzy" and press Enter. Press the Shift key and move your mouse slightly. A single white pixel will light up in the upper-left corner of your screen if your mouse pointer is on a "safe" square. If it's over a mine, the pixel goes out. This little "spy" will guide you safely through every game.

Both of these cheating tricks are explained in *Winning!,* a book of tips on the games in the three Microsoft Entertainment Packs. It's by John Hedtke and published by Peachpit Press.

Winning Without Cheating _____

People sometimes ask me, "Why reveal ways to cheat in these games? Doesn't it spoil the fun?"

Actually, I've found that, now that I know how to cheat in Solitaire, I feel *much better* when I win without cheating! The fact that I know how, and I didn't take advantage of it, gives a fresh pleasure to the mental stimulation of the game.

The Minesweeper trick, since it gives away the location of every single mine, isn't so useful for playing the game, but I find it to be a good way for someone to learn how the game works before seriously playing it.

Another book I've been having fun with lately is *Stupid Windows Tricks,* by Bob LeVitus and Ed Tittle. Somehow an actually useful program crept into this book/disk set: Wallpaper Randomizer, which switches your wallpaper every time you start your PC, so you don't get bored with the same old desktop.

The other programs might earn this book the title of *Windows Nonproductivity Pack:* a video poker game, an app that plays sounds through your speaker, even "roaches" that hide beneath your windows and scurry for cover when you move them. It's published by Addison-Wesley.

Summary

In this chapter, I look at hidden "jokes" behind the Windows interface.

▷ The secret "gang screen" that lists all the programmers and support staff who worked on Windows 3.1, complete with Microsoft's "bear" mascot.

▷ Tricks that allow you to cheat at Solitaire and Minesweeper, which may make you feel more virtuous when you play these games from now on *without* cheating!

Chapter 43
Buying Into Windows Upgrades

In This Chapter

▶ I examine the Windows buying habits of more than 300 companies that were surveyed by IDG Research Services.

▶ The major finding of the survey, in my mind, was that the average company planned to add, by 1993, 50 percent more Windows machines to its existing number, bringing the penetration of Windows to nearly half of all installed PCs — an astonishing growth rate for a product that had first gained corporate acceptance only three years earlier.

When I look into the world of corporate computing, every company I see seems to be grappling with the best ways to roll out Windows to as many desktops as possible. I have a bias towards graphical environments, of course. But confirmation of usage trends has come from a more objective source: a survey of the readers of *InfoWorld* on their Windows habits.

The results of this study, conducted by IDG Research Services, of Natick, Massachusetts, may be very helpful to you if your company is converting PCs to Windows and you've wondered how other folks are proceeding.

For example, the study found that about 82 percent of the companies surveyed are using Windows in some way, and about 30 percent of the PCs in those companies have Windows installed. This figure can give you some ammunition in case you feel your own firm is moving too slowly (or perhaps too quickly) towards Windows conversion.

The subjects were interviewed by telephone in the first quarter of 1992 — before the introduction of Windows 3.1 or the recent fratricidal hardware price wars. But the figures still provide an intriguing snapshot of actual Windows usage by the more than 300 companies represented in the survey's random sample.

For me, the most significant finding is that, by the first quarter of 1993, the respondents predicted that their companies would have Windows installed on about 46 percent of their PCs (up from 30 percent a year earlier). This is a dramatic jump in the Windows installed base, adding 50 percent more users in only one year.

The typical PC running Windows was found to have at least 4MB of RAM. About 73 percent of the respondents' PCs running Windows have 4MB or more, while about 14 percent have 8MB or more. The most common disk-storage capacity on PCs running Windows was 80MB or more, with 40 percent of respondents giving this answer. Another 37 percent reported that 41 to 80MB of disk space was the typical configuration. Another 21 percent used PCs with 40MB or smaller drives, while 2 percent weren't sure.

The movement to ever-faster PCs is certainly reflected in the respondents' answer to the question of what CPU is purchased "most often" to run Windows. While only 17.5 percent reported purchasing 16-bit 386SX machines, a sizable 65 percent purchased full 32-bit 386DX machines. And 14.5 percent reported buying fast 486DX or 486SX boxes. Looking forward, 35 percent of the respondents expected their companies to be purchasing only 486-class machines for Windows use by the first quarter of 1993.

As far as video resolution goes, 30 percent of the PCs running Windows were said to have Super VGA resolution (800 x 600) or better. About 68 percent are running plain VGA, with a few EGA holdouts. I hope to see monitors and video boards with higher resolutions increase their market share, since I personally don't recommend anything less than Super VGA for Windows use (and I find that 1024 x 768 provides even better productivity).

Despite the increasing penetration of Windows, and machines powerful enough to run it, only 10 percent of the companies using Windows had converted to Windows applications exclusively. Eighty-three percent run both DOS and Windows apps, while 7 percent run only DOS apps, using Windows as a kind of DOS menuing system. It looks like we'll have these DOS programs with us for a long, long time.

I hope you've found something here that can provide your own organization with a rationale for your planned acquisitions. Now bring on those Pentiums...

Summary

In this chapter, I describe some of the first reliable research on the penetration of Windows into large U.S. companies.

▶ By early 1993, Windows was expected to be installed on 46 percent of all PCs in these companies, with a phenomenal growth rate suggesting a saturation point by 1995 or 1996, when Windows will be almost universal on the installed base of PCs.

▶ More than one-third of the companies surveyed said that by early 1993, they expected to be purchasing no machines less than 486s for their Windows users, and with further price drops this number should increase even more.

Chapter 44
Gauging Windows Performance

In This Chapter

▶ I examine a utility that can give you an objective measure of the performance of each of your Windows components, perhaps showing you which of various upgrade alternatives would be most cost-effective.

▶ I describe the use of a free utility to determine how much of your time is being wasted simply waiting for your CPU to process Windows applications' tasks before you can regain control of your PC.

When you convert from a character-based application to a Windows application — for example, a graphical word processor — you are likely to find that the Windows app runs the same type of tasks more slowly.

This is primarily due to the difference in display modes. To redraw the screen, a text-mode program needs to write only 4,000 bytes into video memory (80 columns × 25 lines × 2 bytes — one byte for each character and an additional "attribute" byte for the color). To redraw the screen in Windows, a graphical program must write more than 150,000 bytes into video memory, assuming 16-color VGA (640 pixels x 480 pixels x 4 bits of color information, divided by 8 bits per byte).

For this reason, I recommend that companies converting PCs to Windows also upgrade those PCs at the same time. The upgrade expense can usually be cost-justified as part of a long-range company plan. Today, the most common and cost-effective upgrades are to 486 or Pentium systems, or the addition of RAM to bring a Windows system up to 8MB or more.

With the wealth of hardware alternatives available today, however, it's often difficult to know which ones will provide the biggest performance boost in your particular environment.

One of the tools I've found that helps Windows managers sort out the claims from the reality is Personal Measure, a DOS memory-resident program from Spirit of Performance that monitors your PC's activity and reports on how your system has been spending its time.

Since version 1.5, Personal Measure has been completely compatible with Windows 3.*x*. The program sells for $125.

I'm always leery of generic benchmark tests that claim to measure, say, the video performance of Windows. Such tests are often slanted toward the type of operations that predominate in AutoCAD, such as drawing vectors and shapes, instead of the type of operations that Windows requires, namely the constant redrawing of bitmapped typefaces and graphics. I've never seen a business document that required me to draw, for example, 1,000 random ellipses, as several benchmark programs do.

Instead, I find that using a stopwatch on the kind of operations you actually do in Windows can provide more interesting comparisons. For example, when I timed various operations in Windows 3.0's standard and enhanced modes, almost every operation in Microsoft Excel and Windows Paintbrush turned out to be faster in standard mode. But the Print Preview function in Word for Windows was significantly faster in *enhanced* mode. This is a result that I've seen no generic Windows benchmark test predict. (In Windows 3.1, standard and enhanced mode benchmarks come out almost exactly the same, so there is no reason to give up enhanced mode.)

Personal Measure tests your system in much the way that I did — using your own applications. You start Personal Measure from a DOS prompt and then perform the series of Windows actions you want to test. As soon as you exit Windows and give Personal Measure the command to quit, a wide range of performance statistics become available for graphing and printing.

One of the ways Personal Measure reveals bottlenecks in your system is by listing the percentage of time taken by subsystems such as the CPU, disk drive, and printer. If more than 50 percent of the operation you timed was devoted to disk drive activity, you might improve performance with a faster disk drive, a better disk cache, more extended memory, or all three. The best use of Personal Measure is to change only one variable from measurement to measurement, and isolate the results.

Personal Measure is no magic bullet that automatically cures Windows performance issues. You should plan to spend a few hours analyzing the hardware and software variables you wish to test. But having done this, Personal Measure gives you information that is difficult to gain without such a tool.

You can monitor the performance of almost any set of Windows tasks by using a program with a macro language, including Excel, Word for Windows, Ami Pro, and others. You can define an AutoExec macro in the Word for Windows Normal template, for example, that carries out any series of actions every time you start the word processor. Excel similarly allows you to specify in your WIN.INI an

AutoOpen macro that runs when you start Excel. You first save a macro file with an AutoOpen set of commands. Then you insert a line like the following in the Microsoft Excel section of WIN.INI:

```
[Microsoft Excel]
Open=c:\xlmacros\autoopen.xlm
```

You can also automate actions in applications that *don't* have their own macro language by using the Windows Recorder applet.

Ben Myers, president of Spirit of Performance, shared with me some tips on specific enhancements to Windows. If you're still using Microsoft's Windows 3.0 SmartDrive disk cache, he recommends replacing it with Super PC-Kwik from the PC-Kwik Corp. in Beaverton, Oregon. He also suggests reducing disk fragmentation. Personal Measure gives you a clear indication when this fragmentation has advanced to the point where you can gain a subtle, but measurable, 10 to 20 percent improvement in disk operations by running a disk-optimizer program.

One area of Windows performance that can greatly benefit from tuning is Windows applications themselves. Myers examined several Windows programs with his own advanced, proprietary tools, and found wide variations in the methods these programs use to read and write data.

NBI's Legacy word processor, for example, is known to be slow at saving files. Mr. Myers found that this is due to the fact that Legacy reads and writes files only 512 bytes at a time. Microsoft Excel is a little better, using 2048-byte blocks. But this is still inefficient enough that Excel opens and saves files more slowly than some other spreadsheet applications.

Surprisingly, the Excel Setup program is noted for how quickly it installs more than 4MB of files. Mr. Myers found that this is because Setup writes blocks as large as 60,000 bytes. He concludes that Windows developers originally started using small block sizes to conserve memory under Windows 1.*x* and 2.*x*. With today's protected-mode operations, larger block sizes are preferable.

Mr. Myers and his associates often travel to consult with corporate and commercial developers about improving the performance of their programs. Many software publishers would benefit from his experience.

Personal Measure is available from Spirit of Performance, Inc., 73 Westcott Rd., Harvard, MA 01451; 508-456-3889.

Cost-Justify Upgrades with Widget Utility

Sometimes it seems as though companies that buy computer equipment never throw any of it away. Everywhere I go, I see firms trying to get acceptable performance from Windows applications on 16-megahertz 386SX machines and even old 286 systems.

Our experience with Windows 3.x should teach us a hard, cold fact: after a few performance tweaks here and there, nothing improves the performance of Windows like a CPU and video upgrade.

I've been recommending since Windows 3.0 first came out in 1990 that businesses using Windows for job-related tasks purchase nothing less than 25 MHz 386DX machines. Today, if your company is not purchasing 486/33s or better for Windows work, you are buying machines that will become more and more inadequate to handle the demands of Windows NT and future versions of Windows.

Don't misunderstand me — if you are purchasing PCs for home use, or primarily for playing Solitaire or light e-mail reading, a 386SX machine may be fine.

But if you expect people to use Windows to process documents more than one page long, or calculate spreadsheets that contain more than simple addition, you are wasting their time and your company's money.

I sympathize completely with the microcomputer managers out there who are now thinking, "My company will never value people's time enough to buy faster machines to run Windows."

I know how it feels to have to live within a budget. Most companies upgrade their car pools (for purely cosmetic reasons) more often than they upgrade the computers they are paying people to sit in front of and wait for.

Persuading upper management of the need for hardware upgrades can be difficult without quantifiable data. There are usually no hard statistics on what the old machines are costing the company in terms of lost salaries — only subjective complaints.

I mentioned this lack of objective Windows measuring tools to several developers. One company that did something about it is Metz Software. Metz developed a utility called the Metz Widget (a program by Tom Landon). You run the Widget in the background, and it collects hard data on how much time a person spends merely waiting for Windows to catch up. Best of all, Metz is practically giving away this utility (for the duplicating and shipping and cost of the diskette).

The Metz Widget sends a message to Windows every second (you can adjust this interval) and records how long it takes for Windows to reply. The wait represents the time that other Windows applications are keeping the machine to themselves. When you close the Widget, it writes a comma-separated-values (CSV) file, perfect for importing into Excel or 1-2-3. When Windows is simply waiting for keyboard input, cells will be filled with values like 0, 0, 0. But when an application is making the user wait (Excel loading a file, for example), you'll see values like 400, 500, 1000, 1000, 400. The "1000" readings indicate that the application has grabbed the CPU for the whole second of that measurement interval. The user can literally do nothing but wait.

By ignoring the zero values and analyzing the non-zero values, you can assemble quite a persuasive case for upgrades. Take a person whose salary, benefits, and office space cost $50,000 per year. If this person has to wait 10 minutes a day (1/42 of each 7-hour day), it's costing your company more than $1,000 a year in waiting time.

The Metz Widget isn't something you'd want to run all the time. After 4½ hours, you'd have more than 16,000 readings — exceeding the number of rows Excel supports. Running it for an hour or two on each machine, with users' knowledge, should provide plenty of data.

The Metz Widget diskette can be obtained from Metz Software, 4018-148th Ave N.E., Redmond, WA 98052-5516, for $5 shipping by calling 800-767-6292 or 206-869-6292. It is also available as a freeware utility on the diskettes that accompany *Windows Gizmos*.

Summary

In this chapter, tools that can give you detailed and specific measurements of the performance and cost-effectiveness of your Windows system are evaluated.

▶ Personal Measure is a professional-quality package that can isolate bottlenecks and help you compare the strengths and weaknesses of various hardware components you might be considering for upgrades.

▶ Metz Widget is a free utility that records how much of a user's time is spent waiting for elementary tasks to be completed by a CPU before the user can get back to productive work.

Chapter 45

Carrying Windows Around: Removable Hard Drives

In This Chapter

▶ For those of you who have trouble keeping enough free space available on your hard drive to run Windows applications, I examine two ways that you can take advantage of an unlimited amount of disk storage.

▶ These alternatives include removable data cartridges as well as a special high-capacity removable drive that's so small it can be used with a laptop PC.

Windows tends to soak up space on a hard disk more than almost any other PC program. It isn't just Windows itself. It's also the graphics files that Windows encourages you to use. A company logo here, a bitmap there, and pretty soon you're talking real storage space.

I've been testing two different methods the Iomega Corp. has developed for transporting not just bulky Windows data but the Windows environment as well.

The first is the Bernoulli Transportable 90, a 90MB disk drive that uses removable cartridges. At a list price of $1,299, the 90MB model is less expensive than the older, 44MB drives that Iomega discontinued.

As part of my tests, I've taken the Transportable 90 to presentations, with my entire Windows directory and several data files loaded up. By simply inserting a small interface card into a PC at the new location, adding a driver to CONFIG.SYS, and rebooting, that machine recognizes the Transportable 90 as a new drive letter. By changing to that drive, I can start and run my copy of Windows just as it ran before. Try that using floppies.

Bernoulli drives, and similar devices such as the 44 or 88MB removable cartridges from SyQuest Technology, have become a standard feature in typesetting service bureaus, which use them to take large output files output from Windows and Macintosh PostScript publishing programs. But I think many Windows users would find these transportable drives and cartridges invaluable for any job where mobile technical support is required: configuring or diagnosing software, for example.

Another Iomega device with Windows support potential is a 20MB, 3½-inch diskette drive. This drive, originally developed by Insite Technologies of San Jose, California, takes ordinary-looking 3½-inch diskettes. But it uses an optical system (similar to a CD audio player) to read and write diskettes much more densely — hence the name Floptical.

The Floptical drive is unique in that it is the only 20MB diskette drive that also handles 1.44MB and 720K diskettes correctly. The drive detects the format of whatever diskette you place in it, and reads and writes the proper format. The 3½-inch drives list for about $500, and several diskette manufacturers offer special 20MB diskettes for about $20 each (less per megabyte than brand-name 1.44MB diskettes).

Besides the possibility of carrying around Windows data, the Floptical makes Windows backup routines a snap. By installing the 20MB diskette drive as drive B: in a PC, you can leave a diskette in the drive all the time. (Most PCs don't boot up off a diskette in drive B:, only A: or C:, so this doesn't halt the bootup process.) You can then backup any files you've modified since your last bootup by including the following lines in your AUTOEXEC.BAT:

```
:START
XCOPY C:\*.* B:\ /S /M
IF NOT ERRORLEVEL 1 GOTO :OKAY
ECHO Insert a new backup diskette in B:.
PAUSE
GOTO :START
:OKAY
```

This batch file copies from C: to B: all files, from all subdirectories, that are new or modified (the DOS archive bit is set on). When your 20MB diskette fills up, XCOPY sets the errorlevel, which your batch file detects so you can insert a new diskette to continue.

This routine, of course, also works with any formatted 1.44MB diskettes — but they will fill up a lot quicker than 20MB diskettes.

You can easily amend this batch file to use a better backup routine than XCOPY, such as the DOS BACKUP command, or a third-party backup package. My point in giving you this batch file example is that it's so simple to make an automatic backup routine for your Windows files by using drive B: that it's a shame more people don't do it.

When I use a Windows application to save a new version of a file — but I meant to save it under a new name, not wipe out the old file — no undelete utility in the world can help me get the old file back. But my B: drive can.

Contact Iomega Corp. at 1821 West 4000 South, Roy, UT 84067; 801-778-1000.

Summary

In this chapter, I describe two convenient disk storage alternatives distributed by the Iomega Corp.

▶ The Bernoulli Transportable 90 is a 90MB cartridge drive that runs off an add-in board or a parallel port adapter.

▶ The Floptical drive is a 20MB diskette drive that fits within the same form factor as an ordinary 1.44MB drive, but stores over 13 times more data — and also reads and writes normal 1.44MB and 720K diskettes for interchangeability with other machines.

Chapter 46
Monitoring Your Dot Pitch

In This Chapter

▶ I quantify the benefits of a good monitor for prolonged Windows work, with a description of the three factors that make a PC monitor look sharp (rather than fuzzy or muddy) and a utility that can sort out the good from the bad and the downright ugly.

▶ I look at higher-resolution monitors for Windows, particularly a monitor that can display a full-page document on a Windows screen.

One of my readers writes, "When I switch from the standard VGA driver (640 x 480 pixels) to a high-resolution driver (800 x 600), I get better color graphics but poorer text. Can you explain the difference I am seeing?"

Since Windows is a totally bitmapped graphical interface, the clarity of today's color monitors has become increasingly important. A monitor that displays plain DOS text perfectly well may become muddy or fuzzy when displaying Windows.

Because Windows text displayed at 800 x 600 appears physically smaller than text displayed at 640 x 480 (on the same size monitor), it is possible that this is causing the text to look poorer. But my guess is that this is not the problem in this case. A person with normal eyesight quickly adjusts to the slightly smaller appearance of text on an 800 x 600 display — and the increase in available screen area is well worth it.

Some graphics adapter vendors provide Windows drivers that offer both "small fonts" and "large fonts." The latter can be used to enlarge the System font used in menus, for those users who feel the smaller text is too fuzzy to read clearly. But instead of resigning themselves to displays with poor sharpness, Windows users should check the monitors they use — and any monitors they plan to buy — against three criteria: focus, convergence, and dot pitch.

Focus relates to the sharpness of a monitor's electron beam as it paints the face of a cathode-ray tube (CRT). Convergence is how closely the red, green, and blue guns in a color monitor track each other when drawing a color image.

Many monitors can be adjusted to improve the focus, and some allow magnets within the monitor to be realigned to improve the convergence. You should consider having these adjustments made to any monitor that has just been shipped or moved from one place to another.

In one company, I had technicians examine 100 or so VGA displays, and about a dozen of the monitors benefited greatly after the technicians opened the cases and fixed the focus settings. Monitors can also "drift" from their original settings after a year or so of operation, justifying a repeat examination every year. Since opening a monitor's case can void the manufacturer's warranty, you should be careful to use only authorized maintenance personnel.

Dot pitch is the distance between the tiny phosphors that glow on the face of a CRT. Ironically, dot pitch is the one factor that you can't do anything about after you have purchased a monitor — and the factor that has the most impact on Windows.

When one monitor has phosphors spaced more closely together than another monitor, it is said to have a finer dot pitch. The monitor with a coarser dot pitch will display colors less vividly than one with a finer pitch. And, more importantly, the coarser monitor will display less detail in hairlines — such as the text and border lines found in all Windows applications.

Figure 46-1 shows how the red, green, and blue phosphors are arranged on the face of a color monitor. The dot pitch of this monitor is determined by the vertical distance between the centers of two phosphors of the same color — say, red phosphors.

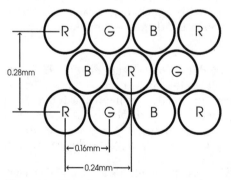

Figure 46-1: The 0.28mm dot pitch of a monitor is measured vertically between the centers of two phosphors of the same color.

Today's monitors usually have a dot pitch of 0.31 or 0.28 millimeters (mm). Beware, however — I've been told that some vendors claim finer dot pitches than this by measuring the distance *horizontally* between two phosphors of the same color. This would allow a 0.28mm monitor to be marketed (deceptively) as a 0.24mm monitor.

A dot pitch that is too coarse can cause small type and lines to look weak, which may be the root of the reader's problem.

Trinitron monitors, by the way, are quite different. Trinitron monitors, based on a technique patented by the Sony Corp., do not have phosphors shaped like dots. Instead, the red-green-blue phosphors on the face of a Trinitron monitor are arranged in thin vertical lines, side by side.

Therefore, a Trinitron monitor does not have a dot pitch, as such. Trinitron monitors are sometimes said to have a "trio pitch," which is the distance measured horizontally from the center of one color stripe to the center of the next stripe of the same color.

It isn't possible to make a direct comparison between the dot pitch of a conventional monitor and the trio pitch of a Trinitron monitor.

What's Best for DOS Isn't Best for Windows

The best monitors for plain DOS text mode may not be the best for working in Windows. Operating in reverse video all the time — as Windows does with its familiar black-on-white display — puts a different burden on monitors than the white-on-black characters common in DOS applications.

A few rules of thumb have developed among professionals in the computer monitor business that can guide us in buying new displays for our GUI work. And some powerful tools for evaluating monitor capabilities that previously were available only to monitor manufacturers and other large businesses are now available to the average person as well.

Let's go back to dot pitch for a minute. Many popular monitors today are sold with a dot pitch of either 0.31mm or 0.28mm, as mentioned earlier. But I have recently seen monitors advertised for sale with dot pitches as coarse as 0.41mm and even 0.51mm.

I realize that the cost of a monitor can represent a major fraction of the total cost of a system. But I can't imagine any way I'd be happy with a monitor for Windows work that had coarser than 0.31mm dot pitch. And I've seen first-hand the improvement that a 0.28mm dot pitch can make in two otherwise identical monitors from the same manufacturer.

Even though dot pitch may be important in a Windows display, it isn't the only factor. All those red-green-blue phosphors appear in tight lockstep on the faces of our monitors only because of a fine mesh grid called a *shadow mask*.

This mask holds the phosphors in position, to be lighted by the CRT's electron beam to form a picture. Each pixel on your display, such as the 640- by 480-pixel resolution of ordinary VGA, actually lights up several individual phosphors. To make a single white pixel on a perfectly black background, you ideally would want to light at least three phosphors: one each of red, green, and blue. Realistically, one pixel may light several more than three phosphors, but the effect is the same — our eyes combine the colors to see "white."

The truth of the matter is that a monitor's shadow mask, which fixes the phosphors in place, can never be perfectly aligned with the ideal position of each row of pixels. The mask will always be a little off, more or less: better in the center of the screen, less good around the corners, and so on.

For this reason, it is not possible to give a hard-and-fast rule about what dot pitch is best for each different monitor size and resolution. The slight misalignment of a monitor's shadow mask, combined with the quality of its focus and convergence, add up to a big question mark about exactly what is *"the"* monitor for Windows.

With that said, I'd like to stick my neck out and give you a yardstick for purchasing displays for Windows users.

Windows is driving a wave of interest in higher and higher resolutions. Since larger monitors seem to become more expensive in proportion to the square of their size, however, many people try to get higher resolutions out of the older, smaller monitors they are used to.

The 14-inch monitors that are now the most common among PC buyers, though, can only go so far. To meet the demand for higher resolutions, 16-inch monitors are now widely available, neatly filling in below the super-expensive 19- and 21-inch giants.

But even a 16-inch monitor has its limits. "Under the best possible conditions," says Bob Diaz, technical support manager for Nanao USA Corp., "you can just barely get 1280 x 1024," and 1024 x 768 is more likely the practical limit on a 16-inch display.

He should know — Nanao makes some of the better high-resolution monitors available.

My recommendations for monitors of various sizes, and the maximum resolution that you should hope to get out of them, thus break down as follows:

Monitor Size	Resolution
14-inch	800 x 600
16-inch	1024 x 768
19-inch	1280 x 960 or 1280 x 1024

And what about dot pitch? At these higher resolutions, I feel you're doing the right thing by looking for monitors with 0.28mm or better. A 14-inch monitor with 0.31mm dot pitch is OK for a plain VGA display. Anything coarser than that is appropriate only for EGA or (ugh) CGA displays, if anyone still uses those for Windows.

The best way to test all these factors on your favorite monitors yourself is with a nifty diagnostic program called DisplayMate. This $149 utility runs monitors through a gantlet of tests that are, frankly, so tough that no monitor made today can pass all of them 100 percent, says its author, Ray Soneira. DisplayMate is used by Nanao and many other video manufacturers to stress-test their own monitors before shipping them — and now you can do the same before you buy them.

Contact Sonera Technologies at 800-932-6323 or 908-747-6886.

Consider a Totally New Type of Monitor

Before you buy any new monitors, however, I'd like to suggest a wholly new type of monitor you should consider.

Those of us who promote the use of personal computers often make grand claims about how these computers make people so much more *productive*.

In reality, during the decade 1980–90 — a period when PCs were installed throughout most companies — statistics show that the productivity of the average U.S. worker changed little, if at all.

I believe this is because most companies simply automated their old paperwork systems without taking advantage of the possibilities inherent in their computers.

In the old days of Selectric typewriters, an executive would dictate a letter to a secretary, who would type a draft. Once the draft had been checked and re-typed, the letter would be sent out.

Today, a business letter can theoretically be produced in half the time, since word processing eliminates the need to ever re-type the entire letter. But now the executive revises each letter *four times* instead of twice, resulting in the same expenditure of time.

A company that wants to really exploit computer technology could make a policy requiring that all documents be edited only in electronic form. All print-ers could be removed from users' desks. Only a final copy of each document need be printed at a central location — all work up to that point could be done on-screen.

Until recently, such a company would be operating at a severe handicap. Most companies have restricted themselves to VGA monitors, which are capable of showing only a "viewport" of a document — 6 inches wide by 3 inches high. Imagine being forced to view all the paperwork on your desk through a 6- by 3-inch porthole!

But today, a solution has appeared that promises to give companies a way to accomplish most or all of their Windows work on-screen, without unnecessary edit-print-edit cycles.

This solution lies in the Full Page Pivot monitor from Radius, Inc.

The Pivot monitor not only displays a full, portrait-mode 8½- by 11-inch docu-ment in color. It easily turns 90 degrees to display documents in landscape mode. When you turn the monitor, Radius' Windows driver automatically re-draws all screen elements so they fit into the new screen proportions.

A monitor like this would be almost unthinkable without the Windows environ-ment, which provides a single video driver for all running applications. Under DOS, a different screen driver would have to be written for every major applica-tion — and there is no guarantee that the mode-switch would work for every DOS mode.

Even so, Radius includes drivers for the DOS versions of WordPerfect, Lotus 1-2-3, AutoCAD (386 and Real Mode), AutoShade, and 3D Studio, as well as sev-eral DOS text modes.

In Windows, the Full Page Pivot supports resolutions of 640 x 480, 800 x 600, and 1024 x 768 noninterlaced. It supports 256 colors in all resolutions, and 32,000 colors in 640 x 480.

The Pivot monitor meets or exceeds most of the criteria for Windows monitors that I've described. It features a dot pitch of 0.28mm, and a refresh rate of 72 Hertz or greater in all resolutions (except the highest resolution, 1024 x 768 with 256 colors, which is supported at 60 Hz). A refresh rate of 70 Hz or better reduces flicker under florescent and other office lighting.

You may be able to find larger landscape-style monitors that can meet these specifications and display as much information vertically as the Pivot by investing in monitors with a noninterlaced 1280 x 1024 resolution at a 70 Hz refresh rate. But these monitors, too, are more expensive than the ordinary VGA and Super VGA boxes that are all too common. If your company's employees spend all day viewing portrait-mode documents, such as scanned-in forms, a portrait monitor can make sense.

The ability to see whole pages in one glance adds about $750 (discounted) to the price of a plain VGA system, which I believe is easily cost-justified in any document-intensive company. The list price for the Pivot monitor is $1,249; the MultiView adapter board is $449.

Contact Radius, Inc., at 1710 Fortune Dr., San Jose, CA 95131; 408-434-1010.

Summary

In this chapter, the interaction between you and the monitor you use to display Windows is my focus (no pun intended).

▶ The focus, convergence, and dot pitch of a monitor are the three crucial elements that make it suitable or unusable for Windows, and you can measure these accurately with DisplayMate, a professional utility.

▶ With the number of documents that businesspeople now must read on computer screens, companies should consider high-resolution monitors or portrait-style monitors such as the Radius Pivot in order to fit an entire page of a form or report onto the Windows display.

Chapter 47
A Gold Mine of Programmers' Tricks

In This Chapter

▶ I examine some of the performance issues that Windows programmers must deal with when attempting to create high-speed but reliable applications.

▶ Much of the leading-edge information that Windows developers need to cope with the demands of the Windows environment comes from a little-known newsletter published by an expert in Windows and OS/2 programming.

Whenever I think that everything about Windows *must* be known by now, I find something else that was not previously documented by anyone.

These Windows features are not limited to the user interface. Many aspects of the Windows Application Programming Interface (API), which programmers use, remain obscure or completely unknown until someone stumbles across them.

Exploiting these features is the business of a technical newsletter called the *Windows Developer Letter* (WDL). Its editor, Asael Dror (pronounced *ah sah ELL DROAR*), has discovered many new techniques that can come in very handy for programmers.

One frustrating thing about Windows 3.x from a programmer's point of view is that it is not a true 32-bit environment. In other words, even in 386 enhanced mode, Windows cannot access all the memory in a system at once, but must deal with memory in 64K chunks known as *segments*. This means that programmers (or the compilers they use) must keep track of many separate segments of memory, rather than simply writing to large memory areas directly. This drags down the performance of Windows applications.

Without going into all the programming details here, Mr. Dror has found "unofficial" techniques for accessing large amounts of memory.

One way to describe this, for those readers who are not C programmers, is that a large block of memory (larger than 64K) can be accessed from a program by using the first address or *selector* of the entire block, in an unorthodox way.

In case you suspect that this undocumented Windows technique has been used by Microsoft applications, Mr. Dror says it has not. His opinion is that accessing large memory objects in this particular way has simply been overlooked until now. Indicating that the method revealed by *WDL* is not totally forbidden, however, a document entitled "Huge Memory Moves" recently appeared on the Microsoft Developer Network CD-ROM (signed by "Dr. GUI"), suggesting some of the same techniques.

Mr. Dror, a former engineer with Chips & Technologies, describes three different programs that access large memory. Each program sorts in descending order the first 1000 integers in an array of 65,536 (a worst-case sort).

Using the conventional method (GlobalAlloc), the first program sorts 1000 integers on a 486/33 in 305 seconds.

With another method (Global32Alloc) — well documented but now discouraged by Microsoft — the second program sorts 1000 integers in only 116 seconds.

But using inline 386 assembly language to manipulate selectors, as WDL recommends, the third program sorts 1000 integers in a mere 52 seconds — six times faster than the normal method!

Volume 1, Number 5 of *WDL,* printed in November 1992, was the first to describe this technique. Volume 2 , Number 1, published in January 1993, includes programming routines known as *macros* so you don't have to code the assembly language yourself.

Mr. Dror feels his method has advantages over using the Win32s API (a subset of the NT API, which can also run on Windows 3.1). He states that Win32s is not available for some 32-bit video device driver calls, for example.

Future issues of *WDL* are expected to reveal how DOS sessions (which benefit from true pre-emptive multitasking under Windows) can communicate with each other and with graphical applications. DOS apps can even use the Windows API to draw into the client area of a Windows app, for example.

WDL subscriptions are $300 a year for 12 issues (including companion diskettes). Back issues are $25. This is expensive, but I think it's well worth it, and Mr. Dror says that most subscribers soon request a complete set once they see the contents of an issue.

Contact *WDL* at 322 Eureka St., San Francisco, CA 94114; (415) 824-8482.

Summary

In this chapter, programming strategies for high-performance Windows applications are examined.

▶ Sometimes, the best way to accomplish a given programming task is not the way Microsoft recommends.

▶ Expert tips that illuminate such misunderstood areas of Windows are provided by the *Windows Developer Letter,* a monthly guide crammed full of programming code samples and revelations of previously unknown Windows shortcuts.

Chapter 48
The Future of 32-Bitness

In This Chapter

▶ I look forward into the 32-bit world that Microsoft and other vendors are bringing Windows into — a world that promises better performance and reliability for graphical applications of all kinds.

▶ Besides Microsoft's 32-bit Application Programming Interfaces (APIs), at least two other development-oriented vendors are specializing in 32-bit tools that offer their own features and support.

Making Windows run better is something that I and a lot of other people are very interested in. We hear a lot about future plans for Windows — how new versions of Windows will be better, how OS/2 is better than Windows, how OS/2 will be better than Windows someday, and so on.

It turns out that producing applications that run "better than Windows" is already possible — and the solution isn't from Microsoft *or* IBM.

This "something better" is the ability to run 32-bit applications under Windows 3.1 or even 3.0. As you already know, on a 386 or better, Windows 3.1 can run in either standard mode or 386 enhanced mode. But even in 386 enhanced mode, Windows uses only 16-bit instructions. The faster and more efficient 32-bit instructions, which take advantage of features unique to 386 and higher processors, are native to Windows NT (New Technology).

That doesn't stop developers from writing 32-bit Windows applications, though. It's a little-known fact that a Windows app can use 32-bit instructions internally. The application need use 16-bit instructions only when communicating with the Windows kernel. This allows such a dual-personality app to take advantage of the speed of 32-bit instructions when recalculating a spreadsheet, say, or repaginating a document. It must slow down to 16-bit instructions only when requesting that Windows display the results, write a file, and so on.

The speed advantage of 32-bit instructions comes from the fact that more work can be performed in a single instruction. It's also possible to address all the memory in a PC as a single large segment instead of as a series of 64K segments. These benefits are collectively known to programmers as "*32-bitness*."

The reason we haven't seen many Windows applications that take advantage of 32-bitness is that dividing an application into two personalities takes time. Time is money when your first priority must be to get a working application out the door. (The fact that 386-class machines and higher have been a minority of the installed base until recently hasn't helped, either.)

All this is changing. Rational Systems, the company in Natick, Massachusetts, that built DOS-extender technology for Lotus 1-2-3 3.x (and many other products) has been shipping a "BigWin" extender to developers for some time. With this product, converting a normal 16-bit Windows application into a dual-personality 32-bit application is a straight forward process.

The developer of an existing Windows application first re-compiles the source code with a 32-bit C compiler, such as the ones available from Zortech, MetaWare, and Watcom (or an updated version of Microsoft C or the OS/2 Software Development Kit). The resulting object code is then linked with BigWin using a 32-bit linker, such as one available from Rational.

The final executable programs that Rational has tested run faster without any change to their underlying code, claims Terry Colligan, Rational's president. He says, for example, that floating-point operations run 400 percent faster, while the application that performs those operations clocks at 250 percent faster (the app must perform operations other than floating-point in order to display anything to the user). Other 32-bit programs have been timed anywhere from 20 to 200 percent faster than the original versions.

Even under the 32-bit Windows NT kernel (and future 32-bit versions of Windows itself), Windows apps with dual personalities will continue to run, says Colligan. This compatibility will buy developers some time to write NT-specific versions of their programs, while still selling 32-bit programs that can run under both NT *and* Windows.

BigWin competes with Microsoft's own Application Programming Interfaces (APIs), which roughly break down as follows:

■ The most capable is Win32, the native API of Windows NT. Win32 allows applications to be *multithreaded,* which means that an application can spawn tasks that run independently of the main program.

■ Win32s is a subset of Win32 that allows applications to run under NT and Windows 3.1. Win32s translates 32-bit programming calls into the 16-bit API that is native to Windows 3.1. But Win32s does not support the multithreading and multiprocessing features of Windows NT.

■ Win32c is a larger subset of Win32 than Win32s. The "c" in Win32c stands for "Chicago," the code name for Microsoft's Windows 4.0 release. Win32c supports most of the Windows NT API — except for features like multiprocessing and security that are unique to NT — for applications running in either NT or Windows 4.0.

Besides Rational Systems, MetaWare, Inc., of Santa Cruz, California, also has its own 32-bit Windows Application Development Kit (ADK).

Both BigWin and MetaWare's ADK require that an application first be run through a 32-bit compiler — such as MetaWare's High C compiler.

But MetaWare's development tools may be significantly less expensive for programmers. If you already have the High C compiler, version 1.7 or later, the new ADK is $495. If not, the ADK, compiler, and 32-bit Source-Level Debugger are available as a package for $1,095 to $1,195.

Rational Systems' BigWin library costs $5,000 plus a royalty payment for each shipping application. MetaWare's tools do not require a royalty payment for applications.

Rational Systems can be reached at 220 N. Main St. Natick, MA 01760; 508-653-6006. MetaWare, Inc., is at 2161 Delaware Ave., Santa Cruz, CA 95060-5706; 408-429-6382.

Summary

In this chapter, the direction of Windows as it heads into a 32-bit future is projected.

▶ Microsoft has committed itself to 32-bit versions of Windows, with both the Win32 API fully implemented in Windows NT, and the Win32c API that is planned to run in Chicago (Windows 4.0) and NT.

▶ Development tools vendors like Rational Systems and MetaWare, Inc., however, are not resting on their laurels, but are continuing to come up with innovative products that offer independent software vendors a choice of development environments.

Part IV

Windows Shareware

Chapter 49

Excellence in Windows Shareware

This book features more than two dozen of the very best programs available free or for a nominal registration from independent Windows programmers. The programs featured in *More Windows 3.1 Secrets* are designed to comple-ment those in *Windows 3.1 Secrets* and *Windows Gizmos,* my two earlier books of undocumented Windows features and Windows software. *Windows 3.1 Secrets* features 44 programs, and *Windows Gizmos* offers 33. But it is not necessary in any way for you to buy those books in order to use the programs featured in this one.

At the time I wrote *Windows 3.1 Secrets,* I thought it encompassed the best Win-dows shareware there would ever be. But I was wrong — a flood of great programs was just beginning! The result was *Windows Gizmos,* which was in-tended to provide readers with a source of the more mature and sophisticated shareware applications that starting appearing in Windows wake. Shareware authors, however, have amazed me by continuing to top themselves. As a result, *More Windows 3.1 Secrets* would not be complete without featuring the Baker's two dozen programs herein — some of which were perfected only weeks before the deadline for publication of this book. Without taking anything away from the programs found in *Windows 3.1 Secrets* and *Windows Gizmos,* I think you'll find that the programs featured in *More Windows 3.1 Secrets* are even more mature, powerful, and fun to use.

How to Use This Software

If you are a new user of Windows:

The next few pages include three sections to help new Windows users: "The Least You Need to Know About DOS," "How to Put An Application on Your Path," and "How to Load an Application At Startup. " Reading these pages should give you everything you need to understand some of the instructions in the chapters that follow.

If you have used Windows for several months or years:

Simply skip the three "new user" sections in this chapter if you already understand DOS, the DOS Path, and loading applications at startup.

Quick Installation Instructions

To install any of the programs on the *More Windows 3.1 Secrets* diskettes:

1. Insert Diskette 1 into the appropriate diskette drive, A: or B:.
2. In the Windows Program Manager, pull down the File menu, then click Run.
3. In the dialog box that appears, type A:\WSETUP if you're using drive A:, or B:\WSETUP if you're using drive B:.

That's it! The WSETUP program allows you to select those programs you wish to install. Simply click each desired program and click Add to add the programs to the list to be installed. When you click the Install button, WSETUP prompts you to change diskettes when necessary.

Some programs require a separate configuration step before you can use them. These programs are the RRKeyCaps font, Sloop Manager, the Video Terminal Screen (VTS) font, and Wiz Manager.

For more details, see the Complete Installation Instructions on the last page of this book, facing the diskettes inside the back cover.

FOR NEW WINDOWS USERS:

The Least You Need to Know about DOS

If you are a DOS beginner or are starting to use Windows after working on another graphical environment, such as a Macintosh, this section is for you.

Windows does not "protect" you from the way DOS stores information on your disk drives. You can see exactly where everything is stored on your drives and organize it as you like. It's sometimes said that DOS is hard to learn. But if you know a few terms, you can use the Windows File Manager (or a similar program) to do everything you need.

1. **Disk Drives.** Most PCs have two or more disk drives for storing information. These drives are identified by the letters A through Z, followed by a colon (:). The first *floppy diskette* drive in your PC is drive A:. The second diskette drive is B:, if you have one. The first *hard drive* is C:, and so on.

2. **Subdividing a disk.** Drives are subdivided into *directories,* also called *folders.* These directories make it easier to find your documents than if everything were stored in one huge list. For example, if you often write memos, you might create a directory called MEMOS. You might create a subdirectory called BOSS for memos to your boss, one called MAILROOM for memos to the mailroom, and so on.

   The *backslash* is a special character in DOS that indicates your level in a drive's directory structure. The directory C:\MEMOS\BOSS has two backslashes in it. This indicates that you are two levels down from the C: drive's main directory, called the *root directory.* The root directory of drive C: is indicated by a backslash with no directory name after it, such as C:\. All other directories *branch* off this main directory. This is why all the directories on a drive are called a *tree.* In Windows, the File Manager initially shows you the directory tree of the current drive, from which you can choose to display any folder.

3. **Storing documents in files.** All documents must be given names. Each document is called a *file,* and DOS allows each *filename* to have from 1 to 8 characters, followed by a period, followed by 0 to 3 more characters called the filename's *extension.* Names like MYFILE.DOC and README.TXT are legitimate DOS filenames.

   A filename can contain any letter or number, plus any of the punctuation marks found on the number keys, 0–9, on your keyboard (except the asterisk). Extensions indicate what type of information is in each file. The extension .DOC probably means a document created by a specific word processor, while .TXT probably means a plain text file that any text-editing program like Windows Notepad can read. Most programs require that you type only the first eight letters when naming a file and will automatically add the proper extension for you.

FOR NEW WINDOWS USERS:

How to Put an Application on Your Path

When you start a program, such as Windows Notepad, Windows looks for a file called NOTEPAD.EXE in a list of directories called the *Path*.

Some of the applications found on the *More Windows 3.1 Secrets* diskettes require that you place their directory on the Path, if you want to start them easily from a File Run dialog box. Fortunately, this is a very simple procedure.

The directories on your Path are usually determined by a line in your C:\AUTOEXEC.BAT file. Your PC reads this file every time you reboot.

You can add a directory to your Path by opening C:\AUTOEXEC.BAT with Windows Notepad. If Windows isn't running, and you have DOS 5.0 or higher, you can type EDIT C:\AUTOEXEC.BAT at a DOS prompt to edit the file. (Don't open AUTOEXEC.BAT in a word processor because it can make the file unreadable.) Once you've opened the file, you should see a line similar to the following:

```
PATH=C:\WINDOWS;C:\DOS;C:\;C:\BAT
```

This line indicates that four directories are on the Path: the Windows directory, DOS, your root directory, and a directory containing batch files. Windows and DOS need to be on the Path to run properly. Your root directory should also be on the Path to help applications find COMMAND.COM and other programs that may be located there.

If you want to add a directory, such as the IniEdit directory (C:\SECRETS2\INIEDIT), to your Path, add a semicolon and the name of the directory to the end of your Path statement. This would make the line shown above look as follows:

```
PATH=C:\WINDOWS;C:\DOS;C:\;C:\BAT;C:\SECRETS2\INIEDIT
```

You must save your changes and reboot your PC for this new Path statement to take effect.

You must make sure that your PATH= statement does not exceed 127 characters (including the word "path" and the equals sign). DOS ignores the PATH= statement after the first 127 characters, which can cause strange behavior. If your Path gets too long, you may have to take some applications off the Path or change their directory names to shorter alternatives.

FOR NEW WINDOWS USERS:

How to Load an Application at Startup _____

You may wish to have several of the programs found on the *More Windows 3.1 Secrets* diskettes load themselves automatically, every time you start Windows. This is also a simple process.

In Windows 3.1 and higher:

The Windows 3.1 Program Manager usually has a group window called StartUp. Any program can be automatically loaded every time Windows starts by placing the program's icon in the StartUp group.

To copy an icon from another Program Manager group window into the StartUp group window, hold down your Ctrl key while dragging the desired icon into StartUp with your mouse. This makes a duplicate copy of the icon in the StartUp group. Dragging an icon without holding down the Ctrl key moves the icon permanently.

After placing the icon in StartUp, click it once to select it, then click File Properties on the Program Manager menu. The Properties dialog box that appears gives you several options. You can start the application minimized (as an icon at the bottom of your screen) or normal (in a window). You can also change the command line that starts the application or select a different icon. The files PROGMAN.EXE and MORICONS.DLL contain numerous icons to choose from.

In Windows 3.0 and higher:

Windows 3.0 does not support a StartUp group in its Program Manager. To load a program automatically, you must add its name to one of two lines in the WIN.INI file, called the LOAD= and RUN= lines.

You can open WIN.INI in Windows Notepad or DOS 5.0's Edit program. (Don't use a word processor.) You should see lines near the top of the file that look as follows:

```
[windows]
load=
run=
```

You add the programs you wish to run as icons to the LOAD= line and the programs you wish to run in normal-sized windows to the RUN= line. For example, to load IconCalc and MegaEdit as icons and Super Resource Monitor in a normal window, find their full filenames and add them to the LOAD= and RUN= lines as follows:

```
[windows]
load=c:\secrets2\odometer\odometer.exe
c:\secrets2\zoom\zoomctrl.exe
run=c:\secrets2\resgauge\resgauge.exe
```

Note that a space is required for each program listed on a line. And you must remember to keep the LOAD= and RUN= lines no more than 127 characters in length, including the words *load* and *run*, and the equals sign. Windows ignores characters after the first 127.

If you run out of space, you can delete the extension .EXE from the LOAD= and RUN= lines, like this:

```
[windows]
load=c:\secrets2\odometer\odometer c:\secrets2\zoom\zoomctrl
run=c:\secrets2\resgauge\resgauge
```

To save even more space, rename the directories to shorter names (and make sure that you adjust any settings in the program to use the new names, if necessary). Or place the directories on your Path, then leave out the directories, and use only the application names, as follows:

```
[windows]
load=odometer zoomctrl
run=resgauge
```

In Windows 3.1 and higher, you can use the StartUp group of Program Manager, as well as the LOAD= and RUN= lines in WIN.INI, to start programs. The programs in WIN.INI are loaded before the programs in the StartUp group. Since the StartUp group starts all Windows programs first and then starts all DOS programs, using the LOAD= or RUN= lines in WIN.INI is the only way to make a DOS program run before a Windows program at startup.

One thing about the LOAD= and RUN= lines is that placing an application here does not necessarily override the way the application itself insists on starting up. The Zoom program, for example, loads only as an icon. It has a configuration dialog box, but this never appears until you double-click Zoom's minimized icon. Placing ZOOMCTRL.EXE on the RUN= line, therefore, loads Zoom as an icon anyway.

Giving You Our Best

I've added my comments to each of the *More Windows 3.1 Secrets* programs. In addition to selecting the best Windows freeware and shareware, I want you to know how the programs work for me, and any tips I can pass along.

Each chapter starts with a section in *italics*. In this introductory section, I describe what I liked about the program that earned it its place in this book. At the end of this section, I define the type of program (utility, game, etc.), what version of Windows it requires (and other requirements it may have), whether the program is freeware or shareware, how to contact the program's author for technical support (if any), and whether there are similar programs in this book, *Windows 3.1 Secrets,* or *Windows Gizmos.*

Following these comments are detailed instructions on each program, which I've based closely on the on-line documentation provided by the programs' authors. In certain cases, I've added comments or illustrations to a program's documentation, to make it clearer for you, the reader. Each program's author, of course, remains the final authority on what his or her program does and how it works, in case there is any discrepancy between what I've printed and how a program actually acts.

How You Can Benefit from Freeware and Shareware

Since most people are not familiar with the concept of shareware, it's important to clarify these often-misunderstood forms of software marketing.

Freeware: Programs at no cost

Freeware programs are programs that have no registration fee. You may use them, and copy to as many other computers as you like, without ever paying for a license to use them.

Freeware programs are usually circulated by their authors with little or no technical support. Fortunately, these programs, because of their simplicity, almost never require technical support. But freeware programs include some quite useful tools and very enjoyable games, so their simplicity is not necessarily a limitation.

There are two kinds of freeware programs: *public-domain* programs and *free, copyrighted* programs.

Public-domain programs are programs to which the author has released all claims. Other people may sell the program or modify it and put their names on it as their own. These programs are often simple utilities and implementations of math algorithms that the author does not wish to support or upgrade in the future.

Free, copyrighted programs are programs to which the author retains all rights. Although the program's author charges nothing for the program and allows others to circulate the program, no one may sell or alter the program without the author's permission.

You may distribute and use free, copyrighted programs on as many computers as you like without ever paying a fee. But you may not sell such programs, or bundle them with a product that is for sale, without permission from the authors of the programs. *More Windows 3.1 Secrets* is authorized by these authors to distribute their programs.

Shareware: Fully functional free trial software

Shareware programs are 100 percent fully functional programs distributed by authors who wish to call attention to the registered versions of the same programs. Shareware programs often are backed with technical support, frequent upgrades that have new features, and customized versions for users with special requests. Shareware authors usually provide these services only to users who register and obtain a license for a nominal fee.

I feel that the concept of shareware is one of the most important distribution techniques available to both program authors and software users. I am a paid-up, registered user of all the shareware programs in *More Windows 3.1 Secrets,* and I have specific permission from all the shareware authors to distribute their programs in this book.

Shareware programs are copyrighted, commercial programs. The only difference between shareware programs and their opposite — retail programs, which are sold through retail channels — is that you have the opportunity to try shareware programs before you invest any money in them.

Compare this with retail programs. Most retail programs cost $100 to $500. As soon as you take a retail program out of a store, you usually cannot get any kind of refund — even if the program doesn't do what it said on the box, or won't even run on your kind of PC.

Most software programmers will never succeed in marketing a retail product. It is often estimated that a company has to have at least $1 million — preferably, more like $5 million — to pay for the advertising, marketing, packaging, and other expenses required to launch a successful shrink-wrapped product.

And because of the high overhead of the retail channel, even the simplest program — with one diskette and a thin manual — cannot be sold for less than a list price of about $40.

Shareware authors, by contrast, *encourage* you to share their programs with as many of your friends and co-workers as you like. This is their main marketing and advertising method. Since shareware authors spend little or nothing on advertising, fancy buildings, and other overhead, they can pass this savings along to you. Most shareware authors' registration fees are a bargain — often only $5, $10, or $15.

And what do you get for your registration fee? Depending on the conditions stated by the on-line documentation for each program, you receive

♦ At the very least, a permanent license to use the program on your PC.

♦ In most cases, the ability to upgrade to a future version of the program, with features that may significantly enhance the version you have.

♦ Technical support, if you have questions or configuration problems regarding your particular type of PC — usually provided by an electronic mail system (in which case you receive a response directly from the authors in a few hours), by regular mail, or, in some cases, by telephone.

♦ Sometimes, a printed manual with more detail or better illustrations than can be provided in the shareware version — and, if you register multiple copies for your company, enough printed materials for each of your staff.

♦ In a few cases, a disk that contains a registered version of the program, along with other "bonus" shareware programs not otherwise listed.

♦ In all cases, the registration of shareware encourages the development of new Windows shareware programs, which could be the next Windows "killer app" — and which you can, again, try out in advance, like all shareware.

As a registered user of each of the shareware programs in this book, I can truly say that the "extras" I have received after registering constantly surprise and impress me. Shareware programs are the world's greatest software bargain.

Crippleware: Programs that do little or nothing

Some people say, "Why should I register for shareware programs I already have?" Or "Why do shareware programs sometimes remind me to register?"

Registering shareware programs encourages the development of more shareware. *Not* registering frustrates programmers into distributing useless programs that do little or nothing. Such programs are called *crippleware*.

Crippleware programs are limited in some essential way that makes them useless, unless you buy what is essentially a retail version. Crippleware programs sometimes cannot save any information or cannot print more than one page or cannot print at all. Some crippleware programs disable themselves or expire after a certain date. Other programs do nothing but display a series of screens that advertise a retail program. These programs are even less valuable than crippleware and are usually called *rolling demos*.

More Windows 3.1 Secrets does not feature, to my knowledge, any crippleware programs. All shareware programs that we support are 100 percent fully functional. This gives you the opportunity to try all aspects thoroughly before making a commitment to use a certain program. (One special case in this book is Makeover, which is a retail package, not shareware. The developers, Playroom Software, have created at my request a free, limited version to allow readers to permanently change their System icons, as described in Chapter 7, "Replace Microsoft's Bland System Icons.")

The existence of shareware programs benefits us all. And the more we register, the more benefits we gain.

Shareware Registration from Outside the U.S.

Most of the shareware vendors in this book request payment "in U.S. funds, drawn on a U.S. bank." This is because U.S. banks charge large fees — sometimes more than the entire registration fee for a shareware package — to accept non-U.S. checks.

If you are outside the U.S. and wish to register a shareware package with a U.S. author, you can send payment in the form of a Postal International Money Order with a U.S. dollar amount. These money orders are available at most post offices around the world and are accepted without a fee by all U.S. post offices and many U.S. banks. If you are in Europe, do not send Eurochecks, which are not accepted by U.S. banks.

The Association of Shareware Professionals

As shareware has grown into an important distribution method for software programmers, many of them have banded together into the Association of Shareware Professionals. This group promotes shareware and encourages high standards of shareware programming, including "no crippling" policies intended to enhance the value of shareware.

If you are a software author, the ASP may help you find distribution channels for your program. Membership fees are very reasonable and should not prevent even casual programmers from joining. For more information, write the Executive Director, Association of Shareware Professionals, 545 Grover Road, Muskegon, MI 49442-9427, or send a message to CompuServe I.D. number 72050,1433.

I am pleased to support the ASP by contributing a portion of my royalties from *Windows 3.1 Secrets, More Windows 3.1 Secrets,* and *Windows Gizmos* to the ASP to further the shareware concept.

Why Have Shareware Registration Notices?

All shareware programs have some kind of pop-up window that lets you know how to contact the author and register the program. Some programs display this window after you click Help About or another menu choice, while others display it automatically when you start or exit the program.

The ASP specifically allows this type of reminder notice. It does not cripple a program in any way, but provides the user with the address of the shareware author and an incentive to register.

I view these reminders like the appeals you sometimes hear on listener-supported radio stations. The appeals are slightly annoying, but the stations could not continue to broadcast without the memberships they receive. Similarly, the shareware authors cannot continue to distribute their programs without the registrations they receive. Reminder notices — which disappear totally after you register a package — are a slight irritation but are well-justified by the full functionality (no crippling) you get in a true shareware package.

The ASP Ombudsman Program

To resolve any question about the role of shareware, registrations, licenses, and so on, the ASP established an ombudsman to hear all parties. Not all the shareware authors who have programs on the diskettes accompanying this book are members of the ASP. But if you have a support problem with an author who is, and you cannot settle it directly with that author, the ombudsman may find a remedy. Remember that you cannot expect technical support for any program unless you are a registered user of that program.

As the association's literature describes it, "ASP wants to make sure that the shareware concept works for you. If you are unable to resolve a shareware-related problem with an ASP member by contacting the member directly, ASP may be able to help. The ASP Ombudsman can help you resolve a dispute or problem with an ASP member, but does not provide technical support for members' products. Please write to the ASP Ombudsman at P.O. Box 5786, Bellevue, WA 98006, or send a CompuServe message to ASP Ombudsman, 70007,3536."

General License Agreement

Each of the shareware programs on the accompanying diskettes has its own license agreement and terms. These are printed in the chapter describing each program or in a text file enclosed with the program on the diskettes. For more information, contact the ASP at the address above for a copy of its General License Agreement, which suggests individual and site license terms for shareware authors and users.

The programs featured in this book are supplied as is. Brian Livingston and IDG Books Worldwide, Inc., individually and together disclaim all warranties, expressed or implied, including, without limitation, the warranties of merchantability and of fitness for any particular purpose; and assume no liability for damages, direct or consequential, which may result from the use of the programs or reliance on the documentation.

The selection and organization of the software on the *More Windows 3.1 Secrets* diskettes, and the information file that installs the software are copyrighted by the author of this book. The *More Windows 3.1 Secrets* diskettes may not be duplicated, sold, or bundled with a product or service that is sold, without permission from the author.

Technical Requirements

When a program featured in this book says it "requires Windows 3.0 or higher," you should always assume that it requires the standard or enhanced modes of Windows. *Real mode,* which exists only in Windows 3.0, is not suitable for running serious programs. Most of the programs featured in this book will not run at all in real mode.

Although many programs say that 1MB of memory is required, most of them (along with other Windows programs) will run much better with 2MB to 4MB of memory. Memory prices are currently low, and adding more memory is usually the best way to get better performance from Windows.

Technical Support

All Windows programs have bugs. This includes all retail Windows software and all shareware featured in *More Windows 3.1 Secrets.* Every program, no matter how simple, has some unexpected behavior or another. This is just the nature of software and is usually fixed with the release of a newer version to deal with the problem.

Because each of the programs featured in *More Windows 3.1 Secrets* is unique and complex, neither Brian Livingston nor IDG Books Worldwide can provide any technical support for these programs.

The shareware authors represented in this book all provide technical support by one means or another. Each chapter describes how to contact the author, how to register, and how to obtain technical support. If you cannot resolve a problem by reading the documentation, the author may be able to help. Remember that by buying this book, you did not license the shareware programs, you only purchased the right to a free trial of each of the programs. Shareware authors usually cannot provide technical support except to registered users. In a few cases, shareware authors provide limited technical support to nonregistered users if they are having difficulty installing a program. In such cases, the policy is described in the text of the shareware chapter.

If a program is listed as freeware, it probably has no technical support. In this case, if a program does not work on your particular PC configuration, you probably will not be able to obtain technical support for it.

Direct Technical Support via CompuServe

The fastest and best method to obtain technical support is usually to contact the shareware author directly, using the CompuServe Information Service (CIS). This electronic mail service should be the first choice for anyone who has a modem attached to his or her PC.

Most shareware authors have an electronic mail address on CompuServe. These numbers are printed at the end of each chapter, if a shareware author has a CIS account.

The advantages of CompuServe for technical support are several:

♦ An electronic mail message can be delivered almost immediately, as opposed to a telephone call, which usually produces a busy signal or a voice-messaging system at most big software companies.

♦ Electronic mail allows the shareware author to send illustrations to help you diagnose a problem, or bug fixes or new versions right to your modem.

♦ CompuServe can be less expensive than telephone calls, especially if you prepare a plain-text message in Notepad and transmit it to CompuServe at the fastest rate of your modem.

♦ CompuServe is available from most countries of the world and can handle a virtually unlimited number of messages 24 hours a day.

To start using CompuServe, call 800-848-8990 in the U.S., Puerto Rico, and the U.S. Virgin Islands, or 614-457-8650 outside these areas. Or write: CompuServe, Customer Service, P.O. Box 20212, 5000 Arlington Centre Blvd., Columbus, OH 43220.

CompuServe will give you a telephone number to call with your PC and modem and they will instruct you how to set your communications software (usually 7 data bits, even parity, and 1 stop bit, often abbreviated 7E1 in computer literature). You can use the Terminal program included with Windows for all communications with CompuServe, or you can use a variety of other packages. In Terminal, you establish your communications parameters by clicking Settings Communications, then File Save to save your settings.

Once you log on to CompuServe, you can type GO MAIL at any prompt to get to the electronic mail service. At that point, type your message; then send it to the CompuServe I.D. number listed in the documentation. Most shareware authors check and respond to their electronic messages once or more each business day.

Electronic mail has advantages for everyone. It's faster than regular mail (even overnight courier!), easier to respond to (no envelopes to tear open). If you have a modem and you haven't tried an electronic mail service, do look into it.

Preventing Viruses

Computer viruses are small programs that copy themselves into other programs and clog up or erase parts of your hard disk. Professionals who have
studied viruses have found that the most common way a computer gets in-
fected is by traveling salespeople who use the same diskette to demonstrate
programs in different companies. Another common problem is passing around
an unprotected diskette to several friends, which exposes the diskette to viruses that may be present on any one PC.

The program files that accompany *More Windows 3.1 Secrets* have been tested
by the latest version of virus-scanning programs from McAfee Associates and
found to be free of viruses. You can ensure that these diskettes remain virus-free
by making sure a write-protect tab remains enabled on each diskette before
inserting it into a drive. Viruses have no way to get into a diskette if it is protected
by a write-protect tab. On a 3½-inch diskette, the write-protect tab is enabled if
the notch is *open*. On a 5¼-inch diskette, the write-protect tab is enabled if the
notch is *closed*. Additionally, the programs on the *More Windows 3.1 Secrets*
diskettes are stored in a compressed form, which is resistant to virus infection.

Shareware programs are generally less prone to viruses than other programs.
This is because shareware authors are aware of viruses and control access to
their programs so viruses cannot get in. Additionally, shareware programs are
handled by far fewer people before release (usually only one person) than retail
programs. Retail programs may pass from hand to hand among dozens of
people in a large software company before being released to the public. By this
means, viruses have found their way into retail software packages from vendors
of spreadsheets, networks, and many other packages.

If you would like to guard against viruses from diskettes or other channels, you
should obtain the Virus Scan utilities from McAfee Associates. These shareware
utilities, as featured in *Windows 3.1 Secrets,* can be obtained directly from
McAfee Associates. A registered version of Scan may be obtained for $25 plus
$9 for a diskette and shipping from: McAfee Associates, 1900 Wyatt Dr., Suite 8,
Santa Clara, CA 95054-1529. You can also call 408-988-3832 or fax 408-970-9727.
Shareware versions of Scan and other McAfee utilities (Clean-up, Vshield, and
others) are also available for downloading from the McAfee Associates bulletin
board system. Call 408-988-4004 with your modem set to 8 data bits, no parity,
and 1 stop bit. Registration entitles you to free upgrades from the bulletin
board for one year. McAfee Associates also has numerous distribution agents in
countries around the world.

The Windows Shareware 100

You can look at the more than 100 freeware and shareware programs featured in *Windows 3.1 Secrets, More Windows 3.1 Secrets,* and *Windows Gizmos* as part of a complementary collection. You do not need to obtain *Windows 3.1 Secrets* or *Windows Gizmos* in order to enjoy any of the programs in *More Windows 3.1 Secrets*. But you may find just the tool or game you seek in *Windows 3.1 Secrets* or *Windows Gizmos,* if it isn't in *More Windows 3.1 Secrets*.

For this reason, I present here a listing, broken into categories, of all freeware and shareware programs in *Windows 3.1 Secrets, More Windows 3.1 Secrets,* and *Windows Gizmos,* for your convenience in finding the perfect program.

Anti-Virus Programs

Viruscan & Clean-up	Virus detectors and removers	*Windows 3.1 Secrets*

Applications

Address Manager	Print your own database, on lists and labels	*Windows Gizmos*
Lathe	Draw any line and watch a 3-D model take shape	*Windows Gizmos*
MathGraf	Graphs even the toughest equations for you	*Windows Gizmos*
MegaEdit	Edit any text file without Notepad's limitations	*Windows Gizmos*
MoneySmith	A full-blown home or business bookkeeping system	*Windows Gizmos*
Parents	Track your lineage and preserve your family tree	*Windows Gizmos*
Recipe Maker	Compute your menu plans and shopping lists	*Windows Gizmos*
Reminder	Keep tabs on your appointments and deadlines	*More Windows 3.1 Secrets*
WindBase	Customizable, easy-to-use Windows database	*Windows 3.1 Secrets*

Calculators

BizWiz	A version of the famous HP-12C financial calculator	*Windows 3.1 Secrets*
IconCalc	A complete calculator, no bigger than an icon	*Windows Gizmos*

Clipboard Utilities

ClipMate	Save and manage your Clipboard text	*Windows Gizmos*
PrintClip	Sends text in the Clipboard to the printer	*Windows 3.1 Secrets*
UltraClip	Work with multiple cut-and-paste graphics	*More Windows 3.1 Secrets*

Clocks and Alarms

ClockMan	Sets alarms and schedules events	*Windows 3.1 Secrets*
PRClock	Watch the time change in cities around the world	*More Windows 3.1 Secrets*
WinClock	Set alarms and never miss another appointment	*Windows Gizmos*
X World Clock	Supports any time zone in the world	*Windows 3.1 Secrets*

Communications

ComReset	Sets communications ports for Windows	*Windows 3.1 Secrets*
RS232 Serial Monitor	Catch modem problems fast	*Windows Gizmos*
Unicom	A great Windows communications program	*Windows 3.1 Secrets*

DOS Replacements

EDOS	Enhances DOS sessions	*Windows 3.1 Secrets*
Exclaim	Replace your DOS sessions with this powerful toolbox	*Windows Gizmos*
WinCLI	A DOS-like Command-Line Interpreter	*Windows 3.1 Secrets*

File & Program Management

ChangeIt	Eliminate tedious editing of Program Manager icons	*More Windows 3.1 Secrets*
Desktop Navigator	Replaces the Windows File Manager	*Windows 3.1 Secrets*
DirNotes for Windows	Break DOS's 8-character filename limit	*Windows Gizmos*
File Commander	Add your own menus to Windows 3.1's File Manager	*Windows 3.1 Secrets*
File Garbage Can	Deletes files securely with drag-and-drop	*Windows Gizmos*
Group Icon	Customize your Program Manager group windows	*Windows Gizmos*
Launch	Starts applications with a click	*Windows 3.1 Secrets*
Plug-In	A terrific enhancement to Program Manager	*More Windows 3.1 Secrets*
RecRun	Runs Recorder macros automatically	*Windows 3.1 Secrets*
RunProg	Runs programs in any size window	*Windows 3.1 Secrets*
Sidebar Lite	The fastest replacement for Program Manager	*Windows Gizmos*
Sloop Manager	A Windows shell to manage files and programs	*More Windows 3.1 Secrets*
Task Manager	Top-rated Windows Task List replacement	*Windows 3.1 Secrets*
WinEZ	The best drop-down menu system for Windows	*Windows Gizmos*
Wiz Manager	Customize File Manager's menus with a batch language	*More Windows 3.1 Secrets*

Games

Bugs!	A fast arcade game to get the keys and escape the *bugs!*	*More Windows 3.1 Secrets*
Checkers	The classic hop-over game, kings and all	*Windows Gizmos*
Chess	Graphical chess for Windows	*Windows 3.1 Secrets*
Code Breaker	A challenging puzzle that changes every time	*Windows Gizmos*
Concentration Solitaire	A clever memory-enhancer requiring your full attention	*More Windows 3.1 Secrets*
Coffee Mug	Avoid this icon or leave rings on your desktop	*More Windows 3.1 Secrets*
Hearts	A cutthroat game where rudeness may pay off	*Windows Gizmos*
Hyperoid	Blast your way through this exciting space game	*Windows Gizmos*
Jewel Thief	A game of wits with jewels and guards	*Windows Gizmos*
Klotz	A better Tetris-like game	*Windows 3.1 Secrets*
Lander	A challenging moon-landing game	*Windows 3.1 Secrets*
Mazemaker	Wind your way through the ever-changing, 3-D hallways	*More Windows 3.1 Secrets*
Mile Bones	Beat your opponent to the finish line and win	*Windows Gizmos*
Odometer	Watch your mouse rack up those inches or centimeters	*More Windows 3.1 Secrets*
Puzzle	A tile game with DDE support	*Windows 3.1 Secrets*
Simon	A game of sound and color	*Windows 3.1 Secrets*
WinPoker	Your own video poker game that never quits	*Windows Gizmos*

Graphics

Big Cursor	Make your mouse pointer more visible	*Windows 3.1 Secrets*
Graphic Viewer	Displays files in different graphics formats	*Windows 3.1 Secrets*
Icon Manager	Icon editor with hundreds of icons	*Windows 3.1 Secrets*
Makeover	Modify the Windows graphical user interface	*More Windows 3.1 Secrets*
MetaPlay	Displays Windows graphics metafiles	*Windows 3.1 Secrets*
Paint Shop	Converts and manipulates graphics files	*Windows 3.1 Secrets*
WinGIF	Converts graphics to Windows formats	*Windows 3.1 Secrets*
Zoom	Give Windows the same cool look as a Mac	*More Windows 3.1 Secrets*

Resource Management

FreeMem	Display Windows's memory and resources	*More Windows 3.1 Secrets*
Resource Gauge	Show the user of the User memory heap, GDI, or both	*More Windows 3.1 Secrets*
Super Resource Monitor	Manage your memory resources	*Windows Gizmos*

Printing Utilities

DirPrint	Print directories from within File Manager or any shell	*More Windows 3.1 Secrets*
WinList	Print out text files and program listings two-up	*More Windows 3.1 Secrets*

Text Editing & Searching

Hunter	Full-text search and retrieval	*Windows 3.1 Secrets*
WinEdit	A much better Notepad	*Windows 3.1 Secrets*
WinPost	On-screen sticky notes	*Windows 3.1 Secrets*

Tools & Utilities

Barry Press Utilities	Switch your printer, match text files, and more	*Windows Gizmos*
DiskCopy	Make perfect diskette copies simply and easily	*Windows Gizmos*
Hex Edit	Change bytes within any file easily	*More Windows 3.1 Secrets*
IniEdit	Modify Windows .INI configurations on the fly	*More Windows 3.1 Secrets*
More Control	Edit .INI settings that Control Panel can't	*More Windows 3.1 Secrets*
PixFolio	Manage your picture library in any graphics format	*Windows Gizmos*
Roger's Rapid Restart	Several ways to exit and restart Windows or reboot	*More Windows 3.1 Secrets*
SnagIt	Prints the screen or any portion of it	*Windows 3.1 Secrets*
Superload	Load applications and configures them	*Windows 3.1 Secrets*
Trash Can	Drag files and delete them	*Windows 3.1 Secrets*
W.BAT	A batch file for Windows	*Windows 3.1 Secrets*
Whiskers	Redefines your mouse buttons	*Windows 3.1 Secrets*
Widget	Track your computer's CPU workload	*Windows Gizmos*
WinBatch	The Windows graphical batch language	*Windows 3.1 Secrets*
WinExit	A way to exit Windows quickly	*Windows 3.1 Secrets*
WinKey	Control your Shift, Caps Lock, and Num Lock keys	*Windows Gizmos*
WinStart	Start up in any Windows mode	*Windows Gizmos*
WordBasic Macros	Macros, ANSI characters, and shortcut keys	*Windows 3.1 Secrets*

TrueType Fonts

RRKeyCaps	Show special keys as characters in your documents	*More Windows 3.1 Secrets*
Video Terminal Screen	Display and print the DOS character set, including line-draw	*More Windows 3.1 Secrets*

Zip File Management

Windows Unarchive	Decompresses ZIP and ARJ files within Windows	*Windows 3.1 Secrets*
ZIP Tools	ZIP file compression and decompression in Windows	*Windows Gizmos*
ZiPaper	Rotate zipped wallpaper for a fresh look	*Windows Gizmos*

Bugs!

Version 1.0
Copyright © Timothy Baldwin

*B*ugs is one of the best kinds of Windows games — a fast arcade game. And Bugs is a game that's harder than it looks. It quickly gets more and more difficult to collect keys (there are two in each room) and exit to the next level of the game. You'll find yourself saying, "Ho, ho, I can beat this," and then having trouble fending off the attack of BUGS!

The free version of this game allows you to play up to 10 rooms. Registered players receive a password that allows you to play up to 30 rooms — much more challenging.

Warning: *Even if you click Turn Off Music on the main menu, Bugs still plays a few tunes at critical moments. So don't click Start if you don't want the person in the next cubicle to know you're playing games!*

Type of Program:	Game.
Requires:	Windows 3.0 or higher.
Registration:	Free. For a password good for playing up to 30 rooms, use the form at the end of this chapter to register with the shareware author.
Technical Support:	Oasis Software provides registered users with technical support by mail, CompuServe, and America OnLine.

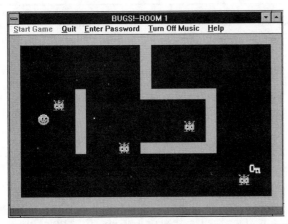

Figure 1: Bugs! is an arcade-style game that's harder than it looks.

Game Objective

Very simple — try and escape from each room before the angry insects catch you. Survive for 30 rooms and you win the satisfaction of knowing that no group of bugs can push you around!

You must do three things to escape from a room:

1. Obtain the first door key by touching it.
2. Obtain the second key the same way.
3. Exit through the door in the right wall.

The second key appears after the first key is touched, and the door opens when the second key is touched. You move around the room by moving the mouse.

Complicating your efforts are the room's bugs, who move about unpredictably and kill by touch. You must avoid them. The number of bugs and their speed increase as the game progresses. The room walls are also deadly to touch.

Fortunately, you have a force field for protection. Click and hold down the mouse button to activate it. Bugs that touch you will be zapped — temporarily stunned and not moving — and cannot hurt you while the field is on. The force uses energy, and a green bar at the bottom of the game area keeps track of how much is left. If it disappears, you can no longer zap any bugs. Recharge by touching power units (they look like a lightning bolt) that appear in some of the rooms. Release the mouse button to deactivate the force field to conserve energy until needed.

You start the game with three lives. More can be found in some of the rooms. Touch the duplicate image of yourself. Room layout and locations of bugs and objects are randomly generated. Some rooms will be easy; others, very difficult. Start the action by clicking over your image in the center of the window.

Password

You must enter a password to play beyond the tenth room. Enter it at anytime by selecting "Enter Password" on the menu bar. "Enter Password" will disappear after you correctly enter the password.

See the "About Bugs" entry in the "Help" menu for details on how you can obtain the password. Please note that the reasonable cost of the password is how I pay for my programming efforts and costs. If you like my game, please send for the password to encourage me to continue! Thank you!

Notes and Strategy

♦ Conserve force field energy. Use only when needed to get through a tough area.

♦ Patience is a virtue! Try waiting in a safe location until the bugs give you an opening to sneak past them.

♦ The game display is infinitely resizable. Play it full screen or itsy-bitsy (to a point, of course!) by resizing the window.

♦ The game "music" is a feeble attempt by me to explore Windows sound functions. I'm no musician! You can turn off the music from the menu bar.

♦ Sometimes the bugs get hungry and eat the keys or other objects. Just click on the mouse button to get them to cough them up.

Problems, Bug Reports, Feedback

Contact me at the address in the About dialog box, or via CompuServe (72240,3372) or America OnLine (OasisSoft).

Tim Baldwin

Registration

Timothy G. Baldwin
Oasis Software
Diggs, VA 23045

[ ] I enclose $5 to register and receive a password to play up to 30 rooms.

Name: _____

Address: _____

_____

_____

City, State, Zip:_____

ChangeIt

Version 1.2
Copyright © Thom Foulks

This simple DOS utility solves an irritating problem in the Windows Program Manager. When you move an application from one drive to another (to free up space on a drive, for example), any icons in Program Manager with command lines that mention the old drive letter turn into blank, generic icons and no longer work. Since the FILENAME.GRP group files that control these icons are in an unreadable format, you can't edit in the correct drive letter with Notepad — you have to laboriously change each icon manually.

CHANGEIT.EXE provides a workaround for .GRP files, as well as .INI and .PIF files. You run CHANGEIT at a DOS prompt (it's better not to use it while Windows is running). You indicate the file you want to change, plus the old and new drive letters, as follows:

```
CHANGEIT filename.ext x: y:
```

This can be much faster than manually editing every icon, especially if you have many icons or many groups. ChangeIt works only in the current directory, and on only one file at a time (no wildcards are allowed) for safety reasons.

I worked with Thom Foulks on part of this problem because it isn't particularly easy editing a .GRP file. That's why ChangeIt can't change directory names, only drive letters — it's a complex proposition. For Windows programmers who have not been able to figure out how to edit .GRP files (because Microsoft's documentation of how .GRP files calculate a "checksum" is inaccurate), Thom has written a description, which is available on CompuServe: type GO WINSHARE, select the File Utilities library, and download the file WCHK.ZIP.

Meanwhile, I hope ChangeIt saves you a little time if you need to move an application and its icons.

Type of Program:	DOS Utility.
Requires:	.GRP, .INI, or .PIF files created by Windows 3.0 or higher.
Registration:	Free. This program requires no registration.
Technical Support:	None.

ChangeIt: Do You Need It?

Here's the situation: (Take your pick....)

A. You've just added a second hard drive, and you want to change your Windows installation from Drive C: to Drive D: ... or

B. You've replaced your Drive C: with a far larger drive, and you want additional partitions (again, moving Windows to some other drive letter) ... or

C. Doublespace or Stacker or one of the other disk compression utilities has fiddled with your drive letters, leaving your Windows files stranded on a drive different from where they were initially installed.

In situations A. and B., it is fairly easy to physically move the files. As an example, if you've kept your Win installation all under a C:\WINDOWS subdirectory, XCOPY can do it for you —

```
XCOPY C:\WINDOWS\*.* D:\WINDOWS\*.* /S/E
```

In situation C., you may have a real nightmare on your hands without hard-nosed detective work to straighten out your Path and a lot of other drive references.

In each case, you will be left with laborious reworking of all your .GRP files, many of your .INI files, and some of your .PIF files, to inform Windows Program Manager where the files are now located. That means using "Change Properties" from Program Manager for .GRPs, editing the .INI files with a text processor, and redoing .PIF files with the PIF Editor.

In each case, ChangeIt can help you. ChangeIt *won't* do everything for you; there are simply too many possibilities.

ChangeIt will look at any .GRP, .INI, or .PIF file and change all references to a given drive letter to a different drive letter. For .GRP files, it will recalculate the file's internal checksum so that the new .GRP file will be acceptable to Program Manager. And it preserves the original file with a .CHG file extension, in case your file-moving hits problems.

ChangeIt will *not* accept wildcards, and will operate on only one file at a time — each change should be tested prior to making another one.

ChangeIt does *not* move files, or copy them — again, there are too many possibilities of how you want your Windows system

ChangeIt will *not* search your drive for files; it must be used from within the directory where the target file resides. (Ever seen a system with 3 — count 'em — MAIN.GRPs? I have. No, I don't know how it got that way.)

ChangeIt will *not* deal with file references maintained separately by various Windows software packages (as example, Word for Windows .DOT files); again, there are too many possibilities.

If only one-third of these comments have been relevant to you, then I urge you to ignore ChangeIt.

For the proper syntax, simply type ChangeIt at the DOS prompt.

ChangeIt is freeware (i.e., you pay nothing for it), and all usage by any user is at that user's sole risk. No user support is provided by the author.

Coffee Mug

Version 1.0
Copyright © Toggle Booleans

*T*his is by far the silliest *Windows program I have ever seen, and yet — because it's absolutely free, requires only 9K of RAM, and will bring a smile to your face — Coffee Mug cried out to be included in* More Windows 3.1 Secrets.

Drag the Coffee Mug icon into your StartUp group, and the next time you start Windows the mug will appear minimized on your icon line. After this, any disturbance — such as dragging an application window over the mug — tips it over, spilling "coffee" on your desktop. Moving the icon drips more coffee on your screen. Even after you click the icon to bring up its System menu, and click Upright Mug to stand the mug back up, moving the icon leaves little "coffee rings" — just like a real coffee cup.

OK, so it isn't Solitaire. But if you run Coffee Mug on your icon line every day, it's likely to remind you not to take your work too seriously — and maybe even help you remember to get up for a real cup of coffee before you get carpal tunnel syndrome. Watch that mug!

Type of Program:	Game.
Requires:	Windows 3.0 or higher.
Registration:	Free. This program requires no registration.
Technical Support:	None.

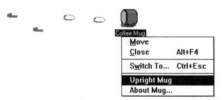

Figure 1: When you start Coffee Mug, your mug is full and your coffee is hot.

Introduction

The Toggle Booleans Coffee Mug pushes the desktop metaphor of computing further than ever before.

Until now there have been notepads, card files, clipboards, and calculators on your Windows desktop, but never has there been a place to put your coffee mug. Now you can finally pick up your coffee mug from wherever you used to keep it and put it where it belongs: on your desktop.

When you start the Coffee Mug, your mug will be full and your coffee will be hot. Be careful, though. If you move a window on top of your coffee mug, you may spill it, which is sure to ruin your day. If this happens, you can upright your mug by selecting Upright Mug from the mug menu. Understandably, your mug will now be a little bit messy and may leave coffee rings behind on your desktop when you move it.

Your coffee will get cold after about 20 minutes. At this point you may wish to get another coffee by closing your coffee mug and starting another.

Coffee Mug Version 1.0 is freeware. It may be copied and distributed freely under the following conditions:

No modifications are to be made to the program or this documentation.

When you're distributing Coffee Mug, the executable file and the documentation file (COFFEE.TXT) must be distributed together.

Disclaimer

The Toggle Booleans Coffee Mug is provided AS IS. Toggle Booleans will in no way be responsible, in financial or any other terms, for damages (both consequential and incidental) resulting from the use or misuse of the Coffee Mug.

For more information about other Toggle Booleans products, write to:

Toggle Booleans
P.O. Box 4204
Station E
Ottawa, Ontario, Canada
K1S 5B2

Concentration Solitaire

Version 2.0
Copyright © Stephen Murphy

---

*H*ere's the classic game of Concentration, in a sprightly Windows version. Unlike the Solitaire game found in Windows, there is always a winning solution in Concentration Solitaire. No frustrating "I-can't-finish-the-game" feelings. You just have to find all the right moves.

Concentration is a great game for developing your memory and, ahem, concentration. But it's also a game that kids of almost any age can enjoy. Try it!

Type of Program:	Card Game.
Requires:	Windows 3.0 or higher.
Registration:	Use the form at the end of this chapter to register with the shareware author.
Technical Support:	Stephen Murphy provides registered users with technical support via CompuServe.

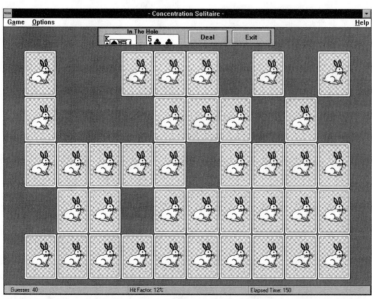

Figure 1: Cards are dealt face down in Concentration Solitaire except for the two "In The Hole."

Welcome to Concentration Solitaire

Thank you for giving Concentration Solitaire a try! This game was originally released about a year earlier in a version done in Visual Basic. The reaction to it was quite good, so I decided to do a faster and slicker version, this time in C.

There is nothing too difficult about the premise of Concentration Solitaire. Simply match up pairs of cards from memory. This does not stop it from being a lot of fun, nevertheless. This software is actually designed for kids, but it's too much fun to be just for kids! Have fun. I hope you enjoy it.

How to Play Concentration Solitaire

From the menu, select Game Deal, or press the Deal button that appears at the top of the screen. Fifty cards will be dealt out face down. It is your job to match them up in pairs. The remaining two cards are dealt face up in the bar at the top of the screen. These cards are said to be "In The Hole" and can be thought of as a head start. They match up just like the other cards except you can see what they are.

To begin play, click a card. When it is clicked, it will turn face up. You must now find its matching pair. The default setting for pair matching is cards of the same value and color. That is, a Queen of Hearts will be matched with a Queen of Diamonds. An Ace of Spades will be matched with an Ace of Clubs. Proceed by clicking on a second card. If this card matches the first card, both cards will move off the screen. If they don't match, they will both turn face down again. Your goal then, is to make 26 matches, at which point you will have an empty screen and the game will be over. It's easy!

Concentration Solitaire keeps track of the lowest number of guesses required to complete a game. If you beat the currently held record for lowest guesses, your name will appear in the Lowest Guesses window, which can be admired by selecting Game Record. Please note that in order to become Low Guess Champion, you must be using the standard value and color pair matching option, and not the easier value-only option.

Options

Deck

From the menu, selecting Options Deck allows you to select a different picture for the deck. Beside each picture is a button. Select the button which corresponds to the picture you want to use and select the OK button. The current picture will be replaced by the one you have selected.

Color

From the menu, selecting Options Color allows you to change the background color of your playing area. Simply click on the new color you wish to use and select OK. The window background will be changed to your new color selection.

Speed

From the menu, selecting Options Speed allows you to control how long it takes unmatched pairs of cards to turn face down again. Some people like to take their time and study the cards while others want them to turn over as fast as possible. Use the scroll bar to vary the speed to your liking. You can also set the speed at which matched pairs are dragged off the screen. If you have a very slow computer, you might want this setting at fast. On the other hand, if you have a monster 486 with a video accelerator, you might want to choose slow so you can see the cards move. Again, this is up to your liking.

Matching

From the menu, selecting Options Matching allows you to determine how pairs are matched. The default setting is for Color and Value. That is to say, pairs must be the same color (Hearts or Diamonds, Clubs or Spades) and they must be the same value (two Aces, for example).

You may set this option to match pairs by Value only, which means any two cards of the same number will match regardless of their color. Six of Clubs and six of Hearts is a match in this case. Because matching by Value is easier, the Lowest Guesses record keeps track of only the Color and Value scores.

All options are saved on exit and will be active next time you run the game.

Required Files

CONCEN.EXE	Main program file
CONCEN.HLP	Windows help file
BWCC.DLL	Borland custom control library
COMMDLG.DLL	Common Dialog Box Dynamic Link Library

BWCC.DLL and COMMDLG.DLL are usually installed in your Windows directory.

Select CONCEN.EXE from Program Manager or File Manager to run Concentration Solitaire.

Registration

This program is released as shareware. Shareware is a process by which software is released to the public. The process begins with a programmer spending many long hours and many dollars on development tools to produce a final product. The product is then released to the general public. The process does not end when you install and use the software on your machine. You are required to hold up your end of the deal. If you find a piece of shareware to be of use or enjoyment to you, you should register that software with its author. That is what keeps the shareware process alive so you will have more fun games and other software to look forward to in the future.

If you enjoy this game, and would like to see more games like it, or if you are a shareware distributor who is making a buck off shareware compilations and would like to put something back into the pot, please send $5 to:

Stephen Murphy
c/o Pigeon Lake Software, Inc.
Box 13, Site 5, RR1
Thorsby, Alberta, Canada
T0C 2P0

Name: _____

Address: _____

City, State, Zip: _____

_____

You will be sent a Registration code, which will eliminate the Registration box that keeps popping up throughout the game.

If you would like to contact the author electronically with bug reports, criticisms, or just general chat, I can be reached on CompuServe at 70661,2461.

DirPrint

Version 1.10
Copyright © Peter Rodwell

This program resolves a Windows problem I have been ranting about since the original publication of Windows 3 Secrets — *the Windows File Manager has no command to print a directory! In DOS, printing a directory listing to a printer is as simple as typing* DIR>LPT1. *But there is no easy way to do this from the File Manager, supposedly a "better" DOS shell. Microsoft has not corrected this oversight for more than three years since the release of Windows 3.0.*

I told readers of Windows 3 Secrets *and* Windows 3.1 Secrets *that they could print directories from File Manager by clicking File Run and adding* COMMAND /C *to the beginning of DOS "internal" commands, and other commands they wanted to redirect to a printer. For example, to print a listing of the* C:\DOS *directory, click File Run and type the following command:*

```
COMMAND /C DIR c:\dos > lpt1
```

Fortunately, Peter Rodwell — a reader of mine in Madrid, Spain — cured this File Manager limitation by developing DirPrint within a few weeks of reading one of my raves. To use DirPrint, you simply click File Run then type x:\path\DIRPRINT. *An easy-to-use dialog box allows you to select any and all files to list to the current printer. (**Tip:** If you move* DIRPRINT.EXE *and* DIRPRINT.TXT *to a directory on your Path, you don't need to type* x:\path\ *before* DIRPRINT.*) Even better, you can run DirPrint with a parameter, such as the following:*

```
DIRPRINT c:\dos
```

In this case, DirPrint will list the C:\DOS *directory to the current printer without any further intervention by you.*

I confess that I became personally interested in planning the implementation of this simple but much-needed utility. The fact that Microsoft continues to leave out of Windows many basic features we take for granted in DOS just bugs the heck out of me. I kibitzed with Peter as I watched early beta versions of DirPrint finally evolve into the useful tool that is included in this book. Besides printing directories, you can now use DirPrint 1.1 to determine how many diskettes will be required to copy any selected set of files. (DirPrint correctly includes the "cluster overhead" required by different diskette formats when it calculates the final number.)

I hope you find many ways to use DirPrint.

Type of Program:	Utility.
Requires:	Windows 3.1 or higher.
Registration:	Free. This program requires no registration.
Technical Support:	None.

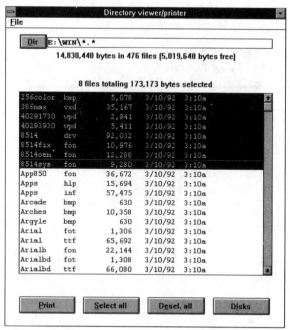

Figure 1: DirPrint displays the contents of the currently selected directory.

Installation

The WSETUP program copies the DirPrint files to a directory and sets up a Program Manager group to display its icons.

Starting DirPrint

Your can start DirPrint in three ways:

1. By double-clicking its icon in the normal way. In this case, DirPrint will display a panel showing the contents of the currently selected directory (its own, if this is the first time you have used it, or the directory which was selected when you last used it).
2. By using the File Run command in Program Manager or File Manager:
   2a.) By typing DirPrint's name (and path, if necessary) without any parameters, in which case DirPrint will start up as though you'd double-clicked its icon.
   2b.) By typing DirPrint's name (and path if necessary) plus the path of the subdirectory you wish to print and optionally a file specifier for the files to be listed (e.g., C:\DOS*.EXE). If no filespec is given, DirPrint automatically adds "*.*" to list all files. In this mode, DirPrint will start up as an icon and will immediately begin to print. When it finishes printing, it automatically terminates.

Operation

Clicking the Dir button opens a dialog box which allows you to move to another disk or directory. Double-clicking a drive or directory name will immediately change disk/directory and redisplay the main listing. This dialog box also allows you to change the file spec by editing the current spec shown in the edit box under the listing.

Clicking file names in the main directory listing "selects" them. A running count of the number of files selected and their total size is displayed. The Select All button selects all entries, while the Deselect button removes all selections. When one or more files are selected, the Disks button is enabled. Clicking this displays a dialog box which shows the total number of diskettes required to store the selected files on different diskette types.

```
Diskettes required to save the
476 files (14,830,440 bytes) selected

Diskette type                    Number

3½" 1.44 Mbytes                    11
3½" 720 kbytes                     21
5¼" 1.2 Mbytes                     13
5¼" 360 kbytes                     41

              OK
```

Figure 2: DirPrint calculates how many diskettes are required to store selected files.

Clicking the Print button starts printing. If files have been selected, you are offered the option of printing a listing of just the selected files or of all files. If either no files are selected or all are selected, printing starts immediately. A small printing dialog box allows printing to be canceled.

Notes

DirPrint can in theory handle directories with up to 4000 entries. Not having that many files in a single directory, I haven't tested it to that limit (which is an arbitrary limit to simplify things; in any case, I think that anyone who has more than 4000 files in a single directory should seriously consider reorganizing his/her hard disk!).

The program creates a small configuration file, called DIRPRINT.GGG, in the Windows subdirectory. It is highly unlikely that a file with this name already exists, but if this is the case, it should be removed before DirPrint is run for the first time. DirPrint will overwrite any file with that name when it terminates.

I "bolted together" this program from other stuff already written, and I have tested it quite thoroughly without finding any problems. It runs fine on my system (a 33 MHz Dell 486) with Windows 3.1 in standard VGA mode; I have not been able to try it with any other screen resolutions or with Windows 3.0. Printing works fine with my LaserJet IIIP with and without PostScript, but that's the only printer I have, so it's the only one used for testing.

If you find any bugs or have any suggestions for improvements, please let me know via CompuServe on 100023,2476.

Finally, my thanks to Brian Livingston of *InfoWorld* for kindly commenting on DirPrint, making a number of useful suggestions and for designing the program's icon, infinitely better than my effort.

The program is in the public domain, so feel free to do with it as you wish. Enjoy!

— Peter Rodwell

FreeMem

Version 1.10
Copyright © Peter Rodwell

There are many, many shareware utilities floating around that report the amount of free memory available in Windows. (Some of them are mentioned below in the Similar Shareware topic.) After testing several of these utilities, I selected FreeMem by Peter Rodwell for this book because it is one utility that not only reports free RAM, but also reports the amount of free disk space on all the hard drives in your system — as bytes, and as a percentage of each drive.

Free RAM is a useful number when you want to watch how much memory each program is consuming under Windows. Some programs, when exited, may not release all the memory they use. In other cases, your system may slow down significantly after you have used up your physical RAM and start swapping programs into virtual memory (a swap file on disk).

The percentage of available disk space is handy to know just before you install a large program or copy a large number of files. Knowing which drive letter contains the most free disk space you can avoid out-of-space problems later on. This feature of FreeMem is easily turned on and off for individual hard drives by clicking FreeMem's System icon and selecting Config FreeMem from the menu.

Type of Program:	Utility.
Requires:	Windows 3.1 or higher.
Registration:	Free. This program requires no registration.
Technical Support:	None.
Similar Shareware:	FreeMem by Metz Software, a program featured in *Windows 3.1 Secrets,* and Super Resource Monitor, a program featured in *Windows Gizmos,* both display the amount of free RAM in Windows as well as Free System Resources (FSR). They do not, however, display free disk space on various drive letters, as FreeMem by Peter Rodwell does.

```
    11,642 kbytes free
C:    503,808 [  2%]
D:  3,309,568 [ 15%]
E:    628,736 [  2%]
F:  9,510,912 [ 30%]
G:  4,194,304 [ 13%]
H:  1,456,128 [  6%]
I:  2,523,136 [ 12%]
J:  2,326,528 [ 11%]
K:  6,449,152 [ 30%]
L:  3,989,504 [ 19%]
M: 26,712,064 [ 27%]
```

Figure 1: When FreeMem is configured to display free disk space, its window includes all the drive letters you select.

```
    2,856 kbytes free
```

Figure 2: You can also turn off the display of drive letters, so FreeMem provides a tiny window reporting on RAM only.

Overview

FreeMem is a small utility that shows the amount of free memory available under Windows (version 3.1 and higher). Optionally, it also shows the amount of space available on your hard disk drive(s), including network drives.

Operation

Start FreeMem in the normal way, by double-clicking its icon. The first time it starts, it will appear as a small window, containing just a window title and a system menu icon, in the upper left of your screen. Its title bar displays the amount of memory available in kilobytes (K). This is updated approximately once per second.

FreeMem's system menu contains three entries:

Stop FreeMem

This stops FreeMem from refreshing its display. Use it if you find that FreeMem is slowing down your system. With FreeMem halted, the display will not reflect any changes to memory/ disk drive space until it is restarted. The Stop option in the system menu changes to Re-Start FreeMem when the program is halted; selecting this option will restart FreeMem.

Configure FreeMem

This allows you to specify which disk drives should be scanned by FreeMem. A panel showing all the active hard disk drives and network drives accessible from your system is displayed. Click the boxes for the disks you want displayed. Clicking a box with a check mark will remove that drive from the display.

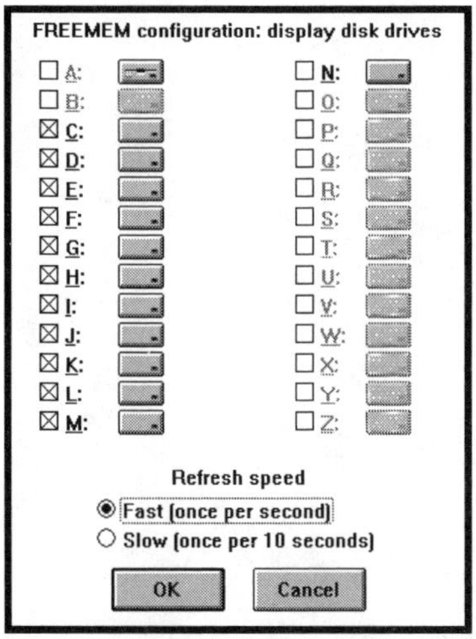

FREEMEM configuration: display disk drives

☐ A:	☐ N:
☐ B:	☐ O:
☒ C:	☐ P:
☒ D:	☐ Q:
☒ E:	☐ R:
☒ F:	☐ S:
☒ G:	☐ T:
☒ H:	☐ U:
☒ I:	☐ V:
☒ J:	☐ W:
☒ K:	☐ X:
☒ L:	☐ Y:
☒ M:	☐ Z:

Refresh speed
◉ Fast (once per second)
○ Slow (once per 10 seconds)

[OK] [Cancel]

Figure 3: Selecting the Configure FreeMem option from the System menu displays a list of hard drives in your PC to choose from.

For each disk drive you select, FreeMem displays

♦ The drive name (i.e., C:).

♦ The amount of free space on that drive, in bytes.

♦ The percentage of free space available.

If the percentage of space available on a drive is less than 10%, the drive details are shown in a sort-of magenta color. If the space is less than 5%, red is used. Otherwise, the details are shown in blue.

You can also select the speed at which FreeMem updates its display: Fast causes an update approximately every second; Slow causes an update approximately every 10 seconds. Use the Slow option if you want to scan a large number of disk drives and you find that FreeMem is slowing down your system.

Select OK to save your changes, or Cancel to keep the original settings.

About FreeMem

This displays the usual panel giving version number, etc.

Configuration File

When the configuration is altered and when you close FreeMem, it saves configuration details in an internal format to a file called FREEMEM.CNF, which it creates in your Windows directory. The details saved are

♦ The refresh speed.

♦ FreeMem's position on the screen — if you move it to a new position, it will appear there the next time you start it.

♦ The disk drives to be displayed.

HexEdit

Version 1.51
Copyright © Al Funk

*H*exEdit *is a great example of a type of program that is widely available for DOS, but is really hard to find for Windows. HexEdit is a utility that allows you to make changes to any file (especially non-text files) by changing the hexadecimal value of individual bytes. HexEdit by Al Funk is the best shareware byte editor for Windows. And it's a good one, with powerful search capabilities and display options.*

Warning: *Changing non-text files, such as executable program files, can permanently disable such programs.* **Always** *make a copy of any file before you touch it with a hex editor. This way, if you make an editing error and your program no longer works, you can delete the edited version, rename the backup copy, and you'll be back to normal.*

Despite the dangers, HexEdit may be the only way to correct some irritating limitations in Windows programs. The captions under the illustrations in this chapter describe one example: how to change some of the default values in NOTEPAD.EXE, *which Microsoft provided no way to alter. (This procedure should not be used on most Windows programs, which do have ways to save your preferred default values.) Remember to make a backup copy first!*

Type of Program:	Hexadecimal Editor.
Requires:	Windows 3.0 or higher.
Registration:	Use the form at the end of this chapter to register with the shareware author.
Technical Support:	Al Funk provides technical support to registered users by mail and CompuServe.

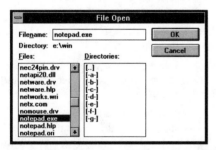

Figure 1: After you make a backup copy of NOTEPAD.EXE, you can click File Open in HexEdit and open the Notepad executable file to change its hard-coded defaults.

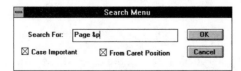

Figure 2: You can change Notepad's default "Page 1, Page 2" footer by searching for "Page &p" in HexEdit's Search Menu dialog box. In Notepad's File Page-Setup dialog box, "&p" represents the current page number, "&f" the filename, "&d" the date, and "&t" the time.

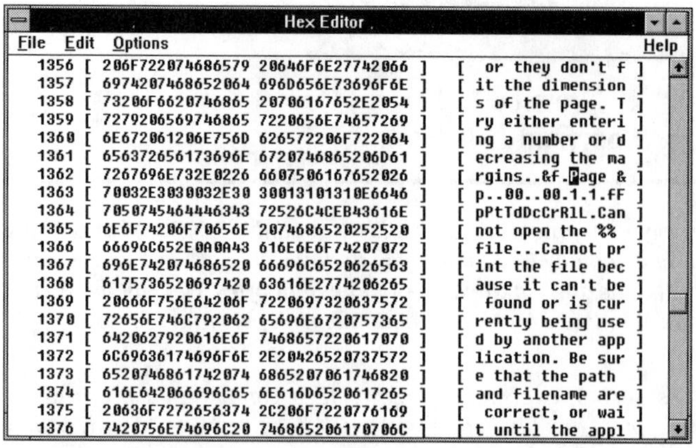

```
┌────────────────────────────── Hex Editor ──────────────────┬─┬─┐
│ File   Edit   Options                                      Help │▲│
│   1356 [ 206F722074686579 20646F6E27742066 ]  [  or they don't f ]│↑│
│   1357 [ 6974207468652064 696D656E73696F6E ]  [ it the dimension ]│ │
│   1358 [ 73206F6620746865 20706167652E2054 ]  [ s of the page. T ]│ │
│   1359 [ 7279206569746865 7220656E74657269 ]  [ ry either enteri ]│ │
│   1360 [ 6E672061206E756D 626572206F722064 ]  [ ng a number or d ]│ │
│   1361 [ 656372656173696E6E 6720746865206D61 ]  [ ecreasing the ma ]│ │
│   1362 [ 7267696E732E0226 6607506167652026 ]  [ rgins..&f.█age & ]│ │
│   1363 [ 70032E3030032E30 300131013100E6646 ]  [ p..00..00.1.1.FF  ]│ │
│   1364 [ 705074546444463 72526C4CEB43616E ]  [ pPtTdDcCrRlL.Can ]│ │
│   1365 [ 6E6F74206F70656E 2074686520252520 ]  [ not open the %%  ]│ │
│   1366 [ 66696C652E0A0A43 616E6E6F6F742070 ]  [ file...Cannot pr ]│ │
│   1367 [ 696E742074686520 66696C6520626563 ]  [ int the file bec ]│ │
│   1368 [ 6175736520697420 63616E2774206265 ]  [ ause it can't be ]│ │
│   1369 [ 20666F756E64206F 7220697320637572 ]  [  found or is cur ]│ │
│   1370 [ 72656E746C792062 65696E6720757365 ]  [ rently being use ]│ │
│   1371 [ 6420627920616E6F 7468657220617070 ]  [ d by another app ]│ │
│   1372 [ 6C69636174696F6E 2E20426520737572 ]  [ lication. Be sur ]│ │
│   1373 [ 6520746861742074 6865206D61746820 ]  [ e that the path  ]│ │
│   1374 [ 616E642066696C65 6E616D6520617265 ]  [ and filename are ]│ │
│   1375 [ 20636F7272656374 2C206F7220776169 ]  [ correct, or wai ]│ │
│   1376 [ 7420756E74696C20 74686520617070 6C ]  [ t until the appl ]│↓│
└─────────────────────────────────────────────────────────────────┘
```

Figure 3: The left side of HexEdit's window shows the NOTEPAD.EXE file in hex values (00 through FF). The right side shows the same information in text form. You can change "Page &p" to "Date &d" to print the current date instead of page numbers in the footer. You cannot change the length of NOTEPAD.EXE or any strings within it.

Overview

HexEdit is not only a hexadecimal viewer but an editor as well (as the name suggests). Thus you can load in any kind of file, view it in hex and text, and make desired modifications. These modifications may be made either through text or hexadecimal entry. Furthermore, the file can be saved.

In addition, there is a character counting facility, which allows the user to get an idea of the number and distribution of characters. There is also a graphical view of alphabetical and punctuation characters.

Searching is possible as well, by either hexadecimal or text characters. There are also limited insertion and deletion functions. There is also a conversion calculator.

This is version 1.51 of HexEdit. It has been tested to a good degree. However, if modifications for bug fixes are necessary, they will be made. In addition, if there is sufficient need (demand) for enhancements, they will be made if there is registration support.

HexEdit is intended for Windows 3.0 with a minimum of approximately 100K of available memory. More memory may be necessary for editing large files. It should be compatible with almost any graphics system. Please let me know if you have problems using HexEdit with any screen or printer device so that any bugs can be fixed.

Mouse Functions

The mouse functions provide for easy location of the caret. Simply point to a potential entry location on either the hex or the text side of the display, and the caret will appear at the beginning of the byte clicked. If the mouse points to a viable location, the caret will be turned on. If not, it will be turned off.

Keyboard Functions

The Hex Editor is completely operable from the keyboard. Key commands are as follows:

ARROWS	See Enter.
BACKSPACE	On the hexadecimal side, moves back one hex digit. On the text side, moves back one byte. No modification will occur.
ENTER	Turn on/off the caret. When the caret is turned on, keyboard typing will place text/numbers at the current caret position. Arrow-key actions will influence entry location. If caret is off, arrow keys will scroll information immediately.
HOME/END	Move caret to beginning or end of the document respectively.
INS/DEL	Inserts or deletes one character from the current caret location, but only if the caret is on. See Enter.
PAGE UP/DN	Page Up and Page Down move information one screenful in the indicated direction.
SPACEBAR	On the text side, spacebar places a space character (ANSI #32). On the hexadecimal side, it moves the caret one hex digit.
TAB	Changes the caret from text side to hex side, or vice versa.

File

The File menu provides options for clearing, opening, and saving. To load a file, simply click the Open option and a Windows dialog box will open prompting you to select the file you wish to open.

Any file may be edited with the exception of certain write-protected, system, or shared files.

To save a duplicate of your file, use the Save As... command with a new filename. Remember, using Save will overwrite your old file. HexEdit will prompt you if you attempt to overwrite.

For information on insertion and deletion, see "Keyboard Functions."

Editing

Search

The Search feature allows you to search for byte information throughout your file. You can type characters into the search dialog directly from the keyboard, or use hexadecimal notation: a pound sign (#) followed by two hexadecimal digits.

Searching may be done from the current caret location (if caret is on). You may also select to ignore or recognize case. Note that any hexadecimal search turns on case sensitivity.

You may continue searching from the last location by selecting the Continue Search option of the Edit menu.

Jump To Line or Displacement

Selecting this menu option brings up a dialog box querying for the location in the file to jump to. If the display is in line mode, enter a line value to jump to. Otherwise, enter a character displacement value (where 0 is the first character). The caret will be turned on and positioned at that location.

Character Count

The Character Count feature brings up either a graph representing all punctuation and letters (the graph is not case sensitive) or a table of the total count of each ANSI character. Counting may begin at beginning or at current caret value.

Options _____

The Options menu allows access to the Display... dialog and the Registration... dialog.

Furthermore, there are two toggle selections available from this menu: Wide Caret and Highlighted Words. Select the Wide Caret toggle to use a block cursor. Select the Highlighted Words toggle to make word boundaries — two bytes equal one hex word — more visible. (This slows down the display, however.) These selections will be saved on exiting the hex editor.

Display

The Display dialog shows statistics about the current file, including size and modification status. You may, at this dialog, select whether to display by displacement (i.e., one count per character/byte) or line (16 bytes per line). The Jump To feature uses this to determine how it will function. Also, the current selection determines how the file will be printed.

Conversion window

The conversion window allows the user to convert between hexadecimal, octal, and decimal numbers. Simply click or select the box desired and type the number to be converted. All numbers are considered to be positive. Click the Convert button or press Enter, and the converted numbers will be displayed in the boxes corresponding to their base.

Click the Done button to close the window. Note that the conversion window can be kept open while the other functions of the hex editor are used.

Printing _____

The procedure for printing is quite straightforward.

To print a range of lines, click the appropriate radio button; then enter the line range in the boxes provided. Alternatively, leave the Print All radio button selected, and the whole file will be printed.

A header may be placed at the top of the file by checking the Header box and entering header text in the appropriate edit box.

Draft mode may be selected by checking its box. Draft mode may or may not function depending on your printer. Draft mode may allow a quicker print or ink-saving mode.

Printing may be aborted by clicking the Cancel button of the print dialog.

Registration _____

HexEdit is a shareware program. Continued usage of this program is restricted to registered users only.

A registration ID may be obtained by sending $10 to the following address, for registration in the U.S.

To register, simply fill in the order blank provided below (and in the file labeled HEXEDIT.TXT) and mail to the appropriate address. (European users, see HEXEDIT.EUR.) You will be given a registration code. The Registration menu option will then be grayed out.

Access to the features of this version of HexEdit is not in any way limited for non-registered users. However, registration is requested of those users who find HexEdit to be a useful program.

To register HexEdit, send in the following form.

HexEdit Registration Version 1.51

Name : _____

Cmpy.: _____

Addr1: _____

Addr2: _____

City : _____ State: _____ Zip:_____

Phone No. (optional) (_____) - _____ - _____

Computer Make: _____ Model:_____

Processor: _____ Memory:_____

DOS version: _____

Name, as will appear in registration box: _____

Organization, as will appear in registration box: _____

Other Comments : _____

_____

CIS ID, if any : _____

copies : _____ @ $10 ea. = $ _____

(OR) Unlimited copies allowed for $75

total = $ _____ . ____

To be paid by check or certified check to:

Al Funk
42 Parkwyn Dr.
Delmar, NY 12054

Requests for information on HexEdit can be sent to the above address or to CompuServe user ID 71505,1277.

To register in Europe and obtain a registration ID, send £10 to:

UNICA Shareware Publishing
39a Hall Street
Stockport, Cheshire, SK1 4DA England,
Or phone with your credit card number +44 (0)61 429 0241. Fax registrations use +44 (0)61 477 2910.

This is version 1.51 of Hex Editor. Updates to this product will be determined by the volume of registration support. Please send any suggestions for improvements with your registration fee. Registered users will be informed of updates to this program and will be entitled to an updated copy as soon as it is available. On-disk copies are available from the author for $2.50 additional (disk+mailing fee).

Requirements: Windows 3.0, 100K free memory + space for loading a file. Most graphics supported.

Written in Turbo Pascal (c) Borland under Windows 3.0 (c) Microsoft Corp.

HexEdit is Copyright 1991,1992 Al Funk. This program is shareware. No fees may be accepted for the distribution of this program in excess of $5.

Modification of this program is not permitted except with the express approval of the author.

IniEdit

Version 1.06s
Copyright © Richard R. Sands

*I*niEdit *is a dream come true for anyone who has to manage two or more Windows configurations — especially network administrators with two or more Windows users. IniEdit allows you to write simple text files that modify your Windows configuration — automatically. You just start Windows from a batch file (or network logon script), which runs the command* x:\path\INIEDIT FILENAME.TXT, *then runs* WIN. *(**Tip**: Move* INIEDIT.EXE *and* INIEDIT.TXT *into a directory on your Path so you won't have to precede the* INIEDIT *command with a drive and directory.)*

The possible uses for IniEdit are endless. You can allow two or more users of the same PC (for example, parents and children, or day and evening work shifts) to have different Program Manager groups by editing the PROGMAN.INI *file that determines which groups are loaded. You can change* WIN.INI, SYSTEM.INI, *and* CONTROL.INI *to match your preferences for fonts, shells, colors, and so on ad infinitum.*

Since these editing changes need to take place before Windows loads, IniEdit is a DOS command-line utility. But I think you'll find it easy to use after perusing Richard Sands's excellent documentation, which follows.

Type of Program:	DOS Utility.
Requires:	Windows 3.0 or higher.
Registration:	Use the form at the end of this chapter to register with the shareware author.
Technical Support:	Richard Sands provides registered users with technical support via mail and CompuServe.

```
IniEdit - Batch .Ini Editor - Version 1.07s
Copyright (C) 1991-1993 Richard R. Sands CIS 70274,103
All rights reserved

Syntax:
       INIEDIT [options] ParamFile [label[ label...]] [options]

Options:                               Default
       /?      This screen
       /B-     Make Backups             /B+
       /C+     Clear screen first       /C-
       /D+     Debug Mode               /D-
       /L+     Show Label List          /L-
       /P-     Don't Pause on Error     /P+
       /W+     Pause on warnings        /W-
```

Figure 1: When you issue the command INIEDIT /? **at a DOS prompt in the IniEdit directory, the utility displays a help screen with the proper syntax.**

Overview

If you often find yourself editing your WIN.INI, SYSTEM.INI, or any other .INI file before you start Windows, then this program is for you!

IniEdit provides batch file editing of your .INI files so you can start up Windows with mnemonic commands. This program reads a text file of editing commands that instruct it to modify the various .INI files by section and keywords. You can change the contents of a line, delete lines, comment, and uncomment them. You may include several labeled sections in your IniEdit script so you can have all of your various Windows configurations in one text file.

Why did I write this program? I have a portable that, at work, is connected to a network; at home it's not. When on the network, I have several utilities I need to load. At home, although the utilities detect the lack of the network, I end up having to click a bunch of OK buttons. I have customized system fonts that I like to use, but as a programmer, I like to boot Windows with the "standard" font to check the dialog box metrics. Sometimes, I want to just start Windows without having to load up all my favorite utilities: get in quick, get out quick. I use different "shell" programs depending on what "type" of environment I want to be in. You get the picture. With IniEdit all of these actions are easily (read, *"I don't have to remember anything"*) written into a menu or batch file.

This program is best used in a batch file, or with your favorite menuing software.

System Requirements

♦ Microsoft Windows 3.0 or higher.
♦ IniEdit has been tested with all DOS versions 2.11 through 5.0. Its memory requirements depend on the size of your largest .INI file (but limited to 4000 lines of text).

Starting IniEdit

IniEdit requires at least one parameter: the Script Filename. The script is a normal ASCII file that contains the commands you want to be executed, and may have any filename extension.

In addition to the script filename, you may place some Switch Options that modify the way IniEdit behaves. For example, the following DOS command line (assuming that you have placed INIEDIT.EXE in a directory on your Path) forces IniEdit to read the text file MYCONFIG.TXT, and execute the commands in the section labeled :NOBEEP, without making a backup .INI file:

```
INIEDIT myconfig.txt NOBEEP /B-
```

The formal syntax for starting IniEdit is as follows:

```
INIEDIT
```
(This will display version, registration, and help screen information.)

or

```
INIEDIT filename.ext {labels} {options}
```

where

`filename.ext`   Is the name of the text file that contains your editing commands.

`labels`   Are optional. A label designates one or more sections of your IniEdit script to be executed. You may have more than 1 label on the command line.

`options`   Are optional, and must be preceded with a slash (/) character. Option switches effect the entire command line. Currently, the options available are:

    `/?` Displays version and help screen.

    `/B-` Disable backup files. Normally, IniEdit will always back up your file before making any edits.

    `/C+` Clears the screen when started. By default, IniEdit will not clear the screen. Having a clear screen is sometimes helpful when debugging your IniEdit scripts.

/D+ Enable "Debug" mode. This will display each line as it is
executed, with additional information so you can track down
any errors in your (or my) logic. When debug mode is on, the
message "Press any key..." is displayed after each statement.

/L+ Shows a list of all labels found in the IniEdit script file. This is
useful if your file requires a user label entered on the command
line. Your batch file can check for a parameter, and, if not
found, then issue switch. This switch returns a DOS Errorlevel
of 1.

/P- Don't pause for a key when an error occurs. Pause on error is
on by default. You can check for errors in your batch file with
the DOS Errorlevel variable.

/W+ Show warnings and wait for a key to proceed. This is off by
default. Warnings are usually available only in debug mode.

Editing Commands _____

All commands to IniEdit are entered into a regular ASCII text file created with your favorite
ASCII editor (or word processor with a "PC ASCII Text" export format).

There are six basic commands:

APPEND	Adds a keyword to a section, whether or not the section exists.
COMMENT	This will change a keyword entry into a comment.
DELETE	This can delete a whole section or just one keyword.
EDIT	This will change the contents of a keyword entry.
EXIT	Quit processing the script file.
INI	Opens an .INI file for editing.
UNCOMMENT	This changes a commented line into a regular line.

Each command is written on its own line. Lines may not wrap, but they may be up to 255
characters (including leading blanks) long. For each command, you may write the whole command (e.g., COMMENT) or just the first three letters (e.g., COM).

For all commands except EXIT and INI, the syntax is identical. You include the command, the
optional text-only .INI filename , the section name enclosed in square brackets, and the
keyword/value pair separated with an equals sign ("="). The .INI filename is assumed to be in the
default Windows directory, so the path and file extension is not required. A typical command
might look like this:

EDIT WIN [Windows] Beep=No

This command will change the Beep keyword under the [Windows] section of the WIN.INI file
to "No." All commands follow this basic format.

Comments are lines starting with a semicolon (;). The line does not have to start in column
one. Comments must be on their own line. This is a remark in the IniEdit script file:

; This is a valid remark

Section Labels are used to "tag" sections of the IniEdit script to be used with a parameter sent
from the command line. This way you can have several different configurations without
having to have them in separate files (as in an old version of IniEdit, version 1.01). All labels
must be on their own line, and be preceded with a colon as with an MS-DOS batch file.

The following is an example IniEdit script file with two sections:

```
; This is TEST.MOD (the .MOD means MODifications)
:FAST
  EDIT Win Load=
  EDIT Win Run=
  EXIT
:SLOW
  EDIT Win Load=C:\AFTERDRK\AD NWSEND EMAIL RESGAUGE BIGDESK
  EDIT Win Run=SkeyWin YaClock
  EXIT
```

Your batch file (or menu program) could issue this command:

```
INIEDIT test.mod SLOW
```

That would execute the section listed under ":SLOW". This command:

```
INIEDIT test.mod FAST
```

would execute the section listed under ":FAST".

Important: Note the EXIT commands at the end of each section. If you don't have one, IniEdit will "fall" through to and execute the next section. (This could be construed as a feature!)

You can place more than one label on the command line. This has the effect of executing each section. The following command will execute two sections:

```
INIEDIT test.mod SLOW FAST
```

You may also have descriptions attached to your labels. Section Labels are always one word, so anything after the first word is considered to be the description. This is very useful when the command-line option **Show Labels** switch (**/L+**) is used:

```
:FAST - Don't load any utilities
```

```
:SLOW - Load all utilities
```

Currently, there are no flow-control statements. The sequence of execution is essentially linear. I was tempted to put in a CALL/GOTO command, but I found it *really* wasn't needed. So far, no one has complained. If you can give me a good situation where you would want one, I'll certainly consider it for the next release.

A Moment of Reflection

As I wrote this program, I considered adding commands for creating and executing some kind of menu system. After some reflection, I decided that the last thing the world needs is a new menu system. If you really need one, I can provide a simple DOS batch file based system with color, nested menus, etc., with all commands using regular batch file commands and one small utility. Again, if you think there is an overriding reason for including these type of commands, let me know and I'll consider it for the next release.

Command Abbreviations

IniEdit version 1.01 allowed the first three characters of the command to be used rather than the whole command (e.g., COM for COMMENT). This is still enabled, but for compatibility with future versions, you are encouraged to use the whole command.

Sample Batch Files

This batch file will start Windows after modifying the various .INI files that I need. It first checks for parameters and, if there are none, displays all the labels in the file. Otherwise, it executes the IniEdit program and checks for any errors. If there are no errors, then Windows is started.

```
@Echo Off
 C:
 cd C:\WIN
 if %1!==! GOTO Error          (check for required parameter)
 INIEDIT WinBoot.Mod %1 %2 %3  (allow user to specify labels)
 if ERRORLEVEL 1 GOTO Done     (check for any errors)
 WIN                           (start Windows)
 GOTO Done                     (and quit)
:Error
 IniEdit WinBoot.Mod /L+       (display list of labels)
:Done
```

Alternatively, I prefer the following batch file. It allows me to set the Windows initialization I want by giving the IniEdit command, but until I need to change the Windows startup I just type WIN. For example:

```
@Echo Off
C:
cd C:\WIN
if %1!==! GOTO Windows         (if no parameters, just run Windows)
INIEDIT WinBoot.Mod %1 %2 %3   (allow user to specify labels)
if ERRORLEVEL 1 GOTO Done      (check for any errors)
:Windows
WIN                            (start Windows)
:Done
```

The Future of IniEdit

I don't think .INI files are going to go away, so this program should be useful for the next few versions of Windows.

Some suggestions that I have not implemented (yet) are some control commands (e.g., GOTO or CALL), some substring handling for modifing portions of a keyword (e.g., remove "clock" from LOAD=Calc Clock Bye), and some screen handling commands for creating prompts /menus; I've even had a request for an OS/2 version.

Depending on additional interest, these types of commands, or other commands could very well appear in future releases of IniEdit.

Command Reference

Documentation conventions

Because square brackets ([ ]) are used to denote Windows section names, in the following examples I show all required values in UPPERCASE and optional values in lowercase. In the following example, only the words EDIT and KEYWORD are required for the EDIT command:

```
EDIT win [section] KEYWORD=value
  ↑    ↑   ↑          ↑          ↑
  |    |   |          |          Argument (not required)
  |    |   |          Section keyword (required)
  |    |   Windows section name (not required)
  |    INI filename (not required)
  Command (required)
```

All keywords must have an equals sign after them, even if nothing follows. For example:

```
EDIT Win [Windows] RUN=
```

APPEND

Syntax:

```
APPEND ini [section] KEYWORD=value
```

Appends (or adds) the contents of the keyword under the [section] heading. If no [section] is provided, then it appends the keyword to the first section that keyword appears under. Otherwise, it appends the keyword after the last keyword matching in the section.

This is provided mostly to handle adding new DEVICE= entries in the SYSTEM.INI file. Since the SYSTEM.INI file contains many entries with the same KEYWORD value, the EDIT command will not work correctly in this case, since EDIT is ambigious. To edit these kind of entries, you need to first try to delete the keyword and then append it:

```
; Edit the DEVICE keyword in the SYSTEM.INI [386Enh] section
INI System
 DELETE [386Enh] DEVICE=vnetware.drv
 APPEND [386Enh] DEVICE=v3com.drv
```

APPEND will not add duplicate lines. Duplicate lines are exact duplicates when all blanks from the line are stripped out, and when made uppercase. I cannot think of any reason why any "keyword=value" would be duplicated exactly within the same file.

While in debug mode (/D+), you may see "warnings" like "keyword not found." These are "soft" errors; IniEdit will add the keyword *and* section if it does not exist.

Example:

```
APPEND system [386Enh] device=special.drv
```

COMMENT

Syntax:

```
COMMENT ini [section] KEYWORD=value
```

Changes the section/line containing the keyword to a comment. This is a non-destructive way of "deleting" keyword entries. If the VALUE entry is present, then an exact match is made. This is useful when using COMMENT with the DEVICE= keywords in the SYSTEM.INI file, since there are multiple occurences of this keyword.

If no [section] label is provided, then COMMENT changes the value of the first keyword under *any* section that matches. See the EDIT entry. This was done for maximum ease of syntax; however, future versions may remove this "feature," as it does not document the script as well.

Keywords not found are "soft" errors and are ignored by IniEdit.

Examples:

```
COMMENT System [boot.description] network.drv=

COMMENT System [386Enh] network=*vnetbios, vnetware.386, vipx.386

COMMENT Win [Clock]
```

DELETE

Syntax:

```
DELETE ini [SECTION] KEYWORD=value
```

Deletes a keyword from the active .INI file. If the keyword is not given, then DELETE deletes the whole section from the .INI file. Note that you must supply the [section] label *and/or* the keyword. If you supply a value entry, then an exact match is performed. This is useful for the SYSTEM.INI's DEVICE= values, which can appear more than once in each section.

Note: This is a hold-over from IniEdit version 1.01. It is best that you use COMMENT and UNCOMMENT rather than DELETE. However, I will continue to keep this command since it seems to be popular.

If no [section] label is provided, then DELETE changes the value of the first keyword under *any* section that matches. See the EDIT entry.

Examples:

```
DELETE Win [Clock]

DELETE Win [Clock] iFormat=

DELETE Win [Clock] iFormat=1

DELETE Win iFormat=1
```

ECHO

Syntax:

```
ECHO any text at all
```

Displays all text following ECHO and performs a carriage-return/line feed. This is provided for optionally notifying the user while long edit commands are being executed.

An ECHO command by itself just writes a blank line.

Examples:

```
Echo Please wait, modifing WIN.INI.

Echo Please wait, modifying SYSTEM.INI.

Echo
```

EDIT

Syntax:

```
EDIT ini [section] KEYWORD=value
```

Changes (or adds) the contents of the keyword under the [section] heading. If no [section] is provided, then it changes the value of the first keyword under *any* section that matches. You *might* be safe saying:

```
EDIT Win Load=Clock
```

But you might have problems with a command like:

```
EDIT Win iFormat=0
```

Several programs use the iFormat keyword, and you could not be *sure* that the iFormat you meant was changed. It would be better to write a statement like this:

```
EDIT Win [Clock] iFormat=0
```

While in debug mode (/D+), you may see "warnings" like "keyword not found." These are "soft" errors; IniEdit will add the keyword *and* the section if it does not exist.

Note: If you are trying to change the value of a keyword that appears more than once in a section (e.g., SYSTEM.INI's DEVICE= keywords), this command will only edit the first item. You should use COMMENT and UNCOMMENT to change those types of entries.

Examples:

```
EDIT system [boot] shell=msdos.exe

EDIT win [desktop] WallPaper=g:\bitmaps\mmonroe.bmp
```

EXIT

Syntax:

```
EXIT
```

Terminates the execution of the current script section. Does not terminate IniEdit, which proceeds to the next label parameter (if any) given on the command line.

This is typically used when you want only a certain portion of a script to be executed. Script sections always have a label to designate the section (except, possibly, for the first section).

EXIT is not required if the section is the last section in the file.

Example:

```
:Label1
   edit win [clock] iformat=1
   EXIT
:Label2
   edit win [clock] iformat=0
```

INI

Syntax:

```
INI file
```

Opens an .INI file for editing. If the file is not found in the Windows directory, IniEdit halts with a hard error. Personally, I like this command since it makes the following lines in the script a little clearer. However, when I have only one EDIT command, I generally just include the .INI file with the command.

This is typically used at the start of a section. This is an optional command since you can include the .INI file on the line of each command.

Example:
```
:Label1
 INI Win
 edit [clock] iformat=1
 edit [desktop] WallPaper=Cube.Bmp
 EXIT
:Label2
 INI System
 ...
```

UNCOMMENT

Syntax:
```
UNCOMMENT ini [section] KEYWORD=value
```

Changes the commented line or section containing the section/keyword to an active statement. This is the complement of the COMMENT command. If the VALUE entry is present, then an exact match made. This is useful when using COMMENT with the DEVICE= keywords in the SYSTEM.INI file since there are multiple occurences of this keyword.

If no [section] label is provided, then UNCOMMENT changes the value of the first keyword under *any* section that matches. See the EDIT entry.

Keywords not found are "soft" errors and are ignored by IniEdit.

Examples:
```
UNCOMMENT System [boot.description] network.drv=

UNCOMMENT System [386Enh] network=*vnetbios, vnetware.386, vipx.386

UNCOMMENT Win [Clock]
```

ERROR MESSAGES

There are two levels of errors: Soft and Hard. A Soft Error will not terminate a program, whereas a Hard Error will.

Soft Errors are warnings. Soft Errors are (usually) ignored during normal execution of the program; they are only reported during Debug Mode (/D+), or if you have the Show Warnings switch (/W+) active. They do not stop the program.

Hard Errors will stop the program and won't make any changes to the current .INI file. If a Hard Error occurs, IniEdit will wait for a key to be pressed, unless the user has specified No Pause On Error (/P-).

Entry Already Exists: [section] keyword=value

A Soft Error, this is reported by the APPEND command. This merely means that the target line already is present.

Exact Match to "[Section] Keyword=Value" not found

A Soft Error, this is reported as a warning by COMMENT and UNCOMMENT if an exact match is specified but not found.

File not found: d:\path\filename.INI

A Hard Error. There was an attempt to open an .INI file that does not exist. Check the path of the filename and spelling.

File not open: d:\path\filename.INI

A Hard Error. An attempt was made to write an .INI file that was not opened. Check the path of the filename and spelling.

Label "xxxx" not found

A Hard Error, since a label parameter supplied on the command line was not included in the IniEdit script file.

No INI file opened!

A Hard Error. A command is about to be executed (any command but EXIT) and there is no .INI file opened. Include the .INI filename, at least, on the first statement of each section.

Parameter file not found: d:\path\filename.ext

A Hard Error. This means you gave an incorrect filename to be used as the IniEdit script. IniEdit makes no assumptions about the file extension you used. Also, check the path of the filename.

Too many lines in d:\path\filename.INI

This is a Hard Error. The .INI file you have tried to edit has grown too large. IniEdit can only edit files up to 4000 lines long. (If you have an .INI file that gets this error, I'd like to see it!)

Too many user parameters

A Hard Error, since you are allowed 15 "User Parameters" to the IniEdit program. I think this should be sufficient for 99% of all users (grin). Each script file may contain many parameters, but this error refers to the number of label parameters written on the INIEDIT command line at execution.

Unknown identifier: xxx

A Hard Error. An unknown command has been encountered in the IniEdit script file. Check your spelling. All execution halts.

Unknown Switch: /x

A Hard Error. You have included a switch that IniEdit does not understand on the command line. Check your batch file or menu program.

You must include a filename

A Hard Error. You must include a filename on the command line to IniEdit. IniEdit does not make any assumptions about what file extension you have used.

Runtime Errors 200-203

These are all Hard Errors. These are Turbo Pascal errors and generally mean you have run out of memory for the program's data. This should not happen if you are launching Windows. If it does, it would mean that you really don't have enough memory to start Windows. Check and make sure that you are not "shelled" out of another program. *Note:* These errors do not ever pause and wait for a key to be pressed.

Legal & Registration Stuff _____

This program is supplied "as is." I make no claims about the suitability of this software on your computer system. I have made my best effort to to keep bugs to a minimum. I cannot be held liable for any claims I've made that are not supported (bugs), nor for any misuse of this program, nor for any damage that may result from using this program.

You may freely distribute the INIEDIT.EXE and INIEDIT.TXT files, as long as INIEDIT.EXE is the unregistered version (any version number ending with an "s"). You may not modify the INIEDIT.EXE or INIEDIT.TXT files in any way.

This is *user-supported* software. A lot of work went into writing this package. If you find this program useful, please send us $20 per copy, or $100 per 10 copies (other deals can be made!). Please send checks only, I cannot accept credit card orders. In return, you will get the latest copy of the program (with no reminder notices), laser-printed documentation, a 286 version, and notification of new updates. You *will* get notified — I keep a database of all registered users.

CORPORATE USERS — IF YOU CONTINUE TO USE INIEDIT, YOU MUST HAVE A FULLY REGISTERED VERSION; AN UNLIMITED-USER SITE LICENSE IS AVAILABLE.

Whether you are registered or not, I am wide open to any enhancements you might offer, bug reports (not *my* programs!), or any comments about anything at all. Best way to do this is to e-mail me via CIS.

Please send check to:

Richard Sands
P.O. Box 3917
Portland, Oregon 97208

Please include the following information with your order:

Your Name: _____

Your Registration Name (e.g., Company, Department, or Name): _____

Where you found the program: *More Windows 3.1 Secrets*

Your CompuServe number, if applicable: _____

Thanks for your support!

— Rick Sands

Makeover

Working Model Version 1.0.06
Copyright © Playroom Software

Makeover is a tool I used in my Incredible Indescribable Doohickies Contest. This contest began with a column I wrote for InfoWorld on Sept. 21, 1992. In this column, I complained that the icons Windows uses for the System Menu (a long dash) and the Document Control Menu (a short dash) are almost impossible for PC support people to describe to Windows users who need help over the phone. These are important icons — the System Menu closes an application (among other functions), and the Document Control Menu performs similiar actions on documents in multiple-document applications. But when speaking with frantic users on the phone, support people are reduced to saying things like, "Click that doohickey in the upper-left corner of the window," which naturally evokes responses like, "What doohickey? Which window?"

The winners of the contest to search for intuitive replacements for these important icons were announced in my columns of Nov. 9 and Nov. 16, 1992. (See the "Replacing Microsoft's Bland System Icons" chapter for more details.) The replacement for the System Menu icon is a door since you can click this icon to switch to other applications, as well as close the current app. The Document Control Menu replacement is a paperclip, a "universal document holder."

Makeover is a $39.95 retail program that allows you to change almost any aspect of Windows you want — buttons, icons, the look of title bars, and more. You can reproduce the look of a Mac, OS/2, Next, and other systems without leaving Windows. When I was preparing this book, Playroom Software suggested developing a free version of ButtonMaker (a major portion of Makeover) that would allow readers to change the System Menu and Document Control Menu icons at will. Playroom also provided a version of OSFrame that allows you to change other aspects of Windows for a trial period of 30 minutes at a time. These are limitations that I ordinarily would not accept in shareware chosen for this book, but Makeover has never been shareware — it is a retail app with a special, free version of ButtonMaker.

This special edition already has several icon replacements ready to go. To change your system icons, run BTNMAKER.EXE from Makeover's Program Manager group. Click File Import-Button-Set, click OK if asked "Replace all buttons?," select DOHICKY1.BTN, and click OK. Back at the main menu, click File Create-Backup-Driver, and save your video driver under a name like VGA.OLD or SUPERVGA.OLD. (ButtonMaker modifies your VGA.DRV or similiar video driver file.) Finally, click File Save to write the changes to your current driver. You need to restart Windows for your changes to take effect.

Type of Program:	Utility.
Requires:	Windows 3.0 or higher.
Registration:	Use the form at the end of this chapter to order the retail version from Playroom Software.
Technical Support:	Playroom Software provides technical support to registered users by phone, mail, and CompuServe.

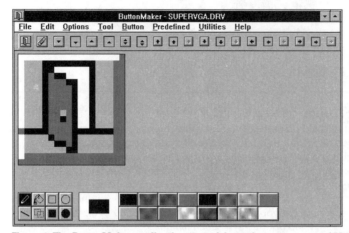

Figure 1: The ButtonMaker application, one of the main components of Makeover, allows you to change your System Menu icons (which are plain dashes in every application) to a door, as shown in the upper-left corner of the window. You can also change your Document Control Menu icons (which are a short dash in applications that support opening multiple documents) to a paperclip, shown at right. Or choose any symbols you want. They look awful when blown up, but can be handy symbols at the small size of a system icon.

Interface... with Your Imagination

Since the release of Windows 3.0, many products have been created to enhance and change the way it works. You can now completely replace the Program Manager or File Manager with better or different programs. And you can replace icons and wallpaper with your own or those created by others. Just about everything in Windows can be configured or customized — *except* the way it looks. Until Makeover, you've been stuck with Microsoft's idea of what your Windows should look like. Sure, you can change your colors and background, but not the general appearance. Now you can subtly enhance the standard appearance, or you can radically change it. The possibilities are virtually limitless.

What ButtonMaker Can Do

ButtonMaker provides a facility for changing the appearance of key components in the Windows interface. Control menu boxes, minimize, maximize, and scroll buttons can be colorized and modified. Predefined button sets are available to make Windows look similar to other Graphical User Interfaces. *More Windows 3.1 Secrets* includes a special, free version of ButtonMaker, which saves changes only to your System Menu, Document Control Menu, and Minimize buttons. The retail package saves changes to all such icons.

What OSFrame Can Do

OSFrame (Operating System Frame) comes with a configuration program that gives you full control over the parameters that are used to create new visual effects. Each screen element can have its color changed, and the depth of the effect can be controlled independently for different screen elements. OSFrame can add 3-D effects to your title bars in several different ways. Three levels of 3-D are available, as well as three special effects that put stripes on the title bar similar to the title bars on another GUI-based computer. Title bar text can be made to appear raised or inset. Three levels of 3-D effect are available for sizing borders, ranging from a light effect to an obvious 3-D effect. The control menus in both application and document windows can have a 3-D effect added so that they match the minimize and maximize buttons. Dialog window borders can have 3-D effects added, also. Borland's chiseled steel dialogs really shine with 3-D dialog borders. OSFrame can now add 3-D effects to menu bars, but not the pulldown menus. *More Windows 3.1 Secrets* includes a free demo version of OSFrame, which changes the Windows environment for a 30-minute trial period. The retail package makes permanent changes.

What Is ButtonMaker?

ButtonMaker provides a facility to modify the title bar buttons and scroll bar buttons. Predefined buttons are provided that help make Windows look similar to other Graphical User Interfaces. Buttons can also be colorized and modified using standard graphic drawing tools.

By combining the effects provided by OSFrame with the custom buttons ButtonMaker applies to your system, you can drastically alter the appearance of Windows.

ButtonMaker achieves its magic by storing the new buttons into the display driver used by Windows to communicate with your video system. The procedure has been thoroughly tested and is completely safe. It does require that Windows be restarted after the new buttons have been applied to the driver, however.

ButtonMaker Keys

Use the following keys in ButtonMaker:

Key(s)	Function
Tab	Moves forward through the tool palette.
Shift Tab	Moves backward through the tool palette.
Left arrow	Selects the button to the left of the current button.
Right arrow	Selects the button to the right of the current button.

Commands

File menu commands

The File menu commands allow you to open and save display drivers. You can also import and export button sets.

Open...
Closes the currently open display driver (see Close below) and presents a dialog box for selection of a new display driver to open.

Open Current Driver
Opens the the display driver that Windows is currently using. This is the same driver that is loaded when ButtonMaker is started up. By editing this driver and restarting Windows, you can quickly and easily change the appearance of Windows.

Close

Closes the currently open display driver. If the currently loaded display driver has been modified, you will be prompted for permission to save the driver. Choosing Save will save the driver to its current name. If you wish to save it to a different name, choose Cancel and then the File, Save As... menu option.

Save

Saves any edits in the the currently open display driver. The original date and time stamp of the driver will be retained.

Save As...

Saves the current display driver to a different name. Do not save the driver to the same name as the driver that Windows is currently using. Doing so will make Windows hang on exit, and may cause the Windows environment to operate erratically.

Save and Restart Windows

Saves any edits in the currently open display driver and restarts Windows immediately. This is the fastest way to activate changes to your title bar and scroll bar buttons. The original date and time stamp of the driver will be retained.

Import Button Set...

Loads a previously exported set of buttons into the current display driver. If the buttons were a different size than those in the current driver, they will be stretched to fit.

Export Button Set...

Saves all of the buttons from the currently loaded display driver into a separate file. The buttons can then be imported into another driver, or can be reloaded into the current driver at a later time.

Create Backup Driver...

Makes a copy of the currently loaded display driver without any modifications. A dialog box is presented to name the new file. It is highly recommended that all program and driver files be backed up before saving changes to them.

Delete File...

Presents a dialog box for selection of a file to be deleted. Use this command to delete un-wanted files without having to switch to another program.

Exit

Closes the currently open display driver (see Close above) and terminates ButtonMaker.

Edit menu commands

The Edit menu commands act on the currently selected button.

Undo

Returns the current button to the way it was before the last drawing action. This command operates as a Redo also since it treats the previous Undo as a drawing action.

Copy

Copies the currently selected portion of the button editing area to the Clipboard.

Paste

Copies the bitmap in the Clipboard to the currently selected portion of the button editing area. The bitmap will be stretched or reduced to fit the current area.

Restore

Returns the currently selected button to its original appearance (when the display driver was opened).

Options menu commands

The Options menu Grid commands allow you to add and remove a grid in the button editing area. The button commands are used for accessing different sizes of buttons in multi-resolution display drivers.

No Grid
Removes a grid from the button editing area.

Black Grid
Puts a black grid on the button editing area.

White Grid
Puts a white grid on the button editing area.

Gray Grid
Puts a medium gray grid on the button editing area.

Light Gray Grid
Puts a light gray grid on the button editing area.

Dark Gray Grid
Puts a dark gray grid on the button editing area.

Primary Buttons
Selects the base size buttons in a multi-resolution display driver. If both of the Alternate Button commands are disabled, you have probably opened a single resolution driver, and this command does nothing. If one of the Alternate Button commands is disabled, you are working with a multi-resolution driver. Select the buttons that match the size of the buttons currently in use on your system.

Alternate Buttons 1
Allows you to select an alternate button size to edit. Even though it is referred to here as an alternate, it can well be the size that you are currently using. You cannot typically change the size of the buttons manually; they are selected when you install a display driver. Select this command if the buttons in the ButtonMaker button bar are not the same size as the one the system is using.

Alternate Buttons 2
This command selects another alternate button size. See Alternate Buttons 1 above.

Color Correction
Some display drivers have problems that cause color translations when ButtonMaker saves a driver or button set. We got tired of waiting for some of the video card makers to fix their problems, so we added this option. Be aware that these problems affect other programs also. The setting of this option is retained from session to session.

Relax Driver Check
If ButtonMaker complains that a file you are attempting to open is not a display driver, and you're pretty sure it is, use of this option may allow the file to be opened. The setting of this option is retained from session to session, so turn it off as soon as possible.

Tool menu commands

The Tool menu commands select a tool to be used for drawing in the button editing area. All of the tools except for Select paint pixels using the colors selected in the color palette. The left button paints using the primary color, and the right mouse button paints using the secondary color. The cursor will change in the editing area depending on the selected tool.

🖉 **Pencil**

Paints the pixel under the cursor. Can also act as a color replacer/translator.

Place the cursor on the pixel to be changed and press the mouse button corresponding to the color desired. Drag the cursor with the mouse button down to draw freehand lines and other shapes.

🖌 **Fill**

Paints the pixel under the cursor and adjacent pixels that are the same color. Two different constraining modes are provided.

Place the cursor on the pixel to be changed and press the mouse button corresponding to the color desired. Hold down a Shift key to limit the fill to horizontally and vertically adjacent pixels of like color. This prevents "spill-through" on diagonal boundaries.

▢ **Rectangle**

Draws an unfilled rectangle or square.

Place the cursor on one corner of the rectangle to be drawn and press the mouse button corresponding to the color desired. Drag the cursor, with the mouse button down, to the opposite corner and release the mouse button. The rectangle will then be drawn.

This tool always draws a rectangle, even if it is only a single pixel. If you picked the wrong starting point, use the Edit Undo command to remove the unwanted rectangle.

◯ **Ellipse**

Draws an unfilled ellipse or circle.

Place the cursor on one corner of where the ellipse is to be drawn and press the mouse button corresponding to the color desired. Drag the cursor, with the mouse button down, to the opposite corner and release the mouse button. The ellipse will then be drawn. The corners, as they are referred to here, are the corners of a rectangle that would contain the ellipse.

This tool always draws an ellipse, even if it is only a single pixel. If you picked the wrong starting point, use the Edit, Undo command to remove the unwanted ellipse.

◥ **Line**

Draws a line between the pixels where the mouse button was depressed and then released.

Place the cursor on one end point of where the line is to be drawn and press the mouse button corresponding to the color desired. Drag the cursor, with the mouse button down, to the other end point and release the mouse button. The line will then be drawn.

This tool always draws a line, even if it is only a single pixel. If you picked the wrong starting point, use the Edit, Undo command to remove the unwanted line.

▦ **Select**

Selects a rectangular area for copying from and pasting to the Clipboard.

Place the cursor on one corner of the rectangle to be selected and press a mouse button. Drag the cursor, with the mouse button down, to the opposite corner and release the mouse button.

■ **Filled Rectangle**

Draws a filled rectangle or square. The area will be outlined and filled using the selected color.

Place the cursor on one corner of where the rectangle is to be drawn and press the mouse button corresponding to the color desired. Drag the cursor, with the mouse button down, to the opposite corner and release the mouse button. The rectangle will then be drawn.

This tool always draws a rectangle, even if it is only a single pixel. If you picked the wrong starting point, use the Edit, Undo command to remove the unwanted rectangle.

◉ **Filled Ellipse**
Draws a filled ellipse or circle. The area will be outlined and filled using the selected color.

Place the cursor on one corner of where the ellipse is to be drawn and press the mouse button corresponding to the color desired. Drag the cursor, with the mouse button down, to the opposite corner and release the mouse button. The ellipse will then be drawn. The corners, as they are referred to here, are the corners of a rectangle that would contain the ellipse.

This tool always draws an ellipse, even if it is only a single pixel. If you picked the wrong starting point, use the Edit, Undo command to remove the unwanted ellipse.

Button menu commands

The Button menu commands select a button for editing. The Application and Document control menus are color reversed when clicked on, but all other buttons have up and down (depressed) images. Windows 3.1 also provides for inactive scroll buttons, which are displayed when a scroll bar cannot be used.

Application Menu (System Menu)
The button that appears in the upper-left corner of all application task windows.

Document Menu
The button that appears in the upper-left corner of document (child) windows in Multiple Document interface applications.

Minimize
The button that reduces a window to an icon.

Maximize
The button that enlarges a window to fill the screen.

Restore
The button that reduces a window from full screen to a sizable window.

Scroll Up
The up scroll button in vertical scroll bars.

Scroll Down
The down scroll button in vertical scroll bars.

Scroll Left
The left scroll button in horizontal scroll bars.

Scroll Right
The right scroll button in horizontal scroll bars.

Predefined menu commands

The Predefined menu commands allow you to quickly apply our predefined button sets to a display driver. You can mix and match using the replacement mode.

Replace all buttons
Sets the button replacement mode so all buttons will be replaced when a predefined button set is selected.

Replace title bar buttons

Sets the button replacement mode so the title bar buttons (control menu, minimize, maximize, and restore) will be replaced when a predefined button set is selected.

Replace scroll buttons

Sets the button replacement mode so the scroll bar buttons (up, down, left, and right) will be replaced when a predefined button set is selected.

Replace current button

Sets the button replacement mode so only the current button will be replaced when a predefined button set is selected.

Windows - Standard

The standard Windows buttons.

Windows - 3-D Ctrl Menus

Standard Windows buttons with 3-D control menu buttons. In some cases the other buttons are enhanced.

Pseudo Mac - Flat

Buttons that do not have a 3-D appearance, and capture the essence of the first popular GUI based computer.

pseudo Mac - 3-D

Buttons that have a 3-D appearance, but still capture the essence.

pseudo NeXT

A really pseudo pseudo that won't fool anyone, but can be fun anyway.

pseudo OSF/Motif 1

Title bar buttons are pretty realistic, but the scroll buttons are like a very early version and more similar to the standard Windows scroll buttons.

pseudo OSF/Motif 2

Same title bar buttons as Motif 1, but the scroll buttons are radically different, and more like the real thing. The backgound of the scroll buttons should be colored to match the scroll bar color.

Utilities menu commands

The Utilities menu provides quick access to global Windows parameters and actions.

OSFrame...

Starts OSFrame, or brings it to the top if it is already running. After you save changes in the current display driver, the new buttons will show up in the OSFrame sample window, giving you a preview of how the new buttons will look.

Control Panel...

Opens the Windows Control Panel program, which is used to control various system components such as fonts, printers, and desktop parameters. The Desktop icon opens a dialog which allows you to change wallpaper, background patterns, and sizing border width.

Windows Setup...

Opens the Windows Setup program, which is used to change display, keyboard, mouse, and network drivers.

Restart Windows

Is equivalent to exiting Windows and then restarting it. This command makes changes to the current display driver take effect, and is the easiest way to see the results of your button changes. This command can be useful if you have modified a system component or setting that requires Windows to be shut down and restarted. It is also useful if an errant program has improperly used up system resources or caused a UAE, and you're concerned about system integrity.

Exit Windows

Leaves Windows and returns you to a DOS prompt.

Procedures

Getting started

ButtonMaker allows you to change the title bar and scroll bar buttons quickly and easily. The ButtonMaker screen has four primary components:

1) The button bar just below the title and menu bars

2) The button editing area below the button bar

3) The tool palette in the bottom-left corner

4) The color palette to the right of the tool palette

When ButtonMaker is executed, it will load the current display driver automatically. You can change the buttons to one of the predefined sets by using the Predefined menu commands. Use the File, Save command to save any changes you have made to the buttons. After saving the current display driver, you must restart Windows before you will see the new buttons as part of the system.

After you have mastered using the predefined buttons, you may want to create your own buttons for an even more customized appearance.

Exporting a button set

In the retail Makeover package, ButtonMaker can export your button creations as a button set so they can be recalled later, or used with other display drivers. A button set is stored in a file with a default extension of .BTN.

Select the File Export-Button-Set... command in the retail package and a dialog box will be presented to name the resulting file. After entering the name in the File Name box and selecting the directory where the file is to be stored, press the OK button. If a file with the same name exits, you will be prompted for permission to overwrite it.

All of the buttons are stored in the file, and the button set file can be used with other display drivers, or shared with other ButtonMaker users.

When naming button sets, you can use the following prefixes to help identify the types of buttons contained in the button set:

W – standard Windows

W3 – Windows with 3-D control menus

M – flat Mac

M3 – 3-D Mac

N – NeXT

O – OSF/Motif 1

X – OSF/Motif 2

Importing a button set

In the Working Model, as well as in the retail Makeover package, ButtonMaker can load a previously exported button set, using the File, Import Button Set... command. You will be presented with a dialog box to select the button set to be imported. Press OK after you have selected the button set file.

If the buttons in the button set file were created for a driver using a different size of buttons, ButtonMaker will stretch or shrink the buttons to fit. This will usually not yield great results, but you can see basically what the buttons look like.

Opening a display driver

To open the current display driver that Windows is using for button modification:

Choose File, Open Current Driver.

Some Windows applications may interfere with opening the current display driver. If you attempt to open the current display driver and get an error message, you are using a utility that has modified your SYSTEM.INI file. You will have to manually open the display driver, and you may have to look at your SYSTEM.INI file to determine the name of the display driver you are using.

To open other display drivers for button modification:

1. Choose File, Open....
2. The Files box contains a list of drivers in the current directory. The initial directory for display drivers is the Windows \SYSTEM subdirectory. To see a list of drivers in another directory, select the directory from the Directories box, or type the name of the directory in the File Name box and press the Open button.
3. Type the name of the display driver you want to open in the File Name box, or select the display driver you want to open in the Files box. You can double click on a file to select and open it in one step.
4. Press the OK button.

You will receive an error message if the file you attempt to open is not a Windows display driver.

Saving a display driver

After applying a predefined button set to a driver, or after you have created your own buttons, you will need to save the display driver that is open.

If you opened the current display driver, you can use the File Save command to save your work. Restarting Windows will activate your button changes.

You can also use File Save-As... to save the modified display driver under a different name. This will create a copy of the original driver, but with the new buttons in it.

If you opened a different driver than you actually want to save the buttons into, you can use the File Export-Button-Set... command to export the buttons into a button set file. They can then be imported into the proper driver.

Selecting and using a drawing tool

Click a tool in the tool palette to select it. You can also use the Tool menu commands.

Before drawing with the tool, you will need to select the colors to be used. Click in the color palette with the left mouse button to select the left button color, and click with the right mouse button to pick the right button color.

Position the mouse cursor to the pixel in the editing area where the drawing action will take place. The mouse cursor will show the tool to be used while the cursor is over the editing area. Click the mouse button that corresponds to the color you want to use, and drag the mouse. If the change is not what you want, use the Edit, Undo command before clicking in the editing area again.

Selecting a button

Click the desired button in the button bar, or use the left and right arrows to select it. Clicking with the mouse is preferable since redrawing a button in the editing area is a relatively time-consuming operation.

Selecting predefined button sets

ButtonMaker provides several different types of predefined buttons. You can use them as they are, mix and match them, or use them as a basis for your own creations.

1. Select the replacement mode. The replacement mode is controlled using the Predefined menu.
2. Select the type of buttons to replace the selected buttons. The button sets are also available on the Predefined menu.

Testing a button

Windows gives visual feedback when the title bar buttons and scroll bar buttons are clicked. The application and document control menus simply have their colors reversed. The rest of the buttons use an "up" image and a "depressed" image to create the illusion that the button has been physically pressed. While you are designing new buttons, it is convenient to see how a button will look when the user clicks it. You can test buttons by clicking them in the button bar. The first time you click a button, it will be selected for editing. Subsequent clicks will show how the button will look when it is clicked. The depressed images will not change when clicked since they are not normally exposed.

Using a grid

Using a grid can make it much easier to draw new buttons. Five different colors of grids are provided. As your new button takes shape, you may want to switch among the colors. The grid color is controlled by the Options menu commands.

Miscellaneous

ButtonMaker hints

The easiest way to use ButtonMaker is to make changes in the current display driver, save the changes, and restart Windows. This way you don't have to worry about changing your display driver using the Windows Setup program, or by doing it manually.

Our predefined buttons are reasonable facsimiles of those used on operating systems they are designed to mock. But, you can creatively combine and colorize the buttons to create your own new look. Try mixing and matching if you want something different without a lot of effort.

After experimenting with colorizing the existing buttons, or creating your own, you will find that certain colors work well for edge and shadow colors. Typically you will use lighter colors like white or light gray for edges. Dark Gray and Black are neutral and work well for shadow colors. Darker versions of a face color don't always work well for shadow colors. Use the Fill tool to experiment with different combinations quickly.

Keep in mind that the Fill tool has two constraining modes. A lot of drawing programs only have one mode, so you may have to get used to the additional flexibility. By default it colors all adjacent pixels, which is very convenient for colorizing buttons like the Mac scroll buttons, but is doesn't work for filling non-rectangular areas, like the inside of the Mac arrows. Use the shift key to constrain the fill.

You can speed up the drawing of the editing area by not having the ButtonMaker main window maximized. The smaller the editing area is, the faster it will draw. There is a practical minimum size of course. ButtonMaker saves its screen location and maximized state on exit.

ButtonMaker license agreement information

Copyright © 1991-1992 Playroom Software. All Rights Reserved.

ButtonMaker is a component of the Makeover for Windows utility program package.

The use of ButtonMaker is covered by the Makeover license agreement. ButtonMaker is copyrighted property belonging to Playroom Software, and may only be used per the terms of the license agreement. Any other use is a violation of United States Federal Copyright laws.

Should you have any questions concerning the agreement, or if you wish to contact Playroom for any reason, please write Playroom Software, 7308-C East Independence Blvd., Suite 310, Charlotte, NC 28227, (704)-536-3093.

What is OSFrame?

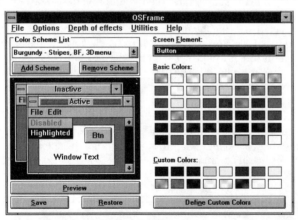

Figure 2: The main OSFrame dialog box allows you to customize the appearance of Windows "furniture" — icons, buttons, title bars, scroll bars, and the like — to suit your imagination or match a non-Windows environment such as a Mac. After using OSFrame to customize your environment you should use OSFrame rather than the Control Panel's Color dialog box to make changes to your Windows color scheme.

OSFrame gives your title bars and borders fully configurable three-dimensional effects. Five levels of 3-D effects are available for title bars, and three levels are available for sizing borders. A stripes effect can also be applied to title bars, and title bar text can be made to appear raised or inset. Six levels of effects are available for dialog window borders.

OSFrame becomes an integral part of Windows after the resident portion (OSFRAMER.EXE) is loaded, and all windows in the system get the special treatment.

The OSFrame control panel is very similar to the Windows Control Panel color settings window. After Makeover is installed, OSFrame should be used to control the colors used by Windows instead of the Control Panel color settings window.

OSFrame Keys

Use the following keys in OSFrame.

Key(s)	Function
Tab	Moves forward through the buttons and fields on the OSFRAME main window.
Shift Tab	Moves backward through the buttons and fields on the OSFRAME main window.
Direction keys	Moves cursor among colors in Basic and Custom Colors palette.
Spacebar	Selects a color highlighted by the cursor in the Basic and Custom Colors palette.

Commands

File menu commands

The File menu commands allow you to export color schemes so that they can be transferred to other computers, and to import previously exported color schemes. You can also close the OSFrame control panel.

Import Scheme...
Loads a color scheme from a previously exported color scheme file. After the file name is specified, you can choose from the color schemes that are contained in the color scheme file. You can also import color schemes from another OSFRAME.INI file. Color scheme files have an OSF filename extension by default.

Export Scheme...
Saves a color scheme to a file that can later be imported by OSFrame, either on this computer system or another. After the file name is specified, you will be prompted for name of the scheme as it will be saved in the file. Multiple color schemes can be saved into a file by exporting to the file multiple times. This allows libraries of color schemes to be created. Color scheme files have an OSF filename extension by default.

Exit
Terminates OSFrame, but leaves OSFRAMER.EXE active. If any scheme changes have not been saved, a prompt allows the exit to be canceled.

Options menu commands

The Option menu commands control miscellaneous OSFrame and OSFramer options.

Auto Preview
Enables updating the system colors immediately when a color is changed or when an effect appearance is changed. Even though the system colors are changed, they are not saved until the Save button is pressed. The state of this option is saved from session to session.

Maximum Compatibility
Most Windows applications coexist with OSFrame peacefully. If an application seems to have a conflict with OSFrame, turn this option on. Enabling this feature disables colored inactive title bar text, title bar text effects, and title bar stripes.

Auto-load OSFRAMER
When enabled, Windows will automatically load OSFRAMER.EXE on startup so that the OSFrame effects become a part of Windows automatically. See Installing OSFRAMER.EXE for more details.

Depth of effects menu commands

The Depth of Effects menu commands control the effects that OSFrame adds to title bars and borders. The first four commands enable certain effects, and the rest of the commands use pop-up menus to control the available options.

Application Control Menus
Enables the 3-D effects for application control-menu boxes. When this option is checked, all of the application control-menu boxes will be shaded to match the minimize and maximize buttons.

Document Control Menus
Enables the 3-D effects for application control-menu boxes. When this option is checked, all of the document control-menu boxes will be shaded to match the minimize and maximize buttons.

Title Bars
Enables 3-D effects or special effects for all title bars. The Depth menu commands are used to control the effect applied to the title bars.

Borders
Enables 3-D effects for all sizing borders. The Depth menu commands are used to control the effect applied to the borders.

Active title bar Text / Inactive title bar text

These commands control the appearance of the effects applied to title bar text in the respective types of windows. There are two types of effects that can be applied to the title bar text. Both effects use a second color that can make the text appear raised or inset. Clicking on the title bar text in the sample window, when title bar text is already selected, will select the secondary text screen element.

None
Title bar text will be unaffected and will appear as it does without OSFrame.

Shadow
Places the secondary text color to the right and bottom of the normal text. Use a light primary text color and a dark secondary color to make the text appear raised. Use a dark primary color and a light secondary color to make the text appear inset.

Edge
Places the secondary text color to the left and top of the normal text. Use a dark primary color and a light secondary color to make the text appear raised. Use a light primary text color and a dark secondary color to make the text appear inset, but be aware that this combination does not seem to yield good results.

Active title bars / Inactive title bars

These commands control the appearance of the effects applied to title bars in the respective types of windows. There are five types of effects that can be applied to the title bars. Most of the effects add a user-controlled color along the top and left sides of a title referred to as the edge, and a user-controlled color along the bottom and right sides referred to as the shadow. The thickness of the edge and shadow can make a big difference in the amount of perceived 3-D effect.

Light
Adds a narrow edge and a narrow shadow.

Medium
Adds a narrow edge and a thick shadow.

Heavy
Adds a thick edge and a thick shadow.

Stripes
Adds horizontal stripes to a title bar. The stripes use the same color as the title text. This option does not add edges or shadows to the title bar.

Light/Stripes
This is a combination of the Light option and the Stripes option. It adds horizontal stripes, a narrow edge, and a narrow shadow to the title bar.

Heavy/Stripes
This is a combination of the Heavy option and the Stripes option. It adds horizontal stripes, a thick edge, and a thick shadow to the title bar.

Active borders / Inactive borders

These commands control the appearance of the effects applied to sizing borders in the respective types of windows. There are three types of effects that can be applied to the borders.

Light
Adds an edge on the left and top sides of borders. The shadow and edge colors are used for the marks that show where the border corners are. This option requires that the border width be set for at least 3; otherwise, the border will not be affected.

Medium
Adds an edge on the left and top sides of borders. The shadow color is used on the right and bottom sides of borders on the right and bottom sides of windows. The shadow and edge colors are used for the marks that show where the border corners are. This option requires that the border width be set for at least 4 to get the full effect.

Heavy
Adds an edge on the left and top sides of borders. The shadow color is used on the right and bottom sides of borders. The shadow and edge colors are used for the marks that show where the border corners are. This option requires that the border width be set for at least 4 to get the full effect. This option can yield a very obvious 3-D effect with proper color selection.

Dialog boxes

These commands control the appearance of the effects applied to dialog window borders. There are six types of effects that can be applied to the borders of dialog windows with title bars. The effects applied to the title bars are controlled by the normal window title bar controls. All six effects also turn on a single type of effect for dialog windows without title bars.

None
All dialog windows appear as they would without OSFrame.

Light
Adds an edge and a shadow to the outside of the dialog frame. This makes the whole dialog appear raised on the screen.

Medium 1
Adds an edge and a shadow to the outside of the dialog frame, and adds a border using the frame color on the inside of the dialog frame.

Medium 2
Adds an edge to the outside of the top and left sides of the dialog frame, adds an edge on the inside of the bottom and right side of the dialog frame, and adds a border using the frame color on the inside of the dialog frame.

Heavy 1
Adds an edge and a shadow to the outside of the dialog frame, adds a border using the frame color on the inside of the dialog frame, and adds an edge on the inside of the bottom and right side of the dialog frame.

Heavy 2
Adds edges and shadows all the way around the dialog frame, and adds an edge on the inside of the bottom and right side of the dialog frame. This creates a prominant 3-D effect.

Heavy 3
Like Heavy 2, but tries to fix an alignment problem with the control menu box. Try Heavy 1 and 2 to see which way looks best to you.

Menu bars

These commands control the appearance of the 3-D effects applied to menu bars. When a menu bar occupies only one line, all three effect levels have the same appearance, but they appear differently when a menu bar occupies more than one line. Pull-down and pop-up menus will not be changed in appearance.

None
Menu bars will be unaffected and will appear as they do without OSFrame.

Light
Adds a thin edge on the top and left sides of the menu bar, and a thin shadow to the bottom and right sides of the menu bar. No additional effects are applied when the menu bar occupies more than one line.

Medium
Adds a thin edge on the top and left sides of the menu bar, and a thin shadow to the bottom and right sides of the menu bar. A dividing line will be placed on a multi-line menu bar using the menu bar shadow and edge colors.

Heavy
Adds a thin edge on the top and left sides of the menu bar, and a thin shadow to the bottom and right sides of the menu bar. A dividing line will be placed on a multi-line menu bar using the menu bar shadow color, the window frame color, and the menu bar edge color.

Utilities menu commands

The Utilities menu provides quick access to global Windows parameters and actions.

Border Width
This command is only available with Windows 3.1 or higher. It allows you to change the width of sizing borders without opening the Windows Control Panel.

Control Panel...
Opens the Windows Control Panel program, which is used to control various system components such as fonts, printers, and desktop parameters. The Desktop icon opens a dialog which allows you to change wallpaper, background patterns, and sizing border width. Sizing border width can be very important to the appearance of an OSFrame color scheme.

Windows Setup...
Opens the Windows Setup program, which is used to change display, keyboard, mouse, and network drivers.

Restart Windows
Is equivalent to exiting Windows and then restarting it. This is useful if you have modified a system component or setting that requires Windows to be shutdown and restarted. It is also useful if an errant program has improperly used up system resources or caused a UAE, and you're concerned about system integrity.

Exit Windows
Leaves Windows and returns you to a DOS prompt.

Push buttons and editing tools

The OSFrame main screen contains push buttons and editing tools for performing most of the color scheme editing operations. These buttons and editing tools are described in the following topics.

Color Scheme List
This drop-down list box lists the currently defined color schemes. The first item in the list is the scheme that the driver defines as its default. OSFrame schemes follow, and schemes defined in the Control Panel follow the OSFrame schemes. The Control Panel schemes have a prefix of <cp>. This allows you to import Control Panel-created schemes into OSFrame for further enhancement.

Please keep in mind that the border depth settings require borders to be at least 4 or 5 units for OSFrame to be able to affect the border appearance. You may need to change your border widths to get the full effect of a color scheme.

Add Scheme
This push button adds the currently defined scheme to the Color Scheme List. If a scheme by the same name already exists, it will be replaced with the currently defined scheme. All of the aspects of a color scheme are saved, including all settings and depth controls.

When the button is pushed, you will be presented with a dialog box asking for the new scheme name. If the current scheme already had a name, it will appear in the name edit box. Enter the new scheme name and press OK to add the scheme to the list. You can abort the operation by pressing Cancel.

After adding a scheme to the list, you will be asked if you want to save it as your permanent color scheme. See the Save Pushbutton topic for more information.

Remove Scheme

This push button removes the currently selected scheme from the Color Scheme List. You will get a dialog box asking for approval to remove the scheme. Press Cancel to abort the scheme removal. Pressing OK will delete the scheme from the list and select the next scheme in the list.

Sample Window

The Sample window shows you approximately what a color scheme will look like. You can select a screen element to have its color changed by simply clicking in the sample window with the mouse. You may find it easier to select certain elements by using the Screen Element drop-down list box. Use the Preview push button to update the system colors to those shown in the sample window for a quick look at the new color scheme.

Preview

This push button updates the system colors to match the currently defined scheme. This feature allows you to quickly try out a color scheme before saving it as your permanent color scheme. Sometimes a color scheme looks a lot different against wallpaper.

When the Settings, Auto Preview menu option is checked, the Preview button will be grayed and cannot be pushed.

Save

This push button makes the currently defined scheme the scheme that will be used when Windows is started. You will be presented with a dialog box asking if you want to make the current scheme the permanent color scheme. It is permanent in the sense that it will be the scheme in use until you select a new scheme, or modify it.

This command updates several files and quite a few parameters. It can take up to a minute to complete, so be patient.

Restore

This push button returns the system colors to the scheme that was in use when the OSFrame configuration program was started. This allows you to preview a color scheme, and then return to your original colors if desired.

Screen Element

This drop-down list box lets you select the screen element whose color is to be changed. You can also select screen elements using the Sample window.

Basic Colors

Selecting a color from this color palette will change the color of the currently selected screen element. Click on a color to select it, or use the arrow keys and press spacebar to select the color.

These are the colors that the display driver provides. The developers of the display driver have determined that these colors can be displayed with reasonable quality by your video card.

Custom Colors

Selecting a color from this color palette will change the color of the currently selected screen element. Click on a color to select it, or use the arrow keys and press <space> to select the color.

You can change the colors contained in this palette by using the Control Panel Color window Define Custom Colors... push button.

Define Custom Colors

This push button presents a dialog box that allows you to create a custom color, or update the colors in the Custom Color palette.

Procedures

Installation

When you run WSETUP on *More Windows 3.1 Secrets* Diskette 1 to install Makeover, the files OSFRAME.INI and OSFRAMER.EXE are copied into your Windows directory. The remaining files are copied into a \MAKEOVER directory, under the drive and directory you specified when you started WSETUP.

OSFRAME.EXE is the configuration program for OSFrame. It becomes your Windows appearance control center. After OSFrame is installed, you should use it any time color settings are changed. Using the Control Panel will not update all of the information that OSFrame uses, and may result in unexpected color schemes.

OSFRAME.INI is where all of the OSFrame configuration information is stored. It should not be edited directly.

OSFRAME.HLP is the help file.

OSFRAMER.EXE is the portion of OSFrame that actually does the work.

Changing a color scheme

A color scheme can easily be customized to better suit you. Click on the screen element you wish to change in the sample window or choose the screen element from the Screen Element drop-down list box. Then select a new color for it from the Basic Colors palette or Custom Colors palette. The sample window will show the result of the color change.

If Auto Preview is enabled, the system colors will also be changed immediately; otherwise, you can press the Preview button to update the system colors.

After you have created a custom scheme that you like, you should save it in the Color Schemes list using the Add Scheme button. You should then make it your active color scheme by pressing the Save button.

Press the Restore button if you wish to restore the colors you started with.

Saving a color scheme

A custom color scheme can be saved by pressing the Add Scheme button. A dialog box will appear that allows you to name the scheme with up to 32 characters. After entering the name, press the OK button and the scheme will be entered into the Color Schemes list. Press the Cancel button to abort the save.

Selecting existing color schemes

To select a color scheme, select one of the color schemes from the Color Schemes drop-down list box. To see what the color scheme looks like, press the Preview button, and the colors will be shown using any open windows. If you like the color scheme, push the Save button and the color scheme will become your active color scheme. If you want to restore the previous colors, push the Restore button.

Changing a color scheme allows you to customize an existing color scheme to suit your taste.

Any schemes that were created using the Control Panel will have a <cp> in front of them. This allows you to import schemes created using the Control Panel.

Removing existing color schemes

Color Schemes created using OSFrame or the Control Panel can be deleted. Any schemes that were created using the Control Panel will have a <cp> in front of them.

To remove a color scheme, select the color schemes from the Color Schemes drop-down list box. Choose Yes to confirm the deletion, or No to cancel.

The Windows Default scheme cannot be deleted.

OSFrame License Agreement Information

Copyright © 1990–1992 Playroom Software. All Rights Reserved.

OSFrame is a component of the Makeover for Windows utility program package.

The use of OSFrame is covered by the Makeover license agreement. OSFrame is copyrighted property belonging to Playroom Software, and may only be used per the terms of the license agreement. Any other use is a violation of United States Federal Copyright laws.

Should you have any questions concerning the agreement, or if you wish to contact Playroom for any reason, please write Playroom Software, 7308-C East Independence Blvd., Suite 310, Charlotte, NC 28227, (704) 536-3093.

The Makeover Working Model

The Makeover Working Model contains working demos of the two anchor components in Makeover. They are limited in various ways, but will let you get a good feel for what the product is about.

All the product information below can be found in the BROCHURE.HLP file. You do need to read the "Running the Demos" section to get started.

Before running any of the enclosed software you must read the license agreement at the end of this chapter, or in MAKEOVER.WRI or LICENSE.TXT.

You also need to read MAKEOVER.WRI because of some preparation that must be done to properly run the software.

It's Not Just Another Pretty Interface...

The retail Makeover package includes ButtonMaker, OSFrame, and these additional utilities that will let you further customize and enhance your environment:

IconMaker modifies icons and cursors in any Windows program or display driver. It allows you to adjust these elements to individual tastes. Icons can be created for use in the Program Manager.

CapsKey changes the behavior of the Caps Lock key. The typewriter mode releases the Caps Lock when a Shift key is pressed along with an alphabetic key, making the keyboard work like a typewriter. Two other alternate modes are provided.

SimpleCalc and **PaperCalc** are convenient calculators that can stay on top of other programs. PaperCalc features a scrollable tape for reviewing calculation entries.

NoiseMaker is a music teaching and entertainment program for basic sight reading and ear training. An on-screen piano keyboard facilitates basic drills including note recognition on the staff and keyboard, and interval training. No additional hardware is required.

Running the Demos

Before you run the demos or do anything else with this software, please read the License Agreement section.

When you run WSETUP to install Makover, it copies the files OSFRAMER.EXE and OSFRAME.INI to your \WINDOWS directory, and adds BTNMAKER.EXE, OSFRAME.EXE, and other icons to a group in Program Manager or equivalent. You will then be set up to play with the OSFrame and ButtonMaker Working Models.

The ButtonMaker Working Model will let you modify all of the title bar and scroll bar buttons, but will only save changes to the System Menu, Document Control Menu, and Minimize buttons. The File Export... command is disabled, and the Clipboard functions (Cut and Paste) are also disabled. ButtonMaker does not have any time limits. After you make changes to buttons with ButtonMaker, you have to restart Windows to see the results. The Utilities Restart-Windows command makes it easy to restart Windows.

Crank up OSFrame and you will get a message that you have about 30 minutes to use it. At the end of the available time, Windows will revert to its normal flat appearance. You can still play with the OSFrame control panel, but your windows will not have the special effects. You will have to restart Windows to get another 30 minutes, but you can do so as many times as you wish. You may want to check out the OSFRAME.HLP file before starting OSFrame. (All of the Makeover components have very complete on-line help.)

The OSFrame Working Model will not allow you to save your color scheme information directly, but you can use the File Export... command to save a color scheme. You can then use File, Import... to reload it. If you create a color scheme that you would like to share, the Export command makes it possible. Please feel free to upload your creations to our library on CompuServe (or anywhere else), so other Makeover users can check them out.

If you want to know more about Makeover, double-click the BROCHURE.HLP icon and Windows Help will appear with an illustrated brochure for Makeover. You can also use File Open... within Help for any other Windows program.

Makeover is not, and never has been, shareware or freeware. Only the Working Model version may be freely distributed. Please remember this if you are sufficiently impressed enough to purchase it. Thanks for giving the Makeover Working Model a try.

License Agreement

This software is owned by Playroom Software and is protected by United States copyright laws and international treaty provisions. You may not modify, reverse engineer, decompile, or disassemble the software.

You may freely distribute the demonstration version of this software, but you may not charge for it other than normal connect-time fees. You may not charge a fee of any kind for any computer-readable media containing this software. The computer archive file, diskette, or other media that contains the software must contain this document and any others originally distributed with the software in unaltered form.

In no event shall Playroom Software or its suppliers be liable for any damages whatsoever (including, without limitation, damages for loss of business profits, business interruption, loss of business information, or other pecuniary loss) arising out of the use or inability to use this Playroom Software product, even if Playroom Software has been advised of the possibility of such damages.

If you do not agree to the terms of this agreement, destroy all of your copies of the software. This is your sole remedy.

Trademarks

Makeover, OSFrame, ButtonMaker, and Playroom Software are trademarks of Playroom Software. Microsoft is a registered trademark, and Windows is trademark of Microsoft Corporation. All other trademarks are acknowledged.

Copyright © 1990–1993 Playroom Software. All Rights Reserved.

Where and How to Buy

The retail price of Makeover is $39.95, and is available directly from Playroom Software (prepaid check or money order only) and is also available through a variety of resellers. Please use the order form at the end of this chapter when ordering from us.

If you would like to purchase using any payment method other than prepaid check or money order, you will need to buy it from a computer software reseller/discounter. Windows Exchange, 800-SOFTWARE, Software Spectrum, Corporate Software, and The Programmer's Shop carry Makeover. Windows Exchange is devoted exclusively to Windows software and accessories. They advertise monthly in *Windows Magazine* and consistently have good prices on everything. Their phone number is 1-800-845-1900 or 313-344-1140. CompUSA carries Makeover on their shelves, and Software Resource distributes Makeover.

Support

If you have questions or problems, please feel free to call. Our hours are 10 a.m.–6 p.m. Eastern time. CompuServe is a very efficient medium for customer support, and we now have our own section on CompuServe. To get to our section, type GO PLAYROOM at any ! prompt, and you'll find us in Section 17 of the WINAPA forum.

Makeover Order Form _____

Please complete, print, and return this form and your remittance to:

Playroom Software
7308-C East Independence Blvd.
Suite 310
Charlotte, NC 28227 USA
(704) 536-3093
CIS:76702,1603

Ship to:

Name: _____

Company: _____

Address: _____

_____

_____

Phone (Day): _____

FAX: _____

Phone (Night): _____

CIS: _____

GEnie: _____

Other: _____

Please send me:

_____ Copies of Makeover on 3.5" diskette @ $39.95 each $ _____

_____ Copies of Makeover on 5.25" diskette @ $39.95 each $ _____

Shipping and handling (U.S.: Free — Anywhere else: $3/copy) $ _____

Subtotal $ _____

Sales Tax (North Carolina residents ONLY add 6%) $ _____

Total $ _____

(U.S. Funds drawn on U.S. Bank)

Payment must be check or money order. If you would like to order using a credit card, please call Windows Exchange (1-800-845-1900 or 313-344-1140), The Programmer's Shop, 800-SOFTWARE, Software Spectrum, Corporate Software, or your favorite dealer. You can also visit CompUSA.

Comments: _____

_____

_____

MazeMaker

Version 2.01
Copyright © Custom Real-Time Software, Inc. (CRTS)

*M*azeMaker — *like Concentration Solitaire, another game in this book — is a challenging puzzle that always has a solution, unlike the Solitaire game that comes with Windows.*

In MazeMaker, you click Up and Down arrows to move from floor to floor in a 3-D maze that changes every time you play. It looks complicated, but you quickly get the hang of it, and there's a great feeling of satisfaction as you watch your pointer get closer and closer to the dollar sign ($) that marks the goal.

MazeMaker has a unique mouse interface. As you move your mouse pointer around in the maze, your pointer is kept from going "through the walls" — a great idea since you couldn't solve the puzzle any other way. But if you move your mouse a great distance, or very rapidly, your mouse pointer is automatically freed from the confines of the game so you can pull down a menu and select your options. This all takes place naturally, without your even having to think about it.

MazeMaker is the type of game that appeals to all ages — grown-ups as well as kids. You can even make the game solve itself, if you would like to get the hang of it before trying the game yourself. It's fascinating to watch the mouse pointer move by itself as the computer figures out the maze . . . the program has to solve it by trial-and-error, too! Try it.

Type of Program:	Game.
Requires:	Windows 3.0 or higher.
Registration:	Use the form at the end of this chapter to register with the shareware author.
Technical Support:	Custom Real-Time Software provides registered users with technical support by mail, phone, and CompuServe.

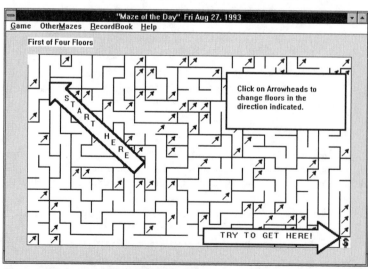

Figure 1: When you start MazeMaker, it creates a unique maze that you solve by moving your mouse pointer up and down through the floors of a "house."

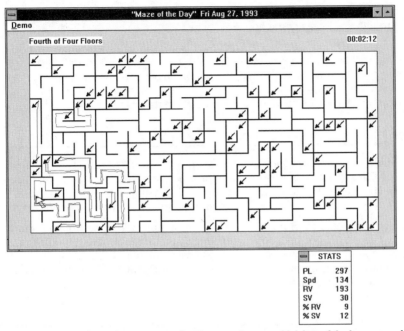

Figure 2: You can have the program solve the maze for you, which is useful when you are learning the game.

Introduction

MazeMaker is a game for Microsoft Windows version 3.0 or higher. You can probably guess that it is a maze game. The intent of the game is to present you with the sort of challenges that a laboratory mouse faces, rather than those of an "adventure"-style game. Thus MazeMaker mazes look more like the ones you might find in a puzzle book, but with some important differences. All but the easiest mazes are three dimensional! And it is nearly impossible to work a maze from the end.

MazeMaker mazes are also more complicated. When MazeMaker is started, it generates the "Maze of the Day." If, at first, you find the Maze of the Day too difficult, try the "EASY Maze of the Day" until you get the hang of it. If you want to be shown how to attempt a maze, select Demo from the Game menu.

After you solve the Maze of the Day, you become eligible to attempt the "Maze of the Week." When you solve this, you can try the "Maze of the Month" and ultimately the "Maze of the Year!"

There are other mazes and options too. You can probably figure them out by exploring the menu options. If not, or if you want more information, look at the text file MAZEMAKR.HLP. (This file may also be viewed while running MazeMaker by selecting HELP.)

General Information

The MazeMaker is capable of generating an assortment of different types of mazes with varying levels of difficulty. When MazeMaker is first started it creates a "Maze of the Day." (You may select the default type of maze; see "Types of Mazes" and "Setup.")

Each maze may be thought of as a house. You must find your way from the entrance to the exit, traveling through the rooms of the house.

There are one or more floors to each maze. Each floor is laid out as a rectangular array of rooms. If there is a wall between rooms, passage between those rooms is prohibited. Conversely, if there is no wall, travel is permitted. Rooms that have an arrow in them are ones that have stairways leading to other floors. Arrows may be up arrows, down arrows, or bi-directional arrows, and they indicate the direction in which travel is permitted.

Maze Travel

Maze travel begins at the upper-left (northwest) corner of the first floor, and the goal is to reach the green dollar sign in the lower-right (southeast) corner of the first floor. All mazes have at least one solution path. Many mazes have some loops and, in these mazes, if a portion of the loop lies along the solution path then there will be more than one solution.

To travel from one room to another on the same floor, just move the cursor to the room you want to go to. To travel from one floor to another, click on an arrowhead to move in the direction indicated. As you travel you will (usually) leave a trail of red "breadcrumbs." On some advanced mazes, floors may be "No Breadcrumb Floors" (xBC) which means that no trail is left on the floors so designated.

The Sticky Cursor

MazeMaker uses a _sticky cursor,_ which resists being pulled through walls. If you pull hard enough, the cursor will change from a transparent arrow to a cross to indicate that you are no longer following the maze path. (You may do this intentionally to select a menu item, or switch to another window.) To regain the arrow cursor and resume travel at the point where you left off, either click the mouse button while the cursor is on the MazeMaker Window or move the cross back to the room where you left the maze. (If you have scrolled a large maze, so the place you would resume from is not visible, you must press the spacebar while MazeMaker is the active Window to get going again.)

Types of Mazes

MazeMaker can create the following types of mazes:

1. SINGLE FLOOR MAZE	One-floor mazes, which are changed daily.
2. EASY MAZE OF THE DAY	Two- or occasionally three-floor mazes, which are changed daily.
3. MAZE OF THE DAY	Four- or occasionally as high as six-floor mazes, which are changed daily.
4. MAZE OF THE WEEK	Seven- through nine-floor mazes, which are changed weekly (every Sunday). There are no breadcrumbs on a few of the floors. You must complete the "Maze of the Day" before you are given the option of selecting this maze type.
5. MAZE OF THE MONTH	Eight- through ten-floor mazes, changed monthly. Larger floors and fewer breadcrumbs than "Mazes of the Week." You must have completed the current "Maze of the Week" before you can try the "Maze of the Month."

6. MAZE OF THE YEAR	Mazes with ten large floors and with hardly any breadcrumbs, which are changed yearly. To be eligible, you must have completed the current "Maze of the Month." Persons attempting these mazes may be considered certifiably insane. Persons solving them may be honored. Call CRTS (201-228-7623) for details.
7. NAMED MAZES	"Maze of the Day"-style mazes. Each named maze is unique. Named mazes may be declared to be "Stock" mazes.
8. CUSTOM MAZES	Mazes where maze parameters (size, breadcrumbs, etc.) are specified. Custom mazes may be declared to be "Stock" mazes.
9. STOCK MAZES	Named or Custom mazes, which are so designated in order that they may be easily selected from a list.

Mazes of the Day/Week/Month/Year are sometimes referred to as "competition mazes" because they are identical on all computers and are intended for competition among pathfinders working throughout the PC world. Some options which might make it easier to solve these mazes are disabled when you work on them.

Maze Selection

The maze generated each time MazeMaker starts is referred to as the "default" maze. Initially, the default maze is the "Maze of the Day." (You may change this from the Game Setup menu option.) You should set the default to a maze type which you find challenging, but not impossible. Beginners may prefer either the Single-Floor Maze or the "EASY Maze of the Day," while people who are good puzzle solvers should probably stick with the standard "Maze of the Day" as their default. You may also choose a Custom maze with parameters you specify as your default.

You may ask the MazeMaker to display a different maze at almost any time. Choose from the Other Mazes menu, which shows the different selections you are permitted to make. Your choice here depends partially upon which mazes you have previously solved. The MazeMaker determines this from the History it keeps and from whom you have told the MazeMaker you are. (The MazeMaker will ask you for your name when you solve a maze. You can sign in anytime using the Record Book/Sign In menu option.)

MazeMaker Etiquette

The MazeMaker may become seriously upset with Pathfinders who set their system clocks to anything other than the correct date. It must be assumed that the reason for doing this is to attempt some maze which the Pathfinder is not presently entitled to work on.

The MazeMaker Menu

The menu presented by MazeMaker normally has four items. They are "Game," "OtherMazes," "RecordBook," and "Help." If the MazeMaker window is sufficiently narrow, though, the menu will merely indicate "Menu." Selecting this little menu will elicit a pop-up menu with four items. In other respects the normal and little menus are identical. If you request a "Demo," you get a Demo Menu until you stop the demo. The Demo Menu is different from the main MazeMaker menu, and is discussed later.

The menu bar occasionally contains non-menu information near its right margin. Specifically, the elapsed time and floor data may be presented in this manner. This will occur when the MazeMaker window is too small to display this information inside the window, or when the MazeMaker window cannot show an entire floor of the maze.

The organization of the MazeMaker menu is as follows:

GAME DEMO (or Ctrl+D) causes the MazeMaker to enter "Demo" Mode. While in Demo Mode, the MazeMaker attempts to solve the maze and you watch! See discussion on Demo Mode below for more information. Demo Mode may not be initiated after you have spent five or more minutes on the maze in progress, nor may it be initiated on Maze of the Week/Month/Year.

GAME HINT (or Ctrl+H) presents a hint from the MazeMaker. Hints are not normally given on "Competition" mazes unless the MazeMaker senses that you are in serious trouble. Hints are limited to five on any maze.

GAME RETURN-TO-START repositions the cursor back to the beginning of the maze (for those who cannot find their own way). This option is disabled on "Competition" mazes.

GAME SWEEP-BREADCRUMBS clears all the breadcrumbs (red stuff) from the maze. Normally, this takes only a few seconds, but it may take a while on larger mazes. This option is disabled on "competition" mazes.

GAME SETUP... presents a dialog box which allows you to customize the way MazeMaker operates. The changes you make are recorded in the MazeMaker data file, and so these changes affect future sessions as well as the present one.

GAME EXIT causes MazeMaker to terminate. Once MazeMaker is terminated, the maze in progress is lost and cannot be restored. To suspend MazeMaker so a maze can be resumed later, shrink MazeMaker to an icon.

OTHER MAZES... Selection of a maze from this menu item causes the maze in progress to be discarded. That is, it cannot be resumed from the point at which you left off. If you wish to start a new maze and be able to continue the maze in progress at a later time, you should shrink the present instance of MazeMaker to an icon and launch another instance of MazeMaker.

OTHER MAZES MAZE-OF-THE-DAY/WEEK/MONTH/YEAR causes a new maze of the type specified to be displayed. The actual menu choice here (and the type that will be drawn) depends upon the mazes that the present "Pathfinder" (the person who has "signed in") has solved. For example, to qualify for the "Maze of the Month," one must have solved both the current "Maze of the Day" and the current "Maze of the Week."

OTHER MAZES STOCK... presents you with a dialog from which you may select an existing Stock maze.

OTHER MAZES EASY-MAZE-OF-THE-DAY causes the "Easy Maze of the Day" to be generated. The maze in progress is lost.

OTHER MAZES SINGLE-FLOOR-MAZE causes the "Single Floor Maze" for the day to be generated. The maze in progress is lost.

OTHER MAZES NAMED... causes the Named Maze Dialog to be initiated. It is used to request that a specific "Named" maze be generated.

OTHER MAZES CUSTOM causes the Custom Maze Dialog to be initiated. Unlike other maze types where the MazeMaker chooses the maze parameters (height, width, etc.), "Custom" mazes are ones where you define the parameters. The Custom Maze Dialog allows you to ask the MazeMaker to generate the type of maze you define.

RECORD BOOK SIGN-IN brings up a dialog screen which allows the current pathfinder (You!) to sign in. You are presented with a list of known pathfinders and you may choose from the list or enter a new name. This menu item may not be selected if the maze in progress is the "Maze of the Week/Month/Year". This dialog is also presented whenever a maze (except Week/Month/Year) is solved. You may want to sign in before you solve a maze if you have already solved the "Maze of the Day" or if you want the MazeMaker to keep track of the mazes you do not solve.

RECORD BOOK COURSE-RECORDS ALL-TIME displays a selection of bests and fastest for the default maze type, and for all non-trivial mazes.

RECORD BOOK COURSE-RECORDS RECENT displays a selection of bests and fastest for the default type, and for all non-trivial mazes among the 100 most recent mazes attempted.

RECORD BOOK HISTORIES THIS-MAZE displays statistics about previous attempts to solve the maze in progress.

RECORD BOOK HISTORIES THIS-PATHFINDER displays information about each maze the current Pathfinder (the one who has signed in most recently) has attempted.

RECORD BOOK HISTORIES THIS-TYPE displays information about each maze, previously attempted, which is of the same type as the maze in progress.

RECORD BOOK HISTORIES COMPLETE displays information about all previous maze attempts.

HELP (or F1) asks the MazeMaker to show you some relevant portion of the MAZEMAKER.HLP file. (The MazeMaker chooses help based upon your sub-menu selection or current situation.) Once you are viewing some text, you may scroll to view any other part of the file or return to whatever you were doing. MAZEMAKER.HLP is a normal ASCII text file, so you can print it out if you wish.

HELP ABOUT displays the usual message about the copyright owner of MazeMaker.

Record Book Information

Obviously, all Record Book Histories contain information only from your own computer and from a single file on that computer. This information is kept in the file MAZEMAKER.DAT in the same directory as the .EXE file. If you manage to have more than one .EXE, then you will have a .DAT file for each .EXE.

The Setup Dialog

The Setup dialog allows you to specify the "Startup Maze," "Maze View," "Stat View," "Program Manager Resizing," and if you would like to start up in "Demo Mode."

The startup, of default, maze is initially the "Maze of the Day." You may choose instead the "EASY Maze of the Day," a "Single Floor Maze," which changes daily, or the "Default Custom Maze." The default custom maze uses the date as a randomizer so it, too, changes daily. The size and other parameters associated with the default custom maze are specified in the dialog associated with the Other Mazes Custom menu item.

The maze view controls the initial shape of the main MazeMaker window each time a new maze is generated. The choices are "Normal" and "Restricted." Normal means that the window will be sized large enough to show an entire floor of the maze, or as much of a floor as is possible. (Except for custom/stock mazes marked "Restricted View Only." These mazes are always shown in a restricted view window which cannot be resized.) Restricted means that the window will be only large enough to show a small number of rooms at one time. It is more difficult to traverse, and more similar to being in an actual maze if the maze view is restricted.

The stat view controls whether an auxiliary "Stats" window is shown. Initially, the stat view is set to "Auto." Alternatively, you may set the stat view to "On" or "Off." On means that a Stats window is displayed in the lower right-hand corner of the screen if the mazeview is normal or directly below the main window if the mazeview is restricted. Off means the Stats window is not displayed. When auto is selected, the MazeMaker decides when it first shows a maze based upon whether any part of the Stats window would obscure a part of the maze. If it would, the Stats are not shown; otherwise, they are shown.

Cursor stickiness controls the force required to pull the "In Maze Cursor" (the transparent arrow) through a wall and change it to a cross. When the cursor changes to a cross, you stop traversing the maze and are free to move the menu, or perform other Windows functions. Set the control to the left to make it easier to pull through walls (make the cursor less sticky); or on the right to make it harder to pull the cursor through walls. Initially, cursor stickiness is set to a middle position.

Program Manager Resizing, when enabled, causes the Program Manager Window to shrink to an icon when MazeMaker is started, and to be restored to its original size when MazeMaker is terminated. (No other control over Program Manager is exercised, so it may be manipulated normally while MazeMaker runs even if this feature is enabled.) Initially, Program Manager Resizing is disabled to be consistent with other Windows programs. You will probably want to enable this option.

You may request that Demo Mode be initiated as soon as the MazeMaker has completed creating the default maze. This may be useful for those who want obvious activity on their Windows Display and invoke MazeMaker from the WIN.INI file.

Named Maze Dialog

The Named Maze Dialog allows one to specify that a "Named" maze be generated. Each unique name causes a corresponding unique "Maze of the Day" style maze to be generated. The dialog allows the maze to be generated. The dialog allows the maze to be designated as a "Stock" maze. Once designated as a stock maze, the name cannot be reselected as a named maze. (Others wishing to try the same maze must select it via the stock dialog.) The Named Maze Dialog may be aborted by selecting the Cancel button.

The Stock Maze Dialog

The Stock Maze Dialog displays a list of available stock mazes, one per line. For each maze, the name, height, width, number of floors, difficulty, and best time are shown. Also shown is an indication of whether some, none, or all the floors are designated as "No Breadcrumb" floors, whether the maze is marked as "Restricted View Only," and whether the maze was originally defined as a "Named" (N) or a "Custom" (C) maze.

Along with the list are three options: OK, List, and Cancel. Cancel aborts the Stock Maze Dialog and restores the cursor to its most recent position in the maze in progress. OK and List each require that an item from the list be selected before they do anything useful. OK causes the selected maze to be generated. List causes a history or previous attempts at the selected maze to be displayed. (After a List is viewed, the dialog is resumed, and the selection may be changed.)

Custom Maze Dialog

The Custom Maze Dialog allows you to specify Width, Height, number of Floors, Difficulty, which floor will not have Breadcrumbs, and whether the maze is a "Restricted View Only" maze. These parameters essentially determine the Type of maze that will be generated. You must also specify a Name. It is the name that determines which of the several Billion (with a B!) mazes of the type you defined the MazeMaker will actually create.

In addition, the dialog allows you to specify that the maze you are defining should become the "Default Custom Maze." You will notice when you begin the dialog that the MazeMaker has filled in all the answers. These are the default values. You are free to change these, of course, to define the type of maze you presently want. And you can also declare that your new values should become the new default by checking the "Make Default" box. This set of values is also used to determine the maze type if you specify "Default Custom maze" as the startup maze. (See "Setup Dialog.")

The Custom Maze Parameters are

Name	A character string which has at least one character and is not the same as an existing "Stock" maze name.
Width	The east-west dimension of the maze specified in rooms (minimum 5, maximum 999).
Height	The north-south dimension of the maze specified in rooms (minimum 5, maximum 999).
Floors	The number of floors the maze has (minimum 1, maximum 10).
	(The product of width, height, and floors — the house size — may not exceed 32,000.)
Difficulty	A parameter used by the MazeMaker when generating the maze, but which is hard to define. (Mazes with low difficulties like one or two are almost certain to be trivial. Increasing the difficulty above 10 percent of the house size is not likely to make the maze significantly harder to solve, and may actually result in an easier maze. The best way to get a feel for the difficulty parameter is to experiment with it. For example if you try a one floor maze with difficulty of one, you will find that the shortest solution path does not stray much from the diagonal.)

No Bread-crumb Floors	Specifies the floor numbers separated by spaces or commas, where no bread-crumbs (red stuff) will be dropped as the maze is traversed. (When left blank, all floors have breadcrumbs. If "all" is specified, none of the floors will have breadcrumbs.)

The Stat Window _____

The "Stat" Window shows statistics which are updated continuously as you work on a maze. These include some or all of the following:

1) PL — The path length, or distance you have traveled (in rooms) since the start of the maze.

2) Spd — Your speed in Rooms per Minute.

3) RV — The number of Rooms you have Visited in this maze.

4) SV — The number of Stairways you have Visited in the current maze.

5) %RV — The percentage of Rooms in the maze that you have Visited.

6) %SV — The percentage of Stairways that you have Visited.

7) Time — The number of hours, minutes, and seconds, you have been working on this maze.

Items 3 through 6 do not appear on "No Breadcrumb" floors. (These numbers, if shown, could be used to determine whether one were retracing one's steps, or not; counteracting the reason for not having breadcrumbs.) Items 4 and 6 are not shown on mazes that have only one floor. (No stairways!) Item 7 appears only if the maze, when first created, requires scrolling. (Otherwise, time is shown in the main window.)

Demo Mode _____

Demo Mode allows you to watch as the computer tries to solve the maze currently displayed. It is initiated by selecting Games Demo from the MazeMaker's main menu, or by selecting the Demo Mode Startup option during Setup. While MazeMaker is operating in Demo Mode, the usual menu is replaced by the Demo Menu. Demo Mode can be exited by selecting Quit from this menu, or by pressing the Esc key on the keyboard.

Demo Mode may not be entered if the current maze is the Maze of the Week/Month/Year, or if more than five minutes have elapsed since the maze was started. No information is recorded in the MazeMaker's history about any maze worked on during Demo Mode.

While Demo Mode is active, the MazeMaker leaves the normal Windows cursor on the screen as well as displaying a Demo Mode Cursor (with a small "D" inside) that traverses the maze. You continue to control the Windows cursor with the mouse, but the computer controls the Demo Mode cursor. You may even switch to another application, but the Demo Mode will continue as if MazeMaker were still active.

Demo Mode attempts to solve the maze with a reasonably intelligent approach, but without actual knowledge of the solution. Half a minute after the maze has been solved, Demo Mode starts over at the beginning (of the same maze) and repeats in this manner until you ask it to stop. Unless the maze is relatively easy, the computer is likely to take different paths each time it attempts to solve the maze.

Demo Mode Menu

There are five options on the Demo Mode Menu:

1) Quit Demo
2) Pause Demo
3) Resume Demo
4) Help
5) Exit MazeMaker

QUIT DEMO causes the MazeMaker to resume normal mode. The Cursor is switched from the Demo Mode Cursor back to the usual MazeMaker cursor, and placed where the Demo Mode left off. The menu is also switched back to the normal menu. Remember, though, that once you have been in the Demo Mode, your result on the present maze will not be recorded in the MazeMaker's History. You may also quit Demo Mode by pressing the Esc key or Ctrl+D if MazeMaker is the active window.

PAUSE DEMO causes the computer to stop moving the Demo Mode Cursor around the maze. The Demo may be resumed later. The spacebar key may also be used to pause the demo if MazeMaker is the active window.

RESUME DEMO causes a paused demo to be resumed. The demo continues just as if it had never been interrupted. The spacebar key may also be used to resume the demo if V is the active window.

HELP enables you to view information contained in the MAZEMAKER.HLP file in the same manner as it does when selected from the main menu.

EXIT MAZEMAKER does just that; it terminates the program. Do not confuse this option with the one that merely quits the Demo Mode.

Multiple MazeMaker Instances

You can create multiple instances of MazeMaker. You may wish to do this if you are in the midst of one maze, and want to begin a second maze without losing what you have done on the first. Multiple instantiation also creates some interesting demos. (For example, try running several restricted view instances in Demo Mode.)

The only limits on multiple instantiation are ones imposed by Windows itself, by the amount of memory that is available, and by the processing power of your CPU. Obviously if some Windows resource (a timer is an example of a Windows resource) is not available, then the new instance will not execute normally or possibly at all. Also each instance requires its own memory, and memory is a finite resource too. MazeMaker always tries to degrade as gracefully as possible.

MazeMaker Memory Requirements

MazeMaker memory requirements are strongly tied to the size of the maze you ask the MazeMaker to generate, and to your video resolution. This is because the MazeMaker asks Windows to keep an exact image of each floor. The image sizes are based upon the number of pixels required to display each room, and the number of rooms. The largest mazes (like the Maze of the Year!) require approximately 4MB free memory for VGA resolution. (Click Help About in the Program Manager to find out how much free memory you have.) If you run out of memory and cannot make more available to V (by terminating other applications, adding "Virtual Memories" and/or reconfiguring your extended memory) you must either ask for smaller mazes or reduce your video resolution. (Video Resolution is a Windows Setup parameter. You might switch down to VGA from Super VGA or from VGA to EGA.)

Disclaimer

MazeMaker is supplied as is. CRTS disclaims all warranties, expressed or implied, including, without limitation, the warranties of merchantability and of fitness for any purpose. CRTS assumes no liability for damages, direct or consequential, which may result from the use of MazeMaker.

MazeMaker is Shareware

MazeMaker is a "shareware program" and is provided at no charge to you for your evaluation. This is a complete program. None of its features are disabled. But MazeMaker is *not* free. If you wish to continue using it, you are required to pay a registration fee. Remember: If you want to be Attorney General someday (or even if you don't), it is against the law to use this program except as authorized by its copyright owner.

Ombudsman Statement

CRTS is a member of the Association of Shareware Professionals (ASP). ASP wants to make sure that the shareware principle works for you. If you are unable to resolve a shareware-related problem with an ASP member by contacting the member directly, ASP may be able to help. The ASP Ombudsman can help you resolve a dispute or problem with an ASP member, but does not provide technical support for members' products. Please write to the ASP Ombudsman at 545 Grover Road, Muskegon, MI 49442 or send a CompuServe message via CompuServe Mail to ASP Ombudsman 70007,3536.

Temporary License

You are granted a temporary license to install and use MazeMaker for evaluation purposes. This license expires 21 days after you first use the game.

Registration

If you find MazeMaker entertaining and wish to continue playing beyond the evaluation period, you must make a registration payment of $15 to CRTS. Upon receipt of the fee, CRTS will send you a registered copy of MazeMaker, which includes a license that permits its unlimited use by one person on one computer at a time. Registered users can submit their records to the MazeMaker National Registry and those that have solved the Maze of the Year! are eligible to win MazeMaker tee-shirts.

A printed copy of the file ORDER.TXT should be filled out and accompany the $15 registration fee.

Network and Site-License arrangements may be made by contacting CRTS.

Support

If you encounter a problem while running MazeMaker (not including frustration!), please contact CRTS. We will endeavor to provide assistance to help solve your problem. If you are writing, be sure to describe your Windows environment (DOS and Windows version numbers, processor type, memory, video configuration, other applications that are running, AUTOEXEC.BAT, CONFIG.SYS, and SYSTEM.INI files; and anything else you think might be relevant) as well as the anomaly exhibited by MazeMaker.

Registered users who are not satisfied with our response, *for any reason,* and who return their *original* MazeMaker Program Disk to CRTS within six months from the date they registered will have their registration fee refunded in full.

Copying and Redistributing

You are permitted and encouraged to provide free copies of MazeMaker to anyone you choose. The only requirement in this regard is that *all* of the files listed below, or their compressed equivalent, must be included unmodified in any copy you make. You may not charge any fee except as provided below.

Anyone distributing MazeMaker for any kind of remuneration must first contact CRTS at the address below for authorization. This authorization will be automatically granted to distributors recognized by the ASP as adhering to its guidelines for shareware distributors, and such distributors may begin offering MazeMaker immediately.

Contacting CRTS

Our address is P.O. Box 1106, West Caldwell, NJ, 07007-1106.

Our phone number is (201) 228-7623.

Our CompuServe ID is 72467,1255.

MazeMaker Files

The following files are supplied with MazeMaker:

1) MAZEMAKR.EXE	A Windows 3.0+ executable file.
2) MAZEMAKR.DAT	File with setup information, stock maze descriptions, and eventually data about mazes you have worked on.
3) MAZEMAKR.HLP	An ASCII file with information about MazeMaker.
4) SETUP.EXE	A Windows 3.0+ program which automates installation of MazeMaker onto your system.
5) SETUP.INF	An information file used by the installation program that tells it what must be done.
6) METER.DLL	A Dynamic Link Library required by the installation program.
7) ORDER.TXT	A form that should accompany your registration fee.
8) README.TXT	This file.
9) VENDOR.DOC	Information file for Shareware Vendors.

Registration

MAZEMAKER REGISTRATION FORM

Remit check or money order to: Ship to: _____

(Payable to CRTS)   _____

MazeMaker REGISTRATION   _____
Custom Real-Time Software
P.O. Box 1106   _____
West Caldwell, NJ, 07007-1106

___ Registered Copies of MazeMaker @ U.S. $15 each $_____

(NJ residents please add 6% sales tax)

Phone Number _____   Indicate Disk Size:

CompuServe ID_____   (5.25") (3.5")

More Control

(includes CP Add-In)
Version 2.0a Copyright © Sloop Software

*M*ore Control and CP Add-In are unique modules that show up as icons in your Control Panel.

More Control allows you to edit several settings in WIN.INI and SYSTEM.INI that are not accessible through the ordinary modules of the Windows Control Panel. This can be useful if you support many PC users in a company and need them to change certain settings frequently, but don't want them opening a whole .INI file in Notepad. Or you might find it useful for your own convenience.

CP Add-In gives the ability to add any command line to the Control Panel. This is very convenient if you frequently need to change one Control Panel setting at the same time that you also use some other application. With CP Add-In, you can do both things right from the Control Panel, like a miniature Program Manager.

More Control and CP Add-In require that several files be located in your \WINDOWS and \SYSTEM directories (which is handled automatically when you run WSETUP to install More Control). Read the following text carefully if you need to uninstall More Control in the future.

Type of Program:	Utility.
Requires:	Windows 3.1.
Registration:	Use the form at the end of this chapter to register with the shareware author.
Technical Support:	Sloop Software provides technical support via mail, CompuServe, Internet, and America OnLine to registered users, and to unregistered users during their trial period.

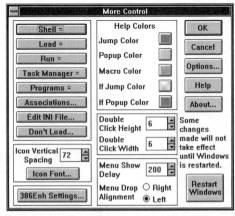

Figure 1: The More Control dialog box, which appears when you double-click the More Control icon in the Control Panel, allows you to edit many settings in WIN.INI and other files that normally are not accessible from a Control Panel module.

Overview

More Control allows you to quickly and easily access many of those settings in WIN.INI and SYSTEM.INI that Microsoft did not see fit to include in the Control Panel dialogs. Easily change the colors used by the Windows help engine in displaying hypertext, the alignment of drop-down menus, the vertical spacing between icons, the font used to display icon titles, plus many other settings. Also, an easy-to-use .INI file editor is included as part of More Control.

This package now includes CP Add-In. This Control Panel module allows you to add any program you want to the Control Panel dialog.

Installation

When you run WSETUP on the *More Windows 3.1 Secrets* Diskette 1 to install More Control and CP Add-In, it copies the files MORECON.CPL, CPADDIN.CPL, and MCSPIN.DLL to your Windows \SYSTEM subdirectory, and copies MORECON.HLP and SETFONT.EXE to your \WINDOWS directory. (MORECON.HLP and SETFONT.EXE can be moved to any directory on your Path, if you prefer.)

That's it. From now on, when you run the Control Panel, you should have an additional icon in the Control Panel window labeled More Control, which will allow you to access the program. You will also have an icon for the CP Add-In program. The on-line help gives full details on both programs' operation.

For more information on the Windows settings affected by More Control, see the files WININI.WRI and SYSINI.WRI in your \WINDOWS directory. Also, refer to the Windows Resource Kit available from Microsoft.

To uninstall More Control, simply delete the files mentioned above, plus the files in the C:\SECRETS2\MORECTRL directory (or whatever directory name you selected when you ran WSETUP). Note that uninstalling More Control will *not* return your system settings to their state before using More Control. There will also be a section labeled [More Control] in WIN.INI that may be deleted.

The More Control Control Panel

The following topics describe the effects of each button in the More Control dialog box (shown in Figure 1).

Shell=

Determines what program is run on Windows startup as the shell. Unless this has been changed, this program would be Program Manager. Of course, given the deficiencies of Program Manager, we highly recommend you check out our shareware Program Manager replacement, Sloop Manager, available on a BBS near you (or in another chapter of this book, *More Windows 3.1 Secrets*). Or use the retail version of Sloop Manager, CEO Desktop Manager (see the file CEOPRESS.TXT in the \MORECTRL directory for full details).

Load=

Allows you to edit the Load= line stored in the WIN.INI file. Any programs listed on this line will be started as icons on the desktop when Windows is started.

Run=

Allows you to edit the Run= line stored in the WIN.INI file. Any programs on this line will be started as windows when Windows is started.

Task Manager=

Determines what program is brought up when you double-click on the desktop. Normally, this program would be the Windows TASKMAN.EXE program (the Task List).

Programs=

Allows you to edit the extensions considered to be applications by Windows.

Associations...

Allows you to modify the associations list stored in WIN.INI. Associations may be added, edited, or deleted.

Edit INI File... Dialog

From this dialog you may easily edit any of the Windows INI files. For information on a control, click the control.

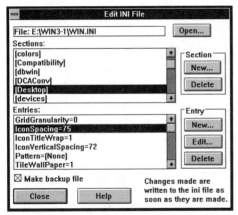

Figure 2: When you click More Control's Edit INI File button, a dialog box allows you to go directly to the section and entry you want to change, instead of having to scroll through the whole file in Notepad.

Sections

This list box displays all sections in the loaded .INI file. Clicking on a section heading will cause the entries in that section to be displayed in the entries list box.

Entries

This list box displays all entries that are included under the section heading selected in the sections list box.

Make backup file

If this check box is selected (checked), whenever an .INI file is opened for editing, a backup file is made of it. This backup has the same name as the .INI file but with the extension .BAK.

Open...

Brings up a dialog box, from which you can select the initialization (.INI) file to be edited.

Section

New...

This button allows you to add a new section to the .INI file. Once it is created, you may add new entries to the new section using the entry new button.

Delete...

This button deletes the section currently selected in the Sections list box. All entries associated with the section are deleted, and the section heading is removed from the .INI file.

Entry

New...

Using this button you may add new entries to a section. A dialog box is displayed in which you may enter the keyword (word on the left of the equals sign) and the value (word on the right of the equals sign).

Edit...

Clicking this button will allow you to edit the currently selected entry. You will be able to change both the keyword and the value.

Delete

This button deletes the currently selected entry in the Entries list box.

Close

The close button terminates your .INI file editing session. Note that any changes made to .INI files will have already been made, since changes are saved as they are made.

Help

The help button brings up the help file.

Note that there is a problem when editing the SYSTEM.INI file. The SYSTEM.INI uses a nonstandard convention, in that more than one line in a section makes use of the same keyword. In this case, the [386enh] section makes use of the keyword DEVICE= multiple times. Due to this, do not attempt to edit the DEVICE= entries using the .INI file editor. Instead, make use of a program such as Notepad.

Don't Load Dialog

Using this dialog, you may specify which Control Panel modules are *not* loaded. For information on a control, click the control.

Figure 3: When you click More Control's Don't Load button, a dialog box allows you to set certain modules *not* to load when you open the Control Panel. This can be handy for PC managers who want certain modules not to appear in some Windows users' Control Panels, such as the Network configuration dialog box.

Load

All modules listed in this list box will be loaded into the Control Panel.

<<Add

Removes the selected Control Panel module from the Don't Load list box and places it in the Load list box.

Remove>>

Removes the selected Control Panel module from the Load list box and places it in the Don't Load list box.

Don't Load

All modules listed in this box will *not* be loaded into the Control Panel.

OK

Accepts all current settings in the dialog and then closes the dialog.

Cancel

Closes the dialog without making any changes to the Windows system settings.

Help

The help button brings up the help file.

Note that if you specify that More Control is not to be loaded, you will have to manually edit the CONTROL.INI file to change what modules are loaded.

Icon Vertical Spacing

Controls the distance (in pixels) maintained between icons. Essentially the same as the Icon Spacing control in the desktop dialog, but controls vertical rather than horizontal spacing.

Icon Font...

Allows you to choose the font to be used to display the titles placed under icons. For this setting to be active, you must have the SetFont program enabled and the file SETFONT.EXE in your Windows directory or on your Path. To enable SetFont, use the Options... button

386 Enhanced Settings

DOS Prompt Exit Instructions — If this setting is enabled, when you start the MS-DOS prompt, a message box appears with instructions on how to exit and switch away from the MS-DOS prompt. Disable this setting if you do not want to see the message. Note that this setting will have no effect if you are running the MS-DOS shell using a batch file.

File Manager System Changes — Indicates whether File Manager automatically receives messages anytime a non-Windows application creates, renames, or deletes a file. If this setting is disabled, a virtual machine can run exclusively, even if it modifies files. Enabling this setting can slow down system performance significantly.

Local Reboot — Specifies whether you can press Ctrl+Alt+Del to terminate applications that cause an unrecoverable error (UAE) in 386 enhanced mode. If this setting is enabled, you can terminate the offending application without restarting the rest of the system. With it disabled, pressing Ctrl+Alt+Del will reboot the computer.

All VM's Exclusive — If enabled, this setting forces all DOS applications to run in exclusive full-screen mode, overriding all contrary settings in the applications' program information files (PIFs). Enabling this setting might prolong the length of the Windows session when you are running network and memory-resident software that is incompatible with Windows.

Help Colors

The settings in this section allow you to set the various colors used by the Windows help engine to display things such as the hypertext links and definitions. The two settings of most concerned are described below.

Jump Color — This is the color used to indicate keywords which jump to new help topics.

Popup Color — This is the color used to indicate keywords which pop up a small box of text describing or defining something.

Double Click Height

Adjusts the amount of movement of the mouse cursor allowed between clicks to be considered a double-click.

Double Click Width

Adjusts the amount of movement of the mouse cursor allowed between clicks to be considered a double-click.

Menu Show Delay

Controls the delay between selecting a submenu and Windows displaying it.

Menu Drop Alignment

Determines whether drop-down menus are aligned on the right or the left of the menu command (useful for languages written right to left).

OK

Accepts all current settings in the dialog and closes the dialog.

Cancel

Closes the dialog without making any changes to the Windows system settings.

Options

Edit INI file icon — Turning on this option will cause an additional icon to appear in the Control Panel. Double-clicking this icon will cause the Edit INI File dialog to be launched. From this dialog you may edit .INI files without having to go through the More Control dialog.

Windows Setup icon — Turning on this option will cause an icon for the Windows Setup program to be placed in the Control Panel. This icon is provided simply for convenience in launching Setup.

Use WIN.INI font settings — This option is used to tell Windows to use the icon title font which has been set in the WIN.INI file. For most cases you should leave this option set on. However, if you wish to use an italic font, you must use the SetFont program. Or, in some display modes, TrueType fonts do not display correctly unless you use the SetFont program. Note that Program Manager does not work that well with the SetFont program, due to the way Program Manager is designed. Just another reason to look at CEO:Desktop Manager, which works fine with SetFont.

Use SetFont program — Activating this option adds SETFONT.EXE to the load line of your WIN.INI file. This is necessary for the icon title font to be set to an italic font or, on some systems, a TrueType font. It is recommend that you do not use this setting if using Program Manager as the Windows shell, as SetFont and Program Manager do not work too well together due to the design of Program Manager.

Help

The help button brings up the help file.

About

The About button brings up a dialog with some information about More Control.

Restart Windows

The Restart Windows button does just what it says; it restarts Windows. Any settings changed in More Control will be saved.

 # CP Add-In

CP Add-In allows you to launch any application from the Control Panel. With CPADDIN.CPL in your \SYSTEM subdirectory, the CP Add-In icon appears when you run the Control Panel. When you double-click CP Add-In, a dialog box like the one in Figure 4 appears. You use the Add, Edit, and Delete buttons to determine what command lines should be available in the CP Add-In dialog box.

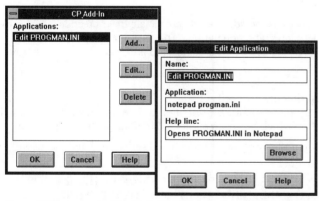

Figure 4: When you double-click the CP Add-In icon in the Control Panel, a dialog box allows you to add, edit, and delete any command lines you might wish to have available to you from within the Control Panel.

Add

When you click the Add button, an Add Application dialog box appears. Type a text description of the program you wish to run in the Name field. Type a command line in the Application field. Finally, type a line of help text in the Help Line field.

Edit

When you select a line in the CP Add-In dialog box and click Edit, an Edit Application dialog box appears. This box allows you to edit the Name, Application, and Help Line fields.

Delete

When you select a line in the CP Add-In dialog box and click Delete, you remove that line from the lines in the CP Add-In dialog box.

More Control License Agreement

The use of More Control is subject to the following terms and conditions.

Title To The Licensed Software. Title to the licensed software is *not* transferred to the end user. The end user is granted an exclusive license to use the software on a *single* computer or computer workstation. *Each* computer or computer workstation must have its own licensed copy of the software.

Copyright protection

More Control is copyrighted material. It is protected by the copyright laws of the United States, the State of Colorado, and other proprietary rights of Sloop Software. You may not make any changes or modifications to More Control. You may not decompile, disassemble, or otherwise reverse-engineer the software in any way.

You may make copies of More Control only under the terms of the section entitled "Limited license to copy the licensed software."

You may use More Control on a trial basis provided you do not violate the protection afforded the licensed software by the copyright laws, and you agree to the terms of the license agreement. If you use More Control on a regular basis, you are obligated to purchase it.

Limited warranty

Sloop Software does not warrant that the licensed software will meet your requirements or that the operation of the software will be uninterrupted or error free. The warranty does not cover any media or documentation which has been subjected to damage or abuse by you.

The software warranty does not cover any copy of the licensed software which has been altered or changed in any way.

ANY IMPLIED WARRANTIES INCLUDING ANY WARRANTIES OF MERCHANTABILITY OR FITNESS FOR A PARTICULAR PURPOSE ARE LIMITED TO THE TERM OF THE EXPRESS WARRAN-TIES. Some states do not allow limitations on how long an implied warranty lasts, so the above limitation may not apply to you.

Other warranties

The warranties set forth above are in lieu of any and all other express or implied warranties, whether oral, written, or implied, and the remedies set forth above are the sole and exclusive remedies.

Limitation of liability

Sloop Software is not responsible for any problems or damage caused by the licensed software that may result from using the licensed software. This includes, but is not limited to, computer hardware, computer software, operating systems, and any computer or computing accessories. End user agrees to hold Sloop Software harmless for any problems arising from the use of the software.

Sloop Software SHALL NOT IN ANY CASE BE LIABLE FOR ANY SPECIAL, INCIDENTAL, CONSEQUENTIAL, INDIRECT OR OTHER SIMILAR DAMAGES ARISING FROM ANY BREACH OF THESE WARRANTIES EVEN IF Sloop Software OR ITS AGENTS OR DISTRIBUTORS HAVE BEEN ADVISED OF THE POSSIBILITY OF SUCH DAMAGES. Some states do not allow the exclusion or limitation of incidental or consequential damages, so the above limitation or exclusion may not apply to you.

In no case shall Sloop Software's liability exceed the license fees paid for the right to use the licensed software, or a sum no greater than one Dollar ($1), whichever is less.

Limited license to copy the software

You are granted a limited license to copy More Control *only for the trial use of others* subject to the terms of this software license agreement described herein, and the conditions described below are met: More Control *must* be copied in an unmodified form and MORECN.ZIP *must* contain the following files:

MOREICON.CPL	More Control Control Panel file
MORECON.EXE	More Control EXE file for stand alone use
MORECON.HLP	More Control help file
CPADDIN.CPL	CP Add-In module
SETFONT.EXE	Used to set the icon title font
MCSPIN.DLL	Spin button dll (required by MC)
INSTALL.EXE	Install program
METER.DLL	Dll for install
SETUP.INF	Setup information
README.TXT	This file
ORDERFRM.TXT	Order form
LICENSE.TXT	License information
VENDOR.DOC	Shareware vendor information
FILE_ID.DIZ	Vendor description file
CEOPRESS.TXT	Information on CEO:Desktop Manager

No fee, charge, or other compensation may be accepted or requested by anyone without the express written permission of Sloop Software.

Public-Domain Disk Vendors may *not charge* a fee for More Control themselves. However, you may include either program on a diskette for which you charge a nominal distribution fee. The purchaser of said diskette must be informed in advance that the fee paid to acquire the diskette does *not* relieve said purchaser from paying the registration fee for either More Control or CP Add-In if said purchaser uses either program.

Operators of electronic bulletin board systems (sysops) may post More Control for downloading by their users without written permission *only as long as the above conditions are met.* A fee may be charged for access to the BBS *as long as no specific fee is charged for downloading* the program files without first obtaining express written permission from Sloop Software to charge such a fee.

The above constitutes the license agreement for More Control. It supersedes any and all previous license agreements.

This program is produced by a member of the Association of Shareware Professionals (ASP). ASP wants to make sure that the shareware principle works for you. If you are unable to resolve a shareware-related problem with an ASP member by contacting the member directly, ASP may be able to help. The ASP Ombudsman can help you resolve a dispute or problem with an ASP member, but does not provide technical support for members' products. Please write to the ASP Ombudsman at 545 Grover Road, Muskegon, MI 49442 or send a CompuServe message via CompuServe Mail to ASP Ombudsman, 70007,3536.

If you are unable to get the More Control icon to appear in the Control Panel, MORECON.EXE is provided. This file lets you run More Control just like a normal application. Please do let us know if you are unable to get the icon to appear, so we can try and track down the problem.

Registration Information

Note that this is a shareware program. As such, you may use it on a trial basis for 30 days. After this time, the program should be registered if it is continued to be used. The cost is $12.50. For a disk with the latest version add an extra $2.00 shipping. The fee is payable to:

Sloop Software
6457 Mesedge Lane
Colorado Springs, CO 80919
(719) 260-0433 voice/fax

Please, check or money orders in U.S. funds only. After registering, you will receive a letter giving you your registration code to eliminate the registration dialog box.

You may also register using GO SWREG on CompuServe; I.D. 945 or 947.

Direct any comments to the above address or e-mail to CompuServe (id 72540,144), Internet (id 72540.144@compuserve.com) or America OnLine (id Sloop Soft). Customer support is available to registered users and to unregistered users during their trial period.

More Control/ICL Builder Registration Form _____

Name: _____

Company: _____

Address: _____

City, State, Zip Code: _____

Country: _____

Optional Info: _____

Obtained program from: _____

Type of machine: _____

Video Type: _____

More Control: ____ copies X $12.50 _____

ICL Builder: ____ copies X $12.50 _____

Both Programs: ____ copies X $20.00 _____

SPECIAL OFFER - CEO:Desktop Manager   only $50.00! _____
(see ceopress.txt for more information, this offer expires 12/31/93)
Add $2.00 ($4.00 overseas) shipping for CEO or for
disk with latest version of MC or ICL Builder   _____

                                 Total _____

Please send payment to:
Sloop Software
6457 Mesedge Lane
Colorado Springs, CO 80919

Checks or money orders in U.S. funds, drawn on U.S. banks only.

Comments:

129.2 ft.

Mouse Odometer

Version 1.0
Copyright © Toggle Booleans

*T*he Mouse Odometer — like Toggle Booleans's other freeware product in this book, Coffee Mug — is a fun diversion for Windows users. It shows you how far your mouse has moved during your current workday, workweek, or even lifetime.

However, I've found a productive use for Mouse Odometer, unlike Coffee Mug. On those occasions when I'm tired and feel like quitting for the day, I can look down at the little icon faithfully adding up my mouse activity and say to myself, "I'll just work a little longer, until I've gone another 100 feet." Call me crazy, but little goals like that keep me going.

You'll probably enjoy Mouse Odometer, though, just for its entertainment and conversational value. Be the first in your office to have one!

Important: *You should "tune" Odometer to your mouse the first time you run it. To do this, move your mouse pointer to the left edge of your screen, then slowly slide your pointer to the right edge, and measure how far your mouse moved on its mouse pad. Do the same thing from the bottom to the top of your monitor. Finally, to enter this information, click the Mouse Odometer icon, select Preferences from the menu that appears, and type in the distance.*

Type of Program: Utility.

Requires: Windows 3.0 or higher.

Registration: Free. This program requires no registration.

Technical Support: None.

Preferences
Distance Settings
Mouse Horizontal Travel `1.0000` in.
Mouse Vertical Travel `1.0000` in.
OK   Cancel
Units
○ Measured in pixels   ○ Measured in centimeters
○ Measured in inches   ○ Measured in meters
○ Measured in feet   ○ Measured in kilometers
● Measured in miles
Update Rate
● High
○ Average
○ Low

Figure 1: When you click the Mouse Odometer icon and select Preferences, this dialog box appears. When you first use the Odometer, measure how many inches it takes to move your mouse slowly from the left edge to the right edge of your screen, then the top to the bottom, and enter your measurements here. This "tunes" Odometer to your mouse.

Overview

Ever wonder how much mileage your mouse accumulates? The Mouse Odometer keeps track of how far the mouse cursor moves and allows you to relate that to how far you actually move the mouse on your desk.

Using Mouse Odometer

The first thing to do is to choose Preferences from the Odometer menu. In the dialog box which appears, enter the distance that your mouse travels in order to move the cursor vertically and horizontally across the screen. The default value is 3.0 inches, which is appropriate for most mice.

The best way to determine the values is to move the cursor to the left side of the screen and then mark the position where your mouse is on your mouse pad. Then move the mouse horizontally until the mouse is at the right side of the screen and measure how far the mouse traveled. Enter the distance, in inches, into the dialog box and then do the same for the vertical distance.

When you start the Mouse Odometer, the default unit of measurement is in terms of pixels. You can also specify inches, feet, miles, centimeters, meters, or kilometers.

If you are running Windows 3.1, it's a good idea to put the Mouse Odometer in your StartUp group. The Odometer remembers the distance traveled from one Windows session to another, so you can see how far your mouse travels in a week or a month, etc. You can reset the Odometer by selecting Reset Counter from the Odometer menu.

The Mouse Odometer, version 1.0, is freeware. It may be copied and distributed freely under the following conditions:

No modifications are to be made to the program or documentation.

The documentation file must be distributed with the program.

If you would like to encourage the development of mostly ridiculous programs like this, please send $10 to the address below. You will receive a copy of the latest version of the Mouse Odometer and a free copy of the Toggle Booleans Screen Blanker! Keep an eye out for other Toggle Booleans products such as the Elvis Detector, the Bit Recycler, and the Coffee Mug desktop metaphor.

For more information about Toggle Booleans products, write to:

Toggle Booleans
P.O. Box 4204
Station E
Ottawa, Ontario
Canada, K1S 5B2

Mouse Warp

Version 2.0c
Copyright © Toggle Booleans

*M*ouse Warp gives you control over a surprising variety of mouse actions. You may never have imagined you would need these features, but once you've tried Mouse Warp I bet you'll find at least one that you'll want to use constantly.

Mouse Warp allows the mouse to "wrap" around the screen. If your mouse is already at the right edge of the screen, and you need to click something on the left, instead of dragging your mouse all the way over there, you can simply push your mouse to the right and watch your pointer wrap around. This takes a little getting used to, but it could be just what you want!

Another great feature (if you need it) is the ability to move the mouse pointer using only your keyboard, not the mouse itself. When this feature is enabled, pressing Ctrl+Arrow keys moves the mouse pointer in the desired direction. This may interfere with some word processors, which use Ctrl+Right Arrow to move right one word, for example. But it might be worth it to you to give up that feature in order to gain keyboard mouse control. (The Keyboard Mouse also takes over Ctrl+Shift+Arrow, Ctrl+Alt+Arrow, Ctrl+A, and Ctrl+Z — check the documentation.)

Mouse Warp also provides alternatives to your normal mouse pointer, in case you need a larger one or an amusing one to enliven your day. You can control the blinking rate of cursors, and even turn blinking off. You can check the exact X-Y coordinates of your mouse with a floating window, in order to select only a certain portion of the screen with a screen-capture utility (such as SnagIt, a program featured in Windows 3.1 Secrets). *And you can associate mouse buttons with certain programs in order to launch them with a click.*

Type of Program:	Utility.
Requires:	Windows 3.0 or higher.
Registration:	Use the form at the end of this chapter to register with the shareware author.
Technical Support:	Toggle Booleans provides technical support for registered users via mail and CompuServe.

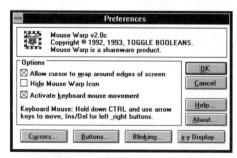

Figure 1: Mouse Warp allows you to control your mouse features, such as wrapping around the screen, using the mouse pointer from the keyboard, changing the mouse pointer, and assigning various actions to the right or middle button.

Overview of New Features

Mouse Warp 2.0 offers the following enhancements and new features over previous versions:

Amazing Cursors
With version 2.0 you have a wide variety of cursors to choose from, including a library of cursor files and even the ability to use any Windows icon as a cursor.

Replace the Hourglass
You can replace the hourglass with one of many shapes, for instance, a sleeping Dr. Watson.

Assign Functions to Unused Buttons
The Buttons dialog allows you to assign functions such as Exit Windows, Double Click, or Start Notepad, to the middle and right buttons.

Coordinate Display
An optional mini display window shows the exact coordinates of the cursor for precision graphics work.

Full Mouse Emulation from the Keyboard
The keyboard mouse is now 100% functional, allowing you to move windows, select menus and double-click, all without even touching the mouse.

Mouse Wrapping

The Mouse Wrapping feature allows the cursor to "wrap" around the edges of the screen. For instance, if you move the cursor past the top of the screen, the cursor will appear on the bottom.

This feature can be particularly useful for systems that use a trackball input device.

Hiding Mouse Warp

Selecting the Hide Icon option will remove the Mouse Warp icon from your desktop. All of the Mouse Warp features will still be active. To bring back the Mouse Warp icon, double-click the Mouse Warp icon in the Program Manager or the MOUSWARP.EXE file in the File Manager.

Keyboard Mouse

When the keyboard mouse is enabled, you can move the mouse cursor solely from the keyboard. To move the mouse, hold down the Ctrl key and press the cursor arrow keys. This will move the mouse eight pixels in the direction you press. For fine movement, hold down the Ctrl and Shift keys, and for huge jumps across the screen, hold down both the Control and Alt keys at the same time.

To simulate a click of the left mouse button, hold down the Ctrl key and press the A key. Similarly, Ctrl+Z will simulate a right mouse click. This can be handy on laptops or for precision graphics work.

Keystroke	Action
Ctrl+Alt+Arrow Key	Moves the cursor 50 pixels
Ctrl+Arrow Key	Moves the cursor 8 pixels
Ctrl+Shift+Arrow Key	Moves the cursor 1 pixel
Ctrl+A	Left click
Ctrl+Z	Right click

Tips

If you find that it takes a long time to traverse the screen using the keyboard mouse, try increasing the keyboard repeat rate from the Control Panel.

Notes

The keyboard mouse in version 2.0 can now serve as a 100% replacement for the mouse. Now you can use the keyboard mouse to select menus, move windows, double-click, or perform any other mouse action.

Note that the required key combinations have changed from version 1.65 to version 2.0.

Selecting Cursors

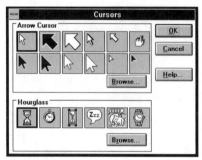

Figure 2: Several different mouse pointers and "wait" icons can be selected from the Cursors dialog box, or you can click the Browse button to select from a library of cursor and icon files.

Mouse Warp allows you to replace the default arrow and hourglass cursors that Windows provides. From the Cursors dialog, you can select from one of twelve arrow cursors and six hourglass cursors.

To select a new cursor, simply click on the cursor image. The cursor will be immediately changed to the selected image so you can try it out. In addition to the built-in cursors, Mouse Warp also provides you with a library of cursors in the form of .CUR files. To select one of the external cursor files, click on the Browse button. The Browse button in the Arrow frame can be used to select a new arrow cursor, whereas the Browse button in the hourglass frame selects a new hourglass cursor. When the Browse button is selected, the standard File Open dialog will appear allowing you to select an external cursor.

Another feature, unique to MouseWarp, is the ability to create a cursor from any Windows icon file. To do so, select the Browse button for the arrow or hourglass cursor and instead of a .CUR file, select any .ICO file. To create your own custom cursor, use an icon editor to draw an icon in the shape you want and then select it as described above. Several public-domain icon editors are available on BBSs and other information services. When you select an icon file, a dialog box will appear asking you to select the "hot spot" for the cursor. Because Windows 3.1 only supports monochrome cursors, the icon will be converted to black and white.

Selecting the Cursor Hot Spot

The Hot Spot dialog box appears after an icon (.ICO) file has been selected as the new cursor. The "hot spot" of a cursor can be thought of as the tip of the cursor, which defines where the cursor points. In the case of the default arrow cursor, the hot spot is the top left-hand corner at the point of the arrow. Windows cursor files (.CUR) contain information about the hot spot location, so when you select a cursor file, you do not need to specify a hot spot.

Icon files, on the other hand, do not contain hot spot information, so before Mouse Warp can use an icon as a cursor, you must specify the hot spot to be used.

The Hot Spot dialog presents a blown-up picture of the selected icon. The gray areas of the icon are the transparent areas of the cursor. The one red dot in the top-left corner defines the hot spot. To change the hot spot, click on a different area of the icon picture. The hot spot indicator will move to the new location.

Button Functions

Most Windows applications do not make use of the middle and right mouse buttons. Mouse Warp allows you assign functions to these buttons. The following list explains the various functions that are available:

Close Application

When the button is pressed, the application underneath the cursor will be closed, as if the Exit option had been selected from the programs menu. As with the Exit option, programs being closed will prompt you if any unsaved modifications have been made.

Double Click

A double-click of the left mouse button will be generated. This can be useful for first-time mouse users who have difficulty performing a double-click.

Exit Windows

You will be returned to the DOS prompt when the button is pressed. As with a normal exit from Windows, any applications that have unsaved modifications will prompt you to save or cancel.

Note that this option does not display a confirmation message.

Exit Windows with Confirm

This option works exactly as if Exit Windows was selected from the Program Manager. You will be returned to the DOS prompt when the button is pressed. As with a normal exit from Windows, any applications that have unsaved modifications will prompt you to save or cancel. Note that the Program Manager need not be running for you to use this function.

Maximize/Restore

This function changes the window state of the window under the cursor. The window under the cursor will be maximized. If the window is already maximized, the window will be returned to the position and size that it was in before it was maximized. This function is equivalent to pressing the Maximize/Restore button in the top-right corner of the window.

Minimize/Maximize

This function changes the window state of the window under the cursor. If the window under the cursor is maximized, it will be minimized. If the window under the cursor is minimized, it will be maximized.

Minimize/Restore

This function changes the window state of the window under the cursor. The window under the cursor will be minimized. If the window is already minimized, the window will be returned to the position and size that it was in before it was minimized. This function is equivalent to pressing the Minimize button of the window.

Press F1 – F10

The F1 through F10 options simulate the pressing of a function key. The Press F1 function can be particularly handy because most applications respond to F1 by providing general or context-sensitive help. For instance, if you have the right button mapped to Press F1 and are using Microsoft Word, pressing the right button will display context-sensitive help for the current function or dialog box.

Start Application

Mouse Warp also provides button functions to start the most frequently used Windows utilities. The following applications are supported and can be associated with either mouse button:

Calculator (CALC.EXE)

Control Panel (CONTROL.EXE)

File Manager (WINFILE.EXE)

Notepad (NOTEPAD.EXE)

Print Manager (PRINTMAN.EXE)

Blinking

With blinking enabled, the mouse will start to blink if you do not move the mouse for two seconds. This makes it easy to find the mouse if you get up from the computer and come back.

To enable blinking, select Fast, Slow, or Custom blinking. The Custom option allows you to specify exactly how often the cursor will blink. Note that on some laptops with LCD or passive matrix screens, blinking can cause the cursor to disappear. This occurs when the screen display cannot keep up with the blink rate. It is recommended that users with such systems use a blink rate of once every five seconds or less.

The Start Blinking After value controls how long Mouse Warp will wait before starting to blink the cursor.

X-Y Display

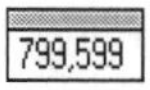

799,599

Figure 3: The X-Y Display window, in this case, shows that the mouse pointer is 799 pixels from the left edge of the screen and 599 pixels from the top.

The X-Y Display window shows the precise location of the cursor, measured in pixels. When used in conjunction with the Keyboard Mouse, it can be a powerful tool for illustrators and graphic artists.

The X-Y Display dialog presents you with the following options:

Show Display Window

When this option is selected, the display window will be shown.

Always On Top

When this option is selected, the X-Y Display window will remain on top and visible when you switch to another application. This is useful when performing detailed editing in an application that is maximized (full screen) and would otherwise cover the display window.

Position

The position options select the location of the display window.

Run Screen Saver Menu Option

The Run Screen Saver option is located in the Mouse Warp menu, which appears when you click once on the Mouse Warp Icon. When this option is selected, the default Windows screen saver will be started. After selecting this option, do not move the mouse; otherwise, the screen saver will be stopped.

Note that this feature will only activate screen savers that use the Windows Control Panel for selection and configuration. This feature may not work with third-party screen savers that use their own configuration system instead of the one in the Control Panel. Most of the professional screen saver packages provide instructions as to how to integrate them into the Windows Control Panel.

If you have selected the Hide Icon option in Mouse Warp, the Run Screen saver option will not be available because the Mouse Warp icon will be hidden. In this case, you might consider assigning the middle or right button of your mouse to "Run Screen Saver" using the Buttons dialog box. Once this is done, you can activate the screen saver with the single click of a button.

License and Disclaimer

Mouse Warp Version 2.0 is shareware. It may be copied and distributed freely under the following conditions:

1) No modifications are to be made to Mouse Warp or the accompanying documentation, including the help file.
2) All files in the original distribution package must be transmitted together.
3) No fee may be charged for the distribution of Mouse Warp other than to cover the cost of the distribution medium or service itself.

Mouse Warp is provided *as is*. Toggle Booleans will in no way be responsible, in financial or any other terms, for damages (both consequential and incidental) resulting from the use or misuse of Mouse Warp.

About Mouse Warp

If you use Mouse Warp regularly, please take the time to register your copy. In return, you will receive the latest version of Mouse Warp as well as a complimentary copy of the Toggle Booleans Screen Saver, which is only available to our registered customers.

To register your copy of Mouse Warp and receive the latest version, send a check or money order for $20 U.S. or $24 Canadian to the address below. International customers, please send an international money order for $20 U.S.

When you register Mouse Warp, send in any suggestions you have for other mouse features, and we'll see if we can include them in the next release. Many of the features added to this version were included at the request of our registered customers.

Toggle Booleans
P.O. Box 4204
Station E
Ottawa, Ontario
Canada, K1S 5B2

Name: _____

Address: _____

_____

City, State, Zip: _____

Plug-In

Version 1.31
Copyright © Plannet Crafters Inc.

*O*ne *of the most common wishes of Windows users is to replace the Program Manager with something more powerful, more customizable. Plug-In could be the answer to your prayers.*

Plug-In works with Program Manager — turning it into a more muscular program-launching system — rather than replacing it entirely. This solves some rare problems with a few Windows applications that won't install properly unless the Program Manager is running somewhere. But you also get all the advantages of the enhanced Plug-In interface.

Plug-In gives you the ability to activate and deactivate group windows (which is easier to deal with than "nesting" groups within groups within groups). It modifies your minimized group window icons, so they don't all look the same. It reports free RAM and Free System Resources in an easy-to-find format. It modifies your mouse pointers and other system cursors. And it does much more than this. Take a look at this chapter, and I'm sure you'll find several features you can benefit from.

Type of Program: Program Manager enhancement.

Requires: Windows 3.1 or higher. (Window 3.0 users, see "Note to Windows 3.0 Users" section in this chapter.)

Registration: Use the form at the end of this chapter to register with the shareware author.

Technical Support: Plannet Crafters Inc. supplies registered users with technical support by phone, fax, mail, CompuServe, Internet, America OnLine, BIX, GEnie, Prodigy, and MCI Mail.

Similar Shareware: Sloop Manager, featured elsewhere in *More Windows 3.1 Secrets,* and Group Icon, featured in *Windows Gizmos,* are other, different Program Manager enhancements.

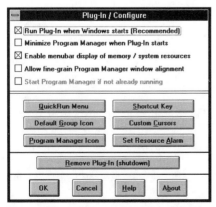

Figure 1: The Plug-In configuration dialog box allows you to customize many aspects of Program Manager, as well as Windows' mouse pointers, cursors, and other features.

Installation Notes

Once WSETUP on the *More Windows 3.1 Secrets* Diskette 1 has unarchived and copied all of Plug-In's files to a directory on your hard disk (e.g., C:\SECRETS2\PLUGIN), run PLUGIN.EXE from Windows. The first time you use it, Plug-In has a built-in install program that copies a few small files to the Windows directory and creates an initialization file. For more information, see the "Some Details about the Installation Procedure" topic later in this chapter.

Keep in mind that Plug-In is fully integrated with Program Manager. To access Plug-In, you use Program Manager's menus!

Once installed, you should refer to

The Quick Tour section in Plug-In's on-line Help.

Configure Plug-In (Options menu in Program Manager).

That's all there is to it! We hope you enjoy the program. The trial license for Plug-In allows you to use it for a period of 21 days, after which time you must register it if you continue using it. When you receive your registration number, simply enter it in the Enter Registration Number dialog.

What Is Plug-In for Program Manager?

Plug-In is a utility that dramatically improves Program Manager.

Plug-In has received press coverage in numerous journals, including *PC Magazine, PC/ Computing, Byte,* and *Windows Magazine.* It is a recipient of the 1993 *Windows Magazine* WinAward for the top 100 Windows products. It won the *Byte* 1993 "User's Choice Award for Shareware of the Year" (Jerry Pournelle, *Byte* Magazine).

Instead of replacing Program Manager, Plug-In simply makes it better. When you run Plug-In, additional items are added to Program Manager's menus, and existing commands are enhanced.

Features include

- ◆ Complete group-file management, including the ability to
  - • Copy groups.
  - • Instantly activate or deactivate groups. (Deactivated groups stay on disk, but are removed from Program Manager.)
  - • Reset all group windows to their original positions.
  - • Dynamically change the StartUp group.
- ◆ The best and easiest way ever to change icons — much better than what Program Manager normally gives you. Allows visual browsing, and includes a Speed List feature to get to your favorite icons in lightning time.
- ◆ Each group can be assigned an icon of its own! In addition, you can change the default group icon.
- ◆ Cursors (the standard pointer and the hourglass/wait cursor) can be replaced with a selection of alternates.
- ◆ An enhanced Run command, including a history list, browse feature, and various runtime options.
- ◆ A single menu choice will install a new Windows application. Just place an installation diskette in a drive — you will be given a chance to view any ReadMe files prior to installation.

- Improved "Exit Windows" dialog also allows you to restart Windows.
- A convenient menu option to "Save Settings Now."
- Enhanced group window commands allow you to minimize all open groups at once, as well as do both vertical and horizontal tiling.
- Free System Resources and available memory are constantly displayed on Program Manager's menu bar, and in Program Manager's icon when it is minimized. (This is fully configurable.)
- An alarm can be set to warn you of low Free System Resources and/or memory.
- Detailed system information includes system resources, memory, system configuration, running applications, Windows up-time, and much more.
- The QuickRun menu provides an easy way to access frequently run applications.
- Full support is provided for Program Manager's Restriction settings. This is particularly valuable for use by corporate system administrators.
- Complete context-sensitive help is available from all dialogs. The help file provides a complete user's guide for Plug-In.
- Supports standard multimedia sound associations for dialogs and alarms.
- Other features include a customizable shortcut key, fine-grained ProgMan alignment, the ability to start ProgMan if not already running, and much more.
- The cost for registration is only $20 plus shipping/handling.

Quick Tour

Plug-In is designed to be extremely easy to use, as it is a natural extension to the Windows Program Manager. Following is a quick tour of some of the more exciting features. Please refer to the help on individual commands for full details.

- First of all, keep in mind that Plug-In becomes an integral part of Program Manager. The commands in Plug-In are all accessed directly through Program Manager's menus.
- Explore the Configure Plug-In dialog box for full control over Plug-In's behavior.
- Take a moment to familiarize yourself with the new commands offered by Plug-In (see "Commands" for full details). Note that there are some totally new commands, as well as some existing commands (e.g., Run and Exit) that have been enhanced by Plug-In.
- Use the Group functions (Groups Copy, Groups Manage, Groups Reposition, Groups StartUp). These are very powerful and provide a number of features missing from Program Manager. And don't forget to take advantage of the external Group utility (see "Using the External Group Utility" for full details).
- The next time you wish to install a new Windows application, use the "Install Application" command (available on the File menu).
- Take a look at the Run command. It has a number of new features, including a history of your last 25 run commands.
- Use the QuickRun menu to gain instant access to your frequently used applications and files.
- Use the Save Settings Now command to organize Program Manager just the way you like and keep it that way! Have fun changing your icons for items and groups (Change Icon) with Plug-In's powerful icon browser.

♦ Notice that you can view your available memory and Free System Resources constantly. When Program Manager is open, this info is displayed on the right side of the menu bar. When Program Manager is minimized, this info is displayed in its icon. Of course, this is all totally configurable. See Configure Plug-In for details.

♦ Use System Info! It's got a lot of information about your Windows environment. It helps you to understand how your system is configured and how your applications are using memory.

♦ If you are running Windows 3.1, you can use the Ctrl+Alt+P key sequence from anywhere (even in a full-screen DOS app) to instantly return to Program Manager! The shortcut key can be changed by selecting Shortcut Key from the configuration dialog box.

♦ Don't forget to take advantage of the two new items in the Windows menu (Tile Horizontally and Minimize All Groups).

Commands

Note: Pressing the Help button or the F1 key while in a Plug-In dialog will bring up the help screen for that dialog.

File Menu

Groups Copy (3.1 only)

Makes a copy of an existing group and adds it to Program Manager.

To copy a group:

1) Select an existing group from the list presented.

2) Enter a description for the new group. This should be unique.

3) Optionally enter a group filename. This is not required, as Plug-In will automatically create a unique filename.

Groups Manage

Allows instant activation and deactivation of individual groups. Deactivated groups remain on disk, but are removed from Program Manager.

Group management is a powerful feature of Plug-In. By controlling which groups are active at any given time, you can reduce clutter in Program Manager.

Following are some scenarios where Group Management is particularly useful:

1) You will find that most Windows applications will create a new group when they are installed. Often, there will be several items in the group, but you may find that you only use one or two of them regularly. You might wish to add the main application item to another group (e.g., Windows Applications) and deactivate the new group. If you ever need any of the other items in the group, simply reactivate it.

2) Some programs/files are not needed on a daily basis. Deactivating less frequently used groups reduces clutter on your Program Manager desktop, saves memory, and reduces the loadtime of Program Manager.

3) If you are using Windows 3.0, each group can consume a large amount of system resources. Deactivating unneeded groups will reduce this resource drain.

Hint: If you hold down the Shift key while closing an existing group (select Close from the group's system menu), the group will be deactivated.

Note: Don't confuse Group Deactivation with the File Delete operation. When you delete a group in Program Manager, it is gone for good (i.e., removed from disk). Plug-In's Group Management allows you to activate and deactivate groups without deleting them from disk.

Using the External Group Utility

The Group Utility is an external program you can use to activate and deactivate groups. Plug-In includes a separate, external utility (GROUP.EXE), which can be used to activate and deactivate groups. You can easily create a single item in a group that will activate/deactivate a specific group. Using this tool, you will have the power and flexibility of nested groups!

Usage:

GROUP ACTivate *groupname*

GROUP DEACTivate *groupname*

GROUP SWITCH *groupname*

Examples:

♦ GROUP ACT WINDOWS APPLICATIONS will activate the group Windows Applications.

♦ GROUP DEACT ACCESSORIES will deactivate the group Accessories.

♦ GROUP SWITCH ACCESSORIES will activate the group Accessories, if it is not activated, and will deactivate it if is currently active.

Notes:

♦ If the group cannot be activated or deactivated, a system beep will be heard.

♦ While using GROUP SWITCH is the easiest and most flexible, the other forms (ACTIVATE and DEACTIVATE) exist because they will execute slightly faster.

♦ You might wish to use the GROUP SWITCH method in a QuickRun menu item to quickly activate and/or deactivate a group.

Refer to QuickRun Menu for more details.

Group Management *vs.* Nested Groups

You may be curious why Plug-In does not support nested groups (i.e., groups within groups). Nested groups are popular in other third-party shells, and are a nice way to organize your programs and files. However, the philosophy of Plug-In is to enhance Program Manager without getting rid of it. As there was not a stable, consistent method of implementing nested groups within the confines of Program Manager, the designers of Plug-In opted to use Group Management instead. After working with the Group Management features, you will find that it provides a high degree of flexibility in organizing your programs and files.

Groups Reposition (Windows 3.1 only)

Repositions all groups to their original positions (at the time of the last save). This command will reposition all the groups to their saved positions. This is particularly useful if you have resized a lot of group windows (through tiling/cascading, etc.) and your Program Manager desktop is a mess.

Note: This command will not reposition the items inside a group, unless you have Auto Arrange enabled (under the Options menu).

Note: This command will also reposition Program Manager's main window to its saved position.

Groups StartUp (Windows 3.1 only)

Changes (or disables) the designated StartUp group that will be executed when Windows starts.

The StartUp group is a special group. All the items contained within it are executed when Windows is started. This is useful for programs or utilities that you always want running. For example, you may wish the File Manager and Calendar to be run whenever you start Windows. Simply copy them to the StartUp group by holding the Ctrl key down while dragging the item from the original group to the StartUp group.

The default StartUp group is named StartUp. However, with the StartUp dialog you can select any group to be the StartUp group. For example, you might wish to assign a different group as your StartUp group while working on a particular project.

If you wish to temporarily disable your StartUp group, simply select No StartUp Group from the StartUp dialog.

Change Icon

Changes the icon for a group or item (also used to browse for cursors).

The Change Icon dialog is a powerful and easy way to change the icon assigned to a group or item.

Please note the usage of the Change Icon dialog in the following situations:

> When changing the icon for an item inside of a group: Select (highlight) the item in the group and then select Change Icon.

> When changing the icon for a group: Select (highlight) the minimized group and then select Change Icon.

> When changing the default group icon: Select the Default Group Icon button in the Configure Plug-In dialog (accessed via the Options menu in Program Manager).

> When browsing for a cursor: Select the Browse button in the Custom Cursors dialog (accessed via the Configure Plug-In dialog).

Note that the title of the Change Icon dialog will reflect the current operation.

Shortcut key: Alt+I

Note: There is a small anomaly ("bug") in Program Manager. When you're changing the icon (or any other property) for an item after its group window has been scrolled, the item may change positions in the group the next time you run Windows. The solution to this problem is to do a Save Settings Now (or save the settings when you Exit Windows) after changing icons or any other property for items that meet the above condition. If you don't save your settings, and your icons are displaced when you next start Windows, simply rearrange your icons in the affected group and do a Save Settings Now. To repeat, this is a bug in Program Manager, not Plug-In!

Note: Don't confuse Plug-In's Change Icon command with the under-powered Change Icon provided inside of Program Manager's Properties dialog.

Editing and Using the Speed List

Use the Speed List to gain lightning-fast access to your icon collection.

The Speed List is a simple helper which lets you get access to your icon collections with lightning speed.

To use a Speed List entry, simply select an item from the drop-down list in the Change Icon dialog. You will instantly be "transported" to the location specified by the Speed List.

To edit the Speed List, select the Edit Speed List button inside the Change Icon dialog. In the Path field, you can enter either a full path to an icon or icon library (e.g., C:\WINDOWS\PROGMAN.EXE), or you can enter a path without a filename (e.g., C:\MYICONS). Selecting the Paste button will paste the currently selected icon or icon library in the Path field.

You may have up to 20 Speed List entries.

Using the Default Icon button

The Default Icon button resets an icon to its original (default) icon.

Item Icon

The default icon for an item is the first icon which appears in an application's executable file. For example, if you change the icon of File Manager and later want to reset it to its original icon, simply select the Default Icon button.

Group Icon

When you're changing a group icon, selecting the Default Icon button will reset the icon to whatever you have defined as the Default Group Icon.

Default Group Icon

When you're changing the Default Group Icon, selecting the Default Icon button will reset the Default Group Icon to Program Manager's default.

Run

An enhanced run command with a history list, browse, and run options.

The Run command is used to start applications and/or open documents.

Each time you enter a run command, it is saved in a history list. Use the drop-down Command Line to access the history list.

You can choose to have the application start in normal, minimized, or maximized states.

If you don't know the name of the application or document, selecting the Browse button will bring up the Browse dialog. If you enter a path without a filename and end it with a backslash, the Browse command will automatically switch to that directory. For example, you could enter C:\WINDOWS\ in the command line and select Browse to view the files in the Windows directory. The Run command has full support for application associations. For example, if you enter README.TXT in the command line, this file will be loaded into NotePad.

Shortcut Key: Alt+R

Using the QuickDOS Feature

QuickDOS executes a DOS command (including DOS internal commands) directly from within the Run dialog.

You can use the QuickDOS feature of the Run Command to quickly execute a DOS command. For example, you can enter DEL C:*.TMP in the Command Line, check the QuickDOS box, and press Enter. This will create a DOS command shell and execute the command line you specified.

Some examples:

1) Enter DIR A:*.DOC in the Command Line and select QuickDOS. Doing a quick directory list in DOS might often be quicker than using File Manager for some tasks.
2) Enter COPY C:\MYDOCS*.DOC A:\SAVEDOCS and select QuickDOS. You might select Run Minimized and put this in the QuickRun menu. Then you could do backups of your documents quickly and in the background (assuming you are running Windows in Enhanced mode).

You can use the QuickDOS feature when you define items in the QuickRun menu.

Install Application

Runs an installation program, while first allowing you to view any ReadMe files.

Most manuals for Windows applications instruct you to select File Run and then enter A:\INSTALL.EXE (or something similar) to start the installation process. With the Install Application command, installing a new program is a cinch!

Just place a diskette in either drive A or B and select the Install Application command. If there are any ReadMe files on the diskette, you will be given a chance to view these before proceeding with the installation (in general, it is highly recommended that you always read the ReadMe files!).

If the installation program is located in another location than drive A or B, a dialog box, Install Path, will prompt you for the location of the installation program and files.

Install Application will look for either SETUP.EXE or INSTALL.EXE. If Plug-In can't find an installation program on your application diskette, please refer to the installation instructions that came with the new product.

Exit Windows

Exit or Restart Windows.

This command will allow you to end your Windows session. You are given the option of saving your Program Manager settings prior to exiting. However, you might find it easier to create your environment the way you like it and select the Save Settings Now command.

Note that the Save Settings option in Program Manager will determine whether Exit or Exit (Save Settings) is the default.

You are also given the option to Restart Windows. This will restart your Windows session without returning to the DOS prompt, and is quicker than exiting Windows and typing WIN again to restart. This can be useful under a number of circumstances. Many (particularly older) applications don't properly free system resources. If you notice your system resources dropping over time, restarting Windows will get back those lost resources. Also, if you find Windows becoming unstable for any reason, restarting it might be prudent.

Note: There is a small anomaly ("bug") in Program Manager. When you're creating or changing the properties for an item after its group window has been scrolled, the item may change positions in the group the next time you run Windows. The solution to this problem is to do a Save Settings Now (or save the settings when you Exit Windows) after changing any properties for items that meet the above condition. If you don't save your settings, and your icons are displaced when you next start Windows, simply rearrange your icons in the affected group and do a Save Settings Now. To repeat, this is a bug in Program Manager, not Plug-In!

Options Menu

Save Settings Now

Saves the current state of Program Manager's desktop configuration.

The only documented way to save your Program Manager settings is to select "Save Settings On Exit." However, you will often find that your Program Manager desktop is a mess when you wish to exit and you don't want it saved.

In general, it is recommended that you do not use Save Settings On Exit (on the Options menu in Program Manager for Windows 3.1). You will find it much "cleaner" to organize Program Manager the way you like and select Save Settings Now to save it. This way you are assured that Program Manager will always start in the same, organized state.

An additional advantage of turning off Save Settings On Exit is that exiting Windows will be faster!

Note: There is a small anomaly ("bug") in Program Manager. When creating or changing the properties for an item after its group window has been scrolled, the item may change positions in the group the next time you run Windows. The solution to this problem is to do a Save Settings Now (or save the settings when you Exit Windows) after changing any properties for items that meet the above condition. If you don't save your settings, and your icons are displaced when you next start Windows, simply rearrange your icons in the affected group and do a "Save Settings Now." To repeat, this is a bug in Program Manager, not Plug-In!

Note: If you find that your Program Manager groups have become a mess (e.g., you tiled/cascaded or otherwise resized the groups) and you want to revert to your clean, saved state, simply select Groups Reposition.

System Info

Displays information on Windows up-time, system configuration, memory utilization, and active Windows applications.

Windows Up Time

The first item tells you how long (in days, minutes, and seconds) Windows has been active. This is the amount of time since you last loaded Windows. Just think ... now you can have a contest with your friends and fellow workers to see who can keep Windows alive the longest!

System

The system information consists of DOS version, Windows version and operating mode, Mouse type, Network type, Video resolution and number of colors supported, and Processor type and whether or not a math coprocessor is present.

Memory

The memory information consists of the percentage free of the USER and GDI heaps and the total amount of memory available. The amount of Free System Resources is calculated as the lower value of the USER and GDI heaps. These heaps should ideally be completely irrelevant to a non-programmer. However, due to limitations on the size of the heaps, it turns out that Windows often runs out of heap space before running out of physical memory. The USER heap is used to store things like windows structures and menus, while the GDI heap is used for graphical things like pens, brushes, regions, bitmaps, etc.

The Detail Button will bring up a dialog of further memory information. Note that this button is enabled for Windows enhanced mode only.

System Info/Memory Details

Provides details on memory configuration and utilization (enhanced mode only).

Physical Memory

This section gives you details on how the actual memory on your computer is being utilized.

Total Memory is the amount of memory installed on your system. The first figure is in kilobytes (1024 bytes is equal to 1K). The second figure is the number of megabytes (1024 kilobytes is equal to 1MB), and may be rounded up or down to adjust for small anomalies in the way the memory is used by your system. If you have an expanded memory (EMS) board, the amount of EMS memory on the board will not be included in this total.

Managed By DOS includes all memory "owned/managed" by DOS before Windows is started. Many things can be included in DOS memory, including DOS itself, Smart Drive, TSRs, etc. If you start DOS applications from within Windows, the memory used by the DOS app is taken from the Windows memory pool.

Managed by Windows includes all memory "owned/managed" by Windows.

Virtual Memory

"Swap File Size" is the actual size of your swap file. A swap file is a disk-based file that is used to swap (or page) chunks of memory when the system is low on memory. A swap file is used by Windows when running in 386-Enhanced mode. Using a swap file can allow you to run many more programs than can actually fit in your physical memory, and is a big benefit of the advanced Intel processors. Swap files are set up using the Control Panel (386 Enhanced icon).

"Swap Threshold" is an indicator of whether or not you are actively swapping to disk. If this value is very small or negative, there is a good chance that you are actively swapping memory. You may not notice much activity until you switch to an application that has been dormant for some time ... at which point you may notice the disk chugging. If it seems that your applications have slowed down substantially, take a look at the swap threshold. While virtual memory (swapping) is of substantial benefit, it does tend to slow things down a bit.

Windows Applications

The list box of Windows Applications shows active Windows apps. If there is an <H> in front of the application's name, this means that its main window is hidden. Various system utilities frequently hide their main windows. As you select each application, the amount of memory it is occupying will be displayed to the right of the list box. Discardable memory is the amount of memory that Windows can get rid of when it needs more memory for another application. Keep in mind that most applications will require a good portion of the discarded memory back when they are made active again.

Configure Plug-In

Configures and customizes Plug-In to suit your specific needs.

Check Box options

Run Plug-In when Windows starts (recommended).

This will configure Plug-In so it automatically starts whenever Windows is started. Under Windows 3.1, Plug-In is added to the StartUp group. Under Windows 3.0, Plug-In is added to the LOAD= line in the WIN.INI file.

If you use lots of different StartUp groups (Groups StartUp), you might wish to start Plug-In via the LOAD= line instead of placing it in each StartUp group.

Default: On

Minimize Program Manager when Plug-In starts

This will force Program Manager to be minimized when Plug-In is started.

Default: Off

Enable menu bar display of memory/system resources.

This will enable the display of memory and system resources on Program Manager's menubar (on the right-hand side). This display is of the form "xx.xxmb/yy%" where *xx.xx*mb represents the number of megabytes of free memory available, and *yy*% represents the percentage of free system resources.

Default: On

Allow fine-grain Program Manager window alignment (Windows 3.1 only)

Windows 3.1 Program Manager uses a technique called "byte alignment" that allows for slightly faster drawing of bitmaps within its main window. However, there is one problem with this method ... the main window of Program Manager cannot be smoothly aligned on the left side of the screen! Our research has shown that the speed benefits of byte alignment in Program Manager are very small on most systems.

To use this feature, check the box, select the OK button, and then position Program Manager's main window exactly where you want it. If you save Program Manager's settings (Save Settings Now), the window will be automatically repositioned to this saved position whenever Plug-In is started.

Default: Off

Start Program Manager if not already running

This will start Program Manager if it is not already running. This setting is only valid if Program Manager is not your Windows shell.

Default: On

Configuration Dialogs

How to Set up and Use the QuickRun Menu

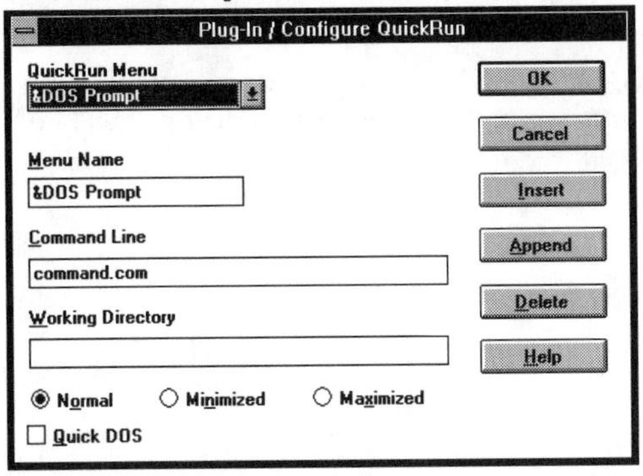

Figure 2: The QuickRun dialog box allows you to place commands on Program Manager pull-down menus.

QuickRun places frequently run applications on a separate menu (QuickRun) in Program Manager.

QuickRun is a drop-down menu which is added to Program Manager's main menu bar. It allows you to define menu items for frequently used commands.

Creating a QuickRun menu item is much like adding an item to Program Manager. You need to define a Command Line, Working Directory (optional), and execution options.

The "Menu Name" is what will appear in the menu to identify an item. You can place an ampersand (&) in front of a character in the "Menu Name" to create a shortcut key for that menu item (i.e., "&DOS Shell" will show up as "DOS Shell" in the menu, and can be accessed quickly by pressing the letter D when the menu is displayed).

An idea for a QuickRun menu item would be to use the External Group Utility as a QuickRun item. For example, you might create an item, Comm Group, which would activate or deactivate your communications group. The command for this would be GROUP SWITCH COMM GROUP.

The QuickRun configuration dialog is accessed through the Configure Plug-In dialog.

You may have up to 25 items in the QuickRun menu.

Default Group Icon

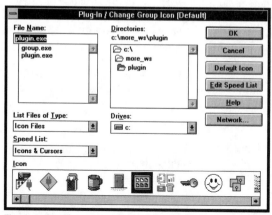

Figure 3: The Group Icon dialog box allows you to select from a wide variety of icons.

Select an icon to be used as the default for groups.

This dialog allows you to select the default icon that will be displayed for a group within Program Manager. If you select Default Icon from within the Change Icon dialog, it will be reset to Program Manager's internal default icon.

Program Manager Icon

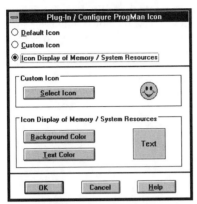

Figure 4: With Plug-In's ProgMan Icon dialog box, you can change the minimized Program Manager icon into a different icon or a convenient Free Ram/Free System Resources gauge.

Configure Program Manager's icon

You are given three choices for configuring the Program Manager icon (the icon displayed when Program Manager's main window is minimized):

1) Default Icon. This just displays Program Manager's default icon.

2) Custom Icon. This will display a custom icon that you have selected using the Select Icon button.

3) Icon Display of System Resources/Memory. This will show you the amount of memory available (top half, in megabytes) and the amount of free system resources (bottom half, as a percentage). You may use the Background Color and Text Color buttons to choose the colors used for this iconic display. Note that you must choose a solid color for the text from the dialogs (some colors are actually made up of patterned combinations of other colors). If you choose a patterned color, you simply won't get what you expected.

Shortcut Key (Windows 3.1 only)

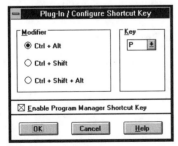

Figure 5: Choose almost any shortcut key you prefer in the Configure Shortcut Key dialog box.

Assign a shortcut key for Program Manager.

This allows you to assign a shortcut key for Program Manager itself. In Windows 3.1, a new feature in Program Manager allows you to assign a shortcut key when you define the properties of an item. However, there is no straightforward way to define a shortcut key for Program Manager itself.

Default: Ctrl+Alt+P

Custom Cursors

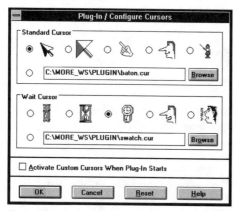

Figure 6: Not only your mouse pointer, but also the depressing Hourglass icon can be modified using Plug-In's amusing Custom Cursors dialog box.

Select Custom Cursors to replace the standard mouse pointer and hourglass. This dialog allows you to select custom cursors to replace the standard mouse pointer and hourglass (wait) cursors.

You can select one of the built-in cursors simply by clicking on it and pressing the OK button. Or you can browse for an individual cursor file (.CUR). Plug-In includes several cursor files (and even more when you register!).

If you select Activate Custom Cursors When Plug-In Starts, the cursors will be changed automatically every time you start Plug-In.

If you wish to revert to the original cursors, simply select the Reset button.

Set Resource Alarm

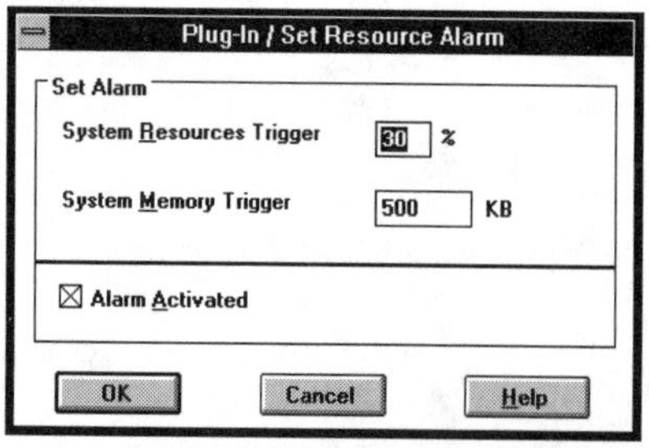

Figure 7: The System Resources and System Memory triggers can be useful to warn you to save your work or restart Windows after your resources fall to unstable levels.

This sets an alarm which will display a dialog box if you are low on either memory or system resources.

It is often handy to be warned of low memory or system resources before it becomes a problem. With the Resource Alarm feature, a dialog box is displayed if either system resources or memory falls below the trigger values.

The Alarm Activated check box is used to enable or disable the alarm.

When the alarm is activated, a dialog box will appear showing the current levels and the trigger values for both system resources and memory. If you press the OK button, the alarm will be reactivated with lowered trigger values (these new trigger values are not retained past the current Windows session). If the system resources were lower than the trigger value, the new trigger value would be 10% less than the present level. If the memory was lower than the trigger value, the new trigger value would be 250K less than the present level. If you wish, you can choose the "Disable Alarm" button to disable the alarm for the remainder of this Windows session (if you want to reenable the alarm, return to the Configuration dialog and press OK).

If you are running in enhanced mode and are using a swap file, you might wish to raise the value of the memory trigger to a higher value.

Note that if you set either trigger (memory or system resources) too low, Plug-In might not be able to get the resources to display the dialog box signifying you are low on resources!

Defaults: System Resources, 30%; Memory, 500K

Remove Plug-In (Shutdown)

Selecting the Remove Plug-In (Shutdown) button will remove Plug-In from memory. Under normal usage, there is no reason to use this button.

Register Me!

Full details and directions on how to register (order) Plug-In for Program Manager.

This brings up the same screen that you see when you first run Plug-In for Program Manager. It contains full instructions on how to register Plug-In. Remember that Plug-In is distributed as shareware, also known as "try-before-you-buy" marketing. If you continue to use this software, you must buy it!

Window Menu

Tile Horizontally (Windows 3.1 only)

Tiles open group windows so that they are wide rather than tall.

The Window Tile menu item in Program Manager will tile your group windows in a vertical (taller rather than wider) fashion. Tile Horizontal allows you to tile the group windows so that they are wide rather than tall.

Minimize All Groups

Minimizes all groups to icons.

This will minimize all open groups to their iconic state. This is particularly convenient if you have several groups open and they are overlapping each other.

Shortcut Key: Alt+N

Help Menu

Plug-In Help Index

Brings up the help file for Plug-In for Program Manager, starting at the Main Index.

About Plug-In

Displays copyright and version information.

This is your standard About box. Nothing exciting. No hidden developer (gang) screens...

User's Guide in On-Line Help

Plug-In contains a complete User's Guide in its on-line help system. You can select the "Help" button (or press F1) in all dialogs to go directly to specific help for that dialog.

Updating from a Previous Version of Plug-In

Note: If you installed an older version of Plug-In, the following steps will retain your current configuration for Plug-In.

1) Shut down Plug-In by clicking the Remove Plug-In (Shutdown) button in the Configure Plug-In dialog (Options menu in ProgMan).

2) Copy the most recent version of Plug-In files into the *same* directory currently used for Plug-In (e.g., C:\PLUGIN). It is OK to overwrite the existing files in this directory.

3) Copy GROUP.EXE to your Windows directory. (Please don't forget to do this!)

4) You are now updated! Simply run PLUGIN.EXE to continue.

International Issues

Plug-In will operate under international versions of Windows. However, there is one thing you must do for proper operation if you are using Windows 3.1: Using NotePad, edit PROGMAN.INI and define your StartUp group under the [Settings] section (e.g., STARTUP=AUTOSTART).

We are planning fully internationalized versions of Plug-In for a future release. Contact us for more details.

Some Details about the Installation Procedure

After you use WSETUP to install Plug-In, if you get a message saying that "Plug-In is being installed from a location that may not be available during later Windows sessions," this means that Plug-In is being run for the first time from either a removable drive (i.e., a floppy drive) or a remote drive (i.e., a network drive). Plug-In sets up its initialization file to point to the location from which it was installed. Because of this, you should not install Plug-In from a floppy drive. However, it is fine to install from a network drive as long as it is always available from within Windows.

The Save Settings On Exit option in Program Manager is turned off during the installation (you can still save on exit if you wish). We recommend that you use Save Settings Now instead. Please refer to the on-line help for further details.

Plug-In sets itself up to load each time Windows is started. This is the best way to get optimal use out of the program. If you decide that you don't want to continue using Plug-In, simply disable the Run Plug-In When Windows Starts option in the configuration dialog.

Plug-In uses five files, which you should move to a directory on your Path if you wish to use them. These are

GROUP.EXE

PLUGINQN.PIF

PLUGINQN.BAT

PLUGINQM.PIF

PLUGINQM.BAT

These files only take up about 7K. They need to be in a directory listed in the Path environment variable. If you do not wish to have these files in your Windows directory, it is acceptable to place them elsewhere, as long as they are on your Path (e.g., you could move them into the directory with the rest of the Plug-In files, if you add this directory to your Path environment variable).

Two other very small files, PLUGIN.INI and PLUGIN.HST, are created and maintained in the Windows directory.

Installing from a CD-ROM Drive

If you are installing Plug-In from a CD-ROM drive, you must first copy all the files to a directory on your hard disk (e.g., C:\PLUGIN). Then run PLUGIN.EXE from the directory on your hard disk.

Obtaining the Most Up-To-Date Version of Plug-In

If, for whatever reason, you want to be *sure* that you have the absolute latest version of Plug-In, you may contact Plannet Crafters directly. We will ship you the latest version for a nominal charge of

$5 (including shipping/handling in the U.S. and Canada)

$8 (including shipping/handling for International orders)

Or you may obtain the latest version directly from the Plannet Crafters bulletin board system (BBS).

The Plannet Crafters BBS

Our bulletin board system (BBS) contains the latest version of Plug-In, as well as other products from Plannet Crafters.

It is available 24 hours a day, and supports baud rates up to 14.4Kbps. The number is (404) 740-8583.

Keeping Backups of Plug-In's Data Files

It is always a good idea to back up your data files! Most of Plug-In's configuration data is kept in one file, PLUGIN.INI, which resides in the Windows directory. Another file, PLUGIN.HST (also in the Windows directory), maintains the history list for the run command. Both of these files are small, and a simple backup procedure is to copy them to a floppy disk on occasion.

While on the topic of backups, you might also wish to keep backups of your group files. Simply copy *.GRP (the group files) and *.G_P (the deactivated group files) from your Windows directory to a floppy disk.

Using Microsoft's MS-Mouse Utility (8.10 or 8.20)

If you wish to use this utility, and also want to make use of Plug-In's custom cursors, you must not use the "growth" feature in the MS-Mouse utility. For more details, refer to the on-line Help.

Note to Windows 3.0 Users

There are a few commands (some of the group functions and tile horizontal) that are available only under Windows 3.1. The unavailable commands will be grayed out (disabled) in the menus.

Plug-In requires two .DLL files which are a part of the Windows 3.1 retail package. These files are COMMDLG.DLL and TOOLHELP.DLL. If you don't have access to these files, you may contact Plannet Crafters and we will help you obtain them.

Please be sure that you have the current versions of these .DLL files on your system. If either of these .DLLs is dated earlier than March 10, 1992, you should try to obtain more current versions.

How to De-Install Plug-In

If you wish to de-install Plug-In from a system, do the following:

1) Disable the Run Plug-In When Windows Starts item in the Config dialog and click the OK button. (If you fail to do this, you must manually remove the Plug-In entry from either the StartUp group or the LOAD= line in the WIN.INI file.)
2) Shut down Plug-In by selecting Remove Plug-In in the Config dialog.
3) In the Windows directory, delete the following files: PLUGINQ?.*, PLUGIN.INI, PLUGIN.HST, GROUP.EXE.
4) Delete all files in Plug-In's home directory (assuming this directory contains *only* Plug-In files!)

How to Contact Plannet Crafters

If you have any questions about Plug-In, please contact us at:

Plannet Crafters Inc.
2580 Runic Way
Alpharetta, GA 30202 USA

Phone: (404) 740-9821 (9a.m. – 6p.m. Eastern U.S. Time)

Fax: (404) 740-1914 (24 hours a day)

BBS: (404) 740-8583 (14.4 Kbps; 24 hours a day)

E-mail addresses:

    CompuServe: 73040,334

    Internet: 73040.334@compuserve.com

    America OnLine: DMandell

    BIX: dmandell

    GEnie: D.MANDELL1

    Prodigy: VSFB48A

    MCI Mail: 572-7179

Thank you for trying Plug-In for Program Manager!

Plug-In for Program Manager Registration Form _____

Name: _____

Title: _____

Company: _____

Address: _____

City: _____ State: _____ Zip: _____

Country: _____

Daytime Phone: _____

E-mail Address: _____

E-mail Service: _____

Where did you obtain this copy?: _____

Disk Size: _____ 3.5"   _____ 5.25"

_____Copy(ies) at $20 each   _____

Shipping Handling

U.S. and Canada $2   _____

International $5   _____

Total   _____

Payment Information (U.S. $ Only!)

_____Cash _____Check/Money Order _____Visa

_____MasterCard _____American Express

Card Number: _____ Expiration Date: _____

Signature: _____

PRClock

Version 2.1
Copyright © Peter Rodwell

If you've ever wondered, "Is it too late to call Tokyo?" PRClock is for you. Peter Rodwell's simple little utility, which sits in the corner of your screen, will give you the answer immediately.

When you first run PRClock, click the System Menu icon once and select PRClock Zones. This displays the dialog box in Figure 1, which allows you to choose the cities you wish to keep track of.

Type of Program:	Time Zone Clock.
Requires:	Windows 3.0 or higher.
Registration:	Free. This program requires no registration.
Technical Support:	None.
Similar Shareware:	X World Clock, a program featured in *Windows 3.1 Secrets*, also displays the time in various cities of the world, as well as sets alarms, but takes up more memory and space than PRClock. If you want a full-blown alarm and scheduling system, check out ClockMan in *Windows 3.1 Secrets* and Reminder elsewhere in this book.

Figure 1: This dialog box, which appears when you click PRClock Zones from the System menu, allows you to select the locations to display and choose between American and international date formats.

Overview

PRClock is a program that displays the time in four different areas of the world — your own time zone plus three others, as well as showing the date in your area.

Operation

PRClock uses your computer's internal clock to display the time. If your computer's clock is wrong, then PRClock will show the wrong time. As most computers do not pretend to be particularly accurate clocks, it's worth checking the time occasionally and resetting it if necessary. Use the DOS TIME command or the Date/Time section of the Windows Control Panel.

You can select the times PRClock displays by selecting the PRClock Zones option on the System menu. This displays a list of some 200+ cities and countries. In Figure 2, the four currently selected zones are displayed — select one of these and then select a time zone from the list. The OK button saves the new configuration; the Cancel button exits the Zones panel without saving the changes. The panel also allows you to select whether the date is to be displayed in MM-DD-YY format (12-31-94) or as DD-MM-YY (31-12-94).

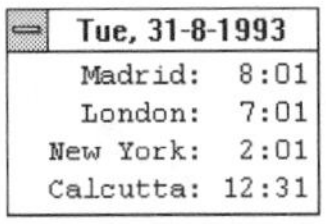

```
╤    Tue, 31-8-1993
    Madrid:   8:01
    London:   7:01
  New York:   2:01
  Calcutta: 12:31
```

Figure 2: PRClock uses a tiny window to keep you informed of the current time in any parts of the world you wish. It even tracks accurately those time zones that are 30 minutes from their neighboring zone, not a full hour, such as Calcutta.

Configuration File

PRClock creates a small configuration file called PRCLOCK.CNF in your Windows directory. In addition to details of the selected time zones and the dates format, this also contains the position of PRClock when it is closed. If you move the clock panel and then close it, it will reappear at the new position when next you start it.

Reminder

Version 2.0
Copyright © Wilson WindowWare, Inc.

Reminder is a program that almost all of us can use. If you've ever said, "Why can't a computer help me track all these events, meetings, and occasions?" then Reminder is for you.

Of course, you must type a few words so that Reminder can help you. But after you get started, I think you'll find that it isn't as bad as you thought it would be. And for those of you lucky enough to have assistants or staff, assigning them to put the group's schedule into Reminder is a great way to use their skills!

Type of Program:	Calendar.
Requires:	Windows 3.0 or higher.
Registration:	Use the form at the end of this chapter to register with the shareware author.
Technical Support:	Wilson WindowWare provides registered users with technical support by telephone, fax, and CompuServe.
Similar Shareware:	ClockMan, a program featured in *Windows 3.1 Secrets,* is a scheduling program with a different feature set than Reminder.

Welcome to Windows Reminder!

Windows Reminder is a new time-management program written exclusively for the new Windows. The program is both simple to use, yet powerful enough to do your work for you without your having to be there!

Functional

Windows Reminder lets you set up and view your appointments as easily as possible. You can visually see the times you have scheduled in the graph display. The graph also allows you to click on the time you want to enter a new item for. Items or tasks are sorted by date and time, which places all items needing attention at the top so you can see what is next on your list. A time is not required so you can still enter a task that needs to be done that day. Enter in a time and Windows Reminder will automatically set the alarm to display your message or run other programs. A repeat option is also provided for daily, weekly, monthly, and end-of-month events. Windows Reminder displays the time and date when running as an icon so you can always track the time.

Set up "To Do" or "Task" lists for yourself and others to keep track of dates, times, and milestones.

Set alarms to remind you of items that have to be done or places you have to be. You can set reminder to chime on the hour, ½, and ¼ hour. If you have Multimedia installed, you will hear the chimes from Control Panel.

Set alarms to start other tasks without your being there.

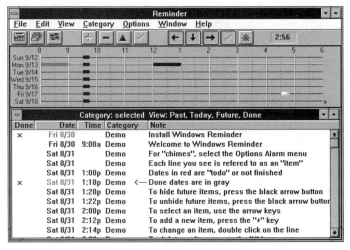

Figure 1: Reminder is a powerful but easy-to-use scheduling program that helps you organize your time.

Generate status reports at any time based on the items you have done and that are still on your list of items that need to be done or need your attention. Collect the time spent on each item for time management reports.

Windows Reminder tracks completed items and creates a log file when you delete your items to a file (see the Options Preference menu to set this.)

Versatile

You can group your items by category for easy viewing and printing of status reports. The category list can be used to schedule what others in your group need to be on top of. This helps with daily assignments and long-term goals by allowing you to schedule different intervals in which to monitor your progress. You can also assign your own personal priorities, like ASAP, by replacing the time field for each item.

As you enter each item, they are sorted automatically by date and time or by your own personal priorities so that you can always see what is next on your list of items to do. For easy viewing, dates are displayed in different colors depending if they are past, present, or future items to do or if they are done so that you can instantly *see* what needs to be done next.

Easy to use

Windows Reminder makes it as simple as possible to enter and edit items by taking full advantage of a control bar with three dimensional buttons, full keyboard support, a Calendar program, Pen Windows support, and a sophisticated On-line Help complete with *Jump Words* for easy access and look-up.

The Windows Reminder control bar gives you quick access to editing and viewing items along with a corresponding key on the keyboard to allow you the same access. The current time is displayed on the right side of the control bar, and an alarm picture is displayed only when there is a time set to go off for the current day. This gives you the added benefit of adding items that have to be done a certain day but have no set time.

The Edit section of the control bar allows you to quickly edit an item. To create a new item to be reminded of, you can choose the + button on the control bar, the + key on the keyboard, the Edit Add menu item, the F5 function key, or double-click on the day you want in the Calendar program.

The View section of the control bar allows you to quickly view the items by past, present, future, and done dates. To view just those items you need to do from the past and today, you just select the left-arrow key (for past) and the down-arrow key (for now or today). If you also want to view what you have done for the same time frame, just press the Check button. You can use the F9–F12 keys to press the same buttons or use the View menu commands. The asterisk at the end is for viewing everything at once by pressing all the buttons down.

Windows Reminder comes with a Calendar program that lets you view the days in a month and scroll to other months and years. It can even print calanders! If Windows Reminder isn't running, Calendar starts it for you by double-clicking on a date. The Enter New Item dialog box opens automatically for you with the selected date already placed in the date field. Any time the Edit Item dialog box is open, you can use Calendar to enter or change the date and time just by clicking the mouse on the date you want and using the right mouse button to select the time.

Powerful Date Transfer and Dynamic Data Exchange (DDE) Windows Reminder data is copied to the Clipboard as tab-delimited text that can then be used with any editor and any spreadsheet program or other program that accepts a tab delimited ASCII file. Windows Reminder also accepts data from the Clipboard that is only space delimited for easy importing.

Windows Reminder supports Dynamic Data Exchange (DDE) as both a Client starting other DDE conversations requesting information and also as a Server so that data can be passed back and forth with other DDE programs. A sample template file for Microsoft Word for Windows and macro sheet for Microsoft Excel is supplied to show you how you can automatically generate different reports with different combinations of monthly and/or items listed by a specific *category*.

Powerful alarm actions

Windows Reminder allows a number of different actions to take place when an alarm goes off. You select the action to take place when you enter your message, and it can be changed at any time. The Run Action automatically starts another Windows or DOS application. Run DDE starts a DDE conversation with another application to run a macro that gathers information from a database or electronic news service that places the information into another application.

When an alarm goes off, your message is displayed for you. You are then given four choices of what you want to do with the message:

1. Do nothing so that you can decide what you want to do with it later.
2. Select the Mark as Done check box to indicate that you no longer need to be reminded of the message.
3. If you are busy when the message is displayed, you can set the Repeat in *?* minutes, a *snooze* option, and press the Reset Time button so the message will be displayed again in the extra time you selected. This is really handy when you are on the phone.
4. Select the Reschedule button to open the message for editing so that you can change the date, time, or any other information. You can reset the item to the next day, week, month, or year, and it also bumps the day to Monday if you use the Business Day option.

When the Run with Prompt or Run DDE with Prompt action item is selected or you select the Option Run menu command, the Run dialog box is open. Here you see the message you had scheduled if it was from an alarm going off, or you can change or enter any command to start up another application or enter in a DDE command. You don't need to run Program Manager or File Manager to start another application.

Late-breaking news

In the new 2.0 version, easier, intuitive, eye-pleasing dialog boxes are part of the new look. Help files are completely reworked. Be sure to go through the help files to learn all about the many new features

Note for Visual Basic programmers: To use the Visual Basic DDE demo program, which illustrates how to access Reminder from a Visual Basic progrm, you need either Visual Basic installed on your system, or at least the file VBRUN100.DLL. The VBRUN100.DLL file may be obtained from any number of BBSs, shareware disk vendors, CompuServe, or by calling our BBS. Because of its size, VBRUN100.DLL is not included with this product. (To connect with the BBS, call 206-935-5198 with your modem. We use USR HST/V.32bis, V.42bis, 14,400+, 8N1. Although we still allow 2400 baud connects as of January 1993, we are considering requiring at least a 9600 baud modem in the future. Connects at 1200 baud and below will not be permitted to log on.)

Overview

Windows Reminder is a Windows application that maintains a "to do" or task list of items that you want to be reminded of. An *item* can be thought of as a specific event such as:

```
Dinner at 6:00 with Fred
Airplane leaves at 8:45.
```

Because a time is not required, you can make a list of errands to do for any day, print the list to carry it with you, or give to others as a reminder.

This list can track items for you, others in your family, or co-workers. If you choose not to delete the item, you will have a log of items accomplished. This comes in handy when you need to give a status report of your work or progress on a project. Reminder can also print reports with details on how long each item took to complete.

Windows Reminder uses DDE — see DDE with Reminder — so you can automatically generate a number of reports such as status of a project, time logged or month-end reports by category or all categories.

Getting Started

The quickest way to get started is to enter an item with the + key. You only need three pieces of information.

1. A date
2. A category
3. A note

A category is set to the default unless you create a category by typing a new one in. Categories allow you to group related items for viewing and reporting purposes.

You can also supply some optional information such as Time, order of importance, and if the item has already been done or not. The Category is used to group or view related items together. How you name your categories will be useful for you to quickly see different items.

For more information on different uses, see the "Reminder Uses" section.

WIN.INI settings

Reminder uses the following setting in WIN.INI. If they are not there, the defaults are used.

[Reminder]

3D	Places 3-D effects in dialog boxes; default is on, 1, off 0.
DialCmd	Dial command that starts with AT; default is ATV1L0DT.
GraphFont	Font name to be used in the graph and report; default is Arial.
GraphSize	Font Size to be used in the graph; default is 12.
HealthTime	Number of minutes to wait before a sound is played; must be 1–59, 0 turns the sound off.
HealthMsg	Health Message played.
Modem	Com port to use and setting; default is COM1,T,2
Path	Full pathname — ending with a backslash (\) — to the data files.
Prefix	Prefix to be placed in front of the dialing number.
ReportSize	Font Size to be used in the Report; default is 12.
RptBars	Default characters used for the day separators found in the Preview dialog.
RptTitle1	Default Title 1 to be used in the Report.
RptTitle2	Default Title 2 to be used in the Report.

Note: See the "Internationalization" section for more uses.

The following alarm settings need to be added to the existing [sounds] section, if one already exists.

Alarm	Sound played when an alarm goes off.
Hourly Chime	Sound played on the hour.
Half Hourly Chime	Sound played on the half hour.
Quarter Hourly Chime	Sound played on the quarter hour.

Here is an example of how to set it up:

[sounds]

Hourly Chime=chord.wav,Hourly Chime

Half Hourly Chime=ding.wav,Half Hourly Chime

Quarter Hourly Chime=chimes.wav,Quarter Hourly Chime

After you type this in and save the WIN.INI file, you can change the sound that is played by using the Control Panel application and selecting the Sound setting.

Note: The chimes will only go off if the Options Alarm dialog box has the check box marked.

Internationalization

Windows Reminder supports Internationalization for the date and time displays. The setting in WIN.INI that Reminder looks for in the [intl] section are:

s1159	a.m. character; default is "a"
s2359	p.m. character; default is "p"
sTime	Time separator; default is ":"

sDate	Date separator; default is "/"
sShortDate	Short date format; default is M/D/Y
iTime	0 = 12, 1=24 hour format; default is 0
iDate	0 = m/d/y;1 = d/m/y;2 = y/m/d; default is 0

The settings in WIN.INI that Reminder looks for in the [Reminder] section are

sDays	Three-character days; default is "badSunMonTueWedThuFriSat". If you want all the days in lowercase, you would have "badsunmontuewedthufrisat".
sDays1	One-letter character used in Calendar; default is "SMTWTFS". If you want all lowercase, you would set the string to "smtwtfs".
1-12	Months used for Calendar; default is 1="January", 12="December". *Note:* a month can be up to 13 characters.

Networks

Reminder uses the following search routine to determine where the data files are.

1. Full path and filename from the command line.
2. Current directory.
3. Checks the WIN.INI file for the [Reminder] PATH= location of the files.
4. Directory where Windows Reminder is loaded from.
5. Directory where Windows was started from.

Reminder Uses

For work:

Meetings, projects, reports, lunch, calls, and auto-dialing.

Reports are generated very quickly, along with a time log of each event. See the "DDE with Reminder" section for more details. Repeat feature for daily, weekly, monthly, yearly, and end-of-month times.

For health at the computer:

The HealthTime feature allows you to set an hour interval that will play a Beep or Sound file. Some examples are *Check your posture* or *Exercise your eyes*. See the "WIN.INI settings" section on how to set this up.

For the home:

Birthdays, anniversaries, Child 1, Child 2, school, practice, vacation, auto-dialing, and ticket schedules.

Child's names can be used as the category entry, so you can see at a glance which child has to be where for what event.

When you are adding birthdays and anniversaries into Address Manager — which is distributed by Wilson WindowWare and featured in *Windows Gizmos* — all you need to do is press the To Reminder button to automatically transfer all the names, birthday, and anniversary information at once.

For other time-related items:

Medications, car-related maintenance, bill paying, and doctor visits.

To create a new category, just enter it in when you enter the item. You also can set up all your categories at once by pressing the F4 key or selecting the Category Add menu. You will be shown a dialog box in which to enter a category name. See the "Category Dialog Box" section for more information.

When you have one or more categories, you can then start adding Items with the + or F5 key.

An item is one line of information that describes what you want to be reminded about.

You attach a category to each item so that you can quickly view all related items at one time. An example of this is all the doctor visits, or meetings in a month. Attaching a category also allows you to quickly generate reports for more than one purpose.

You need at least this information to create an item:

1. Date (defaults to today's date)
2. Category (which you can select from a list)
3. Message

Power users

Highlighting an item and selecting the Phone button on the control bar enables you to quickly dial that number.

After you create your list, you can explore the power of DDE with WinWord, Excel, and Visual Basic to see how to automatically generate reports and time spent on each item.

	Keyboard Commands
Key(s)	**Action**
+	Add a new item.
-	Delete currently selected item.
Enter	Change currently selected item.
Space	Check item as done.
F1	Help.
F4	Add a new category.
F5	Add a new item.
F6	Delete currently selected item.
F7	Change currently selected item.
F8	Check item as done.
F9	View items in the past.
F10	View items for today.
F11	View items for the future.
F12	View items that are done.
Ctrl+Ins	Select the Copy menu.
Shift+Ins	Select the Paste menu.

Menu Commands	
Menu	*Command(s)*
File	Print.
Edit	Add, modify, and delete items.
View	View items.
Category	Add, modify, and delete items.
Options	Customize Reminder for your needs.
Window	Display the windows you want.
Help	Access Help file.

File menu

The file menu gives you access to print your "to do" items. You use the View sub-menus to select what category of items you want selected, and also the past, present, future, and done items. What you see is a list of the items to print. The File Print menu will allow you to further customize your report in the following ways.

To set the default report titles, see the "WIN.INI settings" section. For better looking reports, make the *Start/End report character* and *Day separator character* either a – or = so that a smooth line is made. Otherwise, the selected character will be used. The Suppress same day check box so that the day and date do not repeat. Try the Print Preview menu to see how this looks. To set the date ranges, just supply the beginning and ending dates to print.

Hint: You can enter the dates with the Calendar program. In Calendar, pressing the left mouse button places the selected date in the beginning field, and the right mouse button places the selected date in the ending field.

File menu options:

Print Preview	Before you actually print your list, you have the option to see what the list will look like. If you want more space in between a column, you can then use the Slider Bar to change the margins.
Print	Prints the list that you currently see.
Printer Setup	Set up any new printers you have connected to your computer. This can also be done using the Control Panel and then selecting the printer icon.
Select Printer	Before doing any printing, you should tell Windows Reminder which printer you want to use. All printers that are currently set up in the system will be available for you to choose from. Select the appropriate printer before printing. If you don't do this, Reminder uses the default printer set up through the Control Panel and printer icon.
Exit	Exit the program.

Edit menu

The Edit menu allows you to maintain your items.

Edit menu options:

Copy	Saves only what you have selected to the Clipboard. You can select one or many items with the mouse by holding the mouse button down and dragging. To select separate items not next to each other, hold down the Ctrl key while clicking on the item. See the section "Copying data from Reminder."
Paste	Copies text items from the Clipboard to create new items. See the section "Pasting data to Reminder." *Note:* Don't do this twice unless you want duplicate items.
Copy All	Saves all the items that are displayed. To change which items are displayed, use the View buttons.
Add	(F5) Add or enter a new Item.
Delete	(F6) Delete selected item(s).
Change	(F7) Change a selected item.
Check	(F8) Mark the selected item(s) as done.

View menu

The View menu allows you to easily view your items in different ways.

View menu options:

All items	Shows you *all* items no matter what.
Past	(F9) Shows you items that came before *today*.
Today	(F10) Shows you items for *today* only.
Future	(F11) Shows you items that come after *today*.
Done	(F12) Shows you items that are marked as "done."
Select All	Toggles on and off all the categories at a time. This is useful when you want to select all the categories except one or two.
View All	View *all* the categories.
Individual	The control bar buttons toggle in and out of categories when you press the keys, and the Window caption under the control bar also shows you which iew is currently selected.

Category menu

The Category menu allows you to maintain your categories.

Category menu options:

Add	(F4) Add a new category.
Delete	Displays only the categories not in use so you can delete them.
Change	Change the name of a category.
Defaults	Sets graph color bars of each category and default values when a Category is selected.

Category names are limited to a–z and A–Z, and no spaces. Upper- and lowercase is used only when you create the category the first time. This is used to prevent duplicate categories.

The Personal check box allows you to set this category as personal so that it does not show up on any *automatic* reports by accident.

The Category Defaults menu allows you to set the default values that will automatically be set when a new item is being created. These defaults will also take effect when an item is added from the Clipboard and via DDE. This is where you can set the different colors of each category.

Options

The Options menu allows you to customize Windows Reminder to work the way you like to.

Options menu options:

Alarm	Set the sound and optional chimes. If you have multimedia installed, the setting you have defined in Control Panel are used.
Preferences*	Set the way you like to see the information.
Run	Run other applications and DDE conversations.
Dial	Your modem dials a phone number for you.
Graph	Allows you to set how the Graph is displayed.
Health Msg	Set a sound file to go off every part of an hour. Setting the interval to 0 will turn the sound off. Setting the interval to 20 will have the sound played every 20 minutes. Setting the interval to more than 30 will only play the message once per hour. The sound file can be any *.WAV file that you supply. If it is not on the path, then provide a fully qualified path. Something you might use is *Check your posture*, *Move your neck around*, or *Break time*.

* The Preferences dialog box allows you to customize how Windows Reminder works:

Turn color on and off when you use a black-and-white display.

Turn off the Delete Confirmation dialog box.

Save deleted items to a file. Each item is saved in a file called itemYMM.DEL, where Y is the year and MM is the month. The date you marked the item as done will be saved in the file for report purposes.

Set the date to display the year.

Hint: If the full text of the day is not shown, use the Slider Bar to adjust it.

Choose **not** to display each due item at start up time. This feature can still be overridden with the NAG option on an item-by-item basis.

Set the default setting for Business Day only in the alarm message. When a date is bumped to the next week or month, it will make sure it is not on a Weekend. It does not exclude holidays.

Display the date along with the time in the icon area.

Do **not** display items that do not have a time, such as birthdays.

Close the Calendar program when Reminder closes.

Window menu

The Window menu allows you to display the Calendar program and determine if you want the control bar displayed.

Show Calendar	Starts or displays the Calendar program. If you have your own calendar program you prefer, just add the desired program name after the cal= line in the [reminder] section of the WIN.INI file.

Show control bar   Allows you to show or hide the control bar.

Show Graph   Allows you to show or hide the Graph Schedule.

The Graph Window provides you with many features. While it displays a graph of your scheduled times, it also allows you enter and edit items by clicking in the graph in the desired day and time. If the item is already entered, double-clicking on it will bring up the item for changing. The color of each item depends on the category which can be changed with the Category Defaults menu.

Help menu

The Help file can be entered from Windows Reminder by pressing the F1 key. Extensive use of hot links can be found throughout this help file for easy access to Windows Reminder's operation.

Index   Gets you to this help file.

About   Displays the version number.

Control Bar

Figure 2: The control bar is provided for you to quickly point and click to get different commands to occur.

The first button you see in Figure 2 is for opening the Calendar program. The second button is used for opening the Phone Dialer dialog box. The third button displays and hides the graph that shows scheduled times.

This second group of buttons allows you to edit the currently selected item(s).

The plus sign is used to Add a new item. The minus sign is used to Delete selected item(s). The triangle sign is used to Change a selected item. The check mark sign is used to mark the selected item(s) as done.

The third group of controls are the view item buttons. They allow you to view the items based on the date and if they are "done" or not.

The past sign, the left-pointing arrow, displays items that came before today. The today sign, the down-pointing arrow, displays items that are for today only. The future sign, the right-pointing arrow, displays items that come after today. The done sign, the check mark, displays items that are done. The All sign, an asterisk, displays all items. You will also notice that it pushes down all the other view buttons.

The bell symbol is the alarm indicator. It is displayed automatically when there is a time set to go off some time today. If there are no times set, the alarm picture will not be shown.

The current time on your computer is displayed at the end of the control bar.

Slider Bar

Figure 3: The Reminder slider bar.

You can adjust the width of each column by placing the mouse where the arrows are pointing. The mouse changes to a left and right arrows cursor when you are over an area to slide. You can slide in either the left or right directions, but not less than the text being displayed.

You will need this when you select the Preferences to display both the day and the year. Reminder will remember the position from the previous session, and it will also change how the text is spaced when you print.

Calendar

You can start the Calendar program from the Window Show Calendar menu, from Program Manager, by clicking on the Calendar Icon on the control bar, or clicking the Calendar Icon in the Enter Item dialog. Calendar is a stand-alone program, so Windows Reminder does not need to be running to work, although it is only distributed with Windows Reminder. You can quickly move Calendar out of the way by pressing one of the arrow keys in the direction you want it to move.

Viewing other months and years

To view a different month, use the mouse to click on either the right or left arrows.

To view a different year, use the mouse to click on the inside of the right or left arrows.

Clicking in the middle will bring you back to the current month and year.

Entering a new item with Calendar

You can use Calendar to enter a new item in Reminder by just double-clicking the left mouse button on the date you want. Reminder will open its Enter new item dialog box with the date you picked already inserted! If Reminder isn't running, Calendar will start it for you automatically.

Entering the date with Calendar

To enter a date or change the existing date, just double-click the left mouse button on the date you want.

Entering the time with Calendar

While the Item dialog box is displayed, to enter a new time or change the existing time, just single-click the right mouse button on the time you want. Times between 7:00 a.m. and 11:59 a.m. already default to p.m. unless you put the *a* after the time. If you want p.m. times, then you select a date greater than 12 (which is 24 hour format). If you want 1:00 p.m., select the 13th date, which tells Reminder to use the 13th hour of the day. To get 8:00 p.m., you would select the 20th; just 8 or 8:00 would default to 8:00 a.m..

Closing Calendar automatically

In the Options Preferences, there is a check box that asks you if you want Calendar to close when reminder is closed.

Alarm setting

The way the alarm is set is by providing a time with an item. If the date is today and the time has not already passed, then the alarm picture will be displayed.

If you want to create your own sort options, you can do this by going to the Options Preferences menu and unchecking the Allow only time check box. This will allow you to enter in text such as ASAP, NOW, 1, 2, 3, and it will be sorted by what you have.

Why the alarm picture is not displayed

Here are a few things to check:

1. Verify that your system date has the correct year and the time has the correct a.m. or p.m. setting. You can verify and set your system date and time by running Control Panel and then selecting the Date/Time icon.
2. Check the Action item to make sure it is not set to Nothing.
3. Make sure that the A or P letter is at the end of the time setting: 3:00p.
4. Check the Options Preference menu and make sure the Allow only time box is checked.
5. The alarm will only come on if the date is today and the system time isn't past the current time.
6. If it is today and you think the time has not passed, then check the Options Alarm menu to see if the Advance warning number is not set too high so that the system time you wanted to be warned about is now in the past.

Dialog Boxes

Here is a list of the dialog boxes Windows Reminder uses:

Action	Select which alarms you want to hear.
Alarm Message	What you can do when an alarm goes off.
Category	Allows you to change a category name.
Item	Allows you to enter new items.
Run	Allows you to start other programs.
Dial	Allows you to dial a phone number.
Graph	Allows you to change the graphing options.

Action dialog box

You can select what action to take when an alarm goes off. Here is a list of what each of the different actions gives you control over.

Nothing	Does nothing when the time is reached.
Show Message	Displays the messages you typed in. See the "Alarm Message" section for more information.
Show Item	Opens the Item dialog box.
Run	Runs an application or file extension you supply. This is useful for starting other applications or bringing up a text file for additional notes. You can do this by just entering in the filename like COMMENTS.TXT.
Run with prompt	Same as Run except a dialog box is displayed so that you can change the text, or choose not to run the command. See the "Run dialog box" section for more information.
DDE	Starts a DDE conversation with the specified application.
DDE with prompt	Same as DDE except a dialog box is displayed so you can change the text, or choose not to run the command. See the "Run dialog box" section for more information.

Dial   Displays the phone dial dialog box with the second line of the Item
                        dialog box being the phone number you want to dial.

Alarm message dialog box

You can select what action to take when an alarm you set goes off. Here is a list of what each
of the different actions gives you control over:

Mark as Done   Checks the item as done. Use with the OK button.

Note   Displays the message you entered.

Note 2   Displays the second message line you entered.

Reschedule   Opens the Item dialog box so that you can change the date or time or
                        anything else you need to.

Reset Time   Snooze or Repeat the alarm X minutes from now. Must be used with
                        the Reset Time button.

Business day only   This is for the Reset Day option below only. When it is checked, the
                        day is made to not fall on a weekend. The day is moved to the next
                        business day. This can be set to always be on in the Options Prefer-
                        ences dialog box.

Reset Day   Quickly changes the date for tomorrow, next week, next month, or any
                        number of days with the "other" selection. The "other" option only
                        works for days for now.

Hint: Hold the Shift key down while you press the OK button to stop the rest of the messages
from displaying. When Reminder starts, it checks your past items and items that need to be
done for the day and displays this dialog box. Where this comes in handy is when you exit
Reminder and start it within the same day, or you don't have time to go through all the past
items.

When an alarm goes off, your message is displayed for you. You are then given four choices of
what you want to do with the message. The first is nothing so that you can decide what you
want to do with it later. You can select the Mark as Done check box to indicate you no longer
need to be reminded of the message. If you are busy when the message is displayed, you can
set the Repeat in *?* minutes (snooze) option and press the Reset Time button so the message
will be displayed again in the extra time you selected. This is really handy when you are on
the phone. Selecting the Reschedule button opens the message for editing so that you can
change the date and/or time and any of the other information at one time.

The Reset Day button allows you to quickly change the date to tomorrow, next week, next
month, or any number of days with the "other" selection. The "other" option only works for days
for now. If you check the "Business day only" box, the Reset Day option tells Reminder to
make sure that the day does not fall on a weekend. The day is moved to the next business day.

Category dialog box

Here you can enter in the name of a new category you want to group your items by. This is
handy for viewing what you have done and also what you have to do. You can also use this to
print out a list of items to do for today to take along with you.

Text   Required. Name of category; no spaces are allowed.

Personal   The check box flags this category as personal so that these items will
                        not be included in DDE conversations unless the specific category is
                        asked for. This way, your Birthday items will not be on your reports.
                        To change the name of a category, select the Category Change menu.

From	Old name of the Category.
To	New name of the Category.

Item dialog box

The Item dialog box is used to enter and change items you want to keep track of. ***Hint:*** For an easier way to bring up this dialog with the date and time already filled in, double-click in the Graph at the desired day and time. For far off dates, you can also double-click in the Calendar program.

Done	Check box.
Category	Required. Create new category with the F4 key.
Calendar Icon	When you click this icon, the Calendar program will come up and align itself on the left of the dialog for easy entry.
Date	Required. Format is mm/dd/yy; "/" can be "-". This area is also free-form in that you can enter just one number and it will default to the current month and year. You can also leave out the year and it will default to the current year. ***Hint:*** For an easier way to enter in the date, use the Calendar program with a double-click of the left mouse button.
Time	Not required. This field has two formats depending on what you have selected in the Options Preferences Allow only time option. If you have time selected, The format is hh:00[a|p]. However, this area is also free-form in that you can enter just one number and it will default to the hour you want. The ":00" and "a" or "p" is put in automatically. If it guesses wrong, just put in the "a" or "p" yourself. ***Hint:*** For an easier way to enter the time, use the Calendar program with the right mouse button. ***Note:*** The time will only default if you specify the Options Preferences Allow only time option. This can be turned on and off at any time. The option only affects new items entered or changed. Default times of 12–6 are made into p.m. unless "a" is placed at the end. 12:00 a.m. - 12:59 a.m. are entered as 0:01a - 0:59a. ***Note:*** Not using the time option allows you to make this a Priority, department list, or whatever you want to sort on. See the Alarm setting section for more information.
Length	Not required. This field has one format, but you have to decide if you are going to use whole hours or minutes. You will usually modify this value after you have finished the item so that your reports have the correct amount of time logged. For the graph window, values 1–9 are treated as hours; all other values > 9 are treated as minutes.
Warning	Not required. This field is used to set how far in advance you want to be notified of the event.
Action	Required. Here you are allowed to take the following actions when the alarm goes off.
Note	Required. Free form text. To get additional lines, see the Run option in the Action dialog for more information.
Note 2	Free-form text. The text Note 2 will change depending on the Action item selected. If you select the Dial Action, the word Dial will be displayed.
Notes button	Press this button to enter notes for this item. You can use a filename in the Note 2 line so that if you want, you can start Cardfile or your editor of choice. If nothing is entered in Note 2, the default is to start

	Notepad. After you have added a note, you need to place the full path-name, including the drive letter, of the file in the Note 2 section for easy reference.
Repeat	This is a check box that needs to be set for the repeat feature to be set. It is checked automatically if you select one of the repeat items. You can easily turn off the repeat option by unchecking the Repeat check box.
Nag	This is a check box that you can set to have this item display when you first start Reminder. When this is checked, it will override the Don't display past items on startup option. Setting this Nag switch allows you two functions 1. A repeat item will not be bumped to the next date until it is marked as DONE. 2. Even if the Option Preferences don't display pass items box is checked, this will override it and display it.
Add	Adds the item to your list and works with the Enter key.
Close	Closes the dialog box and works with the Escape key also. *Note:* If the alarm goes off while, editing an item, this dialog box is closed automatically so that you can answer the alarm.

Run dialog box

There are two ways to get to the Run dialog box. The first way is when you set an alarm and you specify the Action of Run with Prompt. You can also get to the Run dialog by selecting the Options Run menu.

Note	Displays the note you entered for this action.
Run	Enter the application or DDE conversation you want.

In the Run line, you can enter any program name with a list of parameters. Here are some items you can enter and their results.

calc	Starts the Calculator application.
test.xls	Starts Microsoft Excel with the TEST.XLS file.

Dial dialog box

There are four ways to get to the Dial dialog box. The first way is when you set an alarm and you specify the Action of Dial. You can also get to the Dial dialog by selecting the Options Dial menu. You can also select the Phone button, on the control bar. The fourth way is to have a DDE Client program send a DDE Execute Command with the name and phone number desired.

Note	Displays the note from the selected item.
Number	Displays the phone number for the selected item or enter the phone number you want dialed.
Prefix	Enter the prefix to be added in front of the phone number. An example you might use is "9" to get an outside line or "*70" to turn off the Call Waiting feature.
Use prefix	Select this if you want to use the prefix.
OK	Dials the number.
Cancel	Closes the dialog box and also works with the Escape key.
Setup	Allows you to change the default setting to your modem.

To change the default dialing string command, ATV1L0DT, that gets sent to the modem, you can create a DialCmd= in the [Reminder] section in the WIN.INI file. The Prefix= line is also kept there.

Graph dialog box

You can display the Graph dialog box by selecting the Window Show Graph menu. To set how the graph looks or is presented, you can select the Options Graph menu or once the graph is displayed, double-click in the left side of the graph where the dates are displayed. Once the Graph Settings dialog box is up, here are what the fields do.

Hint 1: For easy reference, today is displayed with a blue horizontal line.

Hint 2: For items not within the displayed time frame, a « symbol is shown for times before the time and the » symbol is shown for times after the time frame. This way if you have the times set for 8 to 5, and you have something scheduled at 7:00 that night, you will see the » at the end of that day's line.

Hint 3: Double-click in the graph area to bring up the Item dialog with the date and time already filled in. The date and time are determined by the area of the graph you double-clicked on and the default setting provided in the Category Defaults menu.

Hint 4: Double-click on an existing graph item to open the item so that you can see or change it.

Start day	The day the graph starts with. If you select 1st, then today is always displayed at the top. If you select 2nd, then today is always displayed as the second line on the graph. If you select Last, then today is always displayed at the bottom. If you select Center, then today is always displayed in the middle of the graph. If you select Sun or another day, then the day selected will be at the top and today will just fall in line. An example is if you select Mon and today is Wednesday; then Monday would be the first line and today, Wednesday, would be on the third line.
# of days	The number of days you want to see on the graph.
Start time	The starting time of the graph.
End time	The ending time of the graph.
Hour interval*	This can only be set to hour, ½ hour and ¼ hour increments. This setting will affect the time you get in the Item dialog in the time field.
Pen width*	This sets how thick the lines will be on the graph.
Horizontal lines*	This determines if horizontal lines are displayed or not.

* These items will change the sample graph to reflect the changes you are asking for.

Importing and Exporting Data _____

Reminder has a number of ways of importing and exporting data with other applications.

Two ways are to use the Clipboard

Copying data from Reminder transfers data to the Clipboard. When Reminder copies information to the Clipboard, the data is in text (CF_TEXT) format and each field is separated with a Tab. This allows for easy pasting to Word processors and spreadsheet programs. Reminder will place all the items currently viewable into the Clipboard. So, if you want to select just a small amount of data to the Clipboard, you will have to set up the View Category menus and Past, Present, and Future buttons to just display the items you want placed on the Clipboard.

Pasting data to Reminder transfers data from the Clipboard. When Reminder receives information from another application or from the Clipboard, it will look for the following as the minimum amount of data required to make a new item: date, category, note.

Example: 5/15/91. Meeting. Give a status on Project1 to everyone.

You can also supply any of the additional information and it will be accepted.

[done] Only the "x" character is allowed.

date

[time]

category

note

[Tab note 2] Each data field is separated either by a Tab or space.

Note: The Tab is required to separate the first note from the second note.

Warning: To allow a flexible number of fields, you should make sure everything is correct and that you make a backup each day.

Two other ways are to use DDE

Poking data to Reminder
An application sending data to Reminder. Let's say you are in WinWord and have a date for your next meeting listed. You want to be able to select the date and text to be posted to Reminder. So you highlight the text starting at the date to the end of the first message or second message, if you want one. Then just pick the Post to Reminder menu.

Here is a sample macro on how to pass an item from WinWord to Reminder:

```
Sub MAIN
        ChanNum = DDEInitiate("reminder", "items")
        DDEPoke ChanNum, "all", Selection$( )
        DDETerminate ChanNum
End Sub
```

To poke an item to Reminder, you need the following information.

Application = Reminder
Topic = Item
Item = Item
Data = 1/1/93 Holiday New Year's Day

In this example, January 1 of 1993 would have a Category of Holiday, and the text would be "New Year's Day". Address Manager, which is distributed by Wilson WindowWare, uses DDEPOKE to automatically transfer all the names, birthday, and anniversary information into Reminder with the To Reminder button.

Requesting data from Reminder
An application getting data from Reminder. Reminder can pass information back to your application. You can request everything or just a specific type of information. To limit what Reminder will pass you, Reminder will recognize the following one-character formats.

C
Category information.

D
Done information.

M
Month information.

Combining requests together sample.

N
Number of items found; good for building arrarys in spreadsheets.

Category information

For a specific category, you use the C=string command, where "string" is the name of the Category you want.

C=Meeting	Returns only the items with a category of Meeting.
C=Project	Returns only the items with a category of Project.

Hint: Characters can be in upper- or lowercase.

Note: For multiple categories, you just make another Request.

Done information

For a list of the items that were finished or marked as "done," you use the D=V, where D stands for Done and V can be one of the following:

N or 0	For Not done.
Y	For done.

If you do not specify either Y or N, then you will get the items no matter if they are done or not.

d=n	Returns only the items that are NOT done.
d=y	Returns only the items that ARE done.
<none>	Returns all since a preference was not provided.

Hint: Characters can be in upper- or lowercase.

Month information

For a specific month, you use the M=N, where N is the month number, i.e. 1=Jan, 12=Dec.

M=5	Returns all items for the month of May, default to current year.
M=5,3	Returns all items for the month of May, in year 1993.

Note: If you need more than one month, then you just make a separate request for each month. Characters can be in upper- or lowercase

Combining requests

You can combine both the month and done requests together to get the following information.

m=5	Returns all the items in the month of May.
n m=5	Returns the Number of all the items in the month of May.
m=5 d=y	Returns the items done in the month of May.
m=5 d=n	Returns the items not done in the month of May.
m=6	Returns all the items in the month of June.
m=6 c=test	Returns all the items in the month of June with the category of "test."

Hint: Characters can be in upper- or lowercase.

Deleted items are saved to a text file if the Options Preference is selected. Each field is separated with a Tab, and at the end of each line is the actual date you marked the item as done. This makes it easy to generate reports with time-related information. It sets the way you want to see the date displayed, with the day or year. Each item is saved in a file called itemYMM.DEL, where Y is the year and MM is the month.

Items added in this fashion will use the default setting set in the Category Defaults menu.

Working with Other Applications

Reminder has a number of ways of working with other applications.

1. It can start running other applications unattended.
2. It can be a DDE Server application to provide or accept information.
3. It can be a DDE Client to start other DDE applications or retrieve information from other DDE applications.

Starting other applications

Reminder can automatically start up other applications for you at a specific time and run macros for you to further automate your job. See the Run section for complete information.

Reminder can start two different kinds of applications.

1. A regular Windows or MS-DOS application.
2. A Windows application with DDE commands.

To start a regular Windows or MS-DOS application, just supply the name of the program and optional data file to be passed to the application. To start WinWord, just type

```
WinWord
```

In the Note2 section, select the Action to Run, and it's set to start it at the specified time.

Poking data to Reminder

Let's say you are in WinWord and have a date for your next meeting listed. You want to be able to "select" the date, and text to be posted to Reminder. So you highlight in the text starting at the date to the end of the first message or second message if you want one. Then just pick the menu "Post to Reminder" menu.

Here is a sample macro on how to pass an item from WinWord to Reminder.

```
Sub MAIN
        ChanNum = DDEInitiate("reminder", "items")
        DDEPoke ChanNum, "all", Selection$()
        DDETerminate ChanNum
End Sub
```

To poke an item to Reminder, you need the following information.

Application = Reminder

Topic = Item

Item = Item

Data = 1/1/93 Holiday New Year's Day

In this example, January 1 of 1993 would have a Category of Holiday, and the text would be "New Year's Day."

Address Manager, which is distributed by Wilson WindowWare, uses DDEPOKE to automatically transfer all the names, birthday, and anniversary information into Reminder with the To Reminder button.

Requesting data from Reminder

Reminder can pass information back to your application. You can request everything or just a specific type of information.

To limit what Reminder will pass you, Reminder will recognize the following one character formats:

C	Category information
D	Done information
M	Month information
	Combining requests together sample.
N	Number of items found; good for building arrays in spreadsheets.

WinWord Report Sample

For a working example, please see the REMINDER.DOT file.

Here is a sample macro that automatically asks Reminder to divide the information in three parts:

1. What you have done for the month.

2. What you didn't do for the month.

3. What you have planned for next month.

This is all done at the selection of a menu.

```
Sub MAIN
     ChanNum = DDEInitiate("reminder", "items")
     Insert "Here is what I did for the month." + Chr$(10)
     Insert DDERequest$(ChanNum, "m=5 d=y")
     Insert Chr$(11) + " ———————————" + Chr$(10)
     Insert "I did quite a bit of work as you can see."
     Insert "Items that I was not able to get done this month."
     Insert DDERequest$(ChanNum, "m=5 d=n")
     Insert Chr$(11) + " ———————————" + Chr$(10)
     Insert "Items that I have scheduled for next month." + Chr$(10)
     Insert DDERequest$(ChanNum, "m=6")
     DDETerminate ChanNum
     Insert Chr$(10) + " ———————————" + Chr$(10)
     Insert "Let me know if I missed anything." + Chr$(10)
End Sub
```

DDE with Reminder _____

Windows Reminder supports DDE as both a Client and Server.

Reminder as the client

Windows Reminder will work as a DDE Client after you have started a conversation with it using one of the following keywords for the Topic. To start a Windows application with DDE commands, just supply

1. Type of DDE command (examples follow)

2. Name of the program

3. Type of data you want to pass to the program

Enter one of the following keys to send the desired DDE command(s):

=Execute	Execute a command in the other application
=Poke	Poke information to the application
=Request	Request information from the application

Hint: Characters can be in upper- or lowercase.

Note: The "=" is required so that Reminder knows this is a DDE command, rather than a DOS command.

Reminder as the server

Windows Reminder will work as a DDE Server after you have started a conversation with it using one of the following keywords for the Topic. The AppName is always Reminder.

AppName	Topic(s)	Item(s)
Reminder	Items	Used to get data items.

Following are the System topics Reminder supports:

Reminder	System
	Formats
	SysItems
	Status
	Category

Execute command

Reminder can both send and receive the DDE Execute command.

The only Execute command Reminder supports at this time is the "Dial" command. The form it is expecting is

    Dial Name Phone number

where Name is optional. The name field has no purpose other than it is displayed on the Note: line when the dialog box is displayed.

You use the Execute command to tell the other DDE application what to do for you. This can be anything from opening a new WorkSheet or Document to a complex set of tasks to do an entire set of tasks that can also call back to Reminder or Excel, gathering the information, formatting it, and then printing or sending it out via e-mail to others.

Here is how to use the Execute command.

    =Execute AppName TopicName [data]

The following sample will create a new WorkSheet in Excel.

    =E Excel Sheet1 [new()]

Hint: Text can be upper- or lowercase, and you only need one space between words.

Poke command

What you would use the Poke command for is to send a specific bit of information to the other application.

Here is how to use the Poke command:

    =Poke AppName TopicName reference data

The following sample will place the text "Hi" into cell A1 in Sheet1 if the sheet is open:

    =P Excel Sheet1 r1c1 Hi

For more information, see "Poking data to Reminder" or "Pasting data to Reminder."

Hint: Characters can be in upper- or lowercase.

Request command

What you would use the Request command for is to get information from the other application. This can be anything from getting a stock price, month-end total to a phone number of a person you are being reminded to call.

Here is how to use the Request command:

=Request AppName TopicName reference

The following sample will get the value referenced by the name "Total" in the WorkSheet titled "Sheet1" in Excel:

=R Excel Sheet1 Total

If you want to get the "Categories" that Windows Reminder has, you can do so by requesting the following Topic and Item:

Reminder System Category

and Reminder will pass back the Categories with a Tab between each item in the list.

Hint: Characters can be in upper- or lowercase.

Hints and Tips _____

To get additional lines or notes for an Item, just select the Run action item and enter a filename like COMMENTS.TXT. When the alarm goes off, Reminder automatically opens the file or any file with the program that is set up inside of the [extensions] section of the WIN.INI file.

How to get the most out of this program:

♦ Windows Reminder provides you with a program called Cal that prints a monthly calendar with the option of placing your items in each date for a quick, easy reference.

♦ You can use the Calendar program, CAL.EXE, to start Reminder.

♦ Use Calendar to enter dates and time — it's fast and easy.

♦ Use the Graph to enter dates and time — it's fast and easy.

♦ Use the Graph to double-click on entries to open them for viewing or modification.

♦ You can use Reminder to start a DDE conversation with WinWord so that WinWord can get the information from Reminder to put into your report!

♦ Use Address Manager to enter in all your dates and anniversaries quickly.

♦ Use Reminder for tracking length of time each item took to complete.

♦ Saving deleted information to a file allows you to also track when items were marked as done.

Setting the alarm

If the alarm doesn't come on, see the "Alarm setting" section.

Limitations

Although Windows Reminder allows an unlimited number of items, the display area can only display around 900 items. This 900 limit is not exact because it is determined by the amount of text in each item. The 900 item comes from an estimate that each item has an average message length of 30.

Graph displays only 60 days and 150 items. There can only be 64 Categories; each is limited to 20 characters without spaces.

Registration Reminders

Unlicensed copies of Wilson WindowWare products are fully functional. We make them this way so that you can have a real look at them and then decide whether they fit your needs. Our entire business depends on your honesty. If you use it, we expect you to pay for it. We feel that if we treat you right, you will treat us right.

Unlicensed copies of our products do have a pesky registration reminder screen that pops up whenever you start the program. This shouldn't really affect your evaluation of our software.

We're sure that once you see the incredible quality of our software, you will dig out your credit card, pick up the phone, call the nice people at our 800 number, and register the software.

When you pay for the shareware you like, you are voting with your pocketbook, and will encourage us to bring you more of the same kinds of products. Pay for what you like, and voilá, more of what you like will almost magically be developed.

Legal Matters

Of course, the usual disclaimers still apply. We are not responsible for anything at all. Nothing. Even if we are held responsible, the limit of our liability is the licensing fees you paid. The full text of our license agreement is found near the bottom of this file.

Update Policy

It is the policy of Wilson WindowWare to protect faithful customers, and to derive the majority of our income via sales to new customers rather than continually attempting to extract more funds from existing customers. Of course, we must at least cover our costs, or we could not stay in business bringing you new and updated software.

Wilson WindowWare frequently updates it products. There are various kinds of updates, including Major updates, Minor updates, and bug-fix updates.

Minor and bug-fix updates for our shareware products are free — subject only to our reasonable shipping and and handling charges for disks. As we are not in the disk selling business, you may find that shareware vendors specializing in disk sales can easily sell disks cheaper than we can. On the other hand, we *always* have the most recent versions of our software. Our shipping and handling charges for update disks are as follows:

    $10.00 U.S. and Canada for the first product.

    $ 5.00 U.S. and Canada for each additional product.

    $ 9.50 Surcharge for shipping outside of U.S. and Canada.

If you obtain a minor or bug-fix update from CompuServe or other on-line service, a BBS, a shareware disk vendor, or from another source, there is no charge from us (of course, you will have to pay the on-line service fees, disk vendors fees, or at least pay your phone bill for downloading from a BBS). In addition, you may use a single disk to update any number of copies of a product.

The policy and pricing for major shareware updates vary. Depending on the nature of the upgrade, length of time since the previous major upgrade, desirability of new features added, the extent of revisions to the printed manuals (if any), work involved, and possible price changes for new users, we may or may not charge fees.

On-Line Support

Wilson WindowWare has on-line support!

The home of all Wilson WindowWare is on CompuServe, in the WINAPA forum, in the Wilson WindowWare section (#15 currently). Also the latest and greatest downloads are available from DL15 of the WINAPA forum. The Wilson WindowWare section of the WINAPA forum is checked on a daily basis, and all questions will be responded to.

The Fidonet Windows echo is also checked on a fairly regular basis. We only look at the titles of the messages. If you want to leave a message for us, be sure one of the following words are in the title.

Registered users may also call our BBS for the latest versions of our products. 206-935-5198 USR HST/V.32bis V.42bis 14,400+ 8N1

Although we still allow 2400 baud connects as of January 1993, we are considering requiring at least a 9600 baud modem in the future.

Connects at 1200 baud and below will not be permitted to log on.

Association of Shareware Professionals Ombudsman Statement

Wilson WindowWare, the producer of Wilson WindowWare software, is a member of the Association of Shareware Professionals (ASP). ASP wants to make sure that the shareware principle works for you. If you are unable to resolve a shareware-related problem with an ASP member by contacting the member directly, ASP may be able to help. The ASP Ombudsman can help you resolve a dispute or problem with an ASP member, but does not provide technical support for members' products. Please write to the ASP Ombudsman at 545 Grover Road, Muskegon MI 49442 or send a CompuServe message to ASP Ombudsman 70007,3536

The Legalese Section

ADDRESS MANAGER	Copyright © 1990–93 by Wilson WindowWare, Inc.
COMMAND POST	Copyright © 1988–93 by Morrie Wilson.
FILE COMMANDER	Copyright © 1992–93 by Morrie Wilson.
REMINDER	Copyright © 1991–93 by Wilson WindowWare, Inc.
WINCHECK	Copyright © 1990–93 by Wilson WindowWare, Inc.
WINEDIT	Copyright © 1990–93 by Steve Schauer.
WINBATCH	Copyright © 1991–93 by Morrie Wilson.
WINBATCH COMPILER	Copyright © 1991–93 by Morrie Wilson.

Software License

Wilson WindowWare software is not and has never been public-domain software nor is it free software.

Non-licensed users are granted a limited license to use our software on a 21-day trial basis for the purpose of determining whether the software is suitable for their needs. Any use of our software, except for the initial 21-day trial, requires registration. The use of unlicensed copies of our software, outside of the initial 21-day trial, by any person, business, corporation, government agency, or any other entity is strictly prohibited.

A single user license permits a user to use one copy of the licensed software product only on a single computer. Licensed users may use the program on different computers, but may not use the program on more than one computer at the same time.

No one may modify or patch any of our executable files in any way, including but not limited to decompiling, disassembling, or otherwise reverse engineering our software programs.

A limited license is granted to copy and distribute our shareware software only for the trial use of others, subject to the above limitations, and also the following:

1. The software must be copied in unmodified form, complete with the file containing this license information.
2. The full machine-readable documentation must be included with each copy.
3. Our software may not be distributed in conjunction with any other product without a specific license to do so from Wilson WindowWare.
4. Vending of our software products in retail stores (by "shareware rack vendors") is specifically prohibited without prior written authorization. Written authorization will generally require payment of a small royalty on each disk sold.
5. No fee, charge, or other compensation may be requested or accepted, except as authorized below:
   A. Non-profit user groups may distribute copies of our products to their members, subject to the above conditions, without specific permission. Non-profit groups may collect a disk duplication fee not to exceed five dollars.
   B. Operators of electronic bulletin board systems (sysops) may make our products available for downloading only as long as the above conditions are met. An overall or time-dependent charge for the use of the bulletin board system is permitted as long as there is not a specific charge for the download of our software.
   C. Mail-order vendors of shareware software approved by the ASP may distribute our products, subject to the above conditions, without specific permission. Non-approved vendors may distribute our products only after obtaining written permission from Wilson WindowWare. Such permission is usually granted. Please write for details (enclose your catalog). Vendors may charge a disk duplication and handling fee, which, when pro-rated to each individual product, may not exceed eight dollars.

Limited Warranty

Wilson WindowWare guarantees your satisfaction with this product for a period of 90 days from the date of original purchase. If you are unsatisfied with the product within that time period, return the package in saleable condition to the place of purchase for a full refund.

Wilson WindowWare warrants that all disks provided are free from defects in material and workmanship, assuming normal use, for a period of 90 days from the date of purchase.

Wilson WindowWare warrants that the program will perform in substantial compliance with the documentation supplied with the software product. If a significant defect in the product is found, the purchaser may return the product for a refund. In no event will such a refund exceed the purchase price of the product.

EXCEPT AS PROVIDED ABOVE, WILSON WINDOWWARE DISCLAIMS ALL WARRANTIES, EITHER EXPRESS OR IMPLIED, INCLUDING, BUT NOT LIMITED TO IMPLIED WARRANTIES OF MERCHANT-ABILITY AND FITNESS FOR A PARTICULAR PURPOSE, WITH RESPECT TO THE PRODUCT. SHOULD THE PROGRAM PROVE DEFECTIVE, THE PURCHASER ASSUMES THE RISK OF PAYING THE ENTIRE COST OF ALL NECESSARY SERVICING, REPAIR, OR CORRECTION AND ANY INCIDENTAL OR CONSEQUENTIAL DAMAGES. IN NO EVENT WILL WILSON WINDOWWARE BE LIABLE FOR ANY DAMAGES WHATSOEVER (INCLUDING WITHOUT LIMITATION DAMAGES FOR LOSS OF BUSINESS PROFITS, BUSINESS INTERRUPTION, LOSS OF BUSINESS INFORMA-TION AND THE LIKE) ARISING OUT OF THE USE OR THE INABILITY TO USE THIS PRODUCT EVEN IF WILSON WINDOWWARE HAS BEEN ADVISED OF THE POSSIBILITY OF SUCH DAMAGES.

Use of this product for any period of time constitutes your acceptance of this agreement and subjects you to its contents.

U.S. Government Restricted Rights

Use, duplication, or disclosure by the Government is subject to restrictions as set forth in subdivision (b)(3)(ii) of the Rights in Technical Data and Computer Software clause at 252.227-7013. Contractor/manufacturer is Wilson WindowWare, 2701 California Ave. SW, Suite 212, Seattle, WA 98116.

Trademarks

Microsoft and MS-DOS are registered trademarks of Microsoft Corporation.

Windows is a trademark of Microsoft Corporation.

File Commander is a trademark of Wilson WindowWare, Inc.

Command Post is a trademark of Wilson WindowWare, Inc.

WinBatch is a trademark of Wilson WindowWare, Inc.

WinCheck is a trademark of Wilson WindowWare, Inc.

Reminder is a trademark of Wilson WindowWare, Inc.

Address Manager is a trademark of Wilson WindowWare, Inc.

WinEdit is a trademark of Wilson WindowWare, Inc.

Wilson WindowWare Products

Our great line of Windows products includes

Address Manager. Tracks addresses, phone numbers, comments, important dates. Includes dialer and label printer. Supports DDE. $39.95

Command Post. A powerful text-based shell for Windows. Programmable menus, built-in batch language, file viewer, and more. $49.95

File Commander. Allows addition of programmable menu items to the Windows 3.1 File Manager. Make File Manager into a super-powerful shell. $49.95

Reminder. Personal Schedule Manager. Keeps track of "to do" lists, set alarms (which can launch apps), prints reports. Supports DDE. $59.95

WinCheck. Your personal finance manager for Windows. Manages checking, savings, cash, and credit card accounts. Features galore! Supports DDE. Custom Reports. $69.99

WinEdit. Power Programming for the Windows Environment. Full-featured editor, or simple file browser. Super-high speed, super powerful. Winedit comes in three flavors, for novice, intermediate, and advanced users.

WinEdit Lite. Super notepad replacement. $29.95

WinEdit Standard. Programmers' editor. $59.95

WinEdit Pro. Includes full macro language. $89.95

WinBatch. Write your own Windows Batch Files! Dialogs, automatic program control, and powerful data manipulation lets you control your Windows. A must for the power user. $69.95

WinBatch. NOT A SHAREWARE PRODUCT. The WinBatch compiler COMPILER! can compile WinBatch batch files into stand-alone EXE files that may be distributed on a royalty free basis. Great for networks and corporate gurus. Compile your WBT files and then hand them out like candy. $395.00

Premier Support Services

Wilson WindowWare, Inc., a leader in high technology Windows software, is prepared to support software engineering projects with these services:

♦ Programming of custom interfaces to suites of applications running under Microsoft Windows.

♦ Programming custom Electronic Information Systems for the distribution of critical information.

♦ Development of custom functions that extend our Windows Interface Language (WIL) to control customer processes and procedures in manufacturing, process control, communications, networking, and financial analysis.

♦ Migration of business functions to the upcoming Windows NT platform.

Rates begin as low as $125 per hour. Minimums and other considerations apply. Please call 206-938-1743 for more information.

Registration

Registration Fee: $59.95 includes a program, CalPrint, that prints monthly calendars with your items in each day.

Payment options: Checks, American Express, Visa, MasterCharge, EuroCard accepted.

Ordering Information

Licensing our products brings you wonderful benefits. Some of these are

♦ Gets rid of that pesky reminder window that comes up when you start up the software.

♦ Entitles you to one hour free phone support for 90 days (your dime).

♦ Ensures that you have the latest version of the product.

♦ Encourages the authors of these programs to continue bringing you updated/better versions and new products.

♦ Gets you on our mailing list so you are occasionally notified of spectacular updates and our other Windows products.

♦ And, of course, our 90-day money back guarantee.

International Ordering Information

Our International customers may wish to order our products from their favorite dealers. The following shareware vendors will be happy to provide you with registered copies of any of our products. If your favorite vendor is not listed, ask them anyway. If you wish to order direct from Wilson WindowWare, please see the note on the order form for international customers.

Denmark

Pro-Soft
Benloese Skel 4 G,
4100 Ringsted
Denmark
Phone: 53 61 90 42
Fax: 53 61 93 91

France

WindowShare SARL. Pour acquerir la licence de ce logiciel, adressez-vous au specialiste du distribuciel sous MS Windows:

WindowShare SARL
B.P. 2078
57051-METZ cedex 2
France
Fax: (+33)87 32 37 75
Vox: (+33)87 30 85 57
CompuServe: 100031,3257
Minitel: 3615 WinShare

DP Tool Club
102 rue des Fusilles
Villeneuve d'Ascq
B. P. 745 59657
France
Téléphone: 20.56.55.33
Télécopie: 20.56.55.25

Japan

AG-TECH Corp.
Phone: 052-951-2706
Fax: 052-951-4469

KANJI versions of WinBatch, WinBatch Compiler, WinEdit, and File Commander are available from AG-TECH, complete with manuals.

Netherlands

BroCo Software
Ereprisstraaat 26
P.O. Box 446
3760 AK SOEST
The Netherlands
Phone: 31 0 2155 26650
Fax: 31 0 2155 14012

U.K.

Omicron Systems
45 Blenheim Crescent
Leigh-on-Sea
Essex
England SS9 3DT
Phone: 07 02 710 391
Fax: 02 02 471 113

Wilson WindowWare Order Form

Send to: **Wilson WindowWare, Inc.**
2701 California Ave SW #212
Seattle, WA 98116
U.S.A.

or call: 800-762-8383 (U.S.A. Orders Only)
206-938-1740 (Customer Service/International Orders)
206-937-9335 (Technical Support)
206-935-7129 (Fax)

Please allow 1 to 2 weeks for delivery

Name: _____

Company: _____

Address: _____

_____

City:_____ St: _____ Zip: _____

Phone:(_____)_____Country:_____

____ Address Manager(s) @ $39.95 : _____ . ____

____ Command Post(s) @ $49.95 : _____ . ____

____ File Commander(s) @ $49.95 : _____ . ____

____ Reminder(s) @ $59.95 : _____ . ____

____ WinBatch(s) @ $69.95 : _____ . ____

____ WinCheck(s) @ $69.99 :_____.____

____ WinEdit

             Lite(s) @ $29.95 : _____ . ____

             Standard(s) @ $59.95 : _____ . ____

             Pro(s) @ $89.95 : _____ . ____

____ WinBatch Compiler @$395.00 : _____ . ____

____ International Shipping

(except Canada) @ $9.50 : _____ . ____

Total: _____ . ____

Please enclose a check payable to Wilson WindowWare; International customers please see note below. Or you may use Access, Amex, Visa, MasterCharge, or EuroCard. For credit cards, please enter the information below:

Card #:__ __ __ __ - __ __ __ __ - __ __ __ __ - __ __ __ __

Expiration date: ____/____

Signature: _____

Where did you hear about or get a copy of our products?

_____

International customers. Although we do prefer payment by credit card, we can accept non-U.S.-bank checks under certain conditions. The check MUST be in your currency, NOT U.S. DOLLARS. Just look in your newspaper for the current exchange rates, make out your check, and send it to us. We will take care of the rest. No Eurocheques please.

ResGauge

Version 2.0
Copyright © Richard Franklin Albury

*R*esGauge *displays the Free System Resources in your Windows environment — in a convenient form no larger than an icon. (You can also run it in a window of any size.) Free System Resources are important because when Windows has less than 15 or 20 percent free, it becomes impossible to open more applications, and Windows may become erratic.*

The tiny size of the ResGauge icon, which displays the percentage free like a kind of "gas gauge," is very handy when something is using your Free System Resources. Often, a program consumes FSR when loading, and does not free up everything when exiting. This can quickly use all the resources Windows has available. When using ResGauge, you simply run all your programs as usual and track which may not be releasing all their resources. If you find such a program, you can try running your other programs before starting that one. Or you may need to restart Windows — after running the program — to recover resources. Windows never gets much above 70% FSR, so there's no use trying to get to 100% — you can't do it.

Type of Program:	Utility.
Requires:	Windows 3.1 or higher.
Registration:	Free. This program requires no registration.
Technical Support:	None.
Similar Shareware:	Super Resource Monitor, a program featured in *Windows Gizmos*, also displays Free System Resources but requires a larger screen area to display the information than ResGauge.

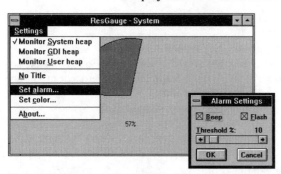

Figure 1: ResGauge can be configured from the Settings menu to beep and flash its icon when Free System Resources fall below a percentage you specify.

What Is ResGauge?

ResGauge is a small and simple, nonintrusive utility that monitors Free System Resources in Windows 3.1. You can easily configure ResGauge to alert you when free system resources drop too low, which lets you save your work before problems occur. Best of all, ResGauge is free, which relieves you of the annoyance of nag screens and the guilt of unregistered shareware.

What Are Free System Resources Anyway?

I'm glad you asked that. The core of Windows is implemented in three distinct *modules*: the system module, the GDI (Graphics Device Interface) module, and the User (interface) module. The GDI and User modules each have a *local heap*: an area of memory in which they allocate memory for their own use. Because a local heap can't exceed 64K, each module is limited in the amount of memory it can allocate for its own use. This gives rise to the notion of Free System Resources, which usually are expressed as the unallocated percentage of the GDI or User modules' local heap. The number you see in the About Program Manager... dialog box is the smaller of these two percentages; this number changes as programs load and free menus, icons, and other interface resources. Not surprisingly, Program Manager in Windows 3.0 was one of the worst offenders in exhausting Free System Resources: Every time you opened a group window, Program Manager would load the program icons but wouldn't free them when the window was subsequently closed. This behavior has been fixed in Windows 3.1.

How Does It Work?

ResGauge is redesigned to work like Clock in Windows 3.1. You can iconize the program and still get information; you can hide the title bar for a cleaner look; you can set the colors, etc. Unlike Clock, however, you can run more than one copy of ResGauge. For this reason, ResGauge doesn't save its window location. Otherwise, each new copy you started would come up over any existing copies.

What's on the System menu?

When you click the minimized ResGauge icon once, the System menu appears, including the following menu item:

♦ Always On Top allows you to keep ResGauge "floating" above other windows, much like Clock does. This is most useful when ResGauge is iconized.

What's on the main menu?

When you double-click the minimized ResGauge icon, the following items appear on the Settings menu in the ResGauge sizable window:

♦ The Monitor System Heap, Monitor GDI Heap, and Monitor User Heap menu items allow you to select which heap you want ResGauge to monitor. The Monitor System Heap setting reports the smaller of the two values reported for the GDI and User heaps. This value is also the same number reported by Program Manager.

♦ No Title removes the menu bar and the title bar from the window. Double-clicking the window or pressing the Escape key allows you to toggle between states. (This behavior was slavishly copied from Clock.) With the title bar gone, mouse users can still size the window and move the window by dragging the window contents. Keyboard users, however, will need to hit Escape to get the title bar back and use the System menu to size or move the window.

♦ Set alarm... opens a dialog box for setting alarm options. The threshold value — the value at or below which the alarm goes off — can be set as high as 99% or as low as 1%, but the default value of 10% seems a good number. ResGauge can be set to beep and/or flash when the alarm is triggered, but if this annoys you, you can disable it at your own risk.

♦ Set color... opens a dialog box for setting the gauge color for the heap you're currently monitoring. If the default gauge colors — pure red for System, pure green for GDI, and pure blue for User — don't appeal to you, you can set them to whatever colors you like.

♦ About... is the usual shameless blurb.

How (and Why) Do I Run More Than One Copy of ResGauge?

ResGauge will either read its configuration file when it starts or use default settings if the file doesn't exist. This scheme obviously doesn't lend itself to running different configurations simultaneously, so Version 1.3 of ResGauge added support for command-line arguments. For Version 2.0 of ResGauge, the command-line support has been simplified. ResGauge monitors the system heap by default, and command-line arguments of GDI and User can be used to have ResGauge monitor the GDI heap or the User heap, respectively. For example:

```
RESGAUGE.EXE GDI
RESGAUGE.EXE USER
```

The case of the argument doesn't matter, but the spelling does, and an invalid argument will result in a warning, as will more than one argument.

How Do I Get Rid of It?

If you're really sure you don't like ResGauge — although I can't imagine why! — the "deinstallation" procedure is also extremely simple: delete the Program Manager icon, delete the ResGauge executable RESGAUGE.EXE, delete RESGAUGE.WRI, and delete the ResGauge initialization file RESGAUGE.INI in your Windows directory.

Who Helped Me?

I wrote this program by myself. Honestly! I did have some helpful suggestions from the following folks, though:

♦ Anthony W. Rairden for the User/GDI/Both options and the alarm threshold idea

♦ Greg Saddler for the Always On Top option

♦ Edward Bauman for the color configuration idea

♦ David Hoos for the no-float/flash fix, some coding suggestions, and the correct spelling of "threshold"

♦ Larry LaBella for displaying both USER and GDI data

I'd like to say in closing that if you have any comments, kudos, complaints, or suggestions, I'd like to hear them. If you have any ideas for any other utilities you'd like to see, please let me know: I'd love to see them.

Richard Franklin Albury
P.O. Box 19652
Raleigh, NC 27619-9652

CompuServe ID: 76477,534
America OnLine: Developer
Internet: rfa20979@usav01.glaxo.com

Roger's Rapid Restart

Version 3.0
Copyright © Plannet Crafters, Inc.

Roger's Rapid Restart answers a question that Windows users have had since the beginning of the environment — "How do I get outta here?!" Searching through layers of windows for the one shell program that can exit Windows is frustrating. With Roger's Rapid Restart (RRR), however, exiting Windows from any application is as easy as pressing Shift+Pause.

You have many, many options besides just exiting Windows, however. You can configure RRR to exit Windows, run a DOS application, and return automatically to the Windows environment as soon as you exit the DOS app. This is great for DOS programs that are incompatible with or just very slow under Windows. You can make RRR exit and restart Windows, which is faster than doing the same thing manually when you need to "restart Windows to make your changes take effect." You can make RRR exit Windows and reboot your PC (after making changes to CONFIG.SYS, for example). You can even configure RRR so it exits Windows without any applications asking whether you want to save any open documents. Of course, you need to be careful — you may want to save those documents you happened to be working on.

The first time you run RESTART.EXE, RRR inserts itself into the LOAD= line of your WIN.INI file, so it will load automatically. To open RRR's main dialog box, simply press your Pause key. (This can be reconfigured to the Ctrl+Alt+Insert key combination.)

RRR will be a convenience that will save you several minutes or hours during its lifetime and yours.

Type of Program:	Utility.
Requires:	Windows 3.0 or higher.
Registration:	Use the form at the end of this chapter to register with the shareware author.
Technical Support:	Plannet Crafters provides technical support to registered users by phone, fax, mail, CompuServe, Internet, America OnLine, BIX/WIX, GEnie, Prodigy, and MCI Mail. Technical support is also provided for unregistered users to properly install and configure the program, by mail and all the above electronic-mail services.
Similar Shareware:	WinExit, a program featured in *Windows 3.1 Secrets,* is a utility that displays a simple icon on the icon line that you double-click to exit Windows quickly, but it doesn't have the customization features of Roger's Rapid Restart.

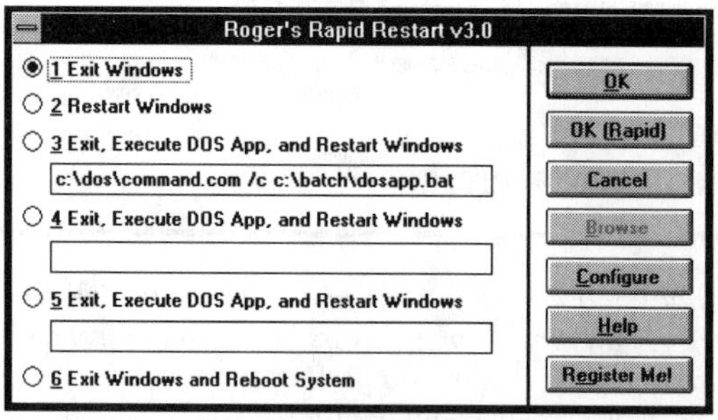

Figure 1: When you run RESTART.EXE and press Pause, this dialog box appears. You determine whether the utility merely exits Windows, restarts it after running a DOS program, or reboots your whole system safely. Then press Shift+Pause to exit Windows.

What Is Roger's Rapid Restart?

Roger's Rapid Restart is a Windows utility that gives you total control over exiting and restarting Windows. It allows you to

- ♦ Exit Windows. This quits Windows and returns you to the DOS prompt. Use Roger's Instant-Action Hotkey to get out of Windows with no questions asked!
- ♦ Restart Windows. This restarts Windows without first going back to the DOS prompt. This is quicker than manually exiting and restarting Windows.
- ♦ Exit Windows, run a DOS application, and restart Windows. This entire process can proceed without any user intervention. This is particularly useful for Windows power-users and developers.
- ♦ Exit Windows and reboot your system. This will exit Windows and perform a soft system reset. This is preferable to simply rebooting from within Windows.

You can utilize our Rapid Restart feature to exit or restart Windows without the delays involved when each application asks if it is OK to exit. This is particularly handy if you are running applications that always ask before terminating (such as a DOS application).You can also run Roger's Rapid Restart with parameters and have full access to its command set.

Why does Roger's Rapid Restart exist?

There are other shareware programs that will exit and/or restart Windows, but they are not as flexible, as unobtrusive or as *quick* as Roger's Rapid Restart (see next section). Under normal circumstances, you must tell your Windows shell (e.g., Program Manager) that you want to exit. It then asks you if you are sure. After asking each program in turn if it wants to exit, the system will finally shut down and return you to the DOS prompt. Developers and power-users often have the need to exit and/or restart Windows on a frequent basis, due to the complexities of their environment. And many people just want a way to exit Windows with no questions asked. Roger's Rapid Restart provides a better, quicker, and more flexible means of getting in and out of Windows. The uses of Roger's Rapid Restart are only limited by your imagination....

What are some common uses for Roger's Rapid Restart?

- ♦ There are many times when it is necessary to restart Windows. Many applications don't release all the system resources in use when they exit, and eventually you will become low on system resources. Or, if you are a developer and your application causes General Protection (GP) faults frequently, you will soon run out of resources. Restarting Windows is quicker and easier than exiting to the DOS prompt and typing WIN again.

- Many people have longed for a way to exit Windows instantly, without having to respond to an intervening dialog box. This is easy with Roger's Instant-Action Hotkey.
- Developers should run the Debug version of Windows to ascertain that their code functions properly with the additional error checking in Debug Windows. However, the Debug version is significantly slower than the retail version. With Roger's Rapid Restart, you can set up commands to change between the retail and debug system binaries with a single keystroke.
- Depending on what you use as a Windows shell, you might occasionally find yourself in a situation where the shell gets a GP fault or is otherwise hung-up. In this situation, you can still exit Windows by using Roger's Rapid Restart.
- There are still a few DOS applications that refuse to operate properly under Windows. Games are a prime example. Many of these can be run by using RRR's command to exit Windows, run a DOS application, and then restart Windows automatically when you are done.
- Even for normal exiting, many users find it more convenient to use Roger's Rapid Restart than to search for the Windows shell on your desktop.
- By utilizing Roger's Rapid Restart to exit Windows and reboot your system, you can set up an unattended system which will safely reboot if needed. You might wish to use this technique if you are dialing into your computer remotely and find a problem.
- You might wish to load, unload, or modify the operation of various TSRs that need to be in place before Windows is started.

Installation Notes

After WSETUP on the *More Windows 3.1 Secrets* Disk 1 has decompressed and copied all of Roger's Rapid Restart's files to a directory on your hard disk (e.g., C:\SECRETS2\RESTART), run RESTART.EXE in Windows.

The first time you run Roger's Rapid Restart, it will add RESTART.EXE to the LOAD= line in your WIN.INI file. This will ensure that the program is always accessible when you need it. If you decide at a later date to discontinue using Roger's Rapid Restart, simply remove RESTART.EXE from the LOAD= line by opening WIN.INI in Notepad, and restart Windows.

Once installed, you can access Roger's Rapid Restart by pressing the activation key from within Windows. (The default activation key is the Pause key.) An alternate method of activating it is to run RESTART.EXE a second time.

Upon startup, Roger's Rapid Restart will display a registration reminder screen (this is not present in the registered version), after which you will not see anything else until you activate the program.

That's all there is to it! We hope you enjoy the program. The trial license for Roger's Rapid Restart allows you to use it for a period of 21 days, after which time you must register it if you continue using it.

The Main Dialog Box

The main RRR dialog box is opened by pressing your Pause key, or by running RESTART.EXE again, after it has already been loaded once (by the LOAD= line in your WIN.INI file, for example). The main dialog box consists of six choices, numbered 1–6. (See Figure 1.) Choices 1, 2, and 6 are fairly self-explanatory. See Notes on exiting and restarting Windows and rebooting your system for more details.

Choices 3–5 are used to exit Windows, execute a DOS application, and return to Windows as soon as the DOS application is finished. Below each of these choices is an edit control box, where you enter the full command-line specification of the DOS application you desire to execute (see "Notes on Executing DOS Apps" for more details).

On the right side of the main dialog box, you will find a number of buttons. Each one is descibed below:

OK   Select this button to perform the choice (1–6) you have selected without using the RapidRestart method.

OK (Rapid)   Select this button to perform the choice (1–6) you have selected by using the Rapid Restart method.

Cancel   Select this button to cancel the dialog without further action.

Browse   Select this button to browse for files when entering a DOS application for choices 3–5. Note that this button will be disabled if you have selected choice 1, 2, or 6.

Configure   Select this button to open the configuration dialog box.

Help   Select this button to enter the help system for Roger's Rapid Restart.

Configuring Roger's Rapid Restart

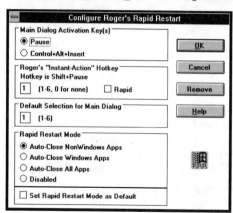

Figure 2: When you click the Configure button in RRR's main dialog box, this dialog box appears, from which you can select the behaviors you want.

Main dialog activation key(s)

The activation key is the key or keys that you press to open the RRR dialog.

The default activation key for RRR is the Pause key. However, you may also choose Control+Alt+Insert as your activation key sequence.

Roger's Instant-Action hotkey

The Instant-Action Hotkey will perform the desired exit/restart/reboot function without first presenting a dialog box. This gives you an easy way to exit Windows instantly.

The Hotkey sequence is the Main Dialog Activation Key(s) with the addition of the Shift key.

Choose 0 to disable this option.

Choose 1–6 to select the desired action. This number corresponds to the choices presented in the main dialog.

You may check the Rapid box if you wish the hotkey to use the Rapid Restart method.

Default selection for main dialog box

This will set the default selection when you bring up the RRR dialog box. This number (1–6) corresponds to the choices presented in the main dialog.

Rapid Restart mode

Rapid Restart is a powerful feature that can greatly speed up the process of exiting and/or restarting Windows. It accomplishes this by bypassing the normal "asking for permission to exit" that Windows normally sends to each active application. Under normal circumstances, this will not cause any problems. However, it is up to you to be sure that you don't have any unsaved files open. For example, let's assume you have configured RRR to use the Rapid Restart mode on Windows apps and you have an unsaved file in Notepad. If you exit Windows using Rapid Restart, you will lose the contents of the file you were editing. Plannet Crafters is *not* liable for *any* damage you inflict upon yourself!

You are given the following four basic options for Rapid Restart Mode.

Auto-close non-Windows apps

This is the default choice and will only auto-close non-Windows applications. It will not auto-close Windows applications.

Auto-close Windows apps

This will only auto-close Windows applications. It will not auto-close non-Windows applications.

Auto-close all apps

This will auto-close all applications, both Windows and non-Windows.

Disabled

This will effectively disable Rapid Restart. If you select Rapid Restart from the main dialog or via the parameter interface, if this option is selected, the effect is the same as a normal exit/restart.

You can choose Select Rapid Restart Mode as Default to set the default button in the main dialog to OK (Rapid).

Remove

This button removes Roger's Rapid Restart from memory.

Two Important Caveats (Please Read)

1. Use care when using the Rapid Restart method, which is selected by pushing the OK (Rapid) button. Depending on the options you have chosen, you could lose unsaved work.

   Rapid Restart is a powerful feature that can greatly speed up the process of exiting and/ or restarting Windows. It accomplishes this by bypassing the normal "asking for permission to exit" that Windows normally sends to each active application. Under normal circumstances, this will not cause any problems. However, it is up to you to be sure that you don't have any unsaved files open.

2. When you enter a DOS application command line in the Exit, Execute DOS App, and Restart Windows options, you must enter the fully qualified path with the file extension! (In other words, EDIT.COM won't work, but C:\DOS\EDIT.COM will.) If you want to

execute a batch file, you must use a secondary copy of COMMAND.COM at the beginning of the command line. For example, to run XYZ.BAT, your command like would look something like this: C:\DOS\COMMAND.COM /C C:\XYZ.BAT.

Exit Windows

You might find using Roger's Rapid Restart easier than searching for Program Manager in order to close Windows. You might also be interested in the "How to get out of Windows with no questions asked!" section below.

Restart Windows

This will Restart Windows without first returning to the DOS prompt. This is faster than exiting and manually restarting Windows, and also requires fewer keystrokes.

Reboot system

This will exit Windows and perform a soft system reset. This is definitely preferable to simply using Ctrl+Alt+Delete from within Windows.

How to get out of Windows with no questions asked!

Many people have been searching for a way to exit Windows instantly without intervening dialogs asking, "Are you sure ..."

With RRR, this is easy! Simply set the Shift+Pause Hotkey Choice to 1. Then, when you want to exit Windows in a flash, just press the Shift+Pause keys! You can also set the Rapid Restart mode to get out even faster.

For more details, please see the section "Configuring Roger's Rapid Restart."

Notes on Executing DOS Apps

This section describes in detail the usage of the Exit, Execute DOS App, and Restart Windows commands.

This will allow you to exit Windows, execute a DOS App, and restart Windows without further intervention.

All commands entered are saved in the RESTART.INI file, and will be available in future sessions.

When you enter a DOS application in the Exit, Execute DOS App, and Restart Windows options, you must enter the fully qualified path with the file extension! (In other words, EDIT.COM won't work, but C:\DOS\EDIT.COM will.)

If you wish to run a batch file, you must use the /C parameter to COMMAND.COM. An example would be C:\DOS\COMMAND.COM /C C:\XYZ.BAT.

If you enter a DOS command improperly, you will usually simply be returned to Windows, although in some circumstances the system will hang (e.g., if you enter C:\XYZ.BAT directly).

Most DOS applications will execute without problems. However, an application that desires to enter 386 protect mode will fail.

Switching between the Debug and Retail Windows Binaries

Windows developers should make use of the Debug Windows binaries during the development process. However, these Debug binaries tend to slow the system down enough to discourage their use. With RRR, you can switch to the Debug binaries with a single keystroke, test your application, and switch back to the retail binaries with another keystroke.

To change from the retail to the debug binaries, enter

```
C:\DOS\COMMAND.COM /C c:\windev\n2d.bat
```

in the Exit Windows, Run DOS App, and Restart Windows command line.

To change from the debug to the retail binaries, enter

```
C:\DOS\COMMAND.COM /C c:\windev\d2n.bat
```

in the Exit Windows, Run DOS App, and Restart Windows command line.

Note: You should obviously replace the diretories and batch filenames in the above examples with pathnames appropriate for your system.

Using Parameters with Roger's Rapid Restart

You can pass parameters to Roger's Rapid Restart and access all of its features. You might wish to create items in Program Manager to do specific exit/restart tasks.

The general syntax for the parameters is

```
RESTART {R}number {dosapp}
```

where {R} is the letter R, which is used to specify Rapid Restart mode; *number* is the command identifier; and {*dosapp*} is the optional DOS application to execute if *number* is 7.

Some examples:

RESTART 1 will exit Windows.

RESTART 2 will restart Windows.

RESTART R2 will restart windows using the Rapid Restart (tm) method.

RESTART 4 will exit Windows, execute the DOS app you have specified in command #4, and restart Windows.

RESTART 7 C:\DOS\EDIT.COM C:\AUTOEXEC.BAT will exit Windows, edit AUTOEXEC.BAT, and restart Windows.

One special parameter is ACTIVATE (only the A is relevant). This will start Roger's Rapid Restart if it is not already running and will instantly activate its dialog box. An example of this is

```
RESTART Act
```

Notes for Users of Roger's Rapid Restart Version 2

Due to popular demand, the default Activation Key has been changed to the Pause key. If you wish to use Control+Alt+Insert, simply change it in the configuration dialog after running RRR. (Press Pause to get to the main dialog the first time.)

User's Guide in On-Line Help

Roger's Rapid Restart contains a complete User's Guide in its on-line help system. You can select the Help button when the main dialog box is displayed.

If You Don't Want RRR to Add Itself to Your LOAD= Line

To get the most benefit out of Roger's Rapid Restart, you should run it when Windows starts. However, you might wish to run RESTART.EXE from your StartUp group as opposed to the

LOAD= line. If you have already installed RRR and want to run it from somewhere else, simply edit the WIN.INI file and remove its entry from the LOAD= line. If you have not yet run RESTART.EXE, simply create a file called RESTART.INI in your Windows directory and add the following lines:

[RRR]
Inst=1

Obtaining the Most Up-To-Date Version of RRR

If, for whatever reason, you want to be *sure* that you have the absolute latest version of Roger's Rapid Restart, you may contact Plannet Crafters directly. We will ship you the latest version for a nominal charge of:

$2 (including shipping/handling in the U.S. and Canada)

$5 (including shipping/handling for International orders)

The Plannet Crafters BBS

Our bulletin board system contains the latest version of Roger's Rapid Restart, as well as other products from Plannet Crafters.

It is available 24 hours a day, and supports baud rates up to 14.4 Kbps. The number is 404-740-8583.

How to De-Install Roger's Rapid Restart

If you wish to de-install Roger's Rapid Restart from a system, do the following:

1. Disable the autoloading of RESTART.EXE when Windows starts up. By default, an entry is added to your LOAD= line in the WIN.INI file. Simply edit WIN.INI and remove this entry.

2. Shut down RRR by clicking the Remove button in the main dialog box.

3. Delete all files in Roger's Rapid Restart's home directory, such as C:\SECRETS2\RESTART (assuming this directory contains *only* RRR files!).

Technical Support

Technical support for Roger's Rapid Restart is available to all registered users. If you are not a registered user, we will provide limited assistance to help you install and become suffi-ciently proficient for proper evaluation.

Technical assistance prior to registration is only available through electronic mail or regular mail.

Full technical support following registration is available by phone. However, we encourage you to use electronic mail to contact us. As you can see below, we have access to most of the common on-line services, and we visit them often. Because it is written, e-mail allows for more concise questions as well as more detailed answers.

This support will be provided for a period of 180 days (6 months) following registration (there is a limit of 30 minutes for phone support).

Additional support and/or training contracts may be purchased. Please contact Plannet Crafters for further information.

For all questions, problem reports, comments, and suggestions, please contact us at:

Mail:
Plannet Crafters, Inc.
2580 Runic Way
Alpharetta, GA 30202 USA

Phone: 404-740-9821 (9 a.m.–6 p.m. Eastern U.S. Time)
Fax: 404-740-1914 (24 hours a day)

Electronic Mail:

CompuServe:	73040,334
Internet:	73040.334@compuserve.com
America OnLine:	DMandell
BIX/WIX:	dmandell
GEnie:	D.MANDELL1
Prodigy:	VSFB48A
MCI Mail:	572-7179

Licenses

Non-registered users of this software are granted a limited license to make an evaluation copy for trial use for the express purpose of determining whether Roger's Rapid Restart is suitable for their needs. At the end of this 21-day trial period, you must either register (purchase) your copy or discontinue using Roger's Rapid Restart.

By registering this software, you will ensure continued support and updates of this product. In addition, registered users will receive a copy of the most current version without the registration reminder screen on startup. Registered users also receive technical support by phone, as well as free upgrades to future versions (shipping/handling extra).

A single Roger's Rapid Restart license entitles you to install and use the program on one computer (with one exception relating to home and work, which is described in detail below). In simple words, every user of Roger's Rapid Restart must be licensed.

Corporate/Site Licenses

All corporate, business, government, or other commercial users of Roger's Rapid Restart must be registered. We offer quantity discounts as well as site and corporate licensing.

Quantity discounts are offered, starting with as few as five copies.

Site licensing agreements allow duplication and distribution of specific number of copies within the licensed institution. Duplication of multiple copies is not allowed except through execution of a licensing agreement. Site license fees are based upon estimated number of users.

Corporate licensing agreements allow unlimited duplication, distribution, and use of Roger's Rapid Restart within the licensed institution.

For more information, please contact Plannet Crafters directly.

ALL PRICES AND DISCOUNTS ARE SUBJECT TO CHANGE WITHOUT NOTICE.

License Agreement

1. Introduction. This agreement explains when and how you may use both shareware and registered copies of software products from Plannet Crafters, Inc. In this agreement:

   ♦ "Program" means the Roger's Rapid Restart software product you have purchased or obtained for evaluation, including both the software and the associated documentation and other materials;

   ♦ "Shareware Copy" means a copy of the Program distributed by us or by our authorized agents for evaluation purposes and which is described as a shareware copy in the Program's sign-on messages;

♦ "Registered Copy" means a copy of the Program purchased from us or from a dealer, and which is not described as a shareware copy in the Program's sign-on messages;

♦ "We" or "us" means Plannet Crafters, Inc, a corporation based in Alpharetta, Georgia, U.S.A.; and

♦ "You" means the end user of the Program.

2. Legal Agreement. This is a legal agreement which allows you, the end user, to use the Program under certain terms and conditions. If you cannot agree to abide by what this agreement says, you should not use or evaluate the Program.

3. Copyright. The Program is copyrighted under U.S. law and international treaty provisions. You agree that your use of the Program is subject to these laws, which prohibit unauthorized copying or duplication of the Program software, documentation, and other materials.

4. Evaluation Period. You may use a Shareware Copy of the Program for an evaluation period of up to 21 days. The purpose of this evaluation period is to allow you to determine whether the program meets your needs before purchasing it. Once the evaluation period has ended, you agree to either purchase a Registered Copy of the Program, or to stop using it. If you have ordered a Registered Copy of the Program from us or from a dealer, you may continue to use your Shareware Copy beyond the end of the 21-day evaluation period until your Registered Copy arrives.

5. Use of the Program. While you are evaluating the Program, you may use it on as many computers as are required to perform your evaluation. Your 21-day evaluation period begins when you first install the Program on one or more computers for evaluation purposes. Once the evaluation period is over and you purchase the program, your use is subject to the following restrictions:

Individual Copies. You agree not to install and use an individual Registered Copy of the Program on more than one computer at a time. However, we agree to an exception to this rule if you meet the conditions described in the rest of this paragraph. You may install your individual copy simultaneously on one computer at work, one computer at home, and one portable computer, if all these computers are used primarily by the same individual, and there is *no possibility* that the computers will be in use at the same time, except while you are actively transferring files between them. If the Program was purchased by your employer, you agree to get your employer's explicit permission before installing the Program on multiple systems as described in this paragraph.

Multi-System Licenses and Network Use. You agree to purchase multiple individual copies or a multi-system license before using the Program simultaneously on more than one computer. When you purchase a multi-system license, you agree not to use the Program on more computers than the number included in your license, as shown on your invoice, the program sign-on screen, or other documents from us. You may install the Program on computers attached to a network, or remove it from one computer and install it on a different one, provided there is *no possibility* that your copy will be installed or used on more computers than it is licensed for. If you have a network, you don't need to include every computer attached to the network in your license, but you must include every computer on which the Program is installed or used, regardless of whether the users of the computer happen to know that the Program is in use on their system. If you have single computers which allow multiple users to use the Program simultaneously, you must count each keyboard or terminal separately when determining how many computers are using the Program. If you have purchased a site license, you may use the Program on any number of computers in the building(s) identified in the license agreement. If you have purchased a corporate license, you may use the Program on any number of computers throughout the corporation. Subsidiaries of a corporation shall not be deemed to have a license to use the Program unless otherwise specified.

6. Making and Distributing Shareware Copies of the Program. You may make copies of your Shareware Copy of the Program to give to others, as long as you include all of the files that you originally received with your Shareware Copy, as listed in the PACKING.LST file included with your Shareware Copy. When you give a Shareware Copy of the Program to another person, you agree to inform them that their copy is to be used for a time-limited evaluation period, and that they must purchase a Registered Copy if they continue to use the Program once the evaluation period has ended. You agree not to sell Shareware Copies of the Program or distribute them to others for any kind of compensation or fee unless you are a shareware disk vendor approved by the U.S.-based Association of

Shareware Professionals, are a non-profit User Group, or have received written permission from us; and your permission to distribute the Program has not been revoked by us; and you charge a fee of U.S $.8 (U.S./Canada) or $12 (International) or less per copy (excluding shipping costs). You also agree not to sell printed copies of any documentation for the Program under any circumstances.

7. Copying Registered Copies of the Program. When you receive a Registered Copy of the Program, you may make copies of the Program software which are necessary for normal backup purposes. However you agree not to make any copies of the printed manual(s) which come with the Program without explicit written permission from us. You also agree not to give your Registered Copy of the Program to others for any purpose. This means that you may not sell or give away copies of a Registered Copy of the Program or any part of it in any way, including bundling or reselling the Program with your own software, or placing such a copy of the Program in any disk library or on any bulletin board or electronic service.

8. LIMITED WARRANTY: The following limited warranty applies to Registered Copies of the Program. It is included here so you understand what your warranty will be when you purchase a Registered Copy. This warranty does *not* apply to Shareware Copies of the Program.

   Satisfaction Guarantee. If you are dissatisfied with any product you buy from us under this Agreement for any reason, you may return it at any time up to 15 days after purchase and we will give you a refund. Refunds will be based on the price you paid, with shipping costs excluded. You must contact us before returning any product for a refund. This satisfaction guarantee does not apply to multi-system licenses for more than 10 computers, or to purchases of more than 10 individual copies at a time.

   Physical Defects. We pledge that the disks and any printed material we send you will arrive free of physical defects which interfere with normal use. If you find such a defect and report it to us within 30 days after you purchase the Program, we agree to replace the defective item(s) at no charge to you as long as the defect was not caused by misuse or abuse.

   Bugs and Program Errors. We don't promise that the Program will be free of bugs or program errors, and you agree that bugs or program errors will not be considered "physical defects" in the program. We agree that if you report a program error or bug to us, we will use our best efforts to correct it. We also agree that if we can verify and correct the error you report, and we then issue a maintenance release for the Program which includes the correction, we will send you a copy of that maintenance release at no charge if you request it. However we will only do this for maintenance releases, not for new major releases or other new versions of the Program.

9. DISCLAIMERS AND LIMITATIONS. And now the full force legal language:

   DISCLAIMER FOR SHAREWARE COPIES. YOU ARE NOT PAYING FOR THE TRIAL USE LICENSE FOR YOUR SHAREWARE COPY OF THE PROGRAM. ACCORDINGLY THE SHAREWARE COPY IS PROVIDED "AS IS" AND WITHOUT WARRANTY OF ANY KIND.

   DISCLAIMER FOR REGISTERED COPIES. EXCEPT FOR THE LIMITED WARRANTY STATED ABOVE FOR REGISTERED COPIES OF THE PROGRAM, WE DISCLAIM ANY AND ALL OTHER WARRANTIES, EXPRESS OR IMPLIED, ORAL OR WRITTEN, INCLUDING ANY IMPLIED WARRANTIES OF MERCHANTABILITY OR FITNESS FOR A PARTICULAR PURPOSE. THE LIMITED WARRANTY ABOVE GIVES YOU SPECIFIC LEGAL RIGHTS, BUT YOU MAY HAVE OTHER RIGHTS, WHICH VARY FROM STATE TO STATE. SOME STATES DO NOT ALLOW A LIMITATION ON HOW LONG A WARRANTY LASTS, SO SUCH LIMITATIONS MAY NOT APPLY TO YOU.

   LIMITATION OF LIABILITY FOR SHAREWARE AND REGISTERED COPIES. IN NO EVENT SHALL WE BE LIABLE FOR ANY INCIDENTAL, CONSEQUENTIAL, OR PUNITIVE DAMAGES WHATSOEVER ARISING OUT OF USE OF THE PROGRAM OR YOUR RELATIONSHIP WITH US, INCLUDING WITHOUT LIMITATION ANY OR ALL DAMAGES FOR LOSS OF PROFITS, BUSINESS INTERRUPTION, LOSS OF INFORMATION OR ANY PECUNIARY LOSS, EVEN IF WE HAVE BEEN ADVISED OF THE POSSIBILITY OF SUCH DAMAGES. SOME STATES DO NOT ALLOW EXCLUSION OR LIMITATION OF LIABILITY FOR INCIDENTAL OR CONSEQUENTIAL DAMAGES; THEREFORE, THE ABOVE LIMITATION MAY NOT APPLY TO YOU. THE REFUND, REPLACEMENT AND TEMPTED REPAIR REMEDIES FOR REGISTERED COPIES STATED IN THE "LIMITED WARRANTY" SECTION ABOVE SHALL BE YOUR SOLE REMEDY FOR ANY AND ALL PROGRAM DEFECTS, PROGRAM ERRORS, OR DOCUMENTATION ERRORS.

Copyright and Trademark Information

Roger's Rapid Restart is copyright © 1991–1992 Plannet Crafters, Inc. All Rights Reserved.

LHA's SFX (Self-Extraction Utility) Copyright © 1991 Yoshi

Plannet Crafters, Roger's Rapid Restart, Rapid Restart, and "Just place your order and wait for space to catch up with time" are trademarks of Plannet Crafters, Inc.

All other product names may be copyright and registered or unregistered trademarks/tradenames of their respective owners.

ASP Ombudsman Information

This program is produced by a member of the Association of Shareware Professionals (ASP). ASP wants to make sure that the shareware principle works for you. If you are unable to resolve a shareware-related problem with an ASP member by contacting the member directly, ASP may be able to help. The ASP Ombudsman can help you resolve a dispute or problem with an ASP member, but does not provide technical support for members' products. Please write to the ASP Ombudsman at 545 Grover Road, Muskegon, MI 49442-9427 or send a CompuServe message via CompuServe Mail to ASP Ombudsman 70007,3536.

Program Credits

"Just Place Your Order and Wait for Space to Catch Up with Time"

This program was produced by Plannet Crafters, Inc. We have specialized in Windows programming since Windows 3.0 was released, and plan to ride the crest of the GUI-Wave into the future....

Plannet Crafters firmly believes that high-quality software products can be produced and marketed by small companies with dedicated employees who don't like much of the bureaucracy that pervades most corporations. We don't wear suits or ties, we avoid overly long meetings, and we make our own hours. However, we work long and hard to produce outstanding software.

We have a growing line of Windows utilities that assist you in making the most of your computer. Look for them!

How to Order/Register Roger's Rapid Restart

Roger's Rapid Restart is being distributed as shareware. This is also known as "try before you buy" marketing. The trial-license agreement provides for an ample evaluation period of 21 days. If you continue to use this software, you must buy it!

We have endeavored to make registration easy and painless. You may register via mail, phone, fax, or electronic mail.

Registered users will receive a copy of the most current version of Roger's Rapid Restart, and a registration code that will remove the registration reminder screen on startup. In addition, registered users also receive technical support by phone, a bonus DOS utility to reboot your system from a batch file, as well as free upgrades to future versions (shipping/handling extra).

For full details on registering, simply click the "Register Me!" buttons present on the Registration Reminder Screen, as well as the main dialog.

If you have any questions relating to registration, please contact Plannet Crafters.

Once registered, the "Register Me!" buttons will not be accessible. If you wish to order additional copies, details are provided on the following page.

Ordering Information

The cost for a single copy of Roger's Rapid Restart is $10, plus an additional charge of $2.00 for shipping and handling in the U.S./Canada, and $5 international.

You may order by phone if you are paying with a Visa, MasterCard, or American Express. Our number is (404) 740-9821 (9 a.m.– 6 p.m. Eastern U.S. Time).

Plannet Crafters, Inc.
2580 Runic Way
Alpharetta, GA 30202 USA

404-740-9821 (9 a.m.– 6 p.m. Eastern U.S. Time)
404-740-1914 fax (24 hours a day)
404-740-8583 BBS (24 hours a day)

CompuServe:	73040,334
Internet:	73040.334@compuserve.com
America OnLine:	DMandell
BIX / WIX:	dmandell
GEnie:	D.MANDELL1
Prodigy:	VSFB48A
MCI Mail:	572-7179

If you wish to order a copy via mail, fax, or e-mail, please include the following:

Name: _____

Address: _____

_____

_____

City, State, Zip: _____

Phone Number: _____

Disk Size (3.5- or 5.25-inch): _____

Product you are registering (Roger's Rapid Restart)

Include check, money order, cash, or credit card number and expiration date, if sending via regular mail; credit card number and expiration date, if sending via fax or email.

RRKeyCaps

Version 5-20-92
Copyright © RoadRunner Computing

I searched high and low for a good TrueType font to print graphical little keyboard keytops in documents. But I wasn't satisfied until I found RoadRunner Computing's RRKeyCaps. Most other keytop typefaces try to achieve fancy 3-D effects with shadows and borders. As the font's author explains in the body of this chapter, these effects just clutter up the fonts and make them difficult to read at the 10-point or 12-point sizes that most documents are set in. RRKeyCaps, by contrast, are clear and simple even at small sizes on low-resolution printers like HP LaserJets. The typeface even prints little mice, with the left or right mouse buttons clicked!

Elizabeth Swoope Johnston developed these TrueType fonts because, in her PC classes for total novices, she found that when she wrote, "Press Enter," some people typed e, n, t, e, r — no matter how many times she explained it. This keycap typeface eliminates all confusion.

Important Installation Instructions: *After running WSETUP on Disk 1, you must open the Control Panel's Fonts dialog box and click the Add button to add RRKeyCaps and RRKeyLetters to your Fonts list so that these typefaces will be available to your Windows applications. WSETUP does not modify your Fonts list, it simply copies the font files RRKEYCAP.TTF and RRKEYLIM.TTF to your Windows directory. See the Installation section below.*

Type of Program:	Typeface.
Requires:	Windows 3.1 or higher.
Registration:	Use the form at the end of this chapter to register with the shareware author and receive an additional typeface (RRKeyLetters) with keycaps for all U.S. keyboard alphabetical characters.
Technical Support:	RoadRunner Computing provides technical support to registered users by CompuServe, GEnie, and mail.
Similar Shareware:	Video Terminal Screen, featured elsewhere in *More Windows 3.1 Secrets,* is another TrueType face, which is a scalable font specifically designed to display all characters of the DOS "PC-8" character set (including line-draw characters).

The RRKeyCaps Character Set

Char	Keycap	Char	Keycap	Char	Keycap	Char	Keycap	Char	Keycap	Char	Keycap
!	F11	1	F1	A	Alt	Q	Enter↵	a		q	SysRq
"		2	F2	B	←Bksp	R	Enter↵	b	↓	r	→
#	F13	3	F3	C	Ctrl	S	⇧Shift	c	CapsLock	s	Spacebar
$	F14	4	F4	D	Del	T	Tab⇥	d	PgDn	t	↑
%	F15	5	F5	E	Esc	U		e	End	u	PgUp
&	▭	6	F6	F	Tab	V	Shift	f	⇥	v	⇧
'	Delete	7	F7	G		W		g		w	
(	▭	8	F8	H		X		h	Home	x	
)	▭	9	F9	I	Ins	Y	Bksp	i		y	
*	▭	:		J	Enter	Z		j	↵	z	
+	+	;	Insert	K		[	🖰	k	Break	{	
,		<		L		\		l	←	|	
-	-	=	🖰	M	Space	]	🖰	m		Alt+	
.		>	>	N		^		n	NumLock	0146	Delete
/		?		O	OMNI	_		o	ScrlLock	0182	¶
0	F10	@	F12	P	Pause	`		p	PrtScr	0255	.

Figure 1: This illustration shows the location of RRKeyCaps characters on your keyboard. To insert an F1 keycap character, for example, change to the RRKeyCaps font in your word processor and press the number 1 on your keyboard. To insert Alt+0146, make sure NumLock is on, then hold down your Alt key, type 0146 on your numeric keypad, and release the Alt key.

The RRKeyLetters Character Set (sample font)

Char	Key	Char	Key	Char	Key	Char	Key	Char	Key	Char	Key
!	[!]	)	[)]	1	[1]	9	[9]	[	[[]	}	[}]
"	["]	*	[*]	2	[2]	:	[:]	\	[\]	~	[~]
#	[#]	+	[+]	3	[3]	;	[;]	]	[]]		
$	[$]	,	[,]	4	[4]	<	[<]	^	[^]	Alt+	
%	[%]	-	[-]	5	[5]	=	[=]	_	[_]	0145	[']
&	[&]	.	[.]	6	[6]	>	[>]	`	[`]	0146	[']
'	[']	/	[/]	7	[7]	?	[?]	{	[{]	0182	¶
(	[(]	0	[0]	8	[8]	@	[@]	|	[|]	0255	.

Figure 2: This illustration shows the location on your keyboard of RRKeyLetters characters, a sample of which are installed with RRKeyCaps. When you register, you receive a version of RRKeyLetters that also supports all alphabetical characters on a U.S. keyboard, A–Z and a–z.

Installation

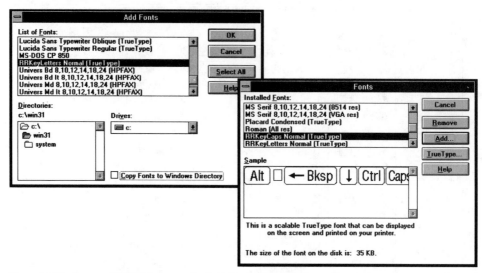

Figure 3: After you run WSETUP to copy the font files to your Windows directory, you must open Control Panel's Font dialog box, click the Add button, select RRKeyCaps Normal and RRKeyLetters Normal, and click OK, so the fonts become part of your list of Installed Fonts.

After you run WSETUP on the *More Windows 3.1 Secrets* Disk 1 to decompress and copy RRKeyCaps to your hard disk, you must do one more thing — add the font RRKeyCaps Normal to the Installed Fonts list in your Control Panel. This allows your Windows applications to "see" this font. To do this, take the following steps:

1. Open the Control Panel by double-clicking its icon in the Program Manager.

2. Double-click the Fonts icon in the Control Panel window.

3. When the Fonts dialog box opens, click the Add button.

4. In the Add Fonts dialog box that opens, you should see a list of fonts in your Windows directory that are available to be added to your Fonts list. Turn *off* the Copy Fonts To Windows Directory box. Select RRKeyCaps Normal from the scrolling list of available fonts and click OK. (You may also select RRKeyLetters, which is a sample font that contains mostly punctuation marks. The complete RRKeyLetters font, with all printable U.S. keyboard characters, is sent to registered users of RRKeyCaps.)

5. When you return to the Fonts dialog box, you should see that the selection you made has been added to the Installed Fonts list. Congratulations! Your selection is now available to all Windows applications that support TrueType. It should not be necessary to restart Windows. (In Microsoft Word for Windows version 1.*x*, you must click File Print-Setup OK for the fonts to be recognized, but this is unusual.)

Overview _____

RRKeyCaps and the matching RRKeyLetters are designed specifically for use in computer documentation and tutorial material for PC compatibles. I have written hundreds of pages of those materials, and I created both fonts after being frustrated with the keycap fonts that currently are available to Windows users.

My keycap and keyletter typefaces are plain 2-D characters that print well and are readable at standard body text sizes (10-12 points). They can be printed at sizes as small as 6 pts. and still be readable. Because they lack embellishments like 3-D or drop shadows, they are not as attractive at larger (display) sizes as typefaces from other vendors, and it is not recommended that you use them as display faces.

Although the current crop of 3-D, drop shadow, and reverse keycap typefaces are quite attractive and interesting, they don't work well at standard text sizes. The reverse keycaps may not reproduce well on typical copy machines, and the lettering in the 3-D and shadow typefaces is hard to read at body text sizes because some of the character height is occupied by the 3-D or drop shadow effect.

Most of the typefaces are cumbersome to use, too. Either you have to compose each key by typing each character (as well as opening and closing characters) and accessing graphics elements using the numeric keypad; or many keys are mapped to characters above 127, which forces you to use the numeric keypad; or the keys aren't mapped logically.

All keys in both of the RR typefaces can be accessed in one or two keystrokes (one of which is Shift). Most of the keys are mapped mnemonically, so you won't need a character map to remember which keycap is mapped to which key or what Alt+*number* combination to use.

There are alternate versions of several keys (Bksp in a text-only and a text-plus-graphic-arrow version; Enter in text-only, graphic-only, and both; Shift in text-only, graphic-only, and both; Tab in text-only, graphic-only, and both; Spacebar and Space; Ins and Insert; Del and Delete) so you can use the version that you prefer.

These typefaces have been designed so you can access them efficiently while developing documentation, without wasted keystrokes and mouse use. With a simple macro or two, you can use these typefaces with barely a hitch in your typing speed.

The following is an RRKeyCaps listing, with a few explanations regarding *why* certain keys were chosen to represent certain keycaps:

A	Alt
B	Backspace
C	Ctrl
D	Del
E	Esc
F	Text-only Tab
I	Ins
J	Text-only Enter
M	Space
O	OMNI (for Northgate Omni keyboard users)
P	Pause
R	Enter/Return
S	Shift
T	Tab
V	Text-only Shift
Y	Text-only Bksp
b	Down-arrow (b for Bottom)
t	Up-arrow (t for Top)
l	Left-arrow
r	Right-arrow

h	Home
e	End
d	PgDn
u	PgUp
c	CapsLock
n	NumLock
o	ScrollLock (this is the only assignment that's *really* weird)
p	PrintScreen
k	Break
s	Spacebar
q	SysRq
f	Graphics-only Tab
j	Graphics-only Enter
v	Graphics-only Shift
;	Insert
'	Delete
1	F1
2	F2
3	F3
4	F4
5	F5
6	F6
7	F7
8	F8
9	F9
0	F10
!	F11 (Shift+1; think, "Shift of F1")
@	F12 (Shift+2)
#	F13 (for Northgate Omni keyboard users)
$	F14 (for Northgate Omni keyboard users)
%	F15 (for Northgate Omni keyboard users)
&	Blank single-width key frame (like Arrow keys)
*	Blank one-and-a-half-width key frame (like Function keys)
(	Blank double-width key frame (like Tab)
)	Blank triple-width key frame (like Enter and Shift)
=	Two-button mouse with no buttons pressed
[	Two-button mouse with left button pressed
]	Two-button mouse with right button pressed
-	Hyphen (This is not a keycap hyphen, but a regular hyphen for use between keycaps, as in Ctrl-Alt-Del, so that you don't have to switch out of the keycap font just to get a hyphen, then switch back in.)
+	Plus (A regular plus sign, for those who prefer to use a plus, rather than a hyphen, between keys, as in Ctrl+Alt+Delete.)

The RRKeyLetters typeface is a set of matching typewriter keys designed to be used with this typeface for combinations like Ctrl+Y. The full set with all alphabetical letters on a U.S. keyboard is available when you register.

Registration

When you register, you'll receive

1. Diskette containing:
   a. RRKeyCaps
   b. Complete matching RRKeyLetters
   c. EPS, CGM, and WPG versions of the four blank keycap templates
2. A printed reference sheet on hard-to-destroy paper that shows the complete character map for both RRKeyCaps and RRKeyLetters on one side and an alphabetical listing of key names, sample keys, and the character to which each is mapped on the second side.
3. Documentation (currently 16 pages excluding table of contents and cover) with installation instructions and detailed instructions for setting up macros, styles, and keyboards (whatever is appropriate) for the most efficient keyboard use of these typefaces in Ami Professional 2.0, Word for Windows 2.0, and WordPerfect 5.1 for Windows.

Registration is $49 for either TrueType and PostScript Type 1 *or* HP bitmaps (with WordPerfect printer driver for bitmaps), or $75 for *both* formats. Shipping is $5.

Elizabeth Swoope Johnston
RoadRunner Computing
P.O. Box 21635
Baton Rouge, LA 70894

Name: _____

Company: _____

Title: _____

Address: _____

_____

City, State, Zip: _____

Country: _____

Phone: _____

E-mail (CIS, GEnie) ID: _____

Item	Qty	Amount
1. TrueType/PostScript Type 1 version (typeface files, blank keycap graphics files, documentation, reference card)	____ x $49	____.00
2. HP bitmaps (8, 9, 10, 11, 12, 13, 14, 16, and 18 pt. fonts in portrait and landscape, WP 5.1 printer driver, blank keycap graphics files, documentation, reference card)	____ x $49	____.00
3. Both items 1 and 2 above	____ x $75	____.00
Software total:		____.00
La. residents add 4% tax, EBR Parish residents add 8% tax:		____ . ____
Handling and shipping:		5.00
Order total:		____ . ____

Terms: Check or Money Order drawn on a U.S. bank in U.S. funds. All orders are prepaid only.

Diskette format (Check one):

___ 3.5" (720K)   ___ 5.25" (1.44MB or 360K)

Comments or questions can be addressed to Elizabeth Swoope Johnston at CompuServe: 76436,2426, or GEnie: E.JOHNSTON6.

Sloop Manager

SLOOPMAN.EXE — Version 1.2d
Copyright © Sloop Software

*S*loop Manager is one of the most ambitious Program Manager replacements in a crowded field. With a little configuration and exploration, you can find yourself using a more powerful and customizable Windows "shell" (the program that runs your StartUp group and launches applications) within minutes.

Important Installation Instructions: *Running the WSETUP program to decompress and copy Sloop Manager to your hard disk does not configure the program for your use. You must also double-click the INSTALL.EXE icon that WSETUP locates in a new Sloop Manager Install group in Program Manager. Sloop Software provides INSTALL.EXE to move files into the proper directories and configure Sloop Manager to your system. See the Installation section below for the correct procedure.*

Type of Program:	Program Manager replacement.
Requires:	Windows 3.1 or higher.
Registration:	Use the form at the end of this chapter to register with the shareware author.
Technical Support:	Sloop Software provides technical support to registered users by CompuServe, Internet, America Online, and phone, and to unregistered users during a 30-day trial period.
Similar Shareware:	Plug-In and WizManager, featured elsewhere in *More Windows 3.1 Secrets,* are Program Manager enhancements with different features than Sloop Manager.

Figure 1: Sloop Manager uses a "folders within folders" metaphor to help you organize your applications and files in a more powerful shell than Program Manager.

Overview

Sloop Manager is the complete graphical replacement for Microsoft's Windows Program Manager. It offers virtually all the features of Program Manager, plus a host of new features.

Features include the ability to

♦ Create folders (groups) within folders

♦ Move or copy items from folder to folder using drag-and-drop

♦ Use a Run command with a Browse button that stores the last 12 commands

♦ Save the location and size of a folder, as well as item positions

♦ Display items as icons or just names in a list box mode

♦ Password-protect individual folders

♦ Use a multi-select capability in adding, deleting, moving, or copying folder items

♦ Use a startup folder that removes the need to edit WIN.INI

♦ Click a command bar for quick access to often-used commands

♦ Customize a popup Run menu

♦ Allow multiple programs to be associated with a single extension

Installation

To install Sloop Manager, or update an older version of Sloop Manager, you must run WSETUP.EXE to decompress the files and INSTALL.EXE to configure the program, as described in the steps below.

Important: If you're installing over an old version of Sloop Manager, it is suggested you backup your SLOOPMAN data directory, just in case there is a problem during the install process.

1. a. **If you are running Program Manager as your Windows shell program:** Insert the *More Windows 3.1 Secrets* Diskette 1 into the appropriate drive. From Program Manager, click File Run, type A:WSETUP or B:WSETUP, and click OK. Select Sloop Manager from WSETUP's list of programs. WSETUP decompresses and copies all Sloop Manager files from Diskette 1 to a directory on your hard drive called SLOOPTMP (under whichever directory you chose when you started Wsetup). But WSETUP does not configure Sloop Manager — to do this, go to Step 2.

1. b. **If you are currently running an older version of Sloop Manager as the shell:** You must first restart Windows with Program Manager as the shell then do Step 1a. To make Program Manager the shell, use Notepad to change the SHELL= line in your SYSTEM.INI to read SHELL=PROGMAN.EXE. Then restart Windows and do Step 1a. Installing or reinstalling Sloop Manager is not possible while Sloop Manager is running as the shell (because it would overwrite files that are in use).

2. **Configure Sloop Manager:** From Program Manager, double-click the INSTALL.EXE icon in the Sloop Manager Install group window. This will start the configuration process, and will install all necessary Sloop Manager files into a directory called C:\WINDOWS\SLOOPMAN (or any other directory name you choose). The INSTALL.EXE program will copy all needed files to the proper directories and, if reinstalling, update the Sloop Manager system to run with the new version.

The INSTALL.EXE program does not create a Program Manager group window for Sloop Manager. To start Sloop Manager if it is not the shell, run SLOOPMAN.EXE in your SLOOPMAN directory. To make Sloop Manager the Windows shell, change the SHELL=PROGMAN.EXE line in your SYSTEM.INI file to read SHELL=C:\WINDOWS\SLOOPMAN \SLOOPMAN.EXE (using the correct directory name for your system).

3. **Remove unnecessary installation files:** After the configuration process runs successfully, delete the SLOOPTMP directory, and all files within it, to save hard disk space. None of the files are needed after INSTALL.EXE is completed. Also delete the Sloop Manager install group window from Program Manager, by minimizing the group, highlighting it, and clicking File Delete.

Should this process fail for any reason, follow the instructions for the manual install process in the file TROUBLE.TXT in the SLOOPTMP directory.

Note that the program will not run under the real mode of Windows 3.0.

Note that you may import any folders created with Sloop Software's separate Folders program, provided it is Folders version 3.1 or later. If you convert an existing Folders system to Sloop Manager, you may delete your \FOLDERS data directory, and the files FOLDERS.EXE, FOLDERS.HLP, and FOLDERS.INI, if you so desire. This will remove Folders from your system, as it is not needed if you have Sloop Manager.

Using Sloop Manager as the Windows Shell

Having Sloop Manager installed as the shell means that whenever Windows is started, Sloop Manager will start up in the same manner as Program Manager does, with the default settings of Windows. To install Sloop Manager as the shell, the file SYSTEM.INI, located in your \WINDOWS directory, needs to be edited. Open the file with a text editor like Notepad. On the first page will be a line which reads shell=*programname,* where *programname* is the name of the current shell. Unless you have already installed a program as the shell, *programname* would normally be PROGMAN.EXE. Change *programname* to read SLOOPMAN.EXE. Save and close the file and restart Windows. Sloop Manager should automatically start up. To remove Sloop Manager as the shell, simply edit SYSTEM.INI again and replace SLOOPMAN.EXE with whatever program you wish to be the shell. (It must be PROGMAN.EXE, WINFILE.EXE, or another program with shell capabilities.)

A special Startup folder may be created to have various programs automatically run upon Windows startup. This folder may be used in lieu of editing the WIN.INI LOAD= and RUN= lines. To use it, first create a folder named Startup. This folder may be located in any other folder. Once it is created, simply move, copy, or add the items you desire to have run on Windows startup. To start an item as an icon, simply use the Properties command and check the Run Minimized check box. Note that the Startup folder only operates when Sloop Manager is the shell.

Commands

The following sections give detailed explanations on the commands available to Sloop Manager and its folders. It is suggested that you read the README.TXT file first and then install the program. Take a look at it and play around before reading through this document. Most of the functions should be self-explanatory. Some commands will work with multiple items selected. In order to select multiple items, hold down the Ctrl key while clicking each item with the mouse. To de-select an item, click it again while holding down the Ctrl key.

File menu

New — This command creates a new folder. Note that you can create subfolders in subfolders, with essentially no limit on nesting folders within folders. Be sure to give each folder a unique name. Changing the case of a letter will not make a name unique.

Open — This command allows you to open (or activate, if already open) any folder on the system, regardless of its location. This allows you to open a specific folder without having to hunt it up.

Save — This command saves any changes made to the folder. Note that some commands will automatically perform a save when executed. They include delete subfolder, rename a subfolder, create a subfolder. The current configuration of a folder may also be saved using this command. The configuration includes the size of the folder, the position of the folder and the location of the items in the folder. Exactly which of these quantities are saved can be set using the Preferences command under the Special menu.

Run — Allows the user to enter a command line to be executed. The last 12 commands entered are stored for easy access.

Exit — Causes the current folder to be closed. If it has not been saved, and changes have been made, you will be prompted on whether or not you want the folder saved.

Edit menu

Add Item — Adds items to the current folder. A dialog box is presented from which you may choose any file on the system. After you choose a descriptive name for the item must be entered. This is the name that will show up under the item's icon. An icon will then appear which represents the item just added. If you double-click this icon, the item may be executed. Multiple items may be added by clicking each file you wish to add in the file list box. Clicking a selected file will deselect it.

Delete —

> **Item** — This command removes the selected item from the folder. It does not delete the file associated with the item. It simply removes it from the folder. If multiple items have been selected, a prompt to delete or not appears for each item selected.
>
> **File and Item** — This command removes the item from the folder and deletes the file associated with the item. As such, use it only when you wish to remove the file completely from the disk. If you wish to only remove the item from the folder, use the Delete Item command. This command does not function with subfolders. If multiple items have been selected, a prompt will appear as to whether or not to delete it for each item selected.
>
> **Subfolder** — Use this command to delete a subfolder. Note that this command completely removes the subfolder. As such, if you have copied it to another folder and wish to be able to still access it from this other folder, use the Delete Item command to remove it from the current folder rather than this command. Also, any subfolders in this subfolder are *not* deleted. So be sure and delete these other subfolders first.

Move — This command moves the currently selected item to the folder specified. In doing so, it is removed from the current folder. Note that if the folder you are moving the item to is open, it must be closed and reopened before the new item will appear. This command will work on any item including subfolders. If multiple items are selected, all items selected are moved. Items may also be moved by dragging them with the mouse to the desired folder, which must also be open.

Copy — Works the same as Move, but does not remove the item from the current folder. If multiple items are selected, all items selected are copied. Use this command to link two or more folders to the same subfolder. Simply create the desired subfolder using the File New command. Then copy the new folder item to whatever other folders you wish to be able to access it. Items may also be copied by dragging them with the mouse to the desired folder. The right mouse button must be held down when releasing the left mouse button for the items to be copied; otherwise, they will be moved.

Properties — This command displays and allows you to edit all the properties associated with an item. These properties include the item's descriptive name, its filename, its command line, its working directory, and its icon. To edit a property, simply type in the new property in the appropriate edit field. To change the item's icon, click on the icon button provided and choose the new icon using the icon browser dialog which appears. Two check boxes are provided to allow the item to be run minimized or maximized on execution. Check whichever option you desire or leave them unchecked for the item to run in a normal window.

Item Icon — Allows you to specify which icon is to be used to represent an item. Icons may be located in .ICO files, .EXE files or .ICL files (icon libraries). This command is the same as that provided by using the Properties command described above and selecting the icon button. It is provided simply so you do not have to go through the Properties command to change the icon.

Special menu

Set Default Icon — This command allows you to associate an icon with a file extension. Doing so will cause the specified icon to be used to display any item with that particular extension unless the item's icon has been set with the Item Icon command. The new associations will not appear until the folder is closed and reopened. This is true for any folder that was open when the changes were made. Once set, any item with the specified extension will appear using the icon associated with that extension.

Arrange Icons — Arranges the folder icons in an orderly manner.

Associate — The associate command is similar to the Associate command in File Manager. It can be used to associate a particular program with a specified file extension. Whenever you execute an item, the program associated with the item's file extension will be run using the item as the data file. Unlike the File Manager's command, multiple programs may be assigned to a single extension. Executing an item with multiple programs assigned to it will cause a list box to appear from which the desired program to be run may be chosen.

Preferences — This command allow the folder to be customized. The aspects of a folder that are saved when using the Save Config command may be set from this command. Also, the folder can be set to minimize or close on execution of an item in the folder. Auto-arrange of icons can be turned on or off from this command. Note that if auto-arrange is on, the icons will be rearranged every time the folder is resized or minimized, so it is recommended it be turned off if saving item positions. Finally, the display mode to be used, icons, or list box may be set from this command and a password may be assigned to the folder by using the Password button.

Edit run menu — (Available only from the main Sloop Manager window.) This command allows you to modify the customizable pop-up Run menu.

Global Options — (Available only from the main Sloop Manager window.) This command allows various global options to be set. These include turning on and off the confirmation of deletes and saves. If either is turned off, the operation will be performed without requesting confirmation from the user. Also, Sloop Manager startup options may be set. Sloop Manager may be set to always start as an icon or as a normal window. In addition, a reopen folders on startup option is available. Selecting it will cause any folders which were opened on exiting Windows to be reopened on Windows startup automatically. Finally, the preference settings given to any new folder upon creation may be set from this command.

Run menu

Displays the pop-up run menu, to allow you to make a selection for execution.

Procedures

Adding items to a folder

1. Select Add Item from the Edit menu.
2. From the dialog box that appears, choose the file you wish to add. Multiple files may be selected by simply clicking each file to be added. To deselect a file, click it again. Use the directory list box on the right to change directories. All highlighted files will be added. Click OK. Note that files may be added from a single directory only.
3. Enter the descriptive name for each item that you wish to have appear under the item icon. Hitting the Cancel button at this point will cause the current item not to be added. Any other items selected will still be added. Note that by double-clicking the File: field of the dialog, you may display the actual filename of the item with its extension.
4. The new item(s) should now appear as an icon in the folder.

Associating programs with file extensions

Application programs may be associated with a particular file extension. For example, Notepad may be associated with .TXT files. Executing a file with a program associated with its extension will cause the associated program to be run using the file as the data file. For instance, if .TXT is associated with Notepad, running the file README.TXT would cause Notepad to run and load the file README.TXT. Sloop Manager provides a command to form such associations. It is similar to the File Manager command, with the exception that it is able to associate more than one program to an extension.

To associate a program, follow these steps:

1. Select the folder item whose filename's extension you wish to associate a program with.
2. From the Special menu, select the command Associate.
3. A dialog box will appear, in which you may enter the name of the program you wish to associate, or the program may be selected using the Browse button.
4. If an association already exists, the option to append the new association will be available. To do so, click the check box 'Append association.' Click OK. This will cause the new association to be added to the list of programs associated with the selected extension.
5. If you wish to overwrite the current association, or if there is no previous association, leave the check box unchecked and click OK.
6. If you wish to view any other associations that have been previously set, click the down arrow at the right of the input box. A list of all other associations that have been set will appear. To close the list, simply click the down arrow again.

Notes: If multiple programs have been assigned to an extension, whenever you execute an item with that file extension, a list box will appear showing all the programs that have been associated with the extension. Simply double-click the program you wish to execute.

To remove a previously set association, follow steps 1 through 3, but on step 3 click the down arrow at the right of the input box. From the list of associations that appears, click the association you wish to remove. The program selection should appear in the input box. Click OK and the association selected will be removed.

Changing an item's icon

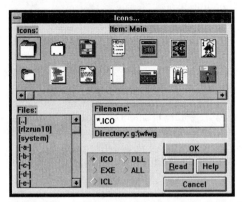

Figure 2: Sloop Manager includes an "icon library" in an .ICL file, plus you can use icons in other files for your items.

1. Select the item whose icon you want to change by clicking it with the mouse.
2. Select Item Icon from the Edit menu. The icon browser dialog will appear.
3. From the dialog box, choose the new icon to be used to represent the selected item. To use an icon in a specific file, select the file using the file list box by clicking the file to be read. The current directory may also be changed from this list box. Use the radio buttons to select the files to be displayed. Click Read to display all icons in the selected file. In the icon list box, select the desired icon and click OK.
4. The item should appear with the new icon.

Changing the properties of an item

1. Select the item whose properties are to be viewed or edited by clicking it with the mouse. Select the Properties command from the Edit menu.
2. The item name, filename, command line and, working directory may be edited by changing the value in the appropriate edit field. Click OK to save the settings. Note that by entering a blank line for the command line or working directory, the default function-ality of the item will be restored. Also, by entering CURRENT DIRECTORY, the directory will not be changed when executing that item.
3. The item icon may be set by clicking the icon button provided. Doing so will bring up the icon browser dialog, from which the new icon may be selected.
4. Finally, the item may be set to run minimized or maximized by clicking the appropriate check box.

Copying items from folder to folder

1. Select the item you wish to copy by clicking it with the mouse. Multiple items may be selected by holding down the Ctrl key while clicking each item.
2. Select Copy from the Edit menu.

3. From the dialog box, select the folder you want the item(s) copied to. Click OK.

4. The item(s) will now be copied to the specified folder.

or

1. Make sure the folder you wish to copy the selected items to is open or is a subfolder of the current folder.

2. Select the items to be copied in the same manner as above, but on the last item selected continue to hold down the left mouse button.

3. Drag the cursor to the folder you wish to copy the items to. The cursor will be a mono-chrome version of the selected item, if only a single item is selected. If multiple items are selected, it will be a generic drag item cursor.

4. While holding down the right mouse button, release the left mouse button while the cursor is over the folder you want to copy the items to. If the cursor is a circle with a line across it, you are over an illegal drop point.

5. Once the left mouse button has been released, the right mouse button may also be released. The selected items will be copied to the specified folder.

Using this command, one can link the same subfolder to two or more other folders. Simply copy the subfolder to the folder you wish to also have access to it.

Creating a new folder

1. Select New from the File menu.

2. Enter the name of the new folder. This name *must* be unique. Upper- or lowercase letters are considered the same. Click OK.

3. A new folder icon representing the new folder should appear in the current folder.

Deleting an item

1. Select the item you wish to delete by clicking it with the mouse. Multiple items may be selected for deletion by holding down the Ctrl key while clicking each item to be deleted.

2. Select Delete Item from the Edit menu.

3. You will be asked if you wish to delete the selected item. Click Yes or No.

4. If you clicked on Yes, the item will be deleted from the folder. Note that if you acciden-tally delete an item, close the folder without saving it. When you reopen it, the item will still be there.

Deleting an item and its file

1. Select the item you wish to delete by clicking it with the mouse. Multiple items may be selected for deletion by holding down the Ctrl key while clicking each item to be deleted.

2. Select Delete File and Item from the Edit menu.

3. You will be asked if you want to delete the selected item and its file. Click Yes or No.

4. If you clicked on Yes, the item will be removed from the folder and the item's associated file will be erased from the disk.

Deleting a subfolder

1. Select the subfolder you wish to delete by clicking it with the mouse.

2. Select Delete Subfolder from the Edit menu.

3. You will be asked if you want to delete this subfolder. Click Yes or No.

4. If you clicked on Yes, the subfolder will be removed from the system. Note that if the subfolder has been copied to other folders, it must be removed from those folders using the Delete Item command.

Note that any subfolders contained in the subfolder being deleted will NOT be deleted. They should be removed through use of this command before deleting the subfolder they are contained within.

Editing the Run menu

A customizable, pop-up Run menu is provided from which programs may be run. A menu editor dialog is supplied to build and maintain this pop-up menu. It may be accessed by selecting the Edit run menu command under the menu command Special. It may be used to add items, including separators and submenus, to update item command lines or to delete items from the Run menu.

Adding run menu items:

1. Select the item from the menu list box you wish the new item to appear under. By selecting the "—— Top of Menu ——" placeholder, a new item may be added at the top of the menu.
2. Select the radio button corresponding to the type of item you wish to add. The new item may be a separator bar, a submenu of the current menu, or just a normal, executable menu item.
3. Fill in the name for the new item and its corresponding command line. The Browse button will bring up a dialog which may be used to select a file for the command line. Note that the command line field should not be modified for separator and submenu item types.
4. Click the Add button and the new item will be added to the Run menu.

Changing an item's command line:

1. Select the item from the menu list box whose command line you wish to change.
2. Type in the new command line. Click the Add button.
3. The item's command line will be updated to the new command line. Note that the Add button is used both to add new items and to modify the command line of old items.

Deleting an item:

1. Select the item from the menu list box you wish to remove from the Run menu.
2. Click the Delete button and the item will be removed from the menu.

Creating submenus:

1. Add a new item for which you have selected the Submenu radio button for the item type. Be sure not to modify the command line when adding the item. Only the name for the submenu needs to be specified.
2. Select the newly added submenu item. The ">>>" button will now be enabled. Clicking this button will allow you to build the menu to be associated with the submenu item added in step 1.
3. To return to the parent menu, click the "<<<" button. You may have as many submenus as you desire and the submenus may have submenus of their own. They may be edited in the exact same manner as the main parent menu.

Once you have made all the desired changes to the Run menu, click the Done button to exit the dialog. The newly edited pop-up Run menu will now be accessible from the main menu Run command, or by clicking the CommandBar with the left mouse button.

Executing an item

    1. Double-click an item's icon to execute it.

or

    2. Click it with the mouse and hit the Enter key.

or

    3. Use the arrow keys to select the item. Hit the Enter key.

Exiting a folder

    1. Select Exit from the File menu, or Close from the System menu.

    2. If changes have been made to the folder since the last save, you will be asked whether or not you wish to save the folder. Clicking Yes will save and exit the folder. Clicking No will exit the folder without saving. Clicking Cancel will cancel the exit operation and return you to the folder.

Global options settings

Various global options may be set using the Global Options command found under the Special menu of the main Sloop Manager window. These options include

Confirmation settings:

Confirm on delete — Checking this box will cause a confirmation box to be presented for the user to confirm the delete. If not checked, the delete will occur automatically.

Confirm save on exit — Normally, upon exiting a folder you are presented with the option of saving any changes that have been made to the folder. If this option is unchecked, the save will be performed automatically upon exit.

Confirm Windows exit — This option controls whether or not to confirm exiting Windows.

Startup settings:

Start SM minimized — Checking this box will cause Sloop Manager to always start as an icon on the desktop.

Start SM normal — This option will cause Sloop Manager to always start as a normal window. Normally, it is not necessary to check this box for SM to start in a normal window.

Reopen folders — Checking this option will cause any folders which were open at the time Windows was exited to be reopened on Windows startup. Note that the folders will not necessarily be opened in the same position or size they were in when Windows was exited.

New folder settings:

All of the options provided under the New Folder Settings heading are used to set the preferences any new folder will be created with. These settings are used only when a new folder is created and once the folder has been created, its preferences settings may be changed using the Preferences command.

Folder icon:

Finally, by clicking the folder icon button, the icon to be used to represent folders may be set. Upon clicking the folder icon button, the icon browser dialog will be presented to allow you to select the desired icon. See the section on changing an item's icon for a description on how to use the icon browser dialog. Once an icon has been selected, all folder icons will be changed to the selected icon.

Having folders open on startup

There are three ways in which you may have specified folders open automatically on Windows startup. The first method is to select the Reopen Folders option in the global options dialog. See Global option settings for information on this option.

The second method involves making use of the startup folder option. By creating a folder named StartUp and placing the folder icons of the folders to be opened in this folder, either by moving or copying them, selected folders may be opened and available on Windows startup. To use this option, simply create a folder named StartUp. Any item, which includes folder and non-folder items, placed into this folder will be run on Windows startup. To have an item start as an icon on the desktop, simply select the Run Minimized option of the Properties dialog for that particular item. To set the order of execution of items, simply arrange the items from left to right, with left being first, and save the folder. By using this option, editing the WIN.INI file may be avoided entirely.

The third, and most awkward method, involves editing the WIN.INI file. First, open the SLOOPMAN.INI file with an editor such as Notepad. Under the section [Folder list], find the folder(s) you wish to have opened on Windows startup. Make a note of the DOS filename to the right of the equal sign. Close this file and open WIN.INI. On the LOAD= or RUN= lines, add the DOS file name you noted from the SLOOPMAN.INI file. Save and close the WIN.INI file. The next time you start Windows, the specified folders should open.

Moving items from folder to folder

1. Select the item you wish to move by clicking it with the mouse. Multiple items may be selected by holding down the Ctrl key while clicking each item.
2. Select Move from the Edit menu.
3. From the dialog box, select the folder you want the item(s) moved to. Click OK.
4. The item(s) will now be moved to the specified folder.

or

1. Make sure the folder you wish to move the selected items to is open or is a subfolder of the current folder.
2. Select the items to be moved in the same manner as above, but on the last item selected continue to hold down the left mouse button.
3. Drag the cursor to the folder you wish to move the items to. The cursor will be a monochrome version of the selected item if only a single item is selected. If multiple items are selected, it will be a generic drag item cursor.
4. Release the left mouse button while the cursor is over the folder you want to move the items to. If the cursor is a circle with a line across it, you are over an illegal drop point. The selected items will be moved to the specified folder.

Opening a folder

1. Select Open from the File menu.
2. Choose the folder you wish to have opened from the list in the dialog box. Click OK.
3. If the folder selected has not been previously open, it will be opened and appear in a second window. If it is already open, it will be made the active window. If is already open and minimized, its icon will be opened into the active window.

Saving a folder

1. Select Save from the File menu.
2. All changes made to the folder will be saved. In order to save a folder's size or position, or the position of the items in the folder, a Save must be executed and the appropriate option must be selected in the Preferences dialog. The exact information saved is determined by the options selected using the Preferences command.

Setting a default icon

1. Select the Default Icon from the Special menu.
3. Choose the item whose file extension you wish to assign a default icon to.
2. Select the icon you want associated with the extension from the icon list box presented. To use an icon in a specific file, select the file in the file list box and click Read. From the icons presented, select the desired icon.
4. To see the new icons, close and reopen the folder.

Note that these associations will apply to all folders, not just the one they are set in. To remove any association previously set, the SLOOPMAN.INI file must be edited. Open it with a text editor like Notepad. Under the section [Icon Extensions], delete the line containing the extension you wish to deassociate. Save the file. The items should now appear using their old icons. To clear all default icons assigned, simply delete the file SLOOPMAN.DFI in your folders data directory.

Setting the folder icon

This procedure may only be performed from the Sloop Manager window.

1. Select the Global Options command from the Special menu.
2. Click the Folder Icon button.
3. From the icon browse box, select the icon to be used as the folder item icon. Click OK.
4. All subfolders and minimized folders will now appear using the selected icon.

Setting the password

1. Select the Preferences command from the Special menu.
2. Click the Password button.
3. Enter the desired password in the input box. Click OK.
4. Once the password is set and saved, every time the folder is opened, the password will need to be entered before the folder will open.

To clear a password, perform steps 1 and 2 above, but instead of entering a password, simply leave the line blank and click OK. The password will then be cleared.

To lock people out of Windows completely, assign a password to the Sloop Manager window. Every time Windows is run, the password will need to be entered correctly; otherwise, Windows will be terminated.

Note that this password scheme is not unbreakable. It will keep out most users, but a determined computer professional will be able to break it.

Using the Browse button

Both the Run command and Associate provide Browse buttons to allow you to select a file to be run or associated. To use the Browse button, simply click it. A browse dialog, essentially identical to the dialog used by the Add Item command, is provided. Find the file in the file list box you wish to make use of and click it. The current directory may be changed using the directory list box on the right. Once you have selected a file, click OK and it will appear in the dialog box of the command being executed (Run or Associate).

Using the CommandBar

A push button command bar is provided for quick access to various main menu commands. Buttons are provided for accessing the New, Open, Save, Add item, Properties, and Item icon commands. Clicking the appropriate button is equivalent to executing that menu command. In addition, by clicking anywhere on the CommandBar itself, the pop-up Run menu may be accessed.

The CommandBar may be turned off from an option in the Global Options dialog. An info bar is provided as well as the CommandBar. The InfoBar displays the actual file name and size of the currently selected folder item. A -1 for the file size indicates that the file path information is incorrect. Like the CommandBar, the InfoBar may be turned off from the Global Options dialog.

Note that by clicking the InfoBar, the Preferences dialog may be brought up.

Using the Preferences command

1. Select Preferences from the Special menu.
2. From the dialog box presented, several options may be set to customize the folder, as explained below.

   Save Configuration options: When executing a Save command, the choices selected here will govern what information about the folder is saved. Information that can be saved include the folder size and position, and the position of the folder items. Any option not selected will not be saved. Note that by deselecting the folder position option, the folder will be free to appear anywhere on the desktop.

   Minimize on use, Close on use options: Selecting one of these will cause the folder to be either minimized or closed when an item in the folder is executed.

   Auto Arrange switch: When this option is activated, the folder item icons will automatically be rearranged whenever the folder is resized or minimized. If you wish to keep the folder items in specific locations at all times, do not use this option.

   Icons off: This option, when set, will cause the folder items to be displayed using only their names. No icons will be displayed. This mode is the list box display mode. If this option is not set, all items will be displayed using icons.

   Show extensions: When in list box display mode, the item file extensions will be displayed as part of the name if this option is set.
3. Once you have chosen the options you wish to be active for this folder, click OK to return to the folder window. Note that a Save or a Save Config must be performed for the preferences to be saved.
4. Finally, a password may be assigned to the folder through the use of the Password button. Clicking it will produce a dialog box in which you may enter the desired password for this folder. The next time the folder is opened, this password will need to be entered before you will be able to access the folder. To clear the password, simply select this function again and enter a blank line for the password.

Using the Run command

1. Select Run from the File menu.
2. In the dialog box that appears, type in the command you wish to execute. Or use the Browse button to select a file to be executed.

3. Click OK. The command entered will be executed. By clicking the 'Run minimized' check box, the program will appear as an icon on the desktop.

Notes: The Run command stores the last 12 commands executed, throwing out duplicates. When the Run command is selected, the last command entered using the Run command will automatically appear in the input box. To execute it, simply click OK. To access the other 11 commands stored, click the down arrow at the right of the input box. A list will appear containing the other 11 commands. Click the command you wish to execute, and then click OK. The command will be run.

Notes on using Icons

Sloop Manager is capable of extracting and using icons from .ICO (icon description files), .EXE (executable programs), and .ICL (icon libraries created by a third-party program) files. An icon library, SLOOPMAN.ICL, is provided with the program for your use. It must be located in the Sloop Manager data directory you specified upon installation for it to be used. Note that you may delete, copy over, or edit (with a program such as Icon Manager or equivalent) this file without impacting Sloop Manager operation.

There may be cases where, for some reason, Sloop Manager cannot extract the icon in the specified file. In order to use such an icon, you will need to convert it into an .ICO file using some utility such as Icon Manager. Once this is done, it may be used by simply specifying the .ICO file.

Some 256- or 32,000-color displays may not display the icons properly when in 256- or 32,000-color mode. If this occurs, try this fix. Open the SLOOPMAN.INI file using an editor like Notepad. Under the section [Defaults] will be a line which reads, COLOR MODE=0. Change the 0 to 256 or 32000 (no comma), whichever is appropriate. This tells Sloop Manager that you are using a 256- or 32,000-color display. Note that the program will not function in other color modes with this setting made. To operate in other color modes, change the setting back to 0 or the mode you wish to use. Acceptable values include 0, 16, 256 and 32000.

Hierarchy of Icons

There is a hierarchy involved when Sloop Manager decides which icon should be used to represent an item. At the top level, if an item has had an icon explicitly set for it using the Item Icon command, this icon will always be used, regardless of any other settings made. Next, if the item does not have an icon set for it, but does have an icon associated with its extension, this icon will be used. If neither of the above is true, but the item is an executable or is associated with an executable, the icon for that executable will be used. Finally, if none of the above holds, the item will appear using the default icon, which is the DOS icon.

Sloop Manager File Structure

Sloop Manager creates and maintains a data file for each folder created. These files end in an .FL1 extension. It is suggested you allow the INSTALL.EXE procedure to create a separate directory for these data files, simply to avoid cluttering up the Windows directory any more than it probably is already. This is not necessary, though, as the files can be maintained anywhere as long as the directory is correctly specified during the install process.

Sloop Manager Getting Confused

Should the SLOOPMAN.INI file get messed up, as will happen if you delete a folder without first deleting its subfolders, it can be repaired. Open SLOOPMAN.INI with a text editor like Notepad. Under the section [Folders List], the name of every folder with its corresponding DOS filename is listed. Make note of the DOS filenames of the folders that should be deleted. Delete those lines. Close the .INI file and go to your Sloop Manager directory. Delete those files whose names you made note of in the .INI file. If you want to save these subfolders, instead of deleting anything, add the file whose name you found to a folder, naming it with the subfolder name.

Keyboard

The keyboard functions essentially the same as for any Windows application. The only unique feature of the keyboard interface involves selecting items and launching applications. Use the arrow keys to move from item to item. Hitting Return will execute the selected item. Note that you may select multiple items by using the mouse only.

Items may also be selected by hitting the first letter of the item's name. Repeatedly hitting a letter will move you through all item's whose names begin with this letter. This interface will work only in icon display mode.

Troubleshooting Information

Automatic install process fails

Should the INSTALL.EXE program fail for any reason, follow the procedure for manually installing the program given below. Note that you will be unable to convert an existing Folders system using the manual install procedure.

If no previous version was installed:

1. From the SLOOPTMP directory created by WSETUP, copy the files SLOOPMAN.EXE, and SLOOPMAN.HLP to your Windows directory. Copy the file SLPMAN.INI to SLOOPMAN.INI in your Windows directory (renaming it SLOOPMAN.INI). Copy the files BWCC.DLL and SMTOOLS.DLL to your Windows \SYSTEM subdirectory.

2. Create a subdirectory of your Windows directory called SLOOPMAN. (***Note:*** This step may be skipped. Any existing directory may be used instead.)

3. Copy the files SLOOPMAN.FL1, SLOOPMAN.ICL, GRPCONV.EXE, and SMTRASH.EXE to the SLOOPMAN data directory created in step 2.

4. Edit the file SLOOPMAN.INI in the following manner, using a text editor such as Notepad: Under the section name [Folders Directory], edit the PATH= line to read: PATH=*directory*\, where *directory* is the directory created in step 2. Note the backslash (\) at the end of the name. An example line would be PATH=C:\WINDOWS\SLOOPMAN\.

5. If you want to use Sloop Manager as the shell, edit the SYSTEM.INI file with an editor, such as Notepad. Change the SHELL= line to read SHELL=SLOOPMAN.EXE.

6. You may convert and install your Program Manager groups into Sloop Manager at this point. Run the program GRPCONV.EXE located in your SLOOPMAN data directory.

7. Finally, from the File Manager, using the Associate command under the File menu, associate SLOOPMAN.EXE with .FL1 files.

If a previous version was installed:

1. If currently using version 1.2x, simply copy the files SLOOPMAN.EXE and SLOOPMAN.HLP from the SLOOPTMP directory to your Windows directory. Copy the file SMTOOLS.DLL to your Windows \SYSTEM directory.

2. If using version 1.1x or earlier, follow the procedure for "No previous version installed." You will be unable to maintain your old version.

That's it. You should now be able to run Sloop Manager as you would any program. Or, if it is installed as the shell, simply restart Windows.

Subfolder item accidentally deleted

Should you accidentally lose a subfolder item, either by deleting it with the Delete Item command rather than the Delete Subfolder command, or through some other misfortune, the folder can be recovered. To recover a lost folder, follow the steps below:

1. Open the file SLOOPMAN.INI with a program such as Notepad. This file should be in your \WINDOWS directory, unless moved by you.

2. Under the section [Folder List], find the name of the folder you wish to recover. To the right of the equal sign will be a DOS filename with a name similar to FLDxxxx.FL1, where xxxx is some number. Make a note of this name. Close the .INI file.

3. From the folder you wish to restore the lost folder to, select the Add Item command. Go to your SLOOPMAN data directory, which was created when the program was installed. Find the file whose name you recorded in step 2. Select it and click OK.

4. In the name input box which appears after you hit OK in step 3, enter the name of the lost folder. Click OK.

A new folder icon representing the lost folder should now appear. It may now be treated in the same manner as any other folder.

Deleting a folder whose password you've forgotten

If you need to delete a folder, but have forgotten the password, the following procedure may be followed to remove it from the Sloop Manager system.

1. Select the folder you wish to delete and execute the Properties command. Make a note of the filename.

2. Delete the item using the Delete Item command. Save the parent folder.

3. Go to your SLOOPMAN data directory and delete the file whose name you made a note of in step 1.

4. Restart Sloop Manager. The folder should now be deleted.

Icons appear scrambled

Should the icons used to display folder items not appear correctly, do the following. First, check what video mode you are running in. Specifically, the number of colors being provided. Sloop Manager supports up to 32,000-color mode. It does not support CGA (4-color) mode.

Should you be running in 256- or 32,000-color mode and the icons are scrambled, try this fix. Edit the file SLOOPMAN.INI with an editor like Notepad. Under the section [Defaults], find the line which reads COLOR MODE=0. Edit it to read: COLOR MODE=256 or COLOR MODE=32000 (notice there is no comma).

This forces the program to run in 256- or 32000-color mode. Note that it will no longer run properly in 16-color mode. To run in 16-color mode, change the 256 in the line to 16, or to 0 for auto-sense mode. If you are still unable to get the icons to appear correctly, contact customer support.

System crash occurs when starting Windows with Sloop Manager as the shell

Provided with the program is a file called SLPMAN.EXE. Copy this file to your \WINDOWS directory. Edit the SYSTEM.INI file with Notepad or equivalent. Change the line which reads SHELL=*whatever* to SHELL=SLPMAN.EXE. Restart Windows. Sloop Manager should now be able to run as the Windows shell.

Uninstalling Sloop Manager

1. Edit the SYSTEM.INI file, found in the Windows directory, using an editor like Notepad.
2. Find the line which reads: SHELL=SLOOPMAN.EXE. Change the line to read: SHELL=PROGMAN.EXE.
3. Save and close the SYSTEM.INI file.
4. Restart Windows. Program Manager should now start as the shell.
5. Delete the SLOOPMAN directory that was created, and the files SLOOPMAN.EXE, SLOOPMAN.HLP, and SLOOPMAN.INI in your \WINDOWS directory. Also, delete SMTOOLS.DLL in the \SYSTEM subdirectory.

Miscellaneous

Trashcan utility

A trashcan program is provided for disposing of folder items. To use the program, execute the file SMTRASH.EXE. This file is initially placed in your SLOOPMAN data directory. Once the program is executed, a trashcan icon will appear on the desktop.

To delete an item from a folder, simply drag the item to the trashcan. Multiple items may dragged and dropped.

Should you wish to recover a deleted item, double-click the trashcan icon. It will open into a window, showing all the items that have been dumped into it during the current Windows session. These items may be dragged out of the trashcan and dropped into a folder to recover them.

The trashcan will automatically empty whenever it is terminated. The trashcan may also be emptied by executing the Empty Trash command under the Trashcan File menu. Finally, the can will automatically empty when the number of items in it exceed 40.

Important note: Dragging an item into the trashcan is equivalent to the Delete Item command under the Sloop Manager Edit menu. It does not delete the item's file from the disk. Also, folders may not be deleted using the trashcan. The delete commands under the Edit menu must be used to delete folders.

Group conversion utility

The group conversion utility is provided to allow you to convert Program Manager groups to Sloop Manager folders. This may be necessary at times, specifically after installing a new program into Windows. While a communication link similar to that used by Program Manager is incorporated into Sloop Manager, some install programs will install only into Program Manager. If you should install such a program, through the use of the group conversion utility, the new group created by the install program may be imported into Sloop Manager.

To make use of the group conversion utility, follow the steps given below:

1. Run GRPCONV.EXE from Windows. This file is initially placed in your SLOOPMAN data directory, but may be moved to any location desired.
2. From the dialog that appears, choose the group to be converted and enter the name for the Sloop Manager folder. Click OK.
3. Once the conversion process is complete, exit and restart Sloop Manager. Do not save Sloop Manager before exiting. If you're using Sloop Manager as the Windows shell, it will be necessary to exit and restart Windows. Note that multiple groups may be converted before exiting by repeating these steps.

Once Sloop Manager has been restarted, there should be a new folder in the main Sloop Manager window containing items equivalent to the items in the Program Manager group.

Customer support

Customer support is available to all registered users of Sloop Manager for as long as you own the program. Support is also available to unregistered users during their 30 day trial period.

Support may be obtained by calling (719) 260-0433 during normal business hours. Please leave a message should we be unable to answer the call immediately. We promise to get back to you that same day, if at all possible.

You may also write us at:

Sloop Software
Customer Support
6457 Mesedge Lane
Colorado Springs, CO 80919 USA

Sending e-mail to CompuServe (72540,144) or Internet (72540.144@compuserve.com) or America OnLine (Sloop Soft). We check CompuServe on a daily basis, allowing for a prompt response to any inquiries.

Please include as many details as possible concerning any problem you may be experiencing, to allow us to fix it as quickly as possible.

This program is produced by a member of the Association of Shareware Professionals (ASP). ASP wants to make sure that the shareware principle works for you. If you are unable to resolve a shareware-related problem with an ASP member by contacting the member directly, ASP may be able to help. The ASP Ombudsman can help you resolve a dispute or problem with an ASP member, but does not provide technical support for members' products. Please write to the ASP Ombudsman at 545 Grover Road, Muskegon, MI 49442 or send a CompuServe message via CompuServe Mail to ASP Ombudsman, 70007,3536.

License agreement

No part of this manual may be reproduced, transmitted, transcribed, stored in a retrieval system, or translated into any language (natural or binary), in any form or by any means, except as described in the following license agreement or without the express prior written consent of Sloop Software.

The use of Sloop Manager is subject to the following terms and conditions:

Title to the Licensed Software. Title to the licensed software is *not* transferred to the end user. The end user is granted an exclusive license to use the software on a *single* computer or computer workstation. *Each* computer or computer workstation must have its own licensed copy of the software.

Copyright protection

Sloop Manager is copyrighted material. It is protected by the copyright laws of the United States, the State of Colorado, and other proprietary rights of Sloop Software. You may not make any changes or modifications to Sloop Manager or this manual. You may not decompile, disassemble, or otherwise reverse-engineer the software in any way.

You may make copies of Sloop Manager only under the terms of the section entitled "Limited license to copy the software."

You may use Sloop Manager on a trial basis provided you do not violate the protection afforded the licensed software by the copyright laws, and you agree to the terms of the license agreement. If you use Sloop Manager on a regular basis, you are obligated to purchase it.

Limited warranty

Sloop Software does not warrant that the licensed software will meet your requirements or that the operation of the software will be uninterrupted or error free. The warranty does not cover any media or documentation which has been subjected to damage or abuse by you.

The software warranty does not cover any copy of the licensed software which has been altered or changed in any way.

ANY IMPLIED WARRANTIES INCLUDING ANY WARRANTIES OF MERCHANTABILITY OR FITNESS FOR A PARTICULAR PURPOSE ARE LIMITED TO THE TERM OF THE EXPRESS WARRANTIES. Some states do not allow limitations on how long an implied warranty lasts, so the above limitation may not apply to you.

Other Warranties. The warranties set forth above are in lieu of any and all other express or implied warranties, whether oral, written, or implied, and the remedies set forth above are the sole and exclusive remedies.

Limitation of Liability. Sloop Software is not responsible for any problems or damage caused by the licensed software that may result from using the licensed software. This includes, but is not limited to, computer hardware, computer software, operating systems, and any computer or computing accessories. End user agrees to hold Sloop Software harmless for any problems arising from the use of the software.

Sloop Software SHALL NOT IN ANY CASE BE LIABLE FOR ANY SPECIAL, INCIDENTAL, CONSE-QUENTIAL, INDIRECT, OR OTHER SIMILAR DAMAGES ARISING FROM ANY BREACH OF THESE WARRANTIES EVEN IF Sloop Software OR ITS AGENTS OR DISTRIBUTORS HAVE BEEN ADVISED OF THE POSSIBILITY OF SUCH DAMAGES. Some states do not allow the exclusion or limitation of incidental or consequential damages, so the above limitation or exclusion may not apply to you.

In no case shall Sloop Software's liability exceed the license fees paid for the right to use the licensed software, or a sum no greater than One Dollar ($1), whichever is less.

Limited license to copy the software

You are granted a limited license to copy Sloop Manager *only for the trial use of others* subject to the terms of this software license agreement described herein, and the conditions described below are met: Sloop Manager *must* be copied in an unmodified form and SLOOPMAN.ZIP *must* contain the following files:

SLOOPMAN.EXE	- The Windows executable program (shareware version only)
SLOOPMAN.WRI	- The program documentation
README.TXT	- Installation information
SLPMAN.INI	- Sloop Manager initialization file for manual install
SLOOPMAN.HLP	- Sloop Manager help file
SLOOPMAN.FL1	- Used for manual install
INSTALL.EXE	- Sloop Manager install program
METER.DLL	- Install link library
SETUP.INF	- Install setup information
SLOOPMAN.ICL	- Sloop Manager icon library
TROUBLE.TXT	- Troubleshooting information
BWCC.DLL	- Link library used by program
SMTOOLS.DLL	- Link library used by command bar
GRPCONV.EXE	- Group conversion utility
SMTRASH.EXE	- Trashcan utility
ORDERFRM.TXT	- Sloop Manager order form
VENDOR.DOC	- Shareware vendor information

No fee, charge, or other compensation may be accepted or requested by anyone without the express written permission of Sloop Software.

Public-Domain Disk Vendors may not charge a fee for Sloop Manager itself. However you may include Sloop Manager on a diskette for which you charge a nominal distribution fee. The purchaser of said diskette must be informed in advance that the fee paid to acquire the diskette does *not* relieve said purchaser from paying the registration fee for Sloop Manager if said purchaser uses Sloop Manager.

Operators of electronic bulletin board systems (sysops) may post Sloop Manager for downloading by their users without written permission *only as long as the above conditions are met*. A fee may be charged for access to the BBS *as long as no specific fee is charged for downloading* Sloop Manager files without first obtaining express written permission from Sloop Software to charge such a fee.

The above constitutes the license agreement for Sloop Manager. It supersedes any and all previous license agreements.

CEO:Desktop Manager for Windows 3.1

Sloop Software is pleased to announce the release of the Windows 3.1 replacement shell, CEO:Desktop Manager. CEO:Desktop Manager is the complete graphical replacement for Microsoft's Windows 3.1 Program Manager. It offers all the major features of Program Manager, plus a host of new features. If you're looking for an easy-to-use replacement with all the features Program Manager should have had, give CEO:Desktop Manager a try. CEO is available as a retail package, with a list price of $79.95.

CEO is based on our popular shareware program, Sloop Manager. It can be used to replace either Folders or Sloop Manager.

CEO's major features include

Consistent interface throughout. No need to make use of two different programs (i.e., Folders and ProgMan) for one job.

Create subfolders (subgroups) within folders, allowing you to create a tree structure of folders and subfolders.

Move or copy items between folders with a simple drag/drop interface. Select a single item to be moved or copied or select multiple items and move or copy all at once.

Display items in folders as icons, text (as in File Manager), or as buttons (as in a toolbar).

Password protection provided for individual folders or can be used to lock people out of Windows completely.

History menu which tracks the last 12 applications launched from any folder. This allows you to quickly re-launch an application you wish to use again after closing it.

Background color used by a folder can be set on a per folder basis. This allows for color-coding of folders.

Link to directory capability which allows you to link a folder to a directory. Once linked, the folder will automatically add and delete items from the folder as files are created or deleted in the directory. This eliminates the need to manually add new items or delete old items.

Add items to folders by dragging files from the File Manager. Launch programs by dropping data files on program icons where the icons may either be icons in a folder or icons on the desktop.

Print files by dropping them on Print Manager.

Multi-select capability provided when adding or deleting items. Add multiple items at once or delete multiple items using two different delete capabilities.

Use any folder as a startup folder when starting Windows. This allows you to start Windows with different startup configurations by just using a command-line parameter when starting Windows.

Launch multiple applications with a single action. All items in a folder may be launched at once or only selected items may be launched by just hitting the Enter key.

Includes run command with browse button. The last 12 commands entered are stored with no duplications for easy access.

Customizable popup run menu provided for quick access to programs accessible from any folder or from the desktop. Easy to use menu editor included for building and maintaining Run menu. Menu items may be set to run minimized or maximized. Also, hotkeys may be assigned to menu items.

Easy-to-use icon selection dialog displays all icons in the specified file in a list box. Scroll back and forth through the icons until you find the one you desire; then double-click it, and the selected item is immediately changed to the icon selected from the list box.

Assign hotkeys to items for quick launching. In addition, programs can be set to automatically inquire for a data file upon execution.

Assign icons to file extensions allowing for automatic use of the specified icon whenever a file with that extension is added to a folder. For example, assign a document icon to the extension .DOC. Any file added with a .DOC extension will automatically appear with the document icon.

Includes associate command similar to File Manager's, but CEO's allows multiple programs to be assigned to a single extension. Executing a folder item with multiple programs assigned to it will cause a list box to appear from which the desired program to be run may be selected.

Global options dialog provides for customizing various aspects of the CEO system. Various confirmation, display, and startup options may be set.

The install program included automatically builds folders from your Program Manager groups and places them in CEO, making for quick and easy setup.

Registration Information

Note that this is a shareware program. As such, you may use it on a trial basis for 30 days. After this time, the program should be registered if it continues to be used. The cost is $35 for the latest version and a printed manual. Please add $2 for shipping and handling ($4 for oveseas orders). The fee is payable to:

> **Sloop Software**
> 6457 Mesedge Lane
> Colorado Springs, CO 80919
> (719) 260-0433 voice/fax
> CompuServe: 72540,144
> America OnLine: Sloop Soft
> Internet: 72540.144@compuserve.com

Customer support is available to registered users and to unregistered users during their trial period. For information on site licenses, see the end of this file.

You may charge your registered version of this program with Visa, Mastercard or American Express, by calling the Software Shopper order line at (800) 847-0309. Outside the United States, call (502) 228-4492 or fax to (502) 228-5121, or mail your order to:

> **Software Shopper**
> The Falsoft Building
> P.O. Box 385
> Prospect, KY 40059

Registration fees and technical support for registered programs are as stated in the author's documentation. Please contact the author for technical assistance with this software. Software Shopper assumes no technical or legal liability for software purchased through the order service.

For upgrades or site licenses, order from Sloop Software directly.

For foreign orders, contact the nearest local distributor or send U.S. funds to our U.S. address.

In Europe, contact:
WindowShare
32, rue des Frieres
57050 METZ
France
Telephone: 87 30 85 57

In Australia, contact:
BudgetWare
PO Box 496
Newtown, NSW 2042 Australia
(02) 519-4233 voice
(02) 516-4236 fax

In Japan, contact:
Personal Data Factory
Shimoueki-cho 451-3
Isesaki-shi
Gunma-ken 372, Japan

Sloop Manager 1.2 Order Form

Name: _____

Company: _____

Address: _____

City, State, Zip Code: _____

Country: _____

Optional Info:

Obtained program from: _____

Type of machine: _____

Video Type: _____

Payment:

SLOOP MANAGER: ____ copies X $35   _____

Shipping/handling charge*:   _____

TOTAL   _____

 Specify disk size: ____ 5.25" ____ 3.5"

*Shipping: $2
$4 overseas

UltraClip

Version 1.7
Copyright © Doug Overmyer

*T*he Windows Clipboard is a neat tool, but it has a severe limitation — it can only hold one piece of text or graphic image at a time. When you copy anything to the Clipboard, any item that was already there is lost.

UltraClip solves that limitation and gives you wide latitude for controlling and managing multiple text items and graphics images. This can help you copy several items from different applications and use them in whatever combination you want in other applications.

Type of Program:	Clipboard enhancer.
Requires:	Windows 3.1.
Registration:	Free. This program requires no registration.
Technical Support:	None.
Similar Shareware:	ClipMate, a program featured in *Windows Gizmos,* allows you to manage multiple Clipboard text items, but not multiple graphics images as UltraClip does.

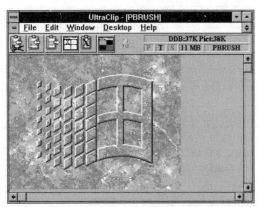

Figure 1: The UltraClip window displays whatever happens to be in the Windows Clipboard — in this case, the WINLOGO.BMP image in Windows 3.1, copied to the Clipboard from Paintbrush — and gives you a great variety of tools to save and manage multiple Clipboard images.

Overview

UltraClip creates and manages a virtual Clipboard for the Windows environment. It lets you do the following:

♦ Create mini-Clipboards that store snapshots of the Windows Clipboard
♦ Create OLE (Object Linking and Embedding) objects with embedded or linked data
♦ View graphical thumbnails for quick retrieval
♦ Track the contents of the Windows Clipboard in an iconic window
♦ Print proofsheets of the thumbnail drawings or graphics from a disk file
♦ Save and retrieve the mini-Clipboard objects as .CLP files

♦ Create mini-clips directly from .BMP, .PCX, .GIF (CompuServe's Graphics Interchange Format), and .WMF (Aldus' Windows Metafile) images stored on disk
♦ Save and restore the current UltraClip desktop and all its objects
♦ Edit and manipulate mini-clips with text objects less than 55K
♦ Edit OLE objects by double-clicking

Constraints

UltraClip stores everything in memory — you'll need sufficient memory to support whatever you wish to store. Large color bitmaps can consume several megabytes, so beware. UltraClip ignores application owner-display formats. Not compatible with the original release of Norton Desktop for Windows 1.0. Printing requires a print driver that supports StretchDIBits.

Upgrades from Earlier Versions

Unfortunately, UltraClip 1.7 does not read the desktop save files used by earlier versions. A slight change in format was needed to accommodate the OLE data streams. If you used a version of UltraClip prior to 1.7, the best strategy would be to export the most needed miniclips as .CLP files and then load them into UltraClip 1.7 as needed.

A Few Terms

Clipboard refers to the Windows Clipboard.

Mini-clip refers to the child windows in UltraClip, which contain mini-Clipboards.

The UltraClip Display Window

UltraClip is an MDI (Multiple Document Interface) application with a button bar and status bar along the top of the window area, and separate windows for each mini-Clipboard.

The status bar is arranged as follows:
Buttons(left to right):

Cut to Clipboard	Copy currently active window to Clipboard, then delete image window
Copy to Clipboard	Copy currently active window to Clipboard
Paste from Clipboard	Create new image window from Clipboard
Delete Window	Remove image window from UltraClip
Clear Clipboard	Delete current contents of Clipboard
Array	Tile the image windows in a grid for easy viewing

In the middle:
A small iconic view of the current contents of the Clipboard, if displayable.

To the right:
Several 3-D boxes giving various pieces of information about the active mini-clip window and system configuration:

Top row:
Format sizes associated with the active mini-clip

Bottom row:
Status of Auto Paste mode(P)
Status of AutoTrack mode(T)
Status of AutoSave mode(S)
Free Global memory
Module/program name of source of data

In the open area are mini-clips, which display thumbnails of the objects currently stored in UltraClip. Each mini-clip has its own window. You can drag these windows around in the display area, iconize them, tile them, or use the other options on the Window menu. If you zoom a mini-clip, the object is displayed full size. If you resize the main window, the mini-clips are retiled automatically.

The Windows Clipboard & OLE

The Clipboard is largely a convention that lets programs share data directly via system memory. When you *copy* to the Clipboard, your application formats various blocks of global memory and turns them over to the Clipboard (the Windows system) to manage. Any application can retrieve those blocks from the system, make copies, and interpret them as best as it can. An application can use both predefined formats and custom formats when creating the data for the Clipboard. Since the various formats usually refer to the same general item, we can collectively call them a Clipboard *object*, which has various formats. When you copy to the Clipboard or empty it, you remove the existing object and replace it with another.

UltraClip allows you to take a snapshot of the Clipboard and preserve it as a mini-clip. These snapshots are also stored in global memory, just like the original, but have a longer life. Together they form a *virtual* Clipboard, where objects persist after a cut or copy, where you can pick and choose one for quick retrieval, and even manipulate its text. You can also save the mini-clips to disk for later retrieval as .CLP files.

OLE is an advanced protocol for sharing data among Windows applications. One approach is to copy OLE data to the Clipboard for pasting into a client application. Ultraclip supports OLE 1.0 in two ways. You can save all the data on the Clipboard as a regular mini-clip (and restore it later), or you can create an OLE mini-clip which actually contains an OLE object. Both linked and embedded objects are supported. There is much more system support for these OLE objects than for simple Clipboard data — the OLE libraries manage the binary data, read and write it to disk, and even control the display. One unique feature of an OLE object is that you can double-click on it and edit the data in the server application (if the application that originally created the object is present).

Using UltraClip

When UltraClip is running, just use the Paste icon or menu option to paste the current contents of the Clipboard into UltraClip. If there is an object on the Clipboard, UltraClip makes a copy, creates a mini-clip, and displays it. You can store as many miniclips as memory and resources allow. If OLE data is present, you can also create an OLE mini-clip — select Edit/ Link or Edit/Embed as desired.

To restore a mini-clip to the Windows Clipboard so that other applications can use it, highlight the window you wish to access, and either click the Copy button, choose Edit/Copy from the menus, or right-click the window's title bar. This will copy the object to the Clipboard, replacing whatever was there before. You can also choose Edit/Cut (or the Cut Button) to copy the object to the Clipboard and delete the mini-clip.

To selectively copy one or more formats (in a particular mini-clip) to the Clipboard, right-click (with your secondary button) anywhere inside the mini-clip. A dialog box with the available formats will appear. Click the formats you are interested in; then click OK to copy the selected formats to the Clipboard. The mini-clip retains a copy of all the formats until you close it, or exit the program. If you chose the wrong format the first time, just repeat the copy.

You can configure several options for UltraClip, using the File/Configure menu option. Choose the startup mode you desire, and it will take effect the next time you start UltraClip.

Clicking the array button arranges the mini-clips in a grid, much like a slide-sorter for your camera. The default sizes the thumbnails to 125 pixels square and fits as many as possible in the current window area. See the "Configuration" section for changing the default.

You can clear the current contents of the Clipboard using the Edit/Clear menu or the Clear button. This may free up some memory, if the Clipboard is currently storing a large image.

When you depress an icon button, the status display box temporarily displays a brief explanation of the action.

You can edit and manipulate the text in a mini-clip if the text size is less than 55K. The Edit/Modify menu option opens an edit window where you can change, add, move, append to Clipboard, and delete text. Double-clicking with the left (primary) mouse button will also open an edit window.

You can edit an OLE mini-clip by double-clicking the object. The host application will start where you can use all its facilities in editing. Before exiting, choose Update to transfer the data back to UltraClip.

The Edit/Append menu choice appends the text object in the active mini-clip to whatever text is on the Clipboard. You can use these options repeatedly to combine text in nearly any fashion.

AutoPaste, AutoTrack, and AutoSave Modes

UltraClip has an Auto Paste mode that will automatically paste every new object placed on the Clipboard (except those copied from UC). To activate AutoPaste, choose the Edit/Start AutoPaste menu option or click the status box with the right mouse button. The status box displays P or _ depending on the current status of AutoPaste.

UltraClip will display an iconic miniature of the current contents of the Clipboard if you configure AutoTrack to be active. This iconic display will also appear when UltraClip itself is iconized, and will be updated whenever the Clipboard changes.

UltraClip uses 3 special icons when there are no public graphic formats on the Clipboard:

　　X — Clipboard is empty
　　T — Clipboard has only Text and non-displayable formats
　　01 — Clipboard has only binary (non-displayable) formats

You can have UltraClip AutoSave the UltraClip desktop every *n* minutes. You set this option in the File/Configuration dialog. When you first start UltraClip, it checks the AutoSave time period. If the period is > 0, it turns on AutoSave. Then, every *n* minutes, UltraClip checks to see if there are any mini-clips on the desktop. If so, it puts up a dialog asking if you really want to overwrite the desktop save file. You have three choices:

♦ Yes: Autosave now runs automatically for the rest of the session.

♦ No: Start counting the minutes and repeat the query process until you answer Yes or Cancel.

♦ Cancel: AutoSave is suspended for the session or until you reactivate it.

You are queried at the start of each session to help ensure that the desktop save file is not accidentally overwritten.

The Mini-Clip Windows

Each mini-clip displays a thumbnail of the object it is *storing* — either a graphic or an unformatted dump of text. When you paste an object into UltraClip, it stores all the available formats as well as building a thumbnail image if a graphic format is found.

If you create an OLE mini-clip, the display is controlled by the OLE libraries as are the available formats. Regretfully, these objects display rather more slowly than the UltraClip thumbnails, which are optimized for speed. The available formats for restoring to the Clipboard are also determined by the OLE system.

If the object contains no displayable formats, the mini-clip displays the program name that put the data on the Clipboard, and the formats that are available for copying. You may have to zoom the window to see all the text, if there are many formats.

The title bar of the mini-clip window displays the origin of the image — the filename if read from disk, or the module that put the object on the Clipboard (if available).

If you zoom a mini-clip, the graphic is redrawn full size. Depending on the size and complexity of the object, this can take a while the first time. The delay is caused by the time needed to create the full image — initially, only the thumbnail is built. The full graphic is cached in memory, though, so you don't need to wait a second time.

Zoomed mini-clips have scroll bars that let you move around the image or scroll through text. Please note that only ten screens of text are maintained for scrolling — this limitation is currently needed for performance reasons. Graphics are available for scrolling, regardless of the image size.

Status Windows

UltraClip displays several pieces of information to help manage the environment. There are status boxes for

♦ AutoPaste status
♦ AutoTrack status
♦ AutoSave status
♦ Free global memory
♦ Source of data in the clip window
♦ Major formats and size stored in the clip object
♦ Iconic Clipboard view

You can right-click several of these status displays, and UltraClip will pop up an expanded view of the status:

♦ Free memory	Free memory + free system resources
♦ Formats	All formats available + global size
♦ Iconic view	All formats on the Clipboard

Drag-and-Drop Interface

There are several ways of getting work done in UltraClip. The menu choices are the most familiar. In addition there are several situations where you can right-click a window to start a particular action — see Mouse Work for a description.

A third approach uses the drag-and-drop object metaphor. The idea is that you select an object and drop it on an icon or area that symbolizes what you want to accomplish. The cursor changes to an up arrow when over an item that will accept a drop. In UltraClip, two objects are droppable: mini-clips and the iconic Clipboard window. Select a mini-clip, then click inside it, and drag — the cursor changes to an up arrow. Here are the players for drag and drop:

Source	Target	Action
mini-clip	Cut button	Copy to Clipboard and delete
	Copy button	Copy to Clipboard
	Delete button	Delete mini-clip
	Array button	Array the open mini-clips
Clipboard	Paste button	Create a mini-clip from Clipboard
(icon)	Clear button	Empty Clipboard contents
	Client area	Create a mini-clip from Clipboard

If you have many palette-intensive mini-clips, you may have to wait a second when you select a new mini-clip — Windows is at work updating the image displays, and will miss the mouse drag if you start too soon.

To edit windows for text, also use drag-and-drop — see next topic.

Manipulating Text

You can edit and manipulate text objects which are less then 55K in size. Two options are available on the Edit menu:

Append to Clipboard: Takes the text object in the active mini-clip and appends it to the text on the Clipboard. The resulting new text object replaces the old one on the Clipboard.

Modify Text: Opens an editing window where you can rearrange, add, and delete text.

You can also open an edit window by double-clicking inside the mini-clip with the left (primary) mouse button. AutoPaste is suspended whenever an edit window is open.

The edit window has several features:

Drag & Drop Editing:

Select a block of text, then move the cursor back over the text, and press. The cursor changes to an up arrow, and you can 'drag' the text to any new position in the text. If you reach the edge of the edit window, the window will automatically scroll the remaining text into view. You can spot your 'drop' by following the caret (a light gray bar) which shows the current insertion point.

If you hold down the Ctrl key when you drop the text, the selected text will be copied to the new spot without deleting the source. Otherwise, the text is moved and the source is deleted.

Important: If you attempt to increase the amount of text beyond 55K, you will find that the additional text is not accepted, and you should see a warning. Save your work, and export the text to the Clipboard for use in a word processor such as Write, which supports large text blocks.

Speed Keys:

The Delete and Backspace keys delete and remove text as you would expect. You can use Ctrl+Home and Ctrl+End to jump to top/bottom of text respectively. Shift+Ctrl+Home and Shift+Ctrl+End jump and select text from the current insertion point to the top or bottom of the text. Ctrl+Insert copies selected text to the Clipboard, while Shift+Insert pastes from the Clipboard.

Adding Text:

You can add text by clicking an insertion point in the existing text, and typing. Hitting the Enter key ends one line and starts the next.

Copy & Paste Buttons:

These buttons copy selected text to the Clipboard, and paste text from the Clipboard respectively. You can also use the speed keys for copy and paste mentioned above. If there are insufficient local resources for the paste operation, a warning message is put up to alert you that the paste failed.

Append Button:

Select a block of text and append it to whatever text is already on the Clipboard. The total size of the new text must be less then 64K. You can use this feature repeatedly to rearrange text in almost any fashion.

UltraClip lets you open multiple edit windows, but only one for a given mini-clip. This feature would, though, let you transfer text fragments from one text object to another (via the Clipboard), with good control over where the text goes in the second window.

Using .CLP Files

Ultraclip can save and read .CLP files that are compatible with the Clipboard Viewer application that comes with Windows. To save a regular mini-clip as a .CLP file, highlight it by clicking on the title bar, and choose File/Save from the file menu. Supply a suitable filename, and your clip object is saved to disk. You can load one or more .CLP files by choosing File/Open, selecting the .CLP file type, and selecting the file/files you wish to load. Each clip object will be loaded into its own window with a thumbnail . You can copy it to the Clipboard or hold for later retrieval (or print a thumbnail sheet).

To save an OLE mini-clip as a .CLP file, copy it first to the Clipboard and paste it as a regular mini-clip which you can then save to disk.

Using .BMP, .PCX, .GIF, and .WMF Files

UltraClip can read Win 3.0 style bitmap files(.BMP), .PCX version 5 files, .GIF single image as well as Aldus-style metafiles (the kind produced by Corel, Arts & Letters, and other draw programs). Choose File/Open, select the file type you are interested in, and highlight the filenames you wish to load. In this situation, UltraClip does a bit more than just load the format into a mini-clip. For .BMP files, both a memory DIB image and a bitmap & palette object are created. You can copy one or all to the Clipboard as needed. PCX and GIF files are translated into a comparable DIB image, and a corresponding bitmap and palette are constructed. For metafiles, UltraClip creates a Picture file as well as a DIB image and bitmap/palette pair. Thus you can use UltraClip to rasterize metafiles and create bitmap objects from DIB and PCX images, if needed.

Text Files

UltraClip will read text files off the disk and create a mini-clip. File size is limited by available memory but editing capacity is much more limited. A text file can contain only printable characters plus CR, LF, Tab, and EOF characters.

The Desktop

The menu options Desktop/Save and Restore let you save the contents of all existing mini-clips to disk and restore them later. This includes OLE mini-clips. You can specify the drive and save the filename using the configure option. Please note that the desktop save file can be very large if you have a number of large objects in memory — it consumes roughly as much disk space as the in-memory images. For example, if UltraClip has reduced your free global memory from 8MB to 5MB, you can expect the desktop save file to use roughly 3 MB of disk space.

Printing Thumbnails

UltraClip includes a simple print option that lets you print 'proof sheets' of the current thumbnails. In the Edit/Configure options dialog, you can specify the grid used to position the printed thumbnails:

> m Across by
>
> n Down with a margin of
>
> x Inches

During printing, new thumbnails are created to optimally fill the available space with a caption built from the filename or module name. Be patient when starting a print — creating a page with 24 or 30 thumbnails is quite system-intensive, considering the scaling and (in most cases) color conversions. Don't try a print without sufficient memory — the Print Manager can consume considerable disk and memory resources. The quality of the output depends somewhat on the printer driver, as does the speed of the operation.

Printing Graphics Directly from Disk

UltraClip will also directly print thumbnail sheets of graphics files residing on the disk without loading them simultaneously into memory. This feature allows you to print thumbnails automatically for a very large number of graphics images — such as might reside on a CD-ROM. Use the File/Print from Disk... menu option to choose the files you wish to print. You can select any bitmap, metafile, or .CLP file that UltraClip can read. In addition to the filename, UltraClip titles each page with the drive/subdirectory where the images were found and a sequential page number.

While much less memory-intensive than printing the images from memory, you must still ensure that the system has sufficient resources.

Memory Checking

UltraClip monitors the free global memory based on a limit you set in the Edit/Configure dialog. When the free memory drops below the specified minimum, you will be prompted before creating new mini-clips. You can defeat this checking by setting the memory limit to 0.

Configuring UltraClip

You can configure UltraClip by choosing Configure from the File menu, or right-clicking the title bar with the mouse. In addition to setting the startup AutoPaste & AutoTrack mode, you can choose a new thumbnail size and printing setup and specify the desktop save filename. Your choices are written to UC.INI and take effect with the next object pasted into UltraClip. Please note that existing thumbnails are not recalculated, so it is best to change that parameter at the beginning or end of a session.

You can temporarily toggle the AutoPaste and AutoTrack mode by right-clicking in the respective status windows. There are also menu options to change the current mode under the Edit menu.

OLE

UltraClip supports OLE in two ways: regular and OLE mini-clips. Regular mini-clips neither embed nor link to objects, but let you store OLE data for embedding and linking in other applications. When you copy OLE formats into UltraClip, it captures the OLE data; when you restore them to the Clipboard, it places copies of the original data back on the Clipboard in the same order and format. The goal is to transparently restore the state of the Clipboard. Of course, if you selectively choose formats to copy to the Clipboard, the copy process will not match the original.

OLE mini-clips actually create an OLE object managed and displayed by the OLE system libraries (and source application). Within UltraClip, these OLE mini-clips behave much like the other windows, although they are completely different internally. There are advantages and disadvantages to using OLE. The OLE mini-clips display much more slowly, contain fewer formats, and are tied to OLE applications. On the plus side, they can be edited from within UltraClip, they require less disk space to store if linked, and they can be automatically updated by the source application.

Manual Configuration Options

There exist several configuration options that you can use to override Ultra-Clip's various safety warnings. You would enter one or more of the following lines in the [UC] section of the UC.INI file (but not the comments inside the curly braces):

```
[UC]
PromptOnClose=0      {no nag exit from UltraClip}
PromptOnSave=0       {no nag before overwriting desktop save file}
AutoRestore=1        {automatically restore the desktop save file when UltraClip starts}
```

Known Peculiarities

Occasionally, AutoPaste may create multiple clip windows when only one is appropriate. Basically, there are two situations: (1) the source application prematurely closes the Clipboard before it is done copying all formats; (2) you close the source application and it replaces the object on the Clipboard with a new one. UltraClip tries very hard to avoid problem number 1, but a slow application can trip it up. This is frustrating — the only fix I know of is to turn off AutoPaste for that application or delete the unwanted (usually incomplete) clip windows. Problem 2 is unavoidable — the "duplicate" object is in fact slightly different from the first, although it may appear identical.

Micrografix Designer 3.1 is unhappy with the MGX_... formats as restored by UltraClip, so they are suppressed, even if present on the Clipboard.

Frame by FrameMaker seems to use a non-standard Clipboard format that fails to render properly in UltraClip. It is possible to create metafiles in advanced drawing applications (such as CorelDRAW) that are simply too complex for Windows to render. Typically, Windows crashes when trying to display these files. One possible workaround is to copy sections of the image to the Clipboard and store them in UltraClip. If, for example, Corel warns you that a given image is 'too complex' for the Clipboard, do not try to display the Clipboard version — rather, clear the Clipboard and start again. If you click a button and nothing happens, check to see that a clip window is highlighted. If not, click a title bar and try the button again.

If you save an object to disk which includes a 'bitmap' format, and then restore it to an environment running in a different graphics mode, the bitmap format will not display properly and may crash the program. This includes both .CLP files and desktop save files. This is unavoidable — the bitmap format is always device specific, and does not transfer between modes such as VGA and SuperVGA. The solution is to use the DIB format, which is device-independent and should display on any graphics adapter.

Disclaimer

UltraClip carries no warranties. You use it entirely at your own risk. You must determine its suitability for your system and needs.

Source Code

UltraClip is written in Borland Pascal.

Acknowledgments

I wish to thank Nord-Jan Vermeer, Nat Johnson, and Christian Gerber, whose many suggestions contributed materially to UltraClip. I appreciate your help a great deal! Thanks also to Ron Burke (editor *Window/DOS Journal*) whose articles inspired drag-and-drop editing, and to Ron Gery (MS Developer Network), whose articles on palettes finally got through!

Copyrights

Arts & Letters is a registered trademark of Computer Support Corporation. CorelDRAW! is a registered trademark of Corel Systems Corporation. Micrografx is a registered trademark of Micrografx, Inc. GIF is a a registered trademark of CompuServe Inc.

Distribution Terms

UltraClip is distributed as freeware — there is no registration fee. If you cannot obtain a copy from an electronic service, I will send one to you for $5 to cover shipping/media/handling. Write to:

Doug Overmyer
1817 San Pedro Avenue
Berkeley, CA 94707
U.S.A.

If you have suggestions, please drop me a note on CompuServe (71021,2535) or Internet: overmyer@netcom.com.

Doug Overmyer

⊞

Video Terminal Screen

Version 3.2 (8-25-93)
Copyright © E.A. Behl

*W*indows *word processors are great tools to document DOS applications, and Windows runs on top of DOS, right? But legions of technical writers have found a big problem with Windows — there is no way to print the line-draw characters and other accented characters that appear in many DOS screens.*

Video Terminal Screen is a way to correct this and make it easy to document all kinds of DOS screens. VTS is a scalable TrueType font, which just happens to contain all the same characters as the IBM PC-8 character set, in exactly the same order. You need to learn how to capture DOS text and paste it into Windows applications without the special characters getting "converted" for you by your Windows app. The following chapter explains each of the steps.

Important Installation Instructions: *After running WSETUP on Disk 1, you must open the Control Panel's Fonts dialog box and click the Add button to add Video Terminal Screen to your Fonts list before this typeface will be available to your Windows applications. WSETUP does not modify your Fonts list, it simply copies the font file VTSR____.TTF to your Windows directory. (The four underscores are an old PostScript convention, which requires that all typeface names be exactly eight characters long.) See the following Installation section.*

Type of Program:	Typeface.
Requires:	Windows 3.1 or higher.
Registration:	Use the form at the end of this chapter to register with the shareware author.
Technical Support:	E.A. Behl Technologies provides registered users with technical support via CompuServe, fax, and phone.
Similar Shareware:	RRKeyCaps, featured elsewhere in *More Windows 3.1 Secrets,* is another TrueType face, which prints small graphical representations of most of the keyboard keytops on a U.S. keyboard, such as Tab and Enter.

The Video Terminal Screen (VTS) Character Set:

32		64	@	96	`	0128	Ç	0160	á	0192	L	0224	α
33	!	65	A	97	a	0129	ü	0161	í	0193	⊥	0225	ß
34	"	66	B	98	b	0130	é	0162	ó	0194	T	0226	Γ
35	#	67	C	99	c	0131	â	0163	ú	0195	⊦	0227	π
36	$	68	D	100	d	0132	ä	0164	ñ	0196	—	0228	Σ
37	%	69	E	101	e	0133	à	0165	Ñ	0197	+	0229	σ
38	&	70	F	102	f	0134	å	0166	ª	0198	╞	0230	µ
39	'	71	G	103	g	0135	ç	0167	º	0199	╟	0231	τ
40	(	72	H	104	h	0136	ê	0168	¿	0200	╚	0232	Φ
41	)	73	I	105	i	0137	ë	0169	⌐	0201	╔	0233	θ
42	*	74	J	106	j	0138	è	0170	¬	0202	╩	0234	Ω
43	+	75	K	107	k	0139	ï	0171	½	0203	╦	0235	δ
44	,	76	L	108	l	0140	î	0172	¼	0204	╠	0236	∞
45	–	77	M	109	m	0141	ì	0173	¡	0205	=	0237	ø
46	.	78	N	110	n	0142	Ä	0174	«	0206	╬	0238	ε
47	/	79	O	111	o	0143	Å	0175	»	0207	╧	0239	∩
48	0	80	P	112	p	0144	É	0176	░	0208	╨	0240	≡
49	1	81	Q	113	q	0145	æ	0177	▒	0209	╤	0241	±
50	2	82	R	114	r	0146	Æ	0178	▓	0210	╥	0242	≥
51	3	83	S	115	s	0147	ô	0179	│	0211	╙	0243	≤
52	4	84	T	116	t	0148	ö	0180	┤	0212	╘	0244	⌠
53	5	85	U	117	u	0149	ò	0181	╡	0213	╒	0245	⌡
54	6	86	V	118	v	0150	û	0182	╢	0214	╓	0246	÷
55	7	87	W	119	w	0151	ù	0183	╖	0215	╫	0247	≈
56	8	88	X	120	x	0152	ÿ	0184	╕	0216	╪	0248	°
57	9	89	Y	121	y	0153	Ö	0185	╣	0217	┘	0249	·
58	:	90	Z	122	z	0154	Ü	0186	║	0218	┌	0250	·
59	;	91	[	123	{	0155	¢	0187	╗	0219	█	0251	√
60	<	92	\	124	|	0156	£	0188	╝	0220	▄	0252	ⁿ
61	=	93	]	125	}	0157	¥	0189	╜	0221	▌	0253	²
62	>	94	^	126	~	0158	₧	0190	╛	0222	▐	0254	■
63	?	95	_	127	⌂	0159	ƒ	0191	┐	0223	▀	0255	□

Figure 1: This illustration shows the character set of Video Terminal Screen, which matches the DOS PC-8 character set, including line-draw characters. Change to the Video Terminal Screen font in your Windows application and press the desired key on your keyboard to insert characters 33–127. To insert characters 0128 and higher, make sure your NumLock is on, hold down your Alt key, press the number on your numeric keypad, and then release both keys.

Installation

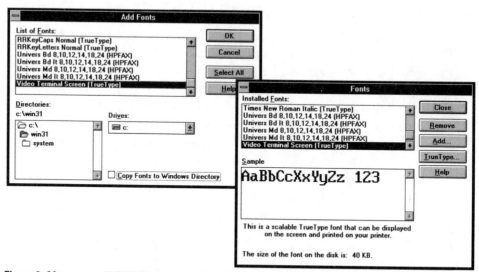

Figure 2: After you run WSETUP to copy the font files to your Windows directory, you must open Control Panel's Font dialog box, click the Add button, select Video Terminal Screen, and click OK so that the font becomes part of your list of Installed Fonts.

After you run WSETUP on the *More Windows 3.1 Secrets* Disk 1 to decompress and copy Video Terminal Screen to your hard disk, you must do one more thing: Add the font to the Installed Fonts list in your Control Panel. This allows your Windows applications to "see" this font. To do this, take the following steps:

1. Open the Control Panel by double-clicking its icon in the Program Manager.
2. Double-click the Fonts icon in the Control Panel window.
3. When the Fonts dialog box opens, click the Add button.
4. In the Add Fonts dialog box that opens, you should see a list of fonts in your Windows directory that are available to be added to your Fonts list. Turn *off* the Copy Fonts To Windows Directory box. Select Video Terminal Screen from the scrolling list of available fonts and click OK.
5. When you return to the Fonts dialog box, you should see that the selection you made has been added to the Installed Fonts list. Congratulations! Your selection is now available to all Windows applications that support TrueType. It should not be necessary to restart Windows. (In Microsoft Word for Windows Version 1.*x*, you must click File Print-Setup OK for the font to be recognized, but this is unusual.)

Overview

Video Terminal Screen (VTS) resembles screen characters of a data terminal or text on an EGA/VGA monitor of a personal computer. Video Terminal Screen is designed for use as a text font for technical documents, such as software programming manuals. The character set is fixed-pitch, so text captured from an actual data session can be imported directly into a document with minimal touch up.

The Video Terminal Screen typeface family consists of three font files, which make available all 253 characters of the PC-8 character set used by IBM PC and compatible personal computers. (There are no characters associated with ASCII 00, 32, or 255). The base (or roman) font file contains all 253 characters, although standard encoding of PostScript Type 1 and TrueType font files do not allow convenient access to all characters.

To make access to the full character set more convenient, two files other than Video Terminal Screen are available: a Low Characters file (with the italic font file attribute) and a Box Characters file (with the boldface font file attribute). The Low Characters file contains the lower 31 characters remapped upward by 64 character positions and the Greek and math characters remapped down by 128 character positions. The Box Characters file contains the box characters remapped down 128 character positions. VTS contains all these characters, but the Low Characters and Box Characters fonts make it easier to access special characters from the keyboard.

Typical of fixed-pitch fonts, Video Terminal Screen has a low aspect ratio, producing a somewhat short and "squatty" appearance. The character set is based on the "standard" 8x16 pixel character set of EGA/VGA card character generators. For the sake of simplicity and memory consumption, each character is an outline of the EGA/VGA pixel pattern. Each pixel is a simple square. Character spacing is provided primarily by virtue of the characters using only the first seven columns of pixels, ensuring that adjacent text characters are separated by at least one pixel width. In this way, when box and graphic characters (which use all eight pixel columns) appear adjacent to each other, they meet to form continuous lines.

Using the VTS Family

The Video Terminal Screen typeface family is designed to conveniently provide full access to the entire IBM-PC character set. Using only the base font file in Microsoft Windows 3.1 or later, almost all characters in the set from ASCII 33 through ASCII 254 are available, using Alt key combinations for characters above ASCII 127. Due to limitations in the Windows implementation of the ANSI standard character set, a few characters are not available. This is not a fault of the font, but a quirk in the way Windows uses some of the ANSI characters. This limitation should not pose a problem for most applications. However, if the more obscure characters are needed out of the set, either or both of the additional font files may be necessary.

The 31 symbol characters from ASCII 01 to 31 in the IBM PC correspond to the ASCII characters Ctrl+A through Ctrl+Underscore (_). The Low Characters file contains these characters, shifted up 64 positions. For instance, the open smiley face character, which corresponds to Ctrl+A in the IBM PC, may be printed by typing an uppercase A in Video Terminal Screen, and then switching the character to italic. The Low Characters file also contains the Greek/math symbols from ASCII 224 through 254, shifted down 128 positions, so that typing a grave accent (the backquote key, with the tilde over it) in italic produces the Greek alpha symbol.

For convenience, the 48 box and geometric characters from ASCII 176 through 223, which appear in their normal positions in the base font file, also are contained in the Box Characters file shifted down by 128 positions. This allows typing the characters from 0 (zero) to the underscore character, then switching to boldface to produce the box characters without using Alt key combinations. This may be useful when Alt key combinations are not allowed, or in non-Windows applications.

Capturing DOS Screens in Windows _____

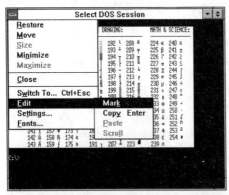

Figure 3: To capture DOS screens as text under Windows' 386 enhanced mode, press Alt+spacebar at a DOS prompt to change to a windowed DOS session and pull down the System Menu. Click Edit Mark, highlight with your mouse or Shift+arrow keys the text you wish to copy to the Clipboard, and then press Enter. In the Clipboard Viewer, you can now save this selection as a .TXT file and open it in a Windows application.

DOS screen captures with the Windows Clipboard are a simple process. Start by running the DOS application from the Windows DOS Prompt icon or in a DOS Window. Press Alt+spacebar to activate the DOS window control box. Select the Edit Mark menu option. Either hold the Shift key down and use the keyboard arrow keys to highlight the portion of the screen to capture, or click and drag the mouse pointer from one corner of the screen to the other. When the desired portion is highlighted, press the Enter key.

Next, open the Windows Clipboard Viewer. Select the File Save As menu option. Enter a filename with .TXT as the filename extension in the File Name box and click the OK button.

Finally, open the Windows Notepad, and select the File Open menu option. Select the filename saved with the Clipboard, adding path information if necessary, and click the OK button.

The file saved by the Clipboard Viewer contains two text variations of the DOS screen. The first variation is untranslated text straight from DOS, and the second is text with high-order characters translated based on a table described in more detail below.

In Notepad, binary header data appears at the top of the file, followed by two text sections, which at first glance may appear to be identical. The first text segment is the segment we are interested in, however. The last step is to carefully delete the unnecessary data from the Clipboard file, and then save the file in Notepad.

The text file can now be opened or imported into a Windows application.

Using VTS with Windows Write _____

To use the captured DOS screen in Write, simply open or import the file saved with Notepad, and select No Conversion when prompted by Write. Highlight the text and select the Format Character menu option. Select Video Terminal Screen from the typeface names and select a point size if desired.

Using VTS with Word for Windows

Open Word for Windows and create a style using VTS as the base font. This makes it easy to recognize the DOS screen text when it is imported. Select the Insert File menu option. Select the file saved with Notepad. When Word prompts for a file type, select "Text Only."

Using VTS with Ventura Publisher

Ventura Publisher does not support the direct use of VTS high-order characters, whether you are using the GEM version or the Windows version. Ventura Publisher has traditionally prohibited use of the characters from ASCII 224 to 255. In addition, Ventura has used the ISO-Latin character coding scheme and remaps characters to follow the ANSI definition under Windows. Thus, the order of nearly all high-order characters are rearranged.

Importing DOS screen captures into Ventura Publisher as text is not impossible, however, just a little more complicated. The Box Characters file of VTS must be installed and included in the Ventura width table.

Open Ventura Publisher, select the File Load menu option, and then select File Type: Text. In the Format box, select WS 4.0/5.0, and select the file saved in the Clipboard Viewer. The WordStar (WS) filter strips the 8th bit off high-order characters, effectively dropping their ASCII value by 128. Once the file is loaded, high-order characters appear as low-order characters. Switch to Text Edit mode and carefully highlight the characters known to have been high-order graphic characters. The last step is to select the Text Bold menu item which changes the highlighted text to box characters.

Using Character Alt+0160 (acute accent á)

In the PC-8 character set, character 160 is the letter *a* with an acute accent (*á*). In Windows, character Alt+0160 is reserved for a nonbreaking space (a space that cannot be used to wrap a word to the next line in a word processor). Therefore, if you type Alt+0160 in the VTS font in Word for Windows and some other word processors, you may see only a space instead of the acute accent *á*.

In Word for Windows 2.0, you can insert the proper character by clicking Insert Field on the main menu. In the scrolling list of field types that appears, select Symbol. Fill in the Field Code box so it looks like this:

```
symbol 0160
```

Then click OK. In the Video Terminal Screen font, this character will appear as the acute accent *á*.

Other word processors may have different methods for inserting this character.

Adjusting the Appearance of VTS

Once the text has been imported, paying attention to line and character spacing will make VTS look just like a screen capture. Word for Windows is discussed specifically, but other word processors have similar controls.

Normally, typesetting adds space above lines of text, called *leading* in typesetting terms, to keep descender strokes of characters such as the lowercase g, j, p, and q from crashing into capital letters, numerals, and lowercase characters with ascender strokes such as the b, d, h, k, and l.

This extra spacing can defeat the ability to make continuous vertical lines with the 179 or 186 characters. To make the graphic characters from adjacent lines connect, set the Line Spacing in Paragraph Format to the same point value as the size of the text. In effect, VTS text at 10 point should have a paragraph line spacing of Exactly - 10pt. Generally, horizontal spacing does not have to be adjusted, however if horizontal lines look dashed instead of continuous, verify that the alignment of the text is flush left and not justified. Justification may stretch the space between characters, defeating the fixed-pitch nature of VTS. If justification is not a problem, you may want to adjust Character Spacing in the Character Format dialog box.

Avoiding Problems Importing DOS Screens in Windows Applications

The most common trouble using VTS in Windows applications is importing text containing high-order characters (those with values above 127) from DOS.

Beginning with Windows Version 3.0, Microsoft heartily endorsed the ANSI typeface character set. The introduction of TrueType technology in version 3.1 married Windows to this standard all the more. In the typeface industry, characters equivalent to the DOS PC-8 single and double box characters just don't exist — most likely because they come from the typesetting world where lines are usually created in some other fashion.

Microsoft recommends that Windows applications handle the transition from PC-8 to ANSI, by using a translation table to change PC-8 box characters to ordinary characters in the ANSI character set, such as hyphens and plus signs. The ANSI assignments for foreign language characters also differ from the PC-8 set, so Microsoft also recommends translating these characters from PC-8 to ANSI as well.

Therefore, as text is imported, Windows applications typically change the value of incoming high-order characters to counterparts in the ANSI character set. For instance, the horizontal line character in the PC-8 character set has a value of 196. This value is routinely changed to 45 (a hyphen) which is the closest thing an ANSI typeface has to offer. Similarly, an incoming character with a value of 160 — the accented *á* in the PC-8 set, is changed to 225 — the corresponding acute accent *á* character in the ANSI character set.

VTS, on the other hand, is a typeface which bucks the ANSI assignments and follows the PC-8 assignment, eliminating the need to change the value of high-order characters from a DOS application. The trick in using VTS with imported text containing high-order characters, then, is to make sure the Windows application doesn't translate the values in the process of importing the DOS text.

Many Windows word processors and other applications have an option for importing text without translation. Write, for instance, asks you directly whether you want to convert a file that is not in the Write format as you import it. Other applications are not always so explicit. Word for Windows, for instance, has several filters for importing text files. However, the correct choice — Text Only — is not an obvious choice. In general, you may have to import the text file several times before determining the method in each application that does not translate high-order characters.

Updating Previous Versions of Video Terminal Screen

The original TrueType Video Terminal Screen files; VTS_____.TTF, VTSLC___.TTF, and VTSBX___.TTF, were incorrectly generated without the PANOSE fixed pitch attribute being set. Although this has no effect on the fonts' appearance or use, Video Terminal Screen may not be listed as a fixed pitch or monospace font in a Microsoft Windows or OS/2 application which differentiates between fixed pitch and proportional spaced fonts.

The new files, dated 8/25/93, have been updated to correct this oversight.

To use the new files, old Video Terminal Screen files must first be deleted and the new files installed. To install the new files, follow the procedure below:

1. Open the Windows Control Panel and select the Fonts icon. Highlight any existing Video Terminal Screen fonts and click the Remove button, selecting the Delete Font File From Disk check box, and clicking the Yes to All button.

2. Click the Add button and select the disk and directory where the new VTS files are located. Highlight the listed Video Terminal Screen fonts and click the OK button.

After installation, Video Terminal Screen should appear correctly as a fixed pitch, monospaced font in Windows and OS/2 applications that check for it.

Thank you for your understanding.

Other TECH/TYPE Typefaces Available from E.A. Behl ___

Since its re-release in November 1992, VTS has become extremely popular in the technical documentation industry for documenting DOS screens. We are proud to announce the recent release of a white-on-black companion typeface to VTS — Reverse Video. Reverse Video has all 253 PC-8 characters and comes in three files just as VTS does. With Reverse Video, you can now highlight text in the DOS screen capture and print it as reverse video characters.

There has been some interest in a *bold* version of VTS — but VTS is fairly dark as it is. As an alternative, we have been developing Video Lite — a "light" variation of VTS, which will allow the distinction between normal and high intensity characters in print.

Alphanumeric is another pixel-based fixed-pitch typeface that resembles the 5 by 8 pixel characters of liquid crystal displays (LCDs) and dot-matrix printers. Alphanumeric contains all 96 standard ASCII characters, many international characters arranged in their PC-8 positions, Greek and math symbols, and several graphic characters.

Dialtone is a key caps typeface for pushbutton telephones. A great typeface for printing telephone dialing instructions with a graphic touch, Dialtone contains the full 12 button dial keys, with number keys in both Metropolitan (letters and numbers) and International (numbers only) styles, the star and pound keys, and the A, B, C, and D keys for military and special purpose dials.

Seven Segment is a typeface containing numerals and symbols made up of seven bars (or segments) arranged in a figure 8 pattern, common in digital alarm clocks and appliances. Numerals with a right decimal point are in the shift-number positions. Seven Segment also includes a limited set of alpha characters including the A, b, c, C, d, E, F, G, h, H, J, L, n, o, P, r, u, U, y, and the Greek Mu (micro) symbol. Punctuation includes the colon (of course), hyphen (dash), underscore, and equal sign.

Also in the planning stages are

♦ A higher resolution equivalent to the VTS family, offering DOS screen captures with greater readability.

♦ A sixteen-segment alpha and numeral typeface, along the same line as Seven Segment but with more alpha characters.

For information, sample sheets, pricing/availability, contact us at the numbers below. To place an order, fill in the order form below and mail it to our address.

License to Use

Video Terminal Screen is provided for non-commercial, evaluation purposes with the book:

More Windows 3.1 Secrets
written by Brian Livingston.

The purchase price of the book does not include a license to use this typeface for other than non-commercial, evaluation purposes.

This typeface may be freely copied and distributed, provided that:

♦ All files are distributed together,

♦ No file is modified or used as the basis for profit, and

♦ No charge of any kind is levied for distribution.

Any other form of commercial distribution is expressly prohibited without the written permission of E.A. Behl.

Video Terminal Screen, in all its variations, and any derivative works, are the exclusive intellectual property of E.A. Behl; protected by copyright law in the United States and by international treaty provisions in many other countries. The base font (Video Terminal Screen - Regular) is Shareware software; it is not released to the Public Domain. This software consists of the following files:

TrueType (MS-DOS) version:

VTS.TXT	Text information and instructions file
VTSNOTES.TXT	Application Tips for using VTS in Windows
ORDERFRM.TXT	Convenient Order Form for VTS and other fonts
VTS____.TTF	253 character set TrueType Font file

This software may be copied and distributed, provided that

♦ All files listed above are distributed together.

♦ The file VTS.TXT must remain unmodified.

Commercial shareware distributors must obtain written permission from E.A. Behl, and pay a $20 duplication fee if any charge whatsoever, including duplication, media, etc., is imposed for its distribution.

Individuals are granted temporary license to use the font software for non-commercial, evaluation purposes only. This license allows the trial use of the font in non-commercial (not-for-profit) applications, for no more than thirty (30) days. To use this font in any form for commercial profit, *the font must be licensed* by the user.

If you find this font of value, you may obtain a license for its continual commercial use, for a nominal, one-time fee. Each license grants permission to install Video Terminal Screen on one low-resolution printer (600 d.p.i. or lower) and/or one high-resolution printer (above 600 d.p.i.), provided both printers are located on the same premises. Registered licensees also receive the Low Characters and Box Characters extended character files, and character mapping tables for each font file. To obtain the extended character files, installation and application instructions, character mapping tables, and a license certificate, use the following order form.

Warranty

This software is licensed as is, with no warranty of any kind, including but not limited to the implied warranties of merchantability and fitness for a particular purpose. The user assumes all risk arising from the use of this software. In no event shall E.A. Behl, its employees, principals, or agents be liable for any direct, indirect, incidental, or consequential losses caused by the use of this software.

Copyrights and Trademarks

Video Terminal Screen
Copyright © 1991–1992, E.A. Behl, Clearwater, FL U.S.A. All rights reserved.

Alphanumeric, Dialtone, Reverse Video, Seven Segment, Video Lite, Video Terminal Screen, VTS, and TECH/TYPE are trademarks of E.A. Behl.

Any trade names referenced herein may be trademarks or registered trademarks of their respective owners, and are included only for reference purposes.

TECH/TYPE Order Form Instructions and Site Licenses

Prices listed on the Order Form are for low-quantity orders. Site licenses are available at a significantly reduced cost. Site License fees are applicable to any one company location and include one complete package of software and documentation, and free updates. To order a Site License, write the word *Site* in the Quantity column followed by the number of users to license.

Number of Users	Price (Effective 5/93)
10	$50
30	100
100	200
Unlimited	500

E.A. Behl Technologies
TECH/TYPE Typefaces for Technology
2663 Red Oak Court
Clearwater, FL 34621-2319

Tel: (813) 789-3550
CompuServe: 70413,1073
Fax: (813) 787-9414

BL/WC-MWS 8/93 TECH/TYPE Order Form

Item	Quantity	Price*	Amount
VIDEO TERMINAL SCREEN (VTS)			
253 PC-8 character set in 3 files.	_____	$10	_____
REVERSE VIDEO			
253 PC-8 character set in 3 files.	_____	10	_____
VIDEO LITE			
253 PC-8 character set in 3 files.			
(Available 9/93 — call to verify)	_____	10	_____
ALPHANUMERIC			
LCD / Dot Matrix character set.	_____	10	_____
DIALTONE			
Pushbutton telephone dial key caps.	_____	8	_____
SEVEN SEGMENT			
Seven segment numeric character set.	_____	8	_____

SHIPPING — U.S. Mail delivery in U.S.A - $2
U.S. 2nd Day (ex AK & HI) - $12
Next Day (2nd Day AK & HI) - $18
International Air Mail delivery - $5   _____

SALES TAX — Florida Purchasers add 6.0% + local
tax, if any.   _____

TOTAL PURCHASE (*Please include check or money order
in U.S. funds.)   _____

Packages include typeface diskette, installation
instructions, license certificate, and character
mapping tables.

DISK PREFERENCE   _____ 3-1/2"   _____5-1/4"

All typefaces supplied on double-density disks and
include both PostScript Type 1 and TrueType format
for PCs.

WinList

Version 1.0
Copyright © Peter Rodwell

*W*inList *is a modest little utility that prints one or more text files — including cover pages, if you wish — with line numbers at the beginning of each line. Peter Rodwell, a programmer, emphasizes that this is helpful for printing code listings. But it really can be useful to any group of people who must collectively edit documents, such as committee reports, political platforms, and so on. Saying, "I'd like to change* he *to* they *in Line 45," is a lot easier than saying, "I'd like to change* he *to* they *in that paragraph down near the bottom of the page."*

At this writing, WinList supports only the Courier New typeface, but it's totally free (the price is right) and easy to use due to its simplicity.

Type of Program:	Printing utility.
Requires:	Windows 3.1 or higher.
Registration:	Free. This program requires no registration.
Technical Support:	None.

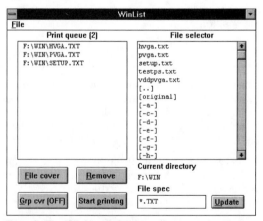

Figure 1: The WinList dialog box allows you to select a group of files to send to the printer by single-clicking filenames in the File Selector box.

Overview

WinList is a program that prints ASCII files from within Windows. It requires Windows 3.1 or later and, obviously, a printer.

WinList is designed for listing program source code files, although it can be used to print any plain ASCII file. It automatically numbers each line as it prints them. Additionally, and optionally, files can be given a cover page, and, if you're listing a group of files, a cover page for the entire group can also be printed.

Installation

The WSETUP program on the *More Windows 3.1 Secrets* Disk 1 decompresses and copies WinList files into a \WINLIST subdirectory beneath which drive and directory you prefer and creates a Program Manager group (if Program Manager or a compatible is running).

When used for the first time, WINLIST.EXE generates a configuration file, called WINLIST.CNF in your Windows directory; it overwrites any file of the same name which already exists there.

Configuration

Choosing the Config option from the File menu displays a dialog box which allows you to set the following parameters:

♦ The manner in which the time is represented (24-hour or 12-hour) on printouts

♦ The date format (DD/MM/YY or MM/DD/YY) on printouts

♦ The Tab stops used in printouts (limited to 5 to 8 spaces)

Change the configuration parameter by clicking the appropriate radio button or, in the case of Tab stops, by typing the appropriate value in the edit box. If you type a Tab stop value that is not within the range 5 through 8, a message advises you of this error.

Click OK to save the config details or Cancel to abandon them.

When you exit WinList, the program also saves the position of its window, so the next time you open it, the window appears at the same position.

Selecting Files

WinList displays two list boxes. The list to the right, headed File selector, is the contents of the currently selected directory. Clicking a filename causes that file's full pathname to appear in the left list box, headed Print queue. The number in brackets in the heading shows how many files are currently in the queue. If you click a subdirectory or drive name in the File selector list, the program switches to the chosen subdirectory or drive and displays its contents.

You can selectively display files in the File selector list by editing the contents of the File spec box. When you first start WinList, it uses the DOS wildcard *.* to display all files; if you want to display only files with the extension .C, for instance, you can change the spec to *.C. When you change the file spec, the "Update" button is activated; click it to update the File selector list with the new file spec.

Both the currently selected drive/path and the file spec are saved in the configuration file when you exit the program and are used automatically the next time you start WinList.

As soon as the first file is added to the print queue, the Start printing button is activated, and remains active as long as there are filenames in the queue.

If you click on a filename in the print queue, both the "File cover" (explained below) and the Remove buttons are activated. The "Remove" button removes the selected file from the queue. (It does *not* delete the file from the disk!)

Cover Pages

WinList offers the option of printing two types of cover page: File and Group.

A file cover page is printed at the start of the printout of an individual file. Click on the filename in the Print queue list and you'll see that the "File cover" and "Remove" buttons are activated.

Click on the "File cover" button to open the file cover dialog box. This displays the filename and, below it, a radio button. Clicking on this will activate or deactivate the printing of a cover sheet for this file only. When activated, two options are available:

♦ Listing date & time: Prints the date and time the file was listed.

♦ File size: Prints the file size, in bytes.

Both options are activated by default when the file cover is activated; you can deactivate them by clicking on the check boxes.

The file cover shows the filename in large type, plus the above text if the options are activated.

When a file cover has been activated, a copyright symbol (a c in a circle) appears at the start of the file's entry in the print queue list.

When more than one file is added to the print queue, the Grp Cvr (Group Cover) button is activated. A group cover is a cover sheet which is printed before the first file is listed. Clicking on this button displays a dialog box which allows the cover to be activated or deactivated, using the Print group cover radio button.

When the group cover is activated, the following options can be selected:

♦ Title: A group title — such as the name of the project — which will be printed on the group cover page.

♦ Listing date & time: The date and time on which the group of files was listed.

♦ List filenames: Causes the names of the files in the group to be listed on the group cover sheet.

You can list files with both a group cover sheet and individual file covers sheets, or with a group cover and no file covers, or a group cover plus file covers for some files only, or with no covers at all.

Printing

Clicking on the Start printing button will — surprise! — start the file printout. Files are printed out in the order in which they appear in the print queue list box; as each file is printed, its entry is deleted from the file queue.

Printing can be canceled at any time by clicking on the Cancel button in the small dialog box which appears once printing starts.

Printout Format

You should ensure that you have selected the printer correctly using the Control Panel before using WinList. Remember to set the correct paper size and to specify no margins.

On each page, WinList prints a header, comprising the filename, the date it was last altered (*not* the date on which it was listed), and the page number.

It adds a line number to the start of each line; if a line of text is longer than one printable line (75 characters), it will continue the line on the next line down, but without a line number.

WinList tries to break the line at the last space before the 75-character limit; if no suitable space is available, it simply breaks the line at the 75th character.

The exact number of lines per page depends on the page size specified in the Control Panel printer setup.

Testing

Due to limited hardware availability, WinList has been tested only on an HP LaserJet IIIP printer, with and without PostScript. Any problems with other printers should be reported to me.

Peter Rodwell
CompuServe: 100023,2476

WizManager

Version 1.1d
Copyright © Mijenix

*W*izManager gives the Windows 3.1 File Manager virtually all the tools you've ever wanted to improve the File Manager interface. With a button bar, a customizable drop-down menu, powerful script and command languages, and more, WizManager gives you more bang for the buck than almost any other Windows program.

Important Installation Instructions: *Running the WSETUP program to decompress and copy WizManager to your hard disk does not configure the program for your use. You must also double-click the INSTALL.EXE icon that WSETUP locates in a new WizManager Install group in Program Manager. Mijenix provides INSTALL.EXE to move files into the proper directories and configure WizManager to your system. See the Installation section below for the correct procedure.*

Type of Program:	File Manager enhancement.
Requires:	Windows 3.1 or higher.
Registration:	Use the form at the end of this chapter to register with the shareware author.
Technical Support:	Mijenix provides registered users with technical support by CompuServe, America OnLine, Internet, phone, and fax.
Similar Shareware:	File Commander, a program featured in *Windows 3.1 Secrets,* is another program that adds menus to the Windows File Manager. The command language used by WizManager is similar to the WinBatch language, which is also documented in *Windows 3.1 Secrets.*

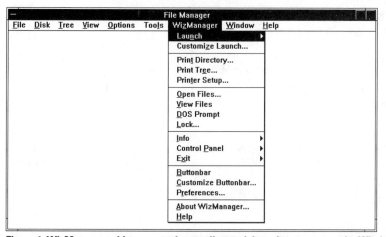

Figure 1: WizManager adds a convenient toolbar and drop-down menu to the Windows 3.1 File Manager.

1: Installing WizManager

To install WizManager, or update an older version of WizManager, you must run WSETUP.EXE on the *More Windows 3.1 SECRETS* Diskette 1 to decompress the files, and INSTALL.EXE to configure the program, as described in the steps below.

1. **Decompress WizManager files:** Insert the *More Windows 3.1 SECRETS* Diskette 1 into the appropriate drive. From Program Manager, click File Run, type A:WSETUP or B:WSETUP, and click OK. Select WizManager from WSETUP's list of programs. WSETUP decompresses and copies all WizManager files from Diskette 1 to a directory on your hard drive called WIZTEMP (under whichever directory you chose when you started WSETUP). But WSETUP does not configure WizManager — to do this, go to step 2.

2. **Configure WizManager:** From Program Manager, double-click the INSTALL.EXE icon in the WizManager Install group window. This will start the configuration process, and will install all necessary WizManager files into a directory called C:\WIZMGR (or any other directory name you choose). The INSTALL.EXE program will copy all needed files to the proper directories and place a WizManager menu item on the Windows File Manager main menu.

3. **Remove unnecessary installation files:** After the configuration process runs successfully, delete the WIZTEMP directory, and all files within it, to save hard disk space. None of the files are needed after INSTALL.EXE is completed. Also delete the WizManager install group window from Program Manager by minimizing the group, highlighting it, and clicking File Delete.

Note: If you wish to install WizManager on a network server, please follow the instructions contained in the Network section of this chapter and in the NETWORK.TXT file on the disk.

If you have any problems installing WizManager, call Mijenix Technical Support at (608) 277-1971 or contact Mijenix though CompuServe mail (75430,1545) or America OnLine mail (Mijenix).

System requirements

WizManager requires the following hardware and software:

Hardware

Any personal computer capable of running Microsoft® Windows™ 3.1.

At least 90K of free RAM, 250K recommended.

700K of free disk space.

Software

MS-DOS™ or PC-DOS™ version 3.3 or later.

Microsoft® Windows™ version 3.1 or Microsoft Windows for Workgroups™ version 3.1. *Note:* WizManager will only run on 16-bit Windows versions.

Microsoft® Windows™ File Manager version 3.1.

Introduction

WizManager is a powerful Windows and Windows for Workgroups File Manager add-on. It appends many features missing in File Manager, and enhances your power to manage your disks and files. WizManager is automatically loaded when File Manager starts and is removed from memory when the latter closes. You do not have to intervene — once installed, WizManager becomes entirely part of File Manager, just like standard features.

WizManager additions are multi-faceted and can be presented as belonging to three major sets of innovative and powerful features:

Fast Access Buttonbar

Command Line Box

WizManager Utilities

The *Fast Access Buttonbar* is completely integrated into File Manager. It allows you to quickly launch any File Manager command without having to browse through File Manager's menus. The customizable Buttonbar is colorful and scrollable, enabling you to access over 50 buttons.

The *Command Line Box* could be called "DOS in Windows." It allows you to enter DOS commands without shelling out to DOS or starting a DOS session. How is it possible? The DOS commands have been rewritten and are completely part of WizManager. Using the Command Line Box, you can execute commands like COPY, DEL, and over 100 other commands without exiting File Manager. You can also launch applications, open files, and execute scripts. With WizManager's Command Line Box, File Manager users get the best of both worlds: Windows *and* DOS.

WizManager also adds many *utilities* to File Manager such as Print Directory, Print Tree, Lock, Customizable Launch Menus, Fast Popup Menu, Direct Access to the Control Panel Options, Exit Windows, Restart Windows, Reboot System, Smart File Open, Access to a File Viewer, etc.

WizManager is the result of listening to the wishes of many File Manager users and implementing those suggestions into a totally compatible software package. With WizManager, using File Manager becomes easier, more useful, and much more enjoyable.

2: Getting Started — What Is WizManager?

WizManager is a powerful Windows and Windows for Workgroups File Manager add-on. It appends many features missing in File Manager, and enhances your power to manage your disks and files. WizManager is automatically loaded when File Manager starts and is removed from memory when the latter closes. You do not have to intervene — once installed, WizManager becomes entirely part of File Manager, just like standard features.

WizManager Components

Figure 2: WizManager screen components.

WizManager's additions to File Manager are multi-faceted. When File Manager is started, WizManager adds many components to File Manager's standard features. This additional power is accessible through

♦ The Fast Access Buttonbar

♦ The Command Line Box

♦ The WizManager Menu

Fast Access Buttonbar

The Fast Access Buttonbar is a long-awaited feature for File Manager users. A buttonbar is to the mouse what key-combination shortcuts are to the keyboard: it accelerates the application and facilitates the access to the functionalities. Instead of browsing through the menus, you can quickly activate a command by simply clicking the appropriate button.

WizManager Buttonbar makes your work with File Manager easier. Tile horizontally or vertically, sort the displayed files, exit File Manager, etc., with just a button click.

WizManager's scrollable Buttonbar displays colorful buttons and lets you access all the File Manager functionalities. Its customization is simple and allows you to display the buttons in your preferred order.

Command Line Box

Added to the Buttonbar is another feature users have been waiting for: a Command Line Box. This Command Line Box is not the simple Run command found in the File menu. Most DOS internal commands and many external commands were rewritten in order to be implemented and available directly in File Manager.

'*Old habits die hard...*' this is especially true for many File Manager users who wish sometimes to quickly type DOS commands like DEL or COPY, start a program, or open a file by simply typing its name instead of using a mouse and menus. All this is possible with WizManager Command Line Box. Because the Command Line Box is part of File Manager, all WizManager DOS commands are executed in Windows, without shelling out to DOS. The result could be called DOS in Windows: it is fast, convenient, and powerful. With WizManager Command Line Box, the File Manager user gets the best of both worlds: Windows *and* DOS.

Menus

WizManager provides many utilities and increases File Manager's capabilities. These utilities can be accessed either through the WizManager menu or by typing their command name in the Command Line Box.

WizManager menu

Figure 2 presents the different commands of the WizManager menu. The WizManager menu is automatically added to the standard File Manager menu bar. WizManager's relative position within the menu bar depends on how many File Manager extensions you are using and the position of the WizManager extension declaration in the [addons] section of File Manager's configuration file (WINFILE.INI).

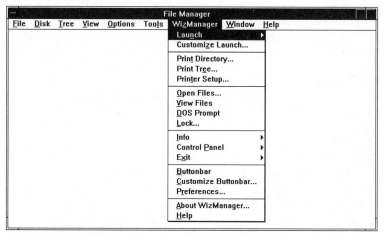

Figure 3: WizManager menu.

WizManager also adds the following menu commands to the standard File Manager Options and Window menus:

Command added to File Manager's Options menu

Save Settings Now
Selecting the Save Settings Now menu item from the Window menu will save the positions and views of all open File Manager directory windows.

Commands added to File Manager's Window menu

Tile Horizontally
Selecting the Tile Horizontally menu item from the Window menu will arrange directory windows on top of each other (horizontally) so that each window is visible and no windows overlap. This command is not added to the Window menu in the Windows for Workgroups version of File Manager as this option already exists.

Tile Vertically
Selecting the Tile Vertically menu item from the Window menu will arrange the directory windows side by side (vertically) so that each window is visible and no windows overlap. This command is not added to the Window menu in the Windows for Workgroups version of File Manager as this option already exists.

Minimize
Selecting the Minimize menu item from the Window menu will minimize all the directory windows to icons.

Restore
Selecting the Restore menu item from the Window menu will restore all the minimized directory windows to their previous size and location.

Quick Tips to Get You Started

Here are a few quick tips to get you started or to give you some indications on how to use WizManager more efficiently.

WizManager Buttonbar

The Buttonbar is a set of shortcuts to File Manager menu commands. Clicking with the left mouse button on any button will immediately start the corresponding command.

Scroll the Buttonbar?

There are two ways to scroll the Buttonbar:

♦ Use the left and right scroll buttons located at the left of the Buttonbar.

♦ Or click with the right mouse button on any button of the Buttonbar. The Buttonbar will scroll the buttons by page until it reaches the last button and then scroll back.

During the scrolling process, the Buttonbar scrolls and displays as many new buttons as your video resolution permits (button page) until it reaches the last set of buttons.

What is this button?

To quickly understand each button's command, a small button information window is displayed underneath each button when the mouse cursor is positioned over the Buttonbar buttons. As long as you stay with the mouse cursor over the buttons limit, the button information window will continue to be updated and displayed. You can scroll the Buttonbar with the right mouse button to display the next page(s) of buttons. The automatic display of the info window can be disabled in the Preferences dialog.

If the Display Info Window is disabled, you can still show the info window by holding down the Shift key while you click with the left mouse button on any button. The same small window showing the command's name will be displayed under the button. You can then release the Shift key and the mouse button and move the mouse over the next buttons to get the information.

When the button you were looking for is found, simply select it with the left mouse button without worrying about the little help window. It will automatically disappear when the command is executed.

Change the order of the buttons?

To customize the Buttonbar, select the Customize Buttonbar command from the WizManager menu. A dialog with a list of the buttons will be displayed. Select a button in the list whose relative position in the Buttonbar you wish to change and click either on the Move Up or Move Down button to move the Buttonbar button further to the front or to the back of the Buttonbar. Repeat with other Buttonbar buttons until you are satisfied. If you wish to reset the entire Buttonbar to its default setting, select the Reset button.

Command Line Box

The Command Line Box is displayed at the left side of the Buttonbar. The caret of the Command Line Box edit field is blinking when the Command Line Box is active and ready to receive your commands.

Quickly switch to the Command Line Box?

To activate the Command Line Box either:

- ♦ Click with the left mouse button in the edit field,
- ♦ Or press Alt+BackSpace.

To return to the File Manager directory window either:

- ♦ Click on a directory or file in the directory tree or directory window,
- ♦ Or press Alt+Enter.

You can have the Command Line Box active and ready at File Manager's startup by selecting this option in the Preferences dialog selected from WizManager's menu.

What is displayed above the Command Line Box?

The current Command Line Box drive and directory is displayed above the edit field. This current directory is independent of File Manager's directory windows. The startup drive and directory can be defined in WizManager Preferences.

Quick outputs from certain commands like PATH, DISKFREE, etc., are displayed next to the Command Line Box current directory.

Error messages are also displayed next to the current directory information, in square brackets [...]. The beep on error feature can be turned on or off in WizManager Preferences.

What commands?

There are over 100 commands available within WizManager, like COPY, DEL, RENAME, ATTRIB, MEM, etc. Most of the WizManager commands accept the same parameters as their DOS equivalent commands and display similar information or confirmation dialogs as their equivalent commands in File Manager.

You can also launch any application by typing its path (if necessary) and filename.

You can open a file by entering its name. The associated application (if set) will be started and your file displayed.

Repeat commands?

You can call any previously entered command (command history) by:

- ♦ Selecting the command from the Command Line Box drop-down list,
- ♦ or using the UP and DOWN keys.

Interrupt a command?

You can press the Esc key (Escape key) at any time to interrupt a WizManager command.

Work with the files displayed in File Manager directory window?

By default, The ' ; ' (semicolon) character symbol (without the quotes) represents in WizManager commands the path of the File Manager active directory window.

This path shortcut symbol is very useful, for it allows you to easily work on the displayed files without specifying the path to the File Manager directory window.

- ♦ For example, if you want to copy all the files with the DOC extension from the File Manager directory window into the current WizManager directory, type

```
copy ;*.exe
```
or
```
copy ;\*.exe if you feel more comfortable keeping a backslash (\)
between the ; and the filename.
```

♦ The ; can also be used as a target directory as in the command:

```
move report.txt ;
```
or
```
move report.txt \;.
```

The path shortcut symbol can be changed in the Preferences dialog.

Access DOS internal commands?

DOS internal commands (COMMAND.COM commands) can be executed by entering a ' = ' (without the quotes) in front of the command, like =COPY or =DEL .

Same command name?

If any WizManager command has the same name as another external command or program, type a ' = ' (without the quotes) in front of the command to execute the external command or program instead of WizManager command. For example, =MEM will execute the DOS MEM command instead of WizManager's MEM command.

Utilities

With WizManager, you also get many utilities. Below you will find hints on what you can do with some of them:

Do you frequently use certain commands or applications?

Use the customizable Launch menus to place your frequently used commands or applications. They will then be only a click away, fast and easily accessible.

Do you wish to quickly minimize all running applications or see which ones are running?

Press the right mouse button anywhere on File Manager and a popup menu will be displayed, listing all the currently active applications in Windows and enabling you to quickly switch to any of them. You can also minimize or restore all the applications, or close any of them. With the pop-up menu you can also access your Launch menus.

Do you need your system information or disk(s) information?

Quickly get your system information or disk(s) information by selecting Info in the WizManager menu.

Do you wish to start multiple files or start a file which doesn't have an association?

A 'smart' association is integrated: Select Open Files from the WizManager menu. With Open Files you can open ALL (more than one at a time) the files selected in File Manager.

In the displayed dialog box you can either open the files according to their associations (extensions), according to a specified association (for example, program associated with the TXT extension), or a specified program name (Browse to find the application path, or enter it directly). All the files can also be sent to the same application.

Do you want to print the directory listing displayed in File Manager?

Select the Print Directory command from WizManager menu. With Print Directory you can print the displayed File Manager directory listing.

Print Directory allows you to either print the list of the files selected in File Manager or the entire directory listing. WizManager also prints Search Result lists. Select the Print Search List command to get a hard copy.

Is your disk full, but you have to find some room for an additional program?
Select the Print Tree command from the WizManager menu. You can specify in the dialog box
that you want all the filenames in each directory printed with the disk directory structure.
You can also select to have the size of each directory printed next to the directory name so
that you can identify which directory is a 'hog' and make some room for your new file(s).

**Do you have to leave your station but you don't want anyone to see or touch your data
while you are gone, and you don't want to turn your computer down?**
Use the Lock command accessible from the WizManager menu. Your system can be safely
locked and restored after typing a user-defined password. This feature permits you to leave
your station, keeping information confidential and secure until you return and enter your
personal password.

There are many more utilities like exiting or restarting Windows, rebooting your system,
accessing the different Control Panel functions directly, etc. As you use WizManager, you will
quickly familiarize yourself with most of them and enjoy the WizManager functionalities.

3: Working with WizManager

Working with the Command Line Box

Introduction

WizManager's Command Line Box is similar to the DOS Prompt, but more powerful. The
Command Line Box, located at the left side of the Buttonbar, allows you to enter WizManager
and DOS commands, start DOS and Windows programs, open files, and execute scripts. The
Command Line Box gives you the power of a command line within File Manager.

Entering commands

You can activate the Command Line Box either by clicking in its edit field with the left mouse
button or by pressing Atl+Backspace. A vertical line (|), called the cursor, flashing in the box
indicates that the Command Line Box is ready to receive and execute commands. This cursor
shows you where to type a command. When you type a character, the cursor moves one
space to the right. If you make a mistake, press the Backspace key to delete the character to
the left of the cursor.

You can type a command in uppercase or lowercase letters. Unless otherwise specified, you
must use a space to separate a command from its parameters. If you want to erase a command, press the Esc key. The Command Line Box is then cleared and the cursor is moved
back to the beginning of the edit field.

To carry out a command, press the Enter key. You can press the Esc key at any time to
interrupt a WizManager command.

Editing commands

The Command Line Box accepts and executes commands entered with the keyboard or
pasted from the Clipboard. To execute a command, press Enter. You can use the following
keys to edit commands.

Press	To
Left Arrow	Move the cursor back one character.
Right Arrow	Move the cursor forward one character.
Ctrl+Left Arrow	Move the cursor to the previous word.
Ctrl+Right Arrow	Move the cursor to the next word.
Home	Move the cursor to the start of the line.
End	Move the cursor to the end of the line.
Delete	Delete the character to the right of the cursor.
Backspace	Delete the character to the left of the cursor.
Esc	Clear the Command Line Box.

Repeating commands

The Command Line Box keeps a list of your commands as you type them. You can use the following keys to view previous commands. To carry out a command again after it is displayed, press ENTER.

Press	To
Up Arrow	Display the previous command in the list.
Down Arrow	Display the next command in the list.
Alt+Down Arrow or F4	Display the list of previously entered commands.
Alt+Up Arrow or F4	Close the list of previously entered commands.
Page Up	Display the newest command in the list.
Page Down	Display the oldest command in the list.

Getting help with a command

On-line Help is available for all WizManager commands. The displayed command Help describes the purpose of the command and provides detailed information of its syntax, parameters, and switches.

To display a command's Help, type the command name followed by the /? switch.

Current directory

The Command Line Box current directory is displayed above the Command Line Box. The current directory is the directory in which you are working at any one time. Each disk drive has its own current directory.

To work with files in a directory that is not current, you have two options:

♦ You can type the path of the other directory.

♦ You can make the other directory current by using the CD (change directory) or ChDir command. The CD command is described in section 5.

To change the current directory to the directory of the active File Manager directory window, use the CD command followed by the File Manager path shortcut symbol: CD ;

File Manager's path shortcut symbol can be set in the Path Shortcut dialog accessible from the Preferences dialog. The semicolon (;) is used, by default, as the path shortcut symbol to File Manager's active directory window.

You can set the Command Line Box current directory at startup by entering the appropriate directory in the Set Startup dialog which can be selected and displayed from the Preferences dialog.

WizManager commands

There are over 100 WizManager commands available from the Command Line Box. Refer to section 5 for detailed information about the different commands.

There are three types of WizManager commands:

Internal commands
WizManager's internal commands are the Windows version of their equivalent DOS commands. Using WizManager internal commands allows you to carry out DOS commands without shelling out to DOS or having to start a DOS session. WizManager internal commands are executed within Windows.

File Manager commands
File Manager commands execute commands specific to File manager or provided by File Manager.

Control Panel commands
Control Panel commands allow you to quickly open Control Panel Options from the Command Line Box.

If any WizManager command has the same name as an external command or program, type a ' = ' (without the quotes) in front of the command to execute the external command or program instead of WizManager command. For example, =MEM will execute the DOS MEM command instead of WizManager's MEM command.

DOS commands

DOS internal and external commands can be carried out from the Command Line Box. Enter the DOS command in the Command Line Box just as you would at a DOS Prompt.

DOS internal commands (COMMAND.COM commands) can be executed by entering a ' = ' (without the quotes) in front of the command, like =COPY or =DEL . If a COMMAND.PIF file is available in the file search path, the DOS internal command will be carried out using the options set in COMMAND.PIF. Refer to the "PIF Editor" chapter of your Windows User's Guide for detailed information on how to customize a PIF file.

Command switches

The execution of any program or opening of a file (from the Command Line Box or from the Launch menus) can be customized with the following switches placed at the end of the command:

Switch	Action
/+	open maximized..i./+ (Command switch);
/-	open minimized..i./- (Command switch);
/=	open restored (normal size)..i./= (Command switch);
/H	open and hide..i./H (Command switch);
/@	make the directory where the application (or file) resides the working directory..i./@ (Command switch);
/;	(semicolon) make the active File Manager directory the working directory.

Command output

The output of a WizManager command is displayed either next to the current directory of the Command Line Box (in blue characters) and/or in a dialog. Each new output or command error message overwrites the previously displayed information.

Error messages

Command execution errors are displayed within square brackets [ ] next to the current directory of the Command Line Box (in blue characters). Other error messages are displayed in a dialog box. Each new output or command error message overwrites the previously displayed information.

Path shortcut to File Manager

The path shortcut symbol (character) is a command parameter prefix which is useful when the current Command Line Box directory differs from the active File Manager directory window directory. The path shortcut symbol represents the full path of the active File Manager directory. It allows you to work on the files displayed in the active File Manager directory window from the Command Line Box with a minimum of keystrokes. To fully specify the path of a file displayed in the active File Manager window, simply enter the path shortcut symbol followed by the filename.

The default path shortcut symbol is the semicolon character (;). The path shortcut symbol can be changed in the Path Shortcut dialog accessible from the Preferences dialog.

Path shortcut examples

In the following examples, the path shortcut symbol is chosen to be the default path shortcut symbol, the semicolon (;).

♦ To change the Command Line Box current directory to the active File Manager directory window, type: cd ;

♦ To change the Command Line Box current directory to the directory CLIENTS located beneath the active File Manager directory window, type: cd ;\clients

♦ To copy all the files from the active File Manager directory window to the A: drive, type: copy ;*.* a:

♦ To create the directory PROJECT in the active File Manager directory window, type: md ;\project

Note: For all commands, entering the path shortcut symbol alone or followed by a Backslash (\) is equivalent, ; for example, typing cd ;\clients is equivalent to typing cd ;clients.

Working with the Buttonbar _____

Access commands through the Buttonbar

WizManager's Buttonbar is a quick way to execute File Manager commands. You don't need to browse through the different menus, all File Manager functions are right under your finger. Click with the left mouse button on any button and the corresponding command will immediately start.

If the Buttonbar is not displayed at the top of File Manager, select Buttonbar from the WizManager menu. This command allows you to display or hide the Buttonbar and the Command Line Box.

Scrolling the Buttonbar

Your video resolution limits the number of buttons displayed simultaneously in the Buttonbar (i.e., there are more buttons available 'behind' the set displayed). Depending on your system video resolution, ten (VGA 640x480 pixels), nineteen (SuperVGA 800x600 pixels), twenty-six (SuperVGA 1024x768 pixels) or thirty-six (SuperVGA 1280x1024 pixels) icons can be simultaneously displayed in the Buttonbar. The higher the horizontal video resolution, the more icons you have available without scrolling. To access the rest of the buttons, simply scroll the Buttonbar.

There are two ways to scroll the Buttonbar:

♦ Use the left and right scroll buttons located at the left of the Buttonbar.

♦ Or click with the right mouse button on any button of the Buttonbar. The Buttonbar will scroll the buttons by page until it reaches the last button and then scroll back.

During the scrolling process, the Buttonbar scrolls and displays as many new buttons as your video resolution permits (button page) until it reaches the last set of buttons.

Buttonbar Buttons

Button	Command	Button	Command
	Sort by Name		Create Directory
	Sort by Type		Delete
	Sort by Size		Rename
	Sort by Date		Properties
	Exit File Manager		Move
	View Names Only		Copy
	View All File Details		Associate
	View Partial Details		Run
	Select Files		Cascade
	Search		Tile Vertically
	View Files		Tile Horizontally

Button	Command	Button	Command
	Open Files		New Window
	Launch Task Manager		Minimize
	Lock		Restore
	Select Drive		View Tree Only
	Print File		View Directory
	Print Directory		View Tree and Directory
	Print Tree		Indicate Expand. Branches
	DOS Prompt		Format Disk
	Control Panel		Disk Copy
	System Information		Label Disk
	Disk Information		Make System Disk
	Font		File Manager Help
	Connect Net Drive (WFW Only)		Share As (WFW Only)
	Disconnect Net Drive (WFW Only)		Stop Sharing (WFW Only)

Customizing the Buttonbar

The Customize Buttonbar dialog displayed when you select the Customize Buttonbar menu item in the WizManager menu allows you to reorganize the Buttonbar's button order. To optimize your work with the Buttonbar, move the most often used buttons to the top of the list and the least often used to the bottom.

See Customize Buttonbar in section 4.

Working with WizManager Utilities

Print Directory and Print Search Results

Selecting the Print Directory menu item in the WizManager menu enables you to print the directory listing of the files in the active File Manager directory window. The displayed Print Directory dialog allows you to print the listing of the selected files or to print the listing of all the files in the File Manager directory window. If the Search Results window is the active File Manager window, a Print Search List menu item is made available in the WizManager menu to print the listing of the selected files or the listing of all the files found. The Print Search Results List dialog is similar to the Print Directory dialog.

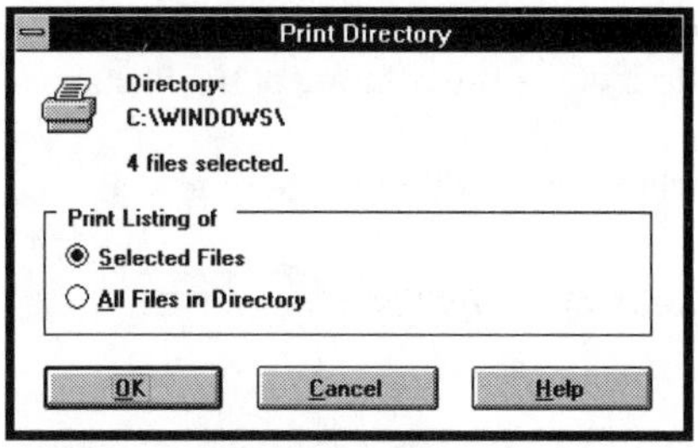

Figure 4: Print Directory dialog.

The path of the files selected in File Manager is displayed at the top of the dialog with the number of selected files underneath.

♦ You can choose to print the listing of only the selected files or the listing of all the files in the directory by selecting the appropriate option in the dialog.

Files are printed in the same order they are displayed in File Manager. Use the View commands to sort the files by name, size, date, or extension (type).

The Print Directory output contains the disk's volume label, one directory or filename per line, including the filename extension, the file size in bytes, the date and time the file was last modified, and the file's attributes. At the end of the listing, the total number of files, the total number of directories, the cumulative size of the files, and the free space remaining on the disk are also printed.

Note: Because of a File Manager problem, the Print Directory or Print Search List menu command is only available from the WizManager menu when at least one file or directory is selected in File Manager's directory window.

Print Tree

Selecting the Print Tree menu item in the WizManager menu enables you to print a selected disk's hierarchical directory structure. The displayed Print Tree dialog allows you to include the printing of the names of the files in each directory and the total size of each directory.

Figure 5: Print Tree dialog.

In the Print Directory dialog

  ♦ Select the appropriate drive from the drop-down list.

  ♦ Check *Print Filenames in Directories* if you wish to include the printing of the filenames in each directory.

  ♦ Check *Print Each Directory Size* if you wish to include the printing of the total size of each directory.

It is possible to check both, *Print Filenames in Directories* and *Print Each Directory Size*.

Printer Setup

Selecting the Printer Setup menu item in the **WizManager** menu opens a printer setup dialog which allows you to set printing options specific to your default printer.

A printer setup dialog can only be displayed if a printer driver has been installed. For information about installing a printer driver, see "Installing a Printer Driver" in your Windows manual.

Open Files

Selecting the Open Files menu item in the WizManager menu opens the Open Files dialog which allows you to select how the selected file(s) in File Manager should be opened and displayed.

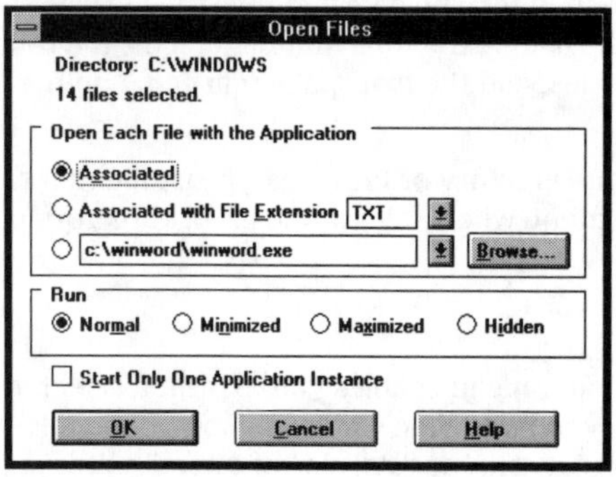

Figure 6: Open Files dialog.

Open Files enables you to open files with a specified application, open files which don't have an association, open files without an extension, etc.

In the Open Files dialog:

♦ Specify which application should open the selected files:

• Selecting Associated will open each file with its associated application.

• Selecting Associated with File Extension will open all the files with the application associated with the specified extension. The extension entered cannot exceed three characters (not including the optional period as first extension character).

• Selecting the third option allows you to enter the path and filename of a specific application which should open all the files. Use the Browse button if you wish to browse through your directories and drives to find the appropriate application.

♦ Specify in the *Run* group how the selected files should be displayed: Normal, Minimized, Maximized, or Hidden.

♦ Check *Start Only One Application* in the dialog if you want to start only one copy of the application and display all the files within this application. Be aware that many applications are not able to display multiple files or generate an error message with this option checked.

The Open Files menu command is only available from the WizManager menu when at least one file is selected in File Manager's directory window.

Fast Open Files

Fast Open Files allows you to have two applications which can be quickly accessed to open or work on the selected files in File Manager. When a Fast Open application is executed, the Open Files dialog is not displayed — the files are directly opened by the specified application.

To set the Fast Open application paths and filenames, select the Preferences menu item in the WizManager menu; then select the Set Fast Open... button in the System Setup group.

♦ To open the selected file(s) in File Manager with the first Fast Open application, hold down the Ctrl key while selecting Open Files from the WizManager menu or from the Buttonbar.

♦ To open the selected file(s) in File Manager with the second Fast Open application, hold down the Ctrl and the Shift keys while selecting Open Files from the WizManager menu or from the Buttonbar.

View Files

Selecting the View Files menu item in the WizManager menu starts the Viewer application set in Preferences and displays the contents of the files selected in File Manager. The Viewer application is an external program, not included with WizManager.

A file viewer is a program which allows you to view the contents of a file. Notepad, the text editor provided with Windows, is probably the simplest file viewer, although its viewing capabilities are limited to small text files. More elaborated file viewers are available, like *Drag And View*™ by Canyon Software™ (shareware) or *Norton Viewer*™, the viewer included in the Norton Desktop for Windows™. These file viewers are able to display the file contents not only of text files but also of formatted files created with word processors, spreadsheets, databases, drawing programs, etc.

To set the file viewer application path and filename, select the Preferences menu item in the WizManager menu; then select the Set Viewer... button in the System Setup group.

The View Files menu command is only available from the WizManager menu when at least one file is selected in File Manager's directory window.

DOS Prompt

Selecting the DOS Prompt menu item in the WizManager menu starts a new DOS prompt (command line) session.

DOS Prompt executes the program named COMMAND.COM through a configuration file named DOSPRMPT.PIF. The latter file is automatically installed in your Windows directory when Windows is installed. DOSPRMPT.PIF controls several facets of the way COMMAND.COM is launched from this command. You can modify (or re-create if necessary) the file using the Windows application PIFEDIT.EXE. Refer to the "PIF Editor" chapter of your Windows User's Guide for detailed information on how to customize a PIF file.

A different PIF file can be used instead of DOSPRMPT.PIF. You can set your preferences by selecting the WizManager Preferences menu command; then select the DOS PIF File... button in the System Setup group.

Lock

Selecting the Lock menu item in the WizManager menu minimizes all running applications and locks Windows until you enter your password in the displayed Unlock dialog.

Lock lets you completely lock your system and restore it after typing a password you previously defined. This feature permits you to leave your station, keeping information confidential or secure until you come back and the defined password is entered.

Figure 7: System Locked dialog.

For maximum confidentiality, during the locking process all applications are minimized leaving only an Enter Password dialog displayed. Applications running in the background which cannot run properly when minimized (for example, certain communication programs) are left untouched.

If you want to set or change your password, select the Preferences menu item in the WizManager menu; then select the Password... button in the System Setup group.

Disk Information

```
─                    Disk Information
Disk:                    C:                    ┌────────────┐
Size:                    43366 kB              │     OK     │
Space used by files:     39964 kB              └────────────┘
Free space left:         3402 kB
Percentage of disk used: 92.2 %
Average file size:       24 kB
Total number of files:   1665  (including 11 hidden)
Total number of directories:  43
─────────────────────────────────────────────────────────
Smallest file, 2 Bytes:
c:\procomm\capture\default.cap

Largest file, 996064 Bytes:
c:\procomm\pw.exe

Largest directory structure, 3 levels:
c:\procomm\aspect\demo
```

Figure 8: Disk Information dialog.

When selecting the Disk Info menu item from the Window menu, the specified drive is scanned and useful information about disk usage and files statistics is retrieved.

Disk Info displays:

Disk size	Total number of files
Space used by files	Total number of directories
Free space left	Smallest file size and path
Percentage of disk used	Largest file size and path
Average file size	Largest directory structure and path

Note: Disk Info and File Manager display inaccurate file space usage of drives which are user space restricted network drives (allocated space). The used space displayed is the unavailable drive space added to the actual file space. The average file size is therefore inaccurate.

System Information

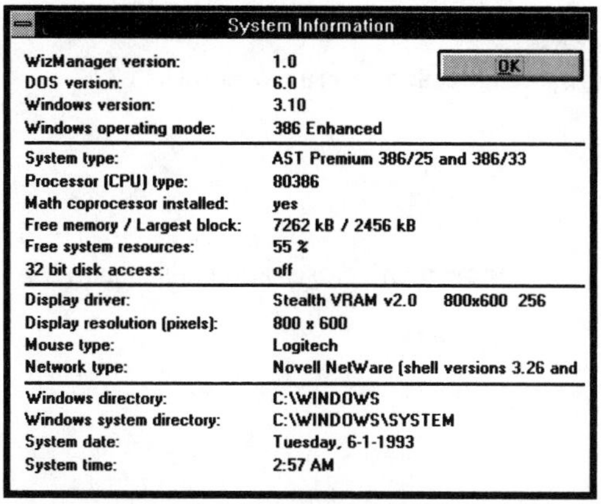

WizManager version:	1.0
DOS version:	6.0
Windows version:	3.10
Windows operating mode:	386 Enhanced
System type:	AST Premium 386/25 and 386/33
Processor (CPU) type:	80386
Math coprocessor installed:	yes
Free memory / Largest block:	7262 kB / 2456 kB
Free system resources:	55 %
32 bit disk access:	off
Display driver:	Stealth VRAM v2.0 800x600 256
Display resolution (pixels):	800 x 600
Mouse type:	Logitech
Network type:	Novell NetWare (shell versions 3.26 and
Windows directory:	C:\WINDOWS
Windows system directory:	C:\WINDOWS\SYSTEM
System date:	Tuesday, 6-1-1993
System time:	2:57 AM

Figure 9: System Information dialog.

Your system is scanned when selecting the System Info menu item from the Window menu and information about your computer and Windows configuration is displayed.

If you have questions about your computer and Windows configuration, System Info is a handy command to use. It instantly displays information about your system in a single dialog box. You are able to see at a glance how much memory you have available, what your CPU, video type, and resolution are, and if you have a coprocessor. It displays the system date and time, WizManager, DOS and Windows versions, whether you are connected to a network, and other critical information.

Control Panel

These commands are available in the WizManager menu, under the Control Panel menu item. Selecting a Control Panel command will start the corresponding Control Panel Option dialog. Refer to the "Control Panel" chapter of your Windows User's Guide for detailed information on how to use the Control Panel options.

Color
Date / Time
Desktop
Drivers
Fonts
International
Keyboard
Mouse
Ports
Printers
Sound
Network
386 Enhanced

Note: The Network option is available only if you have a network installed and started.

The 386 Enhanced option is available only on systems which can run Windows in 386 Enhanced Mode.

Exit

Exit Windows

Selecting the Exit Windows menu item from the Window menu closes and ends all applications running in Windows and exits Windows.

Figure 10: Exit Windows confirmation dialog.

Exit Windows lets you quickly close and terminate Windows. This command executes an orderly shutdown sequence of windows. A confirmation dialog is displayed before proceeding with the closing.

During the process, any running application with unsaved changes will ask for confirmation before closing. If all applications agree to quit, the Windows session is terminated and control returns to DOS.

Restart Windows

Selecting the Restart Windows menu item from the Windows menu exits and restarts Windows.

Figure 11: Restart Windows confirmation dialog.

Restart Windows executes an orderly shutdown sequence of windows, exits and restarts Windows. A confirmation dialog is displayed before proceeding with the restart.

During the process, any running application(s) with unsaved changes will ask for confirmation before closing. If all applications agree to quit, the Windows session is terminated and a new Windows session is created. The restart process is identical to completely exiting Windows and restarting it from the DOS prompt.

A restart is necessary to activate any changes to your SYSTEM.INI file, and may also be used if you wish to restart the system with an altered WIN.INI file, for example.

Reboot System

Selecting the Reboot System menu item from the Window menu exits Windows and reboots (restarts) your system.

Figure 12: Reboot System confirmation dialog.

Reboot System executes an orderly shutdown sequence of windows and completely restarts your computer. A confirmation dialog is displayed before proceeding with the reboot.

During the process, any running application(s) with unsaved changes will ask for confirmation before closing. If all applications agree to quit, the Windows session is terminated and the system is restarted (cold reboot). The Reboot process is identical to turning the power off and back on or pressing the reset button of your computer.

A reboot is necessary to activate any changes to your CONFIG.SYS file, and may also be used if you wish to restart the system with an altered AUTOEXEC.BAT file, for example.

Popup Menu

WizManager's popup menu is displayed when you click with the right mouse button on File Manager. The popup menu provides a fast way for accessing useful features. It displays two Launch menus, four standard menus, and a list of all the tasks currently running in Windows.

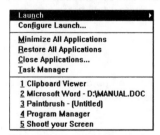

Figure 13: Example of a popup menu.

The popup Launch and standard menus are

Launch	Displays your customized menu items.
Customize Launch	Opens the Customize Launch dialog.
Minimize All Applications	Minimizes all running applications.
Restore All Applications	Restores all running applications.
Close Applications	Prompts before closing each running application.
Task Manager	Opens Windows Task Manager.

If you wish to switch to one of the running applications displayed in the dialog, select it from the dialog's tasks list.

Hidden tasks can be included in the tasks list. Check the appropriate option in WizManager's Preferences. When enabled, a bullet is displayed next to a hidden task in the tasks list to indicate the hidden attribute.

Scripts

A WizManager script file is a text file which contains a sequence of commands which can be executed by WizManager (similar to DOS batch files).

Script files are used to automate repetitive tasks or simplify the execution of multiple commands.

WizManager script files must be unformatted ASCII (text) files and must have the .WIZ extension to be recognized by WizManager. To execute a script file, type its path, filename and extension in the Command Line Box, or in the Run dialog, or double-click its filename in File Manager's directory window. WizManager script files can only be executed if File Manager and WizManager are running.

Because Windows doesn't pass entered parameters along with filenames to associated applications, only parameters entered in the Command Line Box will be transferred for execution.

A script can include

- ♦ Any command which can be executed from the Command Line Box (WizManager commands, DOS commands, filenames, DOS programs, Windows programs, etc.).
- ♦ Replaceable parameters (%0 through %9) which are placeholders for parameters typed at the command prompt (see DOS manual) or entered with the ENTERPARAM or ENTERNEWPARAM script commands.
- ♦ Script Commands.

Script commands

Text included in square brackets [ ] indicates that the script command parameter is optional. Text included in pointed brackets < > indicates that the script command parameter is necessary.

REM

Transforms a line into a comment when placed at the beginning of it. The line is ignored by WizManager.

ENTERPARAM [Text in dialog]

Displays a dialog box which allows the user to optionally enter new parameters which then become usable variables for the replaceable parameters %0 through %9.

If no parameter is entered after ENTERPARAM, 'Enter parameters:' is displayed in the dialog.

Because Windows doesn't pass parameters to associated applications, the ENTERPARAM command is particularly useful when a script is most often used from a File/Run command or is started by double-clicking its name in the File Manager directory window. ENTERPARAM allows the user to still enter parameters in the latter cases. Parameters entered after a script filename are recognized if entered from the Command Line Box.

ENTERPARAM can be used multiple times in a script to prompt the user to enter new parameters for the following lines in the script. The previous parameters (if any) are displayed as default in the dialog.

ENTERNEWPARAM [Text in dialog]
Is equivalent to ENTERPARAM except that previous parameters are not displayed as default.

PAUSE [text to display]
Opens a dialog box which displays the text entered after PAUSE. If no text is entered, then 'Continue?' is displayed as default. OK and Cancel buttons are displayed. Selecting OK (default button) continues the script; selecting Cancel aborts the script.

PAUSE![text to display]
Is equivalent to PAUSE except that an exclamation point icon is displayed.

PAUSE? [text to display]
Is equivalent to PAUSE except that a question mark icon is displayed.

ECHO <text to display>
Is similar to PAUSE except that only an OK button is displayed. ECHO without a text to display parameter is ignored.

ECHO! <text to display>
Is equivalent to ECHO except that an exclamation point icon is displayed.

ECHO? <text to display>
Is equivalent to ECHO except that a question mark icon is displayed.

Script example

Simple (theoretical) script example: EXAMPLE.WIZ

```
REM This is a script example for WizManager
ECHO Please insert a diskette in drive A:
DISKFREE A:
PAUSE? Do you want to proceed with the transfer?
ENTERPARAM Enter the filename of the file(s) to transfer (use wildcards if
necessary):
MOVE %1 a: /N
ECHO! File(s) transferred.
PAUSE? Do you want to delete .BAK files?
ENTERNEWPARAM Enter the path where the .BAK files are located:
DELETE %1\*.bak /P
ECHO! The .BAK files are deleted!
PAUSE? Start Word for Windows?
REM If answered OK, will continue the script.
c:\winword\winword.exe
```

Launch Menus

Customize Launch

Customize Launch allows you to insert, modify, or delete customizable menu items which can be selected in the WizManager menu or in WizManager's popup menu, under the Launch menu item.

Figure 14: Customize Launch dialog.

♦ Insert a new menu item:

1. If you wish to specify the location of the new menu item within the menu items, select the menu item in the menu item list under which you would like to insert a new menu item. If no menu item is selected, the new menu item is inserted at the end of the list.

2. Select the Insert... button and enter the menu item text (optional), the command to execute, the working directory (optional), and the access command (optional) in the displayed dialog.

♦ Modify an existing menu item:

1. Select the menu item to be modified in the menu item list.

2. Select the Modify... button. The menu item text, the command to execute, the working directory, and the access command can then be modified in the displayed dialog.

♦ Delete a menu item:

1. Select the menu item to be deleted in the menu item list.

2. Select OK in the confirmation dialog to delete the menu item.

♦ Set the order of the menu items:

1. Select the menu item to be moved in the menu item list.

2. Select the Move Up button to move the menu item up or the Move Down button to move the menu item down in the list.

3. Repeat steps 1 and 2 for each menu item you wish to move until you are satisfied with the results.

Insert New Menu Item

The Insert Menu Item dialog allows you to specify the different parameters of the new menu item.

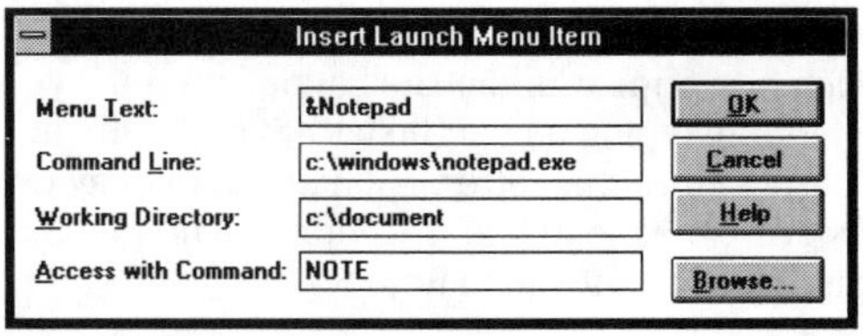

Figure 15: Insert Menu Item dialog.

♦ Menu Text:

Enter the text of the menu item as you wish it to appear under the Launch menu. If you want to choose the command from the menu by typing one of the letters of the menu item text, put an ampersand (&) immediately before that letter. Launch will display the menu item with that letter underlined. Entering the menu text is optional; if no menu text is specified, then the Command Line is displayed as the menu item text.

♦ Command Line:

Enter the command or script to execute, the program to start or the file to open. You can select the Browse button to browse through your directories and drives to select a file. Command switches can be specified.

♦ Working Directory:

Enter the path of the directory which should be the working directory when the command specified in the Command Line is executed. Entering the working directory is optional.

♦ Access with Command:

The command specified in Command Line can also be accessed and executed from the Command Line Box with the command you specify in Access with Command.

The specified command name

• Cannot be longer than 8 characters,

• Cannot contain any space character, and

• Cannot be a WizManager command nor a command already specified in another menu item.

Modify a Menu Item

The Modify Menu Item dialog allows you to modify each parameter of the selected menu item.

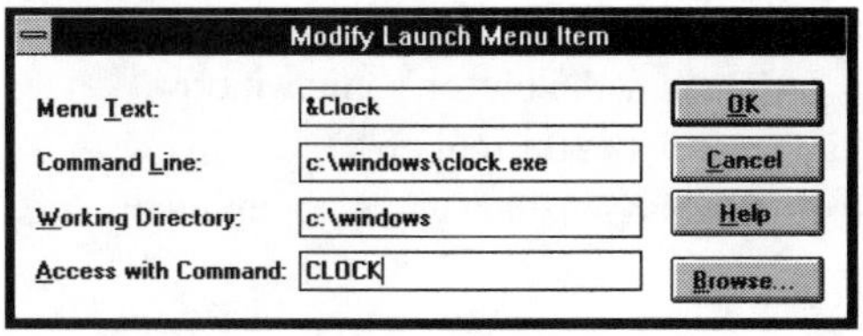

Figure 16: Modify Menu Item dialog.

♦ Menu Text:

Enter the text of the menu item as you wish it to appear under the Launch menu. If you want to choose the command from the menu by typing one of the letters of the menu item text, put an ampersand (&) immediately before that letter. Launch will display the menu item with that letter underlined. Entering the menu text is optional; if no menu text is specified, then the Command Line is displayed as the menu item text.

♦ Command Line:

Enter the command or script to execute, the program to start, or the file to open. You can select the Browse button to browse through your directories and drives to select a file. Command switches can be specified.

♦ Working Directory:

Enter the path of the directory which should be the working directory when the command specified in the Command Line is executed. Entering the working directory is optional.

♦ Access with Command:

The command specified in the Command Line field can also be accessed and executed from the Command Line Box with the command you specify in the Access with Command field.

The specified command name

- Cannot be longer than 8 characters,
- Cannot contain any space character, and
- Cannot be a WizManager command nor a command already specified in another menu item.

Keyboard and Mouse Shortcuts

WizManager shortcut keys

Press	To
Alt+BackSpace	Activate the Command Line Box.
Alt+Enter	Return to the File Manager directory window.

WizManager mouse shortcuts

Press	To
Left Button on Buttonbar Button	Activate the button's function.
Shift+Left Button on Buttonbar Button	Display the button's info window.
Right Button on Buttonbar	Scroll the Buttonbar.
Right Button on File Manager	Display WizManager's popup menu.

4: Customizing WizManager

WizManager Preferences

Selecting the Preferences menu item in the WizManager menu opens the Preferences dialog which allows you to customize WizManager.

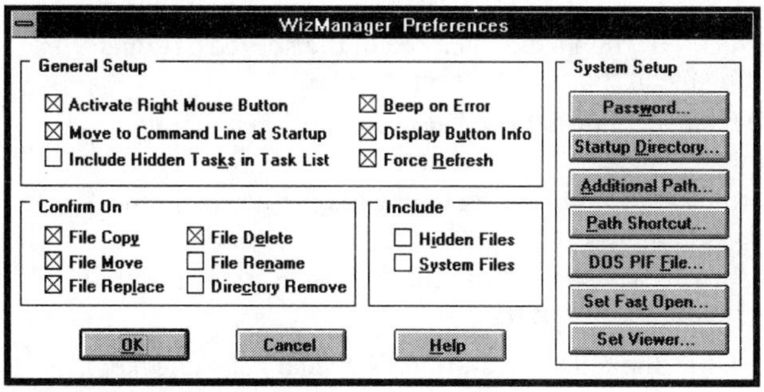

Figure 17: WizManager Preferences dialog.

General Setup

General Setup Check Boxes:

♦ *Activate Right Mouse Button.* Check this box if you want to display the WizManager Popup menu when clicking with the right mouse button anywhere on File Manager.

♦ *Move to Command Line Box at Startup.* Check this box if you want the Command Line Box to be active and ready for command entries when File Manager is started.

♦ *Include Hidden Tasks in Task List.* Check this box if you want to include hidden tasks in WizManager popup menu Task List.

♦ *Beep on Error.* Check this box if you want WizManager to emit a beep when an error is detected.

♦ *Display Button Info.* Check this box to display a help window when the mouse cursor is positioned over a Buttonbar button.

♦ *Force Refresh.* Check this box if you want to force File Manager to refresh its Status Bar and its Directory window each time WizManager performs a COPY, MOVE, or DELETE command.

WizManager's default configuration has the following options automatically checked:

Activate Right Mouse Button

Move to Command Line Box at Startup

Beep on Error

Display Button Info

Confirmations

Confirm On Check Boxes:

♦ *File Copy.* Check this box to have a confirmation dialog displayed each time WizManager's COPY command is used.

♦ *File Move.* Check this box to have a confirmation dialog displayed each time WizManager's MOVE command is used.

♦ *File Replace.* Check this box to have a confirmation dialog displayed before a WizManager's command is executed when a file declared in the source parameter has the same filename as an existing file in the target directory.

♦ *File Delete.* Check this box to have a confirmation dialog displayed each time WizManager's DELETE command is used.

♦ *File Rename.* Check this box to have a confirmation dialog displayed each time WizManager's RENAME or REN commands are used.

♦ *Directory Remove.* Check this box to have a confirmation dialog displayed each time WizManager's RMDIR or RD commands are used.

WizManager's default configuration has the following options automatically checked:

File Copy

File Move

File Replace

File Delete

Include Files

Include Check Boxes:

♦ *Hidden Files.* Check this box if you want WizManager's commands to always include hidden files.

♦ *System Files.* Check this box if you want WizManager's commands to always include system files.

WizManager's default configuration has none of the Include File options checked.

System Setup

Password

The Password dialog allows you to assign a password to unlock WizManager's Lock feature. Lock minimizes all running applications and locks Windows until you enter your password in the displayed Unlock dialog.

Figure 18: Password entry dialog.

To enter a (new) password, select the Preferences menu item in the WizManager menu; then select the Password... button in the System Setup group. The Password dialog displayed allows you to enter the password to unlock your system. You can also type PASSWORD in the Command Line Box to access the password dialog directly.

♦ A password can be any combination of letters, numbers, and/or punctuation. Spaces (spacebar spaces) are accepted. For maximum security, it is strongly recommended NOT to use passwords shorter than four characters. It is also wise NOT to use passwords such as birthdays or first names. These are often the first ones tried by anyone who would try to break into your system.

Entering a new password erases the previously saved password.

Startup Directory

The Startup Directory dialog allows you to assign the Command Line Box current directory when WizManager's Buttonbar is displayed (either at WizManager's startup or later when you select to display the Buttonbar).

Figure 19: Startup Directory dialog.

To enter a new startup directory or to modify an existing one, select the Preferences menu item in the WizManager menu; then select the Startup Directory... button in the System Setup group.

♦ In the Startup Directory dialog, select to either use the directory which is current when the Buttonbar is displayed as the Command Line Box current directory or enter a startup directory in the dialog's edit field.

Additional Path

In addition to the DOS search PATH, WizManager will search the path set in the Additional Path for commands, programs, files, or scripts not found in the current directory.

```
┌─────────────────────────────────────────────┐
│ ▬        WizManager Preferences              │
│ ┌─ Additional File Search Path ────────────┐ │
│ │ ○  None                                   │ │
│ │ ◉  C:\DOCUMENT;F:\BITMAPS;D:\           │ │
│ └───────────────────────────────────────────┘ │
│      ┌────────┐  ┌────────┐  ┌────────┐      │
│      │   OK   │  │ Cancel │  │  Help  │      │
│      └────────┘  └────────┘  └────────┘      │
└─────────────────────────────────────────────┘
```

Figure 20: Additional Path dialog.

To enter an additional path or to modify an existing one, select the Preferences menu item in the WizManager menu; then select the Additional Path... button in the System Setup group.

♦ In the Additional Path dialog, select no additional path or enter a path or set of paths in the dialog's edit field. To specify a set of paths to search, separate the entries with a semicolon (;).

Path Shortcut

The path shortcut symbol represents the path of the active File Manager directory window.

The path shortcut symbol (character) is a command parameter prefix which is useful when the current Command Line Box directory differs from the directory of the active File Manager directory window. The path shortcut symbol represents the full path of the active File Manager directory. It allows you to work on the files displayed in the active File Manager directory window from the Command Line Box with a minimum of keystrokes. To fully specify the path of a file displayed in the active File Manager window, simply enter the path shortcut symbol followed by the filename.

Figure 21: Path Shortcut dialog.

To select a Path Shortcut symbol, select the Preferences menu item in the WizManager menu; then select the Path Shortcut... button in the System Setup group.

The path shortcut symbol can be either:

;   (a semicolon)

+   (a plus sign)

@   (the at character)

or no path shortcut symbol activated.

♦ The default path shortcut symbol is the semicolon character (;). The path shortcut symbol can be changed by selecting another dialog option in the *Select A Path Shortcut Symbol* group.

DOS PIF File

When WizManager opens a DOS Prompt session, it executes the program named COMMAND.COM through a PIF configuration file specified in the DOS PIF File Preferences.

DOSPRMPT.PIF is the default configuration file which is installed in your Windows directory when Windows is installed. DOSPRMPT.PIF is also the default configuration file preset by WizManager. To enter the path and filename of a different configuration file, select the Preferences menu item in the WizManager menu; then select the DOS PIF File... button in the System Setup group.

The DOS PIF configuration file controls several facets of the way COMMAND.COM is launched from the DOS Prompt command. You can set or modify a PIF file using the Windows application PIFEDIT.EXE. Refer to the "PIF Editor" chapter of your Windows User's Guide for detailed information on how to customize a PIF file.

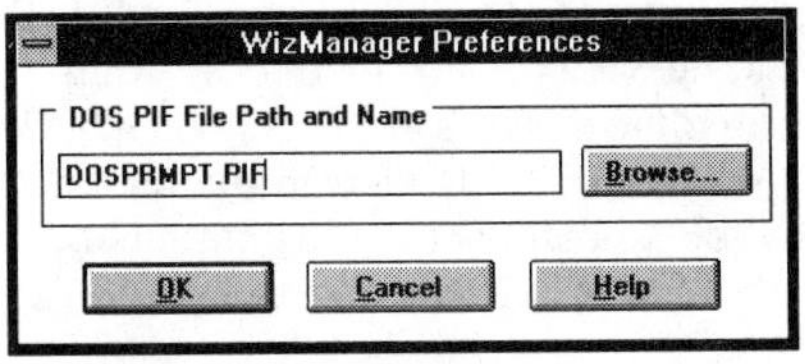

Figure 22: DOS PIF File dialog.

♦ You can set a different path or a different PIF file than DOSPRMPT.PIF in the DOS PIF File Preferences dialog. Enter the PIF path and filename in the edit field or select Browse to browse through your drives and directories and find the appropriate PIF file.

Set Fast Open

Set Fast Open allows you to set two applications which can be quickly accessed to open or work on the selected files in File Manager. When a Fast Open application is executed, the Open Files dialog is not displayed.

To set the Fast Open application paths and filenames, select the Preferences menu item in the WizManager menu; then select the Set Fast Open... button in the System Setup group.

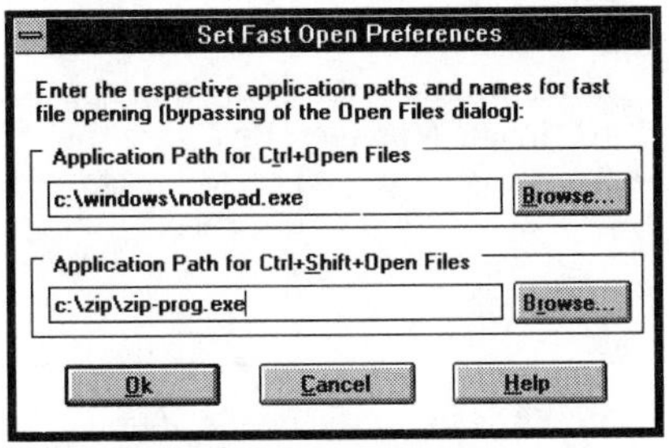

Figure 23: Set Fast Open dialog.

The application specified in the upper edit field is launched and opens the selected files in File Manager when you hold down the Ctrl key while selecting Open Files from the WizManager menu or the Open Files button in the Buttonbar. The second application is selected and launched when you hold down the Ctrl+Shift keys while selecting Open Files from the WizManager menu or the Open Files button in the Buttonbar.

♦ Enter the path and filename of the Fast Open applications in the respective edit fields or select the corresponding Browse button, browse through your drives and directories, and set the appropriate Fast Open application.

Set Viewer

Set Viewer allows you to set the path and filename of a file viewer application. Once the viewer application is set, clicking on the Buttonbar's Viewer button or selecting View files from WizManager's menu will start the viewer application and display the files selected in File Manager.

A file viewer is a program which allows you to view the contents of a file. *Notepad*, the text editor provided with Windows, is probably the simplest file viewer, although its viewing capabilities are limited to small text files. More elaborated file viewers are available, like *Drag And View*™ by Canyon Software™ (shareware) or *Norton Viewer*™, the viewer included in the Norton Desktop for Windows™. These file viewers are able to display the file contents not only of text files but also of formatted files created with word processors, spreadsheets, databases, drawing programs, etc.

Figure 24: Set Viewer dialog.

To set the Viewer application path and filename, select the Preferences menu item in the WizManager menu; then select the Set Viewer... button in the System Setup group.

♦ Enter the path and filename in the dialog's edit field or select the Browse button, browse through your drives and directories, and set the appropriate file viewer application.

♦ Check *Start Only One Viewer Instance* in the dialog if you want to start only one copy of the viewer application to display all the files selected in File Manager. Be aware that many file viewers are not able to display multiple files or generate an error message with this option checked.

Customize Buttonbar

The default order of the buttons in the Buttonbar may not fit your actual needs. If you experience frequent scrolling of the Buttonbar, you should reorganize and customize your Buttonbar.

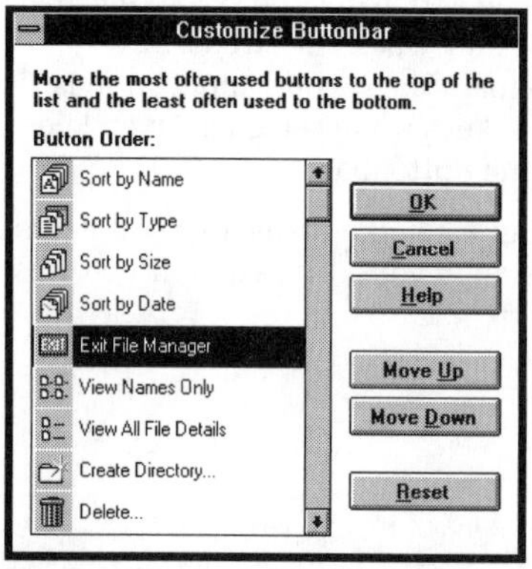

Figure 25: Customize Buttonbar dialog.

To customize your Buttonbar, select the Customize Buttonbar command from the WizManager menu. The displayed Customize Buttonbar dialog allows you to reorganize the Buttonbar's button order. To optimize your work with the Buttonbar, move the most often used buttons to the top of the list and the least often used to the bottom.

♦ To reorganize your Buttonbar:

1. Select the entry in the button list which represents the button you want to move.
2. Select the Move Up or Move Down button to move the button towards the top or the bottom of the button list.
3. Repeat Move Up or Move Down until the button's position in the Buttonbar list is as desired.
4. Repeat procedure 1 to 3 for each button you wish to move.
5. Select OK to save the changes and rebuild the Buttonbar.
6. The Buttonbar now displays the buttons in the order you specified.

If you wish to reset the Buttonbar button order back to its default order, select the Reset button.

5: WizManager Commands Reference

Parts of a Command

A WizManager command has up to three parts. Every command has a command name. Some commands require one or more parameters that identify the object you want WizManager to act on. Some commands also include one or more switches, which modify the action being performed.

Command name
The command name states the action you want WizManager to carry out. Some commands, such as the MEM command, consist only of a command name. Most WizManager commands, however, require more than a name.

Parameters
WizManager sometimes requires additional information, which you specify in one or more parameters after the command name. A parameter defines the object you want WizManager to act on. Some commands require more than one parameter. Parameters are optional for others.

Switches
A switch is a forward slash (/) followed by a single letter or number. You use switches to modify the way a command performs a task.

Naming Files and Directories _____

Rules to follow for naming files and directories:

The name of a file or directory can have two parts: a name and an optional extension. The two parts are separated by a period (for example, YOURFILE.NEW). The name can contain up to eight characters, and the extension can contain up to three characters. The name must start with either a letter or number. It can contain any uppercase or lowercase character except the following:

period (.)	quotation mark (")
slash (/)	backslash (\)
brackets ([ ])	colon (:)
semicolon (;)	vertical bar (I)
equal sign (=)	comma (,)

If you use these characters in a filename, you may get unexpected results. The name cannot contain any spaces. The following names are reserved and cannot be used for files or directories: CON, AUX, COM1, COM2, COM3, COM4, LPT1, LPT2, LPT3, PRN, and NUL.

Examples of valid filenames are LETTER.DOC, MEMO.TXT, BUDGET.93, and 2NDTRY.RPT.

Command Reference _____

The following sections list all WizManager commands — first in alphabetical order and then broken into categories by function. To see the exact syntax of each command, click WizManager Help on the main File Manager menu (after you install and configure WizManager), click Alphabetical Index, and then click the name of the command. Registered users of WizManager also receive a professionally printed, indexed manual with complete descriptions of all WizManager commands.

Commands — Alphabetical index

386	Optimizes Windows for 386 Enhanced Mode.
About	Displays WizManager About Dialog.
Associate	Associates a File with an Application.
Attrib or AttribQ	Changes or Displays File Attributes.
Cascade	Overlaps File Manager Directory Windows.
CD or ChDir	Changes the Current Directory.
Close	Closes Running Applications.
CloseBar	Closes WizManager Buttonbar.
Color	Changes the Windows Screen Colors.
Copy or CopyQ	Copies One or More Files to Another Location.
CustBar	Customizes WizManager Buttonbar.
CustLnch	Allows Customization of Your Launch Menu.
Date	Changes the Date of Your Computer's Clock.
Del, DelQ	Deletes One or More Files.
Desktop	Changes the Look of Your Desktop.
Dir	Displays a Directory Files and Subdirectories.
DiskCopy	Copies One Floppy Disk's Content to Another.

DiskFree or DF	Displays Disk Free Space.
DiskInfo or DI	Displays Disk Information.
DOS	Starts a DOS Prompt Session.
Drivers	Sets Up Optional Drivers.
Erase or EraseQ	Erases One or More Files.
Exit	Exits File Manager.
ExitWin	Exits Windows.
FDetails	Displays All Information on Files and Directories.
FileType	Displays a Specified Group of Files.
FName	Displays Only File and Directory Names.
Fonts	Adds and Removes Fonts.
Format	Formats a Floppy Disk.
Help	Displays WizManager Help Contents.
Indicate	Indicates Expandable Branches in Directory Tree.
Interntl	Specifies International Settings.
Keyboard	Specifies Keyboard Repeat Rate and Delay.
Lock	Locks Windows. (Safety Feature)
MaxFM	Enlarges File Manager to its Maximum Size.
Mem	Displays Free Memory (RAM) and Resources.
MinApp	Reduces All Running Applications to Icons.
MinFM	Reduces File Manager to an Icon.
MinWin	Reduces All Directory Windows to Icons.
MkDir or MD	Creates a Directory.
Mouse	Changes Your Mouse Settings.
Move or MoveQ	Moves One or More Files to Another Location.
NetCon	Connects to a Network Drive.
NetDis or NetDel	Disconnects from a Network Drive.
Network	Specifies Settings for Your Network Connections.
NewWin	Opens a New File Manager Directory Window.
Open	Opens Selected Files in File Manager.
Password	Sets or Changes the Unlock Password.
Path	Displays Search Path.
PDetails	Displays Partial Information on Files and Directories.
Ports	Specifies Serial Ports Communication Settings.
Pref	Sets or Changes WizManager Preferences.
Print	Prints a File.
PrintDir	Prints File Manager Directory Listing.
Printers	Sets Up Printers.
PrnTree	Prints a Disk Directory Structure.
Reboot	Exits Windows and Reboots System.
Refresh	Updates the Active File Manager Directory Window.
Ren, RenQ	Renames a File or Files.

Rename or RenameQ	Renames a File or Files.
RestApp	Restores All Applications to their Original Size.
Restart	Exits and Restarts Windows.
RestWin	Restores All Directory Windows.
RmDir or RD	Removes a Directory.
SaveNow	Saves Positions and Views of Open Directory Windows.
Search	Searches for Files and Directories.
SelDrive	Select Disk Drive.
Select	Selects Files and Directories in a Directory Window.
ShDir or SD	Shares Directory on Network.
SortDate	Sorts Directory Window Files by Last Modification Date.
SortName	Sorts Directory Window Files and Directories by Name.
SortSize	Sorts Directory Window Files by Size.
SortType	Sorts Directory Window Files and Directories by Type.
Sound	Assigns Sounds to System Events.
StopSh or SS	Stops Sharing Directory on Network.
Sys	Copies DOS Operating-System Files onto a Floppy Disk.
SysInfo	Displays System Information.
Task	Displays WizManager Task Menu.
TileH	Arranges Directory Windows Horizontally.
TileV	Arranges Directory Windows Vertically.
Time	Changes the Time of Your Computer's Clock.
Type	Displays the Contents of a Text File.
Ver	Displays WizManager, DOS, and Windows Versions.
Verify	Sets or Displays File Write Verify Status.
Vol	Displays a Disk Volume Label.

Commands — Categorical index

Internal commands

About	Displays WizManager About Dialog.
Attrib or AttribQ	Changes or Displays File Attributes.
CD or ChDir	Changes the Current Directory.
CloseBar	Closes WizManager Buttonbar.
Copy or CopyQ	Copies One or More Files to Another Location.
CustBar	Customizes WizManager Buttonbar.
CustLnch	Allows Customization of your Launch Menu.
Del, DelQ	Deletes One or More Files.
Dir	Displays a Directory Files and Subdirectories.
DiskFree or DF	Displays Disk Free Space.
DiskInfo or DI	Displays Disk Information.
DOS	Starts a DOS Prompt Session.

Erase or EraseQ	Erases One or More Files.
Exit	Exits File Manager.
ExitWin	Exits Windows.
Help	Displays WizManager Help Contents.
Lock	Locks Windows. (Safety Feature)
Mem	Displays Free Memory (RAM) and Resources.
MinApp	Reduces All Running Applications to Icons.
MinWin	Reduces All Directory Windows to Icons.
MkDir or MD	Creates a Directory.
Move or MoveQ	Moves One or More Files to Another Location.
Open	Opens Selected Files in File Manager.
Password	Sets or Changes the Unlock Password.
Path	Displays Search Path.
Pref	Sets or Changes WizManager Preferences.
Print	Prints a File.
PrintDir	Prints File Manager Directory Listing.
PrnTree	Prints a Disk Directory Structure.
Reboot	Exits Windows and Reboots System.
Ren, RenQ	Renames a File or Files.
Rename or RenameQ	Renames a File or Files.
RestApp	Restores All Applications to their Original Size.
RestWin	Restores All Directory Windows.
Restart	Exits and Restarts Windows.
RmDir or RD	Removes a Directory.
SaveNow	Saves Positions and Views of Open Directory Windows.
SysInfo	Displays System Information.
Task	Displays WizManager Task Menu.
Type	Displays the Contents of a Text File.
Ver	Displays WizManager, DOS, and Windows Versions.
Verify	Sets or Displays File Write Verify Status.
Vol	Displays a Disk Volume Label.

File Manager — related commands

Associate	Associates a File with an Application.
Cascade	Overlaps File Manager Directory Windows.
Close	Closes Running Applications.
DiskCopy	Copies One Floppy Disk's Content to Another.
FDetails	Displays All Information on Files and Directories.
FName	Displays Only File and Directory Names.
Format	Formats a Floppy Disk.
FileType	Displays a Specified Group of Files.

Indicate	Indicates Expandable Branches in Directory Tree.
MaxFM	Enlarges File Manager to its Maximum Size.
MinFM	Reduces File Manager to an Icon.
NetCon	Connects to or Disconnects from a Network Drive.
NetDis or NetDel	Disconnects from a Network Drive.
NewWin	Opens a New File Manager Directory Window.
PDetails	Displays Partial Information on Files and Directories.
Refresh	Updates the Active File Manager Directory Window.
Search	Searches for Files and Directories.
SelDrive	Selects Disk Drive.
Select	Selects Files and Directories in a Directory Window.
ShDir or SD	Shares Directory on Network.
SortDate	Sorts Directory Window Files by Last Modification Date.
SortName	Sorts Directory Window Files and Directories by Name.
SortSize	Sorts Directory Window Files by Size.
SortType	Sorts Directory Window Files and Directories by Type.
StopSh or SS	Stops Sharing Directory on Network.
Sys	Copies DOS Operating-System Files onto a Floppy Disk.
TileH	Arranges Directory Windows Horizontally.
TileV	Arranges Directory Windows Vertically.

Control Panel — related commands

386	Optimizes Windows for 386 Enhanced Mode.
Color	Changes the Windows Screen Colors.
Date	Changes the Date of Your Computer's Clock.
Desktop	Changes the Look of Your Desktop.
Drivers	Sets Up Optional Drivers.
Fonts	Adds and Removes Fonts.
Interntl	Specifies International Settings.
Keyboard	Specifies Keyboard Repeat Rate and Delay.
Mouse	Changes Your Mouse Settings.
Network	Specifies Settings for Your Network Connections.
Ports	Specifies Serial Ports Communication Settings.
Printers	Sets Up Printers.
Sound	Assigns Sounds to System Events.
Time	Changes the Time of Your Computer's Clock.

WizManager Installation on a Network Server

WizManager can be installed on a network server so that all connected users can load and run WizManager on their stations. Each computer running WizManager should have a WizManager License. Contact Mijenix for volume discount information.

1. WINFILE.INI SETUP

WizManager WIZMGR.INI file is created during the installation process in WizManager's directory. WIZMGR.INI contains the information and modifications to perform on the WINFILE.INI file in order to have File Manager load and run WizManager (see README2.TXT). WIZMGR.INI is only an information file and is not used by WizManager.

File Manager loads a specified extension when the latter path and filename is provided in WINFILE.INI. This information is stored under the [AddOns] section. Each station which is to run WizManager must have its WINFILE.INI modified by adding a specific entry to the [AddOns] section.

In addition to the [AddOns] section modification, it is necessary to add the [WizManager] section with the path to the WizManager directory as a sole entry. WizManager needs the specified path to launch its memory unit WIZUNIT.EXE at startup.

All the information which should be merged with WINFILE.INI is contained in the WIZMGR.INI file.

If users wish to run WizManager scripts, the following entry has to be added to the users' WIN.INI file under the [Extensions] section:

```
WIZ=[...]\WIZUNIT.EXE ^.WIZ
```

where [...] represents the path to the WizManager directory (an entry example could be WIZ=F:\WIZMGR\WIZUNIT.EXE ^.WIZ).

2. WIZBAR.DLL

It is important that the file WIZBAR.DLL be in the users' file search path.

By default, WIZBAR.DLL is installed in the Windows directory, but it can be installed in any directory declared in the user's file search path.

If WIZBAR.DLL is not found during File Manager's startup process, WizManager will not be loaded and therefore will not be available to the user.

3. MERGEINI.EXE UTILITY PROGRAM

MERGEINI Copyright (c) 1993, Mijenix – Dan Antonuk. All rights reserved.

A useful utility program named MERGEINI.EXE is provided with the registered version of WizManager. MERGEINI is a DOS program which can be used to 'smartly' merge the information contained in WIZMGR.INI with WINFILE.INI.

The MergeIni command syntax is as follows:

```
MERGEINI <SourceFile> <DestinationFile>
```

If any section declared in the <SourceFile> does not exist in the <DestinationFile>, it is automatically created and the related entries are copied from the <SourceFile> to the <DestinationFile>. If a section already exists in the <DestinationFile>, MERGEINI adds or updates the related entries.

MERGEINI can be declared in a login script or batch file so that each user who should have access to WizManager (stored on a file server) would have its WINFILE.INI modified, so that WizManager could be found and loaded when File Manager is launched.

Technical Support

Questions? Problems? Suggestions?

We would like to hear from you if you have any questions, problems, suggestions, or special requests regarding WizManager.

The WizManager User Manual and WizManager Help file have answers to the most commonly asked questions. Try to browse quickly through these sources of information — you should find it useful.

If your questions or problems cannot be answered by the manual or help file, or if you have any suggestions, please contact Mijenix through one of the following channels:

Mijenix
6666 Odana Rd, Ste. 326
Madison, WI 53719
U.S.A.
Tel & Fax: (608) 277-1971
CompuServe: 75430,1545
America OnLine: Mijenix
Internet: 75430,1545@compuserve.com

Due to the oftentimes complex technical nature of WizManager or Windows configurations, technical support by phone is not the most effective and almost always results in a request for follow-up information. Please use one of the other means whenever possible and send us a detailed description of your problem. We will address your concerns promptly. Thank you.

ASP

Mijenix is a member of the Association of Shareware Professionals (ASP). ASP wants to make sure that the shareware principle works for you. If you are unable to resolve a shareware-related problem with an ASP member by contacting the member directly, ASP may be able to help. The ASP Ombudsman can help you resolve a dispute or problem with an ASP member, but does not provide technical support for members' products. Please write to the ASP Ombudsman at 545 Grover Road, Muskegon, MI 49442 or send a CompuServe message via CompuServe Mail to ASP Ombudsman 70007,3536.

!!! Important Installation Notes, Please Read !!!

IF YOU ENCOUNTER ANY PROBLEM DURING OR AFTER THE INSTALLATION, PLEASE NOTIFY MIJENIX. WE WILL TRY TO IDENTIFY AND CORRECT THE PROBLEM. Mijenix's address can be found at the end of this file.

♦ WizManager's Buttonbar uses powerful techniques to provide speed and innovative features. This can push certain Windows video drivers for *accelerated* video boards to the edge. Make sure you have the latest video drivers for your video board. Standard Windows video drivers (VGA and SuperVGA) cause no problem.

If you encounter General Protection Fault (GPF) error messages while running WizManager, start the Windows Setup program and change the video driver of your system to a standard Windows video driver (VGA or Super VGA, for example) and determine whether General Protection Fault messages still appear. If they don't, update the video drivers you were using to the latest available version.

♦ *Do not declare more than four extensions* in the WINFILE.INI [AddOns] section:

Extensions to File Manager are not executable files (.EXE) but Dynamic Link Libraries (.DLL) which are automatically loaded by File Manager when the latter is started and destroyed when File Manager is closed.

How does File Manager 'know' or recognize extensions?

File Manager gets all the necessary information by reading its initialization file WINFILE.INI (not WIN.INI!) which is located in the Windows directory. The different data in WINFILE.INI is sorted by sections (a section title is enclosed in square brackets [...]). The section of interest for recognizing and loading extensions is called [AddOns]. This is where extension paths are declared, one per line, in the form (example):

```
[AddOns]
Extension1=PathToExtension1\extension1.dll
Extension2=PathToExtension2\extension2.dll
```

Each extension will add a top-level menu to File Manager. The documentation for the Windows File Manager Extender Interface states that five top-level menus may be added to the File Manager menu. However, due to what appears to be a bug in Windows File Manager, the fifth menu item does not work properly. Any command selected from the fifth menu item becomes confused with the adjacent File Manager "Window" menu, and the corresponding command from the "Window" menu is executed instead.

What this means is simple:

Do not declare more than four extensions in the [AddOns] section!

You may presently be using File Manager Extensions, like

♦ DOS 6 Tools (Microsoft)
♦ MetzLaunch (Metz TaskManager)
♦ NDW (Norton Desktop)
♦ File Commander (Wilson WindowWare)
♦ FExtend (BarbarSoft)
♦ or others

As File Manager limits you to four extensions, it is up to you to "keep up" and maintain the [AddOns] section of WINFILE.INI. If you have more than four declarations under [AddOns], simply type a ';' (without the quotes) at the beginning of the line(s) you want File Manager to ignore. This lets you keep all the declarations in case you decide later to alter your choices and start only the ones you need.

During the installation of WizManager, the [AddOns] section of WINFILE.INI is updated to include the WizManager library path. This declaration is appended at the end of the [AddOns] section. If more than three other declarations exist above WizManager's line, proceed as explained above to cancel out one or more declarations (use NOTEPAD.EXE for example to edit WINFILE.INI, and modify the [AddOns] entries only).

Windows NT _____

Mijenix will soon port WizManager to the 32-bit world of Windows NT. However, the WizManager version you have installed is a set of 16-bit DLLs written for Windows 3.10 and Windows for Workgroups (WFW); it will not work under Windows NT.

Notice to Users _____

This manual should not be construed as any representation or warranty with respect to the software named herein. Occasionally, changes or variations exist in the software that are not reflected in the manual. Generally, if such changes or variations are known to exist and affect the product significantly, a release note or README file will accompany the manual and/or the distribution disk(s). In that event, please read the release note or README file before using the product.

See the License Agreement and Limited Warranty for complete license and warranty information.

IMPORTANT - BY OPENING THE SEALED SOFTWARE PACKET CONTAINING THE WIZMANAGER SOFTWARE, YOU ACKNOWLEDGE THAT YOU HAVE READ THIS LICENSE AGREEMENT, UNDER-STAND IT, AND AGREE TO BE BOUND BY ITS TERMS. YOU FURTHER AGREE THAT IT IS THE FULL AND COMPLETE AGREEMENT BETWEEN US, SUPERSEDING ALL PRIOR WRITTEN OR VERBAL AGREEMENTS OF ANY KIND.

Mijenix license agreement

This is a legal agreement between you (either an individual or an entity) and Mijenix. By opening the sealed software packet or using Mijenix WizManager software program, you agree to be bound by the terms of this agreement. If you do not understand or do not agree to the terms of this agreement, you must cease using this product immediately.

Mijenix software license

1. GRANT OF LICENSE. This License Agreement permits you to use one copy of the enclosed Mijenix software program (the "SOFTWARE") on a *single* computer. The SOFT-WARE is in "use" on a computer when it is loaded into temporary memory (i.e., RAM) or installed into permanent memory (e.g., hard disk, CD-ROM, or other storage device) of that computer. However, installation on a network server for the sole purpose of internal distribution shall not constitute "use" for which a separate license is required, provided you have a separate license for *each* computer to which the SOFTWARE is distributed.

2. COPYRIGHT. The SOFTWARE is owned by Mijenix or its suppliers and is protected by United States copyright laws and international treaty provisions. Therefore, you must treat the SOFTWARE like any other copyrighted material (e.g., a book or musical recording) *except* that you may either (a) make one copy of the SOFTWARE solely for backup or archival purposes, or (b) transfer the SOFTWARE to a single hard disk provided you keep the original solely for backup or archival purposes. You may not copy the written materials accompanying the SOFTWARE.

3. OTHER RESTRICTIONS. You may not rent or lease the SOFTWARE, but you may transfer the SOFTWARE and accompanying written materials on a permanent basis provided you retain no copies and the recipient agrees to the terms of this Agreement. You may not reverse engineer, decompile, or disassemble the SOFTWARE. If the Software is an update or has been updated, any transfer must include the most recent update and all prior versions.

4. DUAL MEDIA SOFTWARE. If the SOFTWARE package contains both 3.5" and 5.25" disks, then you may use only the disks appropriate for your single-user computer. You may not use the other disks on another computer or loan, rent, lease, or transfer them to another user except as part of the permanent transfer (as provided above) of all SOFTWARE and written materials.

Limited warranty

LIMITED WARRANTY. This program is provided "as is" without any warranty of any kind, either expressed or implied, including, but not limited to, the implied warranties of merchant-ability and fitness for a particular purpose. The entire risk as to the quality and performance of the SOFTWARE is with you, the licensee. Should the SOFTWARE prove defective, you assume the risk and liability for the entire cost of all necessary repair, service, or correction. Some states/jurisdictions do not allow the exclusion of implied warranties, so the above exclusion may not apply to you. This warranty gives you specific legal rights, and you may have other rights which vary from state/jurisdiction to state/jurisdiction.

Mijenix does not warranty the functions contained in the SOFTWARE will meet your require-ments, or that the operation of the SOFTWARE will be error-free or uninterrupted. Mijenix does warrant that the disk(s) on which the program is furnished shall be free from defects in materials and workmanship for a period of ninety (90) days from the date of purchase, so long as proof of purchase is provided.

CUSTOMER REMEDIES. Mijenix's and its suppliers' entire liability and your exclusive remedy shall be, at Mijenix's option, either (a) return of the price paid, or (b) repair or replacement of the SOFTWARE that does not meet Mijenix's Limited Warranty and which is returned to Mijenix with proof of purchase. This Limited Warranty is void if failure of the SOFTWARE has resulted from accident, abuse, or misapplication. Any replacement SOFTWARE will be warranted for the remainder of the original warranty period or thirty (30) days, whichever is longer. Neither these remedies nor any product support services are available outside the United States without proof of purchase from an authorized non-U.S. source.

NO OTHER WARRANTIES. To the maximum extent permitted by applicable law, Mijenix and its suppliers disclaim all other warranties, either express or implied, including, but not limited to, implied warranties of merchantability and fitness for a particular purpose, with regard to the SOFTWARE, the accompanying written materials, and any accompanying hardware. This limited warranty gives you specific legal rights. You may have others which vary from state/jurisdiction to state/jurisdiction.

NO LIABILITY FOR CONSEQUENTIAL DAMAGES. To the maximum extent permitted by applicable law, in no event shall Mijenix or its suppliers be liable for any damages whatsoever (including, without limitation, damages for loss of business profits, business interruption, loss of business information, or any other pecuniary loss) arising out of the use or inability to use this Mijenix product, even if Mijenix has been advised of the possibility of such damages or for any claim by any other party. Because some states/jurisdictions do not allow the exclusion or limitation of liability for consequential or incidental damages, the above limita-tion may not apply to you.

U.S. government restricted rights

The SOFTWARE and documentation are subject to export controls under the United States Export Administration Act, as amended, which Act prohibits exports of certain commodities and technical data, including software, to specified countries. You hereby certify that neither the SOFTWARE nor the documentation will be transmitted or forwarded outside of your country.

If you acquired this product in the United States, this Agreement is governed by the laws of the State of Wisconsin.

Should you have any questions concerning this Agreement, or if you desire to contact Mijenix for any reason, you may write to Mijenix, 6666 Odana Road, Ste. 326, Madison, WI 53719.

Trademarks

Mijenix is a registered trademark of Mijenix.
WizManager is a registered trademark of Mijenix.
Microsoft is a registered trademark of Microsoft Corporation.
Windows is a trademark of Microsoft Corporation.
Windows for Workgroups is a trademark of Microsoft Corporation.
MS-DOS is a registered trademark of Microsoft Corporation.
PC-DOS is a registered trademark of International Business Machines Corporation.
Other trademarks are the property of their respective holders.

Copyright

Copyright © 1993, Mijenix. All rights reserved

No part of this publication may be reproduced, transmitted, transcribed, stored in a retrieval system, or translated into a language or computer language, in any form by any means, electronic, mechanical, magnetic, optical, chemical, manual or otherwise, without the express **written** consent of Mijenix, 6666 Odana Road, Suite 326, Madison, WI 53719, U.S.A.

How to Order WizManager (Registration)

WizManager is distributed as shareware. Shareware is copyrighted software which you can "try before you buy." Shareware is a great concept and we encourage you to try out WizManager and pass along shareware copies to your friends.

Please understand that WizManager is *not* free software. You are welcome to evaluate WizManager for 21 days. If you continue to use WizManager, you should buy the program.

What do you get when you order WizManager?

You get the latest full-featured version of WizManager, a comprehensive user's manual, new release information, the newsletter *Tips & Tricks for File Manager*, and 90 days of free technical support ... and, of course, you'll never have to see the reminder dialog again. Order WizManager today for only $39.95 (plus Shipping and Handling).

You can order WizManager either by sending a check or money order, or by placing a credit card order. Use the order form at the end of this chapter (or print the ORDERFRM.TXT file).

WizManager Order Form

Please send your CHECK or MONEY ORDER to:

        Mijenix
        6666 Odana Road, Ste. 326
        Madison, WI 53719
        Tel/Fax: (608) 277-1971
        CompuServe: 75430,1545
        America OnLine: Mijenix
        Internet: 75430.1545@compuserve.com

Please place CREDIT CARD orders through:

> Public Software Library (PsL)
> P. O. Box 35705, Houston, TX 77235-5705
> U.S.A. Sales: 1-800-242-4775 Overseas : (713) 524-6394
> Fax : (713) 524-6398 CompuServe: 71355,470

THE PsL NUMBERS ABOVE ARE EXCLUSIVELY FOR PLACING ORDERS WITH CREDIT CARDS. MIJENIX CANNOT BE REACHED AT THOSE NUMBERS. IF YOU HAVE QUESTIONS ABOUT THE STATUS OF YOUR ORDER, VOLUME DISCOUNTS, TECH SUPPORT, ETC. PLEASE CONTACT MIJENIX DIRECTLY.

NAME: _____

COMPANY: _____

STREET: _____

CITY: _____ STATE: _____ ZIP: _____

COUNTRY: _____ TEL: _____ FAX: _____

WizManager (item #10869) $ 39.95 U.S. x ___ unit(s) = $ _____

Shipping & Handling:

Continental U.S.	$ 4.00	
AK, HI, CAN, MEX	$ 6.00	
International	$ 12.00	
Express U.S.A.	$ 20.00	$ _____ <
	Subtotal:$ _____ <	
Wisconsin residents add 5.5% sales tax :		$ _____ <
	TOTAL :	$ _____ <

Diskette format: __ 3.5" or __ 5.25"

Payment by: __ MasterCard __ Visa __ AMEX __ Discovery

__ Check (US) __ Certified Check (US) __ Money Order

Card #: _____ Exp. Date: _____

Card Holder Name: _____

Signature: _____

*** NB: Send credit card orders to PsL (NOT to Mijenix) ***

Where did you hear about WizManager? _____

Zoom

Version 1.1
Copyright © Mushy Software

Zoom doesn't fit into any category but Windows Art. Some things have no practical value but are appreciated only for their beauty — and Zoom certainly fits that definition. It doesn't even have any documentation! I created the following description myself, as if you'd need it.

When ZOOMCTRL.EXE is in your Program Manager StartUp group, your Windows applications and dialog boxes gain an animated, "exploding" effect, just like windows have on Macintosh computers. That's it! You may like it or you may hate it, but Zoom just keeps on zooming along.

Not all applications may display the zooming effect, but these spoilsport apps shouldn't distract from the visceral pleasure you'll get from the Windows applets and heavy-duty programs that do. Even more than a screen saver, Zoom brightens your day almost every time you use Windows. And now, if you'll excuse me ... I gotta zoom.

Type of Program:	Art.
Requires:	Windows 3.0 or higher.
Registration:	Free. There is no registration for this program.
Technical Support:	None.

Figure 1: When you click Options on the Zoom window menu, you can select the style and thickness of the Mac-like exploding effect your windows gain.

Overview

Zoom adds an "exploding" effect to Windows applications when they open a new window, very similar to the effect you see on Macintoshes.

To use Zoom, simply put the ZOOMCTRL.EXE icon into your Windows 3.1 StartUp group in Program Manager (or add it to the LOAD= line in your WIN.INI file in Windows 3.0). When you restart Windows, try starting Notepad, Write, the Control Panel, and other applets. Click File Open and other dialog boxes. You should see dotted lines "zooming" out of an origin point, followed by the window of the application itself.

Besides ZOOMCTRL.EXE, Zoom has only one other file: ZOOM.DLL. As long as this file is in the same directory that ZOOMCTRL.EXE is launched from, you'll be fine — the .DLL doesn't need to clutter up your \WINDOWS or \SYSTEM subdirectories.

Configuring Zoom

Click the Options menu item on the ZOOMCTRL window to display the Zoom Options dialog box. In this box, you can select two kinds of effects: Good Looking (which uses dotted lines) and Way Fast Speedy (which uses solid lines). For both effects, you may select or deselect Thick Lines (affectionately known as "James' Thick Lines," for the persistent nag who caused this feature to be implemented). Selecting Thick Lines may slow down the Way Fast Speedy exploding effect, which could be just what you want on a fast 486.

Registration

Zoom is totally free, and totally silly. There is no registration fee, no technical support, and no seriousness allowed. Enjoy!

— Brian Livingston

Index

IDG Books Worldwide License Agreement

Read this agreement carefully before you buy this book and use the programs contained on the enclosed disks.

By opening the accompanying disk package, you indicate that you have read and agree with the terms of this licensing agreement. If you disagree and do not want to be bound by the terms of this licensing agreement, return the book for refund to the source from which you purchased it.

The entire contents of these disks and the compilation of the software contained therein are copyrighted and protected by both U.S. copyright law and international copyright treaty provisions. The individual programs on these disks are copyrighted by the authors of each program respectively. Each program has its own use permissions and limitations. You may copy any or all of these programs to your computer system. To use each program, you must follow the individual requirements and restrictions detailed for each in Part IV of this book. Do not use a program if you do not want to follow its licensing agreement. Absolutely none of the material on these disks or listed in this book may ever be distributed, in original or modified form, for commercial purposes.

Disclaimer and Copyright Notice

Complete Installation Instructions

The programs on the *More Windows 3.1 Secrets* diskettes are stored in a compressed form in order to bring you more than 5 megabytes of programs. You cannot simply copy these diskettes to your hard drive. You must use the WSETUP program located on Diskette 1. You must be running Windows 3.0 or higher in standard or enhanced mode.

STEPS

Installing Your *More Windows 3.1 Secrets* Programs

Step 1. Insert Diskette 1. Place Diskette 1 into your PC's floppy drive — A: or B:, whichever is the correct size.

Step 2. Run the WSETUP program. Using the Windows Program Manager, pull down the File menu and click Run. In the dialog box that appears, type **A:\WSETUP or B:\WSETUP** and click OK. If you use Norton Desktop for Windows as your program manager, you must use NDW Version 2.0 or later.

Step 3. Tell WSETUP what drive and directory to use. The default directory, under which any program directories will be created, is C:\SECRETS2. For example, if you install Concentration Solitaire, WSETUP installs the files into the directory C:\SECRETS2\CONCENTR. You can tell WSETUP at this point to use any valid directory, such as C:\.

Step 4. Install the programs you want. After you select a default directory, you will see a dialog box with a listing on the left of all programs on the diskettes. Click your mouse once on the name of the program you wish to install, then click the Add button. The name will appear in the listing on the right of the dialog box. You can select more than one program to install at a time. WSETUP shows you how much space is required to install each program. When you've finished adding programs to install, click the Install button.

WSETUP installs each program's files then creates a group window for each program in the Program Manager. Because the Program Manager has a limit of 40 group windows, we recommend that you *not* click the Add All button to install all programs. Install one or two at a time and try them before adding more.

WSETUP also creates a file called UNINSTAL.BAT in your default installation directory. This is another good reason to install only one or two programs at a time. If you need to remove a program for any reason, you can run UNINSTAL at a DOS prompt and it will delete the files of each program you installed. WSETUP creates a new batch file every time you install a program, so you can delete only the programs you most recently installed.

Step 5. Configure the programs you installed. Read the first page of the chapter in this book for each program you installed, to see if any additional configuration steps are required. The following programs, for example, require additional steps to configure them:

⇨**Sloop Manager** and **Wiz Manager** require that you run their INSTALL.EXE programs once to configure them.

⇨**RRKeyCaps** and **Video Terminal Screen** are fonts. They require you to run Control Panel's Fonts dialog box and click the Add button to add them to Windows's list of installed fonts.

Step 6. Register for updates. If you like a program, register it with the author. Doing so may bring you a newer, improved version of the program or other benefits, as described at the end of each program's chapter.

That's it. We hope you enjoy running these programs.

IDG BOOKS WORLDWIDE REGISTRATION CARD

RETURN THIS REGISTRATION CARD FOR FREE CATALOG

Title of this book: Infoworld More Windows 3.1 Secrets

My overall rating of this book: ❑ Very good [1]   ❑ Good [2]   ❑ Satisfactory [3]   ❑ Fair [4]   ❑ Poor [5]

How I first heard about this book:

❑ Found in bookstore; name: [6]

❑ Advertisement: [8]

❑ Word of mouth; heard about book from friend, co-worker, etc.: [10]

❑ Book review: [7]

❑ Catalog: [9]

❑ Other: [11]

What I liked most about this book:

What I would change, add, delete, etc., in future editions of this book:

Other comments:

Number of computer books I purchase in a year: ❑ 1 [12]   ❑ 2-5 [13]   ❑ 6-10 [14]   ❑ More than 10 [15]

I would characterize my computer skills as: ❑ Beginner [16] ❑ Intermediate [17] ❑ Advanced [18] ❑ Professional [19]

I use ❑ DOS [20] ❑ Windows [21] ❑ OS/2 [22] ❑ Unix [23] ❑ Macintosh [24] ❑ Other: [25]_____
(please specify)

I would be interested in new books on the following subjects:
(please check all that apply, and use the spaces provided to identify specific software)

❑ Word processing: [26]

❑ Data bases: [28]

❑ File Utilities: [30]

❑ Networking: [32]

❑ Other: [34]

❑ Spreadsheets: [27]

❑ Desktop publishing: [29]

❑ Money management: [31]

❑ Programming languages: [33]

I use a PC at (please check all that apply): ❑ home [35] ❑ work [36] ❑ school [37] ❑ other: [38] _____

The disks I prefer to use are ❑ 5.25 [39] ❑ 3.5 [40] ❑ other: [41]_____

I have a CD ROM: ❑ yes [42]   ❑ no [43]

I plan to buy or upgrade computer hardware this year: ❑ yes [44]   ❑ no [45]

I plan to buy or upgrade computer software this year: ❑ yes [46]   ❑ no [47]

Name: _____   Business title: [48] _____   Type of Business: [49] _____

Address (❑ home [50] ❑ work [51]/Company name: _____)

Street/Suite# _____

City [52]/State [53]/Zipcode [54]: _____   Country [55] _____

❑ **I liked this book!** You may quote me by name in future
IDG Books Worldwide promotional materials.

My daytime phone number is _____

IDG BOOKS

THE WORLD OF
COMPUTER
KNOWLEDGE

❑ YES!

Please keep me informed about IDG's World of Computer Knowledge.
Send me the latest IDG Books catalog.